STRATEGIC MARKETING PROBLEMS

STRATEGIC MARKETING PROBLEMS

Cases and Comments

EIGHTH EDITION

Roger A. Kerin
Southern Methodist University

Robert A. Peterson
University of Texas

PRENTICE HALL, Upper Saddle River, New Jersey 07458

Acquisitions Editor: Whitney Blake
Assistant Editor: John Larkin
Editorial Assistant: Rachel Falk
Editor-in-Chief: James Boyd
Director of Development: Steve Deitmer
Marketing Manager: John Chillingworth
Production Editor: Aileen Mason
Managing Editor: Dee Josephson
Associate Managing Editor: Linda DeLorenzo
Manufacturing Buyer: Kenneth J. Clinton
Manufacturing Supervisor: Arnold Vila
Manufacturing Manager: Vincent Scelta
Design Manager: Pat Smythe
Interior Design: Lee Goldstein
Cover Design: Marjory Dressler
Illustrator (Interior):   Rainbow Graphics, Inc.
Composition: Rainbow Graphics, Inc.

Credits and acknowledgments for materials borrowed from other sources
and reproduced with permission, in this textbook appear on pages 74–75,
86, 89, 92, 101, 103, 121, 123–125, 127, 134–135, 138, 141, 146–150, 152–154,
156–157, 170–174, 217, 229, 253, 254, 255, 267, 272, 273, 275, 276, 277, 278,
280, 281, 309, 310, 312, 313, 329, 338, 339, 340, 343, 344, 347, 348, 353, 367,
368, 369, 370, 371, 374, 375, 376, 394, 395, 398, 399, 400, 402, 404, 405, 420,
421, 422, 423, 424, 426, 427, 428, 432, 440, 441, 446, 450, 454, 463, 465, 466,
468, 470, 471, 474, 481, 485, 486, 487, 489, 492, 524, 525, 528, 529, 543, 544,
546, 548, 549, 550, 555, 556, 570, 571, 573, 576, 577, 598, 599, 618, 634, 636,
638, 644, 646, 647, 648, 649, 652, 653, 654, 657, 658, 659, 660, 666, 667, and 690.

Library of Congress Cataloging-in-Publication Data
Kerin, Roger A.
    Strategic marketing problems : cases and comments / Roger A.
Kerin, Robert A. Peterson. — 8th ed.
        p.   cm.
    Includes indexes.
    ISBN 0-13-632860-1
    1. Marketing—Decision making—Case studies.   2. Marketing—
Management—Case studies.   I. Peterson, Robert A. (Robert Allen),
1944-   .   II. Title.
HF5415.135.K47   1997
658.8'02—dc21   97-13899
                                                            CIP

Prentice-Hall International (UK) Limited, London
Prentice-Hall of Australia Pty. Limited, Sydney
Prentice-Hall Canada, Inc., Toronto
Prentice-Hall Hispanoamericana, S.A., Mexico
Prentice-Hall of India Private Limited, New Delhi
Prentice-Hall of Japan, Inc., Tokyo
Simon & Schuster Asia Pte. Ltd., Singapore
Editora Prentice-Hall do Brasil, Ltda., Rio de Janeiro

Printed in the United States of America

10 9 8 7 6 5 4 3 2 1

To Our Families

Contents

Preface

 Decision making in marketing is first and foremost a skill. Like most skills, it requires tools and terminology. Like all skills, it is best learned through practice. This book is dedicated to the development of decision-making skills in marketing. Textual material introduces concepts and tools useful in structuring and solving marketing problems. Case studies describing actual marketing problems provide an opportunity for those concepts and tools to be employed in practice. In every case study, the decision maker must develop a strategy consistent with the underlying factors existing in the situation presented and must consider the implications of that strategy for the organization and its environment.

The eighth edition of *Strategic Marketing Problems: Cases and Comments* seeks a balance between marketing management content and process. The book consists of eleven chapters and forty-three cases.

Chapter 1, "Foundations of Strategic Marketing Management," provides an overview of the strategic marketing management process. The principal emphasis is on defining an organization's business, mission, and goals, identifying and framing organizational opportunities, formulating product-market strategies, budgeting, and controlling the marketing effort. The appendix to Chapter 1 contains a marketing plan for an actual company, Paradise Kitchens®, Inc. The plan is annotated to focus attention on substantive elements of the plan as well as style and layout elements.

Chapter 2, "Financial Aspects of Marketing Management," reviews basic concepts from managerial accounting and managerial finance that are useful in marketing management. Primary emphasis is placed on such concepts as cost structure, relevant versus sunk costs, margins, contribution analysis, liquidity, operating leverage, and preparing *pro forma* income statements.

Chapter 3, "Marketing Decision Making and Case Analysis," introduces a systematic process for decision making and provides an overview of various aspects of case analysis. A sample case and written student analysis are presented in the Appendix at the end of the book. The student analysis illustrates the nature and scope of a written case presentation, including the qualitative and quantitative analyses essential to a good presentation.

Chapter 4, "Opportunity Analysis and Market Targeting," focuses on the identification and evaluation of marketing opportunities. Market segmentation, market targeting, and market potential and profitability issues are considered in some depth.

Chapter 5, "Marketing Research," deals with the effective management of marketing information. Decisions involved in assessing the value of marketing information and managing the information acquisition process are highlighted.

Chapter 6, "Product and Service Strategy and Management," focuses on the management of the organization's offering. New-offering development, life cycle management, product or service positioning, branding decisions, and brand growth strategies are emphasized.

Chapter 7, "Integrated Marketing Communication Strategy and Management," raises issues in the design, execution, and evaluation of an integrated communication mix. Decisions concerned with communications objectives, strategy, budgeting, programming, and effectiveness, as well as sales management, are addressed.

Chapter 8, "Marketing Channel Strategy and Management," introduces a variety of considerations affecting channel selection and modification as well as trade relations. Specific decision areas covered include direct versus indirect distribution, dual distribution, cost-benefit analysis of channel choice and management, and marketing channel conflict and coordination.

Chapter 9, "Pricing Strategy and Management," highlights concepts and applications in price determination and modification. Emphasis is placed on evaluating demand, cost, and competitive influences when selecting or modifying pricing strategies for products and services and product-line pricing.

Chapter 10, "Marketing Strategy Reformulation: The Control Process," focuses on the appraisal of marketing actions for the purpose of developing reformulation and recovery strategies. Considerations and techniques applicable to strategic and operations control are introduced.

Chapter 11, "Comprehensive Marketing Programs," raises issues in developing integrated marketing strategies. Attention is directed to marketing program decisions for new and existing products and services, including issues related to marketing program implementation and organization.

The case selection in this book reflects a broad overview of contemporary marketing problems and applications. Ninety percent of the cases are dated in the 1990s; 42 percent are dated since 1995. Of the forty-three cases included, thirty deal with consumer products and services, and thirteen have a business-to-business marketing orientation. Sixteen cases introduce marketing issues in the international arena. Marketing of services is addressed in seven cases. Sixty-five percent of the cases are new, revised, or updated for this edition, and many have spreadsheet applications embedded in the case analysis. All text and case material has been classroom tested.

Computer-assisted programs and a student manual are available for use with seventeen of the cases in the book. The manual contains all the materials necessary to use spreadsheets. It includes a sample case demonstration, instructions for use with specific cases, and input and output forms. If this material is not available from your instructor or bookstore, please write to the publisher.

The efforts of many people are reflected here. First, we thank those institutions and individuals who have kindly granted us permission to include their cases in this edition. The cases contribute significantly to the overall quality of the book, and each individual is prominently acknowledged in the Contents and at the bottom of the page on which the case begins. We specifically wish to thank the Harvard Business School, The University of Western Ontario, and the University of Virginia for granting permission to reproduce cases authored by their faculty. Second, we wish to thank our numerous collaborators, whose efforts made the difference between good cases and excellent cases. Third, we thank the adopters of the previous seven editions of the book for their many comments and recommendations for improvements. Their insights and attention to detail are, we hope, reflected here. Finally, we wish to thank the numerous reviewers of this and previous editions for their conscientious reviews of our material. Naturally, we bear full responsibility for any errors of omission and commission in the final product.

Roger A. Kerin

Robert A. Peterson

CHAPTER 1

Foundations of Strategic Marketing Management

 The primary purpose of marketing is to create long-term and mutually beneficial exchange relationships between an organization and the publics (individuals and organizations) with which it interacts. Though this fundamental purpose of marketing is timeless, the manner in which organizations undertake it continues to evolve. No longer do marketing managers function solely to direct day-to-day operations; they must make strategic decisions as well. This elevation of marketing perspectives to a strategic position in organizations has resulted in expanded responsibilities for marketing managers. Increasingly, they find themselves involved in charting the direction of the organization and contributing to decisions that will create and sustain a competitive advantage and affect long-term organizational performance. According to a senior strategic-planning manager at General Electric:

> [T]he marketing manager is the most significant functional contributor to the strategic-planning process, with leadership roles in defining the business mission; analysis of the environmental, competitive, and business situations; developing objectives, goals, and strategies; and defining product, market distribution, and quality plans to implement the business's strategies. This involvement extends to the development of programs and operational plans that are fully linked with the strategic plan.[1]

The transition of the marketing manager from being only an implementer to being a maker of organization strategy has prompted the emergence of strategic marketing management as a course of study and practice. *Strategic marketing management* consists of five complex and interrelated analytical processes.

1. Defining the organization's business, mission, and goals.
2. Identifying and framing organizational opportunities.
3. Formulating product-market strategies.
4. Budgeting marketing, financial, and production resources.
5. Developing reformulation and recovery strategies.

The remainder of this chapter discusses each of these processes and their relationships to one another.

■ DEFINING THE ORGANIZATION'S BUSINESS, MISSION, AND GOALS

The practice of strategic marketing management begins with a clearly stated business definition, mission, and set of goals or objectives. A business definition outlines the scope of a particular organization's operations. Its mission is a written statement of organizational purpose. Goals or objectives specify what an organization intends to achieve. Each plays an important role in describing the character of an organization and what it seeks to accomplish.

Business Definition

Determining what business an organization is in is neither obvious nor easy. In many instances, a single organization may operate several businesses, as is the case with large *Fortune* 500 companies. Defining each of these businesses is a necessary first step in strategic marketing management.

Contemporary strategic marketing perspectives indicate that an organization should define a business by the type of customers it wishes to serve, the particular needs of those customer groups it wishes to satisfy, and the means or technology by which the organization will satisfy these customer needs.[2] By defining a business from a customer or market perspective, an organization is appropriately viewed as a customer-satisfying endeavor, not a product-producing or service-delivery enterprise. Products and services are transient, as is often the technology or means used to produce or deliver them. Basic customer needs and customer groups are more enduring. For example, the means for delivering prerecorded music has undergone significant change over the past 25 years. During this period, the dominant prerecorded music technologies and products evolved from plastic records, to 8-track tapes, to cassettes, and most recently, to compact discs. By comparison, the principal consumer buying segment(s) and needs satisfied have varied little.

Much of the corporate restructuring and refocusing in recent years has resulted from senior company executives asking the question "What business are we in?" The experience of the Domestic Merchandising Group at Sears, Roebuck and Company is a case in point.[3] The company found itself in a competitive environment where discounters and specialty outlets were attracting its traditional middle-class customers. Sears' response was to tinker with its merchandising strategy throughout the 1980s and early 1990s. It promoted itself variously as an upscale, fashion-oriented department store for more affluent customers and as a discounter with budget shops featuring store or private-label brands and discounted prices. Sears then attempted to portray itself as a retailer with "everyday low pricing" and as a collection of "power formats" focusing on popular brands of merchandise. None of these actions improved Sears' performance. Finally, Sears' top management acknowledged that, "We need to much more clearly identify our target customers and needs." Sears decided to focus on "the middle 60 percent of the population that recognizes value." Having refined the company's target customer group and need(s) to be satisfied, the Sears merchandising formula (means) became more focused and effective, thus demonstrating the tight linkage among all three aspects of business definition. The result was that Sears' sales and profits substantially improved in the mid-1990s.

Business Mission

An organization's business mission complements its business definition. As a written statement, a mission underscores the scope of an organization's operations apparent in its business definition and reflects management's vision of what the organization seeks to do. While there is no overall definition for all mission statements, most statements describe an organization's purpose with reference to its customers, products or services, markets, philosophy, and technology.[4] Some mission statements are generally stated such as that for Saturn Corporation, a division of General Motors. Saturn's mission is to:

> Market vehicles developed and manufactured in the United States that are world leaders in quality, cost, and customer satisfaction through the integration of people, technology, and business systems and to transfer knowledge, technology, and experience throughout General Motors.

Others are more specifically written like that for Solartronics Corporation. Solartronics Corporation aspires

> to serve the discriminating purchasers of home entertainment products who approach their purchase in a deliberate manner with heavy consideration of long-term benefits. We will emphasize home entertainment products with superior performance, style, reliability, and value that require representative display, professional selling, trained service, and brand acceptance—retailed through reputable electronic specialists to those consumers whom the company can most effectively service.

Mission statements also apply to not-for-profit organizations. For instance, the mission of the American Red Cross is

> to improve the quality of human life; to enhance self-reliance and concern for others; and to help people avoid, prepare for, and cope with emergencies.

A carefully crafted mission statement that succinctly conveys organizational purpose can provide numerous benefits to an organization including focus to its marketing effort. It can (1) crystallize management's vision of the organization's long-term direction and character, (2) provide guidance in identifying, pursuing, and evaluating market and product opportunities, and (3) inspire and challenge employees to do those things that are valued by the organization and its customers. It also provides direction for setting business goals or objectives.

Business Goals

Goals or objectives convert the organization's mission into tangible actions and results that are to be achieved, often within a specific time frame. For example, the 3M Company emphasizes research and development and innovation in its business mission. This view is made tangible in one of the company's goals: 30 percent of 3M's annual revenues must come from company products that are less than four years old.[5]

Goals or objectives divide into three major categories: production, financial, and marketing. Production goals or objectives apply to the use of manufacturing and service capacity and to product and service quality. Financial goals or objectives focus on return on investment, return on sales, profit, cash flow, and shareholder wealth. Marketing goals or objectives emphasize market share, marketing productivity, sales volume, profit, customer satisfaction, and value. When production, financial, and marketing goals or objectives are combined, they represent a composite picture of organizational purpose within a specific time frame; accordingly, they must complement one another.

Goal or objective setting should be problem-centered and future-oriented. Because goals or objectives represent statements of what the organization wishes to achieve in a specific time frame, they implicitly arise from an understanding of the current situation. Therefore, managers need an appraisal of operations or a *situation analysis*, to determine reasons for the gap between what was or is expected and what has happened or will happen. If performance has met expectations, the question arises as to future directions. If performance has not met expectations, managers must diagnose the reasons for this difference and enact a program for remedying the situation. Chapter 3 provides an expanded discussion on performing a situation analysis.

■ IDENTIFYING AND FRAMING ORGANIZATIONAL GROWTH OPPORTUNITIES

Once the character and direction of the organization have been outlined in its business definition, mission, and goals or objectives, the practice of strategic marketing management enters an entrepreneurial phase. Using business definition, mission, and goals as a guide, the search for and evaluation of organizational growth opportunities can begin.

Converting Environmental Opportunities Into Organizational Opportunities

Three questions help marketing managers decide whether certain environmental opportunities represent viable organizational growth opportunities. They are:

- What might we do?
- What do we do best?
- What must we do?

Each of these questions assists in identifying and framing organizational growth opportunities. They also highlight major concepts in strategic marketing management.

The *what might we do* question introduces the concept of *environmental opportunity*. Unmet or changing consumer needs, unsatisfied buyer groups, and new means or technology for delivering value to prospective buyers represent sources of environmental opportunities for organizations. In this regard, environmental opportunities are boundless. However, the mere presence of an environmental opportunity does not mean that an organizational growth opportunity exists. Two additional questions must be asked.

The *what do we do best* question introduces the concept of organizational capability, or distinctive competency. *Distinctive competency* describes an organization's unique strengths or qualities, including skills, technologies, or resources that distinguish it from other organizations.[6] In order for any of an organization's strengths or qualities to be considered truly distinctive and a source of competitive advantage, two criteria must be satisfied. First, the strength must be imperfectly imitable by competitors. That is, competitors cannot replicate a skill (such as the delivery competency of Domino's Pizza) easily or without a sizable investment of time and money. Second, the strength should make a significant contribution to the benefits perceived by customers and, by doing so, provide superior value to them. For example, the ability to engage in technological innovation that is wanted and provides value to customers is a distinctive competency. Consider the Safety Razor Division of the Gillette Company. Its distinctive competencies lie in three areas: (1) shaving technology and development, (2) high-volume manufacturing of precision metal and plastic products, and (3) marketing of mass-distributed consumer package goods.[7] These competencies were responsible for the Sensor razor, a technological innovation, which sustained Gillette's dominance of the men's and later the women's wet-shaving market in the 1990s.

Finally, the *what must we do* question introduces the concept of success requirements in an industry or market. *Success requirements* are basic tasks that an organization must perform in a market or industry to compete successfully. These requirements are subtle in nature and often overlooked. For example, distribution and inventory control are critical success factors in the cosmetics industry. Firms competing in the personal computer industry recognize that the requirements for success include low-cost production capabilities, access to distribution channels, and continuous innovation in software development.

The linkage among environmental opportunity, distinctive competency, and success requirements will determine whether an organizational opportunity exists. A clearly defined statement of success requirements serves as a device for matching an environmental opportunity with an organization's distinctive competencies. If *what must be done* is inconsistent with *what can be done* to capitalize on an environmental opportunity, an organizational growth opportunity will fail to materialize. Too often organizations ignore this linkage and pursue seemingly lucrative environmental opportunities that are doomed from the start. Exxon Corporation learned this lesson painfully after investing $500 million in the office products market over a ten-year period only to see the venture fail. After the company abandoned this venture, a former Exxon executive summed up what had been learned: "Don't get involved where you don't have the skills. It's hard enough to make money at what you're good at."[8] By clearly establishing the linkages necessary for success before taking any action, an organization can minimize its risk of failure. An executive for L'eggs hosiery illustrates this point when specifying his new-venture criteria:

> [P]roducts that can be sold through food and drugstore outlets, are purchased by women, . . . can be easily and distinctly packaged, and comprise at least a $500 million retail market not already dominated by one or two major producers.[9]

When one considers L'eggs' past successes, it is apparent that whatever environmental opportunities are pursued will be consistent with what L'eggs does best, as illustrated by past achievements in markets whose success requirements are similar. An expanded discussion of these points is found in Chapter 4.

SWOT Analysis

SWOT analysis is a formal framework for identifying and framing organizational growth opportunities. SWOT is an acronym for an organization's *S*trengths and *W*eaknesses and external *O*pportunities and *T*hreats. It is an easy-to-use framework for focusing attention on the fact that an organizational growth opportunity results from a good fit between an organization's internal capabilities (apparent in its strengths and weaknesses) and its external environment reflected in the presence of environmental opportunities and threats. Many organizations also perform a SWOT analysis as part of their goal or objective-setting process.

Exhibit 1.1 displays a SWOT analysis framework depicting representative entries for internal strengths and weaknesses and external opportunities and threats. A strength is something that an organization is good at doing or some characteristic that gives the organization an important capability. Something an organization lacks or does poorly relative to other organizations is a weakness. Opportunities represent external developments or conditions in the environment that have favorable implications for the organization. Threats, on the other hand, pose dangers to the welfare of the organization.

A properly conducted SWOT analysis goes beyond the simple preparation of lists. Attention needs to be placed on evaluating strengths, weaknesses, opportunities, and threats and drawing conclusions about how each might affect the organization. The following questions might be asked once strengths, weaknesses, opportunities, and threats have been identified:

1. Which internal strengths represent distinctive competencies? Do these strengths compare favorably with what are believed to be market or industry success requirements? Looking at Exhibit 1.1 on page 6, for example, does "proven innovation skill" strength represent a distinctive competency and a market success requirement?

2. Which internal weaknesses disqualify the organization from pursuing certain opportunities? Look again at Exhibit 1.1, and note that the organization acknowledges that it has a "weak distribution network and a subpar salesforce." How might this organizational weakness affect the opportunity described as

EXHIBIT 1.1

Sample SWOT Analysis Framework and Representative Examples

Selected Internal Factors	Representative		Selected External Factors	Representative	
	Strengths	Weaknesses		Opportunities	Threats
Management	Experienced management talent	Lack of management depth	Economic	Upturn in the business cycle; evidence of growing personal disposable income	Adverse shifts in foreign exchange rates
Marketing	Well thought of by buyers; effective advertising program	Weak distribution network; subpar salesforce	Competition	Complacency among domestic competitors	Entry of lower-cost foreign competitors
Manufacturing	Available manufacturing capacity	Higher overall production costs relative to key competitors	Consumer trends	Unfulfilled customer needs on high and low end of product category suggesting a product line expansion possibility	Growing preference for private-label products
R & D	Proven innovation skills	Poor track record in bringing innovations to the marketplace	Technology	Patent protection of complementary technology ending	Newer substitute technologies imminent
Finance	Little debt relative to industry average	Weak cash flow position	Legal/ regulatory	Falling trade barriers in attractive foreign markets	Increased U.S. regulation of product-testing procedures and labeling
Offerings	Unique, high-quality products	Too narrow a product line	Industry/ market structure	New distribution channels evolving that reach a broader customer population	Low-entry barriers for new competitors

"new distribution channels evolving that reach a broader customer population"?

3. Does a pattern emerge from the listing of strengths, weaknesses, opportunities, and threats? Inspection of Exhibit 1.1 reveals that low-entry barriers into the market/industry may contribute to the entry of lower-cost foreign competitors. This does not bode well for domestic competitors labeled as "complacent" and the organization's acknowledged high production costs.

■ FORMULATING PRODUCT-MARKET STRATEGIES

In practice, organizational opportunities frequently emerge from an organization's existing markets or from newly identified markets. Opportunities also arise for existing, improved, or new products and services. Matching products and markets to form product-market strategies is the subject of the next set of decision processes.

Product-market strategies consist of plans for matching an organization's existing or potential offerings with the needs of markets, informing markets that the offering exists, having offerings available at the right time and place to facilitate exchange, and assigning prices to offerings. In short, a product-market strategy involves selecting specific markets and profitably reaching them through an integrated program called a *marketing mix.*

Exhibit 1.2 classifies product-market strategies according to the match between offerings and markets.[10] The operational implications and requirements of each strategy are briefly described in the following subsections.[11]

Market-Penetration Strategy

A *market-penetration strategy* dictates that an organization seek to gain greater dominance in a market in which it already has an offering. This strategy involves attempts to increase present buyers' usage or consumption rates of the offering, attract buyers of competing offerings, or stimulate product trial among potential customers. The mix of marketing activities might include lower prices for the offerings, expanded distribution to provide wider coverage of an existing market, and heavier promotional efforts extolling the "unique" advantages of an organization's offering over competing offerings. Coca-Cola uses all of these activities in attempting to achieve its announced goal of increasing its market share from 42 percent to 50 percent of the U.S. soft drink market by the year 2000.[12]

Several organizations have attempted to gain dominance by promoting more frequent and varied usage of their offering. For example, the Florida Orange Growers Association advocates drinking orange juice throughout the day rather than for breakfast only. Airlines stimulate usage through a variety of reduced-fare programs and various family-travel packages, designed to reach the primary traveler's spouse and children.

Marketing managers should consider a number of factors before adopting a penetration strategy. First, they must examine market growth. A penetration strategy is usually more effective in a growth market. Attempts to increase market share when volume is stable often result in aggressive retaliatory actions by competitors. Sec-

EXHIBIT 1.2

Product-Market Strategies

		Markets	
		Existing	*New*
Offerings	*Existing*	Market penetration	Market development
	New	New offering development	Diversification

ond, they must consider competitive reaction. Procter and Gamble implemented a penetration strategy for its Folger's coffee in selected East Coast cities, only to run head-on into an equally aggressive reaction from General Foods' Maxwell House Division. According to one observer of the competitive situation:

> When Folger's mailed millions of coupons offering consumers 45 cents off on a one-pound can of coffee, General Foods countered with newspaper coupons of its own. When Folger's gave retailers 15 percent discounts from the list price . . . , General Foods met them head-on. [General Foods] let Folger's lead off with a TV blitz. . . . Then [General Foods] saturated the airwaves.[13]

The result of this struggle was no change in market share for either firm. Third, marketing managers must consider the capacity of the market to increase usage or consumption rates and the availability of new buyers. Both are particularly relevant when viewed from the perspective of the conversion costs involved in capturing buyers from competitors, stimulating usage, and attracting new users.

Market-Development Strategy

A *market-development strategy* dictates that an organization introduce its existing offerings to markets other than those it is currently serving. Examples include introducing existing products to different geographical areas (including international expansion) or different buying publics. For example, Harley-Davidson engaged in a market-development strategy when it entered Japan, Germany, and France. O. M. Scott and Sons Company employed this strategy when it moved from the home lawn-improvement market to large users of lawn-care products, such as golf courses and home construction contractors.

The mix of marketing activities used must often be varied to reach different markets with differing buying patterns and requirements. Reaching new markets often requires modification of the basic offering, different distribution outlets, or a change in sales effort and advertising.

Like the market penetration strategy, market development involves a careful consideration of competitor strengths and weaknesses and competitor retaliation potential. Moreover, because the firm seeks new buyers, it must understand their number, motivation, and buying patterns in order to develop marketing activities successfully. Finally, the firm must consider its strengths, in terms of adaptability to new markets, in order to evaluate the potential success of the venture.

Market development in the international arena has grown in importance and usually takes one of four forms: (1) exporting, (2) licensing, (3) joint venture, or (4) direct investment.[14] Each option has advantages and disadvantages. Exporting involves marketing the same offering in another country either directly (through sales offices) or through intermediaries in a foreign country. Since this approach typically requires minimal capital investment and is easy to initiate, it is a popular option for developing foreign markets. Procter and Gamble, for instance, exports its deodorants, soaps, fragrances, shampoos, and other health and beauty products to the newly emerging democracies in Eastern Europe and the former Soviet Union. Licensing is a contractual arrangement whereby one firm (licensee) is given the rights to patents, trademarks, know-how, and other intangible assets by their owner (licensor) in return for a royalty (usually 5 percent of gross sales) or a fee. For example, Cadbury Schweppes PLC, a London-based multinational firm, has licensed Hershey Foods to sell its candies in the United States for a fee of $300 million. Licensing provides a low-risk, quick, and capital-free entry into a foreign market. However, the licensor usually has no control over production and marketing by the licensee. A joint venture, often called a strategic alliance, involves investment by both a foreign firm and a local company to create a new entity in the host country. The two companies share ownership, control, and profits of the entity. Joint ventures are popular because one company may not have the necessary financial, technical, or managerial resources to enter a market alone. This approach also often ensures against trade barriers being imposed on the foreign firm by the government of the host company. Japanese companies frequently engage in joint ventures with American and European firms to gain access to foreign markets. A problem frequently arising from joint ventures is that the partners do not always agree on how the new entity should be run. Direct investment in a manufacturing and/or assembly facility in a foreign market is the most risky option and requires the greatest commitment. However, it brings the firm closer to its customers and may be the most profitable approach toward developing foreign markets. For these reasons, direct investment must be evaluated closely in terms of benefits and costs. Direct investment often follows one of the three other approaches to foreign-market entry. For example, PepsiCo first exported Pepsi-Cola to the then Soviet Union in 1972. By early 1997, PepsiCo operated over 30 bottling plants there.

Product-Development Strategy

A *product-development strategy* dictates that the organization create new offerings for existing markets. The approach taken may be to develop totally new offerings (product innovation) to enhance the value to customers of existing offerings (product augmentation), or to broaden the existing line of offerings by adding different sizes, forms, flavors, and so forth (product line extension). Rollerblades are an example of product innovation, as is the introduction of the "Cash Management Account" by Merrill Lynch in the financial services industry. Product augmentation can be achieved in numerous ways. One is to bundle complementary items or services with an existing offering. For example, programming services, application aids, and training programs for buyers enhance the value of personal computers. Another way is to improve the functional performance of the offering. Producers of facsimile machines have done this by improving print quality. Many types of product-line extensions are possible. Personal-care companies market deodorants in powder, spray, and liquid forms; Quaker Oats produces nine flavors of Gatorade; and Frito-Lay offers its Lay's potato chips in a number of package sizes.

Companies successful at developing and commercializing new offerings lead their industries in sales growth and profitability. The likelihood of success is increased if the development effort results in offerings that satisfy a clearly understood buyer need. In the toy industry, for instance, these needs translate into products with three qualities: (1) lasting play value, (2) the ability to be shared with other children, and (3) the ability to stimulate a child's imagination.[15] Successful commercialization occurs when the offering can be communicated and delivered to a well-defined buyer group at a price it is willing and able to pay.

Important considerations in planning a product-development strategy concern the market size and volume necessary for the effort to be profitable, the magnitude and timing of competitive response, the impact of the new product on existing offerings, and the capacity (in terms of human and financial investment and technology) of the organization to deliver the offering to the market(s). More importantly, successful new offerings must have a significant "point of difference" reflected in superior product or service characteristics that deliver unique and wanted benefits to consumers. Two examples from the cereal industry illustrate this view. In 1995, General Mills introduced Fringos, a sweetened cereal flake about the size of a corn chip. Consumers were supposed to snack on them, but they didn't.[16] The point of difference was not significant enough to get consumers to switch from competing snacks such as popcorn, potato chips, or tortilla chips. On the other hand, Nabisco's fat-free Snackwell Cereal Bars became the number one brand in the $700-million snack-bar category in 1996 by delivering a unique and wanted benefit.[17]

The potential for cannibalism must be considered with a product-development strategy.[18] *Cannibalism* occurs when sales of a new product or service come at the expense of sales of existing products or services already marketed by the firm. For example, it is estimated that two-thirds of Gillette's Sensor razor volume came from the company's other razors and shaving systems. Cannibalism of this degree is likely to occur in many product-development programs. The issue faced by the manager is whether it detracts from the overall profitability of the organization's total mix of offerings.

Diversification

Diversification involves the development or acquisition of offerings new to the organization and the introduction of those offerings to publics not previously served by the organization. Many firms have adopted this strategy in recent years to take advantage of perceived growth opportunities. Yet diversification is often a high-risk strategy because both the offering (and often its underlying technology) and the public or market served are new to the organization.

Consider the following examples of failed diversification.[19] Anheuser-Busch recorded 17 years of losses with its Eagle Snacks Division and incurred a $206 million write-off when the division was finally shut down. Rohr Industries, a subcontractor in the aerospace industry, reported a $59.9 million write-off on a mass-transit diversification. Singer's effort to develop a business-machines venture over a ten-year period was abandoned while still unprofitable. Gerber Products Company, which holds 70 percent of the U.S. baby-food market, has been mostly unsuccessful in diversifying into child-care centers, toys, furniture, and adult food and beverages. Coca-Cola's many attempts at diversification—acquiring wine companies, a movie studio, and a pasta manufacturer, and producing television game shows—have also proven to be largely unsuccessful. These examples highlight the importance of understanding the link between market success requirements and an organization's distinctive competency. In each of these cases, a bridge was not made between these two concepts and thus an organizational opportunity was not realized.

Still, diversifications can be successful. Successful diversifications typically result from an organization's attempt to apply its distinctive competency in reaching new markets with new offerings. By relying on its marketing expertise and extensive distribution system, Borden has had success with offerings ranging from milk to glue, and Procter and Gamble with offerings ranging from cake mixes to disposable diapers.

Strategy Selection

A recurrent issue in strategic marketing management is determining the consistency of product-market strategies with the organization's definition, mission and capabilities, market capacity and behavior, environmental forces, and competitive activities. Proper analysis of these factors depends on the availability and evaluation of relevant information. Information on markets should include data on size, buying behavior, and requirements. Information on environmental forces such as social, legal, political, and economic changes is necessary to determine the future viability of the organization's offerings and the markets served. In recent years, for example, organizations have had to alter or adapt their product-market strategies because of political actions (deregulation), social changes (increase in the number of employed women), economic fluctuations (income shifts and changes in disposable personal income), attitudes (value consciousness), and population shifts (city to suburb and northern to southern United States)—to name just a few of the environmental changes. Competitive activities must be monitored to ascertain their existing or possible strategies and performance in satisfying buyer needs. Considerations in the acquisition and management of information are discussed in Chapter 5.

In practice, the strategy selection decision is based on an analysis of the costs and benefits of alternative strategies and their probabilities of success. For example, a manager may compare the costs and benefits involved in further penetrating an existing

EXHIBIT 1.3

Decision-Tree Format

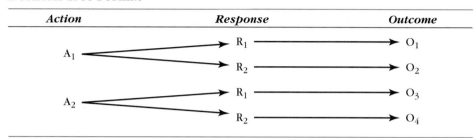

Action	Response	Outcome
A_1	R_1	O_1
	R_2	O_2
A_2	R_1	O_3
	R_2	O_4

market to those associated with introducing the existing product to a new market. It is important to make a careful analysis of competitive structure; market growth, decline, or shifts; and opportunity costs (potential benefits not obtained). The product or service itself may dictate a strategy change. If the product has been purchased by all of the buyers it is going to attract in an existing market, opportunities for growth beyond replacement purchases are reduced. This situation would indicate a need to search out new buyers (markets) or to develop new products or services for present markets.

The probabilities of success of the various strategies must then be considered. A. T. Kearney, a management consulting firm, has provided rough probability estimates of success for each of the four basic strategies.[20] The probability of a successful diversification is 1 in 20. The probability of successfully introducing an existing product into a new market (market-development strategy) is 1 in 4. There is a 50–50 chance of success for a new product being introduced into an existing market (product-development strategy). Finally, minor modification of an offering directed toward its existing market (market-penetration strategy) has the highest probability of success.

A useful technique for gauging potential outcomes of alternative marketing strategies is to array possible actions, the responses to these actions, and the outcomes in the form of a decision tree, so named because of the branching out of responses from action taken. This implies that for any action taken, certain responses can be anticipated, each with its own specific outcomes. Exhibit 1.3 shows a decision tree.

As an example, consider a situation in which a marketing manager must decide between a market-penetration strategy and a market-development strategy. Suppose the manager recognizes that competitors may react aggressively or passively to either strategy. This situation can be displayed vividly using the decision-tree scheme, as shown in Exhibit 1.4. This representation allows the manager to consider actions,

EXHIBIT 1.4

Sample Decision Tree

Action	Response	Outcome
Market-penetration strategy	Aggressive competition	Estimated profit of $2 million
	Passive competition	Estimated profit of $3 million
Market-development strategy	Aggressive competition	Estimated profit of $1 million
	Passive competition	Estimated profit of $4 million

responses, and outcomes simultaneously. The decision tree shows that the highest profits will result if a market-development strategy is enacted and competitors react passively. The manager must resolve the question of competitive reaction because an aggressive response will plunge the profit to $1 million, which is less than either outcome under the market-penetration strategy. The manager must rely on informed judgment to assess subjectively the likelihood of competitive response. Chapters 3 and 5 provide a more detailed description of decision analysis and its application.

The Marketing Mix

Matching offerings and markets requires recognition of the other marketing activities available to the marketing manager. Combined with the offering, these activities form the marketing mix.

A marketing mix typically encompasses activities controllable by the organization. These include the kind of product, service, or idea offered (product strategy), how it will be communicated to buyers (communication strategy), the method for distributing the offering to buyers (channel strategy), and the amount buyers will pay for the offering (price strategy). Each of these individual strategies is described later in this book. Here it is sufficient to note that each element of the marketing mix plays a role in stimulating a market's (buyers') willingness and ability to buy. For example, communications—personal selling, advertising, sales promotion, and public relations—informs and assures buyers that the offering will meet their needs. Marketing channels satisfy buyers' shopping patterns and purchase requirements in terms of point-of-purchase information and offering availability. Price represents the value or benefits provided by the offering.

The appropriate marketing mix for a product or service depends on the success requirements of the markets at which it is directed. The "rightness" of a product, communication, channel, or price strategy can be interpreted only in the context of markets served. Recognition of this fact has prompted the use of regional marketing, whereby different marketing mixes are employed to accommodate unique consumer preferences and competitive conditions in different geographical areas. For instance, Frito-Lay's Tostitos brand of tortilla chips is marketed as a specialty product sold mostly through delicatessens in some northeastern states. The brand's communication and price policies are not aggressive in these states because of fragmented competition. Tortilla chips in southwestern states are a commodity-type product sold by many competitors through supermarkets. The Tostitos brand is therefore supported in that geographical area by more aggressive price and communication programs. Firms that market products and services worldwide often "glocalize" their marketing mixes. That is, global decisions are made in such areas as product development, but decisions related to advertising, pricing, and distribution are arrived at by local (country-specific) marketing managers. A prime example of glocalization is found in the marketing of Swatch watches.[21] In developed countries, Swatch watches are marketed as a fashion item; in less developed countries, the marketing mix emphasizes simple design, affordable cost, and functional qualities.

In addition to being consistent with the needs of markets served, a marketing mix must be consistent with the organization's capacity, and the individual activities must complement one another. Several questions offer direction in evaluating an organization's marketing mix. First, is the marketing mix internally consistent? Do the individual activities complement one another to form a whole, as opposed to fragmented pieces? Does the mix fit the organization, the market, and the environment into which it will be introduced? Second, are buyers more sensitive to some marketing mix activities than to others? For example, are they more likely to respond favorably to a decrease in price or an increase in advertising? Third, what are the costs of performing marketing mix activities and the costs of attracting and retaining buyers?

Do these costs exceed their benefits? Can the organization afford the marketing mix expenditures? Finally, is the marketing mix properly timed? For example, are communications scheduled to coincide with product availability? Is the entire marketing mix timely with respect to the buying cycle of consumers, competitor actions, and the ebb and flow of environmental forces?

Implementation of the marketing mix is as much an art as a science. Successful implementation requires an understanding of markets, environmental forces, organizational capacity, and marketing mix activities with a healthy respect for competitor reactions. These topics are raised again in Chapter 11. An example of an implementation with less than successful results is that of A&P's WEO (Where Economy Originates) program. Prior to implementing the program, A&P had watched its sales volume plateau with shrinking profits, while other supermarket chains continued to increase sales volume and profits. When the WEO program was initiated, it emphasized discount pricing (price strategy) with heavy promotional expenditures (communication strategy). The program increased sales volume by $800 million but produced a profit loss of over $50 million. In the words of one industry observer at the time:

> Its competitors are convinced that A&P's assault with WEO was doomed from the start. Too many of its stores are relics of a bygone era. Many are in poor locations [distribution strategy]. . . . They are just not big enough to support the tremendous volume that is necessary to make a discounting operation profitable [capacity] . . . stores lack shelf space for stocking general merchandise items, such as housewares and children's clothing [product strategy].[22]

The product-market strategy employed by A&P could be classified as a market-penetration strategy. Its implementation, however, could be questioned in terms of internal consistency, costs of the marketing mix activities, and fit with organizational capacity. Moreover, the retail grocery industry was plagued at the time by rising food costs, an environmental force that had a destructive effect on strategy success.

■ BUDGETING MARKETING, FINANCIAL, AND PRODUCTION RESOURCES

The fourth phase in the strategic marketing management process is budgeting. A budget is a formal, quantitative expression of an organization's planning and strategy initiatives expressed in financial terms. A well-prepared budget meshes and balances an organization's financial, production, and marketing resources so that overall organizational goals or objectives are attained.

An organization's master budget consists of two parts: (1) an operating budget and (2) a financial budget. The operating budget focuses on an organization's income statement. Since the operating budget projects future revenues and expenses, it is sometimes referred to as a *pro forma* income statement or profit plan. The financial budget focuses on the effect that the operating budget and other initiatives (such as capital expenditures) will have on the organization's cash position. For example, the 1999 master budget for Saturn Corporation will include an income statement that details revenues, expenses, and profit for its three existing models—a small sedan, a station wagon, and a coupe—and its planned midsize car code-named *Innovate*. Its financial budget will include the $900 million Saturn expects to invest in capital expenditures to manufacture the planned midsize car.[23]

In addition to the operating and financial budget, many organizations prepare supplemental special budgets such as an advertising and sales budget, and related reports tied to the master budget. For example, a report showing how revenues, costs, and profits change under different marketing decisions and competitive and economic conditions is often prepared. As indicated, budgeting is more than an accounting function. It is an essential element of strategic marketing management.

A complete description of the budgetary process is beyond the scope of this section. However, Chapter 2, Financial Aspects of Marketing Management, provides an overview of cost concepts and behavior. It also describes useful analytical tools for dealing with the financial dimensions of strategic marketing management, including cost-volume-profit analysis and the preparation of *pro forma* income statements.

■ DEVELOPING REFORMULATION AND RECOVERY STRATEGIES

Reformulation and recovery strategies form the cornerstone of adaptive behavior in organizations. Strategies are rarely timeless. Changing markets, economic conditions, and competitive behavior require periodic, if not sudden, adjustments in strategy.

Marketing audit and control procedures are fundamental to the development of reformulation and recovery strategies. The *marketing audit* has been defined as follows:

> A marketing audit is a comprehensive, systematic, independent, and periodic examination of a company's—or business unit's—marketing environment, objectives, strategies and activities with a view of determining problem areas and opportunities and recommending a plan of action to improve the company's marketing performance.[24]

The audit process directs the manager's attention to both the strategic fit of the organization with its environment and the operational aspects of the marketing program. Strategic aspects of the marketing audit address the synoptic question "Are we doing the right things?" Operational aspects address an equally synoptic question "Are we doing things right?"

The distinction between strategic and operational perspectives, as well as the implementation of each, is examined in Chapter 10. Suffice it to say here that marketing audit and control procedures underlie the process of defining the organization's business, mission, and goals or objectives, identifying external opportunities and threats and internal strengths and weaknesses, formulating product-market strategies and marketing mix activities, and budgeting resources. The intellectual process of developing reformulation and recovery strategies during the planning process serves two important purposes. First, it forces the manager to consider the "what if" questions. For example, "What if an unexpected environmental threat arises that renders a strategy obsolete?" or "What if competitive and market response to a strategy is inconsistent with what was originally expected?" Such questions focus the manager's attention on the sensitivity of results to assumptions made in the strategy-development process. Second, preplanning of reformulation and recovery strategies, or *contingency plans,* leads to a faster reaction time in implementing remedial action. Marshaling and reorienting resources is a time-consuming process itself without additional time lost in planning.

■ DRAFTING A MARKETING PLAN

A marketing plan embodies the strategic marketing management process. It is a formal, written document that describes the context and scope of an organization's marketing effort to achieve defined goals or objectives within a specific future time period. Marketing plans go by a variety of names depending upon their particular focus. For example, there are business marketing plans, product marketing plans, and brand marketing plans. At Frito-Lay, Inc., for instance, a marketing plan is drafted for a particular business (snack chips), for a product class (potato chips, tortilla chips), and for specific brands (Lay's potato chips, Ruffles potato chips). Marketing plans also have a time dimension. Short-run marketing plans typically focus on a one-year period and are called annual marketing plans. Long-run marketing plans often have a three- to five-year planning horizon.

A formal, written marketing plan represents a distillation of and the attention and thought given the five interrelated analytical processes in this chapter. It is the tangible result of an intellectual effort. As a written document, a marketing plan also exhibits certain stylistic elements. While there is no "generic" marketing plan that applies to all organizations and all situations, marketing plans follow a general format. Appendix A provides an actual example of a condensed marketing plan for Paradise Kitchens,® Inc., a company that produces and markets a unique line of single-serve and microwaveable Southwestern/Mexican-style frozen chili products. This example illustrates both the substance and style of a 5-year marketing plan.

■ MARKETING ETHICS AND SOCIAL RESPONSIBILITY

On a final note, it must be emphasized that matters of ethics and social responsibility permeate every aspect of the strategic marketing management process. Indeed, most marketing decisions involve some degree of moral judgment and reflect an organization's orientation toward the publics with which it interacts.[25] Enlightened marketing executives no longer subscribe to the view that if an action is legal, then it is also ethical and socially responsible. These executives are sensitive to the fact that the marketplace is populated by individuals and groups with diverse value systems. Moreover, they recognize that their actions will be judged publicly by others with different values and interests.

Enlightened ethical and socially responsible decisions arise from the ability of marketers to discern the precise issues involved and their willingness to take action even when the outcome may negatively affect their standing in an organization or the company's financial interests. Although the moral foundations on which marketing decisions are made will vary among individuals and organizations, failure to recognize issues and take appropriate action is the least ethical and most socially irresponsible approach. A positive approach to ethical and socially responsible behavior is evident in Anheuser-Busch's "Know When to Say When" campaign, which advocates responsible drinking of alcoholic beverages.[26] The company spends as much for advertising on this campaign as it does for its flagship brands (Michelob, Busch, and Natural Light). Anheuser-Busch executives acknowledge the potential for alcohol abuse and are willing to forgo business generated by misuse of the company's products. These executives have discerned the issues and have recognized an ethical obligation to present and potential customers. They have also recognized the company's social responsibility to the general public by encouraging safe driving and responsible drinking habits.

NOTES

1. Steve Harrell, strategic planner at General Electric, quoted in Philip Kotler, *Marketing Management,* 9th ed. (Upper Saddle River, NJ: Prentice Hall, 1997): 63.

2. Derek F. Abell, *Defining the Business: The Starting Point of Strategic Planning* (Upper Saddle River, NJ: Prentice Hall, 1980); Roger A. Kerin, Vijay Mahajan, and P. Rajan Varadarajan, *Contemporary Perspectives on Strategic Marketing Planning* (Boston: Allyn and Bacon, 1990).

3. "Strategic Planning," *Business Week* (August 26, 1996): 49; Susan Chandler, "Drill Bits, Paint Thinner, Eyeliner," *Business Week* (September 25, 1995): 84-85; Robert Berner, "Sears' Softer Side Paid Off in Hard Cash This Christmas," *The Wall Street Journal* (December 29, 1995): B4.

4. Jeffrey Abraham, *The Mission Statement Book* (Berkeley, CA: Ten Speed Press, 1995). For examples of mission statements, see Patricia Jones and Larry Kahaner, *Say It and Live It: The 50 Corporate Mission Statements That Hit the Mark* (New York: Currency/Doubleday, 1995).

5. "The Mass Production of Ideas, and Other Impossibilities," *The Economist* (March 18, 1995): 72.

6. Robert A. Pitts and David Lei, *Strategic Management: Building and Sustaining Competitive Advantage* (St. Paul, MN: West Publishing Company, 1996): 6.

7. "Gillette Safety Razor Division: The Blank Cassette Project," Harvard Business School case #9-574-058.

8. "Exxon's Flop in Field of Office Gear Shows Diversification Perils," *The Wall Street Journal* (September 3, 1985): 1*ff*.

9. "Hanes Expands L'eggs to the Entire Family," *Business Week* (June 14, 1975): 57*ff*.

10. This classification is adapted from H. Igor Ansoff, *Corporate Strategy* (New York: Mc-Graw-Hill, 1964), Chapter 6. An extended version of this classification is presented in George Day, "A Strategic Perspective on Product Planning," *Journal of Contemporary Business* (Spring 1975): 1-34.

11. For an extended discussion on product-market strategies, see Roger A. Kerin, Vijay Mahajan, and P. Rajan Varadarajan, *Contemporary Perspectives on Strategic Market Planning* (Boston: Allyn and Bacon, 1990): Chapter 6.

12. Robert Frank, "Soft-Drink Prices May Be Softening on Shelves," *The Wall Street Journal* (September 12, 1996): B10.

13. H. Menzies, "Why Folger's Is Getting Creamed Back East," *Fortune* (July 17, 1978): 69.

14. Warren J. Keegan, *Global Marketing Management,* 5th ed. (Upper Saddle River, NJ: Prentice Hall, 1995): 351-59.

15. "Hasbro, Inc.," in Eric N. Berkowitz, Roger A. Kerin, Steven N. Hartley, and William Rudelius, *Marketing,* 5th ed. (Chicago, IL: Richard D. Irwin, 1997): 656-657.

16. Greg Burns, "Has General Mills Had Its Wheaties?" *Business Week* (May 8, 1995): 68-69.

17. "1995 Edison Best New Products Awards Winners," *Marketing News* (May 6, 1996): Supplement.

18. For an extended treatment of this topic and additional examples, see Roger A. Kerin and Dwight Riskey, "Product Cannibalism," in Sidney Levy, ed., *Marketing Manager's Handbook* (Chicago: Dartnell Company, 1994).

19. These examples are from "How Eagle Became Extinct," *Business Week* (March 4, 1996): 68-69; "Some Things Don't Go Better with Coke," *Forbes* (March 21, 1988): 34-35; and "Gerber Goes Global with 'Superbrand' Concept," *Marketing News* (September 16, 1991): 21.

20. These estimates were reported in "The Breakdown of U.S. Innovation," *Business Week* (February 16, 1976): 56*ff*.

21. Management Briefing: Marketing (New York: Conference Board, January 1990): 5.

22. Robert F. Hartley, *Marketing Mistakes,* 5th ed. (New York: John Wiley & Sons, 1992). Items in brackets added for illustrative purposes.

23. "GM's Saturn Division Plans to Build a Midsize Car to Keep Customers Loyal," *The Wall Street Journal* (August 6, 1996): A4.

24. Philip Kotler, *Marketing Management,* 9th ed. (Upper Saddle River, NJ: Prentice Hall, 1997): 777.

25. For an extensive discussion of ethics in marketing, see Gene Lazniak and Patrick E. Murphy, *Ethical Marketing Decisions: The Higher Road* (Boston: Allyn and Bacon, 1993).

26. This example is based on *Fighting Alcohol Abuse Through Awareness & Education* (St. Louis: Anheuser-Busch Companies, 1994); and "Selling Sobriety," *Dallas Times Herald* (March 19, 1990): A9.

A Sample Marketing Plan

Crafting a marketing plan is hard, but satisfying, work. When completed, a marketing plan serves as a roadmap that details the context and scope of marketing activities including, but not limited to, a mission statement, goals and objectives, a situation analysis, growth opportunities, target market(s) and marketing (mix) program, a budget, and an implementation schedule.

As a written document, the plan conveys in words the analysis, ideas, and aspirations of its author pertaining to a business, product, and/or brand marketing effort. How a marketing plan is written communicates not only the substance of the marketing effort, but also the professionalism of the author. Writing style will not overcome limitations in substance. However, a poorly written marketing plan can detract from the perceived substance of the plan.

■ WRITING AND STYLE CONSIDERATIONS

Given the importance of a carefully crafted marketing plan, authors of marketing plans adhere to certain guidelines. The following writing and style guidelines generally apply:

- Use a direct, professional writing style. Use appropriate business and marketing terms without jargon. Present and future tenses with active voice are generally better than past tense and passive voice.

- Be positive and specific. At the same time, avoid superlatives ("terrific," "wonderful"). Specifics are better than glittering generalities. Use numbers for impact, justifying computations and projections with facts or reasonable quantitative assumptions where possible.

- Use bullet points for succinctness and emphasis. As with the list you are reading, bullets enable key points to be highlighted effectively and with great efficiency.

- Use "A-level" (the first level) and "B-level" (the second level) headings under major section headings to help readers make easy transitions from one topic to another. This also forces the writer to organize the plan more carefully. Use these headings liberally, at least once every 200 to 300 words.

- Use visuals where appropriate. Illustrations, graphs, and charts enable large amounts of information to be presented succinctly.

- Shoot for a plan 15 to 35 pages in length, not including financial projections and appendices. An uncomplicated small business may require only 15 pages, while a new business startup may require more than 35 pages.

- Use care in layout, design, and presentation. Laser or ink-jet printers give a more professional look than do dot matrix printers or typewriters. A bound report with a cover and clear title page adds professionalism.

This appendix is adapted from Eric N. Berkowitz, Roger A. Kerin, Steven W. Hartley, and William Rudelius, *Marketing,* 5th ed. (Chicago: Richard D. Irwin, 1997). Used with permission.

■ SAMPLE FIVE-YEAR ANNOTATED MARKETING PLAN FOR PARADISE KITCHENS,® INC.

The marketing plan that follows for Paradise Kitchens,® Inc. is based on an actual plan developed by the company. The company was founded in 1989, and its products entered distribution in 1990. To protect proprietary information about the company, a number of details and certain data have been altered, but the basic logic of the plan has been preserved. For example, to keep the plan simpler, it does not include details on a line of spicy salsas developed and marketed by the Paradise Kitchens,® Inc. Various appendices are omitted due to space limitations.

Notes in the margins next to the Paradise Kitchens,® Inc. marketing plan fall into two categories:

1. *Substantive notes* elaborate on the rationale or significance of an element in the marketing plan.

2. *Writing style, format, and layout notes* explain the editorial or visual rationale for the element.

As you read the marketing plan, you might consider adding your own notes in the margins related to the discussion in the text. For example, you may wish to compare the application of SWOT analysis and reference to "points of difference" in the Paradise Kitchens,® Inc. marketing plan with the discussion in Chapter 1. As you read additional chapters in the text, you may return to the marketing plan and insert additional notes pertaining to terminology used and techniques employed.

The Table of Contents provides quick access to the topics in the plan, usually organized by section and subsection headings.

Seen by many experts as the single most important element in the plan, the Executive Summary, with a maximum of two pages, "sells" the document to readers through its clarity and brevity.

The Company Description highlights the recent history and recent successes of the organization.

The Strategic Focus and Plan sets the strategic direction for the entire organization, a direction with which proposed actions of the marketing plan must be consistent. This section is not included in all marketing plans.

The Mission statement focuses the activities of Paradise Kitchens for the stakeholder groups to be served.

FIVE-YEAR MARKETING PLAN
Paradise Kitchens®, Inc.

Table of Contents

1. Executive Summary

2. Company Description

Paradise Kitchens®, Inc. was started in 1989 by cofounders Randall F. Peters and Leah E. Peters to develop and market Howlin' Coyote® Chili, a unique line of single-serve and microwaveable Southwestern/Mexican style frozen chili products. The Howlin' Coyote® line of chili was introduced into the Minneapolis-St. Paul market in 1990. The line was subsequently expanded to Denver in 1992 and Phoenix in 1994.

To the Company's knowledge, Howlin' Coyote® is the only premium-quality, authentic Southwestern/Mexican style, frozen chili sold in U.S. grocery stores. Its high quality has gained fast, widespread acceptance in these markets. In fact, same-store sales doubled in the last year for which data are available. The Company believes the Howlin' Coyote® brand can be extended to other categories of Southwestern/Mexican food products.

Paradise Kitchens believes its high-quality, high-price strategy has proven successful. This marketing plan outlines how the Company will extend its geographic coverage from 3 markets to 20 markets by the year 2000.

3. Strategic Focus and Plan

This section covers three aspects of corporate strategy that influence the marketing plan: (1) the mission, (2) goals, and (3) core competence/sustainable competitive advantage of Paradise Kitchens.

MISSION

The mission and vision of Paradise Kitchens is to market lines of high-quality Southwestern/Mexican food products at premium prices that satisfy consumers in this fast-growing food segment while providing challenging career opportunities for employees and above-average returns to stockholders.

> The Goals section sets both the financial and non-financial targets—where possible in quantitative terms—against which the company's performance will be measured.

> Lists use parallel construction to improve readability—in this case a series of infinitives starting with "To . . .".

> The Situation Analysis is a snapshot to answer the question, "Where are we now?"

GOALS

For the coming five years Paradise Kitchens seeks to achieve the following goals:

- Nonfinancial goals
  1. To retain its present image as the highest-quality line of Southwestern/Mexican products in the food categories in which it competes.
  2. To enter 17 new metropolitan markets.
  3. To increase the production and distribution capacity to satisfy future sales while maintaining present quality.
  4. To add a new product line every third year.
  5. To be among the top three chili lines—regardless of packaging (frozen, canned) in one third of the metro markets in which it competes by 1998 and two thirds by 2000.
- Financial goals
  1. To obtain a real (inflation adjusted) growth in earnings per share of 8 percent per year over time.
  2. To obtain a return on equity of at least 20 percent.
  3. To have a public stock offering by the year 2000.

CORE COMPETENCY AND SUSTAINABLE COMPETITIVE ADVANTAGE

In terms of core competency, Paradise Kitchens seeks to achieve a unique ability (1) to provide distinctive, high-quality chilies and related products using Southwestern/Mexican recipes that appeal to and excite contemporary tastes for these products and (2) to deliver these products to the customer's table using effective manufacturing and distribution systems that maintain the Company's quality standards.

To translate these core competencies into a sustainable competitive advantage, the Company will work closely with key suppliers and distributors to build the relationships and alliances necessary to satisfy the high taste standards of our customers.

4. Situation Analysis

This situation analysis starts with a snapshot of the current environment in which Paradise Kitchens finds itself by providing a brief SWOT (strengths, weaknesses, opportunities, threats) analysis. After this overview, the analysis probes ever-finer levels of detail: industry, competitors, company, and consumers.

The SWOT Analysis identifies strengths, weaknesses, opportunities, and threats to provide a solid foundation as a springboard to identify subsequent *actions* in the marketing plan.

SWOT ANALYSIS

Figure 1 shows the internal and external factors affecting the market opportunities for Paradise Kitchens. Stated briefly, this SWOT analysis highlights the great strides taken by the Company in the five years since its products first appeared on grocers' shelves. In the Company's favor internally are its strengths of an experienced management team and board of directors, excellent acceptance of its lines in the three metropolitan markets in which it competes, and a strong manufacturing and distribution system to serve these limited markets. Favorable external factors (opportunities) include the increasing appeal of Southwestern/Mexican foods, the strength of the upscale market for the Company's products, and food-processing technological breakthroughs that make it easier for smaller food producers to compete.

Each long table, graph, or photo is given a figure number and title. It then appears as soon as possible after the first reference in the text, accommodating necessary page breaks. This also avoids breaking long tables like this one in the middle. Short tables or graphs that are less than 1-1/2 inches are often inserted in the text without figure numbers because they don't cause serious problems with page breaks.

Figure 1.   SWOT Analysis for Paradise Kitchens

Internal Factors	*Strengths*	*Weaknesses*
Management	Experienced and entrepreneurial management and board	Small size can restrict options
Offerings	Unique, high-quality, high-price products	Many lower-quality, lower-price competitors
Marketing	Distribution in 3 markets with excellent acceptance	No national awareness or distribution
Personnel	Good work force, though small; little turnover	Big gap if key employee leaves
Finance	Excellent growth in sales revenues	Limited resources may restrict growth opportunities when compared to giant competitors
Manufacturing	Sole supplier ensures high quality	Lack economies of scale of huge competitors
R&D	Continuing efforts to ensure quality in delivered products	

Figure 1. SWOT Analysis for Paradise Kitchens *(continued)*

External Factors	Opportunities	Threats
Consumer/Social	Upscale market, likely to be stable; Southwestern/Mexican food category is fast-growing segment	Premium price may limit access to mass markets
Competitive	Distinctive name and packaging in its markets	Not patentable; competitors can attempt to duplicate product
Technological	Technical breakthroughs enable smaller food producers to achieve many economies available to large competitors	
Economic	Consumer income is high; convenience important to U.S. households	Many households "eating out," and bringing prepared take-out into home
Legal/Regulatory	High U.S. Food & Drug Admin. standards eliminate fly-by-night competitors	

> The Industry Analysis section provides the backdrop for the subsequent, more detailed analysis of competition, the company, and the company's customers. Without an in-depth understanding of the industry, the remaining analysis may be misdirected.

These favorable factors must be balanced against unfavorable ones, the main weakness being the limited size of Paradise Kitchens relative to its competitors in terms of the depth of the management team, available financial resources, and national awareness and distribution of product lines. Threats include the potential danger that the Company's premium prices may limit access to mass markets, no legal patent protection for its foods (although it has registered its Howlin' Coyote® brand), and competition from the "eating-out" and "take-out" markets.

INDUSTRY ANALYSIS: TRENDS IN SPICY AND MEXICAN FOODS

In the past 10 years, hot-spice consumption has doubled in U.S. households. Currently, Mexican food and ingredients are used in 46 percent of American households. Burritos, enchiladas, and taco dinner kits, which had insignificant numbers in 1981, reached 7 percent to 16 percent of American households in 1992.

> Even though relatively brief, this in-depth treatment of the Spicy Southwestern/Mexican food industry in the United States demonstrates to the plan's readers the company's understanding of the industry in which it competes. It gives readers confidence that the company thoroughly understands its own industry.

These trends reflect a generally more favorable attitude toward spicy foods on the part of Americans. Total spice consumption increased 50 percent from 1983 to 1993, according to the American Spice Trade Association. The retail grocery market for Mexican foods (excluding tortilla chips) was more than $4 billion in annual sales in 1994. The Southwestern/Mexican market includes the foods shown in Figure 2.

This summary of sales in the Southwestern/Mexican product category shows it is significant and provides a variety of future opportunities for Paradise Kitchens.

Figure 2.   Foods Included in the Southwestern/Mexican Product Category

Food	1994 U.S. Sales ($1,000,000)	% Change from 1993 to 1994
Dry chili mix	$121	6.0%
Canned chili	578	2.3
Salsa and sauces	1,438	10.3
Mexican foods frozen	602	4.5
Mexican foods canned	353	4.4
Peppers	242	2.5
Chilies	90	0.3
Mexican foods dry	1,259	5.3
Total	$4,681	6.0%

As with the Industry Analysis, the Competitor Analysis demonstrates that the company has a realistic understanding of who its major competitors are and what their marketing strategies are. Again, a realistic assessment gives confidence to readers that subsequent marketing actions in the plan rest on a solid foundation.

COMPETITORS IN SOUTHWESTERN/MEXICAN MARKET

The chili market represents $699 million in annual sales. The products fall primarily into two groups: canned chili (81 percent of sales) and dry chili (17 percent of sales). The remaining 2 percent of sales go to frozen chili products. Besides Howlin' Coyote®, Stouffers and Marie Callender's offer frozen chilies as part of their broad lines of frozen dinners and entrees. Major canned chili brands include Hormel, Wolf, Dennison, Stagg, Chili Man, and Castleberry's. Their retail prices range from $1.09 to $1.49.

Bluntly put, the major disadvantage of the segment's dominant product, canned chili, is that it does not taste very good. A taste test described in the October 1990 issue of *Consumer Reports* magazine ranked 26 canned chili products "poor" to "fair" in overall sensory quality. The study concluded, "Chili doesn't have to be hot to be good. But really good chili, hot or mild, doesn't come out of a can."

Dry mix brands include such familiar spice brands as Lawry's, McCormick, French's, and Durkee, along with smaller offerings such as Wick Fowler's and Carroll Shelby's. Their retail prices range from $1.79 to $1.99. The *Consumer Reports* study was more favorable about dry chili mixes, ranking them from "fair" to "very good." The magazine recommended, "If you want good chili, make it with fresh ingredients and one of the seasoning mixes we tested." A major drawback of dry mixes is that they require the preparers to add their own meat, beans, and tomatoes and take more preparation time than canned or frozen chilies.

The *Consumer Reports* study did not include the frozen chili entrees from Stouffer's or Marie Callender's (Howlin' Coyote® was not yet on the market at the time of the test). However, it is fair to say that these products—consisting of ground beef, chili beans, and tomato sauce—are of average quality. Furthermore, they are not singled out for special marketing or promotional programs by their manufacturers. Marie Callender's retails for $2.97, and Stouffer's retails for under $2.00.

While it is feasible for another food company to match Howlin' Coyote® and create a similar product, no known current companies are in a position to quickly match the offerings. Small companies face technical capacity issues. Large companies view the products as too much outside the mainstream of frozen-food retailing to be attracted to the market, at least initially.

COMPANY ANALYSIS

> The Company Analysis provides details of the company's strengths and marketing strategies that will enable it to achieve the mission and goals identified earlier.

The husband-and-wife team that cofounded Paradise Kitchens®, Inc. in 1989 has 38 years of experience between them in the food-processing business. Both have played key roles in the management of the Pillsbury Company. They are being advised by a highly seasoned group of business professionals, who have extensive understanding of the requirements for new product development.

Currently, Howlin' Coyote® products compete in the chili and Mexican frozen entree segments of the Southwestern/Mexican food market. While the chili obviously competes as a stand-alone product, its exceptional quality means it can complement such dishes as burritos, nachos, and enchiladas and can be readily used as a smothering sauce for pasta, rice, or potatoes. This flexibility of use is relatively rare in the prepared food marketplace.

In its growth strategy, Howlin' Coyote® is retracing a path taken by such enterprising food companies as Snapple Beverages, Celestial Seasonings, and Tombstone Pizza. These companies all broke from the pack of their respective categories and established a new approach. Snapple showed that iced tea and fruit drinks can be fun and highly variable. Celestial Seasonings made tea into a "lifestyle" drink. Tombstone Pizza moved frozen pizza upscale in taste and price, creating the first alternative to "cardboard" home pizzas. Likewise, with Howlin' Coyote®, Paradise Kitchens is broadening the position of frozen chili in a way that can lead to impressive market share for the new product category.

This "introductory over-view" sentence tells the reader the topics covered in the section—in this case customer characteristics and health and nutrition concerns. While this sentence may be omitted in short memos or plans, it helps readers see where the text is leading. These sentences are used throughout this plan.

The higher-level "A heading" of Customer Analysis has a more dom-inant typeface and position than the lower-level "B heading" of Customer Characteristics. These headings introduce the reader to the sequence and level of topics covered.

Satisfying customers and providing genuine value to them is why organizations exist in a market economy. This section addresses the question of "Who are the customers for Paradise Kitchens's products?"

The Company now uses a single outside producer with which it works closely to maintain the consistently high quality required in its products. The greater volume has increased production efficiencies, resulting in a steady decrease in the cost of goods sold.

CUSTOMER ANALYSIS

In terms of customer analysis, this section describes (1) the characteristics of customers expected to buy Howlin' Coyote® products and (2) health and nutrition concerns of Americans today.

Customer Characteristics. Demographically, chili products in general are purchased by consumers representing a broad range of socioeconomic backgrounds. Howlin' Coyote® chili is purchased chiefly by consumers who have achieved higher levels of education and whose income is $30,000 and higher. These consumers represent 57 percent of canned and dry mix chili users.

The household buying Howlin' Coyote® has one to three people in it. Among married couples, Howlin' Coyote® is predominantly bought by households in which both spouses work. While women are a majority of the buyers, single men represent a significant segment. Anecdotally, Howlin' Coyote® has heard from fathers of teenaged boys who say they keep a freezer stocked with the chili because the boys devour it.

Because the chili offers a quick way to make a tasty meal, the product's biggest users tend to be those most pressed for time. Howlin' Coyote®'s premium pricing also means that its purchasers are skewed toward the higher end of the income range. Buyers range in age from 25 to 55. Because consumers in the western United States have adopted spicy foods more readily than the rest of the country, Howlin' Coyote®'s initial marketing expansion efforts will be concentrated in that region.

This section demonstrates the company's insights into a major trend that has a potentially large impact.

Health and Nutrition Concerns. Coverage of food issues in the U.S. media is often erratic and occasionally alarmist. Because Americans are concerned about their diets, studies from organizations of widely varying credibility frequently receive significant attention from the major news organizations. For instance, a study of fat levels of movie popcorn was reported in all the major media. Similarly, studies on the healthfulness of Mexican food have received prominent "play" in print and broadcast reports. The high caloric levels of much Mexican and Southwestern-style food had been widely reported and often exaggerated.

Less certain is the link between these reports and consumer buying behavior. Most indications are that while Americans are well-versed in dietary matters, they are not significantly changing their eating patterns. The experience of other food manufacturers is that Americans expect certain foods to be high in calories and are not drawn to those that claim to be low-calorie versions. Low-fat frozen pizza was a flop. Therefore, while Howlin' Coyote® is already lower in calories, fat, and sodium than its competitors, those qualities are not being stressed in its promotions. Instead, in the space and time available for promotions, Howlin' Coyote®'s taste, convenience, and flexibility are stressed.

5. Product-Market Focus

This section describes the five-year marketing and product objectives for Paradise Kitchens and the target markets, points of difference, and positioning of its lines of Howlin' Coyote® chilies.

MARKETING AND PRODUCT OBJECTIVES

Howlin' Coyote®'s marketing intent is to take full advantage of its brand potential while building a base from which other revenue sources can be mined—both in and out of the retail grocery business. These are detailed in four areas below:

The chances of success for a new product are significantly increased if objectives are set for the product itself and if target market segments are identified for it. This section makes these explicit for Paradise Kitchens. The objectives also serve as the planned targets against which marketing activities are measured in program implementation and control.

- Current markets. Current markets will be grown by expanding brand and flavor distribution at the retail level. In addition, same-store sales will be grown by increasing consumer awareness and repeat purchases. With this increase in same-store sales, the more desirable broker/warehouse distribution channel will become available, increasing efficiency and saving costs.

- New markets. By the end of Year 5, the chili and salsa business will be expanded to a total of 20 metropolitan areas. This will represent 55 percent of U.S. food store sales.
- Food service. Food service sales will include chili products and smothering sauces. Sales are expected to reach $580,000 by the end of Year 3 and $1.2 million by the end of Year 5.
- New products. Howlin' Coyote®'s brand presence will be expanded at the retail level through the addition of new products in the frozen-foods section. This will be accomplished through new product concept screening in Year 1 to identify new potential products. These products will be brought to market in Years 2 and 3. Additionally, the brand may be licensed in select categories.

TARGET MARKETS

The primary target market for Howlin' Coyote® products is households with one to three people, where often both adults work, with household income typically above $30,000 per year. These households contain more experienced, adventurous consumers of Southwestern/Mexican food and want premium quality products.

POINTS OF DIFFERENCE

The "points of difference"—characteristics that make Howlin' Coyote® chilies unique relative to competitors—fall into three important areas:

- Unique taste and convenience. No known competitor offers a high-quality, "authentic" frozen chili in a range of flavors. And no existing chili has the same combination of quick preparation and home-style taste.
- Taste trends. The American palate is increasingly intrigued by hot spices, and Howlin' Coyote® brands offer more "kick" than most other prepared chilies.
- Premium packaging. Howlin' Coyote®'s high-value packaging graphics convey the unique, high-quality product contained inside and the product's nontraditional positioning.

This section identifies the specific niches or target markets toward which the company's products are directed. When appropriate and when space permits, this section often includes a product-market matrix.

An organization cannot grow by offering only "me-too products." The greatest single factor in a new product's failure is the lack of significant "points of difference" that set it apart from competitors' substitutes. This section makes these points of difference explicit.

A positioning strategy helps communicate the company's unique points of difference of its products to prospective customers in a simple, clear way. This section describes this positioning.

Everything that has gone before in the marketing plan sets the stage for the marketing mix actions covered in the marketing program.

This section describes in detail three key elements of the company's product strategy: the product line, its quality and how this is achieved, and its "cutting edge" packaging.

Using parallel structure, this bulleted list presents the product line efficiently and crisply.

POSITIONING

In the past chili products have been either convenient or tasty, but not both. Howlin' Coyote® pairs these two desirable characteristics to obtain a positioning in consumers' minds as very high-quality "authentic Southwestern/Mexican tasting" chilies that can be prepared easily and quickly.

6. Marketing Program

The four marketing mix elements of the Howlin' Coyote® chili marketing program are detailed below. Note that "chile" is the vegetable and "chili" is the dish.

PRODUCT STRATEGY

After first summarizing the product line, the approach to product quality and packaging is covered.

Product Line. Howlin' Coyote® chili, retailing for $2.89 for a 10- or 11.5-ounce serving, is available in five flavors. The five are:

- Green Chile Chili: braised extra-lean pork with fire-roasted green chilies, onions, tomato chunks, bold spices, and jalapeno peppers, based on a Southwestern favorite.
- Red Chile Chili: extra-lean cubed pork, deep-red acho chilies, and sweet onions; known as the "Texas Bowl of Red."
- Beef and Black Bean Chili: lean braised beef with black beans, tomato chunks, and Howlin' Coyote®'s own blend of red chilies and authentic spicing.
- Chicken Chunk Chili: hearty chunks of tender chicken, fire-roasted green chilies, black beans, pinto beans, diced onions, and zesty spices.
- Mean Bean Chili: vegetarian, with nine distinctive bean varieties and fire-roasted green chilies, tomato chunks, onion, and a robust blend of spices and rich red chilies.

Unique Product Quality. The flavoring systems of the Howlin' Coyote® chilies are proprietary. The products' tastiness is due to extra care lavished upon the ingredients during production. The ingredients used are of unusually high quality. Meats are low-fat cuts and are fresh, not frozen, to preserve cell structure and moistness. Chilies are fire-roasted for fresher taste, not the canned variety used by more mainstream products. Tomatoes and vegetables are select quality. No preservatives or artificial flavors are used.

Packaging. Reflecting the "cutting edge" marketing strategy of its producers, Howlin' Coyote® bucks conventional wisdom in packaging. It avoids placing predictable photographs of the product on its containers. (Head to any grocer's freezer and you will be hardpressed to find a product that does not feature a heavily stylized photograph of the contents.) Instead, Howlin' Coyote®'s package shows a Southwestern motif that communicates the product's out-of-the-ordinary positioning. This approach signals the product's nontraditional qualities: "adventurous" eating with minimal fuss—a frozen meal for people who do not normally enjoy frozen meals.

PRICE STRATEGY

Howlin' Coyote® Chili is, at $2.89 for a 10- to 11.5-ounce package, priced comparably to the other frozen offerings and higher than the canned and dried chili varieties. However, the significant taste advantages it has over canned chilies and the convenience advantages over dried chilies justify this pricing strategy.

PROMOTION STRATEGY

Key promotion programs feature in-store demonstrations, recipes, and cents-off coupons.

In-Store Demonstrations. In-store demonstrations will be conducted to give consumers a chance to try Howlin' Coyote® products and learn about their unique qualities. Demos will be conducted regularly in all markets to increase awareness and trial purchases.

Recipes. Because the products' flexibility of use is a key selling point, recipes will be offered to consumers to stimulate use. The recipes will be given at all in-store demonstrations, on the back of packages, and through a mail-in recipe book offer. In addition, recipes will be included in coupons sent by direct-mail or free-standing inserts. For new markets, recipes will be included on in-pack coupon inserts.

Cents-Off Coupons. To generate trial and repeat-purchase of Howlin' Coyote® products, coupons will be distributed in four ways:

- In Sunday newspaper inserts. Inserts are highly read and will help generate awareness. Coupled with in-store

---

This Price Strategy section makes the company's price point very clear, along with its price position relative to potential substitutes. When appropriate and when space permits, this section might contain a break-even analysis.

Elements of the Promotion Strategy are highlighted here with B-headings in terms of the three key promotional activities the company is emphasizing for its product line: in-store demonstrations, recipes featuring its Howlin' Coyote® chilies, and cents-off coupons.

> **Another bulleted list adds many details for the reader, including methods of gaining customer awareness, trial, and repeat purchases as Howlin' Coyote® enters new metropolitan areas.**

demonstrations, this has been a very successful technique so far.

- In-pack coupons. Inside each box of Howlin' Coyote® chili will be coupons for $1 off two more packages of the chili. These coupons will be included for the first three months the product is shipped to a new market. Doing so encourages repeat purchases by new users.
- Direct-mail chili coupons. Those households that fit the Howlin' Coyote® demographics described above will be mailed coupons. This is likely to be an efficient promotion due to its greater audience selectivity.
- In-store demonstrations. Coupons will be passed out at in-store demonstrations to give an additional incentive to purchase.

DISTRIBUTION STRATEGY

> **The Distribution Strategy is described here in terms of both (1) the present method and (2) the new one to be used when the increased sales volume makes it feasible.**

Howlin' Coyote® is distributed in its present markets through a food distributor. The distributor buys the product, warehouses it, and then resells and delivers it to grocery retailers on a store-by-store basis. This is typical for products that have moderate sales—compared with, say, staples like milk or bread. As sales grow, we will shift to a more efficient system using a broker who sells the products to retail chains and grocery wholesalers.

7. Financial Data and Projections

PAST SALES REVENUES

> **All the marketing mix decisions covered in the marketing program have both revenue and expense effects. These are summarized in this section of the marketing plan.**

Historically, Howlin' Coyote® has had a steady increase in sales revenues since its introduction in 1990. In 1994, sales jumped, due largely to new promotion strategies and the opportunities represented by the products' expansion to Western markets. The trend in sales revenues appears in Figure 3.

Figure 3.   Sales Revenues for Paradise Kitchens®, Inc.

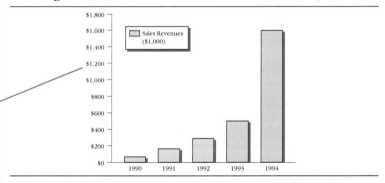

> **The graph shows more clearly the dramatic growth of sales revenue than data in a table would do.**

During the five years since their introduction, Howlin' Coyote® chilies have achieved sales growth of 80 percent annually. New sales-promotion techniques have been so effective that 1994 sales have more than tripled those of 1993.

FIVE-YEAR PROJECTIONS

Five-year financial projections for Paradise Kitchens appear below:

Financial Element	Units	Year 1 1996	Year 2 1997	Year 3 1998	Year 4 1999	Year 5 2000
Cases sold	1,000	195	353	684	889	1,249
Net sales	$1,000	2,832	5,123	9,913	12,884	18,111
Gross profit	$1,000	936	2,545	4,820	6,257	8,831
Operating profit (loss)	$1,000	(423)	339	985	2,096	2,805

These projections reflect the continuing growth in number of cases sold (with 8 packages of Howlin' Coyote® chili per case) and increasing production and distribution economies of scale as sales volume increases.

8. Organization

Paradise Kitchen's present organization appears in Figure 4. It shows the four people reporting to the President. Below this level are both the full-time and part-time employees of the Company.

At present Paradise Kitchens operates with full-time employees in only essential positions. It now augments its full-time staff with key advisors, consultants, and subcontractors. As the firm grows, people with special expertise will be added to the staff.

Figure 4.   The Paradise Kitchens Organization

Because this table is very short, it is woven into the text, rather than given a table number and title.

The Five-Year Financial Projections section starts with the judgment forecast of cases sold and the resulting net sales. Gross profit and then operating profit—critical for the company's survival—are projected and show the company passes break-even and becomes profitable in Year 2. An actual plan often contains many pages of computer-generated spreadsheet projections, usually shown in an appendix to the plan.

The Implementation Plan shows how the company will turn plans into results. Gantt charts are often used to set deadlines and assign responsibilities for the many tactical marketing decisions needed to enter a new market.

The essence of Evaluation and Control is comparing actual sales with the targeted values set in the plan and taking appropriate actions. Note that the section briefly describes a contingency plan for alternative actions, depending on how successful the entry into a new market turns out to be.

Various appendices may appear at the end of the plan, depending on the purpose and audience for them. For example, detailed financial spreadsheets often appear in an appendix.

9. Implementation Plan

Introducing Howlin' Coyote® chilies to new metropolitan areas is a complex task and requires that creative promotional activities gain consumer awareness and initial trial among the target market households identified earlier. The anticipated rollout schedule to enter these metropolitan markets appears in Figure 5.

Figure 5. Rollout Schedule to Enter New U.S. Markets

Year	New Markets Added	Cumulative Markets	Cumulative Percentage of U.S. Market
Today (1995)	0	3	7
Year 1 (1996)	1	4	10
Year 2 (1997)	2	6	18
Year 3 (1998)	3	9	28
Year 4 (1999)	4	13	39
Year 5 (2000)	7	20	55

10. Evaluation and Control

Monthly sales targets in cases have been set for Howlin' Coyote® chili for each metropolitan area. Actual case sales will be compared with these targets and tactical marketing programs modified to reflect the unique sets of factors in each metropolitan area. The speed of the roll-out program may increase or decrease, depending on Paradise Kitchen's performance in the successive metropolitan markets it enters.

CHAPTER 2

Financial Aspects of Marketing Management

 Marketing managers are accountable for the impact of their actions on profits. Therefore, they need a working knowledge of basic accounting and finance. This chapter provides an overview of several concepts from managerial accounting and managerial finance that are useful in marketing management: (1) variable and fixed costs, (2) relevant and sunk costs, (3) margins, (4) contribution analysis, (5) liquidity, and (6) operating leverage. In addition, considerations for preparing *pro forma* income statements are described.

■ VARIABLE AND FIXED COSTS

An organization's costs divide into two broad categories: variable costs and fixed costs.

Variable Costs

Variable costs are expenses that are uniform per unit of output within a relevant time period (usually defined as a budget year); yet total variable costs fluctuate in direct proportion to the output volume of units produced. In other words, as volume increases, total variable costs increase.

Variable costs are divided into two categories, one of which is *cost of goods sold.* For a manufacturer or a provider of a service, cost of goods sold covers materials, labor, and factory overhead applied directly to production. For a reseller (wholesaler or retailer), cost of goods sold consists primarily of the cost of merchandise. The second category of variable costs consists of expenses that are not directly tied to production but that nevertheless vary directly with volume. Examples include sales commissions, discounts, and delivery expenses.

Fixed Costs

Fixed costs are expenses that do not fluctuate with output volume within a relevant time period (the budget year) but become progressively smaller per unit of output as volume increases. The decrease in per-unit fixed cost results from the increase in the number of output units over which fixed costs are allocated. Note, however, that no matter how large volume becomes, the absolute size of fixed costs remains unchanged.

Fixed costs divide into two categories: programmed costs and committed costs. *Programmed costs* result from attempts to generate sales volume. *Marketing expenditures are generally classified as programmed costs.* Examples include advertising, sales promotion, and sales salaries. *Committed costs* are those required to maintain the organization. They are usually nonmarketing expenditures such as rent and administrative and clerical salaries.

It is important to understand the concept of fixed cost. Remember that total fixed costs do not change during a budget year, regardless of changes in volume. Once fixed expenditures for a marketing program have been made, they remain the same whether or not the program causes unit volume to change.

Despite the clear-cut classification of costs into variable and fixed categories suggested here, cost classification is not always apparent in actual practice. Many times costs have a fixed and a variable component. For example, selling expenses often have a fixed component (such as salary) and a variable component (such as commissions or bonus) that are not always evident at first glance.

■ RELEVANT AND SUNK COSTS

Relevant Costs

Relevant costs are expenditures that (1) are expected to occur in the future as a result of some marketing action and (2) differ among marketing alternatives being considered. In short, relevant costs are future expenditures unique to the decision alternatives under consideration.

The concept of relevant cost can best be illustrated by an example. Suppose a manager considers adding a new product to the product mix. Relevant costs include potential expenditures for manufacturing and marketing the product, plus salary costs arising from the time sales personnel give to the new products at the expense of other products. If this additional product does not affect the salary costs of sales personnel, salaries are not a relevant cost.

As a general rule, opportunity costs are also a relevant cost. Opportunity costs are the forgone benefits from an alternative not chosen.

Sunk Costs

Sunk costs are the direct opposite of relevant costs. Sunk costs are past expenditures for a given activity and are typically irrelevant in whole or in part to future decisions. In a marketing context, sunk costs include past research and development expenditures (including test marketing) and last year's advertising expense. These expenditures, although real, will neither recur in the future nor influence future expenditures. When marketing managers attempt to incorporate sunk costs into future decisions affecting new expenditures, they often fall prey to the *sunk cost fallacy*—that is, they attempt to recoup spent dollars by spending still more dollars in the future.

■ MARGINS

Another useful concept for marketing managers is that of *margin*, which refers to the difference between the selling price and the "cost" of a product or service. Margins are expressed on a total volume basis or on an individual unit basis, in dollar terms or as percentages. The three described here are gross, trade, and net profit margins.

Gross Margin

Gross margin, or gross profit, is the difference between total sales revenue and total cost of goods sold, or, on a per-unit basis, the difference between unit selling price and unit cost of goods sold. Gross margin may be expressed in dollar terms or as a percentage.

Total Gross Margin	Dollar Amount	Percentage
Net sales	$100	100%
Cost of goods sold	−40	−40
Gross profit margin	$ 60	60%

Unit Gross Margin		
Unit sales price	$1.00	100%
Unit cost of goods sold	−0.40	−40
Unit gross profit margin	$0.60	60%

Gross margin analysis is a useful tool because it implicitly includes unit selling prices of products or services, unit costs, and unit volume. A decrease in gross margin is of immediate concern to a marketing manager, because such a change has a direct impact on profits, providing that other expenditures remain unchanged. Changes in total gross margin should be examined in depth to determine whether the change was brought about by fluctuations in unit volume, changes in unit price or unit cost of goods sold, or a modification in the sales mix of the firm's products or services.

Trade Margin

Trade margin is the difference between unit sales price and unit cost at each level of a marketing channel (for example, manufacturer → wholesaler → retailer). A trade margin is frequently referred to as a *markup* or *mark-on* by channel members, and it is often expressed as a percentage.

Trade margins are occasionally confusing, since the margin percentage can be computed on the basis of cost or selling price. Consider the following example. Suppose a retailer purchases an item for $10 and sells it at a price of $20—that is, a $10 margin. What is the retailer's margin percentage?

Retailer margin as a percentage of cost is

$$\frac{\$10}{\$10} \times 100 = 100 \text{ percent}$$

Retailer margin as a percentage of selling price is

$$\frac{\$10}{\$20} \times 100 = 50 \text{ percent}$$

Differences in margin percentages show the importance of knowing the base (cost or selling price) on which the margin percentage is determined. *Trade margin percentages are usually determined on the basis of selling price,* but practices do vary among firms and industries.

Trade margins affect the pricing of individual items in two ways. First, suppose a wholesaler purchases an item for $2.00 and seeks to achieve a 30 percent margin on this item based on selling price. What would be the selling price?

$2.00 = 70 percent of selling price

or

Selling price = $2.00/0.70 = $2.86

Second, suppose a manufacturer suggests a retail list price of $6.00 on an item for ultimate resale to the consumer. The item will be sold through retailers whose policy is to obtain a 40 percent margin based on selling price. For what price must the manufacturer sell the item to the retailer?

$$\frac{x}{\$6.00} = 40 \text{ percent of selling price}$$

where x is the retailer margin. Solving for x indicates that the retailer must obtain $2.40 for this item. Therefore, the manufacturer must set the price to the retailer at $3.60 ($6.00 − $2.40).

The manufacturer's problem of suggesting a price for ultimate resale to the consumer becomes more complex as the number of intermediaries between the manufacturer and the final consumer increases. This complexity can be illustrated by expanding the above example to include a wholesaler between the manufacturer and retailer. The retailer receives a 40 percent margin on the sales price. If the retailer must receive $2.40 per unit, the wholesaler must sell the item for $3.60 per unit. In order for the wholesaler to receive a 20 percent margin, for what price must the manufacturer sell the unit to the wholesaler?

$$\frac{x}{\$3.60} = 20 \text{ percent wholesaler margin on selling price}$$

where x is the wholesaler margin. Solving for x shows that the wholesaler's margin is $0.72 for this item. Therefore, the manufacturer must set the price to the wholesaler at $2.88.

This example shows that a manager must work backward from the ultimate price to the consumer through the marketing channel to arrive at a product's selling price. Assuming that the manufacturer's cost of goods sold is $2.00, we can calculate the following margins, which incidentally show the manufacturer's gross margin of 30.6 percent.

	Unit Cost of Goods Sold	Unit Selling Price	Gross Margin as a Percentage of Selling Price
Manufacturer	$2.00	$2.88	30.6%
Wholesaler	2.88	3.60	20.0
Retailer	3.60	6.00	40.0
Consumer	6.00		

Net Profit Margin (Before Taxes)

The last margin to be considered is the net profit margin before taxes. This margin is expressed as a dollar figure or a percentage. *Net profit margin* is the remainder after cost of goods sold, other variable costs, and fixed costs have been subtracted from sales revenue. The place of net profit margin in an organization's income statement is illustrated by the following:

	Dollar Amount	Percentage
Net sales	$100,000	100%
Cost of goods sold	−30,000	−30
Gross profit margin	$70,000	70%
Selling expenses	−20,000	−20
Fixed expenses	−40,000	−40
Net profit margin	$10,000	10%

Net profit margin dollars represent a major source of funding for the organization. As will be shown later, net profit influences the working capital position of the organization; hence the dollar amount ultimately affects the organization's ability to pay its cost of goods sold plus its selling and administrative expenses. Furthermore, net profit also affects the organization's cash flow position.

■ CONTRIBUTION ANALYSIS

Contribution analysis is an important concept in marketing management. *Contribution* is the difference between total sales revenue and total variable costs, or, on a per-unit basis, the difference between unit selling price and unit variable cost. Contribution analysis is particularly useful in assessing relationships among costs, prices, and volumes of products and services.

Break-even Analysis

Break-even analysis is one of the simplest applications of contribution analysis. *Break-even analysis* identifies the unit or dollar sales volume at which an organization neither makes a profit nor incurs a loss. Stated in equation form:

Total revenue = total variable costs + total fixed costs

Since break-even analysis identifies the level of sales volume at which total costs (fixed and variable) and total revenue are equal, it is a valuable tool for evaluating an organization's profit goals and assessing the riskiness of actions.

Break-even analysis requires three pieces of information: (1) an estimate of unit variable costs, (2) an estimate of the total dollar fixed costs to produce and market the product or service unit (note that only relevant costs apply), and (3) the selling price for each product or service unit.

The formula for determining the number of units required to break even is as follows:

$$\text{Unit break-even volume} = \frac{\text{total dollar fixed costs}}{\text{unit selling price} - \text{unit variable costs}}$$

The denominator in this formula (unit selling price minus unit variable costs) is called *contribution per unit*. Contribution per unit is the dollar amount that each unit sold "contributes" to the payment of fixed costs.

Consider the following example. A manufacturer plans to sell a product for $5.00. The unit variable costs are $2.00, and total fixed costs assigned to the product are $30,000. How many units must be sold to break even?

Fixed costs	= $30,000
Contribution per unit	= unit selling price − unit variable cost
	= $5 − $2 = $3
Unit break-even volume	= $30,000/$3 = 10,000 units

This example shows that for every unit sold at $5.00, $2.00 is used to pay variable costs. The balance of $3.00 "contributes" to fixed costs.

A related question is what the manufacturer's dollar sales volume must be to break even. The manager need only multiply unit break-even volume by the unit selling price to determine the dollar break-even volume: 10,000 units × $5 = $50,000.

A manager can calculate a dollar break-even point directly without first computing unit break-even volume. First the *contribution margin* must be determined from the formula:

$$\text{Contribution margin} = \frac{\text{unit selling price} - \text{unit variable cost}}{\text{unit selling price}}$$

EXHIBIT 2.1

Break-even Analysis Chart

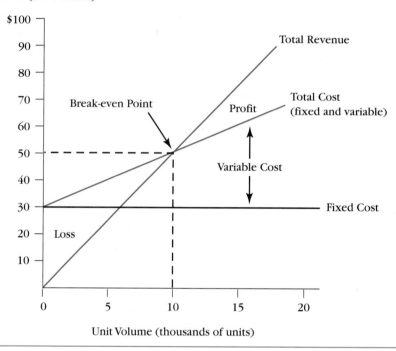

Total Revenue or
Total Cost ($ thousands)

Unit Volume (thousands of units)

Using the figures from our example, we find that the contribution margin is 60 percent:

$$\text{Contribution margin} = \frac{\$5 - \$2}{\$5} = 60 \text{ percent}$$

Then the dollar break-even point is computed as follows:

$$\text{Dollar volume} = \frac{\text{total fixed costs}}{\text{contribution margin}} = \frac{\$30,000}{0.60} = \$50,000$$

In many cases it is useful to develop a graphic representation of a break-even analysis. Exhibit 2.1 provides a visual solution to the problem posed above. The horizontal line at $30,000 represents fixed costs. The upward-sloping line beginning at $30,000 represents the total cost, which is equal to the sum of fixed plus variable costs. This line has a slope equal to $2.00—each unit increase in volume results in a $2.00 increase in the total cost. The upward-sloping line beginning at zero represents revenue and has a slope of $5.00—each unit increase in sales produces a $5.00 increase in revenue. The distance between the revenue line and the total cost line represents dollars of profit (above the break-even point) or loss (below the break-even point).

Sensitivity Analysis

Contribution analysis can be applied in a number of different ways, depending on the manager's needs. The following illustrations show how the break-even points in our example can be varied by changing selling price, variable costs, and fixed costs.

1. What would break-even volume be if fixed costs were increased to $40,000 while the selling price and variable costs remained unchanged?

$$\text{Fixed costs} \; = \; \$40,000$$
$$\text{Contribution per unit} \; = \; \$3$$
$$\text{Unit break-even volume} \; = \; \$40,000/\$3 = 13,333 \text{ units}$$
$$\text{Dollar break-even volume} \; = \; \$40,000/0.60 = \$66,667$$

Note that the difference between the dollar break-even volume calculated from the contribution margin and the result of simply multiplying unit selling price by unit break-even volume (13,333 × $5 = $66,665) is due to rounding.

2. What would break-even volume be if selling price were dropped from $5.00 to $4.00 while fixed and variable costs remained unchanged?

$$\text{Fixed costs} \; = \; \$30,000$$
$$\text{Contribution per unit} \; = \; \$2$$
$$\text{Unit break-even volume} \; = \; \$30,000/\$2 = 15,000 \text{ units}$$
$$\text{Dollar break-even volume} \; = \; \$30,000/0.50 = \$60,000$$

3. Finally, what would break-even volume be if unit variable cost per unit were reduced to $1.50, selling price remained at $5.00, and fixed costs were $30,000?

$$\text{Fixed costs} \; = \; \$30,000$$
$$\text{Contribution per unit} \; = \; \$3.50$$
$$\text{Unit break-even volume} \; = \; \$30,000/\$3.50 = 8,571 \text{ units}$$
$$\text{Dollar break-even volume} \; = \; \$30,000/0.70 = \$42,857$$

Contribution Analysis and Profit Impact

No manager is content to operate at the break-even point in unit or dollar sales volume. Profits are necessary for the continued operation of an organization. A modified break-even analysis is used to incorporate a profit goal.

In simple break-even analysis, contribution per unit is the dollar amount available to pay fixed costs. To modify the break-even formula to incorporate the dollar profit goal, we need only regard the profit goal as an additional fixed cost, as follows:

$$\frac{\text{Unit volume to}}{\text{achieve profit goal}} = \frac{\text{total dollar fixed costs} + \text{dollar profit goal}}{\text{contribution per unit}}$$

Suppose a firm has fixed costs of $200,000 budgeted for a product or service, the unit selling price is $25.00, and the unit variable costs are $10.00. How many units must be sold to achieve a profit goal of $20,000?

$$\text{Fixed costs} + \text{profit goal} \; = \; \$200,000 + \$20,000 = \$220,000$$
$$\text{Contribution per unit} \; = \; \$25 - \$10 = \$15$$
$$\text{Unit volume to achieve profit goal} \; = \; \$220,000/\$15$$
$$= \; 14,667 \text{ units}$$

Many firms specify their profit goal as a percentage of sales rather than as a dollar amount ("Our profit goal is a 20 percent profit on sales"). This objective can be incorporated into the break-even formula by including the profit goal in the contribution-per-unit calculation. If the goal is to achieve a 20 percent profit on sales, each dollar of sales must "contribute" $0.20 to profit. In our example, each unit sold for $25.00 must contribute $5.00 to profit. The break-even formula incorporating a percent profit on sales goal is as follows:

$$\text{Unit volume to achieve profit goal} = \frac{\text{total dollar fixed costs}}{\text{unit selling price} - \text{unit variable costs}}$$

The unit volume break-even point to achieve a 20 percent profit goal is 20,000 units:

$$\text{Fixed costs} = \$200{,}000$$
$$\text{Contribution per unit} = \$25 - \$10 - \$5 = \$10$$
$$\text{Unit volume to achieve profit goal} = \$200{,}000/\$10$$
$$= 20{,}000 \text{ units}$$

Contribution Analysis and Market Size

An important consideration in contribution analysis is the relationship of break-even unit or dollar volume to market size. Consider the situation in which a manager has conducted a break-even analysis and found the unit volume break-even point to be 50,000 units. This number has meaning only when compared with the potential size of the market segment sought. If the market potential is 100,000 units, the manager's product or service must capture 50 percent of the market sought to break even. An important question to be resolved is whether such a percentage can be achieved. A manager can assess the feasibility of a venture by comparing the break-even volume with market size and market-capture percentage.

Contribution Analysis and Performance Measurement

A second application of contribution analysis lies in performance measurement. For example, a marketing manager may wish to examine the performance of products. Consider an organization with two products, X and Y. A description of each product's financial performance follows:

	Product X (10,000 volume)	Product Y (20,000 volume)	Total (30,000 volume)
Unit price	$ 10	$ 3	
Sales revenue	100,000	60,000	$160,000
Unit variable costs	4	1.50	
Total variable costs	40,000	30,000	70,000
Unit contribution	6	1.50	
Total contribution	60,000	30,000	90,000
Fixed costs	45,000	10,000	55,000
Net profit	$15,000	$20,000	$35,000

The net profit figure shows that Product Y is more profitable than Product X. Product X is four times more profitable than Product Y on a unit-contribution basis, however, and generates twice the contribution dollars to overhead. The difference in profitability comes from the allocation of fixed costs to the products. In measuring performance, it is important to consider which products contribute most heavily to the organization's total fixed costs ($55,000 in this example) and then to total profit.

Should a manager look only at net profit, a decision might be made to drop Product X. Product Y would then have to cover total fixed costs, however. If the fixed costs remain at $55,000 and only Product Y is sold, this organization will experience a *net loss* of $25,000, assuming no change in Product Y volume.

Assessment of Cannibalization

A third application of contribution analysis is in the assessment of cannibalization effects. Cannibalization is the process by which one product or service sold by a firm gains a portion of its revenue by diverting sales from another product or service also sold by the firm. For example, sales of Brand X's new gel toothpaste may be at the expense of sales of Brand X's existing opaque white toothpaste. The problem facing a marketing manager is to assess the financial effect of cannibalization.

Consider the following data:

	Existing Opaque White Toothpaste	*New Gel Toothpaste*
Unit selling price	$1.00	$1.10
Unit variable costs	−0.20	−0.40
Unit contribution	$0.80	$0.70

The gel toothpaste can be sold at a slightly higher price, given its formulation and taste, but the variable costs are also higher. Hence the gel toothpaste has a lower contribution per unit. Therefore, for every unit of the gel toothpaste sold instead of a unit of the opaque white toothpaste, the firm "loses" $0.10. Suppose further that the company expects to sell 1 million units of the new gel toothpaste in the first year after introduction and that, of that amount, 500,000 units will be diverted from the opaque white toothpaste, of which the company had expected to sell 1 million units. The task of the marketing manager is to determine how the introduction of the new gel toothpaste will affect Brand X's total contribution dollars.

One approach to assessing the financial impact of cannibalization is shown below:

1. Brand X expects to lose $0.10 for each unit diverted from the opaque white toothpaste to the gel toothpaste.

2. Given that 500,000 units will be cannibalized from the opaque white toothpaste, the total contribution *lost* is $50,000 ($0.10 × 500,000 units).

3. However, the new gel toothpaste will sell an additional 500,000 units at a contribution per unit of $0.70, which means that $350,000 ($0.70 × 500,000 units) in additional contribution will be generated.

4. Therefore, the net financial effect is a positive increase in contribution dollars of $300,000 ($350,000 − $50,000).

Another approach to assessing the cannibalization effect is as follows:

1. The opaque white toothpaste alone had been expected to sell 1 million units with a unit contribution of $0.80. Therefore, contribution dollars without the gel would equal $800,000 ($0.80 × 1,000,000 units).

2. The gel toothpaste is expected to sell 1 million units with a unit contribution of $0.70.

3. Given the cannibalism rate of 50 percent (that is, one-half of the gel's volume is diverted from the opaque white toothpaste), the combined contribution can be calculated as follows:

Product	*Unit Volume*	*Unit Contribution*	*Contribution Dollars*
Opaque white toothpaste	500,000	$0.80	$400,000
Gel toothpaste:			
Cannibalized volume	500,000	0.70	350,000
Incremental volume	500,000	0.70	350,000
Total	1,500,000		$1,100,000
Less original forecast volume for opaque white toothpaste	1,000,000	0.80	800,000
Total	+500,000		+$300,000

Both approaches arrive at the same conclusion: Brand X will benefit by $300,000 from the introduction of the gel toothpaste. The manager should use whichever approach he or she is more comfortable with in an analytic sense.

It should be emphasized, however, that the incremental fixed costs associated with advertising and sales promotion or any additions or changes in manufacturing capacity must be considered to complete the analysis. If the fixed costs approximate or exceed $300,000, the new product should be viewed in a very different light.

■ LIQUIDITY

Liquidity refers to an organization's ability to meet short-term (usually within a budget year) financial obligations. A key measure of an organization's liquidity position is its working capital. *Working capital* is the dollar value of an organization's *current assets* (such as cash, accounts receivable, prepaid expenses, inventory) *minus* the dollar value of *current liabilities* (such as short-term accounts payable for goods and services, income taxes).

A manager should be aware of the impact of marketing actions on working capital. Marketing expenditures precede sales volume; therefore, cash outlays for marketing efforts reduce current assets. If marketing expenditures cannot be met out of cash, accounts payable are incurred. In either case, working capital is reduced. In a positive vein, a marketing manager's creation of sales volume, with corresponding increases in net profit, contributes to working capital. Since the timing of marketing expenditures and sales volume is often lagged, a marketing manager must be wary of marketing efforts that unnecessarily deplete working capital and must assess the likelihood of potential sales, given a specified expenditure level.

■ OPERATING LEVERAGE

A financial concept closely akin to break-even analysis is operating leverage. *Operating leverage* refers to the extent to which fixed costs and variable costs are used in the production and marketing of products and services. Firms that have high total fixed costs relative to total variable costs are defined as having high operating leverage. Examples of firms with high operating leverage include airlines and heavy-equipment manufacturers. Firms with low total fixed costs relative to total variable costs are defined as having low operating leverage. Firms typically having low operating leverage include residential contractors and wholesale distributors.

The higher a firm's operating leverage, the faster its total profits will increase once sales exceed break-even volume. By the same token, however, those firms with high operating leverage will incur losses at a faster rate once sales volume falls below the break-even point.

Exhibit 2.2 illustrates the effect of operating leverage on profit. The base case shows two firms that have identical break-even sales volumes. The cost structures of the two firms differ, however, with one having high fixed and low variable costs and the other having low fixed and high variable costs. Note that when sales volume is increased 10 percent, the firm with high fixed and low variable costs achieves a much higher profit than the firm with low fixed and high variable costs. When sales volume declines, however, just the opposite is true. That is, the firm with high fixed and low variable costs incurs losses at a faster rate than the firm with high variable and low fixed costs once sales fall below the break-even point.

EXHIBIT 2.2

Effect of Operating Leverage on Profit

| | Base Case | | 10% Increase in Sales | | 10% Decrease in Sales | |
	High-Fixed-Cost Firm	High-Variable-Cost Firm	High-Fixed-Cost Firm	High-Variable-Cost Firm	High-Fixed-Cost Firm	High-Variable-Cost Firm
Sales	$100,000	$100,000	$110,000	$110,000	$90,000	$90,000
Variable costs	20,000	80,000	22,000	88,000	18,000	72,000
Fixed costs	80,000	20,000	80,000	20,000	80,000	20,000
Profit	$0	$0	$8,000	$2,000	($8,000)	($2,000)

The message of operating leverage should be clear from this example. Firms with high operating leverage benefit more from sales gains than do firms with low operating leverage. At the same time, firms with high operating leverage are more sensitive to sales-volume declines, since losses will be incurred at a faster rate. Knowledge of a firm's cost structure will therefore prove valuable in assessing the gains and losses from changes in sales volume brought about by marketing efforts.

■ PREPARING A PRO FORMA INCOME STATEMENT

Since marketing managers are accountable for the profit impact of their actions, they must translate their strategies and tactics into *pro forma*, or projected, income statements. A *pro forma* income statement displays projected revenues, budgeted expenses, and estimated net profit for an organization, product, or service during a specific planning period, usually a year. *Pro forma* income statements include a sales forecast and a listing of variable and fixed costs that can be programmed or committed.

Pro forma income statements can be prepared in different ways and reflect varying levels of specificity. Exhibit 2.3 on page 44 shows a typical layout for a *pro forma* income statement consisting of six major categories or line items:

1. *Sales*—forecasted unit volume times unit selling price.

2. *Cost of goods sold*—costs incurred in buying or producing products and services. Generally speaking, these costs are constant per unit within certain volume ranges and vary with total unit volume.

3. *Gross margin* (sometimes called gross profit)—represents the remainder after cost of goods sold has been subtracted from sales.

4. *Marketing expenses*—generally, programmed expenses budgeted to produce sales. Advertising expenses are typically fixed. Sales expenses can be fixed, such as a salesperson's salary, or variable, such as sales commissions. Freight or delivery expenses are typically constant per unit and vary with total unit volume.

5. *General and administrative expenses*—generally, committed fixed costs for the planning period, which cannot be avoided if the organization is to operate. These costs are frequently called overhead.

6. *Net income before (income) taxes* (often called net profit before taxes)—the remainder after all costs have been subtracted from sales.

EXHIBIT 2.3

Pro Forma Income Statement for the 12-Month Period Ended December 31, 19__

Sales		$1,000,000
Cost of goods sold		500,000
Gross margin		$500,000
Marketing expenses		
Sales expenses	$170,000	
Advertising expenses	90,000	
Freight or delivery expenses	40,000	300,000
General and administrative expenses		
Administrative salaries	$120,000	
Depreciation on buildings and equipment	20,000	
Interest expense	5,000	
Property taxes and insurance	5,000	
Other administrative expenses	5,000	155,000
Net profit before (income) tax		$45,000

A *pro forma* income statement reflects a marketing manager's expectations (sales) given certain inputs (costs). This means that a manager must think specifically about customer response to strategies and tactics and focus attention on the organization's financial objectives of profitability and growth when preparing a *pro forma* income statement.

■ **SUMMARY**

This chapter provides an overview of basic accounting and financial concepts. A word of caution is necessary, however. Financial analysis of marketing actions is a necessary but insufficient criterion for justifying marketing programs. A careful analysis of other variables impinging on the decision at hand is required. Thus, judgment enters the picture. "Numbers" serve only to complement general marketing analysis skills and are not an end in themselves. In this regard, it is wise to consider some words of Albert Einstein: "Not everything that counts can be counted, and not everything that can be counted counts."

■ **EXERCISES**

1. Executives of Studio Recordings, Inc., produced the latest compact disc by the Starshine Sisters Band, titled *Sunshine/Moonshine.* The following cost information pertains to the new CD:

CD package and disc (direct material and labor)	$1.25/CD
Songwriters' royalties	$0.35/CD
Recording artists' royalties	$1.00/CD
Advertising and promotion	$275,000
Studio Recordings, Inc., overhead	$250,000
Selling price to CD distributor	$9.00

Calculate the following:

    a. Contribution per CD unit

    b. Break-even volume in CD units and dollars

    c. Net profit if 1 million CDs are sold

    d. Necessary CD unit volume to achieve a $200,000 profit

2. The group product manager for ointments at American Therapeutic Corporation was reviewing price and promotion alternatives for two products: Rash-Away and Red-Away. Both products were designed to reduce skin irritation, but Red-Away was primarily a cosmetic treatment whereas Rash-Away also included a compound that eliminated the rash.

    The price and promotion alternatives recommended for the two products by their respective brand managers included the possibility of using additional promotion or a price reduction to stimulate sales volume. A volume, price, and cost summary for the two products follows:

	Rash-Away	*Red-Away*
Unit price	$2.00	$1.00
Unit variable costs	1.40	0.25
Unit contribution	$0.60	$0.75
Unit volume	1,000,000 units	1,500,000 units

    Both brand managers included a recommendation to either reduce price by 10 percent or invest an incremental $150,000 in advertising.

    a. What absolute increase in unit sales and dollar sales will be necessary to recoup the incremental increase in advertising expenditures for Rash-Away? For Red-Away?

    b. How many additional sales dollars must be produced to cover each $1.00 of incremental advertising for Rash-Away? For Red-Away?

    c. What absolute increase in unit sales and dollar sales will be necessary to maintain the level of total contribution dollars if the price of each product is reduced by 10 percent?

3. After spending $300,000 for research and development, chemists at Diversified Citrus Industries have developed a new breakfast drink. The drink, called Zap, will provide the consumer with twice the amount of Vitamin C currently available in breakfast drinks. Zap will be packaged in an eight-ounce can and will be introduced to the breakfast drink market, which is estimated to be equivalent to 21 million eight-ounce cans nationally.

    One major management concern is the lack of funds available for advertising. Accordingly, management has decided to use newspapers (rather than television) to promote the product in the introductory year in major metropolitan areas that account for 65 percent of U.S. breakfast drink volume. Newspaper advertising will carry a coupon that will entitle the consumer to receive $0.20 off the price of the first can purchased. The retailer will receive the regular margin and be reimbursed by Diversified Citrus Industries. Past experience indicates that for every five cans sold during the introductory year, one coupon will be returned. The cost of the newspaper advertising campaign (excluding coupon returns) will be $250,000. Other fixed overhead costs are expected to be $90,000 per year.

    Management has decided that the suggested retail price to the consumer for the eight-ounce can will be $0.50. The only unit variable costs for the product are $0.18 for materials and $0.06 for labor. The company intends to

give retailers a margin of 20 percent off the suggested retail price and wholesalers' a margin of 10 percent of the retailers' cost of the item.

   a. At what price will Diversified Citrus Industries be selling its product
to wholesalers?

   b. What is the contribution per unit for Zap?

   c. What is the break-even unit volume in the first year?

   d. What is the first-year break-even share of market?

4. Max Leonard, Vice President of Marketing for Dysk Computer, Inc., must decide whether to introduce a mid-priced version of the firm's DC6900 minicomputer product line—the DC6900-X minicomputer. The DC6900-X would
   sell for $3,900, with unit variable costs of $1,800. Projections made by an independent marketing research firm indicate that the DC6900-X would
   achieve a sales volume of 500,000 units next year, in its first year of commercialization. One-half of the first year's volume would come from competitors'
   minicomputers and market growth. However, a consumer research study indicates that 30 percent of the DC6900-X sales volume would come from the
   higher-priced DC6900-Omega minicomputer, which sells for $5,900 (with
   unit variable costs of $2,200). Another 20 percent of the DC6900-X sales vol-
   ume would come from the economy-priced DC6900-Alpha minicomputer,
   priced at $2,500 (with unit variable costs of $1,200). The DC6900-Omega
   unit volume is expected to be 400,000 units next year, and the DC6900-Al-
   pha is expected to achieve a 600,000-unit sales level. The fixed costs of
   launching the DC6900-X have been forecast to be $2 million during the first
   year of commercialization. Should Mr. Leonard add the DC6900-X model to
   the line of minicomputers?

5. The annual planning process at Century Office Systems, Inc., had been arduous but produced a number of important marketing initiatives for the next
   year. Most notably, company executives had decided to restructure its product-marketing team into two separate groups: (1) Corporate Office Systems
   and (2) Home Office Systems. Angela Blake was assigned responsibility for
   the Home Office Systems group, which would market the company's word-
   processing hardware and software for home and office-at-home use by individuals. Her marketing plan, which included a sales forecast for next year of
   $25 million, was the result of a detailed market analysis and negotiations with
   individuals both inside and outside the company. Discussions with the sales
   director indicated that 40 percent of the company sales force would be dedicated to selling products of the Home Office Systems group. Sales representatives would receive a 15 percent commission on sales of home office systems. Under the new organizational structure, the Home Office Systems
   group would be charged with 40 percent of the budgeted sales force expenditure. The sales director's budget for salaries and fringe benefits of the sales
   force and noncommission selling costs for both the Corporate and Home Office Systems groups was $7.5 million.

      The advertising and promotion budget contained three elements: trade
   magazine advertising, cooperative newspaper advertising with Century Office Systems, Inc., dealers, and sales promotion materials including product
   brochures, technical manuals, catalogs, and point-of-purchase displays. Trade
   magazine ads and sales promotion materials were to be developed by the
   company's advertising and public relations agency. Production and media
   placement costs were budgeted at $300,000. Cooperative advertising copy
   for both newspaper and radio use had budgeted production costs of
   $100,000. Century Office Systems, Inc.'s, cooperative advertising allowance

policy stated that the company would allocate 5 percent of company sales to dealers to promote its office systems. Dealers always used their complete co-operative advertising allowances.

Meetings with manufacturing and operations personnel indicated that the direct costs of material and labor and direct factory overhead to produce the Home Office System product line represented 50 percent of sales. The accounting department would assign $600,000 in indirect manufacturing overhead (for example, depreciation, maintenance) to the product line and $300,000 for administrative overhead (clerical, telephone, office space, and so forth). Freight for the product line would average 8 percent of sales.

Blake's staff consisted of two product managers and a marketing assistant. Salaries and fringe benefits for Ms. Blake and her staff were $250,000 per year.

a. Prepare a *pro forma* income statement for the Home Office Systems group given the information provided.

b. Prepare a *pro forma* income statement for the Home Office Systems group given annual sales of only $20 million.

c. At what level of dollar sales will the Home Office Systems group break even?

CHAPTER 3

Marketing Decision Making and Case Analysis

 Skill in decision making is a prerequisite to being an effective marketing manager. Indeed, Nobel laureate Herbert Simon viewed managing and decision making as being one and the same.[1] Another management theorist, Peter Drucker, has said that the burden of decision making can be lessened and better decisions can result if a manager recognizes that "decision making is a rational and systematic process and that its organization is a definite sequence of steps, each of them in turn rational and systematic."[2]

One objective of this chapter is to introduce a systematic process for decision making; another is to introduce basic considerations in case analysis. Just as decision making and managing can be viewed as being identical in scope, so the decision-making process and case analysis go hand in hand.

■ DECISION MAKING

Although no simple formula exists that can assure a correct solution to all problems at all times, use of a systematic decision-making process can increase the likelihood of arriving at better solutions.[3] The decision-making process described here is called DECIDE:[4]

Define the problem.

Enumerate the decision factors.

Consider relevant information.

Identify the best alternative.

Develop a plan for implementing the chosen alternative.

Evaluate the decision and the decision process.

A definition and a discussion of the implications of each step follow.

Define the Problem

The philosopher John Dewey observed that "a problem well defined is half solved." What this statement means in a marketing setting is that a well-defined problem outlines the framework within which a solution can be derived. This framework includes the *objectives* of the decision maker, a recognition of *constraints,* and a clearly articulated *success measure*, or goal, for assessing progress toward solving the problem.

Consider the situation faced by El Nacho Foods, a marketer of Mexican foods. The company had positioned its line of Mexican foods as a high-quality brand and used advertising effectively to convey that message. Shortly after the company's introduction of frozen dinners, two of its competitors began cutting the price of their frozen dinner entrees. The firm lost market share and sales as a result of these price reductions; this loss led to reductions in the contribution dollars available for advertising and sales promotion. How might the problem be defined in this situation? One definition of the problem leads to the question "Should we reduce our price?" A much better definition of the problem leads one to ask: "How can we maintain our quality brand image (objective) and regain our lost market share (success measure), given limited funds for advertising and sales promotion (constraint)?"

The first problem definition asks for a response to an immediate issue facing the company. It does not articulate the broader and more important considerations of competitive positioning. Hence, the problem statement fails to capture the significance of the issue raised. The second definition provides a broader perspective on the immediate issue posed and allows the manager greater latitude in seeking solutions.

In a case study, the analyst is frequently given alternative courses of action to consider. The narrow approach to case analysis is simply to compare these different options. Such an approach often leads to the selection of alternative A or alternative B without regard to the significance of the choice in the broader context of the situation facing the company or the decision maker.

Enumerate the Decision Factors

Two sets of decision factors must be enumerated in the decision-making process: (1) *alternative courses of action,* and (2) *uncertainties* in the competitive environment. Alternative courses of action are controllable decision factors because the decision maker has complete command of them. Alternatives are typically product-market strategies or changes in the various elements of the organization's marketing mix (described in Chapter 1). Uncertainties, on the other hand, are uncontrollable factors that the manager cannot influence. In a marketing context, they often include actions of competitors, market size, and buyer response to marketing action. Assumptions often have to be made concerning these factors. These assumptions need to be spelled out, particularly if they will influence the evaluation of alternative courses of action.

A recent experience of Cluett Peabody and Company, the maker of Arrow shirts, illustrates how the combination of an action and uncertainties can spell disaster. Arrow departed from its normal practice of selling classic men's shirts to offer a new line featuring bolder colors, busier patterns, and higher prices (action). The firm soon realized that men's tastes had changed to more conservative styles (environmental uncertainties). The result? The company posted a $4.5 million loss. According to the company president, "We tried to be exciting, and we really didn't look at the market."[5]

Case analysis provides an opportunity to relate alternatives to uncertainties, and these factors *must* be related if decision making is to be effective. No expected outcome, financial or otherwise, of a chosen course of action can realistically be considered apart from the environment into which it is introduced.

Consider Relevant Information

The third step in the decision-making process is the consideration of relevant information. *Relevant information*, like the relevant costs discussed in Chapter 2, consists of information that relates to the alternatives identified by the manager as being likely to affect future events. More specifically, relevant information might include characteristics of the industry or competitive environment, characteristics of the organization (such as competitive strengths and position), and characteristics of the alternatives themselves.

Identifying relevant information is difficult both for the practicing manager and for the case analyst. There is frequently an overabundance of facts, figures, and viewpoints available in any decision-making setting. Determining what matters and what does not is a skill that is best gained through experience. Analyzing many and varied cases is one way to develop this skill.

Two notes of caution are necessary. First, the case analyst must resist the temptation to consider *everything* in a case as "fact." Many cases, including actual marketing situations, contain conflicting data. Part of the task in any case analysis is to exercise judgment in assessing the validity of the data presented. Second, in many instances relevant information must be created. An example of creating relevant information is the blending together of several pieces of data, as in the calculation of a simple break-even point.

It should be clear at this point that even though the consideration of relevant information is the third step in the decision-making process, relevant information will also affect the two previous steps. As the manager or case analyst becomes more deeply involved in considering and evaluating information, the problem definition may be modified or the decision factors may change.

Upon the conclusion of the first three steps, the manager or case analyst has completed a *situation analysis*. The situation analysis should produce an answer to the synoptic question "Where are we now?" (Specific questions relating to situation analysis are found in Exhibit 3.3 later in this chapter.)

Identify the Best Alternative

Identifying the best alternative is the fourth step in the decision-making process. The selection of a course of action is not simply a matter of choosing Alternative A over other alternatives but, rather, of evaluating identified alternatives and the uncertainties apparent in the problem setting.

A framework for identifying the best alternative is *decision analysis*, which was introduced in Chapter 1. In its simplest form, decision analysis matches each alternative identified by the manager with the uncertainties existing in the environment and assigns a quantitative value to the outcome associated with each match. Managers implicitly use a decision tree and a payoff table to describe the relationship among alternatives, uncertainties, and potential outcomes. The use of decision analysis and the application of decision trees and payoff tables can be illustrated by referring back to the situation faced by El Nacho Foods.

Suppose that at the conclusion of Step 2 in the DECIDE process (that is, enumerating decision factors), El Nacho executives identified two alternatives: (1) reduce the price on frozen dinners, or (2) maintain the price. They also recognized two uncertainties: (1) competitors could maintain the lower price, or (2) competitors could reduce the price further. Suppose further that at the conclusion of Step 3 in the DECIDE process (considering relevant information), El Nacho executives examined the changes in market share and sales volume that would be brought about by the pricing actions. They also calculated the contribution per unit of frozen dinners for each alternative for each competitor response. They performed a contribution analysis because the problem was defined in terms of contribution to advertising and sales promotion in Step 1 of the DECIDE process (defining the problem).

Given two alternatives, two competitive responses, and a calculated contribution per unit for each combination, they identified four unique financial outcomes. These outcomes are displayed in the decision tree shown in Exhibit 3.1 on page 52.

It is apparent from the decision tree that the largest contribution will be generated if El Nacho maintains its price on frozen dinners *and* competitors maintain

EXHIBIT 3.1

Decision Tree for El Nacho Foods

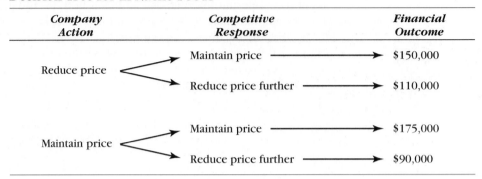

Company Action	Competitive Response	Financial Outcome
Reduce price	Maintain price	$150,000
	Reduce price further	$110,000
Maintain price	Maintain price	$175,000
	Reduce price further	$90,000

their lower price. If El Nacho maintains its price and competitors reduce their price further, however, the lowest contribution among the four outcomes identified will be generated. The choice of an alternative obviously depends on the likelihood of occurrence of uncertainties in the environment.

A *payoff table* is a useful tool for displaying the alternatives, uncertainties, and outcomes facing a firm. In addition, a payoff table includes another dimension—management's subjective determination of the probability of the occurrence of an uncertainty. Suppose, for example, that El Nacho management believes that competitors are also operating with slim contribution margins and hence are most likely to maintain the lower price regardless of El Nacho's action. They believe that there is a 10 percent chance that competitors will reduce the price of frozen dinners even further.[6] Since only two uncertainties have been identified, the subjective probability of competitors' maintaining their price is 90 percent (note that the probabilities assigned to the uncertainties must total 1.0, or 100 percent). Given these probabilities, the payoff table for El Nacho Foods is as shown in Exhibit 3.2.

The payoff table allows the manager or case analyst to compute the "expected value" for each alternative. The expected value is calculated by multiplying the outcome for each uncertainty by its probability of occurrence and then totaling across the uncertainties for each alternative. The expected value of an alternative can be viewed as the value that would be obtained if the manager were to choose the same alternative many times under the same conditions.

The expected value of the price-reduction alternative equals the probability that competitors will maintain prices, multiplied by the financial contribution if competitors maintain prices, plus the probability that competitors will further reduce prices,

EXHIBIT 3.2

Payoff Table for El Nacho Foods

		Uncertainties	
		Competitors maintain price (probability = 0.9)	Competitors reduce price (probability = 0.1)
Alternatives	Reduce price	$150,000	$110,000
	Maintain price	$175,000	$90,000

multiplied by the financial contribution if competitors further reduce prices. The calculation is

$$(0.9)(\$150,000) + (0.1)(\$110,000) = \$135,000 + \$11,000 = \$146,000$$

The expected value of maintaining the price is

$$(0.9)(\$175,000) + (0.1)(\$90,000) = \$157,500 + \$9,000 = \$166,500$$

The higher average contribution of \$166,500 for maintaining the price indicates that El Nacho's management should maintain the price. The contribution is higher because competitors are expected to maintain their prices nine times out of ten. Under the same conditions (same outcomes, same probability estimates), El Nacho would achieve an average contribution of \$146,000 if the price-reduction alternative were chosen. A rational management would therefore select the price-maintenance alternative.

Familiarity with decision analysis is important for four reasons. First, decision analysis is a fundamental tool for considering "what if" situations. By organizing alternatives, uncertainties, and outcomes in this manner, a manager or case analyst becomes sensitive to the dynamic processes present in a competitive environment. Second, decision analysis forces the case analyst to quantify outcomes associated with specific actions. Third, decision analysis is useful in a variety of settings. For example, Ford Motor Company used decision analysis in deciding whether to produce its own tires; Pillsbury used it in determining whether to switch from a box to a bag for a certain grocery product.[7] Fourth, an extension of decision analysis can be used in determining the value of "perfect" information; this topic is discussed in Chapter 5.

Develop a Plan for Implementing the Chosen Alternative

The selection of a course of action must be followed by development of a plan for its implementation. Simply deciding what to do will not make it happen. The execution phase is critical, and planning for it forces the case analyst to consider resource allocation and timing questions. For example, if a new product launch is recommended, it is important to consider how managerial, financial, and manufacturing resources will be allocated to this course of action. If a price reduction is recommended, it will be important to monitor whether the reduced prices are reaching the final consumer and not being absorbed by resellers in the marketing channel. Timing is crucial, since a marketing plan takes time to develop and implement.

As a final note, it is important to recognize that strategy formulation and implementation are not necessarily separate sequential processes. Rather, an interactive give-and-take occurs between formulation and implementation until the case analyst realizes that "what might be done can be done," given organizational strengths and market requirements. Another reading of the discussion on the marketing mix in Chapter 1 will highlight these points.

Evaluate the Decision and the Decision Process

The last step in the decision-making process is evaluating the decision made and the decision process itself. With respect to the decision itself, two questions should be asked. First, *Was a decision made*? This seemingly odd question addresses a common shortcoming of case analyses, whereby a case analyst does not make a decision but, rather, "talks about" the situation facing the organization.

The second question is, *Was the decision appropriate, given the situation identified in the case setting*? This question speaks to the issue of insufficient information on the one hand and the failure to consider and interpret information on the other. In many marketing cases, and indeed in some actual business situations, some of the information needed to make a decision is simply not available. When information is incomplete, assumptions must be made. A case analyst is often expected to make assumptions to fill in gaps, but such assumptions should be logically developed and articulated. Merely making assumptions to make the "solution" fit a preconceived notion of the correct answer is a death knell in case analysis and business practice.

The case analyst should constantly monitor how he or she applies the decision-making process. The mere fact that one's decision was right is not sufficient reason to think that the decision process was appropriate. For example, we have all found ourselves lost while trying to locate a home or business from an address. Eventually we somehow find it, but are again at a loss when later asked to direct someone else to the same address. Analogously, the case analyst may arrive at the "correct" solution but be unable to outline (map) the process involved.

After completing a class discussion of a case, a written case assignment, or a group presentation, the case analyst should critically examine his or her performance by answering the following questions:

1. Did I define the problem adequately?

2. Did I identify all pertinent alternatives and uncertainties? Were my assumptions realistic?

3. Did I consider all information relevant to the case?

4. Did I recommend the appropriate course of action? If so, was my logic consistent with the recommendation? If not, were my assumptions different from the assumptions made by others? Did I overlook an important piece of information?

5. Did I consider how my recommendation could be implemented?

Honest answers to these questions will improve the chances of making better decisions in the future.

■ CASE ANALYSIS

How do I prepare a case? This question is voiced by virtually every student exposed to the case method for the first time. One of the most difficult tasks in preparing a case for presentation—or, more generally, resolving an actual marketing problem—is structuring your thinking process to address relevant forces confronting the organization in question. The previous discussion of the decision-making process should be of help in this regard. The remainder of this chapter provides some useful hints to assist you in preparing a marketing case.

Approaching the Case

On your first reading of a marketing case, you should concentrate on becoming acquainted with the situation in which the organization finds itself. This first reading should provide some insights into the problem requiring resolution, as well as background information on the environment and organization.

Then read the case again, paying particular attention to key facts and assumptions. At this point, you should determine the relevance and reliability of the quantitative data provided in the context of what you see as the issues or problems facing the organization. Valuable insights often arise from analyzing two or more bits of quantitative information concurrently. It is essential that extensive note taking occurs during the second reading. Working by writing is very important; simply highlighting statements or numbers in the case is not sufficient. Behavioral scientists estimate that the human mind can focus on only eight facts at a time and that our mental ability to link these facts in a meaningful way is limited without assistance.[8]

Experienced analysts and managers always work out ideas on paper—whether they are working alone or in a group.

There are three pitfalls you should avoid during the second reading. First, *do not rush to a conclusion*. If you do so, information is likely to be overlooked or possibly distorted to fit a preconceived notion of the answer. Second, *do not "work the numbers"* until you understand their meaning and derivation. Third, *do not confuse supposition with fact*. Many statements are made in a case, such as "Our firm subscribes to the marketing concept." Is this a fact, based on an appraisal of the firm's actions and performance, or a supposition?

Formulating the Analysis

The previous remarks should provide some direction in approaching a marketing case. The marketing case analysis worksheet shown in Exhibit 3.3 provides a framework for organizing information. Four analytical categories are shown, with illustrative questions pertaining to each. You will find it useful to consider each analytical category when preparing a case.

Nature of the Industry, Market, and Buying Behavior The first analytical category focuses on the organization's environment—the context in which the organization operates. Specific topics of interest include (1) an assessment of the structure, conduct, and performance of the industry and competition, and (2) an understanding of who the buyers are and why, where, when, how, what, and how much they buy.

The Organization It is important to develop an understanding of the organization's financial, human, and material resources, its strengths and weaknesses, and the reasons for its success or failure. Of particular importance is an understanding of what

EXHIBIT 3.3

Marketing Case Analysis Worksheet

	Specific Points of Interest
Nature of the industry, market, and buyer behavior	1. What is the nature of industry structure, conduct, and performance?
	2. Who are the competitors, and what are their strengths and weaknesses?
	3. How do consumers buy in this industry or market?
	4. Can the market be segmented? How? Can the segments be quantified?
	5. What are the requirements for success in this industry?
The organization	1. What are the organization's mission, objectives, and distinctive competency?
	2. What is its offering to the market? How can its past and present performance be characterized? What is its potential?
	3. What is the situation in which the manager or organization finds itself?
	4. What factors have contributed to the present situation?
A plan of action	1. What actions are available to the organization?
	2. What are the costs and benefits of action in both qualitative and quantitative terms?
	3. Is there a disparity between what the organization wants to do, should do, can do, and must do?
Potential outcomes	1. What will be the buyer, trade, and competitive response to each course of action?
	2. How will each course of action satisfy buyer, trade, and organization requirements?
	3. What is the potential profitability of each course of action?
	4. Will the action enhance or reduce the organization's ability to compete in the future?

the organization wishes to do. The "fit" between the organization and its environment represents the first major link drawn in case analysis. This link is the essence of the situation analysis, since it is an interpretation of where the organization currently stands. A SWOT analysis like that described in Chapter 1 might be helpful in organizing your thoughts at this point.

A Plan of Action You should be prepared to identify possible courses of action on the basis of the situation analysis. More often than not, several alternatives are possible, and each should be fully articulated. Each course of action typically has associated costs and revenues. These should be carefully calculated on the basis of realistic estimates of the magnitude of effort expected in their pursuit.

Potential Outcomes Finally, the potential outcomes of all courses of action identified should be evaluated. On the basis of the appraisal of outcomes, one course of action or strategy should be recommended. The evaluation, however, must indicate not only why the recommendation was preferred, but also why other actions were dismissed.

Though it is always useful to consider each of the analytical categories just described, the method in which they are arranged may vary. There is no one way to analyze a case, just as there is no single correct way to attack a marketing problem. Just be sure to cover the bases.

Communicating the Analysis

Three means exist for communicating case analyses: (1) class discussion, (2) group presentation, and (3) written report.

Class Discussion Discussing case studies in the classroom setting can be an exciting experience, provided that each student actively prepares for and participates in the discussion. Preparation involves more than simply reading the case prior to the scheduled class period—the case should be carefully analyzed, using the four analytical categories described earlier. Four to five hours of preparation are usually required for each assigned case. The notes developed during the preparation should be brought to class.

Similarly, participation involves more than talking. Other students should be carefully watched and listened to during a class discussion. Attentiveness to the views of others is necessary in order to build on previous comments and analyses. Most class discussions follow a similar format. Class analysis begins with a discussion of the organization and its environment. This discussion is followed first by a discussion of the alternative courses of action and then by a consideration of possible implementation strategies. Knowing where the class is in the discussion is important both for organizing the multitude of ideas and analyses presented and for preparing remarks for the subsequent steps in the class discussion.

Immediately after the class discussion, you should prepare a short summary of the analysis developed in class. This summary, which should include the specific facts, ideas, analyses, and generalizations developed, will be useful in comparing and contrasting case situations.

Group Presentation Group presentation of a case requires a slightly different set of skills. Usually a group of three to five students conducts a rigorous analysis of a case and presents it to classmates. Role-playing may be featured: class members may serve as an executive committee witnessing the presentation of a task force or project team.

If the instructor asks you to form your own groups, do not form groups solely on the basis of friendship. Rather, try to develop a balanced team where various skills complement one another (financial skills, oral presentation skills, and so on).

Seek out individuals who are committed and dependable. Finally, organize the efforts of the group around individual interests and skills.

A polished presentation is very important. Thus, the group should rehearse its presentation, with group members seriously critiquing one another's performance. At the very least, the group should prepare an outline of the presentation (including important exhibits) and distribute it to the class. It is a good idea to use transparencies or other visual aids to highlight important points and unique analyses, but *don't* read transparencies to your audience. For further information, consult a text on oral presentations or guidelines for effective speaking.

Written Report What you need to do to generate a written analysis of a case assignment is similar to what you should do to prepare for class discussion. The only difference is in the submission of the analysis; a written report should be carefully organized, legible (preferably typed), and grammatically correct.

There is no one correct approach to organizing a written case analysis. However, it is usually wise to think about the report as having three major sections: (1) identification of the strategic issues and problems, (2) analysis and evaluation, and (3) recommendations. The first section should contain a focused paragraph that defines the problem and specifies the constraints and options available to the organization. Material in the second section should provide a carefully developed assessment of the industry, market and buyer behavior, the organization, and the alternative courses of action. *Analysis and evaluation should represent the bulk of the written report.* This section should not contain a restatement of case information; it should contain an assessment of the facts, quantitative data, and management views. The last section should consist of a set of recommendations. These recommendations should be documented with references to the previous section and should be operational given the case situation. By all means, commit to a decision!

A case and a written student analysis of it are presented in the appendix at the end of the book. It is recommended that you carefully analyze the case before reading the student analysis.

NOTES

1. Herbert A. Simon, *The New Science of Management Decision* (New York: Harper & Row, 1960).

2. Peter Drucker, "How to Make a Business Decision," *Nation's Business* (April 1956): 38–39.

3. There are a variety of systematic approaches to the decision-making process. For a review, see Ernest R. Archer, "How to Make a Busines Decision: An Analysis of Theory and Practice," *Management Review* (February 1980): 54–61; Beverly Geber, "Decisions, Decisions," *Training* (April 1988): 52–62; and James R. Evans, *Creative Thinking in the Decision and Management Sciences* (Cincinnati, OH: South-Western Publishing, 1991).

4. DECIDE acronym copyright © by William Rudelius. It is used here with permission.

5. "Cluett Peabody & Co. Loses Shirt Trying to Jazz Up the Arrow Man," *Wall Street Journal* (July 28, 1988): 24.

6. An issue that frequently arises in developing these subjective probabilities is how to select them. One source is past experience, in the form of statistics such as A. T. Kearney's probabilities of success for alternative strategies, presented in Chapter 1. Alternatively, case information can be used to develop probability estimates. At the very least, when two possible uncertainties exist, a subjective probability of .5 can be assigned to each. This means that the two uncertainties have an equal chance of occurring. These probabilities can then be revised up or down, depending on case information.

7. These examples and others are found in Jacob W. Ulvila and Rex V. Brown, "Decision Analysis Comes of Age," *Harvard Business Review* (September–October 1982): 130–141.

8. Amitai Etzioni, "Humble Decision Making," *Harvard Business Review* (July–August 1989): 122–126.

CHAPTER 4

Opportunity Analysis and Market Targeting

 The development and implementation of marketing strategy are complicated and challenging tasks. At its pinnacle, marketing strategy involves the selection of markets and the development of programs to reach these markets. This process is carried out in a manner that simultaneously benefits both the markets selected (satisfying the needs or wants of buyers) and the organization (typically in dollar-profit terms).

Within this framework, a necessary first task is opportunity analysis and market targeting. This chapter describes analytical concepts and tools that marketing managers find useful in performing opportunity analyses and selecting market targets.

■ OPPORTUNITY ANALYSIS

Opportunity analysis consists of three interrelated activities:

- Opportunity identification
- Opportunity-organization matching
- Opportunity evaluation

Opportunities arise from identifying new types or classes of buyers, uncovering unsatisfied needs of buyers, or creating new ways or means for satisfying buyer needs. Opportunity analysis focuses on finding markets that an organization can profitably serve.

The case of Reebok International, Ltd., highlights the value of careful *opportunity identification.* In 1981, Reebok was known primarily for its custom running shoes. Consumer interest in running had plateaued, however, and new opportunities had to be identified for the company to grow. Careful investigation revealed that there existed numerous opportunities for product development based on buyer types and needs. In quick succession, Reebok introduced an aerobic dance shoe in 1982; a tennis shoe, a basketball shoe, and a children's shoe in 1984; a walking shoe in 1986; an all-purpose shoe in 1988; step-trainers in 1991; hiking shoes in 1994; and special track and field shoes for 1996 U.S. Olympians. Reebok had identified buyer needs based on athletic activities (tennis, basketball, walking, track and field) and

E X H I B I T   4 . 1

Opportunity Evaluation Matrix: Attractiveness Criteria

Market Niche Criterion	Competitive Activity	Buyer Requirements	Demand/ Supply	Political, Technological, and Socioeconomic Forces	Organizational Capabilities
Buyer type	How many and which firms are competing for this user group?	What affects the willingness and ability to buy?	Do different buyer types have different levels of effective demand? How important are adequate sources of supply?	How sensitive are different buyers to these forces?	Can we gain access to buyers through marketing-mix variables? Can we supply these buyers?
Buyer needs	Which firms are satisfying which buyer needs?	Are there buyer needs that are not being satisfied? What are they?	Are buyer needs likely to be long term? Do we have or can we acquire resources to satisfy buyer needs?	How sensitive are buyer needs to these forces?	Which buyer needs can our organization satisfy?
Means for satisfying buyer needs	What are the strategies being employed to satisfy buyer needs?	Is the technology for satisfying buyer needs changing?	To what extent are the means for satisfying buyer needs affected by supply sources? Is the demand for the means for satisfying buyer needs changing?	How sensitive are the means for satisfying buyer needs to these forces?	Do we have the financial, human, technological, and marketing expertise to satisfy buyer needs?

buyer types (men, women, and children). By doing so, Reebok increased sales from $1 million to more than $3.6 billion in 15 years. In 1997, Reebok's attention turned to opportunities in the global marketplace. The company quickly learned that the English want white cricket shoes only and the Japanese want ultralight running shoes.[1]

Opportunity-organization matching determines whether an identified market opportunity is consistent with the definition of the organization's business, mission statement, and distinctive competencies. This determination usually involves an assessment of the organization's strengths and weaknesses and an identification of the success requirements for operating profitably in a market. A SWOT analysis like that described in Chapter 1 is often employed to assess the match between identified market opportunities and the organization.

The lack of a perceived match between opportunity and organization may account for the fact that the Gillette Company never took advantage of the market opportunity for feminine hygiene sprays, even though it had the aerosol technology and marketing experience in introducing feminine products. The product simply was inconsistent with Gillette's business definition. (This situation allegedly occurred because Gillette executives could not bring themselves to mention certain parts of the female anatomy in their business conversations.[2]) Similarly, no steam locomotive manufacturers entered the field of diesel locomotives, and most manufacturers of safety razor blades do not produce electric shavers. The main cause of such actions is usually unwillingness to modify organizational strategy.

Opportunity evaluation typically has two distinct phases—one qualitative and one quantitative. The qualitative phase focuses on matching the attractiveness of an opportunity with the potential for uncovering a market niche. Attractiveness is dependent on (1) competitive activity; (2) buyer requirements; (3) market demand and supplier sources; (4) social, political, economic, and technological forces; and (5) organizational capabilities. Each of these factors in turn must be tied to its impact on the types of buyers sought, the needs of buyers, and the means for satisfying these needs. Exhibit 4.1 is an opportunity evaluation matrix containing illustrative questions useful in the qualitative analysis of a market opportunity. The quantitative phase yields estimates of market sales potential and sales forecasts. It also produces budgets for financial, human, marketing, and production resources, which are necessary to assess the profitability of a market opportunity.

Opportunity identification, matching, and evaluation are challenging assignments, since subjective factors play a large role and managerial insight and foresight are necessary. These activities are even more difficult in the global arena, where social and political forces and uncertainties related to organizational capabilities in unfamiliar economic environments assume a significant role.

■ WHAT IS A MARKET?

The fact that an opportunity has been identified does not necessarily imply that a market exists for the organization. Although definitions vary, a *market* may be considered to be the prospective buyers (individuals or organizations) willing and able to purchase the existing or potential offering (product or service) of an organization.

This definition of a market has several managerial implications. First, the definition focuses on buyers, not on products or services. People and organizations whose idiosyncrasies dictate whether and how products and services will be acquired, consumed, or used make up markets. Second, by highlighting the buyer's willingness and ability to purchase a product or service, this definition introduces the concept of *effective demand.* Even if buyers are willing to purchase a product or service, exchange cannot occur unless they are able to do so. Likewise, if buyers are able to purchase a product or service but are unwilling to do so, exchange will not occur. These relationships are important to grasp because a marketing strategist must ascertain the extent of effective demand for an offering in order to determine whether a market exists. To a large degree, the extent of effective demand will depend on the marketing-mix activities of the organization. Third, use of the term *offering*, rather than *product* or *service*, expands the definition of what organizations provide for buyers. Products and services are not purchased for the sake of purchase; they are purchased for the values or benefits that buyers expect to derive from them. It is for this reason that the late Charles Revson of Revlon Cosmetics continually reiterated that his company did not sell cosmetics but, rather, hope. This expanded definition of an offering requires strategists to consider benefits provided by a product or service apart from its tangible nature.

Frequently one hears or reads about the automobile market, the soft-drink market, or the health-care market. These terms can be misleading because each refers to a composite of multiple minimarkets. Viewing a market as composed of minimarkets allows a marketer to better gauge opportunities. Consider, for example, the "coffee market." Exhibit 4.2 on page 62 shows how the U.S. coffee market might be broken

EXHIBIT 4.2

Market Structure for Coffee

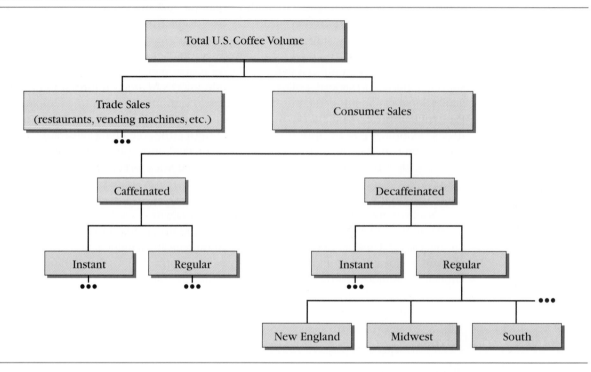

down into multiple markets by a marketing manager for Maxwell House or Folger's. With this breakdown, the manager can more effectively identify who is competing in the caffeinated versus the decaffeinated markets and how they are competing, monitor changes in sales volume for instant decaffeinated coffee, and appreciate differences between buyer taste preferences and competition in the South and in New England. (For these reasons, among others, regional marketing has become popular.[3])

Finally, how a market is defined has a crucial effect on the concept of market share. *Market share* can be defined as the sales of a firm, product, or brand divided by the sales of the "market." Obviously, market definition is critical in calculating this percentage. For example, consider the market share of Brand X, an instant, decaffeinated coffee brand with annual sales of $1 billion. Depending on the definition of the market, the brand's share will range from 12.5 percent to 50 percent, as shown in the following table.

Market Definition	Dollar Sales	Brand X Sales	Market Share
U.S. coffee market	$8 billion	$1 billion	12.5%
U.S. decaffeinated coffee market	$4 billion	$1 billion	25.0%
U.S. instant decaffeinated coffee market	$2 billion	$1 billion	50.0%

■ MARKET SEGMENTATION

A useful technique for structuring markets is *market segmentation*—the breaking down or building up of potential buyers into groups. These groups are typically termed *market segments*. Each segment is thought of as possessing some sort of homogeneous characteristic relating to its purchasing or consumption behavior, which is ultimately reflected in its responsiveness to marketing programs. Market segmentation grew out of the recognition that, in general, an organization cannot be all things to all people.[4]

Although Henry Ford is reputed to have said that buyers of his automobiles could have any color they desired as long as it was black, most marketers today agree that such an undifferentiated marketing strategy is no longer appropriate. The idea that an organization can effectively apply one marketing strategy to all possible buyers is not viable in today's marketing environment.

At the other extreme, unless the organization is highly specialized and sells only to, say, one buyer, it is not feasible to treat each potential buyer as unique. Thus, as Ben Enis has so aptly written, market segmentation "is a compromise between the ineffectiveness of treating all customers alike and the inefficiency of treating each one differently."[5]

Segmentation offers two principal benefits with regard to the development of marketing strategy. First, needs, wants, and behaviors of specific groups of buyers can be more precisely determined. More specifically, the following six fundamental buyer-related questions can be answered for each market segment:

1. Who are they?
2. What do they want to buy?
3. How do they want to buy?
4. When do they want to buy?
5. Where do they want to buy?
6. Why do they want to buy?

Second, resources can be more effectively allocated to marketing-mix activities designed to satisfy the needs, wants, and behaviors of buyer segments. For example, Procter and Gamble markets its Crest toothpaste with different advertising and promotion campaigns directed at six different market segments, including children, Hispanics, and senior citizens.[6]

These advantages, though, are not without their costs. There are research costs associated with identifying appropriate market segments. And designing more than one marketing strategy is likely to increase expenses for such items as offering design, salesperson training, and channel selection.

A variety of measures is useful for segmenting markets. A brief listing includes the following:

- Socioeconomic characteristics, such as sex, age, occupation, income, family life cycle, education, or geographic location
- Buying and usage characteristics, such as end use versus intermediate use, buying for another versus buying for self, size of purchase, or volume of consumption
- Benefits sought from products or services, such as status, economy, taste, or convenience of use

Increasingly, marketers are complementing these measures with attitudinal and life-style measures to better understand why and how people buy, use, or consume their products and services. Segmentation research at Frito-Lay, Inc. is a case in point. In addition to studying consumer socioeconomic characteristics, buying and usage behavior, and product benefits sought, the company has identified two attitudinal and life-style market segments that consume snack chips. "Indulgers" are consumers who know they should limit their fat consumption but cannot, and those who simply don't care. This segment represents 47 percent of snack chip consumers who are heavy users of snack chips. The other 53 percent of consumers are "compromisers," who restrict their snack chip intake because of nutrition concerns.[7]

In selecting the measures to use for segmenting a particular market, the manager must depend on his or her knowledge of their relative contributions to buyer behavior and effective demand. Whichever measures are selected must satisfy a number of important requirements. First, the measures should assist in the identification of distinct groups of prospective buyers. Second, the groups identified should be economically accessible to a product or service organization through existing or possible marketing programs. Finally, the groups should be large enough in terms of sales volume potential to support the costs of the organization serving them. Frito-Lay, Inc. executives believed the "compromiser" segment met all three requirements and targeted this group for a complete line of "better-for-you" products. The most successful of these was Baked Lay's low-fat potato crisps which posted sales of $250 million in its first full year on the market.[8]

■ OFFERING-MARKET MATRIX

A useful procedure for investigating markets is to construct an *offering-market matrix*. Such a matrix relates offerings to selected groups of buyers. Exhibit 4.3 shows an illustrative matrix for hand-held calculators. Four possible user groups (or market segments) are business, scientific, home, and school. Displaying offerings and user groups in this manner facilitates identification of gaps in the calculator market. In other words, it makes it easier to identify which user groups are not being satisfied. Furthermore, competitors and their product offerings can be assigned to specific

EXHIBIT 4.3

Offering-Market Matrix for Hand-Held Calculators

Computational Characteristics	Market Segments (User Groups)			
	Business	*Scientific*	*Home*	*School*
Simple (arithmetic operations only)				
Moderate (arithmetic operations, squares, and square roots)				
Complex (all of the above plus trigonometric functions)				
Very complex (all of the above plus programmable features)				

cells in the matrix. Knowing where competitors are active provides a basis for determining whether a market opportunity exists. Identification of gaps in the market and knowledge of competitive activities in specific offering-market cells should assist the marketing manager in gauging the effective demand for an organization's offering and the likelihood of developing a profitable marketing program. Regardless of whether the organization is investigating a potential or an existing market, development of an offering-market matrix is often a prerequisite for market targeting.

■ MARKET TARGETING

After a market has been segmented, it is necessary to select the segment(s) on which marketing efforts will be focused. *Market targeting* (or target marketing) is merely the specification of the segment(s) the organization wishes to pursue. Once the manager has selected the target market(s), the organization must decide which marketing strategies to employ.

For example, recognizing that Wal-Mart and Home Depot were targeting the home-improvement "do-it-yourselfer" segment for home repairs and remodeling, Payless Cashways targeted the professional remodeler segment. Once decided, the company modified its merchandise assortment, changed its credit and delivery policies, and added a sales force to call on contractors. The result? Sales to professionals grew to 45 percent of Payless's revenues, up from 25 percent of sales in previous years. Profits also improved.[9]

Two frequently used market targeting approaches are *differentiated marketing* and *concentrated marketing*. In a differentiated marketing approach, the organization simultaneously pursues several different market segments, usually with a unique marketing strategy for each. An example of this type of marketing is the strategy of *Time* magazine. It publishes more than 200 different U.S. editions and more than 100 international editions, each targeted at its own geographic and demographic segments. In a concentrated approach, the organization focuses on a single market segment. An extreme case would be one in which an organization marketed a single product offering to a single market segment. More commonly, an organization will offer a product line to a single segment. For many years Gerber proclaimed that "babies are our only business." Today, Gerber further segments the "baby" segment into infants (one year old or less) and toddlers (12 to 30 months) and provides specially prepared foods for each subsegment.[10]

■ MARKET SALES POTENTIAL AND PROFITABILITY

An essential activity in opportunity evaluation is the determination of market sales potential and profitability. Estimating a market's sales potential for offerings is a difficult task even for a seasoned marketing executive. Markets and offerings can be defined in numerous ways that can lead to different estimates of market size and dollar sales potential. This was illustrated earlier in the description of market structure and resulting market shares in the U.S. coffee industry. For innovative offerings or new markets, marketing analysts must often rely almost entirely on judgment and creativity when estimating market sales potential. Therefore, it is understandable that market sales potential estimates vary greatly for high-definition television (HDTV) and electric automobiles. The underlying technology for both offerings is still evolving as is the physical form. In such dynamic settings, measures for identifying prospective market segments are uncertain.

Estimating Market Sales Potential

Market sales potential is a quantitative approximation of effective demand. Specifically, *market sales potential* is the maximum level of sales that might be available to all organizations serving a defined market in a specific time period given (1) the marketing-mix activities and effort of all organizations, and (2) a set of environmental conditions. As this definition indicates, market sales potential is not a fixed amount. Rather, it is a function of a number of factors, some of which are controllable and others not controllable by organizations. For instance, controllable marketing-mix activities and marketing-related expenditures of organizations can influence market sales potential. On the other hand, consumer disposable income, government regulations, and other social, economic, and political conditions are not controllable by organizations, but do affect market sales potential.

Three variables are commonly considered when estimating market sales potential.[11] These include: (1) the number of prospective buyers (B) who are willing and able to purchase an offering; (2) the quantity (Q) of an offering purchased by an average buyer in a specific time period, typically one calendar year; and (3) the price (P) of an average unit of the offering. Market sales potential is the product of these three variables:

Market sales potential = B × Q × P.

Though simple, this expression contains the building blocks for developing a more complex formulation through what is called the *chain ratio method*, which involves multiplying a base number by several adjusting factors that are believed to influence market sales potential. An application of this method by Coca-Cola and Pepsi-Cola is shown in the following calculation of cola-flavored carbonated soft drink potential in a South American country:

$$
\begin{array}{l}
\text{Market sales} \\
\text{potential for} \\
\text{cola-flavored} \\
\text{carbonated soft} \\
\text{drinks in a} \\
\text{country}
\end{array}
=
\left[
\begin{array}{l}
\text{Population aged 8 years and over} \times \text{proportion} \\
\text{of the population who consume carbonated} \\
\text{soft drinks on a daily basis} \times \text{proportion of} \\
\text{the population preferring cola-flavored} \\
\text{carbonated soft drinks} \times \text{the average number} \\
\text{of carbonated soft drink occasions per day} \times \\
\text{the average amount consumed per consump-} \\
\text{tion occasion (expressed in ounces)} \times 365 \text{ days} \\
\text{in a calendar year} \times \text{the average price per} \\
\text{ounce of cola}
\end{array}
\right.
$$

The chain ratio method serves three important purposes. First, it yields a quantitative estimate of market sales potential. Second, it highlights factors that are controllable and not controllable by organizations. Clearly, a country's population aged 8 years and older is an uncontrollable factor. However, the other factors are controllable or can be influenced to some degree. For example, organizations can influence the proportion of a population who consumes carbonated soft drinks through primary demand advertising and the cost of cola drinks through pricing. If either of these two factors change, market sales potential changes, other things being equal. Finally, it affords a manager flexibility in estimating market sales potential for different buyer groups and different offerings. For example, by including another factor such as the proportion of the population preferring diet colas, the potential for this offering can be calculated.

Sales and Profit Forecasting

Sales and profit forecasting follow the estimation of market sales potential. A *sales forecast* is the level of sales a single organization expects to achieve based on a chosen marketing strategy and an assumed competitive environment. An organization's forecasted sales are typically some fraction of estimated market sales potential.

Forecasted sales reflect the size of the target market(s) chosen by the organization and the marketing mix chosen for these target market(s). Forecasted sales also reflect the assumed number of competitors and competitive intensity in the chosen target market(s). For example, suppose an organization's target market represents one-fourth of 1 million prospective buyers for a particular offering. The marketing channel chosen for the offering provides access to about three-fourths of these buyers and the communication program (advertising) reaches these same buyers. Suppose further that the average purchase rate is 20 units of an offering per year and the average offering unit price is $10.00. Using a version of the chain ratio method, forecasted sales might be calculated as follows:

Total Estimated Prospective Buyers	1 million
times	
Target Market (25% of total buyers)	$\times .25$
times	
Distribution/Communication Coverage (75% of target market)	$\times .75$
times	
Annual Purchase Rate (20 units per year)	$\times 20$
times	
Average Offering Unit Price ($10.00)	$\times \$10.00$
Forecasted Sales	$37.5 Million

The $37.5 million sales forecast does not consider the number of competitors vying for the same market target nor does it consider competitive intensity. Therefore, this sales forecast should be adjusted downward to reflect these realities.

Forecasting sales, like estimating market sales potential, is not an easy task. Nevertheless, the task is central to opportunity evaluation and must be undertaken. For this reason, sales forecasting is addressed again in Chapter 5 in the context of marketing research and also in Chapter 6 in reference to product and service life cycles.

Finally, a *pro forma* income statement should be prepared showing forecasted sales, budgeted expenses, and estimated net profit (Chapter 2). When completed, the marketing analyst can review the identified opportunities and decide which can be most profitably pursued given organizational capabilities.

NOTES

1. Reebok's growth is detailed in Eric N. Berkowitz, Roger A. Kerin, Steven W. Hartley, and William Rudelius, *Marketing*, 5th ed. (Chicago: R. D. Irwin, 1997): 233–237.

2. W. Corley, "Gillette Co. Strategizes as Its Rivals Slice at Fat Profit Margins," *The Wall Street Journal* (February 2, 1972): 1*ff*.

3. For an extensive discussion of regional marketing, see S. McKenna, *The Complete Guide to Regional Marketing* (Homewood, IL.: R. D. Irwin, 1992).

4. For a recent and comprehensive treatment of market segmentation, see James H. Myers, *Segmentation and Positioning for Strategic Marketing Decisions* (Chicago: American Marketing Association, 1996).

5. Ben M. Enis, *Marketing Principles: The Management Process*, 2nd ed. (Pacific Palisades, CA: Goodyear, 1977): 241.

6. "Make It Simple," *Business Week* (September 9, 1996): 96–104.

7. "Salting Away Big Profits," *U.S. News & World Report* (September 16, 1996): 71–72.

8. "Frito-Lay Named New Product Marketer of 1995," *Marketing News* (May 6, 1996): Special Supplement.

9. C. Palmeri, "Remodeling Your Business," *Forbes* (August 16, 1993): 43.

10. "Baby Food Is Growing Up," *American Demographics* (May 1993): 20-22.

11. Portions of this discussion are based on Donald R. Lehmann and Russell S. Winer, *Analysis for Marketing Planning*, 4th ed. (Chicago: Richard D. Irwin, 1997): Chapter 6; and Philip Kotler, *Marketing Management*, 9th ed. (Upper Saddle River, NJ: Prentice Hall, 1997): Chapter 4.

Sorzal Distributors

Sorzal Distributors is an importer and distributor of a wide variety of South American and African artifacts. It is also a major source of southwestern Indian—especially Hopi and Navajo—authentic jewelry and pottery. Although the firm's headquarters is located in Phoenix, Arizona, there are currently branch offices in Los Angeles, Miami, and Boston.

Sorzal (named after the national bird of Honduras) originated as a trading post operation near Tucson, Arizona, in the early 1900s. Through a series of judicious decisions, the firm established itself as one of the more reputable dealers in authentic southwestern jewelry and pottery. Over the years, Sorzal gradually expanded its product line to include pre-Columbian artifacts from Peru and Venezuela (see Exhibit 1) and tribal and burial artifacts from Africa. Through its careful verification of the authenticity of these South American and African artifacts, Sorzal developed a national reputation as one of the most respected importers of these types of artifacts.

In the late 1980s Sorzal further expanded its product line to include items that were replicas of authentic artifacts. For example, African fertility gods and masks were made by craftspeople who took great pains to produce these items so that only the truly knowledgeable buyer—a collector—would know that they were replicas. Sorzal now has native craftspeople in Central America, South America, Africa, and the southwestern United States who provide these items. Replicas account for only a small portion of total Sorzal sales; the company agreed to enter this business only at the prodding of the firm's clients, who desired an expanded line. The replicas have found most favor among gift buyers and individuals looking for novelty items.

Sorzal's gross sales are about $12 million and have increased at a constant rate of 20 percent per year over the last decade, despite a recession and little price inflation. Myron Rangard, the firm's national sales manager, attributed the sales increase to the popularity of Sorzal's product line and to the expanded distribution of South American and African artifacts:

> For some reason, our South American and African artifacts have been gaining greater acceptance. Two of our department store customers featured examples of our African line in their Christmas catalogs last year. I personally think consumer tastes are changing from the modern and abstract to the more concrete, like our products.

Sorzal distributes its products exclusively through specialty shops (including interior decorators), firm-sponsored showings, and a few exclusive department stores. Often the company is the sole supplier to its clients. Rangard recently expressed the reasons for this highly limited distribution:

> Our limited distribution has been dictated to us because of the nature of our product line. As acceptance grew, we expanded our distribution to specialty shops and some exclusive department stores. Previously, we had to push our products through our own showings. Furthermore, we just didn't have the product. These South Amer-

EXHIBIT 1

Pre-Columbian Water Vessel From Peru

ican artifacts aren't always easy to get and the political situation in Africa is limiting our supply. Our perennial supply problem has become even more critical in recent years for several reasons. Not only must we search harder for new products, but the competition for authentic artifacts has increased tenfold. On top of this, we must now contend with governments' not allowing exportation of certain artifacts because of their "national significance."

The problem of supply has forced Sorzal to add three new buyers in the last two years. Whereas Sorzal identified 5 major competitors a decade ago, there are 11 today. "Our bargaining position has eroded," noted David Olsen, Director of Procurement. "We have watched our gross margin slip in recent years due to aggressive competitive bidding by others."

"And competition at the retail level has increased also," injected Rangard. "Not only are some of our specialty and exclusive department store customers sending out their own buyers to deal directly with some of our Hopi and Navajo suppliers, but we are often faced with amateurs or fly-by-night competitors. These people move into a city and dump a bunch of inauthentic junk on the public at exorbitant prices. Such antics give the industry a bad name."

In recent years several mass-merchandise department store chains and a number of upper-scale discount operations have begun to sell merchandise similar to that offered by Sorzal. Even though product quality was often mixed and most items were replicas, occasionally an authentic group of items was found in these stores, according to company sales representatives. Subsequent inquiries by both Rangard and Olsen revealed that other competing distributors had signed purchase contracts with these outlets. Moreover, the items were typically being sold at retail prices below those charged by Sorzal's dealers.

In early January, 1997, Rangard was contacted by a mass-merchandise department store chain concerning the possibility of carrying a complete line of Sorzal products and particularly a full assortment of authentic items. The chain was currently selling a competitor's items but wished to add a more exclusive product line. A tentative contract submitted by the chain stated that it would buy at 10 percent below Sorzal's existing prices, and that its initial purchase would be for no less than $250,000. Depending on consumer acceptance, purchases were estimated to be at least $1 million annually. An important clause in the contract dealt with the supply of replicas. Inspection of this clause revealed that Sorzal would have to triple its replica production to satisfy the contractual obligation. Soon after Sorzal executives began discussing the contract, Sorzal's president, Andrew Smythe, mentioned that accepting the contract could have a dramatic effect on how Sorzal defined its business. Smythe added:

> The contract presents us with an opportunity to broaden our firm's position. The upside is that we have the potential to add $1 million in additional sales over and above our annual growth. On the other hand, do we want to commit such a large percent of our business to replicas? Is that the direction that the market is going? What effect will this contract have on our current dealers, and, I might add, our current customers?
>
> I want you both (Rangard and Olsen) to consider this contract in light of your respective functions and the company as a whole. Let's meet in a few days to discuss this matter again.

Jones•Blair Company

In early January 1996, Alexander Barrett, President of Jones•Blair Company, slumped back in his chair as his senior management executives filed out of the conference room. "Another meeting and still no resolution," he thought. After two lengthy meetings, the executive group still had not decided where and how to deploy corporate marketing efforts among the various architectural paint coatings markets served by the company in the southwestern United States. He asked his secretary to schedule another meeting for next week.

■ THE U.S. PAINT INDUSTRY

The U.S. paint industry is divided into three broad segments: (1) architectural coatings, (2) original equipment manufacturing (OEM) coatings, and (3) special purpose coatings. Architectural coatings consist of general purpose paints, varnishes, and lacquers used on residential, commercial, and institutional structures, sold through wholesalers and retailers, and purchased by do-it-yourself consumers, painting contractors, and professional painters. Architectural coatings are commonly called shelf goods and account for 43 percent total industry dollar sales. OEM coatings are formulated to industrial buyer specifications and are applied to original equipment during manufacturing. These coatings are used for durable goods such as automobiles, trucks, transportation equipment, appliances, furniture and fixtures, metal containers and building products, and industrial machinery and equipment. OEM coatings represent 35 percent of total industry dollar sales. Special purpose coatings are formulated for special applications or environmental conditions, such as extreme temperatures, exposure to chemicals, or corrosive conditions. These coatings are used for automotive and machinery refinishing, industrial construction and maintenance (including factories, equipment, utilities, and railroads), bridges, marine applications (ship and offshore facilities such as oil rigs), highway and traffic markings, aerosol and metallic paints, and roof paints. Special purpose coatings account for 22 percent of total industry dollar sales.

The U.S. paint industry is generally considered to be a maturing industry. Industry sales in 1995 were estimated to be slightly over $13 billion. Average annual dollar sales growth was forecasted to approximate the general rate of inflation through 2000.

Outlook for Architectural Paint Coatings and Sundries

Industry sources estimated U.S. sales of architectural paint coatings and sundries (brushes, rollers, paint removers and thinners, etc.) to be $10-plus billion in 1995. Ar-

The cooperation of Jones•Blair Company in the preparation of this case is gratefully acknowledged. This case was prepared by Professor Roger A. Kerin, Edwin L. Cox School of Business, Southern Methodist University, as a basis for class discussion and is not designed to illustrate effective or ineffective handling of an administrative situation. Certain names and selected market and sales data have been disguised and are not useful for research purposes. Copyright © 1996 by Roger A. Kerin. No part of this case may be reproduced without written permission of the copyright holder.

chitectural coatings are considered to be a mature market with long-term sales growth projected in the range of 1 to 2 percent per year. Demand for architectural coatings and sundries reflect the level of house redecorating, maintenance, and repair, as well as sales of existing homes, and to a lesser extent new home, commercial, and industrial construction. Industry sources also noted that the demand for architectural coatings and sundries is affected by two other factors. First, the architectural coating segment faced competition from alternative materials, such as aluminum and vinyl siding, interior wall coverings, and wood paneling. Second, paint companies had developed higher quality products that reduced the amount of paint necessary per application and the frequency of repainting. Counteracting these factors, industry observers foresaw increasing demand for paint sundries due to a trend toward do-it-yourself painting by household consumers.

U.S. paint manufacturers are under growing pressure to reduce emissions of volatile organic compounds (VOCs) from paints and to limit the consumption of solvents. The Environmental Protection Agency (EPA) has proposed a three-step plan for the reduction of VOCs in architectural and industrial maintenance coatings. The first phase of the plan, which will take effect in 1996, requires a 25 percent reduction in VOC content from the base year of 1990. VOCs must be reduced by 35 percent (from the 1990 base year) in 2000 and 45 percent in the third phase in 2003. Compliance with EPA regulations has further eroded historically low profit margins in the paint industry.

Consolidation and Competition in the Architectural Coatings Segment

Slow sales growth, the necessity for ongoing research and development, and recent compliance with governmental regulations have fueled merger and acquisition activity in the U.S. paint industry since 1990. Companies seeking growth and a higher sales base to support increasing costs are making acquisitions. Companies that were unwilling or unable to make capital and R&D commitments necessary to remain competitive sold their paint businesses. Industry sources estimate that the number of paint companies is currently 600, or about 40 percent fewer companies than in 1975. The number of paint companies is presently declining at a rate of 2 to 3 percent per year. Merger activity in 1994 and 1995 generally involved the purchase of small companies by larger firms to boost their specific market or geographic presence. Still, because of readily available technology and difference in paint formulations associated with regional climatic needs, a small number of regional paint manufacturers, such as Jones•Blair Company, have competed successfully against paint manufacturers that distribute their products nationally.

Major producers of paint for the architectural coatings segment include Sherwin-Williams, Benjamin Moore, the Glidden unit of Imperial Chemicals, PPG Industries, Valspar Corporation, Grow Group, and Pratt & Lambert. These producers account for upwards of 60 percent of sales in the architectural coatings segment. They market paint under their own brand names and for retailers under private, controlled, or store brand names. For example, Sherwin-Williams markets the Sherwin-Williams brand and produces paint for Sears.

About 50 percent of architectural coatings are sold under private, controlled, or store brands. Sears, Kmart, Wal-Mart and Home Depot are major marketers of these brands. In addition, hardware store groups such as True Value and Ace Hardware market their own paint brands.

Specialty paint stores, lumberyards, and independent hardware stores that sell architectural paint and paint sundries have been able to compete in the paint business despite the presence of mass merchandisers (such as Sears) and home improvement centers (such as Home Depot). Industry sources estimate that specialty paint stores account for about 36 percent of paint and sundry sales; hardware and lumber-yards account for 14 percent. Furthermore, specialty paint and hardware stores and lumberyards in nonmetropolitan areas have outdistanced mass-merchandisers and home improvement centers as sources for paint and paint sundries. This is largely attributable to a lack of home improvement centers and mass-merchandiser distribution in these areas and paint store, hardware, and lumberyard customer relations and service. However, Wal-Mart has been an effective competitor in many nonmetropolitan areas.

Exhibit 1 shows store patronage by do-it-yourself painters and professional painters for 1991 and 1993. As indicated, home centers (including wholesale home

EXHIBIT 1

Store Patronage By Type of Buyer: Do-It-Yourselfer and Professional Painter

Where Do-It-Yourselfers Most Often Buy Paint & Sundries

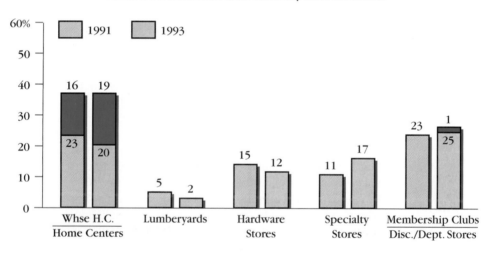

Where Professional Painters Purchased Majority of Paint/Varnish/Stain

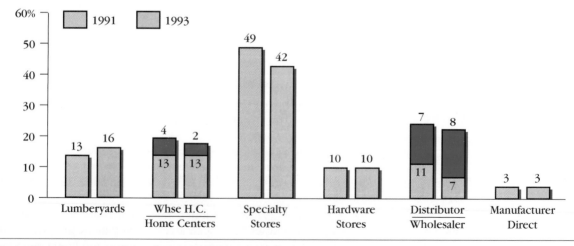

Source: Home Improvement Research Institute. Reprinted from *National Home Center News*, "10 Forces Reshaping the Retail Home Improvement Market," © 1996. Used with permission.

centers) and mass merchandisers (including membership clubs such as Sam's) represent the two most frequently patronized categories of retailers shopped by do-it-yourself painters for paint and sundry items. Specialty paint stores and lumberyards were the most frequently patronized retail stores by professional painters for paint products and sundry items.

Architectural Coatings Purchase Behavior

Approximately 50 percent of architectural coatings dollar sales are accounted for by do-it-yourselfer painters. Professional painter purchases account for 25 percent of dollar sales. The remainder of architectural coatings dollar sales result from government, export, and contractor sales.

Almost 60 percent of annual architectural coatings sales are for interior paints. Exterior paint represents 38 percent of sales. Lacquers and all other applications make up the balance of sales. Slightly less than one in four households purchase interior house paint in any given year. The percentage of households purchasing exterior house paint is considerably less than that for interior paint. The popularity of do-it-yourself painting, particularly for interior applications, has increased the paint and sundry item product line carried by retail outlets. Paint industry consumer research indicates that the average dollar paint purchase per purchase occasion is about $74.00. The average dollar sundry purchase per purchase occasion is about $12.00.

Recent research by the Home Improvement Research Institute indicates that do-it-yourself painters first choose a retail outlet for paint and paint sundries, then choose a paint brand. This research also identified four steps in the do-it-yourself decision process for home improvement products, including paint. The results of this research are summarized in Exhibit 2.

"Paint has become a commodity," commented Barrett. "Do-it-yourself purchasers all too often view paint as paint—a covering—and try to get the best price. But there are a significant number of people who desire service as well in the form of in-

EXHIBIT 2

Consumer Buying Decision Process for Home Improvement Products

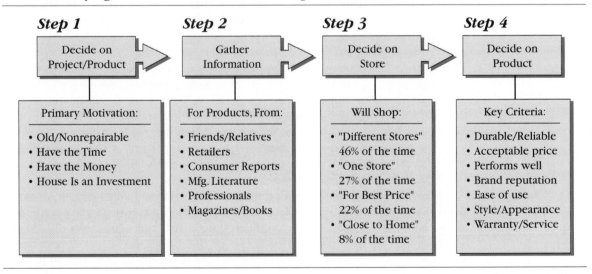

Source: Home Improvement Research Institute. Reprinted from *National Home Center News*, "10 Forces Reshaping the Retail Home Improvement Market," © 1996. Used with permission.

formation about application, color matching, surface preparation, and durability," he added. He conceded that "once paint is on the wall, you can't initially tell the difference between premium-priced and competitively priced paint."

"There is a difference between painting contractors and professional painters, however," he continued. "Pot and brush guys [professional painters] do seek out quality products, since their reputation is on the line and maintenance firms don't want to have to paint an office each time a mark appears on a wall. They want paint that is durable, washable, and will cover in a single coat. They also look to retailers who will go the extra mile to give them service. Many request and get credit from stores. They appreciate being able to get to stores early in the morning to pick up paint and supplies. They deal with stores that can mix large quantities of custom colors and expect to work with knowledgeable store employees who can give them what they want. It is not surprising to me that paint stores remain the preferred outlet for paint and sundries for professional painters. Contractors simply want a coating in many instances and strive for the lowest price, particularly on big jobs."

■ JONES•BLAIR COMPANY SERVICE AREA

Jones•Blair Company markets its paint and sundry items in over 50 counties in Texas, Oklahoma, New Mexico, and Louisiana from its plant and headquarters in Dallas, Texas. The eleven county Dallas–Fort Worth (DFW) metropolitan area is the major business and financial center in the company's southwestern service area.

Competition at the retail level has accelerated in recent years. Sears and Kmart have multiple outlets in DFW, as do Sherwin-Williams and Home Depot. Competition for retail selling space in paint stores, lumberyards, and hardware stores has also increased. "Our research indicates that 1,200 of these outlets now operate in the 50-county service area, and DFW houses 450 of them," noted Barrett. "When you consider that the typical lumberyard or hardware store gets 10 percent of its volume ($65,000) from paint and the typical paint store has annual sales of $400,000 with three brands, you can see that getting and keeping widespread distribution is a key success factor in this industry. Over 1,200 outlets were in operation in the area in 1995; about 600 were situated in the DFW area."

Competition at the paint manufacturing level has increased as well. The major change in competitive behavior has occurred among paint companies that sell to contractors serving the home construction industry. These companies have aggressively priced their products to capture a higher percentage of the home construction market. "Fortunately, these companies have not pursued the 400 or so professional painting firms in DFW and the 200 professional painters outside the DFW area or the do-it-yourselfer market as yet," said Barrett. "They have not been able to gain access to retail outlets, but they may buy their way in through free goods, promotional allowances, or whatever means are available to them in the future."

"We believe that mass merchandisers control 50 percent of the do-it-yourselfer paint market in the DFW metropolitan area. Price seems to be the attraction, but we can't quarrel with their quality," noted Barrett.

The estimated dollar volume of architectural paint and allied products sold in Jones•Blair's 50-county service area in 1995 was $80 million (excluding contractor sales). DFW was estimated to account for 60 percent of this figure, with the remaining volume being sold in other areas. Do-it-yourself household buyers were believed to account for 70 percent of non-contractor-related volume in DFW and 90 percent of non-contractor-related volume in other areas. A five-year summary of architectural paint and allied product sales in the Jones•Blair service area is shown in Exhibit 3.

EXHIBIT 3

Architectural Paint and Sundry Sales Volume, Excluding Contractor Sales (in Millions of Dollars)

Year	Total Dollar Sales	DFW Area Sales	Non-DFW Area Sales
1991	$75.7	$50.9	$24.8
1992	76.4	50.8	25.6
1993	77.6	50.5	27.1
1994	78.4	50.7	27.7
1995	80.0	48.0	32.0

■ JONES•BLAIR COMPANY

Jones•Blair Company is a privately held corporation that produces and markets architectural paint under the Jones•Blair brand name. In addition to producing a full line of architectural coatings, the company sells paint sundries (brushes, rollers, thinners, etc.) under the Jones•Blair name, even though these items are not manufactured by the company. The company also operates a very large OEM coatings division, which sells its products throughout the U.S. and worldwide.

Company architectural paint and allied products sales volume in 1995 was $12 million, and net profit before taxes was $1,140,000. Dollar sales had increased at an average annual rate of 4 percent per year over the past decade. Paint gallonage, however, had remained stable over the past five years. "We have been very successful in maintaining our margins even with increased research and development, material and labor costs, but I'm afraid we're approaching the threshold on our prices," Barrett said. "We are now the highest-priced paint in our service area." In 1995, paint cost-of-goods sold, including freight expenses, was 60 percent of net sales.

Distribution

The company distributes its products through 200 independent paint stores, lumberyards, and hardware outlets. Forty percent of its outlets are located in the eleven-county DFW area. The remaining outlets are situated in the other 39 counties in the service area. Jones•Blair sales are distributed evenly between DFW and non-DFW accounts. Exhibit 4 shows the account and sales volume distribution by size of dollar purchase per year.

EXHIBIT 4

Account and Sales Volume Percentage Distribution by Dollar Purchase per Year

Dollar Purchase/Year	Retail Accounts			Dollar Sales Volume		
	DFW	Non-DFW	Total	DFW	Non-DFW	Total
$50,000+	7%	10%	17%	28%	28%	56%
$25,000–$50,000	14	20	34	13	13	26
Less than $25,000	19	30	49	9	9	18
Total	40%	60%	100%	50%	50%	100%

EXHIBIT 5

Jones•Blair Company Print Advertisement

Retail outlets outside the DFW area with paint and sundry purchases exceeding $50,000 annually carry only the Jones•Blair product line. However, except for 14 outlets in DFW (those with purchases greater than $50,000 annually), which carry the Jones•Blair line exclusively, DFW retailers carry two or three lines, with Jones•Blair's line being premium priced. "Our experience to date shows that in our DFW outlets, the effect of multiple lines has been to cause a decline in gallonage volume. The non-DFW outlets, by comparison, have grown in gallonage volume. When you combine the two, you have stable gallonage volume," remarked Barrett.

Promotional Efforts for Architectural Coating Sales

Jones•Blair employs eight sales representatives. They are responsible for monitoring inventories of Jones•Blair paint and sundry items in each retail outlet, as well as for order taking, assisting in store display, and coordinating cooperative advertising programs. A recent survey of Jones•Blair paint dealers indicated that the sales representatives were well liked, helpful, professional, and knowledgeable about paint. Commenting on the survey findings, Barrett said, "Our reps are on a first-name basis with their customers. It is common for our reps to discuss business and family over coffee during a sales call, and some of our people even 'mind the store' when the proprietor has to run an errand or two." Sales representatives are paid a salary and a 1-percent commission on sales.

The company spends approximately 3 percent of net sales on advertising and sales promotion efforts. Approximately 55 percent of advertising and sales promotion dollars are allocated to cooperative advertising programs with retail accounts. The cooperative program, whereby Jones•Blair pays a portion of an account's media costs based on the dollar amount of paint purchased from Jones•Blair, applies to newspaper advertising and seasonal catalogs distributed in a retailer's immediate trade area. Exhibit 5 shows an example of a Jones•Blair Company cooperative print advertisement. The remainder of the advertising and sales promotion budget is spent on in-store displays, corporate brand advertising, outdoor signs, regional magazines, premiums, and advertising production costs.

■ PLANNING MEETING

Senior management executives of Jones•Blair Company assembled again to consider the question of where and how to deploy corporate marketing efforts among the various architectural paint coatings markets served by the company. Barrett opened the meeting with a statement that it was absolutely necessary to resolve this question at the meeting in order for the tactical plan to be developed. The peak painting season was soon approaching and decisions had to be made.

Vice-President of Advertising: Alex, I still believe that we must direct our efforts toward bolstering our presence in the DFW do-it-yourselfer market. I just received the results of our DFW consumer advertising awareness study. As you can see [Exhibit 6 on page 80], awareness is related to paint purchase behavior. Industry research on paint purchase behavior indicates that a large number of do-it-yourselfers choose a store before selecting a brand. However, a brand name is also important to consumers because they do think about paint they have seen advertised when choosing a brand. This becomes very important in those stores carrying multiple brands. It seems to me that we need an awareness level of at least 30 percent among do-it-yourselfers to materially affect our sales.

Preliminary talks with our ad agency indicate that an increase of $350,000 in corporate brand advertising beyond what we are now spending, with an emphasis on television, will be necessary to achieve this awareness level. Furthermore, this television coverage will reach non-DFW consumers in some 15 counties as well.

Vice-President of Operations: I don't agree. Advertising is not the way to go, and reference to the DFW area alone is too narrow a focus. We have to be competitive in the do-it-yourselfer paint market, period. Our shopper research program indicated that dealers will quickly back off from our brand when the customer appears price-sensitive. We must cut our price by 20 percent on all paint products

EXHIBIT 6

Percentage of DFW Population Who Were Aware of Paint Brands and Purchased Paint in the Last 12 Months

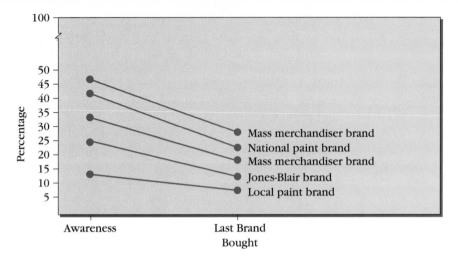

Awareness Question: "What brands come to mind when you think of paint?"

Last Brand Bought: "What paint brand did you purchase the last time you bought paint?"

Note: Sample size was N = 400. Percentages are subject to a 5-percent sampling error.

to achieve parity with national paint brands. Look here. In today's newspaper, we advertise a price-off special on our exterior paint, and our price is still noticeably higher than a mass merchandiser's everyday price. With both ads on the same page, a customer would have to be an idiot to patronize one of our dealers.

Vice-President of Sales: Forget the DFW market. We ought to be putting our effort into non-DFW areas, where half of our sales and most of our dealers exist right now. I hate to admit it, but our sales representatives could be more aggressive. We have only added five new accounts in the last five years; our account penetration in non-DFW areas is only 16 percent. I'm partially at fault, but I'm ready to act. We should add one additional sales representative whose sole responsibility is to develop new retail account leads and presentations or call on professional painters to solicit their business through our dealers. I've figured the direct cost to keep one rep in the field at $60,000 per year, excluding commission.

Vice-President of Finance: Everyone is proposing a change in our orientation. Let me be the devil's advocate and favor pursuing our current approach. We now sell to both the home owner and the professional painter in DFW and non-DFW markets through our dealers. We have been and will continue to be profitable by judiciously guarding our margins and controlling costs. Our contribution margin is 35 percent. Everyone suggests that increasing our costs will somehow result in greater sales volume. Let me remind you, Alex, we have said that it is our policy to recoup noncapital expenditures within a one-year time horizon. If we increase our advertising by an incremental amount of $350,000, then we had better see the incremental sales volume as well. The same goes for additional sales representatives and, I might add, any across-the board cut in prices.

Mr. Barrett: We keep going over the same ground. All of you have valid arguments, but we must prioritize. Let's think about what's best for all of us.

Increased advertising seems reasonable, since national paint firms and mass merchandisers outspend us tenfold in absolute terms. You are right in saying people have to be aware of us before they will buy, or even consider, Jones•Blair. But I am not sure what advertising will do for us given that about 75 percent of the audience is not buying paint. Your reference to DFW as being our major market has been questioned by others. Can't we take that $350,000 of incremental advertising and apply it toward newspapers and catalogs in non-DFW areas?

The price cut is a more drastic action. We might have to do it just to keep our gallonage volume. It would appear from our sales representatives' forecast that gallonage demand for paint in our service area will not increase next year and we can't increase our prices this year. Any increases will have to come out of a competitor's hide. Moreover, since our costs are unlikely to decline, we must recoup gross profit dollars from an increase in volume. Is this possible?

The idea of hiring additional representatives has merit, but what do we do with them? Do they focus on the retail account side or on recruiting the professional painter? Our survey of retail outlets indicated that 70 percent of sales through our DFW dealers went to the professional painter, while 70 percent of our sales through our non-DFW outlets went to do-it-yourselfers. These figures are identical to the 1990 survey of retail outlets. Our contractor sales in DFW and other areas are minimal. We would need a 40-percent price cut to attract contractors, not to mention the increased costs, expertise, and headaches of competitive bidding for large jobs.

Now that I've had my say, let's think about your proposals again. We're not leaving until we agree on a course of action.

Pharmacia & Upjohn, Inc.
Rogaine Hair Regrowth Treatment

On February 9, 1996, the U.S. Food and Drug Administration (FDA) approved Rogaine Hair Regrowth Treatment for sale without a physician's prescription. Rogaine, the only medically proven hair regrowth treatment at the time for men and women with common hereditary hair loss, had been sold as a prescription drug in the United States since 1988. Cumulative sales of Rogaine in the United States since its introduction exceeded $700 million. Worldwide cumulative Rogaine sales exceeded $1 billion (see Exhibit 1).[1]

With Rogaine's patent about to expire in four days, FDA approval of Rogaine as a nonprescription, or over-the-counter (OTC), drug was welcome news to Pharmacia & Upjohn, Inc., the manufacturer of the product. According to a company official, "We are pleased with the FDA's decision switching Rogaine from prescription to OTC sales. OTC availability of Rogaine is a welcome convenience for millions of men and women who experience common hair loss. We are pursuing an aggressive timetable to make Rogaine quickly and widely accessible to consumers."[2] The launch of nonprescription Rogaine was scheduled for April 1996. At that time, prescription-only Rogaine would be discontinued, since both prescription and nonprescription Rogaine had identical formulations. The company also requested the FDA to approve a three-year period of marketing exclusivity for nonprescription Rogaine under provisions of the Waxman-Hatch Amendment to the U.S. Food, Drug and Cosmetic Act. These provisions allow pharmaceutical companies to petition the FDA for a three-year marketing exclusivity if they pay for new research that is necessary to convert a prescription drug to nonprescription use. FDA response to this petition was expected in late March or April 1996.

In anticipation of FDA approval for nonprescription Rogaine following a positive recommendation by an FDA advisory committee in November 1995 and a favorable FDA response to the petition for a three-year marketing exclusivity, company officials had already outlined the marketing program for the brand scheduled for an April 1996 launch.[3] Rogaine would be targeted at men and women aged 25 to 49. The brand would be positioned as the only product available without a prescription that

---

[1] Sales figures are based on information provided in "Rogaine Will Be Sold Over-the-Counter," *PR Newswire*, February 12, 1996; estimates made by Bear, Stearns, & Company and Prudential Securities industry analysts; and data reported in "For Rogaine, No Miracle Cure—Yet," *Business Week* (June 4, 1990), p. 100, and "Blondes, Brunettes, Redheads, and Rogaine," *American Druggist* (June 1992), pp. 39–40.

[2] "Rogaine Will Be Sold Over-the-Counter," *PR Newswire,* February 12, 1996.

[3] This description is based on "Rogaine Will Be Sold Over-the-Counter," *PR Newswire*, February 12, 1996; Michael Wilke, "New Rivals Push Rogaine to Jump-Start Its OTC Ads," *Advertising Age* (April 15, 1996), p. 45; Michael Wilke, "Rogaine, Nicorette Seek Edge from FDA," *Advertising Age* (February 19, 1996), p. 4; "OTC Rogaine Receives FDA Advisory Committee Recommendation," *PR Newswire*, November 17, 1995; Sean Mehegan, "Hair Today," *BRANDWEEK* (April 8, 1996), pp. 1, 6.

EXHIBIT 1

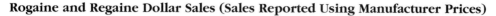

Rogaine and Regaine Dollar Sales (Sales Reported Using Manufacturer Prices)

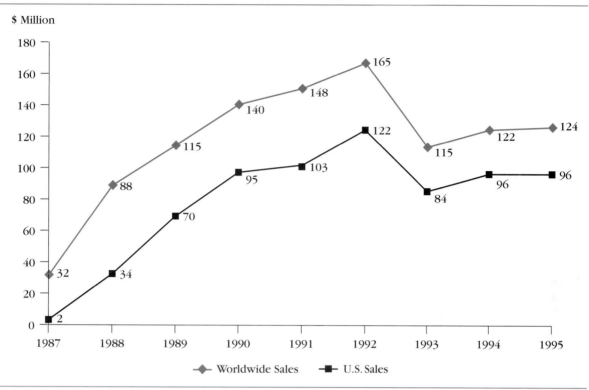

is medically proven to regrow hair. Separate packages—Rogaine for men and Rogaine for women—would be sold. Each package would feature labeling and include a brochure designed to help prospective users accurately identify themselves as Rogaine candidates. The suggested retail price for one bottle, which is equivalent to a one-month supply, would be $29.50. This price was approximately one-half the price of prescription Rogaine for a one-month supply. Distribution would be expanded to locate Rogaine in the pharmacy or hair-care section of food, drug, and mass-merchandise retail outlets. Marketing spending during the first six months of the brand introduction, estimated at $75 million, would support Rogaine and the company's relaunched nonprescription Progaine shampoo. More than half of the $75 million expenditure would be devoted to consumer advertising. The spending level represented the largest consumer and trade promotion campaign for a nonprescription product in the company's history. According to industry sources, company officials were telling retail store buyers of health and beauty aids that the brand had a retail sales potential of $250 million-a-year.

On April 5, 1996, the FDA notified Pharmacia & Upjohn, Inc. that its request for a three-year period of marketing exclusivity for nonprescription Rogaine had been denied.[4] In addition, by April 9, 1996, the FDA had approved three competing generic versions of Rogaine containing 2-percent solutions of minoxidil—the active chemical ingredient in Rogaine that stimulates hair regrowth—for sale without a prescrip-

---

[4] This discussion is based on "Generic Versions of Rogaine Ok'd," *The Dallas Morning News* (April 9, 1996), p. 4D; "Pharmacia & Upjohn Files Lawsuit Over OTC Rogaine Exclusivity," *PR Newswire*, April 12, 1996; "Rogaine Awarded Temporary Restraining Order," *PR Newswire*, April 15, 1996.

tion. Generic products, which are supposed to be medically equivalent to brand-name products, are typically priced 25 percent to 50 percent less than brand-name products and not advertised. On April 12, 1996, Pharmacia & Upjohn, Inc. filed a lawsuit against the FDA in Federal District Court in Grand Rapids, Michigan. The company asked the Court to reverse the FDA's ruling on the matter of market exclusivity for nonprescription Rogaine and to order the FDA to defer approval of competing nonprescription products containing minoxidil. On April 15, the Court issued a temporary restraining order prohibiting the FDA action. A preliminary hearing was set for April 30, to hear the Pharmacia & Upjohn, Inc. motion for a preliminary injunction which sought to extend injunctive relief until a full trial had been held.

The conversion of Rogaine from a prescription to nonprescription status and the FDA's possible denial of a three-year marketing exclusivity for Rogaine, along with approval of generic products, raised a variety of related market and marketing questions. First, what unit and dollar sales potential for the product category as a whole might be expected now that a minoxidil treatment for hair regrowth no longer required a prescription? Pharmacia & Upjohn, Inc. believed sales of $1 billion for Rogaine were possible over five years given its marketing program and assuming no competitive products. However, less optimistic views existed. One industry analyst believed "there is enough vanity out there, that a lot of people will try it, at least initially." However, another analyst noted that "those who are truly motivated have probably already tried it."[5]

Second, how might the loss of U.S. patent protection and marketing exclusivity that Rogaine had enjoyed since its introduction and competition from generic products affect sales of the Rogaine brand? There were no comparable situations to draw upon in the pharmaceutical industry to answer this question for a product like Rogaine.[6] For instance, pharmaceutical industry analysts estimate that it was common for patented prescription drugs to lose up to 60 percent of their volume within six months after their patent expired due to generic competition. However, this situation was typical of prescription drugs and not necessarily prescription drugs converting to a nonprescription status upon expiration of their patent. In another situation, Nicorette Gum, a smoking cessation product, lost its marketing exclusivity in June 1994. But with increased advertising and no direct branded or generic competition, except nicotine patches, the Nicorette brand saw dollar sales increase almost 6 percent in 1995. Unlike Nicorette Gum, if Rogaine lost its marketing exclusivity, it could face competition from generic or branded products with a 2-percent solution of minoxidil in 1996. These products were manufactured by Bausch & Lomb, Alpharma, and Lemmon Company, a division of Israeli-based Teva Pharmaceutical Industries. A Bausch & Lomb spokesperson said, "We do see a market for minoxidil as viable and would very much like to be a player." Lemmon Company manufactures generic drugs and private-label products and has announced that it intended to have a generic and private-label versions of minoxidil available by mid-1996. The company has also initiated discussions with other companies to offer a branded product. In addition, Merck was testing its prostate medicine, Proscar, for hair growth which would be in pill form. This product could be submitted for FDA approval within a year and be on the market by 1999. Finally, would the U.S. marketing strategy developed for nonprescription Rogaine prior to the FDA's recent rulings need to be modified? If so, how? Nonprescription Rogaine was already being

---

[5] Laurie McGinley, "Baldness Drug Cleared for Sale Over Counter," *The Wall Street Journal* (February 13, 1996), p. B3; Michael Wieke, "OTC Status Might Not Be Boon to Rogaine," *Advertising Age* (January 29, 1996), p. 10.

[6] The following discussion is based on Patricia Winters, "Prescription Drug Ads Up," *Advertising Age* (January 18, 1993), pp. 10, 50; "Rogaine, Nicorette Seek Edge from FDA," *Advertising Age* (February 19, 1996), p. 4; Sean Mehegan, "Hair Today," *BRANDWEEK* (April 8, 1996), pp. 1, 6.

shipped to retailers and the consumer advertising and sales promotion program was ready to be implemented.

■ TREATMENTS FOR BALDING

There are about 300,000 hairs on the scalp of a person considered to have a "full" head of hair.[7] The exact number of hairs on a person's head depends on the number of hair follicles, which is established before birth. On average, a person will shed 100 to 150 hairs per day from the scalp and a new hair begins to emerge from the follicle. However, many people experience permanent hair loss on the scalp. Called *androgenetic alopecia*, both men and women can have this condition. With male pattern baldness, the most common form of *alopecia*, normal hair is lost initially from the temples and crown, where it is replaced by fine, downy hair. The affected area gradually becomes wider as the line of normal hair recedes. This process of hair loss is inherited and the typical progression in men is shown in Exhibit 2. Women also experience hair loss, a condition referred to as diffuse hair loss. This condition is manifested by thinning hair all over the head, rather than the progression typical of male pattern baldness, although young women and women who have passed menopause occasionally exhibit this progression.

Survey research indicates that 38.6 percent of women say they would seek treatment if they were losing their hair compared with 30.4 percent of men who say they would seek treatment.[8] However, this research also reported that at most 13.3 percent of surveyed women who were experiencing hair loss actually sought some form of treatment while at most 9.9 percent of men experiencing hair loss actually sought treatment. People with hair loss and who seek remedies have numerous options to treat this condition. The most popular treatments involve prescription and

EXHIBIT 2

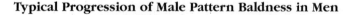

Typical Progression of Male Pattern Baldness in Men

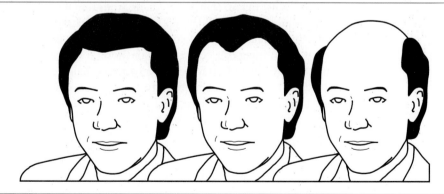

---

[7] This material is based on Charles B. Clayman, ed., *The American Medical Association Encyclopedia of Medicine* (New York: Random House, 1989), pp. 88, 504; William G. Flanagan and David Stix, "The Bald Truth," *Forbes* (July 22, 1991), pp. 309–310; "Baldness: Is There Hope?," *Consumer Reports* (September 1988), pp. 533–547; Gary Belsky, "Beating Hair Loss," *MONEY* (March 1996), pp. 152–155; "Hair Loss: Does Anything Really Help?," *Consumer Reports* (August 1996), pp. 62–63.

[8] Laurie Freeman, "Upjohn Takes a Shine to Balding Women," *Advertising Age* (February 27, 1989), p. S1. These statistics are based on a Gallup Organization survey of 1,000 adults in the United States.

EXHIBIT 3

The Amount U.S. Adults Are Willing to Spend for the Treatment of Balding

Amount	Men	Women
$1,000–$10,000	11.3%	11.1%
$600–$1,000	7.1	5.3
$300–$599	13.5	9.7
$100–$299	14.2	13.5
$99 or less	27.0	28.5
Don't Know	26.9	31.9
	100.0%	100.0%

Source: Gallup Organization Survey of 1,000 U.S. adults commissioned by *Advertising Age*. Reported in Laurie Freeman, "Upjohn Takes a Shine to Balding Women," *Advertising Age* (February 27, 1989), p. S1. Reproduced with the permission of *Advertising Age*.

nonprescription hair shampoos, lotions, and conditioners. These hair-thickening products are often used to treat thinning hair. It is estimated that there are 40 million balding men and 20 million women with thinning hair in the United States and they spend over $300 million annually on these kinds of products. Exhibit 3 shows the amount of money men and women say they are willing to spend per year for the treatment of balding. Hairpieces or wigs, hair transplants, and drugs, such as minoxidil, can be used when hair loss is prominent. American consumers spend about $1.3 billion annually for these treatments. Another $100 million is spent for elixirs, teas, horse-hoof ointments and the like to treat hair loss.

Hairpieces or Wigs

Hairpieces (or toupees) and wigs are worn by over two million Americans. About $400 million is spent annually for these products, including periodic cleaning and styling. Hairpieces and wigs can be made from real human hair or from synthetic material, usually nylon. Hairpieces made from human hair usually last no more than one year. Synthetic hair will last up to two years. The cost of a small filler hairpiece made from human hair for a balding man's crown can be purchased for as little as $325; a full women's wig can cost $2,000 or more. A typical man's hairpiece made of human hair costs from $1,000 to $3,500. Synthetic hairpieces for men cost between $1,800 and $2,500. Hairpieces require maintenance every six to eight weeks with the average cost for adjusting, cleaning, and styling running between $50 and $100. Spirit gum or a double-faced tape is used to hold the hairpiece or wig on the scalp.

Hair Transplants

A hair transplant consists of a surgical cosmetic operation in which hairy sections of the scalp are removed and transplanted to hairless areas. One or a combination of the following procedures may be used. "Punch grafting" is the most common procedure. With this procedure, a punch is used to remove small areas of bald scalp (about 1/4 inch across), which are replaced with areas of hairy scalp. The grafts are taped into position until the natural healing process takes effect. "Strip grafting" is a procedure whereby strips of bald skin are removed from the scalp and replaced with strips of hairy scalp which are stitched into position. "Flap grafting" is similar to strip grafting, except that flaps of hairy skin are lifted from the scalp, swiveled, and stitched to replace areas of bald skin. This procedure is typically used to form a new hairline. "Male pattern baldness reduction" consists of cutting out areas of bald scalp and then stretching surrounding areas of hairy scalp to replace the bald area. Hair transplants, no matter how successful, do not last indefinitely. As time passes, transplanted areas become bald.

About $800 million is spent each year for hair transplants in the United States. Hair transplant procedures of the grafting variety cost patients $3,500 to $15,000. Male pattern baldness reduction often costs $2,000 to $3,500 per procedure plus the transplant fee. These procedures are usually not covered by medical insurance.

Drugs

Although many topical ointments and elixirs are promoted, only one product had been approved by the FDA as a drug to restore hair growth for men and women prior to April 1996. Rogaine Hair Regrowth Treatment, produced by Pharmacia & Upjohn, Inc., received FDA approval for use by men in the United States in August 1988 and for women in August 1991. Rogaine is a 2-percent solution of minoxidil that is applied twice daily to areas of the scalp that has thinning hair or no hair. Clinical tests conducted by the company indicated that hair growth appeared to be more pronounced for men under 30 years of age and those in the early stages of the male pattern baldness progression. An estimated 35 percent of men under 30 years of age experience hair loss. The properties of minoxidil and its use as a topical ointment for hair growth are such that if not applied twice daily, hair loss results. In other words, minoxidil is a life-time treatment if its effects on hair growth and retention are to be permanent.

Until February 1996, treatment with Rogaine required a physician's prescription. A one-month supply of the product then cost a patient $50 to $60 and up to $125 if the product was used in high concentrations, or if mixed with other drugs such as Retin-A. In addition, periodic physician office fees raised the annual patient cost for treatment. Rogaine was not typically covered by medical insurance.

In February 1996, the FDA approved Rogaine as a nonprescription drug. This decision reversed a 1994 FDA ruling that denied nonprescription status for Rogaine. At that time, FDA officials testified that the drug was most effective when applied during the early stages of baldness, but that the drug was not a cure. The group leader of the FDA's dermatology group said Rogaine was a "marginal product" in curing baldness.[9] In approving Rogaine as a nonprescription drug in 1996, the FDA reported that Rogaine resulted in "meaningful" hair growth in 25 percent of men and 20 percent of women.[10] "Meaningful" hair growth was defined by the FDA as "new individual hairs that covered some or all of the thinning areas but weren't as close together as hairs on the rest of the head." A larger percentage of users saw "minimal" hair growth in which "some new hairs were seen but not enough to cover thinning areas."

In clinical tests conducted by Pharmacia & Upjohn, Inc., 26 percent of mostly white men between the ages of 18 and 49 with moderate hair loss reported moderate to dense hair regrowth and 33 percent reported minimal regrowth after using Rogaine for four months.[11] By comparison, 11 percent of men in the 18–49 age group who used a placebo (a liquid without a 2-percent solution of minoxidil) reported moderate to dense hair regrowth while 31 percent reported minimal regrowth after four months of treatment. Clinical tests with mostly white women aged 18–45 with mild to moderate hair loss yielded different results. In these tests, 19 per-

---

[9] "Upjohn's Rogaine Fails to Win Vote of FDA Panel in Nonprescription Bid," *The Wall Street Journal* (July 28, 1994), p. A2.

[10] Laurie McGinley, "Baldness Drug Cleared for Sale Over Counter," *The Wall Street Journal* (February 13, 1996), p. B3.

[11] Based on Rogaine product literature prepared by Pharmacia & Upjohn, Inc.

cent of women reported moderate hair regrowth and 40 percent reported minimal regrowth after using Rogaine for eight months. In a control group which received a placebo, 7 percent of women reported moderate regrowth and 33 percent had minimal regrowth after eight months of use.

According to a Rogaine marketing executive: "We have been very clear about what the drug delivers, that this is not a quick-fix product, that it needs the commitment to be used twice a day, every day, and it's a drug that must be used for four to six months—and for some individuals for up to a year before any results are seen."[12] Furthermore, Rogaine treated only male pattern baldness. This condition accounts for 95 percent of all hair loss cases among men and women in the United States. In addition, the drug is most likely to regrow hair on top of the head or crown, not on a receding frontal hairline.

■ PHARMACIA & UPJOHN, INC.

Pharmacia & Upjohn, Inc. was created with the merger of Pharmacia AB of Sweden and The Upjohn Company of the United States in November 1995.[13] The merger resulted in the new company becoming the world's ninth largest pharmaceutical firm. Pharmacia & Upjohn, Inc. reported net sales of $6.949 billion and net earnings of $924 million (excluding charges related to the merger) for the year ending December 31, 1995.

Pharmacia & Upjohn, Inc. is a provider of human health care products and related businesses, and operates on a global scale. Its corporate management center is located in London, England, with major research and manufacturing centers in the United States, Sweden, and Italy. Pharmaceutical products account for 90 percent of company sales; diagnostic and biotech/biosensor products produce 10 percent of company sales. Almost 70 percent of company sales are made outside of the United States.

The company's ongoing research and development effort, supported by a $1 billion annual budget, focused on developing new products and line extensions. In 1995, the company had 25 new products or line extensions expected to be submitted for regulatory approvals in the 1995–1997 period.

Human Health Care Business

With the merger, Pharmacia & Upjohn, Inc. announced its commitment to achieving and maintaining leading positions in a number of therapeutic areas. The largest of these were oncology, metabolic diseases, critical care, infectious diseases, central nervous system/neurology, women's health, and nutrition. Exhibit 4 shows the company's net sales by major therapeutic group for 1994 and 1995.

Prescription Pharmaceutical Sales. About 84 percent of company pharmaceutical sales are for prescription products. These products are marketed directly to health care providers worldwide by technically trained representatives who call on physicians, pharmacists, hospital personnel, Health Maintenance Organizations (HMOs) and other managed health care organizations and wholesale drug outlets. Product advertising literature and sales efforts for prescription pharmaceuticals are directed mostly toward health care professionals. This practice is necessary because of long-

---

[12] "Rogaine: Promises, Promises, Promises," *Advertising Age* (October 3, 1993), p. S14.

[13] This company overview is based on *The Upjohn Company Annual Report: 1994* and *Pharmacia & Upjohn, Inc. Annual Report 1995*.

EXHIBIT 4

Pharmacia & Upjohn, Inc. Year-to-Year Comparison of Consolidated Net Sales by Major Therapeutic Product Groups (U.S. Dollars in Millions)

Product Grouping	1995 Sales	% Change	1994 Sales
Infectious Disease	$687.1	10.3%	$622.9
Metabolic Disease	635.9	(2.1)	649.4
Critical Care and Thrombosis	579.7	12.8	514.1
Central Nervous System	571.8	.3	570.3
Oncology	566.2	6.7	530.6
Women's Health	541.2	6.1	509.9
Nutrition	399.0	8.1	369.0
Ophthalmology	296.0	5.3	281.0
Other Prescription Pharmaceuticals	957.7	(12.8)	1,098.1
Consumer Health Care	441.5	(2.1)	451.2
Animal Health	383.1	14.0	336.2
Chemical & Contract Manufacturing	199.9	17.1	170.7
Total Pharmaceuticals	6,259.1	2.6	6,103.4
Biotech/Biosensor	437.0	13.5	385.0
Diagnostics	253.0	17.1	216.0
Consolidated Net Sales	$6,949.1	3.6%	$6,704.4

Source: Pharmacia & Upjohn, Inc. 1995 Annual Report, p. 37.

standing FDA regulations that require virtually all prescription drug advertising to list all product use side effects and contraindications. Complete disclosure of such information for the great majority of prescription pharmaceutical products was often cost prohibitive for television and print advertisements directed at consumers due to time and space requirements and technical language.

In 1995, sales of Infectious Diseases products were led by the Cleocin (Dalacin outside the U.S.) family of antibiotic products. Sales of Metabolic Diseases products were led by Genotropin, a growth hormone. Critical Care and Thrombosis product sales were led by Solu-Medrol, an injectable steroid, and other Medrol products. Sales of Central Nervous System agents were led by Xanax, an anti-anxiety agent, Halcion, a sleep-inducing agent, and Sermion for senile dementia. Farmorubicin, which treats solid tumors and leukemias, and Adriamycin, a cancer drug, led sales of Oncology products. Sales in the Women's Health product category were led by Depo-Provera, an injectable contraceptive. Sales of Nutrition products were led by the non-U.S. sales of Intralipid, a fat emulsion for intravenous nutrient delivery, while Healon, for cataract surgery, led sales of Ophthalmology products.

Nonprescription Pharmaceutical Sales. Pharmacia & Upjohn, Inc. also manufacturers and distributes many other familiar products which do not require a prescription, including Motrin IB Tablets and Caplets, used as an analgesic; Kaopectate products, for diarrhea; Cortaid products, which are anti-inflammatory topical products containing hydrocortisone; the family of Unicap vitamin products; Dramamine products which are anti-motion sickness medicines, Mycitracin, an antibiotic ointment for treatment of minor skin infections and burns; and nonprescription laxative products, Doxidan and Surfak. The company also manufactures Nicorette Gum, a smoking cessation product, which is marketed under a license to SmithKline Beecham.

Competition in the human health care business is intense. There are at least 50 competitors in the United States that market prescription and nonprescription pharmaceutical products. Companies compete on the basis of product development and their effectiveness in introducing new or improved products for the treatment and prevention of disease. Other competitive features include product quality, pricing to and through marketing channels, and the dissemination of technical information and medical support advice to health care professionals. Advertising and sales promotions directed at consumers and trade promotions provided to retailers are important in marketing nonprescription pharmaceutical products. For this reason, these products are often referred to as "advertised remedies."

Development of Rogaine Hair Regrowth Treatment[14]

The development of Rogaine can be traced to the mid-1960s when researchers at The Upjohn Company observed that a drug, originally thought to be a possible antacid agent, lowered the blood pressure in laboratory animals. Subsequent research produced a drug, given the generic name minoxidil, which proved to be a potent agent for lowering high blood pressure in humans. Assigned the trade name Loniten, the drug was given FDA approval for marketing in 1979.

Clinical research on minoxidil as an antihypertensive drug led to an unexpected discovery in 1971 when investigators noticed unusual hair growth in some patients who were taking minoxidil orally. Then, in 1973, a patient taking minoxidil for hypertension began to grow hair on a previously bald spot on his head. Additional clinical trials of minoxidil and related studies were conducted between 1977 and 1982 with more than 4,000 patients. The primary clinical study at 27 different testing sites tracked 2,326 patients who were nearly all white men in good health, aged 18 to 49 and diagnosed as exhibiting a moderate degree of hair loss. This study concluded that a 2-percent minoxidil solution applied twice daily to the head offered the best safety and effectiveness profile for this group. The safety and effectiveness of this solution for people under 18 was not tested (Rogaine is not recommended for persons under 18 years of age). Some side effects of the drug included itching and skin irritation to the treated areas of the scalp. In terms of effectiveness, 48 percent of the patients said they had achieved moderate to dense hair growth after one year of use. Investigators at the time judged that 39 percent of the patients achieved moderate to dense hair growth after one year of use. These data were submitted to the FDA in 1985. The FDA approved the 39 percent moderate to dense hair growth claim. In 1986, The Upjohn Company began selling the 2-percent minoxidil solution outside the United States under the trade name Regaine. However, more stringent and time-consuming review procedures by the FDA slowed the approval process in the United States.

Continued study on minoxidil led company researchers to draw two basic conclusions:

> First, it was clear after four months that topical minoxidil could grow hair on some scalps. Second, efficacy seemed to be related in many cases to the age of the patient, the extent of his baldness and how long he had been bald. Younger men who were not as far into the balding process seemed to respond better to the drug. There are exceptions to this finding, however, and the correlation of age to efficacy has not been scientifically established.[15]

In 1987, the Company established the Hairgrowth Research Unit to determine the mechanism of action of minoxidil, develop new and better minoxidil analogs, and in-

---

[14] This description is based on *The Upjohn Company Annual Report: 1988*, pp. 10–11; Steven W. Quickel, "Bald Spot," *Business Month* (November 1989), pp. 36–43; "Baldness: Is There Hope?" *Consumer Reports* (September 1988), pp. 533–547.

[15] *The Upjohn Company Annual Report: 1988*, p. 11.

vestigate other agents that affect hair growth or loss. At the time, researchers could only theorize why minoxidil stimulated hair growth in some patients. According to the company's director of dermatology:

> The most plausible theory is that minoxidil somehow stimulates the matrix cell of the hair follicle to regrow when it is destined to turn off. It's an overcoming of the genetic propensity to shut down. But we don't know how minoxidil modifies the metabolic activity of that cell.[16]

Two noteworthy developments occurred in 1988. First, an eight-month clinical study on Rogaine use for female hair loss was completed. The study was submitted to the FDA and ultimately led to agency approval to market the minoxidil solution to women in August 1991. Pregnant women and nursing mothers were advised not to use Rogaine, however. Second, in August 1988, the FDA granted approval to market the solution to men in the United States. However, the Regaine name was replaced with the Rogaine name because an FDA official believed the Regaine name suggested that the minoxidil solution would result in complete hair growth. During this time, minoxidil had received considerable publicity in the consumer and marketing media and in the financial community as a miracle cure for baldness. For example, Wall Street financial analysts believed Rogaine's ability to reverse male pattern baldness in men would rapidly produce $400 to $500 million in annual sales.[17]

■ PRESCRIPTION DRUG MARKETING PROGRAM FOR ROGAINE HAIR REGROWTH TREATMENT

The initial marketing plan for prescription Rogaine for men in the United States was developed concurrently with the FDA approval process. The announced marketing objective for Rogaine was "to maximize sales of Rogaine in the new U.S. market."[18] Since Rogaine had FDA approval as a prescription drug, Upjohn's initial attention was placed on educating its sales force who called on physicians, dermatologists, and other health care professionals. Rogaine was introduced to the medical community by its sales force and through advertisements in medical journals and periodicals. A company spokesperson said, "We couldn't begin marketing Rogaine to consumers until we felt the awareness level was adequate in the medical community."[19]

Consumer Advertising Program

Consumer advertising for Rogaine, targeted at 25- to 49-year-old males, began in November 1988 (see Exhibit 5 on page 92 for an age and income summary for U.S.

---

[16] "Baldness: Is There Hope?" *Consumer Reports* (September 1988), p. 544.

[17] "The Hottest Products: Baldness Treatment," *ADWEEK* (November 7, 1988), p. 6; "For Rogaine, No Miracle Cure—Yet," *Business Week* (June 4, 1990), p. 100. The Upjohn Company neither confirmed nor denied these sales projections.

[18] *The Upjohn Company Annual Report: 1988*, p. 11. The following material is based on Stuart Elliott, "Upjohn Turns to Women to Increase Rogaine Sales," *Advertising Age* (January 2, 1992), p. 4; "Rogaine for Women Gets $20M in Support," *Advertising Age* (January 6, 1992), p. 1; "New Hope for the Hair-Impaired," *Business Week* (August 17, 1992), p. 105; "For Rogaine, No Miracle Cure—Yet," *Business Week* (June 4, 1990), p. 100; "Britain Approves Upjohn Hair Drug," *The New York Times* (April 6, 1990), p. 4; Laurie Freeman, "Can Rogaine Make Gains Via Ads?" *Advertising Age* (September 11, 1989), p. 12; Stephen W. Quickel, "Bald Spot," *Business Month* (November 1989), pp. 36-37*ff*; Laurie Freeman, "Upjohn Takes a Shine to Balding Women," *Advertising Age* (February 27, 1989), p. S1; Patricia Winters and Laurie Freeman, "Nicorette, Rogaine Seek TV OK," *Advertising Age* (November 27, 1989), p. 31; "Minoxidil," *Vogue* (September 1989), p. 56; "Hair Today: Rogaine's Growing Pains," *New York* (October 30, 1990), p. 20; "Blondes, Brunettes, Redheads, and Rogaine," *American Druggist* (June 1992), pp. 39–40.

[19] Steven W. Quickel, "Bald Spot," *Business Month* (November 1989), p. 40.

EXHIBIT 5

Age and Income of Persons in the United States

Age Category	Persons (millions)	Less than $2,500	$2,500- $4,999	$5,000- $9,999	$10,000- $14,999	$15,000- $24,999	$25,000- $49,999	$50,000- $74,999	$75,000- or more
					Percent Distribution by Income Level				
Males									
15–24	17.4	28.1	15.1	22.0	14.9	14.8	4.9	.3	—
25–34	21.3	3.1	3.7	10.0	13.8	28.6	34.4	4.7	1.7
35–44	19.0	2.6	2.8	6.5	8.3	20.1	41.8	11.8	6.0
45–54	12.4	3.0	2.4	6.3	8.5	18.4	39.3	13.9	8.1
55–64	10.2	3.1	4.1	10.8	11.2	21.1	33.1	10.1	6.4
65 and over	12.5	1.9	5.8	24.7	20.9	24.2	16.0	3.9	2.6
Total Males	92.8								
Females									
15–24	17.5	31.0	19.7	22.8	13.1	10.5	2.7	.1	—
25–34	21.6	15.7	8.8	16.5	15.3	25.0	17.2	1.2	.4
35–44	19.6	14.9	7.6	14.8	13.8	23.0	22.2	2.7	1.0
45–54	13.3	14.7	7.9	15.3	14.2	21.7	22.2	3.0	1.0
55–64	11.2	17.0	14.8	20.4	14.5	17.0	13.0	2.5	.8
65 and over	17.5	5.0	19.4	37.0	16.7	13.8	6.8	.9	.5
Total Females	100.7								

Source: U.S. Bureau of the Census, *Current Population Reports.*

males and females). This start date, two months earlier than planned, was prompted by slow prescription sales due to low trial. The television campaign began on November 23, 1988. The print campaign featured advertisements in popular consumer magazines and newsstand business publications.

Television and print advertising messages emphasized a soft-sell that urged consumers to "see your doctor . . . if you're concerned about hair loss." These advertisements contained no mention of Rogaine since federal regulations at the time prohibited the use of brand names in prescription-drug advertising to consumers. However, The Upjohn Company name appeared in the advertisements. With a U.S. sales rate of $4 million per month for the first quarter of 1989, a decision was made to revamp the advertising campaign. The new campaign featured a bald man standing before his bathroom mirror. Like the earlier messages, viewers were again urged to see their doctor. Sales in the U.S. improved, reaching $70 million for 1989. A third advertising campaign was developed and launched in February 1990 with print advertisements featuring the Rogaine name for the first time with FDA approval. Advertisement copy emphasized that Rogaine was the only FDA-approved product for hair growth with the headline: "The good news is there's only one product that's proven to grow hair . . . Rogaine." Companion television advertising, however, did not mention Rogaine. Rogaine U.S. sales in 1990 totaled $95 million. This campaign continued in 1991; however, the Rogaine name now appeared in television advertisements with FDA approval. Year-end Rogaine sales totaled $103 million in 1991. Industry sources estimated that the amount spent on consumer-measured media advertising for Rogaine was $4,914,500 in 1989, $9,347,500 in 1990, and $3,443,000 in 1991.[20]

Price–Sales Promotion Program

A one-year supply of Rogaine could cost a user between $600 and $720 depending on pharmacist margins.[21] The total out-of-pocket cost to patients, including periodic physician office fees, could be as high as $800 to $900 per year, since patients were advised to visit their physicians twice per year after the initial consultation.

A variety of price incentives and sales promotion activities were also implemented to stimulate physician visits. For instance, rebates were offered to people who received a Rogaine prescription from their physician. The patient would either get a certificate worth $10 toward the purchase of the first bottle of Rogaine, or $20 for sending in the box tops from the first four bottles used. Selected barbershops and salons were also provided information packets to be given to customers worried about hair loss, including 150,000 copies of informational videos. Consumer advertising also included an 800 number to call to receive information about the product. By 1991, some one million calls had been made to The Upjohn Company. It has been estimated that The Upjohn Company spent between $40 and $50 million annually to market prescription Rogaine since its introduction through 1991. This cost included professional and consumer advertising, the price–sales promotion program, and selling expenses.

In September 1991, the price–sales promotion program for Rogaine was the subject of a day-long Congressional hearing in Washington, D.C.[22] Several members of Congress expressed criticism of the practice of using consumer rebates and cash in-

---

[20] *Measured media* refers to newspapers, consumer magazines and Sunday magazines, outdoor billboards, network, spot, syndicated and cable television, and network and spot radio. *Unmeasured media* include direct mail, co-op advertising, couponing, catalogs, and business publications.

[21] Although pharmacy margins varied, pharmacists typically obtained a gross profit margin of 10 percent based on the selling price to the consumer, based on "Blondes, Brunettes, Redheads, and Rogaine," *American Druggist* (June 1992), p. 40.

[22] Steven W. Colford and Pat Sloan, "Feds Take Aim at Rogaine Ads," *Advertising Age* (September 16, 1991), p. 47.

centives to market a prescription drug. An FDA official said, "We are concerned about this kind of tactic." Commenting on prescription drug consumer advertising in general, FDA Commissioner Dr. David Kessler commented, "We believe the public, in general, is not well-served by ads for prescription drugs." An FDA spokesperson later said the agency ". . . will let [the current Rogaine campaign] continue as it is, though we are not going to tip our hand as to what might happen in the future."

Even though the FDA and some physicians did not favor prescription drug advertising, consumer response to prescription drug advertising was generally favorable. A survey of 2,000 adult U.S. consumers reported that 40 percent said they had talked to a physician because of an advertisement they had seen, 72 percent of consumers in the survey said the advertising was an educational tool and 71 percent thought prescription drug advertising was worthwhile.[23]

Rogaine for Women[24]

FDA approval for Rogaine use by women was granted in August 1991 and the advertising and promotion program directed at women began in February 1992. The female-market entry plan mirrored the marketing program for males, including the same price and reference to the Rogaine name in advertisements. Extensive use of consumer print advertising appeared in *Cosmopolitan, People, US, Vogue,* and *Woman's Day,* as well as other magazines. The advertising copy for Rogaine advertising directed toward women differed from that used for men, however, because the topic of hair loss was discussed among men, but less often among women. According to an Upjohn Company official, women who suffer from hair loss "feel very much alone because no one talks about it."[25] This view materialized in the message conveyed in Rogaine print advertisements for women. For example, a woman in a Rogaine print advertisement said: "Finally I can do a lot more about my hair loss than just sit back and take it." The advertisement concluded by saying: "Take the control you've always wanted, and do it now." Television commercials also appeared in major U.S. metropolitan markets during daytime, early evening, and weekend programs on local stations and cable networks. In the television commercials, a woman portraying a news reporter says: "On this job, you cannot do a story until you get the facts. So when I heard about Rogaine with minoxidil, I wanted to get all the facts for myself."

The price–sales promotion program included a $10 incentive to visit a physician or dermatologist and an 800 number to call to receive an informational brochure about the product. Brochures were made available at drugstores and doctors' offices. An extensive professional effort evident in journal advertising, direct mail, and sales-staff support launched the product, including new print and video materials for pharmacists. The total marketing budget (including advertising) for the female market launch in 1992 was reported to be $20 million. U.S. sales of Rogaine in 1992 rose to $122 million due to the expanded customer base for the product. Total consumer advertising for Rogaine was $12,569,600 in 1992 according to industry sources.

---

[23] "Upswing Seen in R_x Drug Ads Aimed Directly At Consumer," *American Medical News* (June 1, 1990), pp. 13, 15.

[24] This discussion is based on "Blondes, Brunettes, Redheads, and Rogaine," *American Druggist* (June 1992), pp. 39–40; Steven W. Colford and Pat Sloan, "Feds Take Aim at Rogaine Ads," *Advertising Age* (September 16, 1991), p. 47; Stuart Elliott, "Upjohn Turns to Women to Increase Rogaine Sales," *Advertising Age* (January 2, 1992), p. 4.

[25] Stuart Elliott, "Upjohn Turns to Women To Increase Rogaine Sales," *Advertising Age* (January 2, 1992), p. 4.

Rogaine was marketed to both women and men as a prescription drug through 1995.[26] Two additional advertising campaigns directed at women appeared during this period and a new advertising campaign for men was launched. Advertising expenditures also increased. According to a company spokesperson, aggressive advertising that urged consumers to initiate a dialogue about hair loss with their physician was essential to maintaining sales of Rogaine. The spokesperson said: "A lot of physicians won't bring up the subject of hair loss in front of a patient."[27] Advertising in measured media was $34,579,800 in 1993, $32,404,000 in 1994, and $40 million in 1995 according to industry sources. With over $21 million spent on cable television alone in 1995, Rogaine was ranked as the fifth most-advertised brand in this medium in the United States. In addition, the company created the first-ever infomercial for a prescription drug in 1995. The 30-minute infomercial was targeted toward women and hosted by actress Cindy Williams, who interviewed a licensed dermatologist, a hair designer and stylist, and a company marketing executive. The company also established a Worldwide Web site for the product, which was another industry first.

During this three-year period, company attention also was placed on building a Rogaine prospect and user database to support a relationship marketing program. This program proved to be useful for targeting prospects and users for direct mail and telemarketing. A result of this effort was that people who started the Rogaine treatment tended to stay with it for a longer period of time. Also, Rogaine's price-sales promotion program continued. Rogaine sales in the United States declined to $84 million in 1993, then rose and plateaued at $96 million in 1994 and 1995.

Product and Market Development

The company continued its product and market development efforts on Rogaine since its introduction in 1988. For example, a different concentration of minoxidil had been examined which would require only one application per day rather than two. This development could improve the product's convenience of use because, as one former company executive conceded, "It's hard to use something twice a day, come hell or high water."[28] Also, an easier-to-use gel was introduced to Europe. In early 1989, the nonprescription Progaine hair-thickener shampoo product line was introduced for use by men and women. These products did not promote hair growth, but served as a treatment for thinning hair. It was believed these products would benefit from the sound-alike name and be considered a companion to Rogaine. In December 1995, the company submitted a new drug application to the FDA for a Rogaine 5-percent minoxidil formulation to treat common hair loss. Marketing clearance for this prescription-only hair regrowth treatment was expected in late 1996.

Market development on a global scale also continued. By April 1996, Rogaine (Regaine in non-U.S. markets) was marketed in more than 80 countries and more than 3 million people had used the product. FDA approval of nonprescription Rogaine meant that the product was approved for sale without a prescription in 13 countries, including Denmark, The Netherlands, New Zealand, Spain, the United King-

---

[26] This discussion is based on Emily DeNitto, "Rogaine Raises Women's Interest," *Advertising Age* (February 28, 1994), p. 12; "Rogaine: Promises, Promises, Promises," *Advertising Age* (October 3, 1993), p. S14; Emily DeNitto, "Rogaine Fashions New Ads for Women," *Advertising Age* (February 28, 1994), p. 12; Jeffrey D. Zbar, "Upjohn Database Rallies Rogaine," *Advertising Age* (January 23, 1995), p. 42; Joshua Levine, "Scalped," *Forbes* (November 6, 1995), p. 128; "Rogaine Opens New Category for Infomercials: Pharmaceuticals," *Advertising Age* (March 11, 1996), p. 10A; "Top 80 Brands on Cable TV," *Advertising Age* (March 25, 1996), p. 34.

[27] Yumiko Ono, "Prescription-Drug Makers Heighten Hard-Sell Tactics," *The Wall Street Journal* (August 29, 1994), pp. B1, B7.

[28] "For Rogaine, No Miracle Cure—Yet," *Business Week* (June 4, 1990), p. 100.

dom, and the United States. Rogaine (Regaine) sales outside the U.S. were $30 million in 1995 in the face of competition from generic brands and substitute products in non-U.S. markets.

■ OVER-THE-COUNTER MARKETING PROGRAM FOR ROGAINE HAIR REGROWTH TREATMENT

The nonprescription drug marketing plan for Rogaine called for the prescription drug marketing program to be phased out by April 1996. Production, distribution, advertising, and promotion for prescription Rogaine had stopped by April 3, 1996.

Marketing Program for Nonprescription Rogaine

The marketing program planning process for nonprescription Rogaine had begun in late 1995. Its mission was to create a new product category called the "Hair Regrowth Category." The reported expenditure for the marketing program was $75 million. More than half of this amount would be designated for consumer advertising to create awareness and trial of the product. Principal elements of the program are outlined below.[29]

Rogaine Targeting, Product Positioning, and Packaging. Like the prescription drug marketing program, the target market for Rogaine would be men and women aged 25 to 49. Rogaine would be positioned as the only product medically proven to regrow hair.

Separate packaging for men and women would be prepared even though the product was identical. Rogaine For Men would be packaged in a light blue carton. Rogaine For Women would be packaged in a salmon-pink carton. Each carton would contain a brochure with gender-based instructions for use and address possible consumer questions. Single-packs with one 60 milliliter Rogaine bottle, twin-packs with two bottles, and triple-packs with three bottles would be sold. One bottle contained sufficient solution for one month's use. The bottles would be tamper-evident and child-resistant. Rogaine For Men would come with dropper and sprayer applicators. Rogaine For Women would have an extended sprayer for ease of application with longer hair.

Rogaine Advertising and Promotion. A multi-pronged advertising and promotion program was designed for Rogaine. The advertising objectives for Rogaine were to raise consumer awareness of the brand's recently approved nonprescription status, encourage product trial, and communicate user expectations. Initially, one new 30-second television advertisement for Rogaine For Men and one 30-second television advertisement for Rogaine For Women would be created. According to a company spokesperson, "Men and women experience the physical and psychological effects of hair loss differently. Also, men and women respond differently to Rogaine. So Rogaine advertising, like Rogaine packaging, will address the gender-specific concerns of Rogaine users."[30] The brand manager for Rogaine added that advertising will take an educational slant, emphasizing the fact that "this is the only product medically proven to regrow hair."[31] The Rogaine For Men television commercial would air dur-

---

[29] This discussion is based on "Rogaine Will Be Sold Over-the-Counter," *PR Newswire* (February 12, 1996); "OTC Rogaine Introduced," PR Newswire (April 8, 1996); "New Rogaine TV Commercials Begin," *PR Newswire* (April 22, 1996); Sean Mehegan, "Hair Today," *BRANDWEEK* (April 8, 1996), pp. 1, 6; Sean Mehegan, "Rogaine/Progaine," *MEDIAWEEK* (April 8, 1996), p. 38; Michael Wilkie, "New Rivals Push Rogaine to Jumpstart Its OTC Ads," *Advertising Age* (April 15, 1996), p. 45.

[30] "New Rogaine TV Commercials Begin," *PR Newswire* (April 22, 1996).

[31] Sean Mehegan, "Hair Today," *BRANDWEEK* (April 8, 1996), p. 6.

ing evening prime time, sports, cable sports, late-night, and syndicated programs. The Rogaine For Women television commercial would air during evening prime time and day schedules on network, cable, and syndicated programs.

The planned media schedule for Rogaine was designed so that 92 percent of the target market would see Rogaine television advertisements seven times in a four-week period following the brand's introduction as a nonprescription drug. Print advertisements were scheduled to reach 77 percent of the target audience. The advertising agency executive responsible for Rogaine said, "If there still are consumers who don't know about Rogaine, how to apply it, how it works, and the fact that it is available without a prescription, this new ad campaign will take care of that."[32]

The advertising program for Rogaine would be complemented by an extensive consumer and trade promotion campaign. An estimated 40,000 physicians would receive a mailing announcing Rogaine's nonprescription status. More than 20,000 pharmacists would be mailed a Rogaine Pharmacy Kit. Items in the kit would include an educational brochure and video for pharmacists, consumer education brochures, and an announcement easel for the pharmacy counter. Free-standing inserts (FSIs), in-store circular ads, and coupons would comprise the consumer promotion program.

Direct marketing efforts would be employed with the objective of encouraging product compliance and repeat usage, and to reinforce user expectations. Planned periodic mailings to users would include money-saving coupons, a newsletter with hair care and styling suggestions, and comments from users, dermatologists, and other authorities. Consumers could join the direct marketing program by returning an enrollment card from the Rogaine package or by calling a Rogaine toll-free number.

Rogaine Distribution and Pricing. Planned distribution for Rogaine would include pharmacy or hair care sections of food, drug, and mass-merchandise retail outlets. This placement was based on Pharmacia & Upjohn, Inc. marketing research which indicated that consumers would look for and expect to find Rogaine in these sections.

Nonprescription Rogaine would be priced at about one-half of prescription Rogaine. A single-pack suggested retail price for Rogaine would be $29.50. Twin-packs would be priced at $55.00 and triple-packs would be available in some stores with a suggested retail price of $75.00. The retailer margin on Rogaine would be about 20 percent of the suggested retail price. Commenting on the expanded distribution and pricing, a senior company executive said: "The availability of OTC Rogaine is welcome news for the millions of men and women in this country who experience common hereditary hair loss. Instead of going to a doctor's office, they can simply walk into a food store, drug store, or mass merchandiser outlet and purchase Rogaine without a prescription at its full prescription strength. It's much more convenient and because the price is now lower, it's much more affordable."[33]

Hair Regrowth Category Development: Rogaine and Progaine

The launch of nonprescription Rogaine focused on creating a brand with $250 million-a-year in retail sales at the suggested retail prices in what Pharmacia & Upjohn, Inc. officials coined as the "Hair Regrowth Category" of products. In this regard, the concurrent relaunch of Progaine shampoo represented an effort to synergize the Rogaine/Progaine brand names into a system of hair care. The Progaine relaunch in-

---

[32] "New Rogaine TV Commercials Begin," *PR Newswire* (April 22, 1996).
[33] "OTC Rogaine Introduced," *PR Newswire* (April 8, 1996).

volved a package redesign and a new formula with added proteins, conditioners, and hair-thickening agents. To bolster the linkage between Rogaine and Progaine, coupons for Progaine would be inserted in Rogaine cartons. The two products also would be located side-by-side in the hair-care aisle in retail stores. Progaine retail shampoo sales in 1995 were about $2 million. Total U.S. retail sales of shampoos in 1995 approached $1.5 billion.[34]

■ APRIL 30, 1996: THE FEDERAL DISTRICT COURT RULING

On April 30, 1996 the Federal District Court ruled in favor of the FDA.[35] This meant that Rogaine would not have a three-year marketing exclusivity and three competing generic products had approval for sale without a prescription in the United States.

This development raised a variety of issues related to the marketing opportunity for FDA-approved nonprescription hair regrowth products containing a 2-percent minoxidil solution, and the Rogaine brand in particular. For example, how might the unit and dollar sales potential of the hair regrowth category be affected? Pharmacia & Upjohn, Inc. believed sales of $1 billion were possible over five years for Rogaine when it was the only hair regrowth product containing a 2-percent minoxidil solution. Might this sales figure for the category as a whole need revision and by how much? A useful starting point might be to revisit the sales history of prescription Rogaine. This would involve simulating the trial and repeat purchase patterns for prescription Rogaine and determining how these patterns might have contributed to sales growth.

Relatedly, the absence of marketing exclusivity and the presence of generic products changed the competitive landscape for Rogaine. No longer would Rogaine hold a monopoly position as the sole supplier of a hair regrowth product with a 2-percent minoxidil solution. Rather, prospective users of this product could now try a competitive product and current Rogaine users could switch to another product. The effect on Rogaine sales required further attention.

Nonprescription hair regrowth product category sales and Rogaine's share of these sales would depend, in large measure, on the marketing program for nonprescription Rogaine. Developed in anticipation of a favorable FDA response to its petition for a three-year marketing exclusivity, this program was being currently executed. At issue at this time was how the marketing plan should be modified, if at all.

---

[34] Pat Sloan, "Brand Scorecard: Premium Products Lather Up Sales," *Advertising Age* (July 24, 1995), p. 24.

[35] "Court Allows Sale of Generic Forms of Rogaine," *The New York Times* (May 1, 1996), p. 40.

Duncan Industries
Market Opportunities in the European Union

In September 1996, Mark Duncan, President of Duncan Industries, had just finished reading a feasibility report on entering the European market in 1997. Duncan Industries manufactured surface automotive hoists, a product used by garages, service stations, and other repair shops to lift cars for servicing (Exhibit 1 on page 100). The report, prepared by the company's marketing manager, Pierre Gagnon, outlined the opportunities in the European Union and the entry options available.

Mr. Duncan was not sure if his company was ready for this move. While the company had been successful in expanding sales into the U.S. market, Mr. Duncan wondered if this success could be repeated in Europe. He thought that, with more effort, sales could be increased in the United States. On the other hand, there were some positive aspects to the European idea. He began reviewing the information in preparation for the meeting the following day with Mr. Gagnon.

■ DUNCAN INDUSTRIES

Mr. Duncan, a design engineer, had worked for eight years for the Canadian subsidiary of a U.S. automotive hoist manufacturer. During those years, he had spent considerable time designing an above-ground (or surface) automotive hoist. Although Mr. Duncan was very enthusiastic about the unique aspects of the hoist, including a scissor lift and wheel alignment pads, senior management expressed no interest in the idea. In 1986, Mr. Duncan left the company to start his own business with the express purpose of designing and manufacturing the hoist. He left with the good wishes of his previous employer who had no objections to his plans to start a new business.

Over the next three years, Mr. Duncan obtained financing from a venture capital firm, opened a plant in Lachine, Quebec, and began manufacturing and marketing the hoist, called the Duncan Lift (Exhibit 1).

From the beginning, Mr. Duncan had taken considerable pride in the development and marketing of the Duncan Lift. The original design included a scissor lift and a safety locking mechanism which allowed the hoist to be raised to any level and locked in place. As well, the scissor lift offered easy access for the mechanic to work on the raised vehicle. Because the hoist was fully hydraulic and had no chains or pulleys, it required little maintenance. Another key feature was the alignment turn plates that were an integral part of the lift. The turn plates meant that mechanics could accurately and easily perform wheel alignment jobs. Because it was a surface lift, it could be installed in a garage in less than a day.

This case was prepared by Professor Gordon H. G. McDougall, Wilfrid Laurier University, as the basis for class discussion rather than to illustrate either effective or ineffective handling of an administrative situation. Used by permission.

EXHIBIT 1

Examples of Automotive Hoists

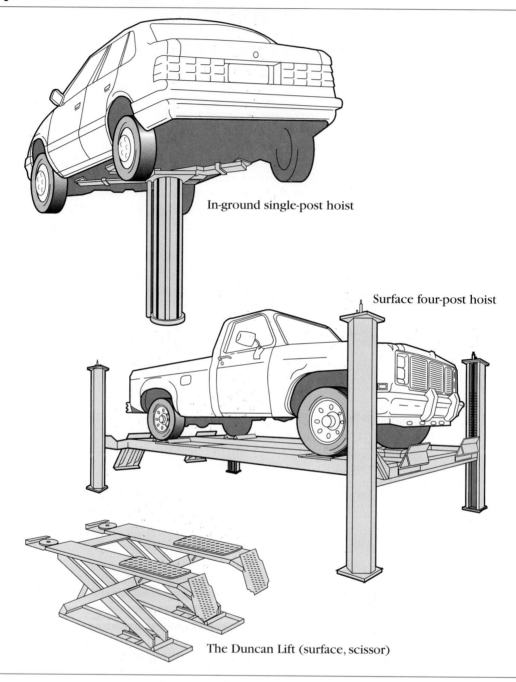

In-ground single-post hoist

Surface four-post hoist

The Duncan Lift (surface, scissor)

Mr. Duncan continually made improvements to the product, including adding more safety features. In fact, the Duncan Lift was considered a leader in automotive lift safety. Safety was an important factor in the automotive hoist market. Although hoists seldom malfunctioned, when they did, it often resulted in a serious accident.

The Duncan Lift developed a reputation in the industry as the "Cadillac" of hoists; the unit was judged by many as superior to competitive offerings because of

EXHIBIT 2

Duncan Industries Selected Financial Statistics (1993–1995)

	1993	1994	1995
Sales	$6,218,000	$7,454,000	$9,708,000
Cost of sales	4,540,000	5,541,000	6,990,000
Contribution	1,678,000	1,913,000	2,718,000
Marketing expenses*	507,000	510,000	530,000
Administrative expenses	810,000	820,000	840,000
Earnings before tax	361,000	583,000	1,348,000
Units sold	723	847	1,054

Marketing expenses in 1995 included advertising ($70,000), four salespeople ($240,000), marketing manager and three sales support staff ($220,000).

Source: Company records.

its design, the quality of the workmanship, the safety features, the ease of installation, and the five-year warranty. Mr. Duncan held four patents on the Duncan Lift including the lifting mechanism on the scissor design and a safety locking mechanism. A number of versions of the product were designed that made the Duncan Lift suitable (depending on the model) for a variety of tasks, including rustproofing, muffler repairs, and general mechanical repairs.

In 1988, Duncan Industries sold 23 hoists and had sales of $172,500. During the early years the majority of sales were to independent service stations and garages specializing in wheel alignment in the Quebec and Ontario markets. Most of the units were sold by Mr. Gagnon, who was hired in 1988 to handle the marketing side of the operation. In 1990, Mr. Gagnon began using distributors to sell the hoist to a wider geographic market in Canada. In 1992, he signed an agreement with a large automotive wholesaler to represent Duncan Industries in the U.S. market. By 1995, the company sold 1,054 hoists and had sales of $9,708,000 (Exhibit 2). In 1995, about 60% of unit sales were to the U.S. with the remaining 40% to the Canadian market.

■ THE INDUSTRY

Approximately 49,000 hoists were sold each year in North America. Hoists were typically purchased by any automotive outlet that serviced or repaired cars including new car dealers, used car dealers, specialty shops (for example, muffler shops, transmission, wheel alignment), chains (for example, Firestone, Goodyear, Canadian Tire), and independent garages. It was estimated that new car dealers purchased 30% of all units sold in a given year. In general, the specialty shops focused on one type of repair, such as mufflers or rust proofing, while "non-specialty" outlets handled a variety of repairs. While there was some crossover, in general Duncan Industries competed in the specialty shop segment and, in particular, those shops that dealt with wheel alignment. This included chains such as Firestone and Canadian Tire as well as new car dealers (for example, Ford) who devote a certain percentage of their lifts to the wheel alignment business and independent garages who specialized in wheel alignment.

The purpose of a hoist was to lift an automobile into a position where a mechanic or service person could easily work on the car. Because different repairs required different positions, a wide variety of hoists had been developed to meet specific needs. For example, a muffler repair shop required a hoist where the mechanic could gain easy access to the underside of the car. Similarly, a wheel alignment job required a hoist that offered a level platform where the wheels could be adjusted as well as providing easy access for the mechanic. Mr. Gagnon estimated that 85% of Duncan Industries' sales were to the wheel alignment market to service centers like Firestone, Goodyear, and Canadian Tire and independent garages that specialized in wheel alignment. About 15% of sales were made to customers who used the hoist for general mechanical repairs.

Firms purchasing hoists were part of an industry called the automobile aftermarket. This industry was involved in supplying parts and service for new and used cars and was worth over $54 billion at retail in 1995 while servicing the approximately 14 million cars on the road in Canada. The industry was large and diverse; there were over 4,000 new car dealers in Canada, over 400 Canadian Tire stores, over 100 stores in each of the Firestone and Goodyear chains, and over 220 stores in the Rust Check chain.

The purchase of an automotive hoist was often an important decision for the service station owner or dealer. Because the price of hoists ranged from $3,000 to $15,000, it was a capital expense for most businesses.

For the owner/operator of a new service center or car dealership the decision involved determining what type of hoist was required, then what brand would best suit the company. Most new service centers or car dealerships had multiple bays for servicing cars. In these cases, the decision would involve what types of hoists were required (for example, in-ground, surface). Often more than one type of hoist was purchased, depending on the service center/dealership needs.

Experienced garage owners seeking a replacement hoist (the typical hoist had a useful life of 10 to 13 years) would usually determine what products were available and then make a decision. If the garage owners were also mechanics, they would probably be aware of two or three types of hoists but not very knowledgeable about the brands or products currently available. Garage owners or dealers who were not mechanics probably knew very little about hoists. The owners of car or service dealerships often bought the product that was recommended and/or approved by the parent company.

Competition

Sixteen companies competed with Duncan Industries in the automotive lift market in North America: 4 Canadian and 12 U.S. firms. Hoists were subject to small import duties. In 1996, duties on hoists entering the U.S. market from Canada were 1.2% of the selling price; from the U.S. entering Canada the import duty was 3.4%. With the advent of the 1988 U.S.–Canada Free Trade Agreement, the duties between the two countries were being phased out over a 10-year period. For Mr. Duncan, the import duties had never played a part in any decisions—the fluctuating exchange rates between the two countries had a far greater impact on selling prices.

A wide variety of hoists were manufactured in the industry. The two basic types of hoists were in-ground and surface. As the names imply, in-ground hoists required a pit to be dug "in-ground" where the piston that raised the hoist was installed. In-ground hoists were either single post or multiple post, were permanent, and obviously could not be moved. In-ground lifts constituted approximately 21% of total lift sales in 1995 (Exhibit 3). Surface lifts were installed on a flat surface, usually concrete. Surface lifts came in two basic types, post lift hoists and scissor hoists. Surface lifts, compared to in-ground lifts, were easier to install and could be moved, if necessary. Surface lifts constituted 79% of total lift sales in 1995. Within each type of hoist (for example, post lift surface hoists), there were numerous variations in terms of size, shape, and lifting capacity.

EXHIBIT 3

North American Automotive Lift Unit Sales, by Type (1993–1995)

	1993	1994	1995
In-ground			
Single post	5,885	5,772	5,518
Multiple post	4,812	6,625	5,075
Surface			
Two post	27,019	28,757	28,923
Four post	3,862	3,162	3,745
Scissor	2,170	2,258	2,316
Other	4,486	3,613	3,695
Total	48,234	50,187	49,272

Source: Company records.

The industry was dominated by two large U.S. firms, AHV Lifts and Berne Manufacturing, who together held approximately 60% of the market. AHV Lifts, the largest firm with approximately 40% of the market and annual sales of about $60 million, offered a complete line of hoists (that is, in-ground, surface) but focused primarily on the in-ground market and the two post surface market. AHV Lifts was the only company that had its own direct sales force; all other companies used (1) only wholesalers or (2) a combination of wholesalers and company sales force. AHV Lifts offered standard hoists with few extra features and competed primarily on price. Berne Manufacturing, with a market share of approximately 20%, also competed in the in-ground and two post surface markets. It used a combination of wholesalers and company salespeople and, like AVH Lifts, competed primarily on price.

Most of the remaining firms in the industry were companies who operated in a regional market (for example, California, British Columbia) and/or who offered a limited product line (for example, four post surface hoist).

Duncan had two competitors that manufactured scissor lifts. AVH Lifts marketed a scissor hoist that had a different lifting mechanism and did not include the safety locking features of the Duncan Lift. On average, the AVH scissor lift was sold for about 20% less than the Duncan Lift. The second competitor, Mete Lift, was a small regional company with sales in California and Oregon. It had a design that was very similar to the Duncan Lift but lacked some of its safety features. The Mete Lift, regarded as a well-manufactured product, sold for about 5% less than the Duncan Lift.

■ MARKETING STRATEGY FOR DUNCAN INDUSTRIES

As of early 1996, Duncan Industries had developed a reputation for a quality product backed by good service in the hoist lift market, primarily in the wheel alignment segment.

The distribution system employed by Duncan Industries reflected the need to engage in extensive personal selling. Three types of distributors were used: a company sales force, Canadian distributors, and a U.S. automotive wholesaler. The company sales force consisted of four salespeople and Mr. Gagnon. Their main task was to service large "direct" accounts. The initial step was to get the Duncan Lift approved by large chains and manufacturers and then, having received the approval, to sell to individual dealers or operators. For example, if General Motors approved the hoist, then Duncan Industries could sell it to individual General Motors dealers. Duncan Industries sold directly to the individual dealers of a number of large accounts including General Motors, Ford, Chrysler, Petro-Canada, Firestone, and Goodyear. Duncan Industries had been successful in obtaining manufacturer approval from the big three automobile manufacturers in both Canada and the U.S. As well, Duncan Industries had also received approval from service companies such as Canadian Tire and Goodyear. To date, Duncan Industries had not been rejected by any major account but, in some cases, the approval process had taken over four years.

In total, the company sales force generated about 25% of the unit sales each year. Sales to the large "direct" accounts in the United States went through Duncan Industries' U.S. wholesaler.

The Canadian distributors sold, installed, and serviced units across Canada. These distributors handled the Duncan Lift and carried a line of noncompetitive automotive equipment products (for example, engine diagnostic equipment, wheel balancing equipment) and noncompetitive lifts. These distributors focused on the smaller chains and the independent service stations and garages.

The U.S. wholesaler sold a complete product line to service stations as well as manufacturing some equipment. The Duncan Lift was one of five different types of lifts that the wholesaler sold. Although the wholesaler provided Duncan Industries with extensive distribution in the United States, the Duncan Lift was a minor product within the wholesaler's total line. While Mr. Gagnon did not have any actual figures, he thought that the Duncan Lift probably accounted for less than 20% of the total lift sales of the U.S. wholesaler.

Both Mr. Duncan and Mr. Gagnon felt that the U.S. market had unrealized potential. With a population of 264 million people and over 146 million registered vehicles, the U.S. market was almost 10 times the size of the Canadian market (population of 30 million, approximately 14 million vehicles). Mr. Gagnon noted that the six New England states (population over 13 million), the three largest mid-Atlantic states (population over 38 million), and the three largest mid-eastern states (population over 32 million) were all within a day's drive of the factory in Lachine. Mr. Duncan and Mr. Gagnon had considered setting up a sales office in New York to service these states, but they were concerned that the U.S. wholesaler would not be willing to relinquish any of its territory. They had also considered working more closely with the wholesaler to encourage it to "push" the Duncan Lift. It appeared that the wholesaler's major objective was to sell a hoist, not necessarily the Duncan Lift.

Duncan Industries distributed a catalogue-type package with products, uses, prices and other required information for both distributors and users. In addition, Duncan Industries advertised in trade publications (for example, *Service Station & Garage Management*), and Mr. Gagnon traveled to trade shows in Canada and the U.S. to promote the Duncan lift.

In 1995, Duncan Lifts sold for an average retail price of $10,990 and Duncan Industries received, on average, $9,210 for each unit sold. This average reflected the mix of sales through the three distribution channels: (1) direct (where Duncan Industries received 100% of the selling price), (2) Canadian distributors (where Duncan Industries received 80% of the selling price), and (3) the U.S. wholesaler (where Duncan Industries received 78% of the selling price).

Both Mr. Duncan and Mr. Gagnon felt that the company's success to date was based on a strategy of offering a superior product that was primarily targeted to the needs of specific customers. The strategy stressed continual product improvements, quality workmanship, and service. Personal selling was a key aspect of the strategy; salespeople could show customers the benefits of the Duncan Lift over competing products.

■ THE EUROPEAN UNION MARKET

Against this background, Mr. Duncan had been thinking of ways to continue the rapid growth of the company. One possibility that kept coming up was the promise and potential of markets in the European Union. The fact that Europe became a single market in 1993 suggested that it was an opportunity that should at least be explored. With this in mind, Mr. Duncan asked Mr. Gagnon to prepare a report on the possibility of Duncan Industries entering the European Union. The highlights of Mr. Gagnon's report follow.

History of the European Union

The European Union (EU) had its basis formed from the 1957 "Treaty of Rome" in which five countries decided it would be in their best interest to form an internal market. These countries were France, Spain, Italy, West Germany, and Luxembourg. By early 1996, the EU consisted of 15 countries (the additional ten were Austria, Belgium, Denmark, Finland, Greece, Ireland, The Netherlands, Portugal, Sweden, and the United Kingdom) with a population of over 370 million people. Virtually all barriers (physical, technical, and fiscal) in the EU were scheduled to be removed for companies located within the EU. This allowed the free movement of goods, persons, services, and capital.

In the last ten years many North American and Japanese firms had established themselves in the EU. The reasoning for this was twofold. First, these companies regarded the community as an opportunity to increase global market share and profits. The market was attractive because of its sheer size and lack of internal barriers. Second, there was continuing concern that companies not established within the EU would have difficulty exporting to the EU due to changing standards and tariffs. To date, this concern had not materialized.

Market Potential

The key indicator of the potential market for the Duncan Lift hoist was the number of passenger cars and commercial vehicles in use in a particular country. Four European Union countries had more than 20 million vehicles in use with Germany having the largest domestic fleet of 41 million vehicles followed in order by Italy, France, and the United Kingdom (Exhibit 4). The number of vehicles was an important indicator since the more vehicles in use meant a greater number of service and repair facilities that needed vehicle hoists and potentially the Duncan Lift.

EXHIBIT 4

Number of Vehicles and Population in Five European Union Countries

Country	Vehicles in Use (Thousands) in 1993		1995 New Vehicle Registrations (thousands)	1995 Population (thousands)
	Passenger	Commercial		
Germany	38,325	2,842	3,209	81,500
France	24,385	4,890	1,973	58,000
Italy	29,600	2,746	1,610	57,200
United Kingdom	20,344	3,991	1,911	58,300
Spain	13,440	2,783	910	39,200

An indicator of the future vehicle repair and service market was the number of new vehicle registrations. The registration of new vehicles was important as this maintained the number of vehicles in use by replacing cars that had been retired. Again, Germany had the most new cars registered in 1995 and was followed in order by France, the United Kingdom, and Italy.

Based primarily on the fact that a large domestic market was important for initial growth, the selection of a European country should be limited to the "Big Four" industrialized nations: Germany, France, the United Kingdom, or Italy. In an international survey companies from North America and Europe ranked European countries on a scale of 1 to 100 on market potential and investment site potential. The results showed that Germany was favored for both market potential and investment site opportunities while France, the United Kingdom, and Spain placed second, third, and fourth respectively. Italy did not place in the top four in either market or investment site potential. However, Italy had a large number of vehicles in use, had the fourth largest population in Europe, and was an acknowledged leader in car technology and production.

Little information was available on the competition within Europe. There was, as yet, no dominant manufacturer as was the case in North America. At this time, there was one firm in Germany that manufactured a scissor-type lift. The firm sold most of its units within the German market. The only other available information was that 22 firms in Italy manufactured vehicle lifts.

■ INVESTMENT OPTIONS

Mr. Gagnon felt that Duncan Industries had three options for expansion into the European market: licensing, joint venture, or direct investment. The licensing option was a real possibility as a French firm had expressed an interest in manufacturing the Duncan Lift.

In June 1996, Mr. Gagnon had attended a trade show in Detroit to promote the Duncan Lift. At the show, he met Phillipe Beaupre, the marketing manager for Bar Maisse, a French manufacturer of wheel alignment equipment. The firm, located in Chelles, France, sold a range of wheel alignment equipment throughout Europe. The best-selling product was an electronic modular aligner which enabled a mechanic to utilize a sophisticated computer system to align the wheels of a car. Mr. Beaupre was seeking a North American distributor for the modular aligner and other products manufactured by Bar Maisse.

At the show, Mr. Gagnon and Mr. Beaupre had a casual conversation wherein both explained what their respective companies manufactured. They exchanged company brochures and business cards, and both went on to other exhibits. The next day, Mr. Beaupre sought out Mr. Gagnon and asked if he might be interested in having Bar Maisse manufacture and market the Duncan Lift in Europe. Mr. Beaupre felt the lift would complement Bar Maisse's product line and the licensing would be of mutual benefit to both parties. They agreed to pursue the idea. Upon his return, Mr. Gagnon told Mr. Duncan about these discussions and they agreed to explore this possibility.

Mr. Gagnon called a number of colleagues in the industry and asked them what they knew about Bar Maisse. About half had not heard of the company but those who had commented favorably on the quality of its products. One colleague, with European experience, knew the company well and said that Bar Maisse's management had integrity and would make a good partner. In July 1996, Mr. Gagnon sent a letter to Mr. Beaupre stating that Duncan Industries was interested in further discussions and enclosing various company brochures including price lists and technical information on the Duncan Lift. In late August 1996, Mr. Beaupre responded stating that Bar Maisse would like to enter a three-year licensing agreement with Duncan Industries to manufacture the Duncan Lift in Europe. In exchange for the manufacturing rights, Bar Maisse was prepared to pay a royalty rate of 5% of gross sales. Mr. Gagnon had not yet responded to this proposal.

A second possibility was a joint venture. Mr. Gagnon had wondered if it might not be better for Duncan Industries to offer a counter proposal to Bar Maisse for a joint venture. He had not worked out any details, but Mr. Gagnon felt that Duncan Industries would learn more about the European market and probably make more money if they were an active partner in Europe. Mr. Gagnon's idea was a 50–50 proposal where the two parties shared the investment and the profits. He envisaged a situation where Bar Maisse would manufacture the Duncan Lift in their plant with technical assistance from Duncan Industries. Mr. Gagnon also thought that Duncan Industries could get involved in the marketing of the lift through the Bar Maisse distribution system. Further, he thought that the Duncan Lift, with proper marketing, could gain a reasonable share of the European market. If that happened Mr. Gagnon felt that Duncan Industries was likely to make greater returns with a joint venture.

The third option was direct investment where Duncan Industries would establish a manufacturing facility and set up a management group to market the lift. Mr. Gagnon had contacted a business acquaintance who had recently been involved in manufacturing fabricated steel sheds in Germany. On the basis of discussions with his acquaintance, Mr. Gagnon estimated the costs involved in setting up a plant in Europe at: (1) $250,000 for capital equipment (welding machines, cranes, other equipment), (2) $200,000 in incremental costs to set the plant up, and (3) carrying costs to cover $1,000,000 in inventory and accounts receivable. While the actual costs of renting a building for the factory would depend on the site location, he estimated that annual building rent including heat, light, and insurance would be about $80,000. Mr. Gagnon recognized these estimates were guidelines but he felt that the estimates were probably within 20% of actual costs.

■ THE DECISION

As Mr. Duncan considered the contents of the report, a number of thoughts crossed his mind. He began making notes concerning the European opportunity and the future of the company:

- If Duncan Industries decided to enter Europe, Mr. Gagnon would be the obvious choice to head up the "direct investment" option or the "joint venture" option. Mr. Duncan felt that Mr. Gagnon had been instrumental in the success of the company to date.

- While Duncan Industries had the financial resources to go ahead with the direct investment option, the joint venture would spread the risk (and the returns) over the two companies.

- Duncan Industries had built its reputation on designing and manufacturing a quality product. Regardless of the option, Mr. Duncan wanted the firm's reputation to be maintained.

- Either the licensing agreement or the joint venture appeared to build on the two companies' strengths; Bar Maisse had knowledge of the market and Duncan Industries had the product. What troubled Mr. Duncan was whether this apparent synergy would work or would Bar Maisse seek to control the operation.

- It was difficult to estimate sales under any of the options. With the first two (licensing and joint venture), it would depend on the effort and expertise of Bar Maisse; with the third, it would depend on Mr. Gagnon.
- Duncan Industries' sales in the U.S. market could be increased if the U.S. wholesaler would "push" the Duncan lift. Alternatively, the establishment of a sales office in New York to cover the eastern states could also increase sales.

As Mr. Duncan reflected on the situation he knew he should probably get additional information—but it wasn't obvious exactly what information would help him make a yes or no decision. He knew one thing for sure—he was going to keep this company on a "fast growth" track, and at tomorrow's meeting he and Mr. Gagnon would decide how to do it.

Mary Kay Cosmetics
Asian Market Entry

In February 1993, Curran Dandurand, senior vice president of Mary Kay Cosmetics, Inc.'s (MKC) global marketing group, was reflecting on the company's international operations. MKC products had been sold outside the United States for over 15 years, but by 1992, international sales represented only 11% of the $1 billion total. In contrast, one of MKC's U.S. competitors, Avon Products, Inc., derived over 55% of its $3.6 billion retail sales from international markets in 1992.

Dandurand wondered how MKC could expand international operations and which elements of MKC's culture, philosophy, product line, and marketing programs were transferable. She wanted to define the critical success factors for MKC internationally and establish a marketing strategy for future international expansion. Specifically, she was currently evaluating two market entry opportunities: Japan and China. The first was a mature but lucrative market where cosmetics marketing and direct selling were well-known and accepted. The second was a rapidly growing and changing but relatively unknown market with substantially lower individual purchasing power.

■ THE COSMETICS AND DIRECT SELLING INDUSTRIES

MKC competed in both the cosmetics and direct selling industries. A decade of mergers, acquisitions, takeovers, buyouts, and sell-offs had dramatically changed the shape of the global cosmetics industry. Powerful multinational marketing companies such as Colgate-Palmolive, Procter & Gamble, Estée Lauder, Gillette, and Unilever (Elizabeth Arden and Chesebrough-Pond's) had increased their market shares, many pharmaceutical companies had exited the industry, and Japanese companies such as Kao and Shiseido were gaining strength internationally.

In 1992, worldwide retail sales of facial treatments and color cosmetics products exceeded $50 billion, with the United States accounting for $16 billion. The top four companies in the U.S. cosmetics market in 1992 were Procter & Gamble with $4.3 billion cosmetics retail sales, Estée Lauder, Avon, and Revlon. L'Oreal, a subsidiary of Nestlé, dominated the world market with $5.9 billion in retail sales, followed by Procter & Gamble, Avon, Unilever, Shiseido, Revlon, Colgate-Palmolive, Estée Lauder, SmithKline Beecham, and Gillette.

Research Associate Nathalie Laidler prepared this case under the supervision of Professor John A. Quelch as the basis for class discussion rather than to illustrate the effective or ineffective handling of an administrative situation. Confidential data have been disguised.

In 1992, the value of sales to consumers by the U.S. direct selling industry was estimated at $14 billion. Products of all types were sold to consumers in their homes by independent salespeople, many of whom worked on a part-time basis. Retail sales by the U.S. direct selling cosmetics industry were estimated at $5 billion in 1992. Cosmetics companies used two approaches to direct selling: the repetitive person-to-person method, used by Avon, in which a salesperson regularly visited customers in their homes and sold products one to one; and the party plan method, in which a salesperson presented and sold products to a group of customers attending a "party" or "show" in one of the customer's homes. The party plan method was used by MKC.

Other large international direct selling organizations included Amway, which sold a variety of household and personal care products and recorded retail sales of over $3.5 billion in 1992, and Tupperware, which sold household products through the party plan method and had retail sales of over $1 billion. International sales for Amway and Tupperware accounted for 60% and 75% of their total sales respectively.

■ MKC OPERATIONS AND PHILOSOPHY

Incorporated in Texas in 1963 by Mary Kay Ash, MKC was a direct selling cosmetics company with 1992 estimated retail sales of $1 billion, net company sales of $624 million, cost of goods sold of $148 million, and earnings before interest and taxes of $110 million.[1] (Exhibit 1 depicts the growth in MKC net revenues, operating cash flow, and number of consultants between 1986 and 1992.) MKC sold a range of skin care, personal care, and cosmetics products through approximately 275,000 independent salespeople worldwide, known as "beauty consultants," who purchased products from the company and resold them at skin care classes or facials held in homes that were attended by four to six, or one to two, potential customers respectively.

The company's powerful culture was based on offering unlimited opportunities for women in business, coupled with a distinctive compensation and recognition plan. Mary Kay Ash's charismatic personality and drive had been central to the company's rapid growth and success, and, for many beauty consultants, she represented a caring and successful role model. In 1993, MKC defined its mission as promoting business opportunities for women, teaching women how to care for their skin and use cosmetics, offering skin care systems as opposed to individual products, and providing unsurpassed personal service to its customers. (Exhibit 2 on page 112 outlines what the company considered to be its competitive advantages and points of difference with respect to both potential beauty consultants and cosmetics consumers.)

Product Line

In 1992, MKC manufactured a relatively narrow line of 225 SKUs (stockkeeping units), including different color shades.[2] Product policy emphasized skin care "systems" that included several related items formulated for specific skin types or skin conditions. (Table A on page 113 reports the number of products—excluding different shades within color product categories—and percentage of 1992 sales for each of the eight product categories in which MKC competed.)

---

[1] Net company sales were defined as sales of MKC products by the company to its sales consultants. Retail sales are defined as those sales made by consultants to consumers.

[2] In 1992, Avon had an estimated 1,500 SKUs.

EXHIBIT 1

Mary Kay Cosmetics—Net Revenues, Operating Cash Flow, and Number of Consultants, 1986–1992

Net Revenues

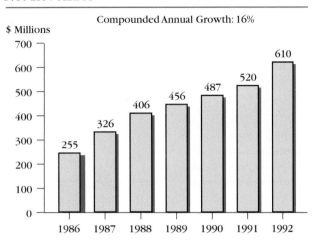

Operating Cash Flow

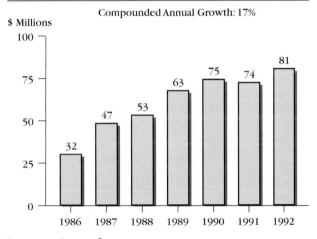

Beauty Consultants

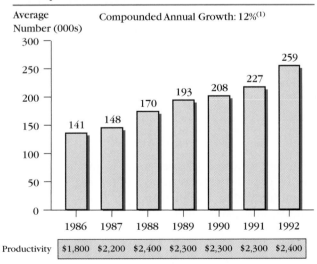

Note: (1) Based on year-end numbers of Beauty Consultants.

E X H I B I T   2

The Mary Kay Cosmetics Career and Consumer Program

The Mary Kay Career

- The Mary Kay career path allows a woman to advance into a management/training position if she so wishes. She cannot buy her way into these positions, but can earn them based on her proven ability to sell and build a team.

- The Mary Kay career path provides the opportunity to earn higher part-time and full-time compensation more quickly than other direct sales companies and most corporations.

- The company does not compete with its Consultants by offering products at retail locations, salons, or via "Buying Club" discounts.

- The company provides advanced training and the presentation and sales tools to allow a Consultant to offer her customers value-added services and information. "She is a teacher of skin care and glamour." In addition the Consultant receives training on leadership and aspects of running a successful business.

- The company supports a Consultant's business by offering business-building programs:
    - Direct Support (consumer direct mail program) to retain and increase current customer business.
    - Leads for new customers and recruits generated by company advertising, direct mail, and sampling programs.

- A Mary Kay Consultant is in business for herself, but never by herself. She receives ongoing training (product knowledge, business and leadership skills), recognition, and motivation from the company and her Director. The Director forms a mentorlike relationship and encourages ongoing involvement and success on the part of the Consultant.

- The unit concept of the sale force organization taps into the Japanese desire to belong to a group and compete with others based on team activities.

The Mary Kay Consumer Program

- Mary Kay Cosmetics offers women self-improvement and self-esteem enhancement through skin care and glamour education provided by a certified Beauty Consultant.

- Consumers are taught how to care for their skin and basic glamour application skills within a unique training class that provides:
    - Individualized analysis of their skin type.
    - Individual vanity tray and mirror that allows the customer to apply each product as it is explained and demonstrated.
    - The ability to try all products prior to purchase via hygienic, single-use samplers.
    - Hands-on glamour application training.
    - Fun, social interaction and entertainment aspect of a skin care class.

- Consumers are offered advanced training including the ColorLogic Glamour System, Advanced Glamour, Skin Wellness, Nail Care, etc.

- On-the-spot delivery of product is provided for most products.

- Enrollment in a unique gift-with-purchase program (Direct Support).

- 100% satisfaction guarantee or full refund.

- Products' packaging are designed to be as environmentally friendly as possible (refillable compacts, recycled/recyclable cartons).

- Ongoing advice and service from a trained expert.

- Skin care products designed for particular skin types and skin conditions.

- Unique glamour system designed to take the guess work out of selecting glamour shades.

- Customers have the opportunity to earn valuable product discounts or unique gifts by hostessing a skin care class.

- Value-added services and further education are provided through high-quality brochures, and newsletters given free of charge to customers.

MKC regularly involved its sales force in product policy decisions, sending them samples of prospective new products for evaluation. Virtually all MKC products were manufactured in a single plant near Dallas, considered to be the most efficient cosmetics production facility in the world.

Sales Force

Four basic levels of independent contractors were included in the MKC sales force: beauty consultants, sales directors, senior sales directors, and national sales directors.

Table A   Number of Products and Percentage of 1992 Sales

	Number of Products	% Sales (1992)
Skin care (cleansers, creams, moisturizers, foundations)	27	46
Glamour (lipsticks, eye colors)	24	30
Fragrances	9	10
Nail care	12	5
Body care	5	3
Sun care	7	2
Hair care	5	1
Men's skin care	6	1

Promotions were made from within and based entirely on performance, as defined by volume sales and recruitment of new salespeople. Virtually all MKC beauty consultants were female, and new consultants were recruited by existing salespeople whose compensation and advancement were partly dependent on their recruiting success.

A new MKC beauty consultant had to purchase a Beauty Consultant Showcase, which cost around $100. Consultants bought MKC products at a 40% to 50% discount off the retail selling price, depending on volume. A minimum wholesale order of $180 had to be placed once every three months for a consultant to remain active. If a consultant terminated her association with MKC, the company would, if requested, buy back all her MKC inventory at 90% of the price she had paid for it.

In addition to the margins made on product sales, salespeople received a 4% to 12% commission on the wholesale prices of products purchased by those beauty consultants they had recruited. This commission, which increased with the number of recruits achieved, encouraged consultants to devote time to recruiting and training other consultants. To be promoted to sales director, a consultant had to recruit 30 active consultants; to become a senior sales director one of the director's recruits had to become a sales director herself; and to become a national sales director, a director had to motivate at least 10 of the consultants in her group to become sales directors. Nonmonetary rewards and recognition incentives, for which MKC was renowned, included pink Cadillacs, diamonds, and furs.

Communications

MKC developed programs, manuals, and sales training aids for its sales force. Since the emphasis was on "teaching skin care and glamour" to consumers, beauty consultants had to be taught how to teach. A new recruit would attend three "classes" given by an experienced consultant, study the "Beauty Consultant's Guide," and sit through an orientation class organized by her unit director prior to her being enrolled as an MKC beauty consultant. Weekly training sessions covered product information, customer service, business organization, and money management. Each year, some 15% of the MKC sales force traveled to Dallas at their own expense for a three-day seminar where sales and recruiting achievements of top-performing consultants were recognized. Queens of Sales and Recruiting were crowned by Mary Kay Ash and well-known entertainers made guest appearances. Workshops on every aspect of building and managing the business were conducted by consultants and directors that had developed a particular expertise. In addition, many national directors held their own yearly "jamborees" patterned after the Dallas event.

MKC also supported its consultant sales force with consumer print advertising, placed in women's magazines. (Exhibit 3 on page 114 reproduces some examples of recent MKC print advertisements in the United States.)

EXHIBIT 3

Reproductions of Mary Kay Cosmetics Print Advertisements in the United States: 1992

Challenges Facing MKC in 1993

In 1993, MKC was facing a mature U.S. cosmetics market, an increasing number of competing direct selling organizations, and potentially maximum historical penetration in some areas of the United States. At the same time, MKC's international subsidiaries' sales growth had been modest. Given that competitors such as Avon and

Amway had been very successful internationally, MKC executives could see no reason why MKC could not do the same. They believed that the MKC culture could be transferred internationally and that Mary Kay Ash's charisma, motivation, and philosophy were likely to appeal to women throughout the world.

■ INTERNATIONAL OPERATIONS

In early 1993, MKC products were sold in 19 countries. The company had 100%-owned subsidiaries in nine countries: Argentina (which also served Uruguay and Chile), Australia (with additional sales to New Zealand), Canada, Germany, Mexico, Taiwan, Spain, Thailand, and Russia. MKC was also planning to enter Italy, Portugal, the United Kingdom, and Japan or China in the near future. In addition, distributors existed in Costa Rica, Singapore, Malaysia, Brunei, Bermuda, Guatemala, Sweden, Norway, and Iceland.

Historically, international expansion had been opportunistic, based largely on personal contacts. The first two markets entered, Australia and Argentina, were not chosen for strategic reasons but in response to approaches to the company from local entrepreneurs. An international division with separate back-room operations, based in Dallas, had evolved to support the international businesses; this ensured the latter received adequate attention but duplicated functions and resources at headquarters.

In 1992, MKC initiated an organizational change that resulted in the formation of global resource groups to support sales subsidiaries worldwide, thereby consolidating the human resource, legal, finance, manufacturing, and marketing functions. (Exhibit 4 on page 116 depicts the new organizational structure.) The global marketing group, headed by Dandurand, provided subsidiaries with product development and marketing support, advertising, public relations and consumer promotion materials, and controlled the quality, consistency, and image of the Mary Kay brand around the world. Dandurand anticipated that marketing communication strategies would gradually become more locally driven. She explained:

> Once we have firmly established consistently high quality and clearly communicated the desired image for our company and brand, the local subsidiaries will be given more autonomy to develop their own marketing communication programs.

In addition, regional sales headquarters were established for Asia/Pacific, Europe, and the Americas (excluding the United States) to support the country subsidiaries within those regions more effectively and to facilitate MKC's future international expansion.

To illustrate the challenges MKC faced internationally, the evolution of each of four MKC subsidiaries is briefly described:

Canada The Canadian market was similar to the United States both in product requirements and organization, and U.S. sales directors were allowed to go to Canada to recruit and build sales areas. The Canadian subsidiary had been operating for 15 years. However, in 1993, market research indicated that MKC was perceived by some Canadian consumers as out of date. A salaried country manager with a marketing and sales staff ensured local contact with the Canadian consultants and the efficient order processing and delivery of MKC products.

Australia The Australian subsidiary began with the acquisition of an existing direct selling company in the early 1970s. In 1992, MKC had low brand awareness and a poor image. All products were imported from the United States and the U.S. pricing

EXHIBIT 4

Mary Kay Cosmetics Organization, 1992

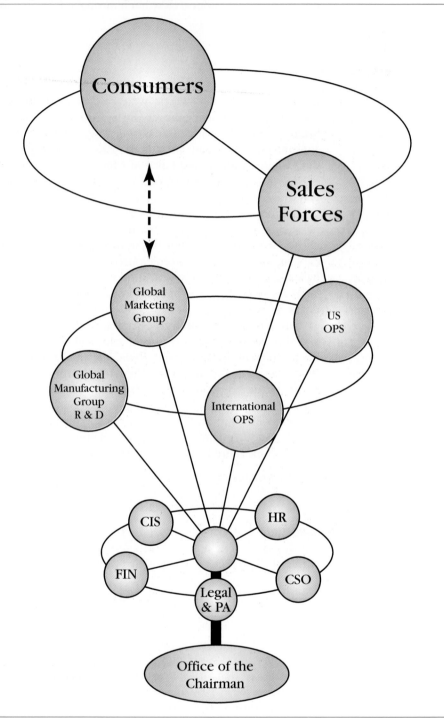

Note: CIS = Customer Information System, CSO = Chief Scientific Officer, OPS = Operations (incl. manufacturing), FIN = Finance, HR = Human Resources.

strategy had been replicated without much adaptation to local market conditions. Nutri-Metics, an Australian competitor, had successfully used a hybrid of party plan and door-to-door direct selling methods, backed by media advertising, catalog sales, and Buying Club sales.[3] Unlike MKC, Nutri-Metics did not hold skin care classes, and salespeople could buy in and remain "active" with lower purchase commitments than were required of MKC consultants.

Mexico In 1988, MKC established a subsidiary in Mexico headed by a husband-and-wife team who had previously worked for the direct selling party-plan cosmetics company, Jafra. The couple became salaried employees with performance incentives. The new Mexican subsidiary also benefited initially from U.S. sales directors who went to Mexico to recruit consultants. Three thousand new consultants joined the company in the first three months. After four years, brand awareness was high, the brand image was positive, and sales force size exceeded 6,200.

Taiwan The Taiwan subsidiary, launched in July 1991, emphasized intensive training for new consultants. Chinese women were characterized as typically entrepreneurial, independent, and hardworking, with a strong drive to make money. The local country manager had previous experience in direct selling with both Avon and Tupperware. In 1992, rapid expansion had generated $3.3 million in sales through 1,800 consultants. Sales were expected to triple in 1993. All products were shipped from Dallas.

MKC also had established subsidiaries in Germany, with an estimated 1,500 consultants in 1993, and in Argentina, which, despite periodic hyperinflation throughout the 1980s, was profitable in 1992. Poor results in the United Kingdom had resulted in the subsidiary being closed in 1985 after four years of operation, though there were plans to reopen in 1993. (Exhibit 5 presents data on MKC sales, number of directors, and number of consultants by subsidiary.)

Dandurand believed that MKC's limited international success was due partly to the direct application of the U.S. marketing strategy, products, and communications to different subsidiaries without sufficient local modifications. Other factors con-

EXHIBIT 5

Mary Kay Cosmetics Net Sales and Headcount, 1989 and 1992

	Net Sales ($000s)		Consultant Count		Director Count	
	1989	1992	1989	1992	1989	1992
United States	$404,990	$559,719	171,073	232,692	4,689	5,837
Argentina	3,638	12,450	5,142	6,675	152	152
Australia	9,494	7,812	4,161	4,143	122	116
Canada	24,811	25,386	9,866	10,597	167	283
Germany	1,210	5,131	583	1,306	9	26
Mexico	4,598	8,586	2,640	6,241	25	89
Taiwan	0	3,133	0	1,064	0	13
Distributors	3,333	4,690				

[3] Buying Clubs enabled women to purchase products such as cosmetics at a discount for their personal consumption rather than for resale. Individuals were not required to purchase a minimum level of inventory to enroll in the club. The most successful clubs offered broad product lines.

straining growth included low consumer brand awareness and insufficient marketing resources to develop it. Dandurand explained:

> In some countries, cultural barriers impede the use of the party plan and door-to-door selling. The size of a typical home may be smaller than in the United States, or a party for unfamiliar guests may be considered an invasion of privacy. In addition, the time required for a two-hour skin care class is sometimes an obstacle.

Future International Expansion

A strategic planning process in early 1993 identified a "great teachers" strategy to differentiate MKC worldwide from other retail and direct selling competitors and to build on the company's proven capabilities in this area. Greater emphasis would be placed on sales force training and on adapting MKC's positioning, the product range, and marketing communications mix to local market needs. A standard core product line would be supplemented with products developed specifically for each local market. Products would either be imported from the United States or manufacturing and/or final packaging would be subcontracted in individual country markets as was currently done in Mexico and Argentina. In particular, MKC was currently looking for a European manufacturing site to support its planned market entry into several European countries.

A country manager who wanted products adapted would have to seek the approval of the MKC regional president who, in turn, would meet with the international marketing and manufacturing managers. MKC regional presidents were all equity holders and therefore both advocates for the interests of the countries in their region as well as representatives of the headquarters' perspective.[4]

MKC executives believed that the company's values were transferable. Dandurand elaborated:

> Telling women they can achieve, making them believe in themselves and giving them caring and respect, is an international message. However, the message needs to be tailored to each market and communicated effectively and I'm not sure whether or not additional role models are needed in each foreign market for the company to be successful.

It was recognized that one or two charismatic leaders could generate massive growth in number of consultants and product sales.

Avon's International Strategy

Avon had become a successful international cosmetics company. Each country subsidiary was run by a country manager who had considerable decision-making authority so long as agreed-upon performance objectives were achieved. On average, 60% of the Avon products sold by a foreign subsidiary came from a common core line, while 40% were adapted to local markets. The company placed a heavy emphasis on merchandising with 18 three-week marketing campaigns used to promote specific consumer events such as Mother's Day, and 26 two-week drive periods supported by specific sales brochures each year. Avon sales consultants had to deal with the complexity of a product line of 1,500 SKUs. In contrast to MKC, Avon employed salaried sales managers who oversaw the company's independent salespeople.

In 1992, Avon eliminated its regional headquarters in favor of a single global support group based in New York. Many Avon subsidiaries were large enough to afford their own strong functional staffs and therefore no longer needed backup from re-

---

[4] As a private company, MKC had a compensation plan for senior executives that worked like a partnership.

gional headquarters. MKC executives believed that their lower product line turnover ought to permit a more streamlined and lower-cost central support group than Avon's.

Avon had been more willing than MKC to adapt its marketing programs internationally, adjusting prices according to the level of consumer buying power in individual countries. Avon hired strong local nationals as country managers, giving them specific strategic direction, generous resource allocations, and clear profit-and-loss responsibility. The Avon culture was considered "hard-nosed" and numbers-driven—return on equity and return on assets being especially important—but local country managers who delivered enjoyed considerable autonomy. According to some MKC executives, MKC had a more caring orientation and placed greater emphasis on support systems, mentoring, training, and recognition of consultants.

■ MKC IN ASIA

MKC's Taiwanese subsidiary had, by 1992, become profitable and promised good future sales growth. As part of the recent reorganization, an Asia/Pacific regional manager would shortly establish a base in Hong Kong from which to build MKC sales in Asia.

Asia was evolving as one of the fastest growing and most dynamic regions of the world. Its share of world GDP was scheduled to reach 32% by the year 2000, up from 24% in 1988. The choice between a Japanese or Chinese market entry would, Dandurand believed, impact MKC's long-term market position in Asia. She began to compare the two countries on some key characteristics to help make the decision (Table B). She wanted to build on MKC's past international experience and current competitive advantages to develop a market entry strategy that fit with the MKC culture and the local market environment and that would enable MKC to establish a firm base from which to build its Asian operations.

Table B   Key Characteristics of Japanese and Chinese Markets

	Japan	*China*
Population, 1992	124 million	1,139 million
Estimated population, 2020	137 million	1,541 million
Population distribution (0–24; 25–49; 50+):		
1993	32%; 37%; 31%	42%; 39%; 19%
2000	29%; 35%; 36%	40%; 39%; 21%
Urban population, 1992	77%	27%
Population/square mile	865	315
Gross domestic product (US$ billion)	3,370	371[a]
1993 GDP growth % (estimated)	2.3%	10.1%
1994 GDP growth % (estimated)	3.2%	9.5%
1990 per capita GNP	$14,311	$325
Average hourly compensation (US$)	$14.41	$0.24
Penetration of:		
Televisions	1 per 1.8 persons	1 per 8 persons
Radios	1 per 1.3	1 per 9
Telephones	1 per 2.3	1 per 66
1992 advertising expenditure per capita	$220	$0.86

[a] *In early 1993, China's GDP was reestimated at $1,700 billion by the International Monetary Fund on the basis of purchasing power parity. This meant the Chinese economy was the third largest in the world.*

■ JAPAN

The Cosmetics Industry

In 1992, there were 1,100 cosmetics manufacturers in Japan but five companies accounted for 69% of domestic sales. Domestic production exceeded $9 billion in factory sales in 1991 and included local production by foreign firms, estimated at 18% of total domestic production. Imports represented 5% of total sales in 1991, up from 3% in 1989; over 45% of imports came from France, of which 27% consisted of fragrances and cologne. In addition, Japanese tourists purchased around $500 million of cosmetics at duty-free shops each year. Table C summarizes the size of the Japanese cosmetics market and the sources of product.

Table C   Japanese Cosmetics Market Size and Sources of Shipments

$ Millions (manufacturer shipments)	*1989*	*1990*	*1991*
Imports:	265	318	460
From the United States	41	57	89
Local production	8,983	8,433	9,072
Exports	128	147	214
Total market	9,120	8,604	9,318

The Japanese cosmetics market was mature, recording average annual value growth of 3% between 1988 and 1992, compared with a growth rate of 4.4% in the United States. Major consumers of cosmetics were women in their 20s and 30s. Foreign-made cosmetics were considered high-status products. Issues impacting the industry in 1992 included the end of manufacturers' control over the prices at which their products were resold by retailers and a continuing decrease in the number of independent cosmetics retailers. Strict Ministry of Health regulations governing imports and the manufacture of cosmetics involved lengthy approval processes. In many cases, common ingredients approved for use in cosmetics outside Japan were prohibited by the Ministry of Health, requiring reformulations of most products.

The Direct Selling Industry

In 1992, Japan was the largest direct selling market in the world with an estimated $19.2 billion in retail sales. Direct selling enabled consumers to bypass inefficient wholesale and retail distribution systems which some viewed as inefficient and non-price competitive. Japanese women who left business in order to have children came back into a company with no tenure and had to start up the corporate ladder from scratch. Consequently, direct selling, which could be done part time, was an attractive second career for mothers seeking to reenter the work force. According to the Japan Direct Selling Association, 1,120,000 women engaged in direct selling in 1992.[5]

Amway had been in Japan since 1977 and, by 1991, recorded sales of US$1.2 billion with a product line that included home care, personal care and food products, housewares, cosmetics, and gifts. The company had a sales force of 1,000,000 people, developed primarily through word-of-mouth. Training was conducted by direct distributors who sponsored new distributors. Compensation consisted of a 30% commission and a bonus based on the sales of sponsored distributors. Conventions were held every year for training purposes and to recognize outstanding perfor-

---

[5] In 1992, the total Japanese population was 124 million, of whom 41% were women over 15 years of age.

mance. In 1990, only seven other foreign companies generated more revenues in Japan than Amway. Reasons for this success were: an effective distribution system based on company-owned warehouses; high-quality, value-oriented products; good relations with dedicated distributors; and a philosophy that emphasized human relationships, fulfillment of dreams, and financial freedom.

Consumers

In the 1990s, an increasing percentage of Japanese women were going on to further education and working outside the home. In 1992, over 50% of the 51.8 million Japanese women aged over 15 years were employed, predominantly on a part-time basis. They earned lower salaries than men and preferred more flexible work schedules. Women's activities outside the home were increasing as were their expectations of equality. Many women were marrying later and having fewer children. (Exhibit 6 summarizes the results of a 1990 attitude study of 1,000 Japanese women.)

Annual cosmetics expenditures were above US$260.00 per household in 1992. Forty percent of all cosmetics sales were to women in their 20s and 30s (26% of all Japanese women over the age of 15). The heaviest users were 8.8 million women aged between 20 and 29 (14% of all Japanese women over the age of 15). These heavy users were less price sensitive and more interested in high-quality cosmetics. Working women spent, on average, 25% more on cosmetic purchases than women who did not work outside the home. A fair complexion and fine-textured skin were considered hallmarks of beauty in Japan, so skin care products accounted for 40% of all cosmetic sales. The growing sales of skin care products were also fueled by the increasing average age of the Japanese population; 23% of the population would be aged over 65 years by the year 2010, compared with 14% in 1992.

Fifty-four percent of facial skin care users and 40% of shaded makeup users purchased all or some of their products from direct sales companies. Corresponding figures in the United States were 25% and 22%, respectively. Nineteen percent of Japanese skin care users and 20% of shaded makeup product users purchased only from direct salespeople. Japanese women purchased, on average, 16.2 skin care items a year at a price of $32.97 per purchase. In the United States, an average 20.1 annual

EXHIBIT 6

1990 Survey of Japanese Women

Age Group	Important Job Attributes	Points of Dissatisfaction at Work
19–24	Realize own potential and develop own capabilities.	Low bonus, too much overtime, inability to display or develop one's capabilities.
25–29	Able to continue after marriage and children, availability of nursery facilities, flexible time schedule to take care of children.	Feel job has no value.
30–39	Availability of nursery facilities, flexible time schedule, contributes to local community.	Low bonus, too many minute duties.
40–43	Job encourages and promotes women.	Inadequate social benefits.
44–49	Within close vicinity.	

Note: Data based on a study of 1,000 Japanese women between 15 and 65 years of age.

Source: Adapted from a survey by *Pola Cultural Center*, 1990.

purchases were made at $9.05 per purchase. Thus, the average Japanese woman spent almost three times more on skin care than the average American woman. In the area of shaded makeup, Japanese women made 13 purchases per year compared with 27 in the United States, but price differentials between the two countries resulted in almost equal annual expenditures. (Exhibit 7 summarizes Japanese consumer buying behavior for skin care and shaded makeup products.) In addition to functional product benefits, Japanese consumers placed a special emphasis on the visual appeal of product packaging.

Japanese consumers believed that they had sensitive skin as MKC confirmed when it ran extensive trials with Japanese women who had recently arrived in the United States. Pink was seen as a color more appropriate for children and teenagers so the classic MKC pink was muted on potential packaging and caps retooled to present a more upscale image. It was felt that redesigned packages might also appeal to U.S. consumers and that the potential existed for a global packaging redesign.

Products

Skin care products accounted for 40% of all cosmetics sales in Japan in 1992. (Exhibit 8 on page 124 details sales of major cosmetics product categories over time.) In the skin care category, sales of skin lotion increased by 12%, face wash and cleansing products by 4%, while cold cream, moisture cream, and milky lotion decreased by 1%. In 1992, Kao and Shiseido dominated the Japanese skin care market. Makeup accounted for 23% of cosmetics sales but its share had been declining since 1986. Foundation products accounted for more than 50% of makeup sales.

Foreign manufacturers were more successful in selling makeup than skin care products while the reverse was true for domestic companies. Dandurand explained:

> In Japan, makeup products are associated with status, image, and dreams. Japanese women tend to aspire to look like the Western women on the cosmetics ads and so foreign brands, with the attached status, are more popular for color cosmetics. When it comes to skin care products, Japanese women tend to be more pragmatic. They believe that they have very delicate skins that require highly scientific products especially made for them by Japanese manufacturers who understand their needs better.

Distribution

Cosmetics were distributed in Japan through three main channels: franchise systems, general distributorships, and door-to-door sales.

Franchise systems were based on contracts between manufacturers and retailers, also known as chain stores, whereby a manufacturer's affiliated distribution company provided retailers with a full range of products, marketing support, and product promotions. In addition, trained beauty consultants were provided by manufacturers at each outlet. This enabled manufacturers to maintain control over the selling process and to provide consumers with individualized service. Franchise systems accounted for 40% of cosmetic sales in 1992 but were expected to decline. A variation of the franchise system was the direct selling franchise system whereby manufacturers dealt directly with retail accounts without going through a distribution company. This method was used by many foreign manufacturers who focused their marketing efforts, supported by face-to-face counseling, on a limited number of prestige shops and department stores.

General distributorships were the conventional channels whereby products flowed from manufacturer to wholesaler to retailer, and the manufacturer and retailer were not connected directly. The manufacturer provided full marketing support via advertising and promotion for products that tended to be lower-priced and less sophisticated. The volume share of cosmetics sold through this channel was estimated at 30% in 1992 and expected to increase.

EXHIBIT 7

Japanese Cosmetics Consumer Buying Behavior, April 1991–January 1992

Product Category	Penetration: Percentage Purchasing	Market Share (Unit)	Market Share (Value)	Distribution Share Retail	Distribution Share Direct	Average $ Spent per Purchase	Average Frequency of Purchase (10 Months)
Skin Care							
Cleansing	41.7	10.5	7.2	58.0	42.0	39.13	2.2
Cold and massage	19.1	3.2	3.1	43.1	56.9	36.40	1.6
Clear lotion	81.5	29.5	25.3	53.6	46.1	70.54	2.9
Milky lotion	52.9	10.9	9.9	57.4	42.6	42.29	1.7
Moisture cream	40.4	8.7	14.0	45.2	54.8	78.49	1.7
Mask	23.2	4.5	4.8	50.5	49.5	47.27	1.7
Whitening powder	2.1	0.4	0.6	73.4	26.6	64.72	NA
Essence	31.6	7.4	12.6	56.0	44.0	90.80	1.9
Foundation	78.9	24.8	22.5	66.1	33.9	64.59	2.5
Glamour							
Lipstick	68.9	38.8	47.3	65.5	34.5	33.93	1.7
Eye shadow	21.3	9.8	9.9	76.7	23.3	23.05	1.4
Eyeliner	11.6	4.9	3.9	65.3	34.7	16.58	1.7
Mascara	11.9	4.8	4.8	79.8	20.2	19.99	1.7
Eyebrow	20.6	8.7	6.3	70.7	29.3	20.00	1.5
Blusher	21.5	8.7	9.3	61.4	38.6	21.26	1.4
Manicure	25.9	16.0	6.1	75.6	24.4	11.72	1.9
Fragrance	16.8	8.3	12.4	63.2	36.8	36.38	1.8

Source: Adapted from *Cosmetics and Toiletries Marketing Strategies, Fuji Keizai,* 1992.

123

EXHIBIT 8

Japanese Cosmetics Market: Growth by Subcategory (billion yen)

Value of Factory Shipments	1986	1987	1988	1989	1990	1990/89
Skin Care Products	452.5	430.0	455.2	484.4	500.8	103.4%
Face wash cream/foam	41.4	42.7	46.8	51.0	53.0	
Cleansing cream/foam/gel	27.7	28.7	32.9	35.6	37.2	
Cold cream	22.5	18.2	18.4	16.8	16.7	
Mositure cream	87.9	68.7	79.0	75.9	75.3	
Milky lotion	64.6	60.6	63.0	64.6	62.1	
Skin lotion (freshener)	134.0	142.1	142.5	159.1	178.4	
Face mask	26.1	22.3	22.3	23.2	24.3	
Men's	10.2	10.2	11.6	11.8	10.7	
Other	38.1	36.5	38.7	46.4	43.1	
Makeup Products	306.8	308.8	300.3	301.9	295.8	98.0
Foundation	154.3	157.1	160.0	161.8	158.3	
Powder	19.6	18.2	18.9	18.8	18.5	
Lipstick	44.2	49.3	48.3	46.4	48.2	
Lip cream	9.7	9.2	10.0	8.6	9.1	
Blush	15.5	14.1	11.9	11.4	11.2	
Eye shadow	26.0	27.5	22.3	22.7	19.9	
Eyebrow/eyelash	15.2	15.0	15.1	16.9	15.8	
Nail care	17.8	15.4	11.8	13.5	13.0	
Other	4.5	3.0	2.0	1.8	1.8	
Hair Care Products	335.5	362.2	392.1	403.5	413.4	102.5
Fragrances	22.1	21.1	18.7	18.8	20.9	111.1
Special Use (Suncare, shaving, bath products)	27.3	27.9	30.2	31.1	33.7	108.6
Total	1,144.0	1,146.6	1,196.2	1,239.6	1,263.9	102.0

Source: Adapted from *The Complete Handbook of Cosmetics Marketing 1992, Shukan Shogyo.*

Door-to-door sales or home visiting systems enabled manufacturers to bypass the costly, complex retailing network. This direct selling system, which had worked well in the past, was facing problems in 1992: fewer women were staying at home, and direct selling companies were finding it increasingly difficult to attract sales personnel. In 1982, this channel had represented 25% of cosmetic sales; by 1992, it represented 19%. Some direct selling companies were diversifying into other ways of reaching the consumer. For example, Pola, a major Japanese direct selling cosmetics company, had started marketing its products in variety shops, aesthetic salons, and by mail order. Avon and Noevir, also a large Japanese direct selling cosmetics company, and Menard, had opened retail stores and Salon outlets. Other channels included beauty parlors and barber shops. (Shares of cosmetics sales in Japan by distribution channel and by consumer age group are given in Exhibit 9.)

Competitors

The top five domestic cosmetics manufacturers in 1992 were Shiseido with 27% of the market; Kao with 16%; Kanebo with 11%; Pola with 8%; and Kobayashi Kose with 7%. These companies spent, on average, 4% of sales on research and development, double the level spent by the major foreign manufacturers. Shiseido, founded in

EXHIBIT 9

Japanese Cosmetic Sales by Distribution Channel and Consumer Age Group, 1990

	Percentage Women 1985	Percentage Women 1990	Change 1985–1990	1990 Teens	1990 20s	1990 30s	1990 40s	1990 50s
Department store	22.8	25.2	2.4	37	30	19	19	24
Cosmetic store	44.6	37.5	(7.1)	26	48	33	37	43
Drug/pharmacy	12.7	22.3	9.6	25	20	29	18	18
Door-to-door	19.6	12.0	(7.6)	1	7	19	16	12
Supermarket	15.6	18.1	2.5	22	11	21	22	15
Beauty salon	3.7	6.1	2.4	3	7	4	7	9
Convenience store	NA	2.9		12	2	1	1	1
Variety shop	NA	1.7		5	2	2		
Others	NA	8.4		2	9	13	10	5

Source: Adapted from a survey by Marketing Intelligence Corp.

1872 as Shiseido Pharmacy, entered the cosmetics business in 1902. Ninety years later, Shiseido products were sold through 25,000 chain stores and 9,000 retail beauty consultants. Kao, Kanebo, and Kobayashi Kose also operated nationwide networks. Foreign companies such as Max Factor, Revlon, and Clinique entered the Japanese market in the early 1980s and pursued selective distribution through a limited number of prestigious department stores. (Exhibit 10 summarizes sales data for the major Japanese and foreign cosmetics manufacturers, and Table D profiles the major direct selling cosmetics companies.)

EXHIBIT 10

Major Cosmetics Companies in Japan, 1990

Company	Total Sales $ Million	Skin Care	Makeup	Hair Care	Fragrances	Men's Cosmetics
Top 5 Cosmetics Companies						
Shiseido	$1,963.3	49%	31%	3%	3%	10%
Kanebo	1,331.2	39	36	5	3	12
Pola	704.1	54	28	2	3	2
Kose	553.8	51	36	5	1	3
Kao	470.8	46	42	2	0	10
Top 5 Foreign Cosmetics Companies						
Max Factor	440.8	37	54	1	2	1
Avon	303.8	35	30	4	0	0
Revlon	92.3	25	52	10	7	0
Clinique	80.7	72	25	1	0	0
Chanel	76.1	21	21	0	58	0

Source: Adapted from *Cosmetics and Toiletries Marketing Strategies, Fuji Keizai;* 1992.

Table D   Manufacturer Sales of Major Direct Selling Cosmetics Companies in Japan—1990

	Sales Growth 1989–90	Total Sales 1990 ($ million)[a]	Facial Skin Care (%)	Makeup (%)	Hair Care (%)	Fragrances (%)	Men's Cosmetics (%)
Pola	2.4%	$704	54%	28%	2%	3%	2%
Nippon Menard	(2.3)	373	67	23	1	1	2
Avon[b]	1.9	304	35	30	4		
Noevir	2.8	292	64	24	4	4	4
Oppen	0.0	213	64	24	3	1	1
Aistar	0.0	185	100				
Naris	12.0	110	58	26		1	2
Yakult	1.7	50	56	22	4	2	2

[a] *Total company figures. Some companies were engaged in other businesses in addition to cosmetics; therefore, percentages of cosmetic sales do not add to 100%.*

[b] *Avon percentages total 69% because Avon also sold jewelry and lingerie.*

Pola was established in 1946 and had $740 million in sales in 1991. With 180,000 "Pola Ladies," 20,000 salespeople, and 6,500 retail outlets, Pola ranked third in cosmetics sales and first in direct sales of cosmetics in Japan. Originally targeted at older women, Pola had begun recently to focus on younger women with its moderately priced product line. Pola provided in-depth training for its staff, ranging from one month for a "Pola Lady" to over a year for sales research staff at company headquarters. The compensation structure for Pola Ladies had 21 levels: "Class 1" salespeople who sold up to $370 monthly made a 25% margin and no commission. A "Super Million Lady" salesperson, with monthly sales over $37,000, earned a 35% margin, a $400 jewel allowance, and $800 in bonus. In 1991, Pola spent $28.5 million on media advertising, of which newspaper ads accounted for 9%, magazine ads for 28%, and television commercials for 63%.

Nippon Menard was established in 1959 and had $373 million in sales in 1990, of which 67% was derived from skin care products and 23% from makeup. Organized into 33 sales companies and sold through over 12,000 retail outlets and 160,000 beauty specialists, it ranked eighth among cosmetics companies and second among direct selling cosmetics companies. Main brands included Entals, Delphia, and Ires, positioned at lower price points and targeted at women in their 20s and 30s, and Eporea, positioned at a high price point and targeted at older women. Beauty specialists followed a series of four training classes and could advance through seven levels from "beginner" to "special" depending on their monthly sales. A beginner beauty specialist, who achieved monthly sales of $300 to $450, earned a commission of 30% but no bonus. At the other extreme, a "special" beauty specialist sold over $23,000 per month and earned a 38% commission plus between $350 and $1,000 in bonus. In 1991, Menard spent a total of $25 million on advertising, of which 6% was on newspaper ads, 11% on magazine advertising, and 83% on television commercials.

Noevir was established in 1978 and had $292 million in sales in 1990, of which 64% was derived from skin care products and 24% from makeup. It operated on a consignment basis with 580 sales companies selling to two levels of 109,000 agencies, through 200,000 sales people. It ranked ninth among cosmetic companies and third among direct selling cosmetic companies. In 1992, Noevir had two subsidiaries, Sana and Nov; Sana sold through 5,000 skin care retail outlets and 400 makeup retail outlets, and Nov sold through 2,000 pharmaceutical outlets. Sana targeted younger women while Nov's product line included hypo-allergenic cosmetics recommended by dermatologists. In 1991, Noevir spent $8 million on advertising —13% on magazine ads and the remainder on television commercials.

Avon was established in Japan in 1973 and had $325 million in sales in 1991, of which 65% was derived from cosmetics. Avon sold through mail-order catalogs and 350,000 Avon Ladies. In 1992, Avon had successfully floated 40% of the subsidiary's equity on the Tokyo stock exchange. It ranked thirteenth among cosmetics companies and fourth among direct selling cosmetics companies. The company targeted women in their 30s and 40s and, unlike other direct selling companies, Avon's products were not regularly demonstrated to consumers by Avon Ladies.

Avon, Menard, Pola, Noevir, and Amway also offered "buying club" programs. Most recruited salespeople on the basis of providing an opportunity to make extra income, but only Amway heavily stressed advancement into management based on recruiting and sales performance. Most competitors offered thorough product training at little or no cost; the training was more extensive than that provided by most U.S. direct selling organizations. Sales presentations typically were made one-to-one, but other than through catalogs and brochures, little instruction was provided to consumers. (Exhibit 11 profiles the characteristics of consumers using the principal brands, and Exhibit 12 on page 128 reproduces competitor print advertisements.)

MKC in Japan

MKC began assessing the Japanese market in 1988 with a comparative study of products and competition. It was determined that the typical Japanese woman's skin care regimen involved a seven-stage process as opposed to three steps in the United States, and that whitening products, not widely available in the United States, were

EXHIBIT 11

Customer Profiles of MKC's Principal Potential Competitors in Japan, 1992

	Menard	*Pola*	*Noevir*	*Avon*	*Amway*
Educational Background					
Current student	0.0%	2.7%	2.0%	1.1%	2.1%
College	11.1	17.3	14.3	32.6	27.7
Senior high school	63.9	62.7	63.3	53.7	63.3
Junior high school	25.0	17.3	20.4	12.6	6.4
Marital and Employment Status					
Married—not working	27.8	32.9	22.9	44.2	39.1
Married—working	69.4	53.4	70.9	40.0	36.7
Unmarried	2.8	13.7	6.2	15.8	23.9
Age					
15–19	0.0	2.7	0.0	2.1	0.0
20–29	8.3	18.7	14.3	15.8	38.3
30–39	11.1	17.3	30.6	28.4	17.0
40–49	41.7	25.3	30.6	32.6	25.5
50–59	38.9	36.0	24.5	21.1	19.1
Occupation					
Not employed	27.8	32.0	22.4	43.2	38.3
Employed	72.2	65.3	75.5	55.8	59.6

Source: Company reports.

EXHIBIT 12

Competitor Print Advertisements: Japan 1993

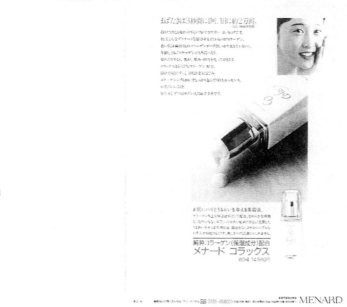

very popular in Japan.[6] In 1989, a comparative pricing study was undertaken and relationships established with an ingredient supplier and a private-label manufacturer who might produce an estimated 20% of the product line, tailored to the Japanese market, including whitening products and wet/dry foundation cake. In 1992, MKC proceeded with lengthy product approval processes involving the Japanese Ministry

---

[6] In the United States a typical skin care regimen included a cleanser, a toner, and a moisturizer. In Japan, several different cleansers and moisturizers were typically used in a single skin care regimen.

of Health. By year end, over $1 million had been invested in preparing to enter the Japanese market.

There was concern that MKC would be a late entrant in a mature, complex, fragmented, and highly competitive market. Dandurand believed that it would take three to five years before MKC would turn a profit and take market share from competitors. On the other hand, 1993 might be an opportune time for MKC to launch in Japan since, increasingly, women wished both to raise children and be involved in activities outside the home, and an economic recession created more demand for part-time employment to supplement household incomes. Some MKC executives believed that success in Japan was essential to the company's future in the countries of the Pacific Rim.

■ CHINA

China covered 3.7 million square miles and was divided into 22 provinces, 3 municipalities (Beijing, Shanghai, and Tianjin), and 5 autonomous regions (Guangxi, Zhuang, Nei Mongol, Ningxia Hui, Xinjiang Uygur, and Tibet). The population was estimated at 1.1 billion in 1992 and was predicted to grow to 1.5 billion by the year 2020. Eighty percent lived in the eastern half of the country depicted in Exhibit 13. The urban

EXHIBIT 13

Map of Eastern China

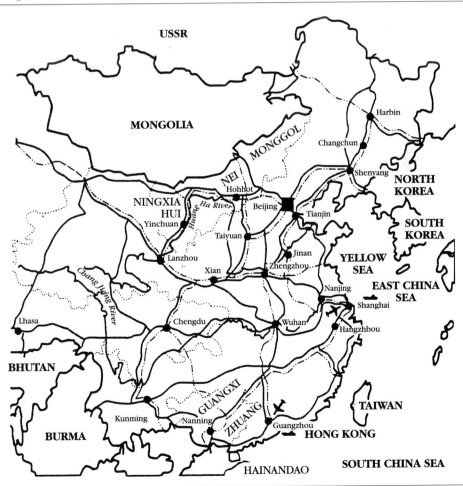

population was estimated at 310 million, the female population at 545 million, and the female population living in urban areas at around 156 million. In the second half of the twentieth century, China experienced one of the fastest demographic transitions in history. Mortality rates decreased and average life expectancy rose from 42 years in 1950 to 70 in 1992. Fertility rates fell from an average of 6 children per woman in 1950 to 2.3 in 1992. Trends towards urbanization and a shift in population from the agricultural to the service sector were expected to continue in the 1990s.

In 1979, the "Open Door Policy" heralded a series of wide-ranging economic reforms: agriculture was decollectivized; the development of private and semiprivate enterprises to produce goods was permitted; free market pricing and more liberal foreign exchange conversion were introduced; and foreign investment became more acceptable. These economic reforms had the greatest impact on the coastal provinces where economic free zones were established to facilitate foreign investment. Guandong province, for example, had experienced the fastest growth in East Asia in the 1980s. Overall, China's GNP had increased by 9% annually during the 1980s, while consumption had increased by 6.6%. In 1990, 70% of industrial growth was attributed to private, cooperative, and foreign ventures.

Since 1988, a higher-income, urban middle class had emerged with household earnings over $125 a month and saving rates estimated at 35%. By the year 2000, it was estimated that 41 million households would have incomes of over $18,000 per annum. Retail sales had increased nearly fivefold since 1980 with the number of retail outlets increasing from 2 million in 1980 to 12 million in 1992, most being private enterprises. All types of goods were available in the major cities, and the adoption rate of new products was rapid. In 1992, China was viewed as a sellers' market but experts believed that more sophisticated marketing skills and product differentiation would become increasingly important.

In assessing the political and economic risks of investing in China, multinational companies had three main concerns. First, some thought political instability was likely to follow the retirement or death of China's long-standing Premier Deng Xiaoping. Political struggles between conservatives and reformers might delay further economic reforms. Second, the Chinese government was not granting its people political freedom commensurate with their increasing economic freedom. Progress on human rights was essential to China maintaining most-favored nation status as a trading partner with the United States. Third, multinationals importing finished goods into China faced not only high tariffs but also the likely devaluation of the Chinese currency which would further increase the retail prices of their goods.

During the 1980s, cosmetics and toiletries became an important branch of China's light industry, and the number of cosmetics factories in China increased sixfold between 1982 and 1990. In 1992, the cosmetics market was estimated at $825 million (manufacturer sales), with skin care products dominant. There were approximately 3,000 cosmetics producers in China manufacturing limited product lines; about half were located in Shanghai. Many local brands were available as import tariffs on cosmetics averaged 100%. In 1991, the Chinese Ministry of Commerce initiated a professional training program for two million cosmetics managers, purchasers, and sales clerks with the objective of teaching them how to appraise the quality of cosmetics and skin conditions of consumers.

Consumers

There was a growing difference in purchasing power and consumer behavior between the urban and rural populations in China, with the urban population becoming increasingly prosperous and demanding, and the rural consumer evolving less quickly. Consumer habits also varied by region: northerners appeared to be more concerned with clothing and appearance while southerners bought more household products and consumer electronics. Brand names were highly appreciated by Chinese consumers who would pay up to four times more for foreign or joint venture brands, such as Ritz Crackers and Sony televisions, than for the equivalent local products.

Eighty-seven percent of Chinese women worked and many held two jobs: one state job and one independent job. Urban workers were generally employed in factories or workshops, employment assignments being allocated by local labor bureaus. Safety standards in factories were poor but compensation was adequate. The wage range from lowest grade to highest grade was a factor of three, and a sum equal to 10% of total wages was typically available for bonuses. Virtually all housing, medical, and transportation costs and midday meals were subsidized by Chinese government work units. Around 40% of the household income of a two-income urban household was typically spent on food and housing; the remainder was disposable income.

Government-subsidized housing units were small; 200 square feet was the typical size of a one-bedroom urban apartment. A workers' committee still managed each apartment building. A few apartments were also available for purchase; US$5,000 could purchase a two-bedroom apartment in Guangzhous in early 1993. Housing conditions were better in Guangzhou and Beijing than in Shanghai. Young workers, especially women, tended to live with their parents until they married. Once married, they would live with the husbands' parents or take their own apartments.

Female workers were entitled to 56 days of pregnancy leave and most factories had nurseries and kindergarten facilities. The Chinese government wished to encourage women to spend more time at home and therefore established the "Period Employment" system whereby women could elect to take three months maternity leave at 100% pay and/or up to seven years off at 70% of basic pay to aid in childraising. In 1992, an estimated 66% of Chinese women over the age of 25 were married.

A 1991 consumer study concluded that the average Chinese female urban consumer was 32 years old, married with one child, worked in a state factory, and earned the equivalent of $50 a month. She typically controlled the family budget and was concerned about the rising cost of living. Attracted to foreign brands, she considered skin care and cosmetics important, particularly those that prevented freckles and promoted cleanliness.

Chinese women were greatly interested in learning; education was held in very high esteem in Chinese culture. Chinese colleges and universities were increasingly asserting their independence; MKC might be able to sponsor skin care courses and sell products to the enrolled students and/or secure product endorsements from medical schools.

By 1992, differences in buying power and buyer behavior were evident across the various regions of China. The three most important regional markets were: Guangzhou, Beijing, and Shanghai. (Table E on page 132 summarizes key characteristics of these three metropolitan markets.)

Guangzhou Hong Kong's influence was strongly felt in Guangzhou, whose economy was driven by the private sector. More interested in spending their disposable incomes on food, drink, eating out, and entertaining, Guangzhou consumers were wealthier but characterized as less cosmopolitan and sophisticated than other urban Chinese consumers. Described as flashy and ostentatious, Guangzhou consumers were also known as generous and free-spending. Many companies viewed the Guangzhou consumer market as very similar to Hong Kong's and believed that consumer characteristics of the two markets would continue to converge.

Beijing Beijing consumers were generally characterized as conservative and serious. Less concerned with appearances than Shanghai consumers, they spent less on clothing and personal care products. However, Beijing, being the home of senior

Table E Characteristics of Three Principal Regional Markets in China: 1992

	Guangzhou	*Beijing*	*Shanghai*
Location	South (100 miles north of Hong Kong)	North (China's capital)	East Coast by Yangtze River
Population	6 million = city	4 million = city	13.5 million = city
	25 million = province	11 million = province	60 million = province
Region characteristics	Low-cost manufacturing base for Hong Kong. Most flexible for business approvals and hiring.	Government ministries. Second-largest retail center and strong industrial base.	8.5% of China's industrial output. Cultural and commercial capital.
Foreign companies	Avon, Colgate, P&G and Amway	Shiseido, L'Oreal	Johnson & Johnson, Unilever
Consumer characteristics	Unrefined. Main interest is food and family. But more interested in glamour.	Rigid, bureaucratic. More cerebral.	Elegant, vain, tough negotiators, seek quality.
Typical wage level	$200/month, highest consumer goods spending in China. Flooded by foreign consumer goods.	$80/month but rising level of affluence in the last two years.	Over $100/month. Highest spending on clothing, cosmetics, jewelry. (Estimates = 30% disposable income).

government and Party officials, had an elite group of consumers interested in luxury goods and designer labels. Also characterized as straightforward and honest, advertisements based on fact and information were well-received. Before making a major purchase, Beijing consumers would be well-versed on the technical aspects of the product. On the other hand, these consumers also appeared to be more willing to try new products, and new brands launches were often initially more successful than in Shanghai.

Shanghai Being the largest city, Shanghai was the commercial and cultural center of China. Shanghai consumers were characterized as proud and very concerned about their appearances. While not the wealthiest consumers in China, they were known as the best dressed and smartest looking. Shanghai consumers spent a significantly greater proportion of their disposable income on clothing, jewelry, and personal care products than their counterparts elsewhere in China, and premium-priced products and brands moved better in Shanghai than anywhere else. Shanghainese acknowledged and even took pride in the historical European and Western influences on their city and personal habits. Housing conditions however, were distinctly worse in Shanghai than in most other cities in China.

Shanghai was also the manufacturing center of China, and Shanghai goods were recognized as among the best in China. As a result, Shanghai consumers were more loyal to their local brands than were other Chinese consumers. Considered the most influential market in China, it was believed that a successful launch in Shanghai was likely to be able to be extended to the rest of China, whereas a marketing program which worked in Beijing or Guangzhou would not necessarily work in Shanghai.

Products

Within the skin care category of the Chinese cosmetics market, the main product claims being made were prevention and removal of wrinkles; reduction of premature aging; absorption into and the effect upon functions of the skin; environmental protection; making skin snow-white, smooth, and more elastic; healing acne; and purifying pores. Within the makeup category, Avon's Cake Foundation claimed to complement oily skins and give complexions a smooth, matte finish.

Packaging was much more basic than in the United States or Japan. Skin care products were mainly marketed in plastic or glass jars with decorated or colored caps. Labels were applied or jar screened (stamped directly onto the jar) and carried both English and Chinese copy. Outer packaging was less common and varied widely in the quality of carton and liners used. Inserts ranged from instructions on thin paper in Chinese only to color brochures with pictures and illustrations in both English and Chinese.

Distribution

State-owned department stores with 280,000 outlets accounted for 40% of all consumer product retail sales. Collectively owned stores, of which there were 1.2 million, accounted for 32%, while 8 million individually owned stores accounted for 20% of retail sales. The remaining sales were made through 330 joint venture stores (5% of sales) and direct-selling companies (3%). In general, the Chinese distribution system was more accessible to U.S. companies than the Japanese system. However, it was even more fragmented.

Cosmetics displays in stores tended to be confusing and cluttered with many brands. In department stores however, imported brands were sold in separate cases from domestic products. Three price tiers existed: imported brands such as Dior retailed at 8 times the retail prices of China-manufactured brands of Western/Chinese joint ventures and at 15 times those of local brands. Cosmetic companies rented cosmetic cases and shelf space from the department stores and paid the wages of the department store clerks.

Advertising

In 1992, per capita advertising spending in China was less than $1.00 but was expected to increase by 174% between 1992 and 1995. Newspapers were small and fragmented and rarely used for print advertising. Regional or provincial television channels were more popular than the single national channel, and advertising on the national television channel was more liable to censorship. A satellite television channel broadcast from Hong Kong, Star TV could be accessed by 4.8 million households in China and advertising costs through this channel averaged $0.50 per 1,000 people.

The cost of television advertising varied according to the status of the advertiser. The cost of a 30-second prime time advertisement on provincial television in Guangzhou province in May 1993 was $200 for a local company, $500 for a joint venture partnership, and $2,000 for a foreign importer. In Guangzhou City, these costs were about 40% of those for advertising to the entire province. For a foreign importer, the cost of a 30-second prime time advertisement on Chinese national television was $4,000 compared to $9,000 on Hong Kong television.

Competitors

Foreign competitors in China in 1992 included Avon, Johnson & Johnson, Kao, Unilever, L'Oreal, Procter & Gamble, Revlon, and Shiseido. However, their combined sales accounted for only 3% of the market. (Exhibit 14 on page 134 lists the main

EXHIBIT 14

Partial Listing of Skin Care Cosmetics Products Sold in China, 1992

Brand/Product	Manufacturer
Avon Rich Moisture Face Cream	Avon (joint venture)
Avon Skinplicity	Avon (joint venture)
Ballet Pearl Beautifying Cream	Cosmetic Factory of Nanjing China
Ballet Pearl Cream	China Light Industrial Products Import and Export
Ballet Silk Peptide UV Defense Cream	Nanjing Golden Ballet Cosmetic Co. Ltd.
Bong Bao Maifanite Face-beautifying Honey	Dongyang Mun Cosmetics Works, Zhejiang Provence
Bong Bao Maifanite Pearl Cream	Dongyang Mun Cosmetics Works, Zhejiang Provence
Dabao Instant Anti-wrinkle Cream	Beijing Sanlu Factory
Lan Normolee Moisturizing Cream	International Gottin Cosmetics
Lorensa U.S.A. Retin-A Nourish Cream	Lorensa Cosmetics U.S.A.
Lychee Brand Pianzihuang Pearl Cream	Made in chemical factory for domestic use, Zhangzhou, Fujian, China
	Supervised by Pharmacy Industry Corporation, Fujian, China
Maxam Cleansing Lotion	Maxam Cosmetics (joint venture with S.C. Johnson)
Maxam	Maxam Cosmetics (joint venture with S.C. Johnson)
Meidi Beautiful Youth Nourish Cream	Grand Blom Co. Ltd., Hong Kong
Monica Beauty Skin Cleanser	Formulated in France
Montana Anti-wrinkle Cream	Concord Group U.S.A. (joint venture)
Montana Bleaching Cream	Concord Group U.S.A. (joint venture)
Qinxiang Day Cream	Guangzhou Cosmetic Factory
Rhoure Ulan Cream	Guangzhou First Lab Cosmetics Industry
	Thailand First Lab Chemical Products Co. Ltd.
Ruby Nourishing Cream	S.C. Johnson (joint venture)
Smiss Natural Silk Cream	Wuxi Novel Daily Chemical Co. Ltd.
Ximi	—
Yue-Sai Protective Moisturizer	—
Ying Fong	Nan Yuan Ying Fong Group Co.

Source: Company research.

cosmetics products and brands available in China in 1992; Exhibit 15 provides comparative pricing data for the major cosmetics product segments.)

In 1992, Avon was the first and only direct selling cosmetics company in China. Avon had established a joint venture with the Guangzhou Cosmetics Factory (GCF) in which it owned 60% of the equity. GCF owned 35%, with the remaining 5% split between two Hong Kong business partners who had provided introductions to Chinese government officials. Avon operated only in the southern province of Guangdong. Sales in 1991 were about $4 million and rose to $8 million in 1992. Avon offered a full product line of 170 items (including a product that was a skin toner, moisturizer, and cleanser all in one), selling for an average of $4.00 each. Sales of skin-whitening products were especially strong. It was estimated that half the items were imported.

EXHIBIT 15

Indexed Retail Prices of Domestic and Imported Cosmetics in China by Product Category, 1992

Product	Domestic Products			Imported Products		
	Shanghai	Guangzhou	Beijing	Shanghai	Guangzhou	Beijing
Moisturizer	100	45	121	703	341	418
Cleanser	163	57	70	459	354	366
Toner	43	72	NA	340	368	NA
Mask	NA	104	NA	NA	400	NA
Day cream	48	55	76	345	351	373
Night cream	57	100	88	354	397	385
Pearl cream	45	84	NA	341	381	NA
Nourishing cream	55	58	83	352	354	380
Hand/body lotion/cream	37	43	68	333	340	364
Eye cream	NA	69	88	NA	366	385
Anti-aging cream	18	23	53	315	320	350
Whitening lotion	39	22	80	335	318	377
Lipstick	85	59	41	381	356	337
Cheek color	NA	72	NA	NA	368	NA
Foundation	71	128	NA	367	425	NA
Nail polish	40	72	32	337	368	328
Perfume	117	98	NA	413	394	NA

Source: Company reports.

In 1993, Avon used television advertising to promote product benefits and print advertising to recruit salespeople. Products were sold by about 15,000 Avon Ladies, mostly part-timers, who kept their regular state jobs to retain their housing subsidies, medical benefits, and pensions. Salespeople sold Avon products for whatever markup they could achieve. On average, they were believed to earn a 30% margin on product sales. Avon distributed its products through 10 branch depots located throughout Guangdong. Two hundred sales managers, who were salaried employees, oversaw 4,500 Franchise Dealers, who in turn managed the sales representatives. A training program for the Franchise Dealers included classes on product benefits, cosmetics and skin care, and general business management.

Avon positioned itself as offering consumers service, quality, reliability, and product guarantees; the latter, in particular, was a new concept for the Chinese consumer. Typical Avon consumers were urban women, aged between 20 and 35 years. Many were thought to live with their parents and spend their wages on Western goods. Compared with other imported brands, Avon was thought to be popular with younger women because Avon products were reasonably priced, and purchase—either at work or at home—was considered convenient. In addition, Avon Ladies gave their good customers a 10% to 20% discount on volume purchases and received "finders fees" for recruiting salespeople.

By 1993, Avon had achieved a beachhead in China, but several problems were evident. Inflation was forcing frequent pay increases for Avon's trained salaried employees, many of whom were receiving attractive job offers from other direct marketing firms. Avon's salaried employees were also demanding that the company provide housing as state-owned enterprises had traditionally done. In addition, Avon executives did not receive the permanent discount off of the standard 30%–40% retail turnover tax and the temporary exclusivity for the direct marketing of cosmetics in Guangzhou that executives believed they had negotiated with the provincial government.[7]

Shiseido had established a joint venture company, Shiseido Liyuan Cosmetics Co., with Beijing Liyuan in 1987. Products were sold under the brand name Huazi and cumulative sales during the first five years after the launch were estimated at $80 million. Shiseido positioned itself as offering high quality, technologically sophisticated products. The company offered 15 items at prices ranging from $4 to $6, in four product categories: eye makeup, hair care, nail care, and skin care.

MKC in China

In addition to choosing a location, MKC could choose to enter the Chinese market either by designating a licensed distributor or negotiating a joint venture agreement with a Chinese partner. Joint ventures were the most common structures Western companies used for entering China. Negotiations always involved government bodies and took an average of two years to complete. Successful joint ventures, such as those set up by Pepsi and Colgate-Palmolive, emphasized a careful search for the right partner, an in-depth market feasibility study, patience and a long-term commitment to the investment, and a strong focus on training and developing local management. MKC could also choose to build a manufacturing facility as Gillette and Amway had, expand and upgrade an existing production facility as Avon had done, subcontract manufacturing, or simply import products from the United States. It was estimated that the construction of a one-million-square-foot manufacturing plant would take two years and cost over $20 million.

Timing was considered critical in the decision to enter the Chinese market: Avon was still marketing only in the South; the number of cosmetics competitors was increasing; and the retail infrastructure was expected to continue to improve substantially.

■ MARKET ENTRY DECISION

One critical issue in deciding which markets to enter and in what order, was the acceptability and potential success of MKC's party plan approach to sales in the two markets. In Japan, Tupperware had pioneered the use of party plans, which were subsequently successfully used by a number of companies. By 1992, party plans had become an established and accepted sales technique in Japan. On the other hand, to date, no company had attempted the party plan approach in China. In 1992, MKC conducted a number of focus groups to help determine the acceptability and potential success of this sales approach. Initial findings suggested that the party plan method would be well-received in China. However, most homes were small, and in Shanghai living conditions were particularly difficult such that people did not, as a rule, entertain in their homes. In terms of consultant recruiting, results indicated that Chinese women were highly entrepreneurial, placed an emphasis on learning and self-development, and were strongly attracted to a flexible financial opportunity that would enable them to supplement their state salaries. The focus group results indicated that Chinese women were interested in cosmetics and very eager to learn more about products and how best to use them. Dandurand believed that MKC could implement a successful party plan operation in China but that resources would be needed to explain and communicate the concept to both potential consultants and consumers.

---

[7] "Avon Calling," *Business China*, Economist Intelligence Unit, July 12, 1993, pp. 1–2.

Marketing Mix Options

Product line Dandurand believed that it was essential for MKC to enter any market with both skin care and makeup products. She explained: "The two product groups both depend on consumer education. First, we teach consumers how to care for their skin and demonstrate the available treatments, then how to use glamour products to enhance their natural beauty."

Individual products in both lines would require local adaptation. Developing a product line to meet the exacting government regulations and demanding consumers of Japan would require roughly three times as much time and resources as developing a line for the Chinese market. Some MKC executives argued that the product line should be adapted as little as necessary. They believed that, with the exception of certain shades of makeup, the current product line was already global in appeal.

Positioning Assuming MKC would be marketing both the skin care and makeup products, Dandurand had to decide whether the company should be positioned as a "glamour provider," offering makeup products and expertise combined with some skin care products, or as a "skin treatment" expert that also provided makeup products. Other decisions would include the level of emphasis to place in MKC communications on the career opportunities and consumer training aspects of the MKC organization, and what messages to use to communicate them. To help with the latter, MKC conducted recruitment research in Taiwan, Japan, and China in early 1993. The results of this study are given in Exhibit 16 on page 138.

In Japan, Dandurand believed that competitive differentiation was key to success but was unsure what the basis of differentiation should be and which age group to target. One suggested modification of MKC's U.S. strategy was a buying club, similar to those offered by Avon, Menard, and Noevir. This would accelerate the recruitment of consultants, would be more consistent with competition, and would offer women the discounts on products and purchase convenience that they wanted. However, some MKC executives argued that this approach was inconsistent with MKC's emphasis on offering consultants a career opportunity and professional consumer training, and that it would not differentiate MKC from other direct selling companies operating in Japan.

Pricing Even taking product development costs into account, it was estimated that unit margins obtained on products sold in Japan would be twice as high as for corresponding products sold in China. Dandurand, however, pointed out that start-up costs, office overheads, and advertising expenditures, could be somewhat lower in China and that a Chinese market entry was expected to break even within 24 months as opposed to three to five years for Japan.

Dandurand wondered how MKC products should be priced in relation to both domestic and foreign competitors, particularly Avon, to support her positioning decision, and whether to replicate the U.S. consultant compensation scheme or to adopt consultant compensation that matched competitors' programs and local economies.

Promotion In either market, consultant recruitment programs would have to be developed, backed by print advertising, public relations, and public service workshops on women's issues. In Japan, MKC was considering establishing a toll-free number, distributing videos, organizing career opportunity seminars, and/or developing a traveling showroom to target consumers in the suburbs. Dandurand wondered what the best way to reach potential consultants and consumers in China might be.

EXHIBIT 16

Recruitment Study in Taiwan, Japan, and China, 1993

	Taiwan	*Japan*	*China*
Ideal Life Aspirations	Would like to work as long as they can take care of family. Personal fulfillment and increased knowledge are important.	Key aspiration is to get married and be a good mother/wife. Lead fulfilling and satisfying personal lives and enjoy themselves.	Most women have government-sponsored jobs. Would like to reduce the number of nonproductive hours of work, expand their knowledge and feel more productive.
Jobs and Careers	Career: perceived as involving risk, long-term commitment and higher financial rewards. Job: no risk, short-term way to make money. To work is to gain self-confidence.	Career: image of independence not positive. Do not feel that it is possible to combine career and family. Job: Should be enjoyable and flexible, a hobby to pass time. Interest was not in earning an income.	Career: Sounded far-fetched, an alien concept. Job: Only vehicle to earn money. Earning money perceived as a way to become independent, gain social acceptance and self-esteem.
Role Model Images	Self-confident, independent but not tough. Good relationship with family. Nice environment and surroundings.	Good mother figure. Happy family. Children playing. Husband and wife.	Pretty, youthful, well dressed. Romantic and relaxing life. Nice environment and surroundings. Career women type only prominent among younger, white-collar workers.

Source: Based on in-depth focus groups.

To build the necessary level of MKC brand awareness among consumers in Japan would require at least $3 million per year in advertising. To create comparative brand awareness levels in one region of China might require $100,000 in advertising per year for the first three years.

In order to compare the economics of the two market entry options, Dandurand made the preliminary calculations summarized in Exhibit 17.

EXHIBIT 17

Preliminary Estimates of the Economics of Market Entry: Japan and China

	Japan	*China*
Average retail unit price US$	$25.00	$9.00
Average MKC wholesale unit price	$12.50	$4.50
Cost of goods	$2.30	$1.20
Freight and duty	$0.75	$1.28
Gross margin	$9.45	$2.02
Product development costs/year	$0.9 million	$0.1 million
Start-up investment costs	$10.0 million	$2.0 million
Promotion and advertising costs/year	$3.0 million	$0.1 million

DowBrands Ziploc™
The Case for Going International

In October 1990, Stewart James, vice-president of international for DowBrands, Inc., was reviewing the success of Ziploc™ brand zippered bags outside the United States:

> The jury is still out. In Canada, we're at about break even. In Latin America, we've built a plant—we've put a stake in the ground for Ziploc™—but have yet to show operating profits. We're in the process of buying back a joint venture in Japan, after which we should make some money. We sell some product in Europe through our own organization, but none of our European subsidiaries is convinced that there is much of a future for Ziploc™; and some recent market research seems to support the conclusion that it will never be more than a niche product in those countries. Sometimes in these cases, the only way to find out for sure is to make a commitment and go for it.
>
> In my view, DowBrands should grow Ziploc™ at all costs, and this means taking it to the rest of the world. It is our number 1 product in sales and profitability, and my experience has shown that estimating volume potential where behavioral changes are required is a very difficult question to research anyway. We are the low-cost producer in this category, and for a product that is as much a production art as it is a science, we are still far ahead on the learning curve. We are facing increased competition and margin erosion in the U.S. market, and now is the time to go forth in the international arena. The only problem is: how do we get the rest of the organization fired up about this opportunity?

■ DOWBRANDS, INC.

As a separate corporate entity, the DowBrands subsidiary of the Dow Chemical Company was only 5 years old, although its genesis was with the marketing of Saran Wrap™ in 1953. Saran Wrap™, a thin plastic film, was originally conceived to protect military arsenal stored at the end of World War II, but someone discovered it made an excellent wrap for the preservation of fresh and/or leftover foods. In time, Dow added other food-care products and such cleaning products as Dow Bathroom Cleaner™ to the line.

The parent company was a successful, $18 billion, multinational chemical company, but the consumer-products portion had never reached what many executives believed was its full potential. Dow spent $1 billion for research and development, and its inventors—dubbed "the molecule movers"—had an excellent track record for inventing new chemical compounds, but the company had been less successful in realizing the full market potential from those inventions. A notable example was a moisture-absorbing technology that Dow developed but sold to Procter & Gamble. It became one of P&G's most profitable products ever. Dow believed that the rewards of such inventions were reaped more by the successful marketer than by the successful inventor. Based on the idea that a dollar in sales of a specialty product would deliver more profit than a dollar of basic commodity sales, an ongoing discussion at DowBrands was how to exploit markets for its inventions.

The mission for the consumer-products division was to become a *technology-driven* packaged-goods concern, with the basis for excellence coming from highly protected technical advantages. The importance of good marketing skills could not be ignored, however, so in 1985 Dow bought the Texize Division of Morton Thiokol, which not only made and manufactured a line of complementary cleaning products, but also employed personnel skilled in the design and marketing of consumer packaged goods. Texize was combined with the consumer-products division to form the new DowBrands business unit. In 1989, DowBrands acquired the European operations of the First Brands Company, which marketed the well-known Glad brand of plastic bags and wraps in the United States. Its Glad and Albal brands of household wrappers were well established in Europe. (See Exhibit 1 for a listing of major Dow-Brands products sold internationally.)

Division sales for 1990 were forecast at $1 billion, with food care representing about a third of this amount and international sales about 20%. Ziploc™ sales at retail were about $300 million and represented about 70% of the division's food-care business. The president and chief executive officer of DowBrands reported to the chairman of the board of DowBrands.

Ziploc™ Storage Bags

With the rise of private automobiles, home refrigerators and freezers, and large supermarkets in the United States after World War II, shopping trips for groceries became less frequent than daily, and the need arose for a way to protect fresh food (and leftovers) from becoming stale and hard. The need was met by aluminum foil, wax paper, and plastic wraps, augmented in 1962 by small plastic bags. The plastic

EXHIBIT 1

Selected DowBrands International Division Products[a]

Canada:	Dow bathroom cleaner; Glass Plus; Fantastik spray cleaner, bathroom cleaner, and upholstery cleaner; K2r, Spray'N Wash, Spray'N Starch; Ziploc™, Saran Wrap™, Handi-Wrap™, Stretch'N Seal
Italy:	Domopak brand aluminum foils, aluminum containers, plastic wraps, food and garbage bags
Brazil:	Zipy (Ziploc™), Mr. Magic (Fantastik lemon), Thunder (Dow bathroom cleaner)
Argentina:	Radiante brand cleaners
Japan:	Reed/Ziploc™ food bags and microwave cooking bags
Hong Kong:	Ziploc™
Singapore:	Ziploc™
Europe:	Albal aluminum foils and containers, Albal food and garbage bags; Glad aluminum products, plastic film, food and garbage bags

a Ziploc™ is a trademark of DowBrands, Saran Wrap™ and Handi-Wrap™ are trademarks of the Dow Chemical Company. "Glad" is used under license to DowBrands.

Source: Company records, dated 3/24/90.

bag (using a thin polyethylene film) was first introduced as a wrap for sandwiches, and it grew in sales at over 15% a year. Dow tried to protect its own plastic-wrap business with the Handi-Wrap™ sandwich bag, but was unsuccessful in coming up with a form and packaging that were competitive. At the same time, the use of plastic bags for large storage (garbage, leaves, and the like) was introduced; this market grew at 10% a year.

In 1966, Dow R&D personnel saw a custom bag with a plastic "zipper" at a trade show; the zipper used a unique technology that allowed the open end of a plastic bag to be closed by gently pressing a plastic ridge on one edge into a plastic track on the opposing edge. Not only did the zipper offer a convenient, reusable closure, but consumers believed it also served to seal out hostile air more thoroughly than traditional twist-tie closures then in use. Dow obtained exclusive rights to the manufacture of zippered bags for grocery-store distribution, but lack of consistent quality led to high consumer returns, and the project was dropped.

Dow continued to work on perfecting the manufacture of zippered bags while looking for untapped applications for nonzippered bags, especially at the premium end of the price spectrum. By 1970, Dow had determined that "unique, leak-proof seal" was a more important benefit to stress to consumers than "convenient/easy-to-use"; in fact, the zipper seal was perceived as *not* easy to use, because beginning the zippering process was not always easy, and determining whether the zipper had "caught" or closed fully enough to make a perfect seal was not always clear. Dow changed the name of the product to Ziploc™ and introduced it nationally in 1972 with heavy advertising to educate consumers about the benefits and use of the zipper system.

A number of favorable elements in the climate helped Ziploc™ sales take off in 1973—increased U.S. disposable income, which reduced the importance of the premium price and a shortage of glass products for food storage and freezing. New positioning for the storage bag included nonfood uses, and in 1975 Ziploc™ storage bags led the market with a 33% share. A Ziploc™ sandwich bag was also introduced in 1975. A premium pricing strategy was effected by (1) offering fewer bags at the same price as competitors' packages while (2) continuing to advertise heavily and consistently to demonstrate zipper-seal benefits. While competitors tended to offer consumer and trade discounts, Dow did neither; it used its advertising to build strong consumer loyalty.

When consumer research revealed that a third of Ziploc™ bags were used in freezers, a bag especially designed for this harsh environment was offered in 1980. A period of high inflation in 1981–1983 led to an advertising theme of cutting high food costs through the use of high-quality storage protection. Consumers still complained about the difficulty of using the zipper, however, and in 1983 a new, wide-track seal was developed. Nevertheless, market research showed that, given products of equal "ease of use," to claim "ultimate in food protection" would still capture more business.

In 1984, continued consumer-behavior research confirmed three distinct uses for Ziploc™: storage (refrigerator and cupboard), lunch bag/box sandwiches, and freezer. In addition, the Ziploc™ positioning was changed to focus on an end benefit of fresh, good-tasting food. The zipper feature was no longer the chief focus, but was used to support the "fresh" promise. Advertisements differentiated the three product types (storage, sandwich, and freezer), and Dom DeLuise was selected as the Ziploc™ spokesperson.[1]

---

[1] DeLuise is a well-known television comedian whose ample frame was augmented by his notorious love of good food. Advertisements showing DeLuise peering into a refrigerator, cooing over "my precious little [. . . sausage. . . , . . . coq-au-vin. . . . and the like]" protected by Ziploc™, were designed to create viewer involvement in a low-salience product.

Dow continued to make product improvements and line extensions, including pint-sized freezer bags for single servings, jumbo bags for nonfood use, wide-track zippers on freezer bags, "grip strips" for easier opening on all products, "pleated" bags for easier use, "write-on labels" for freezer bags, and "Microfreez" bags for storing, reheating, and cooking in the microwave oven (which were not successful).

Dow management believed that a consumer "information overload" was forming by the late 1980s (because of the proliferation of new products) that would lead to a "big brand" era. Because consumers had less time or desire to experiment than in the past, this trend would benefit major brands that had established good recall based on dependability and value. Hence, in 1989 Dow advertising began to emphasize Ziploc™'s quality heritage. A new advertisement campaign focused on "put your trust in a Ziploc™ bag," and new package graphics were aimed at improving the product's positioning of high quality.

By 1990, zippered bags had obtained a 70% share of the $600 million U.S. retail storage/freezer/sandwich bag market (60% of 365 million cases). Ziploc™ accounted for about half of the total dollar market (about 40% of the total unit market); it was the seventeenth largest-selling nonfood item in U.S. food stores.

Competitors were First Brands' Glad bags (about 25% of the total dollar market, split between zippered and regular products), private-label bags (about 20% of the dollar market, roughly split between zippered and regular), and Reynolds Metals' Sure-Seal Zippered Bags and Mobil Oil's twist-tie Baggies, which together accounted for the remainder. First Brands had bought the Glad business from Union Carbide in 1986 and, soon after, introduced a bag with a unique seal that changed colors when the bags had been properly sealed. Despite Reynolds' small share, Dow was watching its Sure-Seal brand carefully, because whereas Ziploc™'s strategy had consistently been to use consumer advertising and promotions with few trade incentives, Reynolds' strategy was apparently to round out its protective-packaging line, rather than make early profits, by offering a parity product with heavy trade and consumer promotion. This strategy yielded Reynolds a price advantage versus Ziploc™ of 30 to 40 cents for a package of 20 quart storage bags. Glad had responded with heavy trade promotions, while Ziploc™ maintained its strategy of heavy advertising, reminding consumers of its premium protection.

By summer 1990, Glad seemed to be maintaining its share, while Sure-Seal had gained 5 share points, mostly from Ziploc™. The group brand manager for Ziploc™ bags, Dawn Miller, responded to this threat by a consumer deal offering "get three for the price of two." Response was great, but Miller was concerned by eventual price erosion of Ziploc™. The possibility of introducing a lower-priced "fighter brand" was rejected, since the slotting allowances of almost $500,000 would reduce the return to an unacceptable level. As Miller said,

> Our main task will be to continue improving the product through performance features. However, this is tricky, since the production process is so complex: one small change might affect many other parts of the production process. It is far from a trivial act to tinker with any part of it! Gone is the time when we were the only product on the market, able to establish and hold our premium positioning through advertising alone. Consumers understand our concept well: Ziploc™ is a high-quality, low-volume storage product, almost like a disposable Tupperware, only better, because it seals better while taking up less room.
>
> The challenge is whether we can continue to add value to command a premium price. While we may be the low-cost producer because we can make the bags faster, I wonder whether the large investment required to support our automated factories offsets this advantage. If a price war starts, we will learn fast how far our cost advantage extends! I know that there is a segment for whom quality or price/value is no issue, but I am concerned that this segment is a shrinking one. This is an interesting time to be in this job!

First Brands/Europe Acquisition, 1989

The acquisition of the First Brands/Europe wholly owned subsidiary (FBE) in early 1989 was consistent with DowBrands' strategic plan to increase international sales to $230 million by 1995. The strategic objective was to become a leader in the food-care/disposables (fcd) category in Japan, Latin America, and Europe, with Europe targeted as a priority area.[2]

In assessing world opportunities, the DowBrands strategic planners noted that, because no large plastics or hydrocarbon firms were selling fcds outside the United States, given Ziploc™'s U.S. position, it could be considered the strongest premium fed brand in the world. Unlike other DowBrands categories, the worldwide fcd market was serviced mostly by small regional manufacturers whose strengths seemed to be more in manufacturing than in marketing; only First Brands/Europe appeared to have built any meaningful multinational business. The planners also based Dow's strong future potential in this category on its superior and protectable technology.

Europe seemed to be especially attractive. Although household expenditures for fcds were just half ($10.62 per household) those of the United States ($20.43), the number of 1987 households in the five countries of France, Italy, Germany, Spain, and the United Kingdom exceeded that of the United States (100 million in Europe versus the United States' 91 million). Moreover, annual fcd growth rate in Europe was attractive (10% compared to 3% in the United States). The leading four competitors held only 30% of the business (versus 70% in the United States).

The premium category was of special interest. It consisted of products that offered the extra benefits of convenience or product strength, such as Ziploc™, drawstring garbage bags, and pleated food bags. Industry experts estimated that these products had high gross margins (50% or better), but that selling expenses were also high (typically 35%). The premium fcd business was estimated to be 36% of all fcd sales dollars in the United States (annual growth was 10%), but it was only a "few millions dollars" in Europe (less than 1% of the fcd market). The gross margin potential differed substantially by country, as did trade margins, as the following table indicates:

	Average Price/ Nielsen Unit ($)	Estimated Average Trade Margin (%)
Germany	1.06	36
United Kingdom	.98	40
France	2.20	27
Italy	1.22	33

Source: Company records.

The DowBrands planners expected such factors as increasing numbers of European homemakers in the work force and the growing penetration of large refrigerators and freezers to push this segment's growth. Appendix A gives selected data on major European markets.

FBE had sales of $96 million in 1988 with pretax profits of $3 million. It marketed a full line of fcds with strong shares in France and Spain (the Albal brand) and in Scandinavia and Belgium (the Glad brand). The Glad brand was sold in all the European countries except Ireland. Over 40% of FBE's business was in France, 30% in Spain and Portugal, and the rest in Germany (private label only), Scandinavia, and the Benelux countries. Of its 312 employees, 200 were in manufacturing and the rest in sales and administration. FBE had a plastic bag and wrap factory in Germany and an

---

[2] The term fcd, as used here, covers all nondurable products used to transport, store, freeze, and dispose of food, including foils, wraps, papers, and bags.

aluminum-rewinding plant in France. Some 54% of its dollar sales were in aluminum foil (the most important fcd in Europe), 14% in garbage bags, 13% in food bags, 8% in plastic wraps, and 11% in other products. Branded sales represented 75% of FBE's total sales.

DowBrands planners summed up their arguments for acquiring First Brands/Europe this way:

> The acquisition appeal is due to First Brands' strength in France and Spain, two of DowBrands target markets where we currently have no position. It also has a leading position in food bags and wraps in Scandinavia and Belgium. It is unique in Europe because it has pioneered the premium product segment by introducing both state-of-the-art zippered food bags and drawstring trash bags into France. Together with Domopak [DowBrands' existing operation in Italy] this acquisition would form a potent food care/disposables company, competing for the strongest position in the category in Europe.

(See Appendix B for the planners' detailed comments on FBE's strengths.)

Upon the acquisition of FBE in March 1989, DowBrands created a new position of managing director for Europe, which reported to the vice-president of international. Under the managing director were regional managers for four country subsidiaries, each with a full-function organization (Italy, France, Spain, and Germany); the German subsidiary was also responsible for sales organizations in Scandinavia, the Benelux countries, and the United Kingdom. In the managing director's headquarters were the European managers for manufacturing, marketing research and business development, human resources, and so on.

Stewart James

As vice-president and Global Product director, James had responsibility for all DowBrands' businesses abroad. Reporting to him were the general managers of the company's operations in Canada, South America (headquarters in Sao Paulo and a plant in Rio de Janeiro, Brazil), the Pacific Rim (headquarters in Tokyo), and Europe (the former First Brands/Europe companies; headquarters in Germany).

James, 40, came to his job in October 1989 from previous positions in marketing and sales at DowBrands and at a southeastern food manufacturer; his most recent assignment had been vice-president of sales for DowBrands. While he had had no prior experience in international sales, he was perceived by his colleagues as accomplished, aggressive, and well suited to lead DowBrands into the international arena because of his energy and all-consuming desire to succeed.

He made these comments in the most recent DowBrands newsletter:

> We're going to do about $235 million this year—that's in excess of 20% of Dow-Brands overall sales. But I'm not so concerned about that increasing in terms of percentage as I am in terms of the quality of our business. My vision for the future is that we should, given our size, be considered a multinational company and not a global package good company at this time.
>
> My vision is to build critical mass in the top strategic countries. Strategic countries are those countries that have a large concentrated urban population and gross domestic product and have the type of homemakers that can afford to buy our products. . . . For example, Japan, with half the population of the States and a higher gross domestic product per capita income than the United States, is a tremendous opportunity. We must stop thinking of Japan as a $20 million market and then go to Taiwan, Korea and Hong Kong, etc., etc. Instead, we ought to think of Japan as a potential $100 million market 5 years from now and therefore use these other satellite countries to feed that investment. The top strategic countries are the ones that count and the ones that in the long term will enable us to do other things.

■ FINDINGS FROM CONSUMER RESEARCH ON THE FCD MARKET IN EUROPE

In the fall of 1987, the U.K. office of DowBrands had conducted a set of comparison "awareness and usage" surveys for fcd products in Great Britain, France, and Germany in order to set priorities for the Ziploc™ opportunities in those three countries. (Spain had been eliminated as a possible candidate in an earlier study.) Data were collected regarding the types of uses for fcds, perceptions regarding strengths and weaknesses of the existing brands of wrappings, and those brands' respective images. About 425 in-depth home interviews conducted in each country asked what had been wrapped (fish, meat, and so on), for where (refrigerator, freezer, and so on), what material was used (aluminum foil, plastic, and so on), and how frequently respondents usually performed such an action (for example, "wrapped fish for the freezer with aluminum foil less than three times a month"). A summary report was issued in May 1988; following are selected findings from that report.

Overall, the extrapolated monthly "fcd occasions" ranged from 1.3 billion in Germany to 1.1 billion in the United Kingdom to 0.8 billion in France. Exhibit 2 gives the extrapolation calculations for this study, Exhibit 3 presents a breakdown by materials and destinations, and Exhibit 4 on page 148 is a summary graph of destination and materials combined. (The second part of Exhibit 4 compares the usage of bags in these countries with earlier data from the United States.) As shown in Exhibit 5 on page 149, the 10 most frequent specific uses varied considerably by country.

The researchers clustered respondents psychographically based on their answers to a number of life-style questions. The relative size of the six clusters for each country and their use of major fcd materials are shown in Exhibit 6 on page 150.

Respondents were asked to name what material they would have used as an alternative if the material actually used had not been available (the materials were aluminum, plastic wraps, plastic bags, and rigid containers). In France, the biggest "winner" was rigid containers; in Germany, aluminum; and in Great Britain, aluminum. Plastic bags did not show a material "win" in any country. Exhibit 7 on page 151 details the substitution data within each country.

A test of "satisfaction with each wrap" compared with use revealed that, in France, aluminum foil was highest in use and in satisfaction; in Germany, plastic wrap

E X H I B I T   2

Extrapolated Number of Monthly FCD Occasions for Total Population in Each Country[a]

	D	F	GB
Percentage of households represented by survey:	85	92	84
Household universe (millions) represented:	21.9	19.4	17.8
Average number of occasions per month, per household:	80.9	48.3	65.6
Extrapolated numbers (millions) of:			
Monthly foodcare occasions for the total household population:	1,771	937	1,167
Monthly fcd usage occasions (aluminum, wraps, or bags):	1,332	834	1,063
Monthly fcd usage occasions using rigid containers or other materials:	439	103	104

[a] "D" was the international symbol for West Germany, "F" was France, and "GB" was Great Britain.

Source: Company records, dated May 1988.

EXHIBIT 3

FCD Usage Occasions, Weighted Incidence: Shares of the Total Number of Usage Occasions/Month

	Germany %	France %	Great Britain %
Base 100% =	36,919	21,436	30,816
Materials			
Aluminum	23	56	30
Wraps	33	14	35
Bags	17	15	21
Containers	25	11	13
Other	2	4	1
	100	100	100
Destination			
Freezer	19	21	15
Refrigerator	64	62	33
Kitchen	9	2	6
Oven	1	4	10
MWO	—	1	9
Out of home	7	10	27
	100	100	100

Kitchen = out in the open in the kitchen; MWO = microwave oven.

Source: Company records, dated May 1988.

was highest in use but rigid containers were highest in satisfaction; and in Great Britain, plastic wrap had the highest use but plastic bags had the highest satisfaction, higher than in the other two countries.

In general, homemakers in all three countries displayed average-to-high levels of satisfaction with all materials across the majority of destinations and use occasions. German homemakers tended to be less satisfied with substitutes than those in France and Great Britain. A summary of the three most important material attributes is given in Exhibit 8 on page 152. A perceptual map of users of each of the fcds in each country is reproduced in Exhibit 9 on page 153.

Respondents were shown a number of "photoprompts" of the major fcd brands and asked, for a number of image items (for example, "high quality," "good value for money," and so on), which brands were best or worst for that image or feature. In Germany, the Melitta and Frapan brands were positioned closely together at the quality end of the high/low quality spectrum for all fcds; in France, again for all fcds, the Propsac, Handy Bag, Sopalin, and Albal (foil and bags only) brands were perceived as "national brands with high availability"; not surprisingly, the major brands in all countries were associated with "high availability," and retailers' (private) brands were associated with "not available everywhere." In all countries, respondents perceived most positively those brands that they "currently use" and/or the one they designated as the "leading brand." In Great Britain, however, retailers' brands often had a good image, especially with respect to "good value for the money."

In general, the researchers concluded that the greatest opportunity for Ziploc™ in Great Britain was for the sandwich-bag market, but in France and Germany, it was for Ziploc™ freezer bags. They were encouraged that one of the most important fcd attributes discovered for all countries was "airtight closure," a major Ziploc™ selling

E X H I B I T   4

FCD Usage Occasions Summary

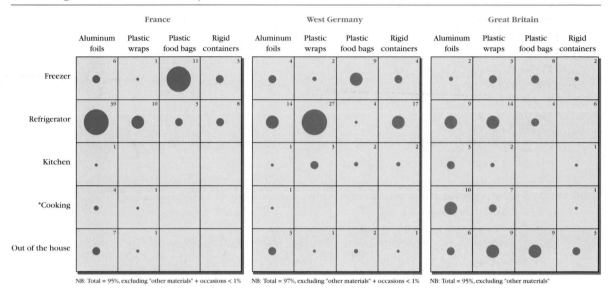

NB: Total = 95%, excluding "other materials" + occasions < 1%   NB: Total = 97%, excluding "other materials" + occasions < 1%   NB: Total = 95%, excluding "other materials"

Source: Opportunity study, 1987.

Comparison of Destination of Bags in Four Countries[a]

	France	West Germany	Great Britain	United States[b]
Base (usage occasions):	(3,119)	(5,914)	(6,294)	(45,647)
	%	%	%	%
Refrigerator	24	27	18	22
Freezer	76	61	37	15
Microwave	—	—	1	—
Oven	—	1	1	—
Out of home	—	11	43	63
	100	100	100	100

[a] *Europe, 1987; United States, 1984.*
[b] *U.S. data from diary panel, 1984.*

Source: Company records, dated May 1988.

feature; they also noted the importance given to "keeping food fresh and tasty" and "isolating odors well."

The Decision

James was familiar with the marketing research results, but he felt that they might not provide enough support for launching an aggressive Ziploc™ program in Europe:

> As detailed and well executed as it is, the research only shows that there is promise in Europe, especially in the large markets of France, Germany, and the United Kingdom. It has the usual defect in that it shows more about what *is* with respect to current products and segments than what *might be* the prospects for an emerging premium segment. The detailed study was not carried out in Spain, since refrigerators tend to be small and freezers nonexistent, and everyday shoppers apparently don't

EXHIBIT 5

Recap FCD Usage Occasions: The 10 Most Frequent Individual Occasions by Country (weighted incidence)

	Germany	France	Great Britain
Base 100% =	36,919	21,436	30,816
Occasions within 10 most frequent in at least two countries	%	%	%
Cheese/refrigerator	12.7	14.7	7.9
Veg-fruit/refrigerator	10.4	6.8	3.2
Raw meat/freezer	4.8	7.7	3.1
Bread-cakes/out house	3.6	2.5	3.1
Veg-fruit/freezer	4.1	4.3	3.6
Raw meat/refrigerator	2.3	8.6	—
Sandwiches/out house	—	4.3	21.6
Cooked meat/refrigerator	—	10.9	6.3
Leftovers/refrigerator	—	10.7	6.0
Other frequent occasions specific to one country			
Deli meat/refrigerator	18.4		
Bread-cakes/kitchen	6.1		
Bread-cakes/refrigerator	5.3		
Bread-cakes/freezer	4.5		
Fish/refrigerator		2.6	
Veg-fruit/microwave			3.1
Raw meat/oven			6.9
Total top 10	72.2	73.1	64.8

Source: Company records, dated May 1988.

perceive the need for the superior protection of Ziploc™. And, frankly, this is the attitude that some of our people still have about food-shopping habits even in France and Germany. So, you can picture the resistance I am getting from my management in Europe against making the kind of investment spends we will need to do to build the premium segment of zippered bags.

We have to use imagination: we might have done more research in Spain, and we should do it in the rest of Europe, all with an open mind for spotting opportunities. When you ask customers to relate current usage to new ideas, they have great difficulty in doing that. I wonder if the typical A&U [attitude and usage] studies are up to the task. What they do do is to give my European management the wrong kind of ammunition. And these people remind me that we can't expect the same high profit margins abroad that we have here in the States and that start-up expenses will be high. But even with a lower margin in Europe, I still see Ziploc™ improving the overall margin mix after the expenses of the sell-in are absorbed. . . .

How would I go? I need to hammer, hammer, hammer my vision. Perhaps I should set up a "President of Ziploc™" in Europe. The Glad people there are not convinced; with $130 million in sales, they don't need it. They say, "Look how long it took to develop the Ziploc™ business in Canada." I must show them success stories in Europe. That's why we bought Europe, and now it's time to act.

EXHIBIT 6

Usage of Material Types by Cluster Groups

Cluster Sizes	NF	EG	HO	OP	EXP	RE
Germany (D)	13	16	16	20	12	23
France (F)	18	15	23	14	16	14
Great Britain (GB)	12	18	38	14	9	9
Aluminum						
D index:	99	47	118	91	128	118
Share:	13	8	19	18	15	27
F index:	123	109	82	77	130	80
Share:	22	16	19	11	21	11
GB index:	76	93	106	104	134	84
Share:	9	17	40	15	12	8
Wraps						
D index:	84	84	89	138	113	87
Share:	11	13	14	28	14	20
F index:	83	103	113	48	142	100
Share:	15	15	26	7	23	14
GB index:	73	98	84	125	113	159
Share:	9	18	32	18	10	14
Bags						
D index:	46	58	99	121	108	137
Share:	6	9	16	24	13	32
F index:	61	69	97	101	131	156
Share:	11	10	22	14	21	22
GB index:	96	82	96	113	60	178
Share:	12	15	36	16	5	16

An earlier awareness and usage study uncovered six cluster groups based on an analysis of the pattern of respondents' answers. The groups were described as follows:

RE = Role enhancer: High positive association with all items relating to home cooking, make own foods, home care, and so on, but negative with "spend most of the day away from home." High awareness and usage of fcd brands. (Not found in Spain.)

EXP = Experimentalist: High purchase of recently launched products. Tend to be "away from home most of day." High microwave ownership.

OP = Own produce preserver: High scores for freezing produce grown by self or bought directly from producer. Not experimental. High deep freezer ownership.

HO = Home oriented: High scores for "home" and "cooking" items. Not necessarily high for "freezing." Tend to be nonworking.

EG = Easy going: Lowest scores for home-oriented items. Tendency to score low on freezing items. Often spend day away from home. Youngest group.

NF = Nonfreezing: Lowest scores on freezing times. May have high home-oriented scores. Low freezer ownership. Older group, lower social class.

The entries following "cluster sizes" show the percentages of each cluster by country (for example, the NF cluster represents 13% of the German sample but 18% of the French sample). An index is the ratio of a cluster's share of usage compared to its size (for example, the NF cluster in France uses 22% of aluminum, which, compared with its 18% of the sample, yields an index of 123.)

Source: Company records, dated May 1988.

EXHIBIT 7

Substitution Between Materials

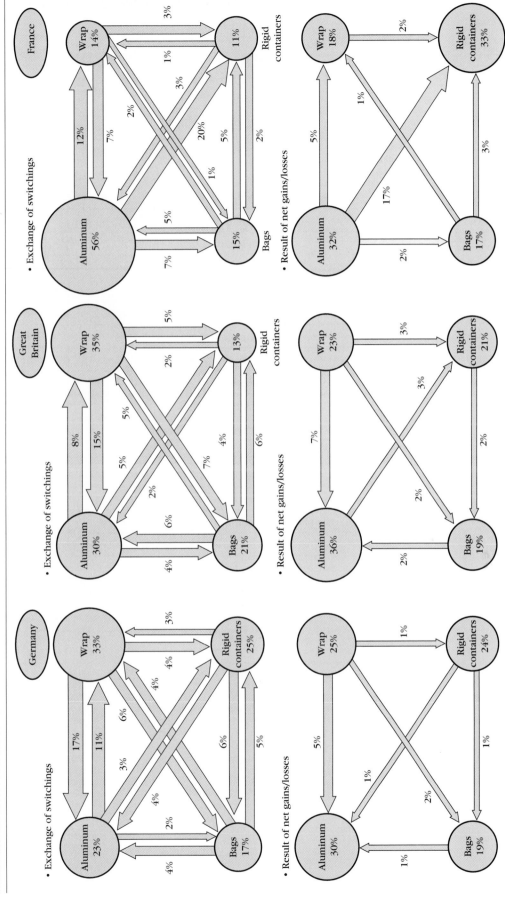

The question was: "If the material you used had not been available when you did that occasion, what would you have used instead?"

EXHIBIT 8

Importance of FCD Material Attributes in Three European Countries (% for Least, Second/Third, Most Important)

	Least			Second/third			Most		
Important attribute in:	F	D	GB	F	D	GB	F	D	GB
Keeps food fresh and tasty				●	●	●	•	●	●
Isolates odors well	•	•	•	●	●	●	●	●	·
Easy to handle	•	•	•	●	•	•	•	•	·
Very hygienic		•		•	•	•	•	●	•
Airtight closure	•	•	•	•	•	●	•	•	•
Space saving	·	·	·	•	•	•	•	•	•
Prevents food spoiling		•	•	•	●	•	•	•	•
Resistant	•		•	•	•	•	•	•	•
Moisture proof	•	•	•	•	•	•	•	•	·
Safe with all foods	•	•		•	•	•	•	•	•
Good value for money	•	•	•	•	•	•	•	•	•
Can recognize contents	•	●	•	•	•	•	•	•	•
Inexpensive	•	•	•	•	●	•	•	•	•
Adapts itself well around shapes	•	•	•	•	•	•	•	•	•
Stays in place once wrapped	•	•	•	•	•	•	•		•
Easy to dispense	•	•	•	•	•	•	•	•	•
Safe for the environment	•	•	•	•	•			•	
Reusable	●	●	●	•	•	•		•	•

The sizes of the circles are relative to "keeps food fresh and tasty" in Germany, which received the greatest percentage response across all questions and countries.

Source: Company records, dated May 1988.

E X H I B I T   9

Images of FCD Materials

Images of FCD materials

Analysis of correspondence based on users of aluminum foil (A), plastic wrap (W), plastic food bags (B), and permanent (PC) and disposable (DC) rigid containers in each country.

Axis 1 (vertical) and 2 (horizontal) variance explained = 86%.

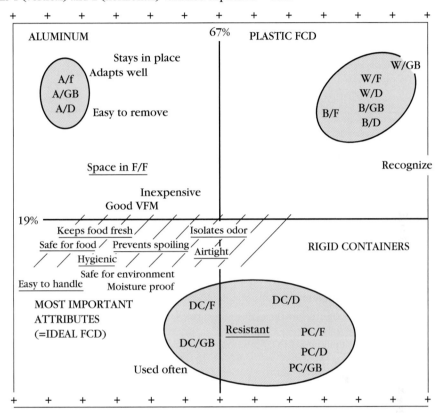

Source: Company records, dated May 1988.

Selected Data on Major European Markets[a]

Demographic Profiles of the 5 Major European Countries

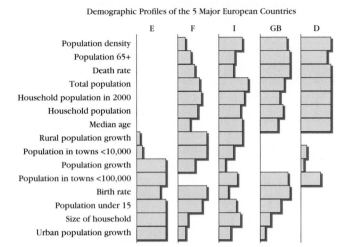

Notes: See definition of each indicator in data table below.

The graph above highlights differences among countries by using, for each indicator, the minimum and maximum values as the edge of a constant scale.

	E	F	I	GB	D	USA
Population density (per km², 1988)	78	102	191	233	246	26
Population 65+ (%, 1988)	12.6	13.6	14.0	15.5	15.3	12.3
Death rate (deaths per 1,000, 1988)	8.3	10.1	9.9	11.8	11.7	8.8
Total population (millions)	39.2	55.8	57.5	56.9	61.0	248.0
Household population in 2000 (estimated millions)	15.2	23.8	23.1	22.1	25.8	106.0
Household population (millions, 1987)	11.7	21.1	20.4	21.2	25.8	90.5
Median age (1988)	32.5	34.3	36.2	35.5	38.2	32.4
Rural population growth (average annual 1980-85)	−1.7	.2	−.5	−1.8	−1.8	.7
Population in towns <10,000 (%)	26	50	33	23	26	NA
Population growth (total % change 1986/90)	33	19	10	8	9	33
Population in towns >100,000 (%)	42	16	27	36	33	NA
Birth rate (births per 1,000, 1988)	13.1	13.6	11.0	13.4	10.6	15.3
Population under 15 (%, 1988)	21.7	20.4	17.7	18.7	14.7	21.5
Size of household (average number of persons)	3.76	2.77	3.4	2.72	2.32	2.67
Urban population growth (average annual 1980-85)	1.4	.4	.3	.2	.1	.9

[a] *"E" is the international symbol for Spain and "I" for Italy.*

Sources: Trends & Opportunities Aboard, 1988 AmericanDemographics Inc.—"EBM '87," European Basic Data, G.F.K.

APPENDIX A *(Continued)*

Socioeconomic Profiles of the 5 Major European Countries and the USA

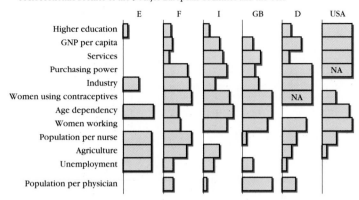

Notes: See definition of each indicator in data table below.

The graph above highlights differences among countries by using, for each indicator, the minimum and maximum values as the edge of a constant scale.

The indicator population per physician is isolated because of the peculiarity shown.

	E	*I*	*F*	*GB*	*D*	*USA*
Higher education (% enrollment in)	26	26	27	20	29	57
GNP per capita ($)	4,290	6,520	9,540	8,460	10,940	16,690
Services (% labor force in)	46	48	56	59	50	66
Purchasing power Index, 1986 (100—AV.16 European countries)	57	109	112	86	133	NA
Industry (% labor force in)	37	41	35	38	44	31
Women using contraceptives (% married 15-49)	59	76	79	83	NA	68
Age dependency (ratio, # of 0-14, 15-64, 65+)	52	46	52	52	43	51
Women working (% women 15-64)	27	41	53	56	52	62
Population per nurse	280	250	110	120	170	180
Agriculture (% labor force in)	17	12	9	3	6	4
Unemployment rate, 1985	22.0	10.6	9.9	11.5	7.3	7.1
Population per physician	390	750	460	1,991	420	500

APPENDIX A   *(Continued)*

Foodcare Appliances Ownership – 1987
• In the five major European countries • By multiownership groups

Country (Household millions) →	D (25.8)	GB (21.2)	F (21.1)	I (20.4)	E (11.7)
None of the three appliances	3	2	3		3
Refrigerator only	20	21	26	20	
Combined refrigerator-freezer only	18	33	30	59	52
Separate refrigerator only	49	36	29	9	41
Both types of freezers	10	8	12	12	13 / 1

% Housewives owning

	D	I	GB	F	E
Separate deep freezer	(59)	(44)	(41)	21	4
Combined refrigerator-freezer	28	(41)	(42)	(71)	(42)
Any freezer	(77)	(77)	(72)	(80)	46

Source: Europanel, January '87

Selected Details of First Brands/Europe Strengths, 1989

France:	First Brands/Europe has a solid No. 2 position in the $300 million French market, the largest food care/disposables market in Europe. And at just under 12% growth over the last 4 years, France is Europe's second fastest growing market. FBE's sales force has done a good job in getting its products onto French supermarket shelves and the consumer awareness of the Albal brand is the best among all fcd brands in France. FBE's French business originated with the acquisition of the Albal trademark from the French national aluminum company in 1985. Following this, FBE added plastic wraps and bags into what was previously an aluminum-based business. FBE's plastics business and its overall share of the French market have grown steadily ever since.
Spain:	Spain's fcd market is $60 million and is the fastest growing European market at over 12% a year. FBE has become increasingly enthusiastic about the growing Spanish market and purchased the operating business from its distributor in October 1988. They are the market leader with Albal in aluminum and with Glad in wraps and bags.
Premium Bags:	FBE launched a zipper-closure food bag in France in late 1987, under the brand name AlbaZip. This product is identical to the colored-zipper Glad Lock product that competes with Ziploc™ in America. This market is still very small, but after only months on the market, AlbaZip has already captured more than half of the premium food bag market. The key competitors, by the way, are utilizing bags with the outdated Mini-Grip-style zipper. Both the Ziploc™ and the Glad Lock closures (used on AlbaZip) are overwhelmingly preferred by the consumer. FBE has also recently launched a premium drawstring trash bag into France called Lock-Up. Premium trash bags represent a promising growth area for us throughout Europe.
Competitors:	There are no dominant leaders across the continent [see table attached]. Only FBE has a major position in more than one country. The significant role played by private labels is evident, especially in the United Kingdom and, to a lesser extent, in France. FBE is a major private label supplier in Germany (and also in France and Spain). Melitta's dominant share in Germany gives it the overall lead in these five markets. When combined with our strong position in Italy, the marriage of FBE and Domopak not only puts us in a solid position in three of the five key Western European markets, but it also positions DowBrands well to compete effectively in Europe in 1992.

Source: Company records, dated 11/23/88.

Western Europe Competitive Environment, 1987

France ($306M)		United Kingdom ($281M)		Germany ($245M)		Italy ($163M)		Spain ($60M)	
Leaders	Share (%)	Leaders	Share (%)	Leaders	Share (%)	Leaders	Share (%)	Leaders	Share (%)
ELF/Aquitaine (Handy Bag)	22	Polylina	17	Melitta	45	Cuki	22	FBE	37
FBE	12	Br. Alcan	11	Pely	6	Domopak	21	Reynolds	21
Akzo (Propsac)	11	HD. Plastics	3	Kraft	5	Comiset	2		
Private label	36		65		22		N/A		N/A

Share of Total, Five Countries

Melitta	10.8%
ELF/Aquitaine	6.3
FBE	8.6
Domopak	8.2
Private label	32.7
Total	66.6%

M = millions.

Source: Company records, dated 11/23/88.

CHAPTER 5

Marketing Research

Effective management of information is a prerequisite for successful decision making. Put simply, the better the information, the better the decision because information reduces uncertainty, and the less uncertainty, the less risky a decision.

Marketing managers are faced with three information-related tasks. They must first determine the kind and amount of information necessary for making a correct decision. They must then compare the costs of acquiring this information with its value in reducing uncertainty. Finally, managers must be able to organize, interpret, and evaluate information as it relates to the decision at hand.

Marketing research is one source of information for the marketing manager. Although definitions vary, marketing research can be thought of as a systematic procedure for providing marketers with actionable decision-making information. As such, marketing research facilitates decision making by providing information that is useful in both the identification and the solution of marketing problems.

Typically, the marketing manager is not directly involved in the practice of marketing research. Technical functions such as data collection, sampling, scaling, and statistical analysis are more likely to be performed by marketing-research specialists. Still, it is imperative that the marketing manager be familiar with the process, procedures, and techniques of marketing research. Only this familiarity will enable the manager to ascertain the true value of the information provided by marketing research.[1]

Because the decision-making process directly interfaces with the marketing-research process (the latter being a subset of the former), the marketing manager must be able to evaluate the following:

- Value of marketing-research-based information
- Marketing-research information-acquisition process

■ APPRAISING THE VALUE OF INFORMATION

From a conceptual perspective the value of information is reflected by the extent to which information can reduce decision-related uncertainty. Alternatively, the value of information is reflected by the degree to which the chances of making a correct decision are increased by use of information. Implicit in this perspective is the notion that the information being referred to is incremental information. Hence, information value implicitly refers to the value of incremental information—discrete units of information not currently available to the decision maker.

Given this perspective, information is potentially more valuable in certain decision situations than in others. Since the value of information may be defined as information benefits minus information costs, value increases as benefits increase or costs decrease. Additionally, though, information is potentially more valuable in a decision situation in which there is a great deal of uncertainty present and the consequences of an incorrect decision (the amount at stake) are substantial.

Quantitative Appraisal

As indicated in Chapter 3, decision analysis can be used to determine the value of information. Decision analysis is used to link together uncertainties in the environment and the alternatives available to a manager, and it can be extended to identify the upper limit to spend for research information as well.

In the El Nacho example in Chapter 3, decision analysis was used to determine that El Nacho management should maintain its prices, given the subjective probabilities of competitor actions and the attendant outcomes (payoffs) assigned to each alternative competitive reaction linkage. The analysis used to arrive at that decision is reconstructed in Exhibit 5.1.

Exhibit 5.1 also shows how the expected monetary value of "perfect" information (EMVPI) can be calculated. Simply speaking, EMVPI is the difference between what El Nacho would achieve in contribution dollars if its management knew for certain what competitors would do and the average contribution dollars realized without such information. In other words, if El Nacho knew for certain that competitors would maintain their price, the "maintain price" alternative would be selected. If El Nacho management knew for certain that competitors would reduce their price, however, the "reduce price" alternative would be chosen. Assuming El Nacho man-

E X H I B I T 5 . 1

Decision Analysis and the Value of Information

		Payoff Table Uncertainties	
		Competitors maintain price (probability = 0.9)	*Competitors reduce price (probability = 0.1)*
Alternatives	A$_1$: Reduce price	$150,000	$110,000
	A$_2$: Maintain price	$175,000	$90,000

Calculation of Expected Monetary Value (EMV):

$\text{EMV}_{A_1} = 0.9(\$150,000) + 0.1(\$110,000) = \$146,000$

$\text{EMV}_{A_2} = 0.9(\$175,000) + 0.1(\$90,000) = \$166,500$

Calculation of Expected Monetary Value of Perfect Information (EMVPI):

$\text{EMV}_{\text{certainty}} = 0.9(\$175,000) + 0.1(\$110,000) = \$168,500$

$\text{EMVPI} = \text{EMV}_{\text{certainty}} - \text{EMV}_{\text{best alternative}}$

$\text{EMVPI} = \$168,500 - \$166,500 = \$2,000$

agement faced this decision ten times and knew what competitor reaction would be each time, El Nacho management would make the appropriate decision each time. The result would be an EMV of $168,500. The difference of $2,000 between $168,500 and $166,500 (the best alternative without such information) is viewed as the upper limit to pay for "perfect" information.

Qualitative Appraisal

A question still remains: What constitutes good decision information? Intuitively, certain types of information would seem to be more valuable than others. Therefore, we need to address those explicit characteristics that make information valuable for decision making.

One such characteristic is the cost of information. Although cost (especially absolute cost) may be an overriding concern in determining whether a particular kind or form of information is to be utilized in a specific decision context, cost probably should not be the only characteristic taken into account. The value of information for decision making can also be evaluated according to five other characteristics. To be maximally useful for decision making, information must possess the characteristics of (1) accuracy, (2) currency, (3) sufficiency, (4) availability, and (5) relevancy. The extent to which information possesses these characteristics determines its practical value in the decision-making process.

Accuracy refers to the degree to which information reflects reality. In other words, information must closely approximate the true state of affairs. While no one would disagree with this statement, frequently there is a tendency to overlook the more subtle question "How much accuracy is required for a given decision to be correctly made?" Specifically, the level of accuracy required is best viewed in a relative context: What is the consequence of making an incorrect decision? If a television manufacturer is in the process of launching a new high-definition television (HDTV)—the success or failure of which may determine the future of the firm—there is a need for highly accurate decision information. Alternatively, if the decision relates to whether a restaurant should offer flat or round toothpicks, less accurate information will suffice. Hence, the accuracy criterion should be considered in a relative sense: How accurate must the data be for the specific decision at hand? In brief, information accuracy must be assessed relative to the importance of the decision and the probability and consequences of an incorrect decision.

Currency is the degree to which information reflects events in the present time period. Information must be up to date. Information on clothing styles or automobile travel in the early 1990s may be obsolete for decision making today. The clothing fashion cycle is so rapid that what was in style last fall is "ancient history" this year. Likewise, gasoline and oil price fluctuations can quickly render automobile travel information obsolete. Because of the rapidity with which environmental changes influence marketing, there is little likelihood that stale information will be decision-actionable.

Sufficiency refers to whether there is enough information to make a correct decision. The extent to which information is useful for decision making depends on its completeness and its detail. If information is not sufficient, complete, or detailed enough to permit a decision to be made, it is of little value to a decision maker. Although aggregated information on the existence or size of a market may be available, the lack of detailed information on its geographical, demographic, or attitudinal composition may preclude effective decision making as to what, if any, marketing activities should be directed toward that market.

Availability refers to having information accessible (in hand) when a decision is being made. A marketing manager faced with making a promotion budget decision by the end of July needs appropriate information before then. Even perfect information would be of no value if it was not available until August 1. Information must be available when a decision is being made. Tomorrow is too late.

Relevancy refers to the pertinency and applicability of information to the decision issue at hand. This is perhaps the single most important characteristic of information. Even if information possesses all the other characteristics of good information, it is of no use unless it is relevant. Although trade-offs frequently must be made among the other characteristics—the requirement of accuracy, for example, is often relaxed to ensure availability—relevancy should be the one characteristic immune to compromise. It is the one information ingredient essential for successful decision making.

Bad information—information that does not possess the characteristics just mentioned—may be worse than no information at all. Even if a decision maker does not have information, there is always a chance of making a correct decision. Though good information does not ensure good decisions (judgment is still required), bad information will normally result in poor decisions. The decision maker has little opportunity to make a correct decision if the underlying information is incorrect. The decision to introduce a new recipe for Coca-Cola is a classic example of how bad information can lead to a poor decision. Coca-Cola marketing research focused heavily on taste tests (which favored the new recipe over the old) but failed to consider the emotional bond to the original Coca-Cola. As a result, marketing-research experts have labeled the research effort "bad research," and industry executives have criticized Coca-Cola for neglecting to use a "large dose of judgment" in designing the research and interpreting the results.[2]

■ MANAGING THE INFORMATION-ACQUISITION PROCESS

The manager should play an active role in the marketing research information-acquisition process. Specific responsibilities are as follows:

1. Delineating information requirements by defining the problem to be studied
2. Devising the best way to obtain the information
3. Determining the amount to spend for the information
4. Deciding on the types of analysis and interpretation that will best solve the problem
5. Developing actionable marketing strategies from the information

Delineating Information Requirements

The most critical and difficult task a manager faces is the specification of information needed to make a decision. Specification of the kinds and amounts of information needed is based on an understanding of the problem confronting the manager. Consider the situation faced by the Gerber Products Company after it introduced a cereal for infants. Despite optimistic sales forecasts, actual sales performance was disappointing. Was the problem a less-than-expected sales volume, or was this merely evidence of a still more basic problem? If low sales volume was defined as the problem, then a manager would ask the fairly general question "Why has the sales volume failed to meet the forecasts?" Alternatively, if low sales volume was viewed as a result of more basic underlying factors, such as the marketing mix, market capacity, or competitive behavior, information could be gathered on all or any of these factors. Gerber executives chose to begin by examining existing company information on the distribution of the cereal, and they learned that the item was being distributed through only 25 percent of the outlets originally planned for it.[3]

This example illustrates two important points. First, issues facing organizations many times represent the tip of the iceberg; they are symptomatic of more fundamental problems. By addressing the sales-volume question, executives could collect information on a wide variety of topics. However, specification of the problem in terms of factors that could influence sales volume would enable a more disciplined and productive information-collection process to be implemented. This means that a model must be specified that identifies both the factors influencing the problem under investigation and the relationships among these factors. The idea of models and model building should not connote highly sophisticated or mathematical representations of a phenomenon. Simple (not simplistic) models often provide valuable insight and structure for thinking about a problem. For example, sales volume for a new product can be modeled as follows (emphasis in original):

> The number of people in the target market *times* the fraction who become aware of the product *times* the fraction who find it available *times* the share of purchases that triers devote to the new brand *times* the sales rate for the product class.[4]

Second, implicit in the Gerber example is the idea that existing or readily available information is sought out first. Once a problem has been defined, existing sources of information should be examined first. Not only is this information readily available, but it is often the most inexpensive and relevant information available. Only if it is inadequate should additional data be collected.

Devising the Best Means for Obtaining Information

The cost of information will depend on the means for obtaining it. The best means for getting the information necessary for decision making depends on the manager's information requirements, potential or available funds, time constraints, and an appraisal of the usefulness of information once obtained. Managers are often called on to decide whether information should be (1) generated internally, either from available organizational data or from data collected by the organization's personnel, or (2) acquired from external sources, either through standardized information services provided by them or through data collection carried out by them especially for the problem under investigation. Internal and external information sources often complement each other. It is not uncommon to get conflicting information from the two sources, however, and managers sometimes obtain redundant information when both sources are used.

As a generalization, Japanese executives are prone to rely on information gathered by themselves rather than by marketing research professionals, either inside or outside their organizations. Moreover, much of this information is in the form of "soft data," that is, impressions garnered from consumers who have purchased and used the products and from intermediaries (wholesalers and retailers) that sell the products and those of competitors. American and European executives are more likely to rely on marketing research professionals, either inside or outside their organizations, for "hard data" in numerical form produced by customer surveys and various kinds of syndicated, consumer-tracking data services. Increasingly, these two approaches to gathering information are converging. American and European marketing executives are spending more time with customers and intermediaries; Japanese executives have recognized efficiencies in gathering information through large-scale data collection efforts.[5]

Determining the Cost of Information

Information has a monetary cost in that the acquisition of data must be paid for as a direct expense. The actual amount spent for information is often related to the financial loss of making a poor decision. For instance, it is common for movie studios in the United States to spend upward of $200,000 on test screenings (sneak previews), audience research, and advertising research before a new film is released. Why? The cost of a "flop" is roughly equivalent to the $54 million necessary to produce and market a typical movie today.[6]

Information also has a time cost in that the time spent to gather information dictates when the decision can be made. The cost of time is an opportunity cost, described in Chapters 1 and 2. Thus, the expenditure of time in acquiring information is a relevant cost. For example, Campbell Soup Company "spent" 18 months testing a blended fruit juice called Juiceworks. By the time the company had completed its testing, three competing brands had been introduced, so Campbell dropped the product.[7] An important determinant in evaluating expenditures of money and time for information acquisition is the value of the information. Therefore, the manager must evaluate its accuracy, currency, sufficiency, availability, and relevancy to arrive at a decision about the amount of money and time that should be allocated to obtaining it.

Deciding on the Types of Analysis and Interpretation

Since marketing managers must ultimately make a decision based on the information provided by research, they should be involved in specifying the types of analyses performed on it. For example, a manager should specify how the information should be organized. A manager examining the sales of a product might find it useful to have sales data organized by geographical location of the sale, the type of intermediary selling the product, buyer characteristics, and so forth.

An important consideration in specifying the type of analysis is the selection of those factors that best present the information and assist the manager in focusing on critical aspects of the decision to be made. In this way, the manager can ensure that information is relevant—that he or she is not inundated with an impressive volume of meaningless information. Marketing research practice at Ocean Spray Cranberries, Inc., is a case in point. The Ocean Spray marketing manager for whom research is being conducted is expected to draft a "usage of results" statement when requesting research. This statement is used by the research department in developing a research program to assure that what is expected is ultimately delivered.[8]

Deciding how to interpret marketing research data is often a difficult task, even after the manager has specified how research data are to be presented. Consider the research conducted by Brown-Forman Distillers Corporation on Frost 8/80, a new brand of whiskey that was clear as opposed to being amber or pale brown like other whiskeys. The firm employed eight research firms and spent $500,000 studying virtually every aspect of the product and its potential market. The product failed despite development and marketing expenditures of $6.5 million. In retrospect, the executive who directed the sales for the brand placed the blame on the interpretation of research data:

> The research we had done probably was all right, but we misread it. The brand came off high on "uniqueness," and we interpreted this to mean the people would be anxious to try it. As it turned out, uniqueness was our biggest problem. The product looked like vodka but tasted like whiskey. It upset people. They didn't know what to make of it. As far as I'm concerned, that was it in a nutshell.[9]

Developing Actionable Strategies

A final responsibility of the manager is the development of actionable marketing strategies based on the information gathered. Even though this responsibility is considered last in this discussion, it follows directly from specifying the information requirements and permeates every aspect of the information-acquisition process. A quote from Mark Twain sums up the importance of knowing in advance the reason for collecting information: "Collecting data is much like collecting garbage. You must know in advance what you are going to do with the stuff before you collect it."[10]

If the information obtained is not actionable, in that it does not lend itself to effective decision making, then its costs have exceeded its value. By specifying in advance, either implicitly or explicitly, what various informational inputs will lead to in terms of specific actions, the manager can ensure that the entire marketing research information-acquisition process becomes a worthwhile venture.

NOTES

1. J. Walker Smith, "Beyond Anecdotes: Towards a Systematic Model of the Value of Marketing Research," *Marketing Research* (March 1991): 3–14.

2. For an extended description of the Coca-Cola example, see Robert F. Hartley, *Marketing Mistakes,* 5th ed. (New York: John Wiley & Sons, Inc., 1992): 294–310.

3. "The Low Birthrate Crimps the Baby-Food Market," *Business Week* (July 13, 1974): 44–50.

4. J. D. C. Little, "Decision Support Systems for Marketing Managers," *Journal of Marketing* 43 (1979): 9–27.

5. This discussion is based on Calvin I. Hodock, "The Decline and Fall of Marketing Research in Corporate America," *Marketing Research* (June 1991): 12–22; Johny K. Johansson and Ikujiro Nonaka, "Marketing Research the Japanese Way," *Harvard Business Review* (May–June 1987): 16–18, 22; and "Marketing in Japan: Taking Aim," *The Economist* (April 24, 1993): 74.

6. "Lights, Camera, Less Action," *Business Week* (July 1, 1996): 50–51.

7. "A Test for Market Research," *Newsweek* (December 28, 1987): 32–33.

8. John Tarsa, "Ocean Spray Marketing Research: Delivering Insights in a Customer/Supplier Relationship," *Marketing Research* (September 1991): 5–11.

9. F. Klein, "An Untimely End," in *Paths to Profit,* ed. J. Barnett (Princeton, NJ: Dow Jones Books, 1973): 36–42.

10. This quote, attributed to Mark Twain, is found in William Rudelius, W. Bruce Erickson, and William Bakula, Jr., *An Introduction to Contemporary Business* (New York: Harcourt Brace Jovanovich, 1976): 142.

South Delaware Coors, Inc.

Larry Brownlow was just beginning to realize the problem was more complex than he had thought. The problem, of course, was giving direction to Manson and Associates regarding what research should be completed by February 20, 1990, to determine market potential of a Coors beer distributorship for a two-county area in southern Delaware. With data from this research, Larry would be able to estimate the feasibility of such an operation before the March 5 application deadline. Larry knew his decision on whether to apply for the distributorship was the most important career choice he had ever faced.

■ LARRY BROWNLOW

Larry was just completing his M.B.A. and, from his standpoint, the Coors announcement of expansion into Delaware could hardly have been better timed. He had long ago decided the best opportunities and rewards were in smaller, self-owned businesses and not in the jungles of corporate giants. Because of a family tragedy some three years earlier, Larry found himself in a position to consider small business opportunities such as the Coors distributorship. Approximately $500,000 was held in trust for Larry, to be dispersed when he reached age 30. Until then, Larry and his family were living on an annual trust income of about $40,000. It was on the basis of this income that Larry had decided to leave his sales engineering job and return to graduate school for his M.B.A.

The decision to complete a graduate program and operate his own business had been easy to make. Although he could have retired and lived off investment income, Larry knew such a life would not be to his liking. Working with people and the challenge of making it on his own, Larry thought, were far preferable to enduring an early retirement.

Larry would be 30 in July, about the time money would actually be needed to start the business. In the meantime, he had access to about $15,000 for feasibility research. Although there certainly were other places to spend the money, Larry and his wife agreed the opportunity to acquire the distributorship could not be overlooked.

■ COORS, INC.

Coors' history dated back to 1873, when Adolph Coors built a small brewery in Golden, Colorado. Since then, the brewery had prospered and become the fourth-largest seller of beer in the country. Coors' operating philosophy could be summed

This case was prepared by Professor James E. Nelson and doctoral student Eric J. Karson, of the University of Colorado, as a basis for class discussion and is not designed to illustrate effective or ineffective handling of an administrative situation. Certain data have been disguised. Copyright by the Business Research Division, College of Business and Administration and the Graduate School of Business Administration, University of Colorado, Boulder, Colorado 80309-0419.

up as "hard work, saving money, devotion to the quality of the product, caring about the environment, and giving people something to believe in." Company operation is consistent with this philosophy. Headquarters and most production facilities are still located in Golden, Colorado, with a new Shenandoah, Virginia, facility aiding in nationwide distribution. Coors is still family operated and controlled. The company had issued its first public stock, $127 million worth of nonvoting shares, in 1975. The issue was enthusiastically received by the financial community despite its being offered during a recession.

Coors' unwillingness to compromise on the high quality of its product is well known both to its suppliers and to its consuming public. Coors beer requires constant refrigeration to maintain this quality, and wholesalers' facilities are closely controlled to ensure that proper temperatures are maintained. Wholesalers are also required to install and use aluminum can recycling equipment. Coors was one of the first breweries in the industry to recycle its cans.

Larry was aware of Coors' popularity with many consumers in adjacent states. However, Coors' corporate management was seen by some consumers to hold anti-union beliefs (because of a labor disagreement at the brewery some ten years ago and the brewery's current use of a nonunion labor force). Some other consumers perceived the brewery to be somewhat insensitive to minority issues, primarily in employment and distribution. These attitudes—plus many other aspects of consumer behavior—meant that Coors' sales in Delaware would depend greatly on the efforts of the two wholesalers planned for the state.

■ MANSON RESEARCH PROPOSAL

Because of the press of his studies, Larry had contacted Manson and Associates in January for their assistance. The firm was a Wilmington-based general research supplier that had conducted other feasibility studies in the south Atlantic region. Manson was well known for the quality of its work, particularly with respect to computer modeling. The firm had developed special expertise in modeling such things as population and employment levels for cities, counties, and other units of area for periods of up to ten years into the future.

Larry had met John Rome, senior research analyst for Manson, in January and discussed the Coors opportunity and appropriate research extensively. Rome promised a formal research proposal (Exhibit 1 on page 168) for the project, which Larry now held in his hand. It certainly was extensive, Larry thought, and reflected the professionalism he expected. Now came the hard part—choosing the more relevant research from the proposal—because he certainly couldn't afford to pay for it all. Rome had suggested a meeting for Friday, which gave Larry only three more days to decide.

Larry was at first overwhelmed. All the research would certainly be useful. He was sure he needed estimates of sales and costs in a form allowing managerial analysis, but what data in what form? Knowledge of competing operations' experience, retailer support, and consumer acceptance also seemed important for feasibility analysis. For example, what if consumers were excited about Coors and retailers indifferent, or the other way around? Finally, several of the studies would provide information that could be useful in later months of operation, in the areas of promotion and pricing, for example. The problem now appeared more difficult than before!

It would have been nice, Larry thought, to have had some time to perform part of the suggested research himself. However, there just was too much in the way of class assignments and other matters to allow him that luxury. Besides, using Manson and Associates would give him research results from an unbiased source. There would be plenty for him to do once he received the results anyway.

E X H I B I T   1

Research Proposal by Manson and Associates

January 16, 1990

Mr. Larry Brownlow
1198 West Lamar
Chester, PA 19345

Dear Larry:

It was a pleasure meeting you last week and discussing your business and research interests in Coors wholesaling. After further thought and discussion with my colleagues, the Coors opportunity appears even more attractive than when we met.

Appearances can be deceiving, as you know, and I fully agree some formal research is needed before you make application. Research that we recommend would proceed in two distinct stages and is described below.

Stage One Research, Based on Secondary Data and Manson Computer Models:

Study A: National and Delaware Per-Capita Beer Consumption for 1988–1992.
Description: Per-capita annual consumption of beer for the total population and for population age 21 and over in gallons is provided.
Source: Various publications, Manson computer model
Cost: $1,000

Study B: Population Estimates for 1986–1996 for Two Delaware Counties in Market Area.
Description: Annual estimates of total population and population age 21 and over are provided for the period 1986–1996.
Source: U.S. Bureau of Census, *Sales Management Annual Survey of Buying Power,* Manson computer model
Cost: $1,500

Study C: Estimates of Coors' Market Share for 1990–1995.
Description: Coors' market share for the two-county market area based on total gallons consumed is estimated for each year in the period 1990–1995. These data will be projected from Coors' nationwide experience.
Source: Various publications, Manson computer model
Cost: $2,000

Study D: Estimates of Number of Liquor and Beer Licenses for the Market area, 1990–1995.
Description: Projections of the number of on-premise sale operations and off-premise sale operations are provided.
Source: Delaware Department of Revenue, Manson computer model
Cost: $1,000

Study E: Beer Taxes Paid by Delaware Wholesalers for 1988 and 1989 in the Market Area.
Description: Beer taxes paid by each of the six presently operating competing beer wholesalers are provided. These figures can be converted to gallons sold by applying the state gallonage tax rate ($.06 per gallon).
Source: Delaware Department of Revenue
Cost: $200

Study F: Financial Statement Summary of Wine, Liquor, and Beer Wholesalers for Fiscal Year 1988.
Description: Composite balance sheets, income statements, and relevant measures of performance for 510 similar wholesaling operations in the United States are provided.
Source: Robert Morris Associates Annual Statement Studies, 1989 ed.
Cost: $49.50

Stage Two Research, Based on Primary Data:

Study G: Consumer Study.
Description: Study G involves focus-group interviews and a mail questionnaire to determine consumers' past experience, acceptance, and intention to buy

EXHIBIT 1 *(continued)*

Coors beer.[a] Three focus-group interviews would be conducted in the two counties in the market area. From these data, a questionnaire would be developed and sent to 300 adult residents in the market area, utilizing direct questions and a semantic differential scale to measure attitudes toward Coors beer, competing beers, and an ideal beer.
Source: Manson and Associates
Cost: $6,000

Study H: Retailer Study.
Description: Group interviews would be conducted with six potential retailers of Coors beer in one county in the market area to determine their past beer sales and experience and their intention to stock and sell Coors. From these data, a personal-interview questionnaire would be developed and executed at all appropriate retailers in the market area to determine similar data.
Source: Manson and Associates
Cost: $4,800

Study I: Survey of Retail and Wholesale Beer Prices.
Description: In-store interviews would be conducted with a sample of 50 retailers in the market area to estimate retail and wholesale prices for Budweiser, Miller Lite, Miller, Busch, Bud Light, Old Milwaukee, and Michelob.
Source: Manson and Associates
Cost: $2,000

Examples of the final report tables are attached [Exhibit 2, pages 170–174]. This should give you a better idea of the data you will receive.

As you can see, the research is extensive and, I might add, not cheap. However, the research as outlined will supply you with sufficient information to make an estimate of the feasibility of a Coors distributorship, the investment for which is substantial.

I have scheduled 9:00 A.M. next Friday as a time to meet with you to discuss the proposal in more detail. Time is short, but we firmly feel the study can be completed by February 20, 1990. If you need more information in the meantime, please feel free to call.

Sincerely,

John Rome
Senior Research Analyst

---

[a] *A focus-group interview consists of a moderator's questioning and listening to a group of 8 to 12 consumers.*

E X H I B I T   2

Examples of Final Research Report Tables

Table A
National and Delaware Residents' Annual Beer Consumption per Capita, 1988–1992 (Gallons)

	U.S. Consumption		Delaware Consumption	
Year	Based on Entire Population	Based on Population Age 21 and Over	Based on Entire Population	Based on Population Age 21 and Over
1988				
1989				
1990				
1991				
1992				

Source: Study A.

Table B
Population Estimates for 1986–1996 for Two Delaware Counties in Market Area

County	Entire Population					
	1986	1988	1990	1992	1994	1996
Kent						
Sussex						

County	Population Age 21 and Over					
	1986	1988	1990	1992	1994	1996
Kent						
Sussex						

Source: Study B.

Table C
Estimates of Coors' Market Share for 1990–1995

Year	Market Share (%)
1990	
1991	
1992	
1993	
1994	
1995	

Source: Study C.

EXHIBIT 2 *(continued)*

Table D
Estimates of Number of Liquor and Beer Licenses for the Market Area, 1990–1995

Type of License	1990	1991	1992	1993	1994	1995
All beverages						
Retail beer and wine						
Off-premise beer only						
Veterans beer and liquor						
Fraternal						
Resort beer and liquor						

Source: Study D.

Table E
Beer Taxes Paid by Beer Wholesalers in the Market Area, 1988 and 1989

Wholesaler	1988 Tax Paid ($)	1989 Tax Paid ($)
A		
B		
C		
D		
E		
F		

Source: Study E

Note: Delaware beer tax is $0.06 gallon.

Table F
Financial Statement Summary for 510 Wholesalers of Wine, Liquor, and Beer in Fiscal Year 1988

Assets	Percentage
Cash and equivalents	
Accounts and notes receivable, net	
Inventory	
All other current	
Total current	
Fixed assets, net	
Intangibles, net	
All other noncurrent	
Total	100.0

EXHIBIT 2 *(continued)*

Table F *(continued)*

Liabilities	*Percentage*
Notes payable, short term	
Current maturity long-term debt	
Accounts and notes payable, trade	
Accrued expenses	
All other current	
Total current	
Long-term debt	
All other noncurrent	
Net worth	____
Total liabilities and net worth	100.0
Income Data	
Net sales	100.0
Cost of sales	
Gross profit	
Operating expenses	
Operating profit	
All other expenses, net	____
Profit before taxes	
Ratios	
Quick	
Current	
Debt/worth	
Sales/receivables	
Cost of sales/inventory	
Percentage profit before taxes, based on total assets	

Interpretation of Statement Studies Figures:
RMA recommends that Statement Studies data be regarded only as general guidelines and not as absolute industry norms. There are several reasons why the data may not be fully representative of a given industry:

1. The financial statements used in the Statement Studies are not selected by any random or statistically reliable method. RMA member banks voluntarily submit the raw data they have available each year, with these being the only constraints: (a) The fiscal year-ends of the companies reported may not be from April 1 through June 29, and (b) their total assets must be less than $100 million.
2. Many companies have varied product lines; however, the Statement Studies categorize them by their primary product Standard Industrial Classification (SIC) number only.
3. Some of the industry samples are rather small in relation to the total number of firms in a given industry. A relatively small sample can increase the chances that some of our composites do not fully represent an industry.
4. There is the chance that an extreme statement can be present in a sample, causing a disproportionate influence on the industry composite. This is particularly true in a relatively small sample.
5. Companies within the same industry may differ in their method of operations, which in turn can directly influence their financial statements. Since they are included in our sample, too, these statements can significantly affect our composite calculations.
6. Other considerations that can result in variations among different companies engaged in the same general line of business are different labor markets, geographical location, different accounting methods, quality of products handled, sources and methods of financing, and terms of sale.

For these reasons, RMA does not recommend that Statement Studies figures be considered as absolute norms for a given industry. Rather, the figures should be used only as general guidelines and in addition to the other methods of financial analysis. RMA makes no claim as to the representativeness of the figures printed in this book.

Source: Study F (Robert Morris Associates, © 1989).

EXHIBIT 2 *(continued)*

Table G
Consumer Questionnaire Results

	Percentage		*Percentage*
Consumed Coors in the past:		Usually buy beer at:	
Attitudes toward Coors:	%	Liquor stores	
Strongly like		Taverns and bars	
Like		Supermarkets	
Indifferent/no opinion		Corner grocery	
Dislike			
Strongly dislike			
Total	100.0	Total	100.0
Weekly beer consumption:		Features considered	
Less than 1 can		important when buying beer:	
1–2 cans		Taste	
3–4 cans		Brand name	
5–6 cans		Price	
7–8 cans		Store location	
9 cans and over		Advertising	
Total	100.0	Carbonation	
Intention to buy Coors:		Other	
Certainly will		Total	100.0
Maybe will			
Not sure			
Maybe will not			
Certainly will not			
Total	100.0		

Semantic Differential Scale, Consumers[a]

	Extremely	*Very*	*Somewhat*	*Somewhat*	*Very*	*Extremely*	
Masculine	—	—	—	—	—	—	Feminine
Healthful	—	—	—	—	—	—	Unhealthful
Cheap	—	—	—	—	—	—	Expensive
Strong	—	—	—	—	—	—	Weak
Old-fashioned	—	—	—	—	—	—	New
Upper-class	—	—	—	—	—	—	Lower-class
Good taste	—	—	—	—	—	—	Bad taste

[a] *Profiles would be provided for Coors, three competing beers, and an ideal beer.*

Source: Study G.

EXHIBIT 2 (*continued*)

Table H
Retailer Questionnaire Results

	Percentage		*Percentage*
Brands of beer carried:		Beer sales:	
Budweiser		Budweiser	
Miller Lite		Miller Lite	
Miller		Miller	
Busch		Busch	
Bud Light		Bud Light	
Old Milwaukee		Old Milwaukee	
Michelob		Michelob	
		Others	
Intention to sell Coors:			
Certainly will		Total	100.0
Maybe will			
Not sure			
Maybe will not			
Certainly will not			
Total	100.0		

Semantic Differential Scale, Retailers[a]							
	Extremely	*Very*	*Somewhat*	*Somewhat*	*Very*	*Extremely*	
Masculine	—	—	—	—	—	—	Feminine
Healthful	—	—	—	—	—	—	Unhealthful
Cheap	—	—	—	—	—	—	Expensive
Strong	—	—	—	—	—	—	Weak
Old-fashioned	—	—	—	—	—	—	New
Upper-class	—	—	—	—	—	—	Lower-class
Good taste	—	—	—	—	—	—	Bad taste

[a] *Profiles would be provided for Coors, three competing beers, and an ideal bear.*

Source: Study H.

Table I
Retail and Wholesale Prices for Selected Beers in the Market Area

Beer	*Wholesale Six-Pack Price[a] (dollars)*	*Retail Six-Pack Price[b] (dollars)*
Budweiser		
Miller Lite		
Miller		
Busch		
Bud Light		
Old Milwaukee		
Michelob		

[a] *Price at which the wholesaler sold to retailers.*

[b] *Price at which the retailer sold to consumers.*

Source: Study I.

■ INVESTING AND OPERATING DATA

Larry was not completely in the dark regarding investment and operating data for the distributorship. In the past two weeks he had visited two beer wholesalers in his home town of Chester, Pennsylvania, who handled Anheuser-Busch and Miller beer, to get a feel for their operation and marketing experience. It would have been nice to interview a Coors wholesaler, but Coors management had instructed all of their distributors to provide no information to prospective applicants.

Although no specific financial data had been discussed, general information had been provided in a cordial fashion because of the noncompetitive nature of Larry's plans. Based on his conversations, Larry had made the following estimates:

Inventory		$240,000
Equipment:		
Delivery trucks	$150,000	
Forklift	20,000	
Recycling and miscellaneous equipment	20,000	
Office equipment	10,000	
Total equipment		200,000
Warehouse		320,000
Land		40,000
Total investment		$800,000

A local banker had reviewed Larry's financial capabilities and saw no problem in extending a line of credit on the order of $400,000. Other family sources also might loan as much as $400,000 to the business.

To get a rough estimate of fixed expenses, Larry decided to plan on having four route salespeople, a secretary, and a warehouse manager. Salaries for these people and himself would run about $160,000 annually, plus some form of incentive compensation he had yet to determine. Other fixed or semifixed expenses were estimated as follows:

Equipment depreciation	$35,000
Warehouse depreciation	15,000
Utilities and telephone	12,000
Insurance	10,000
Personal property taxes	10,000
Maintenance and janitorial services	5,600
Miscellaneous	2,400
	$90,000

According to the two wholesalers, beer in bottles and cans outsold keg beer by a three-to-one margin. Keg beer prices at the wholesale level were about 45 percent of prices for beer in bottles and cans.

■ MEETING

The entire matter deserved much thought. Maybe it was a golden opportunity, maybe not. The only thing certain was that research was needed, Manson and Associates was ready, and Larry needed time to think. Today is Tuesday, Larry thought—only three days until he and John Rome would get together for direction.

Soft and Silky Shaving Gel

On Friday, January 3, 1997, Phoebe Masters, the newly appointed Product Manager for hand and body lotions at Ms-Tique Corporation, was faced with her first decision one day after her promotion. She had to decide whether to introduce a new package design for the company's Soft and Silky Shaving Gel. The major questions were whether a $5^{1}/_{2}$-ounce or a 10-ounce aerosol container should be introduced and whether she should approve additional funds for a market test. Timing was critical because the incidence of women's shaving would increase during the spring months and reach its peak during the summer months.

■ THE COMPANY AND THE PRODUCT

Soft and Silky Shaving Gel is marketed by Ms-Tique Corporation, a manufacturer of women's personal-care products with sales of $122.5 million in 1996. The company's line of products includes facial creams, hand and body lotions, and a full line of women's toiletries. Products are sold by drug and food-and-drug stores through rack jobbers. Rack jobbers are actually wholesalers that set up retail displays and keep them stocked with merchandise. They receive a margin of 20 percent off the sales price to retailers.

Soft and Silky Shaving Gel was introduced in the spring of 1983. The product was viewed as a logical extension of the company's line of hand and body lotions and required few changes in packaging and manufacturing. The unique dimension of the introduction was that Soft and Silky Shaving Gel was positioned as a high-quality women's shaving gel. The positioning strategy was successful in differentiating Soft and Silky Shaving Gel from existing men's and women's shaving creams and gels at the time. Moreover, rack jobbers were able to obtain product placement in the women's personal-care section of drug and food-and-drug stores, thus emphasizing the product's positioning statement. Furthermore, placement apart from men's shaving products minimized direct price comparisons with men's shaving creams, since Soft and Silky Shaving Gel was premium-priced—with a suggested retail price of $3.95 per $5^{1}/_{2}$-ounce tube. Retailers received a 40 percent margin on the suggested retail selling price.

Soft and Silky Shaving Gel has been sold in a tube since its introduction. This packaging was adopted because the company did not have the technology to produce aerosol containers in 1983. Furthermore, the company's manufacturing policy was and continues to be to utilize existing production capacity whenever possible. As of early 1997, all products sold by Ms-Tique Corporation were packaged in tubes, bottles, or jars.

This case was prepared by Professor Roger A. Kerin, Edwin L. Cox School of Business, Southern Methodist University, as a basis for class discussion and is not designed to illustrate effective or ineffective handling of an administrative situation. Certain names have been disguised. Copyright © 1997 by Roger A. Kerin. No part of this case may be reproduced without written permission of the copyright holder.

Soft and Silky Shaving Gel Income Statement for the Year Ending December 31, 1996

Sales		$1,862,000
Cost of goods sold (incl. freight)[a]		392,000
Gross profit		$1,470,000
Assignable costs:		
Advertising and promotion costs	$577,220	
Overhead and administrative costs	210,780	788,000
Brand contribution		$ 682,000

[a] For analysis purposes, treat the cost of goods sold and freight cost as the only variable cost.

Soft and Silky Shaving Gel had been profitable from the time of its introduction. Although the market for women's shaving cream and gels was small, compared to men's shaving cream and gels, Soft and Silky's unique positioning had created a "customer franchise," in the words of Heather Courtwright, the Soft and Silky brand assistant. "We have a unique product for the feminine woman who considers herself special." Soft and Silky Shaving Gel sales were $1,862,000 in 1996 with a 980,000 unit volume (see Exhibit 1).

■ WOMEN'S SHAVING

Research on women's shaving commissioned by Masters' predecessors over the past decade had produced a number of findings useful in preparing annual marketing plans for Soft and Silky Shaving Gel. The major findings and selected marketing actions prompted by these findings are described below.

Methods of Hair Removal and Shaving Frequency

Women use a variety of methods for hair removal. The most popular method is simply shaving with razors and soap and water. Shaving with razors and shaving cream and gels is the next most used method, followed by shaving with electric razors. Women typically have their own razors and purchase their own supplies of blades. Approximately 42 million women shave with a razor; 15 million women use electric shavers.

Over 80 percent of women shave at least once per week, and women who work outside the home shave more frequently than those who do not. On average, women shave ten times per month and shave nine times more skin than men per shaving occasion (men shave 5.33 times each week on average). Shaving frequency varies by season, with the summer months producing the greatest shaving activity (see Exhibit 2 on page 178). Accordingly, in-store promotions and multipack deals were scheduled during the summer.

Attitudes Toward Shaving

Women view shaving as a necessary evil. When queried about their ideal shaving cream or gel, women typically respond that they want a product that contains a moisturizer, reduces irritation, and makes shaving easier. It appears that four out of five women use a moisturizer after shaving.

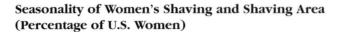

**Seasonality of Women's Shaving and Shaving Area
(Percentage of U.S. Women)**

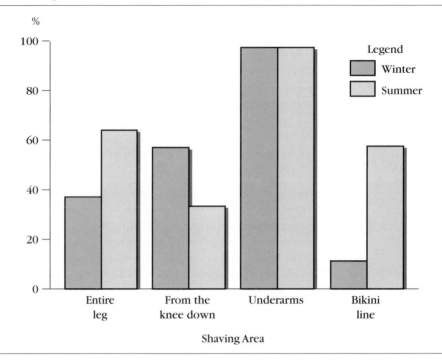

These specific findings resulted in a change in the Soft and Silky Shaving Gel ingredient formulation in 1987. Prior to 1987, the product contained only aloe. In 1987, three additional moisturizers were added to the product, including vitamin E. These ingredients were emphasized on the package and in-store promotions and media advertising.

Market Size and Competitive Products

Industry sources estimate the U.S. dollar value of women's "wet shaving" products to be over $150 million in 1996, at manufacturer's prices. Sales growth has been in the range of 3 to 5 percent per year since 1991. Razors account for the bulk of sales growth and annual sales.

Historically, women who used shaving cream or gels had few "women's-only" products to choose from. However, since 1991, a vibrant women's shaving cream and gel category has emerged due to new-product activity, increased advertising and promotion, and improved shaving technology. Some industry analysts pointed toward the introduction of Gillette's Sensor Razor for Women as one important growth stimulant. Other analysts cited improvements in the quality of shaving creams and gels for women and increased advertising. Until 1993, only two competitive products were normally available in the drug and food-and-drug stores served by Ms-Tique Corporation rack jobbers. These products were S. C. Johnson's Skintimate (formerly called Soft Sense) and Soft Shave, a lotion sold by White Laboratories. By late 1996, seven brands existed in the women's shaving cream or gel category even though all were not stocked by stores that carried Soft and Silky Shaving Gel. Exhibit 3 shows representative brands, sizes, forms (cream, gel, lotion), and typical retail prices. Ms-Tique Corporation advertising and promotion for Soft and Silky Shaving

EXHIBIT 3

Representative Women's Shaving Products

Brand (Manufacturer)	Size[a]	Form	Price/Price Per Oz.
Skintimate (S. C. Johnson)	7 oz.	Gel	$2.48/$.35
Skintimate (S. C. Johnson)	10 oz.	Cream	$2.48/$.25
Satin Care (Gillette)	7 oz.	Gel	$2.30/$.33
Hers (Medtech Labs)	7.5 oz.	Cream	$2.17/$.29
Soft Shave (White Labs)	10 oz.	Lotion	$2.29/$.23
Barbasol Pure Silk (Pfizer)	7 oz.	Cream	$1.99/$.28
Aveeno (Ryoelle Labs–Div. of S. C. Johnson)	7 oz.	Gel	$3.39/$.48
Inverness Ultra-Lubricating Shaving Gel (Inverness Corp.)	6 oz.	Gel	$2.15/$.36
Soft and Silky Shaving Gel (Ms-Tique Corp.)	5.5 oz.	Gel	$3.95/$.72

[a] *Several manufacturers also sold smaller 2, 2$^1/_2$, and 2$^3/_4$ ounce sizes designed for travel purposes.*

Gel had responded to the increase in competition. Expenditures had increased each year since 1993, reaching 31 percent of sales in 1996.

By 1996, the dominant packaging for women's shaving cream or gels had become the aerosol container. Only a few shaving gels and brands were sold in tubes or plastic bottles, including Soft and Silky Shaving Gel, Soft Shave lotion, and Inverness Ultra-Lubricating Shaving Gel.

■ NEW PACKAGE DESIGN

The idea for a new package design was provided by Masters' brand assistant, Heather Courtwright. She originally proposed the new package to Masters' predecessor in July 1996. Her recommendation was based on four developments. First, unit sales volume for Soft and Silky Shaving Gel had declined and then plateaued in recent years (see Exhibit 4 on page 180). Second, the growth of Soft and Silky Shaving Gel had strained manufacturing capacity. In the past, production of Soft and Silky Shaving Gel had been easily integrated into the firm's production schedules. However, growth in the entire line of hand and body lotions, coupled with Soft and Silky Shaving Gel sales, had overburdened production capacity and scheduling. Moreover, inspection of shipping records indicated that the product's fill rate (that is, Ms-Tique Corporation's ability to supply quantities requested by retailers) had dropped, leading to out-of-stock situations and lost sales. Third, the company had no manufacturing capacity-expansion plans for the next three years. And finally, the aerosol packaging had become the dominant design for women's shaving creams and gels by 1996.

Courtwright's observations prompted a preliminary study of outsourcing opportunities for a new package design. Her study included visits to several firms specializing in "contract filling" and requests for production proposals. A contract filler purchases cans, propellants, caps, and valves from a variety of sources and then assembles these components, including the product fill (that is, shaving gel), into the final container. The production method is called pressure filling. In this method, the cap and valve are inserted in the can and then sealed. At the same time, a vacuum is

EXHIBIT 4

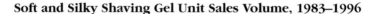

Soft and Silky Shaving Gel Unit Sales Volume, 1983–1996

Unit Volume

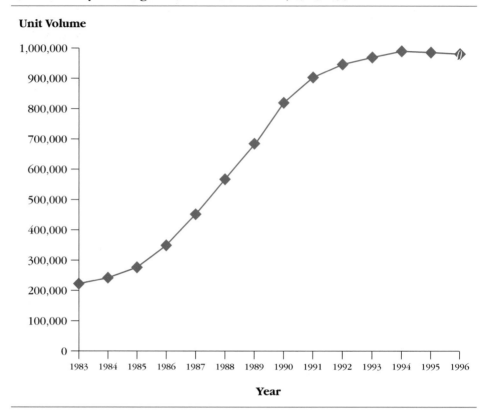

Year

created in the container. The product fill and propellant are then injected under high pressure through the valve into the can.

Her review of supplier proposals led her to choose one that was capable of meeting production requirements and providing certain "value-added" features. For example, the chosen supplier could deliver a propellant with no chlorofluorocarbons (CFCs), which are harmful to the earth's ozone layer. Also, the container's bottom would be rust-proof and leave no rust ring when wet. This feature was desired because most women shave in the bathtub or shower and tend to leave a wet can on the tub's porcelain, which can leave a rust stain. In addition, the supplier could produce and ship product directly from its manufacturing facility at a lower per unit cost than the tube container and was prepared to maintain an adequate safety stock of inventory. The only drawback in the supplier's proposal was that only $5^{1}/_{2}$- and 10-ounce containers could be produced without making significant and expensive changes in its equipment. The typical sizes for women's shaving creams and gels were 7-ounce and 10-ounce containers.

The estimated total cost of producing and delivering to retailers a 10-ounce aerosol can of shaving gel was $0.29. A minimum order of 100,000 10-ounce cans would be required. Courtwright believed the suggested retail price would be set at $4.25 per 10-ounce can, reflecting Soft and Silky's premium-price strategy. The estimated total cost of producing and delivering to retailers a $5^{1}/_{2}$-ounce aerosol can of shaving gel was $0.24, and the suggested retail price would be $3.50. A 100,000-unit minimum order would be required. A one-time set-up charge for the Soft and Silky

Shaving Gel production line and package graphics was $5,000, due and payable by Ms-Tique Corporation upon the signing of the supply agreement. This charge would be the same whether one or both sizes were produced.

■ PRELIMINARY TESTS

In November 1996, Courtwright received authorization from Masters' predecessor to spend $25,000 to assess consumer response to the proposed container. Her proposal was approved on the basis of the cost data provided and the recognition that use of a contract filler would require no incremental investment in company manufacturing capacity.

Courtwright commissioned a large marketing research firm to conduct four focus-group studies.[1] Two focus groups would involve current users of Soft and Silky Shaving Gel, and two focus groups would involve users of shaving creams and gels other than Soft and Silky Shaving Gel and soap and water users. The principal information sought from these focus group studies was as follows:

1. Are present customers and noncustomers receptive to the new package?

2. At what rate would present customers convert to the aerosol can, and would noncustomers switch over to Soft and Silky Shaving Gel?

3. Where, in drug and food-and-drug stores, would customers and noncustomers expect to find the aerosol can?

4. Is the suggested retail price acceptable?

In addition, the marketing research firm was asked to examine analogous situations of package changes and report its findings.

In late December 1996, the marketing research firm presented its findings to Courtwright, two days after Masters' predecessor resigned to take a position with another company. There were five principal findings from the focus groups:

1. Customers and noncustomers were unanimously in favor of the aerosol can. The 10-ounce can was the favorite, since it would require fewer purchases.

2. Twenty percent of Soft and Silky Shaving Gel customers said they would convert to the 10-ounce can; 25 percent said they would convert to the $5\frac{1}{2}$-ounce can.

3. One-fourth of the noncustomers said they would switch over to the aerosol can irrespective of can size. These consumers' preference for the aerosol over the tube package was their principal reason (in addition to price) for not buying Soft and Silky Shaving Gel previously.

4. Customers expected to find the aerosol can next to the tube container. Noncustomers expected to find the aerosol container stocked with women's toiletries.

5. The pricing was acceptable and actually favored by current customers. Noncustomers thought the suggested retail price was somewhat high, but liked the value-added features and would try the product.

In addition to these findings, the marketing research firm presented ten case histories in which marketers of men's shaving cream had introduced a new package. (There was no distinction made with respect to size of package, whether the pack-

---

[1] A *focus-group* interview consists of a moderator's questioning and listening to a group of 8 to 12 consumers.

EXHIBIT 5

Soft and Silky Shaving Gel Sales Forecasts by Size and Type of Container

Forecast A: Low estimate for 5^1/$_2$-ounce aerosol package addition

5^1/$_2$-oz. tube package volume		4,300,000 ounces
5^1/$_2$-oz. aerosol package volume:		
Cannibalized volume	1,072,587	
Net new volume	150,000	1,222,587
		5,522,587 ounces

Forecast B: High estimate for 5^1/$_2$-ounce aerosol package addition

5^1/$_2$-oz. tube package volume		4,200,000 ounces
5^1/$_2$-oz. aerosol package volume:		
Cannibalized volume	1,172,587	
Net new volume	250,000	1,422,587
		5,622,587 ounces

Forecast C: Low estimate for 10-ounce aerosol package addition

5^1/$_2$-oz. tube package volume		4,500,000 ounces
10-oz. aerosol package volume:		
Cannibalized volume	872,587	
Net new volume	400,000	1,272,587
		5,772,587 ounces

Forecast D: High estimate for 10-ounce aerosol package addition

5^1/$_2$-oz. tube package volume		4,800,000 ounces
10-oz. aerosol package volume:		
Cannibalized volume	572,587	
Net new volume	750,000	1,322,587
		6,122,587 ounces

age change was from aerosol to nonaerosol, or vice versa, or previous sales performance.) Two statistics were highlighted: first-year sales with the combined packages and the cannibalization rate for the existing package. According to the report,

> It is difficult to draw one-to-one comparisons between the experience of other shaving creams and gels and that of Soft and Silky Shaving Gel, given its unique market position. We have tried to do so after examining ten product-design changes. Our estimates [Exhibit 5] are broken down into a "high" and a "low" forecast for each package size. Seven out of the ten products studied experienced the "high" situation presented; three experienced the "low" situation. We see the 10-ounce package as producing the largest increase in ounces sold. Even with the cannibalism effect operating, we believe that an additional package will produce higher sales, in ounces, than the Soft and Silky Shaving Gel forecasted volume of 5,372,587 ounces (976,834 5^1/$_2$-ounce tubes) for 1997. Only a market test can indicate what will actually occur.

■ THE PACKAGING AND TEST MARKET DECISION

Courtwright presented the research firm's findings to Phoebe Masters on January 3, 1997, one day after Masters became Product Manager for hand and body lotions. Masters listened attentively as Courtwright summarized the research findings and recommended that a market test be conducted to determine the best package size.

Courtwright's test-market recommendation included a proposal to introduce the new package design in a limited cross-section of drug and food-and-drug stores, including heavy-volume and low-volume stores, that presently carried Soft and Silky Shaving Gel. Test stores would be isolated geographically from nontest stores. The new package would be placed among women's toiletries, and the test would run for three months, beginning April 1, 1997. The April 1 start date was necessary to assure that adequate supply of the new package was available. One-half of the stores would carry the $5^1/_2$-ounce container, and the other half would carry the 10-ounce container. The test would include a full complement of promotional aids, including newspaper ads and point-of-purchase displays, and would approximate a full-scale introduction.

Courtwright's estimated cost for the test market was $15,000, which included the cost of gathering marketing research data on the cannibalization rate and incremental sales growth. In addition, the $5,000 supplier set-up charge would have to be paid. However, Courtwright negotiated a 20,000 unit minimum order for each package size for the test market. No other incremental costs would be charged against the products. Sales and marketing efforts for the existing tube package would remain unchanged during the course of the test.

Late in the evening of Friday, January 3, 1997, Masters found herself considering whether the $5^1/_2$-ounce or the 10-ounce container should be introduced. She believed it unwise to introduce both sizes, given the uncertainty of market acceptance, and packaging practices of most competitors. She also wondered whether Courtwright's test-market proposal should be adopted. Masters was confident that, given the product's sales history, the existing Soft and Silky Shaving Gel package would produce sales of 976,834 units (a .32 percent decrease from 1996) in 1997 if no new package was introduced. She was also confident that a new package would simultaneously cannibalize the existing package and generate incremental unit volume. Therefore, she knew that her decision on the package sizes and test market would have to focus on what was best for the Soft and Silky Shaving Gel product line, assuming an aerosol container would be marketed alongside the original tube container.

Masters also sensed that the new package had become a pet project for Courtwright. Courtwright had championed the idea for six months in addition to working on a variety of other assignments. Furthermore, she had heard that Courtwright felt that she, not Masters, should have been promoted to Product Manager for hand and body lotions given her association with the line for five years. Given the situation, Masters believed that her handling of this decision would affect her working relationship with Courtwright.

MacTec Control AB

"The choices themselves seem simple enough," thought Georg Carlsson, "either we enter the U.S. market in Pennsylvania and New York, we forget about the U.S. for the time being, or we do some more marketing research." The difficult part was the decision.

Georg was president of MacTec Control AB, a Swedish firm located in Kristianstad. Georg had begun MacTec in 1980 along with his wife, Jessie. MacTec had grown rapidly and boasted some 30 employees and annual revenues of about $2.8 million by 1990. Since 1985, MacTec had been partly owned by the Perstorp Corporation, whose headquarters were located nearby. Perstorp was a large manufacturer of chemicals and chemical products, with operations in 18 countries and annual revenues of about $600 million. Perstorp had provided MacTec with capital and managerial advice, as well as chemical analysis technology.

■ MACTEC'S AQUALEX SYSTEM

MacTec's product line centered about its Aqualex System, a design of computer hardware and software for the monitoring and control of pressurized water flows. Most often these water flows consisted of either potable water or sewage effluent, as these liquids were stored, moved, or treated by municipal water departments.

The Aqualex System employed MacTec's MPDII microcomputer (see Exhibits 1 and 2 on page 186) installed at individual pumping stations where liquids are stored and moved. Often these stations were located quite far apart, linking geographically dispersed water users (households, businesses, etc.) to water and sewer systems. The microcomputer performed a number of important functions—it controlled the starts, stops, and alarms of up to four pumps; monitored levels and available capacities of storage reservoirs; checked pump capacities and power consumptions; and recorded pump flows. It could even measure amounts of rainfall entering reservoirs and adjust pump operations or activate an alarm as needed. Each microcomputer could also be easily connected to a main computer to allow remote control of pumping stations and produce a variety of charts and graphs useful in evaluating pump performance and scheduling needed maintenance.

The Aqualex System provided a monitoring function that human operators could not match in terms of sophistication, immediacy, and cost. The system permitted each individual substation to control its own pumping operations; collect, analyze, and store data; forecast trends; transmit data and alarms to a central computer; and receive remote commands. Alarms could also be transmitted directly to a pocket-sized receiver carried by one or more operators on call. A supervisor could continually monitor pumping operations in a large system entirely via a computer

EXHIBIT 1

Information on the MPDII Microcomputer

MPDII CONTROLS AND MONITORS THE PUMPING STATIONS

An MPDII microcomputer is installed at a pumping station and works as an independent, intelligent computer. When required, it can go on-line with the central computer and report its readings there.

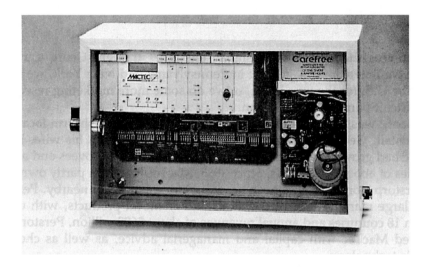

HERE ARE SOME OF THE FUNCTIONS OF THE MPDII:

- It governs the starts, stops, and alarms of up to four pumps, controlled by an integrated, piezo-resistive pressure-level sensor.
- It checks the sump level.
- It checks pump capacity and changes in pump capacity.
- It activates an alarm when readings reach preset deviation limits.
- It registers precipitation and activates an alarm in case of heavy rain.
- It constantly monitors pump power consumption and activates an alarm in case of unacceptable deviation.
- It registers current pump flow by means of advanced calculations of inflow and outfeed from the sump.
- It can register accumulated time for overflow.
- It switches from forward to reverse action, even by remote command.
- It stores locally the last nine alarm instances with time indications. These may be read directly on an LCD display.
- It can be remotely programmed from the central computer.

An MPDII does a great job, day after day, year after year.

terminal at a central location and send commands to individual pumps, thereby saving costly service calls and time. The system also reduced the possibility of overflows that could produce disastrous flooding of nearby communities.

MacTec personnel would work with water and sewage engineers to design and install the desired Aqualex System. Personnel would also train engineers and operators to work with the system and would be available 24 hours a day for consultation. If needed, a MacTec engineer could be physically present to assist engineers and op-

EXHIBIT 2

Computerized Monitoring and Control of Water Treatment Plants

The Aqualex System cuts operating and maintenance costs for water treatment plants.

The System takes over most of the monitoring and control of the plant by means of computerized controls. This frees resources for use in planned and efficient maintenance work, type of work that cannot be automated.

The Aqualex System is based on a number of intelligent computer sub-stations. These are placed at the pumping stations, sewage treatment plant, waterworks, etc. and are on-line to the central computer.

The computer sub-stations can independently handle local process control, store readings and analyze trends. They carry on advanced communication with the central computer to transmit readings and alarms and receive remote commands.

The central computer has the capacity to process the readings received from the sub-stations and present them in the form of reports and trends. Alarms can also be transmitted to one or more pocket-sized receivers with alarm code displays.

The operator on call can monitor the entire system at home by means of a portable home terminal. This terminal also has the capacity for remote commands, which saves many costly service calls.

The Aqualex System does the job of many people with high precision and reliability.

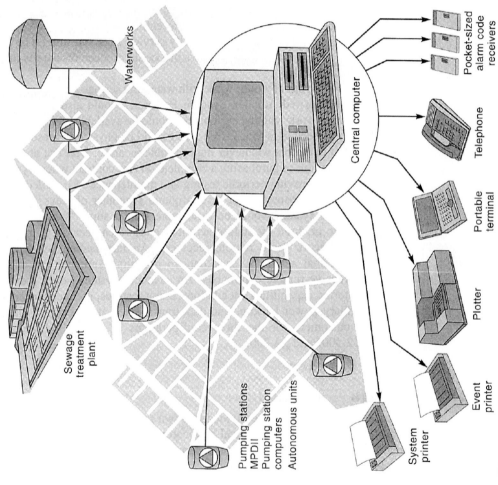

Waterworks

Sewage treatment plant

Pumping stations
MPDII
Pumping station computers
Autonomous units

Central computer

Pocket-sized alarm code receivers

Telephone

Portable terminal

Plotter

System printer

Event printer

erators whenever major problems arose. MacTec also offered its clients the option of purchasing a complete service contract whereby MacTec personnel would provide periodic testing and maintenance of installed systems.

An Aqualex System could be configured a number of ways. In its most basic form, the system would be little more than a small "black box" that monitored two or three lift station activities and, when necessary, transmitted an alarm to one or more remote receivers. An intermediate system would monitor additional activities, send data to a central computer via telephone lines, and receive remote commands. An advanced system would provide the same monitoring capabilities but add forecasting features, maintenance management, auxiliary power backup, and data transmission and reception via radio. Prices to customers for the three configurations in early 1989 were about $1,200, $2,400, and $4,200.

■ AQUALEX CUSTOMERS

Aqualex customers could be divided into two groups—governmental units and industrial companies. The typical application in the first group was a sewage treatment plant having some 4 to 12 pumping stations, each station containing one or more pumps. Pumps would operate intermittently and—unless an Aqualex or similar system was in place—be monitored by one or more operators who would visit each station once or perhaps twice each day for about a half hour. Operators would take reservoir measurements, record running times of pumps, and sometimes perform limited maintenance and repairs. The sewage plant and stations typically were located in flat or rolling terrain, where gravity could not be used in lieu of pumping. If any monitoring equipment were present at all, it typically would consist of a crude, on-site alarm that would activate whenever fluid levels rose or fell beyond a preset level. Sometimes the alarm would activate a telephone dialing function that alerted an operator some distance from the station.

Numerous industrial companies also stored, moved, and processed large quantities of water or sewage. These applications usually differed little from those in governmental plants except for their smaller size. On the other hand, there was a considerably larger number of industrial companies having pumping stations, and so, Georg thought, the two markets often offered about identical market potentials in many countries.

The two markets desired essentially the same products, although industrial applications often used smaller, simpler equipment. Both markets wanted their monitoring equipment to be accurate and reliable, the two dominant concerns. Equipment should also be easy to use, economical to operate, and require little regular service or maintenance. Purchase price often was not a major consideration—as long as the price was in some appropriate range, customers seemed more interested in actual product performance than in initial outlays.

Georg thought that worldwide demand for Aqualex Systems and competing products would continue to be strong for at least the next ten years. While some of this demand represented construction of new pumping stations, many applications were replacements of crude monitoring and alarm systems at existing sites. These existing systems depended greatly on regular visits by operators, visits that often continued even after new equipment was installed. Most such trips were probably not necessary. However, many managers found it difficult to dismiss or reassign monitoring personnel that were no longer needed; many were also quite cautious and conservative, desiring some human monitoring of the new equipment "just in case." Once replacements of existing systems were complete, market growth would be limited to new construction and, of course, replacements of more sophisticated systems.

Most customers (as well as noncustomers) considered the Aqualex System to be the best on the market. Those knowledgeable in the industry felt that competing products seldom matched Aqualex's reliability and accuracy. Experts also believed that many competing products lacked the sophistication and flexibility present in Aqualex's design. Beyond these product features, customers also appreciated MacTec's knowledge about water and sanitation engineering. Competing firms often lacked this expertise, offering their products somewhat as a sideline and considering the market too small for an intensive marketing effort.

The market was clearly not too small for MacTec. While Georg had no hard data on market potential for Western Europe, he thought that annual demand could be as much as $9 million. About 40 percent of this came from new construction, whereas the rest represented demand from replacing existing systems. Industry sales in the latter category could be increased by more aggressive marketing efforts on the part of MacTec and its competitors. Eastern European economies represented additional, new potential. However, the water and sewer industries in these countries seemed less interested than their Western counterparts in high-technology equipment to monitor pumping operations. Additionally, business was often more difficult to conduct in these countries. In contrast, the U.S. market looked very attractive.

■ MACTEC STRATEGY

MacTec currently marketed its Aqualex System primarily to sewage treatment plants in Scandinavia and other countries in Northern and Central Europe. The company's strategy could be described as providing technologically superior equipment to monitor pumping operations at these plants. The strategy stressed frequent contacts with customers and potential customers to design, supply, and service Aqualex Systems. The strategy also stressed superior knowledge of water and sanitation engineering along with up-to-date electronics and computer technology. The result was a line of highly specialized sensors, computers, and methods for process controls in water treatment plants.

This was the essence of MacTec's strategy, having a special competence that no firm in the world could easily match. MacTec also prided itself on being a young, creative company without an entrenched bureaucracy. Company employees generally worked with enthusiasm and dedication; they talked with one another, regularly, openly, and with a great deal of give and take. Most importantly, customers—as well as technology—seemed to drive all areas in the company.

MacTec's strategy in its European markets seemed to be fairly well decided. That is, Georg thought that a continuation of present strategies and tactics should continue to produce good results. However, an aspect that would likely change would be to locate a branch office having both sales and manufacturing activities somewhere in the European Community (EC), most likely The Netherlands. The plan was to have such an office in operation well before 1992, when the 12 countries in the EC (Belgium, Denmark, France, Germany, Greece, Ireland, Italy, Luxembourg, The Netherlands, Portugal, Spain, United Kingdom) would mutually eliminate national barriers to the flow of capital, goods, and services. Having a MacTec office located in the EC would greatly simplify sales to these member countries. Moreover, MacTec's presence should also avoid problems with any protective barriers the EC itself might raise to limit or discourage market access by outsiders.

Notwithstanding activities related to this branch office, Georg was considering a major strategic decision to enter the U.S. market. His two recent visits to the United States had led him to conclude that the market represented potential beyond that for Western Europe, and that the United States seemed perfect for expansion. Industry experts in the United States agreed with Georg that the Aqualex System outperformed anything used in the U.S. market. Experts thought that many water and sewage engineers would welcome MacTec's products and knowledge. Moreover, Georg thought that U.S. transportation systems and payment arrangements would present few problems. The system would be imported under U.S. Tariff Regulation 71249 and pay a duty of 4.9 percent.

Entry would most likely be in the form of a sales and service office located in Philadelphia. The Pennsylvania and New York State markets seemed representative of the United States and appeared to offer a good test of the Aqualex System. The two states together probably represented about 18 percent of total U.S. market potential for the system. The office would require an investment of some $200,000 for inventory and other balance sheet items. Annual fixed costs would total upward of $250,000 for salaries and other operating expenses—Georg thought that the office would employ only a general manager, two sales technicians, and a secretary for at least the first year or two. Each Aqualex System sold in the United States would be priced to provide a contribution margin of about 30 percent. Georg wanted a 35 percent annual return before taxes on any MacTec investment, to begin no later than the second year. At issue was whether Georg could realistically expect to achieve this goal in the United States.

■ MARKETING RESEARCH

To this end, Georg had commissioned the Browning Group in Philadelphia to conduct some limited marketing research with selected personnel from the water and sewage industries in the city and surrounding areas. The research had two purposes: to obtain a sense of market needs and market reactions to MacTec's products and to calculate a rough estimate of market potential in Pennsylvania and New York. Results were intended to help Georg interpret his earlier conversations with industry experts and perhaps allow a decision on market entry.

The research design itself employed two phases of data collection. The first consisted of five one-hour interviews with water and sewage engineers employed by local city and municipal governments. For each interview, an experienced Browning Group interviewer scheduled an appointment with the engineer and then visited his office, armed with a set of questions and a tape recorder. Questions included:

1. What procedures do you use to monitor your pumping stations?

2. Is your current monitoring system effective? Costly?

3. What are the costs of a monitoring malfunction?

4. What features would you like to see in a monitoring system?

5. Who decides on the selection of a monitoring system?

6. What is your reaction to the Aqualex System?

Interviewers were careful to listen closely to the engineers' responses and to probe for additional detail and clarification.

Tapes of the personal interviews were transcribed and then analyzed by the project manager at Browning. The report noted that these results were interesting in that they described typical industry practices and viewpoints. A partial summary from the report appears below:

> The picture that emerges is one of fairly sophisticated personnel making decisions about monitoring equipment that is relatively simple in design. Still, some engineers would appear distrustful of this equipment because they persist in sending opera-

tors to pumping stations on a daily basis. The distrust may be justified because potential costs of a malfunction were identified as expensive repairs and cleanups, fines of $10,000 per day of violation, lawsuits, harassment by the Health Department, and public embarrassment. The five engineers identified themselves as key individuals in the decision to purchase new equipment. Without exception, they considered MacTec features innovative, highly desirable, and worth the price.

The summary noted also that the primary use of the interview results was to construct a questionnaire that could be administered over the telephone.

The questionnaire was used in the second phase of data collection, as part of a telephone survey that had contacted 65 utility managers, water and sewage engineers, and pumping station operators in Philadelphia and surrounding areas. All respondents were employed by governmental units. Each interview took about ten minutes to complete, covering topics identified in questions 1, 2, and 4 above. The Browning Group's research report stated that most interviews found respondents to be quite cooperative, although 15 people refused to participate at all.

The telephone interviews had produced results that could be considered more representative of the market because of the larger sample size. The report had organized these results about the topics of monitoring procedures, system effectiveness and costs, and features desired in a monitoring system:

> All monitoring systems under the responsibility of the 50 respondents were considered to require manual checking. The frequency of operator visits to pumping stations ranged from monthly to twice daily, depending on flow rates, pumping station history, proximity of nearby communities, monitoring equipment in operation, and other factors. Even the most sophisticated automatic systems were checked because respondents "just don't trust the machine." Each operator was responsible for some 10 to 20 stations.
>
> Despite the perceived need for double-checking, all respondents considered their current monitoring system to be quite effective. Not one reported a serious pumping malfunction in the past three years that had escaped detection. However, this reliability came at considerable cost—the annual wages and other expenses associated with each monitoring operator averaged about $40,000.
>
> Respondents were about evenly divided between those wishing a simple alarm system and those desiring a sophisticated, versatile microprocessor. Managers and engineers in the former category often said that the only feature they really needed was an emergency signal such as a siren, horn, or light. Sometimes they would add a telephone dialer that would be automatically activated at the same time as the signal. Most agreed that a price of around $2,000 would be reasonable for such a system. The latter category of individuals contained engineers desiring many of the Aqualex System's features, once they knew such equipment was available. A price of $4,000 per system seemed acceptable. Some of these respondents were quite knowledgeable about computers and computer programming while others were not. Only four respondents voiced any strong concerns about the cost to purchase and install more sophisticated monitoring equipment. Everyone demanded that the equipment be reliable and accurate.

Georg found the report quite helpful. Much of the information, of course, simply confirmed his own view of the U.S. market. However, it was good to have this knowledge from an independent, objective organization. In addition, to learn that the market consisted of two, apparently equal-sized segments of simple and sophisticated applications was quite worthwhile. In particular, knowledge of system prices considered acceptable by each segment would make the entry decision easier. Meeting these prices would not be a major problem.

A most important section of the report contained an estimate of market potential for Pennsylvania and New York. The estimate was based on an analysis of discharge permits on file in governmental offices in the two states. These permits were required before any city, municipality, water or sewage district, or industrial company could release sewage or other contaminated water to another system or to a lake or river. Each permit showed the number of pumping stations in operation. Based on a 10 percent sample of permits, the report had estimated that governmental units in Pennsylvania and New York contained approximately 3,000 and 5,000 pumping stations for waste water, respectively. Industrial companies in the two states were estimated to add some 3,000 and 9,000 more pumping stations, respectively. The total number of pumping stations in the two states—20,000—seemed to be growing at about 2 percent per year.

Finally, a brief section of the report dealt with the study's limitations. Georg agreed that the sample was quite small, that it contained no utility managers or engineers from New York, and that it probably concentrated too heavily on individuals in larger urban areas. In addition, the research told him nothing about competitors and their marketing strategies and tactics. Nor did he learn anything about any state regulations for monitoring equipment, if indeed any existed. However, these shortcomings came as no surprise, representing a consequence of the research design proposed to Georg by the Browning Group some six weeks ago, before the study began.

■ THE DECISION

Georg's decision seemed a difficult one. The most risky option was to enter the U.S. market as soon as possible; the most conservative was to stay in Europe. In between was the option of conducting some additional marketing research.

Discussion with the Browning Group had identified the objectives of this research as to rectify limitations of the first study as well as to provide more accurate estimates of market potential. (The estimates of the numbers of pumping stations in Pennsylvania and New York were accurate to around plus or minus 20 percent.) This research was estimated to cost $40,000 and take another three months to complete.

Bateson Battery Chargers

Ed Warren left his office early, filled with enthusiasm. His meeting with Mark Mercer had gone well, the field test of a Rejuvenator prototype had exceeded everyone's expectations, and the project now appeared to be back on schedule. "Rejuvenator" was the name chosen by the project team for an innovative battery charger two years ago, in October 1990, when Warren was still working in Corporate Marketing. Mercer, too, was an original team member, having left his job as Manufacturing Engineer in the Bateson Battery Division. Charlene Becker became the third and last team member, coming to the team from Corporate Finance in November 1990.

The three team members had volunteered for an assignment to design several Rejuvenator models and investigate marketing feasibility. Each saw the project as a splendid opportunity to advance his or her own career at Bateson. If the project was a "go," team members would undoubtedly remain with the new division, at high levels of responsibility. On the other hand, if the project was abandoned, each would still have gotten a great deal from a challenging experience—not to mention numerous contacts with and widespread visibility among high-level Bateson executives.

Initial efforts related to the project had involved the concurrent design, testing, product costing, and market analysis for the Rejuvenator. The first three activities had taken place largely inside the company, but market analysis had consisted mostly of studies prepared by commercial marketing research firms. These studies, which ranged in price from $2,000 to $5,000, had helped Warren and his fellow team members "decipher the multitude of applications for battery chargers and the numerous routes available for marketing such a product." Nevertheless, a decision concerning the choice of market targets and subsequent market research was yet to be made as of December 1992.

■ BATESON CORPORATION

Bateson Corporation is a large manufacturer of automotive and related products with its headquarters in Cleveland, Ohio. Sales revenues for 1991 were over $2.2 billion. Subsidiaries and divisions of the company are located primarily in the United States, with major manufacturing facilities at several locations in California, Florida, Ohio, Michigan, and Indiana. Total employment in December 1992 was over 20,000 people. Major product lines include automotive headliners, carpeting, hoses, interior paneling, seals, and batteries. Almost 70 percent of Bateson's sales revenues come from automotive products.

Bateson's strategy in the United States for many of its automotive products could be described as defensive, oriented toward maintaining market share and controlling

This case was written by Associate Professor James E. Nelson, of the University of Colorado at Boulder. He thanks Professor Roger A. Kerin, of the Southern Methodist University, for his helpful comments in writing this case. The case is intended for educational purposes rather than to illustrate either effective or ineffective decision making. Some data as well as the identity of the company are disguised. Copyright © 1992 by James E. Nelson.

fixed and variable costs. The U.S. market for automotive parts has reached maturity, with limited growth forecast for the future. Still, the market is characterized by a good deal of change based on emerging technologies and on styling and design modifications initiated by automobile manufacturers.

In contrast to the U.S. market, Europe and eastern Asia were seen by senior Bateson executives as opportunities for growth. The company had joint-venture or license agreements with several companies located in several countries in Europe. These firms manufactured and marketed Bateson products under their own brand name and paid Bateson a fee for the privilege. However, with the coming of the new European Community in 1992, Bateson had decided in late 1989 to let these agreements expire at the end of December 1991. Construction of a Bateson manufacturing facility in Frankfurt, Germany, was completed in the summer of 1991, and an office and sales staff were in place soon thereafter. Bateson Europe was fully operational on January 1, 1992.

Bateson also had manufacturing plants and sales offices in Malaysia and Korea. Similar operations were tentatively planned for Mexico and, perhaps, Brazil. In total, almost 30 percent of Bateson's 1991 sales revenues came from international operations, with about one-half coming from foreign production and one-half from U.S. exports. International revenues were expected to grow steadily as the company became increasingly global in its orientation and culture.

Product strategy at Bateson was evolving as well. Early products (pre-World War II) were simple in design and manufacture and had rather long life cycles. Mercer described the six-volt battery on his bookshelf as a mainstay of the Bateson product line for over 20 years. He had found it in his grandfather's 1948 Plymouth. Bateson products had become much more complex and sophisticated, and most new models have a life cycle of between two and five years. Opinions varied, but most industry experts viewed Bateson products as "about average" in terms of quality and price. Although this position was barely acceptable in the United States, the company had found it necessary to raise its design and production standards in Europe.

Bateson Battery Division

The Battery Division (where work on the Rejuvenator had begun) generated almost $200 million in sales for 1991. Over 2,000 employees work as production operators, engineers, accountants, salespeople, and managers in the division. Over 1,000 different models of batteries are manufactured and marketed. Most models are the conventional, lead-acid batteries that are commonly found under the hoods of automobiles and light trucks. Most of these batteries are sold as "replacement" batteries to large retail chains (automotive specialty stores and mass merchandisers) and to wholesalers. About 10 percent of Bateson's models are used in agricultural, construction, and marine applications. Another 10 percent are nickel-cadmium batteries used in a variety of applications.

Much of Bateson's revenues from the entire line of automotive products come from sales made directly to original equipment manufacturers such as Ford, Nissan, Honda, and Hyundai. However, a majority of battery revenues came from aftermarket sales to chain retailers such as Northern Automotive, AutoZone, and Western Auto, to mass merchandisers such as Sears and JCPenney, and to wholesale distributors that sell to smaller, independent retailers. Price and sales terms have seemed to be the most influential factors when the large retailers select suppliers. Most of the division's 60 salespeople were formerly engineers. Most are experienced and capable, with average tenure with Bateson being about ten years. All are paid a salary plus a commission (based on sales volume and averaging about 60 percent of a salesperson's total compensation).

Bateson Battery Charger

In 1988, a Bateson engineer had developed a microchip design for a battery charger whose performance was based directly on properties of the discharged battery. The design incorporated a pulsing current that changed in magnitude and direction over the charging time period. The consequence was that electrochemical processes in the battery were much improved—the lives of working batteries could be greatly extended, and, in fact, many batteries thought to be worn out could be brought back to normal operation. The design was granted a U.S. patent in 1989. As of December 1992, similar patents were pending in the European Community (under the European Patent Treaty), Spain, India, and Japan.

As Warren saw it, the charger's ability to extend (perhaps even double) the lives of operational batteries and to recondition old batteries were its two primary advantages. He had roughed out a short promotion piece using a simple graphics package that stressed these points (Exhibit 1).

"Our advantage is unlikely to be in costs," said Warren when Becker had summarized her product cost estimates. Each battery charger model was projected to cost about $150,000 in tools and fixtures in order to begin production. Bateson policy required that this investment be recovered within two years after the product entered the market. Fixed costs for each model were estimated at $100,000, exclusive of marketing expenditures and tools depreciation. Variable costs for each model would be between $12 and $500, depending on the charger's size and features, as long as production runs of 2,000 were scheduled. Becker and Mercer had concluded that runs of this size would be feasible. They had also concluded that Bateson's investments and its fixed and variable costs for each model would be little different from those faced by existing competitors. "Our chip for the charger adds only a dollar or so over a conventional design in terms of variable costs, as long as we sell 50,000 units over the model's life cycle," Becker had estimated.

Apart from investments and costs, the selling price for a Bateson charger would depend on many factors. Competitors' prices at the retail level varied "all over the map" according to Becker. For example, a small, conventional battery charger for motorcycles sold to consumers for about $18, whereas a typical model for automobiles sold for $30. At the middle of the spectrum, high-capacity chargers for electric-powered golf carts retailed for almost $400. At the top end were very high-capacity chargers used by automobile dealers and repair shops that were priced at $800 to $2,000. Bateson's prices for any application would be near competing prices, although the team thought that their charger's technological advantage should command some sort of price premium.

■ BATTERY CHARGER MARKETS

In December 1992, the team faced a decision: Which market or markets should Bateson focus on for purposes of making a later, go/no-go decision on the product? The issue was extremely complex because of the enormous diversity of battery use. Rechargeable batteries are used in products ranging from electric toothbrushes to golf carts to space shuttles. The team had already ruled out applications in the first and last categories, focusing initially on seven disparate markets. For the sake of analysis, Warren divided all potential buyers into two groups: end users and commercial markets.

End Users

End users consist of consumers who purchase battery chargers for their own personal use. A research study conducted by a marketing research firm and purchased by the team described this market as follows:

E X H I B I T   1

Mock-up of Rejuvenator Promotional Piece

THE REJUVENATOR™
The New Age for Rechargeable Lead Acid Batteries

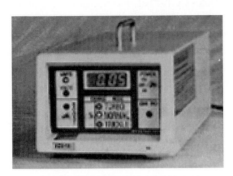

Important News For All Users
of Lead Acid Batteries, 12V and 6V

- ✔ Auto and Truck Dealers
- ✔ Antique car owners
- ✔ Boat Marinas
- ✔ Farmers
- ✔ Maintenance shops
- ✔ Pro golf shops
- ✔ Service facilities
- ✔ Taxi companies

THE REJUVENATOR™
new and patented battery
CONDITIONER/CHARGER
can extend a battery's service life to
twice the manufacturer's rated life.
It will restore, recondition, and
maintain lead-acid batteries.
***The TCS-15 should be used on
ALL 6 Volt and 12 Volt
lead-acid batteries.***

INCREASED BATTERY LIFE EXPECTANCY

THE REJUVENATOR Conditioner/Charger has demonstrated, with its newly patented Pulse Amplitude Circuit, it can recondition sulfated batteries. When returned to service, these batteries are good for one or more additional life cycles. A life cycle is the manufacturer's rated lifetime.

EXTENSIVE TESTING

Formal and field tests were conducted by qualified battery and electrochemical experts. The batteries tested were discarded due to internal sulfation with loss of power, cranking performance and electrical capacity. THE REJUVENATOR was successful in reconditioning and charging 90% of these batteries (excluding those with physical damage). With THE REJUVENATOR, performance levels were equal to or above new ratings.

GOOD BATTERIES FROM BAD

THE REJUVENATOR has passed, with high ratings, every field test by independent experts. Sophisticated testing concludes that this device conditions and charges batteries when conventional chargers fail. Further, charge levels and specific gravities show impressive gains. The typical reaction from test users has been, *"When and where can I buy THE REJUVENATOR?"*

End users buy battery chargers from mass merchandisers and specialty stores, primarily for automotive applications. The purchase often is made based on an emergency (a dead battery), in winter, and in snowbelt states. Purchasers tend to be unaware of product features and product performance and instead rely on clerks or on-package information in making their choice. Purchasers usually buy one or two battery chargers over a 20-year period.

The same study went on to describe distribution channels for battery chargers sold to end users as follows. The channel with the largest sales volume consists of automotive specialty stores. These stores sell parts and accessories for almost all makes and models of automobiles. Trade association data identified the largest chain in terms of number of stores to be Northern Automotive, with almost 900 retail stores in operation in 1991. The largest in terms of sales volume was Pep Boys, Inc., which had 1991 sales of over $900 million (from only 300 stores). Other major chains include AutoZone, Chief, and Western Auto. In addition to these large chains, there are numerous independent automotive specialty stores. These stores usually buy parts and accessories from wholesalers who service market areas as large as several states. Because of wholesalers' margins and other factors, prices in independent stores are often slightly higher than prices in the chains. In 1991, chains and independents totaled almost 50,000 stores and sold almost $32 billion in automotive parts and accessories.

About 40 percent of the end user market comes almost completely from large mass merchandisers such as Kmart, Sears, Wal-Mart, and JCPenney. Stores in these chains usually contain an automotive department or section that sells merchandise similar to the products offered in specialty stores. However, mass merchandisers usually offer a larger selection of products, including battery chargers. Mass merchandisers often carry three or four brands of battery chargers, while specialty stores usually carry only one or two. Mass merchandisers might devote two or three times more shelf space to chargers than specialty stores do. Mass merchandisers generally consider automotive departments as attractive operations, with sales growth rates twice that of the average department and with equally attractive gross profit margins.

The marketing research report concluded that both types of channels expect about a 33 percent retail margin based on their selling price. Both types of channels expect battery chargers to turn over about six times per year. Chain members in both channels usually buy their merchandise directly from manufacturers, often on the basis of an annual, blanket purchase order that guarantees a minimum purchase quantity. Negotiations for these contracts are quite intense, as Bateson's existing salesforce could attest. Independent stores usually buy from wholesalers. Bateson's sales personnel consider wholesalers easier to deal with because they generally represent a much smaller sales volume than the chains.

Commercial Markets

The picture was more complicated on the commercial side. A second research study conducted by another marketing research firm and purchased by the team divided this market into five smaller markets: transportation fleets (automobiles and trucks), golf carts, boats, light aircraft and helicopters, and automobile dealers and repair shops. However, each market is characterized by its purchase of battery chargers as part of a business activity.

Transportation fleets include public and private buses, over-the-highway tractors, delivery vehicles, rental cars, rental trucks, corporate cars, police cars, school buses, and taxis—a diverse group to say the least. Secondary data were used to conclude that the largest single segment is rental cars and corporate cars with approximately 7 million vehicles estimated to be on the road. The remaining segments contain upward of 3 million vehicles. Fleets usually buy vehicles at least once each year and generally sell their vehicles after one to three years of use. Purchases of battery chargers are usually made directly from a manufacturer or a wholesaler. The battery chargers themselves might be identical to those used by end users; however, they are more likely to be high-capacity models that are capable of charging a fully discharged battery in ten minutes or less.

Golf cart owners, including golf courses, represent another market. About one-half of the 700,000 golf carts in operation in the United States are estimated to be electric. These split into two equal-sized groups: those owned by individuals and those owned by public and private golf courses. The study described the application as follows:

> An individual owner of an electric golf cart almost always owns a battery charger for the vehicle. Golf courses typically own one charger for every four carts. Carts themselves generally require charging after one or perhaps two rounds of golf. Batteries used in carts often are light duty units purchased in used condition from a golf cart dealer. In addition to the batteries and the carts themselves, dealers also sell battery chargers at the rate of one per cart. The total number of dealers and courses that provide electric carts is about 10,000.

These battery chargers are much different from those for the end-user market. To charge the six or eight batteries in a golf cart requires a high-capacity charger and four to ten hours of uninterrupted charging. Chargers used by golf courses usually have an even higher capacity and can complete a charge cycle on several carts at once in much less time.

Boat owners, including marinas, constitute another market. Secondary data estimated the number of boats in the United States that require a battery to be about 10 million; the number of marinas, boat dealers, and marine motor repair shops total about 10,000. Battery chargers used in marine applications are often the same models used in the end-user market. However, some large marinas and dealers located near large bodies of water also use one or more high-capacity chargers identical to those used by transportation fleets and by automobile dealers and repair shops.

Private or civil aircraft, small commercial airlines (fixed wing passenger and freight and helicopters), airports and heliports, aircraft service and repair facilities, and other aviation services comprise yet another market. The U.S. market contains about 350,000 privately owned and small commercial aircraft. The number of airports and heliports totals about 20,000; the number of repair and other aviation services also totals about 20,000. In addition, a field test in Texas had demonstrated the Bateson charger's performance in the aircraft market. The test report summary read:

> A total of 39 batteries were brought in for testing. All had failed standard maintenance inspections. Eight had obvious physical damage such as cracked cases and were discarded. All of the remaining 31 batteries were charged with the Rejuvenator system and then returned to the maintenance hangar for a full Federal Aviation Authority "deep-cycle" test. Every one of the 31 batteries passed the test and was returned to full service.

The test concluded with the service manager asking to purchase the prototype charger!

The last commercial market—automobile dealers and repair shops—is clearly the largest. The U.S. market contains about 100,000 new and used car dealers and about 300,000 repair shops. Dealers and repair shops usually own several high-capacity chargers, each capable of rapid recharging of dead batteries on as many as ten vehicles at once. Dealers and shops also might own one or two end-user models. Almost all dealers and many of the larger repair shops stock and sell replacement batteries. In contrast to the other commercial markets, the number of automobile dealers and repair shops has been slowly declining.

■ MOTOR VEHICLE BATTERIES

The number of motor vehicle batteries shipped in the United States in 1991 was estimated by the team to be around 80 million units. About 65 million units were known to be replacement batteries, sold because an existing battery on a car, truck, bus, or other motor vehicle had failed. Battery failures were growing in number because vehicle owners were keeping their vehicles for longer periods of time before disposal—the average age of a vehicle on U.S. highways increased from 4.8 years in 1970 to 6.9 years in 1991. The average life of an automobile battery is about three years.

The cost to the owner for a replacement battery varies "all over the map," according to Becker. Depending on application, battery quality, retail outlet, and other factors, the cost of a replacement battery for a car or light truck could range from $30 to $80. "The only thing I can say for sure," Becker had said, "is that this cost is almost always important to the vehicle's owner. If we can restore the old battery, we come off as a hero."

Bateson could also look like a hero to state government environmentalists in the United States who were worried about the disposal each year of some 65 million batteries. A data-base search undertaken by a Bateson librarian found numerous environmentally oriented articles addressing battery disposal. The 1990 Clean Air Act, other national legislation, and over 2,000 bills introduced into state legislatures in 1991 also evidenced the nation's concern over hazardous automotive waste. The primary issue related to discarded batteries is water pollution caused by the batteries' lead plates and terminals. If half of the 65 million wornout batteries could be restored and the other half recycled, this pollution problem could be eliminated.

Increasing pressure for restoring and recycling motor vehicle batteries is likely to come from the state of California. The state's Air Resources Board—comparable to the federal Environmental Protection Agency—adopted a regulation that requires 2 percent of all new-car sales in California in 1998 to be "zero emissions vehicles." The requirement rises to 5 percent in 2001 and to 10 percent in 2003 and beyond. The only way to meet the quota is for automobile manufacturers to develop and market battery-powered vehicles. Consequently, General Motors, Ford Motor Company, Toyota, Nissan, BMW, and almost all major automobile manufacturers began extensive research and development efforts for zero emission vehicles in 1990. The Bateson technology would be applicable to charger designs for these vehicles.

■ BATTERY CHARGER COMPETITORS

A third study commissioned from an outside marketing research firm had researched battery charger competitors. The resulting report described competing products in the end-user market as "almost indistinguishable" from one another in terms of performance, price, packaging, and warranty. Quite simply, most battery charger designs had not changed in years. In addition, products on the commercial side that are targeted to fleets, boats, aircraft, and auto repair shops are often almost identical to one another, differing only in terms of capacity and durability. The report described the situation as follows:

> Conventional battery chargers utilize an extremely simple concept, which is considered common domain. A few patents have been granted worldwide for design modifications that purport to extend lead-acid battery life. More patents have been granted for designs that reduce charging time.

Given this relatively primitive technology, the team thought that the Bateson battery charger should be quite appealing.

Most battery charger manufacturers in the end-user market compete on the basis of offering "standard" product performance at a low price, the latter feature assured by the use of established designs, long production runs, and limited marketing activities. No competitor advertises to end users. Instead, competitors rely on their salesforces to promote products to automotive specialty chains, mass merchandisers, and wholesalers.

All battery charger manufacturers in the United States are smaller than Bateson in terms of sales revenues and employees. The study estimated that upward of several hundred companies actually manufacture battery chargers in the United States, with about 70 firms competing in the markets described earlier. Many firms target only one or two specialized niches. For example, Rolls Battery Engineering and American Monarch are well known for their golf cart chargers. Kussmaul Electronics Company and Vanner specialize in high-capacity chargers used in the automobile dealer and repair shop market. Teledyne Battery Products targets the aircraft market. Numerous other firms promote their expertise in specialized applications in any market—on the basis of custom engineering, minimum orders of ten units or more, and delivery within four weeks.

The largest manufacturer of chargers for lead-acid batteries was thought by the team to be Schauer Manufacturing Company. Schauer was founded in 1907 and had its headquarters in Cincinnati, Ohio. Schauer employed about 250 people and was expected to sell around $12 million worth of battery chargers in 1991. The company was recognized by industry experts as a full-line manufacturer of chargers, listing 42 standard models in its 1991 catalog. Five models were targeted to end-user markets and sold in numerous automotive specialty and mass-merchandiser stores; the balance serviced a number of customers in the automobile dealer and repair shop market, transportation fleet market, and marine market.

The report concluded with a short section summarizing market size. The discussion began with a caveat stating that because of the diversity and fragmentation of the battery charger industry, any sales estimate was bound to be approximate at best. The report's sales estimate for 1991 was $220 million at manufacturer prices for charger applications in the seven markets. Sales were thought to be growing at 4 percent per year.

■ DECISIONS

Ed Warren's meeting with Mark Mercer had begun with a short discussion of the $220 million figure. Clearly the number represented sufficient potential for Bateson—a 10 percent market share would increase sales for the Battery Division by 11 percent. However, just as clearly, a failed market entry consisting of, say, a half-dozen models would have a disastrous effect on Bateson's bottom line. Moreover, a failed entry might upset Bateson's existing customers and could produce negative repercussions for current products.

Warren and Mercer had roughed out their estimates of the numbers of models needed to cover 90 percent of the units sold in the seven markets under consideration. Five models would cover 90 percent of the end-user market (automotive specialty stores and mass merchandisers). Eight models were thought to be enough to satisfy the needs of 90 percent of both the transportation fleet market and the automobile dealer and repair shop market, because the same models could be used for both. Golf carts would require five models (however, these could duplicate those intended for the end-user markets and the automotive markets). The marine and aircraft markets would each require five different models.

They had placed these estimates against a schedule prepared by Charlene Becker that summarized her estimates of manufacturers' sales revenues, Bateson's contribution margins per unit, and Bateson's marketing costs for the seven markets (Exhibit 2 on page 200). Her estimates of Bateson unit contribution margins reflected a weighted average or composite of the models that Bateson would offer to each market. Estimates of Bateson's marketing costs consisted primarily of salesforce and other promotion expenditures, all of which could be considered fixed for pur-

EXHIBIT 2

Estimates for Battery Charger Markets (Dollars at Manufacturer Level)

Markets	1991 Market Sales (thousands)	1991 Market Unit Sales (thousands)	Bateson's Average Unit Contribution Margin	Bateson's Marketing Costs (thousands)	Number of Bateson Models
Specialty shops	$48,000	2,400	$5	$1,500	5[a]
Mass merchandisers	32,000	1,600	5	1,100	5[a]
Fleets	50,000	140	200	500	8[b]
Golf carts	14,000	50	200	300	5
Marine	12,000	70	50	500	5
Aircraft	4,000	15	200	200	5
Automotive	60,000	170	200	1,000	8[b]
Total	$220,000				

[a] Same models used in specialty shop and mass-merchandiser markets.

[b] Same models used in fleets and automotive markets.

poses of analysis. The existing salesforce would be used if Bateson targeted only the end-user markets; another salesforce or independent sales representatives would be needed if Bateson entered any commercial market.

Warren and Becker had agreed that these numbers were quite crude and had concluded that more marketing research was needed. However, before additional research could be undertaken, the team would have to narrow the number of markets to no more than two or three. Once they felt comfortable with specific market opportunities for the Rejuvenator, they would commission additional studies.

An outside supplier or suppliers would again be called on to design and execute these additional studies. Warren had described several possibilities to Mercer, as follows:

1. *Focus groups of users.* This research would gather qualitative data from small groups of either end users or mechanics, depending on the market. Some five to seven groups from each market would be needed, each group costing about $5,000. Data would consist of group members' reactions to the Rejuvenator name and product concept, their knowledge of and likes and dislikes concerning existing chargers, their beliefs about product performance and price, and their purchase and usage behaviors.

2. *Focus groups of corporate buyers.* This research would gather qualitative data from small groups of corporate buyers in each market under consideration. Some three or four groups from each market would be needed, each group costing about $7,000. Data would consist of group members' reactions, much as described for end users.

3. *Surveys of users.* This research would use a probability sample of 300 to 400 users (either end users or mechanics, depending on the market). Each survey would cost about $15,000 for a nationally representative sample. For end users, a telephone survey would be used; for mechanics, personal interviews. Data would consist of respondents' attitudes and beliefs about battery chargers, interest in purchasing a Rejuvenator charger, usage and purchase behaviors, and demographic characteristics.

4. *Surveys of corporate buyers.* This research would use a probability sample of 200 to 300 purchasing agents employed by large retailers and wholesalers

in the seven markets. The survey would use personal interviews and cost about $15,000. Data would consist of reactions to the topics described in the preceding study.

5. *Use tests*. This research would place approximately 100 Rejuvenator chargers in the field with either end users or mechanics, depending on the market. Chargers would be used for a four-month period, and data would be collected on actual product performance as well as on user reaction, likes and dislikes, and so forth. The cost would be about $200 per user, not including the chargers themselves.

6. *Test markets*. This research would test actual end-user market reaction under competitive conditions for a four-month period. Two or three market areas would be chosen. Placement of the Rejuvenator charger in retail stores would be guaranteed by the research supplier. Bateson would supply shelf tags, other promotional materials, and limited training for retail salespeople. Data would be collected on actual sales and market share, competitive reaction, and buyer reaction to three different price points, buyer satisfaction, and demographics. The cost would be approximately $100,000 per market, excluding costs of the chargers themselves.

7. *Competitive analysis*. This research would identify major competitors and their marketing strategies in each chosen market and would describe their relative strengths and weaknesses and their expected reactions to a Rejuvenator market introduction. The cost would be about $15,000.

"All things considered," Warren thought as he opened his car door, "the week could hardly have gone better. We've got a great product, good results from the field, and fine numbers from Charlene." His thoughts were interrupted by a question from out of nowhere.

It was his boss, Noah Reddy. "Have you guys decided on markets for that battery charger yet?" The tone was supportive, with no overtones of "What are you doing leaving the office at four on a Friday?"

"Not yet. But we should have an answer by Tuesday," he replied. Warren knew that Reddy expected not only a decision but the team's reasoning behind it. The weekend would be an ideal time for the team to choose markets and support its choice and also rough out a research program for the chosen markets. Noah would like that.

"See if we can't set something up for around 3:00 on Tuesday," was Noah's only response.

CHAPTER 6

Product and Service Strategy and Management

 The fundamental decision in formulating a marketing mix concerns the offering of an organization. Without something to satisfy target market wants and needs, there would be nothing to price, distribute, or communicate. In essence, the ultimate profitability of an organization depends on its product or service offering(s). Accordingly, issues in the development of a product and service strategy are of special interest to all levels of management in an organization.

The three basic kinds of offering-related decisions facing the marketing manager concern (1) modifying the offering mix, (2) positioning offerings, and (3) branding offerings. Aspects of each decision are described in this chapter.

In certain ways, offering decisions are extensions of product–market matching strategies described in Chapter 1. Like other marketing-mix decisions, offering decisions must be based on consideration of organization and marketing objectives, organization resources and capabilities, customer needs and wants, and competitive forces in the marketplace.

■ THE OFFERING PORTFOLIO

The Offering Concept

Before proceeding to a discussion of offering-related decisions, we should define the term *offering*. In an abstract sense, an *offering* consists of the benefits or satisfaction provided to target markets by an organization. More concretely, an offering consists of a tangible product or service (a physical entity) plus related services (such as delivery and setup), warranties or guarantees, packaging, and the like.

Use of the term *offering* rather than *product* or *service* has numerous benefits for strategic marketing planning. By focusing on benefits and satisfaction offered, it establishes a conceptual framework. This framework is potentially useful in analyzing competing offerings, identifying the unmet needs and wants of target markets, and developing or designing new products or services. It forces a marketer to go beyond the single tangible entity being marketed and to consider the entire offering, or extended product or service.

In a broader view, an organization's offerings are an extension of its business definition. Offerings illustrate not only the buyer needs served, but also the types of customer groups sought and the means (technology) for satisfying their needs.

The Offering Mix

Seldom do organizations market a solitary offering; rather, they tend to market many product or service offerings. The typical supermarket contains over 30,000 different products; General Electric offers over a quarter million. Banks provide hundreds of services to customers, including computer billing, automatic payroll deposits, checking accounts, and loans of numerous kinds. Similarly, hospitals maintain a complete "inventory" of services ranging from pathology to obstetrics to food services. The totality of an organization's offerings is known as its product or service *offering mix* or *portfolio*. This mix usually consists of distinct offering lines—groups of offerings similar in terms of usage, buyers marketed to, or technical characteristics. Each offering line is composed of individual offers or items.

Offering decisions concern primarily the width, depth, and consistency of the offering portfolio. Marketing managers must continually assess the number of offering lines (the width decision) and the number of individual items in each line (the depth decision). Although these decisions depend, in part, on the existing competitive or industry situation, as well as organizational resources, they are perhaps most often determined by overall marketing strategy. The options are many. At one extreme, an organization can concentrate on one offering; at the other, it can offer complete lines to its customers. In between, it can specialize in high-profit and/or high-volume offerings. Furthermore, managers must consider the extent to which offerings satisfy similar needs, appeal to similar buyer groups, or utilize similar technologies (the consistency decision).

Increasingly, organizations have turned to "bundling" as a means to enhance their offering mix. *Bundling* involves the marketing of two or more product or service items in a single "package." For example, AT&T sells computer hardware, software, and maintenance contracts together. Bundling is based on the idea that consumers value the package more than the individual items. This is due to benefits received from not having to make separate purchases and enhanced satisfaction from one item given the presence of another. Moreover, bundling often provides a lower total cost to buyers and lower marketing costs to sellers. For instance, Microsoft Corporation sold a "bundle" of spreadsheet and word-processing software in its Microsoft Office package for $750 prior to its introduction of Windows 95. Priced separately, items in the bundle cost a buyer $2,190.[1]

■ MODIFYING THE OFFERING MIX

The first offering-related decision confronting the manager is whether to modify the offering mix. Rarely, if ever, will an organization's offering mix stand the test of changing competitive actions and buyer preferences, or satisfy an organization's desire for growth. Accordingly, the marketing manager must continually monitor target markets and offerings to determine when new offerings should be introduced and existing offerings modified or eliminated.

Additions to the Offering Mix

Additions to the offering mix may take the form of a single offering or of entire lines of offerings. An example of adding a complete line of offerings is General Mills' introduction, several years ago, of salty snack items called Whistles, Bugles, and Daisies.

Whatever the reason for considering new offerings, three questions should direct the evaluation of this action:

- How consistent is the new offering with existing offerings?
- Does the organization have the resources to adequately introduce and sustain the offering?
- Is there a viable market niche for the offering?

First, in evaluating the consistency of the new offering with existing offerings, offering interrelationships—whether substitute, complementary, or whatever—must be carefully taken into account. This is necessary to avoid situations where sales of the new offering may excessively cannibalize those of other offerings. Eastman Kodak did not originally introduce 35mm cameras and camcorders because of the potential for cannibalizing its core products—cameras. Today, a similar situation exists with electronic imaging cameras, which could cannibalize sales of existing cameras.[2] Determining a new offering's consistency also involves considering the degree to which the new offering fits the organization's existing selling and distribution strategies. For example, will the new offering require a different type of sales effort, such as new sales personnel or selling methods? The Metropolitan Life Insurance Company faced such a situation when it added automobile insurance to its line of life and health insurance, since the sales task for auto insurance differs from that for life insurance. Or will the new offering require a different marketing channel to reach the target market sought? Both the cannibalization question and the question of fit with sales and distribution strategies raise a fundamental third question relating to the buyers sought for the new offering. Will the new offering satisfy the target markets currently being served by the existing offering mix? If it will, then the sales and distribution issue may be settled, but the cannibalization question remains. If it will not, then the situation is just the opposite.

The second issue arising from the addition of new offerings relates to the adequacy of an organization's resources. In particular, the financial strength of the organization must be objectively appraised. New offerings often require large initial cash outlays for research, development, and introductory marketing programs. Gillette, for example, spent $200 million on research and development alone to produce the Sensor razor; introductory marketing programs for grocery products often approach $20 million.[3] Other costs of sustaining the new offering before it returns a profit to the organization must also be measured. These costs will be determined, in part, by the speed and magnitude of competitive response to new offerings in the market and by market growth itself. The experience of Royal Crown Company, the maker of RC Cola, is a case in point. The company pioneered the first can in 1954, the first diet cola in 1962, and the first caffeine-free cola in 1980. All three offerings achieved a respectable market presence only to lose it when larger competitors such as Coca-Cola and Pepsi-Cola introduced competitive products.[4]

Finally, one must determine whether a market niche exists for the new offering. Important questions here are whether the new offering has a relative advantage over existing competitive offerings and whether a distinct buyer group exists for which no offering is satisfactory. Careful market analysis is necessary to answer these questions.

New-Offering Development Process

Marketing managers are often faced with new-offering decisions. In dealing with the often-chaotic process of developing and marketing new offerings, most managers attempt to follow some sort of structured procedure.[5] This procedure typically includes four multifaceted steps: (1) idea generation/idea screening, (2) business analysis, (3) market testing, and (4) commercialization.

Briefly, the process is as follows. New-offering ideas are obtained from many sources—employees, buyers, and competitors—through formal (marketing research) and informal means. These ideas are screened, both in terms of organizational definition and capability and from the viewpoint of prospective buyers. Ideas deemed incompatible with organizational definition and capability are quickly eliminated. The match between prospective buyers and offering characteristics is assessed through questions such as the following. First, does the offering have a *relative advantage* over existing offerings? Second, is the offering *compatible* with buyers' use or consumption behavior? Third, is the offering *simple* enough for buyers to understand and use? Fourth, can the offering be *tested* on a limited basis prior to actual purchase? Fifth, are there *immediate benefits* from the offering, once it is used or consumed? If the answers to these questions are yes and the offering satisfies a *felt need*, then the new-offering idea passes on to the next stage. At that point, the idea is subjected to a business analysis to assess its financial viability in terms of estimated sales, costs, and profitability. Those ideas that pass the business analysis are then developed into prototypes, and various testing procedures are implemented. Marketing-related tests may include product concept or buyer preference tests in a laboratory situation, or even field market tests. Offering ideas that pass through these stages are commercially introduced into the marketplace in the hope that they will become profitable to the organization. A study by Booz, Allen, and Hamilton, Inc., an internationally recognized management consulting firm, indicated that it takes an average of seven ideas to generate one successful new product. This study also reported that the two major factors contributing to the success of new offerings were (1) a fit with market needs and (2) a fit with the internal strengths of the organization.[6]

Although the stages just outlined are relatively straightforward from a managerial perspective, two require further elaboration: the business analysis and testing stages. Sales analysis and profit analysis are two fundamental aspects of the business analysis stage. Forecasting sales volume for a new offering is an enormously difficult task; nevertheless, preliminary forecasts must be made before further investigation of the offering is warranted. For the most part, profitability analyses are related to investment requirements, break-even procedures, and payback periods. Break-even procedures can be used to determine estimates of the number of units that must be sold to cover fixed and variable costs. An extension of this procedure—and one that is frequently used in evaluating new offerings—is to compute the payback period of the new offering. *Payback period* refers to the number of years required for an organization to recapture its initial offering investment. The shorter the payback period, the sooner an offering will prove profitable. Usually the payback period is computed by dividing the fixed costs of the offering by the estimated incoming cash flows from it. Though widely used, the method is limited in that it does not distinguish among offering investments according to their absolute sizes. A final method often used is to calculate the common return on investment (ROI). ROI equals the ratio of average annual net earnings (return) divided by average annual investment, discounted to the present time. Like the payback method, the ROI method does not distinguish among offering alternatives according to their riskiness. Risk must still be subjectively assessed.

Test marketing is a major consideration in the development and testing stage. A test market is a scaled-down implementation of one or more alternative marketing strategies for introducing the new offering. Test markets provide several benefits to managers. First, they generate benchmark data for assessing sales volume when the product is introduced over a wider area. Second, if alternative marketing strategies are tested, the relative impacts of the two programs can be examined under actual market conditions. In a similar vein, test markets allow the manager to assess the incidence of offering trial by potential buyers, repeat-purchasing behavior, and quantities purchased. A manager should remember, however, that test markets of new offerings inform competitors of the organization's activities and thus may increase the magnitude and speed of competitive response. This happened to the Clorox Company. Its Wave laundry detergent with bleach was test-marketed for five years, only to be dropped after competitors introduced their own detergents with bleach supported by extensive marketing resources.[7]

Life-Cycle Concept

An important managerial tool related to the development and management of offerings is the concept of the life cycle. A *life cycle* plots sales of an offering (such as a brand of coffee) or a product class (such as all coffee brands) over a period of time. Life cycles are typically divided into four stages: (1) introduction, (2) growth, (3) maturity-saturation, and (4) decline. Exhibit 6.1 shows the general form of a product life cycle and the corresponding stages.

The sales curve can be viewed as being the result of offering trial and repeat-purchasing behavior. In other words,

$$\text{Sales volume} = (\text{number of triers} \times \text{average purchase amount} \times \text{price})$$
$$+ (\text{number of repeaters} \times \text{average purchase amount} \times \text{price})$$

Early in the life cycle, management efforts focus on stimulating trial of the offering by advertising, giving out free samples, and obtaining adequate distribution. The vast majority of sales volume is due to trial purchases. As the offering moves through its life cycle, an increasing share of volume is attributable to repeat purchases, and management efforts focus on retaining existing buyers of the offering through offering modifications, enhanced brand image, and competitive pricing.

Anticipating and recognizing movement into advanced stages of the life cycle are crucial to managing the various stages. Movement into the maturity-saturation stage is often indicated by (1) an increase in the proportion of buyers who are repeat purchasers (that is, few new buyers or triers exist), (2) an increase in the standardization of production operations and product–service offerings, and (3) an in-

EXHIBIT 6.1

General Form of a Product Life Cycle

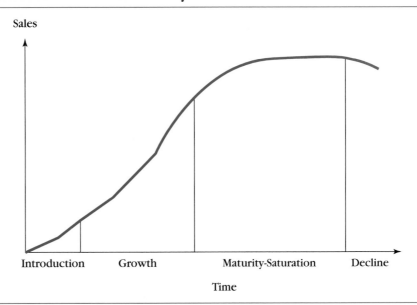

crease in the incidence of aggressive pricing activities of competitors. As the offering enters into and moves through this stage, management efforts typically focus on finding new buyers for the offering, significantly improving the offering, and/or increasing the frequency of usage among current buyers. Ultimately, the decline stage must be addressed. The decision criteria at this stage are outlined in the following discussion on modifying, harvesting, and eliminating offerings.

Services often follow a life cycle very similar to the product life cycle described above. As a service firm approaches maturity, it typically modifies its operations to attract new buyers. Examples include McDonald's with its expanded menu and barbershops that evolve into hair-stylist operations featuring hair-cutting services for men and women. Often service firms expand their geographical scope by reproducing facilities through franchising and licensing agreements to become multisite operators.

Modifying, Harvesting, and Eliminating Offerings

Modifying offerings is a common practice. Firms must always be on the lookout for new ways to improve the value their offerings provide consumers in terms of quality, functions, features, and/or price.

Modification decisions typically focus on trading up or trading down the offering. *Trading up* involves a conscious decision to improve an offering—by adding new features and higher-quality materials or augmenting the offering with attendant services—and raising the price. Examples of augmenting products with services are found in the computer industry. Manufacturers of computers enhanced the image and suitability of their products through programming services, information-system assistance, and user training. *Trading down* is the process of reducing the number of features or quality of an offering and lowering the price.

The dichotomy between trading up and trading down has been blurred in recent years as a result of competitive and cost pressures. In particular, many organizations have modified their offerings downward while maintaining or increasing the price. For example, many distillers have reduced the alcohol content of their beverages without changing prices. Some airlines have added more seats, thus reducing leg room, and eliminated certain extras without lowering fares. Consumer-packaged-goods firms have reduced the content of packages without reducing prices—a practice called *downsizing*.

Although modification decisions typically arise in the maturity-saturation stage of the life cycle, modifications might be appropriate earlier in the life cycle to stimulate trial. For example, several producers of convection ovens recognized early in the introduction phase that the oven had to be augmented with cookbooks to assist buyers in scheduling meals and preparing a variety of foods.

The elimination of offerings as a specific decision is given less attention than new-offering or modification decisions. However, the elimination decision has grown in importance in recent years because of the realization that some offerings may be an unnecessary burden in light of potential opportunities. As an alternative to total elimination, management might consider harvesting the offering when it enters the late-maturity or decline stage of the life cycle. *Harvesting* is the strategic management decision to reduce the investment in a business entity in the hope of cutting costs and/or improving cash flow.[8] In other words, the decision is not to abandon the offering outright but, rather, to minimize human and financial resources allocated to it. Harvesting should be considered when (1) the market for the offering is stable, (2) the offering is not producing good profits, (3) the offering has a small or respectable market share that is becoming increasingly difficult or costly to defend from competitive inroads, and (4) the offering provides benefits to the organization in terms of image or "full-line" capabilities, despite poor future potential.

Outright abandonment, or elimination, means that the offering is dropped from the mix of organizational offerings. Generally speaking, if the answer to each of the following questions is "very little" or "none," then an offering is a candidate for elimination.

1. What is the future sales potential of the offering?
2. How much is the offering contributing to the overall profitability of the offering mix?
3. How much is the offering contributing to the sale of other offerings in the mix?
4. How much could be gained by modifying the offering?
5. What would be the effect on channel members and buyers?

■ POSITIONING OFFERINGS

A second major offering-related decision confronting the manager concerns the positioning of offerings. *Positioning* is the act of designing an organization's offering and image so that it occupies a distinct and valued place in the target customer's mind relative to competitive offerings. There are a variety of positioning strategies available, including positioning by (1) attribute or benefit, (2) use or application, (3) product or service user, (4) product or service class, (5) competitors, and (6) price and quality.[9]

Positioning Strategies

Positioning an offering by attributes or benefits is the strategy most frequently used. Positioning an offering by attributes requires determining which attributes are important to target markets, which attributes are being emphasized by competitors, and how the offering can be fitted into this offering-target market environment. This kind of positioning may be accomplished by designing an offering that contains appropriate attributes or by stressing the appropriate attributes if they already exist in the offering. This latter tactic has been employed by a number of cereal manufacturers, who have emphasized the "naturalness" of their products in response to the growing interest in nutrition among a sizable number of cereal buyers.

In practice, operationalizing the positioning concept requires the development of a matrix relating attributes of the offering to market segments. Using toothpaste as an example, Exhibit 6.2 on page 210 shows how particular attributes may vary in importance for different market segments.[10] Several benefits accrue from viewing the market for toothpaste in this manner. First, the marketing manager can spot potential opportunities for new offerings and determine if a market niche exists. Second, looking at offering attributes and their importance to market segments permits subjective estimation of the extent to which a new offering might cannibalize existing offerings. If two offerings emphasize the same attributes, then they can be expected to compete with each other for the same market segment. Alternatively, if the offerings have different mixes of attributes, they probably will appeal to different segments. For this reason, Procter and Gamble's introduction of Crest tartar-control-formula toothpaste for adults did not have a major adverse effect on its sales of the existing Crest toothpaste for children. Third, the competitive response to a new offering can be judged more effectively using this framework. By determining which brands serve specific markets, one can evaluate offerings in terms of financial strength and market acceptance.

Organizations can also position their offerings by use or application. Arm &

EXHIBIT 6.2

Attributes and Marketing Segment Positioning

| | Market Segments | | | |
| | Children | Teens, Young Adults | Family | Adults |
Toothpaste Attributes				
Flavor	*			
Color	*			
Whiteness of teeth		*		
Fresh breath		*		
Decay prevention			*	
Price			*	
Plaque prevention				*
Stain prevention				*
Principal brands for each segment	Aim, Stripe	Ultra Brite, McCleans	Colgate, Crest	Topol, Pearl Drops

Note: An asterisk (*) indicates principal benefits sought by each market segment.

Hammer used this approach to position its baking powder as an odor-destroying agent in refrigerators and a water softener in swimming pools. Public television was originally positioned as a source of educational and cultural programming.

Positioning by user is a third strategy. This strategy typically associates a product or service with a user group. Federal Express positions its delivery service for the busy executive. Certain deodorant brands position themselves for females (Jean Naté by Charles of the Ritz), whereas others focus on males (Brut by Fabergé).

Products and services can be positioned by product or service class as well. For example, margarine brands position themselves against butter. Savings associations position themselves as "banks."

An organization can position itself or its offerings directly against competitors. Avis positions itself against Hertz in the rental car business. Sabroso, a coffee liqueur, positions itself against Kahlua. For many years, the National Pork Producers Council positioned their product as being like poultry: "Pork: The Other White Meat." Often a political candidate will position himself or herself against the opponent.

Finally, positioning along a price-quality continuum is also possible. Hewlett-Packard consciously prices its line of office personal computers below Compaq and IBM in an attempt to convey a "value" position among corporate buyers. Ford Motor Company, on the other hand, has pursued a quality positioning stance evidenced by its "Quality Is Job One" advertising program.

The challenge facing a manager is deciding which positioning strategy is most appropriate in a given situation. The choice of a strategy is made easier when the following three questions are considered. First, who are the likely competitors, what positions have they staked out in the marketplace, and how strong are they? Second, what are the preferences of the target consumers sought and how do these consumers perceive the offerings of competitors? Finally, what position, if any, do we already have in the target customer's mind? Once answered, attention can then be focused on a series of implementation questions:

1. What position do we want to own?

2. What competitors must be outperformed if we are to establish the position?

3. Do we have the marketing resources to occupy and hold the position?

The success of a positioning strategy depends on a number of factors. First, the position selected must be clearly communicated to targeted customers. Second, as the development of a position is a lengthy and often expensive process, frequent positioning changes should be avoided. Finally, and perhaps most important, the position taken in the marketplace should be sustainable and profitable.

Repositioning

Repositioning is necessary when the initial positioning of a product, service, or organization is no longer competitively sustainable or profitable or when better positioning opportunities arise. However, given the time and cost to establish a new position, repositioning is not advisable without careful study.

Examples of successful repositionings include the efforts of Johnson & Johnson's Baby Shampoo and Carnival Cruise Lines. Johnson & Johnson repositioned its shampoo from one used for babies to a shampoo for adults who wash their hair frequently and therefore needed a mild shampoo. This repositioning led to almost a five-fold increase in market share for the shampoo. Carnival Cruise Lines repositioned itself from a vacation alternative for older people to a "Fun Ship" for younger adults and families. After expanding its service offering to include Las Vegas-style shows, Camp Carnival, and Nautica Spa programs, Carnival became the largest and most successful company in the cruise industry.

■ BRANDING OFFERINGS

Branding offerings is a third responsibility of marketing managers. A brand name is any word, "device" (design, sound, shape, or color), or combination of these that are used to identify an offering and set it apart from competing offerings. The major managerial implication of branding offerings is that consumer goodwill, derived from buyer satisfaction and favorable associations with a brand, can lead to *brand equity*—the added value a brand name bestows on a product or service beyond the functional benefits provided.[11] This value has two distinct advantages for the brand owner. First, brand equity provides a competitive advantage, such as the Sunkist label that signifies quality citrus fruit and the Gatorade name that defines sports drinks. A second advantage is that consumers are often willing to pay a higher price for a product or service with brand equity. Brand equity, in this instance, is represented by the premium a consumer will pay for one brand over another when the functional benefits provided are identical. Duracell batteries, Coca-Cola, Kleenex facial tissues, Louis Vuitton luggage, Lexus cars, and Microsoft software all enjoy a price premium arising from brand equity.

Branding Decisions

Two branding decisions commonly confront marketing managers. The first relates to the strategy used to assign brands to multiple offerings or multiple lines of offerings. A manufacturer must decide whether to assign one brand name to *all* of the organization's offerings (such as General Electric), to assign one brand name to *each line* of offerings (Sears' appliances are Kenmore, and Sears' tools are Craftsman), or to assign individual names to *each offering* (Tide, Cheer, and Oxydol are all laundry detergents sold by Procter and Gamble). The branding strategy selected will depend on the consistency of the offering mix. If the offerings are related in terms of needs satisfied, then a common (family) brand strategy is often favored. A common brand name for offerings is also likely to be selected if the organization wishes to establish dominance in a class of product or service offerings, as in the case of Campbell's soups. The decision to use a single brand name has certain advantages and disadvantages. Among the advantages is the fact that it is usually easier to introduce new offerings when the brand name is familiar to buyers—an outgrowth of brand equity. However, a single brand name strategy can have a negative effect on existing offerings if a new offering is a failure.

The second branding decision relates to supplying an intermediary with its own brand name. From the intermediary's perspective, the decision is whether or not to carry its own brands. Distributors favor carrying their own brands for a number of reasons.[12] By carrying a private brand, a distributor avoids price competition to some extent, since no other distributor carries an identical brand that consumers can use for comparison purposes. Also, any buyer goodwill attributed to an offering accrues to the distributor, and buyer loyalty to the offering is tied to the distributor, not the producer. If a distributor desires a private brand, it must locate a producer willing to manufacture the brand. A marketing manager is then placed in the position of having to decide whether to be the producer. A potential producer of private brands, or distributor brands, should consider a number of factors when making this decision. If a producer has excess manufacturing capacity and the variable costs of producing a distributor's brand do not exceed the sale price, the possibility exists for making a contribution to overhead and utilizing production facilities. Even though a distributor's brand will often compete directly with a producer's brand, the combined sales of the brands and the profit contribution to the producer may be greater than if a competitor obtained the rights to produce the distributor brand. For these reasons and others, firms such as H. J. Heinz, Borden, Ralston Purina, and Dial produce private brands of pet foods, dairy products, cereals, and bar soap for their distributors.[13] However, a great danger in producing private brands is the possibility of becoming too reliant on private-brand revenue, only to have it curtailed when a distributor switches suppliers or builds its own production plant. Overreliance on distributor brands will also affect trade relationships between a producer and distributor. As a generalization, the influence of a producer, in terms of price and channel leadership, is inversely related to the proportion of its output or revenue obtained from a distributor's brand.

Brand Growth Strategies

An organization has four strategic options for growing its brands (see Exhibit 6.3).[14] The options are dictated by whether a marketing manager wishes to extend existing brands or develop new brands and whether the manager chooses to deploy these brands in product classes presently served or not served by the organization.

The most frequently employed brand growth strategy is a *line extension strategy*. Line extensions occur when an organization introduces additional offerings with the same brand in a product class that it currently serves. New flavors, forms, colors, different ingredients or features, and package sizes are examples of line extensions. As an example, Campbell Soup Company offers regular Campbell soup, home-cooking style, chunky, and "healthy request" varieties, more than 100 soup flavors, and several different package sizes in the prepared soup product class. Line extensions respond to customers' desire for variety. They are also used to eliminate gaps in a product line that might be filled by competitive offerings or to neutralize competitive inroads. This strategy can also lower advertising and promotion costs because the same brand is used on all items, thus raising the level of brand awareness. Line extensions do involve risk. Notably, there is a likelihood of product cannibalism occurring rather than incremental volume gains as buyers substitute one item for another in the extended product line. Also, proliferation of offerings within a product

EXHIBIT 6.3

Brand Growth Strategies

		Product/Service Class Served By the Organization	
		New Product Class	*Existing Product Class*
Brand Name	*New Brand*	New Brand Strategy	Fighting/Flanker Brand Strategy
	Existing Brand	Brand Extension Strategy	Line Extension Strategy

line can create production and distribution problems and added costs without incremental sales. As an example, just under 8 percent of personal-care and household products sold in the United States account for 84.5 percent of total sales. Such statistics have led companies that market these products to prune their product lines in the mid-1990s.[15]

Strong brand equity makes possible a *brand extension strategy*, the practice of using a current brand name to enter a completely different product class. This strategy can reduce the risk associated with introducing an offering in a new market by providing consumers the familiarity of and knowledge about an established brand. For instance, the equity in the Tylenol name as a trusted pain reliever allowed Johnson & Johnson to successfully extend this name to Tylenol Cold & Flu and Tylenol PM, a sleep aid. Fisher-Price, an established name in children's toys, was able to extend its name to children's shampoo and conditioners and baby bath and lotion products. Transferring an existing brand name to a new product class requires great care. For example, research indicates that the perceptual fit of the brand with and the transfer of the core product benefit to the new product class must exist for a brand extension to be successful. This happened with Tylenol and Fisher-Price, and both ventures produced sizable sales volume gains for the brands. However, it did not with Levi business attire and Dunkin Donuts cereal. Both efforts failed. Even successful brand extensions involve a risk. Too many uses for one brand name can dilute the meaning of a brand for consumers. Some marketing analysts claim this has happened to the Arm & Hammer brand given its extension to toothpaste, laundry detergent, cat litter, air freshener, carpet deodorizer, antiperspirant, and other product classes.[16]

A recent variation on brand extensions is the practice of *co-branding*, the pairing of two brand names of two manufacturers on a single product. For example, Hershey Foods has teamed with General Mills to offer a co-branded breakfast cereal called Reese's Peanut Butter Puffs and with Nabisco to provide Chips Ahoy cookies using Hershey's chocolate morsels. Citibank co-brands MasterCard and Visa with American Airlines and Ford. Co-branding benefits firms by allowing them to enter new product classes and capitalize on an already established brand name in those product classes.

In situations in which an organization concludes that its existing brand name(s) cannot be extended to a new product class, a new brand strategy is appropriate. A *new brand strategy* involves the development of a new brand and often a new offering for a product class that has not been previously served by the organization. Examples of successful new brand strategies include the introduction of Prego spaghetti sauce by Campbell Soup, and Aleve, a nonprescription pain reliever, by Roche Holding, Ltd. In both examples, existing company brand names were not deemed extendable to the new product classes for which they were targeted.

A new brand strategy may be the most challenging to successfully implement and the most costly. The cost to introduce a new brand in some consumer markets ranges from $50 million to $100 million. In many ways, this strategy is akin to diversification, with all the attendant challenges associated with this product-market strategy. The marketing of Eagle brand snacks by Anheuser-Busch described in Chapter 1 is an example of a new brand strategy failure. Launching a new brand (Eagle) in a product class new to the company (salty snacks) meant competing with Frito-Lay, the market leader, and its well-entrenched brands. Without a cost/price or quality advantage, focused distribution, effective advertising, promotion, or sales effort, the Eagle brand never achieved more than a modest market share and operated at a loss for 17 years before its demise in 1996.[17]

Sometimes new brands are created for a product class already served by the organization when a line extension strategy is deemed inappropriate. These brands expand the product line to tap specific consumer segments not attracted to an organization's existing products/brands or represent defensive moves to counteract competition. As the name suggests, a *flanker brand strategy* involves adding new brands on the high or low end of a product line based on a price–quality continuum. The Marriott Hotel group has done this to attract different traveler segments. In addition to its medium-priced Marriott hotels, it has added Marriott Marquis hotels to attract the upper end of the traveler market. It has added Courtyard hotels for the economy-minded traveler and the Fairfield Inn for those with a very low travel budget. Each brand offers a different amenities assortment and a corresponding room rate. A *fighting brand strategy* involves adding a new brand whose sole purpose is to confront competitive brands in a product class being served by an organization. A fighting brand is typically introduced when (1) an organization has a high relative share of the sales in a product class, (2) its dominant brand(s) is susceptible to having this high share sliced away by aggressive pricing or promotion by competitors, or (3) the organization wishes to preserve its profit margins on its existing brand(s). Frito-Lay successfully used its Santitas brand tortilla chip as a fighting brand to confront lower price and lower quality regional tortilla chip brands. This was done without changing the premium price and quality of its flagship Doritos and Tostitos brand tortilla chips. Similarly, Kodak introduced its Funtime brand of film priced 20 percent below its dominant Kodak brand to compete against lower-priced film sold by Fuji and Konica.

Like line extensions, fighting and flanker brand strategies incur the risk of cannibalizing the other brand(s) in a product line. This is particularly likely with lower-priced brands. However, advocates of these brand strategies argue that it is better to engage in *preemptive cannibalism*—the conscious practice of stealing sales from an organization's existing products or brands to keep customers from switching to competitor's offerings—than lose sales volume.[18]

NOTES

1. "It's Not As Easy As 1-2-3 Anymore," *Business Week* (October 14, 1991): 112–114.

2. J. Rigdon, "Kodak Tries to Prepare for Filmless Era Without Inviting Demise of Core Business," *The Wall Street Journal* (April 18, 1991): B1, B5; "Kodak's New Focus," *Business Week* (January 30, 1995): 62–67.

3. "Pinning Down Costs of Product Introductions," *The Wall Street Journal* (November 26, 1990): B1; "Blade Runner," *The Economist* (April 10, 1993): 68; "Role of New Products Puts Scope on SKUs," *Advertising Age* (October 9, 1995): 18–19.

4. "Royal Crown Co. to Launch A 'Premium' Cola," *The Wall Street Journal* (June 13, 1995): B10.

5. For an extended treatment of the new product development process, see C. Merle Crawford, *New Products Management*, 5th ed. (Chicago: Richard D. Irwin, 1997).

6. *New Products Management for the 1980s* (New York: Booz, Allen, and Hamilton, 1982). Also see "FLOPS," *Business Week* (August 16, 1993): 76-82.

7. B. Johnson, "Wash-day Washout," *Advertising Age* (June 3, 1991): 24.

8. Philip Kotler, *Marketing Management*, 8th ed. (Upper Saddle River, NJ: Prentice Hall, 1994): 371.

9. Much of the following discussion is based on Rajeev Batra, John G. Myers, and David A. Aaker, *Advertising Management*, 5th ed. (Upper Saddle River, NJ: Prentice Hall, 1996): 190-201.

10. This example is adapted from Russell Haley, "Benefit Segmentation: A Decision Oriented Research Tool," in Ben Enis and Keith Cox (eds.) *Marketing Classics*, 7th ed. (Boston: Allyn and Bacon, 1991): 208-215.

11. For an extended discussion on brand equity, see David Aaker, *Managing Brand Equity* (New York: Free Press, 1991); Kevin Keller, "Conceptualizing, Measuring, and Managing Customer-Based Brand Equity," *Journal of Marketing* (January 1993): 1-22; R. Kenneth Teas and Terry H. Grapentine, "Demystifying Brand Equity," *Marketing Management* (Summer 1996): 25-29; and Betsy Morris, "The Brand's the Thing," *Fortune* (March 4, 1996): 72-86.

12. For an extended discussion of distributor brands, see Walter Salmon and K. Omar, "Private Labels Are Back in Fashion," *Harvard Business Review* (May-June 1987): 99-106. Also see John A. Quelch and David Harding, "Brands Versus Private Labels: Fighting to Win," *Harvard Business Review* (January-February 1996): 99-109.

13. "Big Companies Add Private-Label Lines That Vie With Their Premium Brands," *The Wall Street Journal* (May 21, 1993): B1.

14. For different views on brand growth strategies, see John A. Quelch and David Kenny, "Extend Profits, Not Product Lines," *Harvard Business Review* (September-October 1994): 153-60; Edward M. Tauber, "Brand Leverage: Strategy for Growth in a Cost-Controlled World," *Journal of Advertising Research* (August-September 1988): 26-30; "Attack of the Fighting Brands," *Business Week* (May 2, 1994): 125; and David A. Aaker and Kevin Lane Keller, "Consumer Evaluations of Brand Extensions," *Journal of Marketing* (January 1990): 27-41.

15. "Make It Simple," *Business Week* (September 9, 1996): 96-105.

16. "Missteps Mar Church & Dwight's Plans," *The Wall Street Journal* (April 28, 1995): B5.

17. "How Eagle Became Extinct," *Business Week* (March 4, 1996): 68-69.

18. For an extended discussion on product cannibalism and preemptive cannibalism, see Roger A. Kerin and Dwight Riskey, "Product Cannibalism," in Sidney Levy, ed., *Marketing Manager's Handbook* (Chicago: Dartnell Company, 1994).

Zoëcon Corporation
Insect Growth Regulators

In January 1986, Zoëcon Corporation executives met to assess future growth and profit opportunities for its Strike® brand insect growth regulator (IGR) called Strike ROACH ENDER®. The meeting was prompted by a recent change in top management and corporate objectives, which now emphasized a focus on high financial-return businesses and products.

The first item on the agenda was the marketing program for Strike ROACH ENDER. This product had been in a consumer test market for six months in four cities: Charleston, South Carolina; Beaumont, Texas; Charlotte, North Carolina; and New Orleans, Louisiana. The results of the test market and future directions for the product were to be discussed. Ideas had already surfaced in informal meetings, however. Some executives believed Zoëcon (pronounced Zoy-con) should expand distribution of Strike ROACH ENDER to 19 cities in April 1986, with the intent of distributing the product nationally in April 1987. Other executives felt that Zoëcon should concentrate its effort on opportunities in the professional pest control market. Still other executives held the view that Zoëcon should reconsider any plans to market the product itself. Rather, these executives said Zoëcon should sell its IGR compound to firms actively engaged in reaching the consumer insecticide market. These firms included d-Con Company, S. C. Johnson and Son (Raid), and Boyle-Midway Division of American Home Products (Black Flag).

Further discussions indicated that some alternatives were mutually exclusive and others were not. For example, Zoëcon could sell to the consumer market under the Strike name or through other firms and also distribute its IGR to professional pest control operators. However, if Zoëcon was able to sell its IGR compound to, say, d-Con, then selling Strike ROACH ENDER would be infeasible. According to one Zoëcon executive, "The decision is basically how can we best allocate our technical, financial, and marketing resources for our IGR compounds."

■ ZOËCON CORPORATION

Zoëcon Corporation was founded in 1968 in Palo Alto, California, by Dr. Carl Djerassi to research endocrinological methods of insect population control. Djerassi was a pioneer in the development of chemical methods for human birth control, which subsequently led to the introduction of the birth control pill. The name Zoëcon is a combination of the Greek words *zoe* for life and *con* for control.

Zoëcon Corporation was acquired in 1983 by Sandoz, Ltd., a Swiss-based producer of pharmaceuticals, agrichemicals, and colors and dyes. Zoëcon's mission was to be the marketing arm of Sandoz, Ltd., in the animal health and insect control areas.

This case was prepared by Dr. Larry Smith, graduate student, under the supervision of Professor Roger A. Kerin, of the Edwin L. Cox School of Business, Southern Methodist University, as a basis for classroom discussion and is not designed to illustrate effective or ineffective handling of an administrative situation. Certain names and data have been disguised. The cooperation of Zoëcon Corporation in the preparation of this case is gratefully acknowledged. Copyright © 1986 by Roger A. Kerin. No part of this case may be reproduced without written permission of the copyright holder.

EXHIBIT 1

Selected Zoëcon Products and Applications

Brand/Product	Target Insects and Rodents
Consumer	
Strike ROACH ENDER®	Cockroaches, fleas, ticks, mosquitoes,
Strike FLEA ENDER®	spiders, crickets
VAPORETTE® flea collars	
Methoprene	
Roach traps	
Insect strips	
Animal Health	
VET-KEM®—flea collars, dips, flea aerosols and foggers, flea powders, flea shampoos	Fleas, ticks, sarcoptic mange
ZODIAC®—flea collars, dips, flea aerosols and foggers, flea powders, flea and regular shampoos	
STARBAR®—flybait; cattle dusts, sprays, and dips; swine dusts, sprays, and dips; insect strips; rodenticides; pet products; Altosid® feed-through	Houseflies, cattle hornflies, grubs, lice, mosquitoes, rats and mice, fleas, ticks, and sarcoptic mange
Pest Control	
SAFROTIN®	Cockroaches, fleas, houseflies, pharoah's
PRECOR®	ants, stored-product pests, tobacco moths,
GENCOR®	cigarette beetles, mosquitoes, and blackflies
FLYTEK®	
PHARORID®	
DIANEX®	
KABAT®	
ALTOSID®	
TEKNAR®	

Source: Company records. STRIKE, ROACH ENDER, FLEA ENDER, VAPORETTE, VET-KEM, ZODIAC, STAR-BAR, SAFROTIN, PRECOR, GENCOR, FLYTEK, PHARORID, DIANEX, KABAT, ALTOSID, and TEKNAR are trademarks of Sandoz, Ltd.

Zoëcon sells (1) animal health products to small-animal veterinarians and clinics, (2) pest control chemicals for farm animals, (3) insecticides for household pets and pest control to supermarkets, pet stores, veterinarians, and pest control companies, and (4) products and chemical compounds to firms engaged in marketing pest control products to the consumer market. For example, Zoëcon produces the chemicals for the Black Flag Roach Motel sold by Boyle-Midway. The company recorded $100 million in sales from these products and a 25 percent pretax profit on sales. A partial list of company products and applications is shown in Exhibit 1.

■ INSECT CONTROL

The use of chemical toxins to control insect pests is commonplace. Although these toxins are potentially harmful to people as well as insects, recent advances in chemistry have reduced the threat to people. Surviving insects, however, may produce successive generations that are resistant to toxins.

Public concern over the toxic effect of agricultural and household insecticides has remained widespread despite the advances in chemistry. In particular, consumers have evidenced increasing concern that safer household insecticides be used where children and pets might come in contact with the residual chemicals. The demand for safer compounds caused a change in the focus of research and development from new insect adulticides, which kill adult insects, to chemical compounds that disrupt insect reproduction.

Insect Life Cycles

Insects reproduce by laying eggs. The life patterns after hatching from the egg vary among different insect species. The flea has a complete metamorphic cycle, passing in sequence through the egg, larval, and pupal stages to the adult stage in 23 days. Cockroach metamorphosis is incomplete. Wingless nymphs hatch from eggs and grow by shedding their exoskeletons, molting six times through six nymphal stages, called instars. Molting of the sixth instar produces winged, sexually mature adult roaches in 74 days.

Metamorphosis is controlled by the insect's endocrine system. In fleas, hormones regulate development and transition from larval to pupal to adult stages. Analogously, in roaches, molting is initiated when the brain produces a neurohormone that activates prothoracic gland production of a molting hormone. Additionally, a juvenile hormone is produced by the brain in decreasing amounts, until at the sixth and final molt no juvenile hormone is produced. This molting produces sexually mature adult cockroaches up to two inches long.

The life cycle of the cockroach is shown in Exhibit 2. It begins with formation of about 40 eggs in a capsule called an ootheca. The adult female produces one

EXHIBIT 2

Normal Life Cycle of the Cockroach

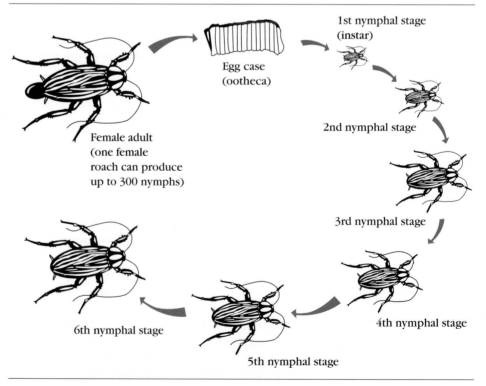

Egg case (ootheca)

1st nymphal stage (instar)

2nd nymphal stage

3rd nymphal stage

4th nymphal stage

5th nymphal stage

6th nymphal stage

Female adult (one female roach can produce up to 300 nymphs)

ootheca every 23 days over an average life span of 150 days, for a total of about 260 roaches. Research on cockroaches indicates that a roach population will increase geometrically if ample food, water, and shelter are available. Research also indicates that roaches are omnivorous and have a particular liking for beer.

Insect Growth Regulators

Insect growth regulators are effective against insects that are problems as adults, such as cockroaches. Roaches have been shown to carry bacteria, viruses, fungi, and protozoa, which cause diseases such as food poisoning, diarrhea, dysentery, hepatitis B, polio, and encephalitis. They are also capable of carrying organisms causing cholera, plague, typhus, leprosy, and tuberculosis. Furthermore, in susceptible individuals, cockroach contaminations may produce allergic reactions similar to hay fever, asthma, food allergies, and dermatitis.

Insect growth regulators are synthetic analogs of the natural insect juvenile hormones produced in the normal sequence of metamorphosis. The concentration of juvenile hormone produced decreases with each molting, to permit emergence of an adult insect after the pupal stage (for fleas) or after the last nymph stage (for roaches). If the larva or nymph is exposed to an IGR during the stage prior to molting, however, subsequent development into an adult is prevented or altered. Fleas exposed to an IGR during the larval stage pupate but fail to emerge to continue the reproductive cycle. Similarly, cockroaches exposed to an IGR in the sixth instar molt will become deformed, sexually immature adults incapable of reproducing.

As chemicals, IGRs are much less toxic than compounds typically used in household insecticides. Because they are synthetic chemical analogs of juvenile hormones specific to insects, they are not physiologically active in human or animal endocrine systems.

IGRs are extremely effective in eliminating insect populations. Only a few tenths of a milligram per square foot is required for effective control of insect reproduction. When an IGR is combined with an adulticide, many insects are killed and those that survive are prohibited from reproducing. In time, an insect infestation is controlled and, ideally, eliminated.

A unique feature of IGRs is that the immediate effects of an application are not observable. That is, since an IGR affects the reproductive cycle of an insect, it does not kill insects that come in contact with the compound. Controlled tests of a cockroach IGR indicate that a significant reduction in roach population occurs after 120 days and continues with applications spaced at 120-day intervals. When the IGR is combined with an adulticide, adult roaches and nymphs are killed upon contact with the adulticide. Short-term residual effects of the adulticide can repel roaches from treated areas, however. Therefore, the adulticide can hamper the effect of an IGR, since insects avoid treated areas.

■ PREMISE INSECTICIDE MARKET

The premise insecticide market is divided into two segments: the consumer market and the professional pest control market. The distinction is based on distribution systems and product forms. Insecticides for the consumer market are packaged in easy-to-use, do-it-yourself containers sold mostly through supermarkets. The professional pest control market consists of sales of insecticides, often in diluted form, to professional applicators. Orkin and Terminix are examples of professional applicators.

Consumer Market

Estimated annual sales for all consumer-disbursed insecticides in 1985 were $400 million at manufacturers' prices. Sales were forecasted to grow at an average rate of 10 percent per year through 1990. S. C. Johnson and Son, Inc. captured 45 percent of this market with its Raid brand. The Boyle-Midway Division of American Home Products accounted for 12 percent of the market with Black Flag, and d-Con Company captured 10 percent. No other company had a market share greater than 8 percent.

Supermarkets accounted for 70 percent of insecticide sales, followed by drugstores (9 percent) and a host of other retailers such as home improvement centers and house and garden outlets (21 percent). Aerosol sprays, including foggers, were the preferred method for applying insecticides and accounted for 74 percent of retail sales. Liquid sprays followed with 14 percent. Solids, strips, pastes, traps, and baits generated 12 percent of retail sales. Differences in packaging were based on consumers' preferences for quick-kill, residual control, or a margin of safety. Quick-kill dominated the consumer mindset, hence the popularity of aerosols and liquids that allowed for a "chase and squirt" routine when a roach was seen.

The consumer market was further subdivided into insect-specific insecticides. Ant and roach killers captured 40 percent of the market, flying insect killers 20 percent, flea killers 11 percent, and other insect-specific products 29 percent.

As expected, household insecticide sales were seasonal and varied by geography. The six-month period from May through October was the prime sales time for insecticides; 75 percent of annual sales were made during this period. The southern tier of 14 states (from the East Coast to the West Coast) accounted for 50 percent of annual sales.

Insecticides sold to the consumer market are heavily promoted. In 1983, the most recent year for which advertising expenditures were available, manufacturers spent $28.6 million for magazine, newspaper, television, radio, and outdoor advertising. For example, it was estimated that S. C. Johnson and Son spent $1.4 million to advertise Raid Ant & Roach Killer, Roach and Flea Killer, and Roach Traps. Boyle-Midway spent almost $3 million to advertise its Black Flag Roach & Ant Killer and Roach Motel. Past history of product introductions indicated that a minimum $10 million promotion investment was required to successfully launch a new product when consumers were familiar with the brand name.

Professional Pest Control Market

The professional pest control market produced revenues of $2.5 billion in 1985. Revenues were forecasted to be $3.7 billion in 1990, representing an annual average growth rate of 8 percent. About 6 percent of the revenues produced by pest control operators (PCOs) were accounted for by chemical compound cost.

The majority (52 percent) of professional pest control revenues resulted from general insect control (for example, of cockroaches, fleas, or ants). Termite control accounted for 21 percent of professional pest control revenues. The remaining 27 percent were from specialty pest control applications, especially rodent control.

This market was dominated by many small PCOs. There were an estimated 14,000 PCOs, of which only two (Orkin and Terminix) had annual sales greater than $100 million. About 28 PCOs had annual sales greater than $3 million, whereas over 6,000 had revenues under $50,000 annually.

Insecticides were sold to PCOs through distributors. These distributors purchased insecticides in bulk quantities (cases and pallets) from producers and then sold them to PCOs in smaller quantities. These distributors typically received an average gross margin of 27 percent on the selling price to PCOs. Although percentages varied, industry sources estimated that the producer's average gross profit on chemicals sold to the professional pest control market was 51 percent. By comparison, the average gross profit on insecticides sold to the consumer market was 55 percent.

Producer marketing expenses associated with selling to the professional pest control market were small in comparison to the costs of selling to the consumer market. As a general rule, about 27 percent of sales were spent for marketing to PCOs. Most of these expenses were for trade advertising and sales efforts.

■ ZOËCON PRODUCT DEVELOPMENT AND MARKETING

From its beginning, Zoëcon made a large commitment to ongoing research on IGRs. By the mid-1970s, Zoëcon research scientists, who comprised more than 25 percent of the company's employees, had synthesized more than 1,250 IGRs, and 175 patents had been issued for these inventions.

Development and Marketing of Flea Compound

The first commercialized IGR, methoprene, was introduced in 1974 for mosquito control. This IGR was made available in a variety of product forms over the years for multiple control uses. In 1980, Zoëcon obtained EPA approval for the use of methoprene under the trade name PRECOR® as a flea control compound. Given the company's already established trade relations with PCOs, veterinary clinics, and pet stores, Zoëcon began selling its flea control compound to these outlets. By 1985, Zoëcon executives estimated that the company had captured 80 percent of all flea product sales made through these outlets. Some company executives attributed the success of PRECOR to the fact that PCOs, veterinarians, and pet store sales personnel could explain the unique benefits and application of methoprene.

The early success of PRECOR led Zoëcon to look for opportunities outside of PCOs, animal clinics, and pet stores. Market analysis revealed that supermarkets accounted for a rapidly growing percentage of flea product sales volume. Since Zoëcon had no significant experience dealing with supermarkets, it approached the makers of d-Con, Black Flag, and Raid products about including PRECOR in their products. Only d-Con expressed interest. In 1981, d-Con introduced Flea Stop, a fogger for fleas containing only PRECOR—no adulticide was included among the ingredients. Flea Stop sold well in supermarkets, given the sales and marketing support provided by d-Con.

PRECOR's success prompted Zoëcon to again approach the makers of Black Flag and Raid in 1982. No agreement could be reached, however. This setback resulted in the decision by Zoëcon to develop its own brand for sales through supermarkets. In early 1983, Zoëcon introduced Strike FLEA ENDER®, which includes PRECOR and an adulticide, in 19 cities that accounted for the majority of flea product sales. By late 1983, Strike FLEA ENDER had captured 11 percent of flea product sales in those cities. This success led to an agreement with S. C. Johnson and Son, in December 1983, to include PRECOR in its Raid Flea Killer Plus. This agreement allowed Zoëcon to continue marketing PRECOR under the STRIKE brand name. Strike FLEA ENDER had an 18 percent market share in 1985; however, the product had not yet achieved its profit objective.

Development and Marketing of Roach Compound

Continuing research efforts resulted in the development of hydroprene, an IGR that was particularly useful for preventing normal cockroach maturation. This discovery was viewed as a major breakthrough in the creation of synthetic chemical analogs of naturally occurring insect juvenile hormones. In early 1984, Zoëcon obtained EPA

EXHIBIT 3

Strike ROACH ENDER Print Advertisement

registrations for hydroprene. By late 1984, the company was marketing hydroprene under the GENCOR® trade name only to PCOs, since pet stores and veterinary clinics had little or no use for this compound.

In late 1984, Zoëcon executives responsible for Strike FLEA ENDER proposed that a hydroprene-based product with the name Strike ROACH ENDER® be introduced to supermarkets. This proposal requested that Strike ROACH ENDER, which would contain hydroprene and an adulticide, be introduced in the same 19 cities where Strike FLEA ENDER was being sold. Top management believed that an opportunity existed but that Strike ROACH ENDER should be test-marketed before an investment in all 19 markets was made. Accordingly, a test market plan was drafted in early 1985.

Test-Marketing Strike Roach Ender

Two objectives were set for the test market: to determine consumer acceptance of the product and to qualify the trade and consumer marketing program. The four cities chosen for the test were Charlotte, North Carolina; Charleston, South Carolina; Beaumont, Texas; and New Orleans, Louisiana. These cities were considered representative of the 19-city market where 80 percent of roach insecticides were sold. The cities contained 1.17 million households, or 5.3 percent of the 22 million households in that market area. The test market ran from May through October 1985. Product shipments to supermarkets in the four cities began in April.

Segmentation and Positioning Research on roach insecticide users indicated that three segments existed, based on the primary benefit sought. The primary target market for Strike ROACH ENDER was the "end problem permanently" segment. A secondary market was the "product that lasts" segment. The "convenience/low cost" segment was not considered a primary or secondary target.

Strike ROACH ENDER was positioned as a scientific breakthrough with unique qualities desired by the targeted segments. A print advertisement for the product is shown in Exhibit 3.

Product Packaging and Price Strike ROACH ENDER was packaged in a 10-ounce aerosol spray and a 6-ounce fogger. The retail price for the aerosol was $4.49 and for the fogger was $3.99. These prices were 50 to 75 percent higher than those of existing roach insecticides. The premium price was justified on the basis of the product's unique compound and long-lasting effect. The higher price also provided supermarkets with a higher margin than they received from competitive products. Price and cost data are shown in Exhibit 4.

Consumer and Trade Promotion Television and newspaper advertising was used to build consumer awareness, and cents-off coupons were employed to stimulate product trial. The consumer promotion and media strategy focused on 25- to 54-year-old women living in households of three or more. A "blitz" strategy was used, with the heaviest promotion scheduled for the first three months of the test. A public relations effort was also launched, featuring press kit mailings to newspapers, guest ap-

EXHIBIT 4

Strike ROACH ENDER Package Economics

	10-oz. Aerosol	6-oz Fogger
Price to trade[a]	$3.14	$2.79
Cost of goods sold[b]	1.41	1.26
Zoëcon's gross profit	$1.73	$1.53

[a] Price to trade is the price at which Zoëcon sells directly to the retailer.

[b] Cost of goods sold includes the cost of the can, solvent, propellant, active ingredients, and freight. Note that the cost of goods sold represents virtually all of the variable costs associated with the product forms.

EXHIBIT 5

Strike ROACH ENDER Trade Promotion

pearances on local radio and television talk shows, and an 800-number consumer hotline to answer consumers' questions.

The trade promotion included discounts for first-time supermarket buyers, a calendar to assist buyers in coordinating store promotion with consumer advertising, freestanding in-store displays, and sales aids. Exhibit 5 shows a Strike ROACH ENDER trade promotion.

Test-Market Expenditures and Results The cost of the test market was $1,478,000. An itemized summary is shown in Exhibit 6.

Results of the test market were tracked by an independent marketing research firm. At the end of the test in November 1985, 57 percent of the households in the test cities were aware of the product, 6 percent of the households in the test cities had tried the product, and 30 percent of those households that had tried the prod-

EXHIBIT 6

Summary of Marketing Expenses for the Strike ROACH ENDER Test Market

Activity	*Expense*
Promotion and advertising[a]	$1,016,000
Setup/auditing[b]	377,000
Marketing research[c]	65,000
Miscellaneous[d]	20,000
	$1,478,000

[a] Includes consumer advertising and promotion to supermarket buyers.

[b] Includes point-of-purchase materials, monitoring of shelf placement, sales aids, and free goods.

[c] Includes consumer tracking studies (for example, product awareness and purchase behavior).

[d] Includes public relations campaign.

uct had repurchased during the test period. The average number of units purchased by all trier households was 1.3 units. Households that repurchased bought an average of 3.5 units in addition to their initial purchase. Sixty-six percent of Strike ROACH ENDER sales were of the aerosol spray; 34 percent were of foggers. This breakdown was identical for first purchases and subsequent purchases. Product shipments data indicated that 11,700 cases (at 12 units per case) of 10-ounce aerosol units and 6,300 cases (at 12 units per case) of 6-ounce fogger units were shipped to supermarket warehouses in the four cities during the test period.

■ JANUARY MEETING

When Zoëcon executives met in January 1986, the first item on the agenda was to review the test-market results and prepare marketing plans for 1986. Different points of view had already been expressed in informal discussions among Zoëcon executives. One position advanced was that Strike ROACH ENDER distribution should be expanded to the 19 cities where Strike FLEA ENDER was being sold. Marketing research indicated that these 19 cities accounted for 80 percent of roach insecticide volume. These executives reasoned that the up-front investment in marketing research, public relations, and set-up/auditing costs would not have to be repeated in the expanded distribution. Rather, the primary direct costs associated with the rollout to all 19 cities would be for promotion and advertising.

A second view was that Zoëcon should direct its resources to PCOs. These executives noted that GENCOR® (hydroprene) had been well received by PCOs in late 1984 and many PCOs were promoting its benefits to their customers. These executives felt that an ongoing investment of $500,000 per year above the 27 percent of sales typically budgeted for trade advertising and sales efforts would accelerate its use.

A third opinion was that Zoëcon should pursue opportunities for selling hydroprene to the makers of d-Con, Black Flag, and Raid for use in their products. This strategy had worked in the past for PRECOR (methoprene). A product cost analysis performed on Strike ROACH ENDER indicated that the cost of goods sold for the 10-ounce aerosol package without hydroprene would be $0.80. For the 6-ounce fogger package without hydroprene, the cost of goods sold would also be $0.80. Furthermore, Zoëcon could realize a 50 percent gross margin on hydroprene sold to another insecticide marketer with no investment in marketing or sales. These costs would be absorbed by the marketer of the product—d-Con, Black Flag, or Raid. Executives favoring this option believed the test-market experience could be used to interest insecticide marketers in the product. Specific aspects of the proposal, including the price for hydroprene, would have to be developed if this option was adopted. Executives favoring the continued marketing of Strike ROACH ENDER cautioned that this action could spell the end for Zoëcon's presence in the consumer market.

Zoëcon executives present at the January 1986 meeting were acutely aware of the importance of the decision they faced. Moreover, the peak season for roach insecticides was approaching, and a decision needed to be made quickly.

Frito-Lay's® Dips

In late 1986, Ben Ball, Marketing Director, and Ann Mirabito, Product Manager, had just completed the planning review for the line of dips sold by Frito-Lay, Inc. Frito-Lay's® Dips were a highly profitable product line and had shown phenomenal sales growth in the past five years. Sales in 1985 were $87 million, compared with $30 million in 1981.

A major issue raised at the planning meeting was where and how Frito-Lay's® Dips could be developed further. Two different viewpoints were expressed. One view was that the dip line should be more aggressively promoted in its present market segment. This segment was broadly defined as the "chip dip" category. The other view was that Frito-Lay should also actively pursue the "vegetable dip" category. The company had recently introduced a shelf-stable, sour cream–based French onion dip nationally, and 1986 sales were forecasted to be $10 million. The new dip was the first sour cream–based dip introduced by Frito-Lay. Some executives felt that this dip could provide a bridge to the vegetable dip category, which could be further developed.

Frito-Lay executives had yet to decide how much emphasis to place on each category in 1987. Furthermore, expense budgets would need special consideration. More aggressive marketing would require higher marketing investment or at least a reallocation of funds, while at the same time the gross margin and profit contribution of dips would have to be preserved.

■ DIP CATEGORY

Dips are typically used as an appetizer, snack, or accompaniment to a meal. Dip popularity has risen in recent years as a result of the convenience of use, multiple uses, and "grazing" trends in the United States. Dips can be served along with chips, crackers, or raw vegetables.

The market for dips is highly fragmented and difficult to measure; however, upward of 80 percent of dip sales are accounted for by supermarkets. According to industry estimates, total dip retail dollar sales volume through supermarkets was $620 million in 1985. Two-thirds of this dollar volume was captured by prepared dips; the remaining one-third was accounted for by dip mixes for at-home preparation. About 55 percent of the prepared dips sold in supermarkets required refrigeration. The major competitors in this segment were Kraft, Borden, a large number of regional dairies, and numerous store brands. Refrigerated dip retail prices were typically in the range from $0.07 to $0.15 per ounce. About 45 percent of prepared dips were "shelf stable" (that is, they were packaged in metal cans and required no refrigera-

This case was prepared by Jeanne Bertels, graduate student, under the supervision of Professor Roger A. Kerin, of the Edwin L. Cox School of Business, Southern Methodist University, as a basis for class discussion and is not designed to illustrate effective or ineffective handling of an administrative situation. The cooperation of Frito-Lay, Inc. is gratefully acknowledged. Selected financial and market data have been disguised or approximated and are not useful for research purposes. Copyright © 1986 by Roger A. Kerin. No part of this case may be reproduced without the written permission of the copyright holder.

tion). These dips could be displayed virtually anywhere in a supermarket, though they were typically located near snack foods. Frito-Lay was the major competitor in shelf-stable dips, followed by regional chip manufacturers. Shelf-stable dip retail prices were in the range from $0.13 to $0.20 per ounce. By comparison, prices of dip mix were typically $0.09 per ounce (including the cost of a sour cream mixer or base).

Exhibit 1 shows a breakdown of the $620 million sales of dips in supermarkets by product type. Industry research indicates that dip dollar sales are growing at 10 percent per year, but this growth has come about because of price (inflationary) increases. No real growth is evident. Virtually all of the growth in 1984 and 1985 was accounted for by cheese-based dips, which captured market share from other dip flavors.

Flavor Popularity and Usage

Sour cream-based dips are the most popular flavor. Sour cream-based prepared dips and dip mixes account for about 50 percent of total dip sales. Cheese-based dips are the second most popular segment and account for about 25 percent of total dip sales. Bean and picante dips account for about 10 percent of total dip sales, and cream cheese-based dips account for the remaining 15 percent.

Dips are most frequently used with salty snacks, such as potato chips and corn chips. Whereas about 67 percent of total dip sales are linked to salty snack usage, virtually all bean and picante dips are consumed with salty snacks. One-fourth of cream cheese-based dip volume and 85 percent of cheese-based volume are linked with chip usage. Shelf-stable dips and many dip mixes are located adjacent to salty snack foods in supermarkets. Dry soup mixes are typically shelved with canned soups. Approximately 33 percent of all dip sales ($207 million) are linked to vegetable usage, and most of this volume is sold through supermarkets. Vegetable dips are located throughout supermarkets, in produce, soup mix, salad dressing, and snack sections, since they are viewed as a complementary as opposed to a primary product. Two brands—Libby's Dip Mixes and Bennett's Toppings/Dips—are located in the produce section, but each is sold only on a regional basis. Numerous local brands are also shelved in the produce section.

The popularity of Mexican food, including nachos, has fueled the growth of cheese-based dips in particular. New product introductions and accompanying market expenditures have also stimulated trial and acceptance of Mexican-style dips. For instance, Kraft, a major competitor in cheese dips, added Mexican flavors to both new and existing product lines in 1984. New products included Kraft Nacho Cheese Dip and Kraft Premium Jalapeno Cheese Dip. Kraft also added a Mexican zest to two of its popular products: Velveeta Mexican process cheese spread features jalapeno peppers, and Kraft Cheese Whiz is offered in variations of hot salsa and mild salsa. Kraft competes primarily in the refrigerated segment of the dip market. In late 1985, however, Kraft entered the shelf-stable market with Kraft Nacho Dip and Kraft Hot Nacho Dip.

Dip Substitutes

Even though the market for dips is large, it is estimated that about 20 percent of all dip volume consumed by households in the United States is homemade. In addition, many consumers use refrigerated salad dressings for dips, especially for vegetables. It is estimated that 35 percent of refrigerated salad dressing volume is used for dips. These refrigerated salad dressings are typically located in the produce section of supermarkets and include such brands as Marie's, Bob's Big Boy, Marzetti's, and Walden Farms, as well as a few local brands in different areas of the country. Market research indicates that refrigerated salad dressings sold in the produce section of supermarkets account for $67 million in retail sales annually. Retail sales of refrigerated salad dressings have been growing at a compound annual rate of 18 percent since 1978.

EXHIBIT 1

Estimated 1985 Supermarket Dip Sales at Retail Prices

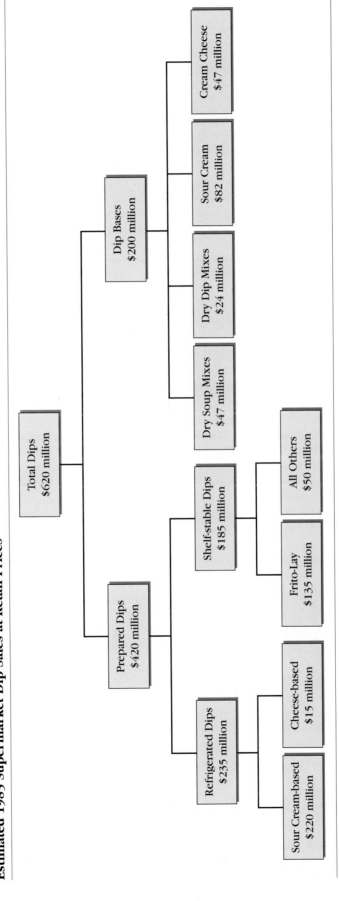

Source: Frito-Lay, Inc. company records.

Competitive Activity

Competitive activity in the dip market accelerated in 1984 and 1985. During these two years, numerous new products were introduced, and advertising expenditures increased. Industry sources estimated that dip competitors combined (excluding Frito-Lay) spent $58 million for consumer advertising alone in 1985. This figure was 25 percent higher than in 1984.

Equally noteworthy is the fact that large, well-financed companies began to aggressively pursue the dip market. For example, Campbell Soup introduced a nacho soup/dip and a line of vegetable dip mixes in 1985, and Lipton expanded its line of vegetable dip mixes and upgraded its packaging in 1985. According to Ann Mirabito, "These companies, coupled with Borden, Kraft, and regional chip manufacturers, have dramatically altered the competitive environment for chip dips in the past two years."

■ FRITO-LAY, INC.

Frito-Lay, Inc. is a division of PepsiCo, Inc., a New York-based diversified consumer goods and services firm. Other PepsiCo, Inc. divisions include Pizza Hut, Taco Bell, Pepsi Cola Bottling Group, Kentucky Fried Chicken, and PepsiCo Foods International. PepsiCo, Inc., recorded net sales of over $8 billion in 1985.

Frito-Lay is a nationally recognized leader in the manufacture and marketing of salty snack foods. The company's major salty snack products and brands include potato chips (Lay's®, O'Grady's®, Ruffles®, Delta Gold®), corn chips (Fritos®), tortilla chips (Doritos®, Tostitos®), cheese puffs (Cheetos®), and pretzels (Rold Gold®). Other well-known products include Baken-Ets® brand fried pork skins, Munchos® brand potato chips, and Funyuns® brand onion-flavored snacks. In addition, the company markets a line of nuts, peanut butter crackers, processed beef sticks, Grandma's® brand cookies and snack bars, and assorted other snacks. Frito-Lay's net sales in 1985 approached $3 billion.

Given the nature of its products, Frito-Lay competes primarily within what is termed the salty snack food segment of the snack food market. In 1985, Frito-Lay captured about 33 percent of the salty snack food tonnage sold in the United States.

The Dip Business

The first two dips introduced by Frito-Lay were Frito-Lay's® Jalapeno Bean Dip and Enchilada Bean Dip. These dips, marketed in the 1950s, were viewed as a logical complement to the company's Fritos® corn chips. A Picante Sauce Dip was introduced in 1978 to complement the newly introduced Tostitos® tortilla chips. These three dips were the only Frito-Lay dips sold until 1983.

Dip popularity accelerated extension of the dip product line in 1983. In late 1983 and early 1984, Frito-Lay introduced a number of cheese-based dips, including Mild Cheddar, Cheddar and Herb, Cheddar and Jalapeno, and Cheddar and Bacon, all of which were packaged in nine-ounce cans like the Mexican-style dips. According to Ben Ball, "Cheese dips were an extension of Frito-Lay's tortilla chip business and were a response to the Mexican food phenomenon sweeping the country." These new dips were shelf stable and were sold under the Frito-Lay's® brand name. Ball commented, "There was some discussion about whether or not we should use the Frito-Lay's® brand name with the cheese dips. However, we chose to stay with the Frito-Lay's® name to trade off the company's equity in salty snacks and capitalize on the company's strengths in marketing and distribution." The cheese dips, like their predecessors, were displayed in the salty snack section of supermarkets.

EXHIBIT 2

Dollar Sales of Frito-Lay's® Dips (in Millions of Dollars)

Year	Mexican Dips	Cheese Dips	Sour Cream Dip	Total Dips
1986 (forecast)	$41	$48	$10	$99
1985	39	48	—	87
1984	40	55	—	95
1983	38	5	—	43
1982	35	—	—	35
1981	30	—	—	30

In 1986, Frito-Lay introduced its first sour cream-based, shelf-stable dip. This dip carried the Frito-Lay's® brand name and was displayed in the salty snack section of supermarkets. Its French onion flavor was viewed as an ideal accent for the company's potato chips. Industry data indicated that about 50 percent of salty snack volume sold in the United States was accounted for by potato chips. In addition, this onion dip was also deemed suitable as a vegetable dip.

Frito-Lay's dip sales for the period 1981–1985 are shown in Exhibit 2. Jalapeno Bean Dip and Picante Sauce Dip showed consistent, although slow growth in these years. Enchilada Bean Dip was dropped from the Mexican dip line in mid-1985 as a result of falling sales. Sales trends indicated that Mexican dips would show a 4 percent increase in sales in 1986. Cheese dips, by comparison, represented a huge success and outsold Mexican dips in their introductory year. Nevertheless, total dollar sales of dips declined in 1985, and forecasted 1986 sales of cheese dips would be unchanged from the previous year. Ann Mirabito attributed the decline to three factors. First, the novelty of shelf-stable cheese dips had passed. Mirabito commented, "We had good initial penetration for the products; however, with the passage of time, we settled down to a core group of customers." Second, she believed that increased competitive activity had played a part in slowing Frito-Lay's dip volume growth. Third, discontinuance of Enchilada Bean Dip had had an unexpected effect. It had been expected that consumers would switch to Frito-Lay's other Mexican dips. "They didn't, and we lost customers," Mirabito noted. Nevertheless, dips were a highly profitable product line. Exhibit 3 on page 232 shows the 1985 income statement for the dip product line.

Dip Distribution and Sales Effort

Frito-Lay distributes its products through 350,000 outlets nationwide. In 1985, 34,000 outlets were supermarkets, 47,000 were convenience stores, and 20,000 were nonfood outlets. The remainder of Frito-Lay's 350,000 outlets were small grocery stores, liquor stores, service stations, and a variety of institutional customers. The great majority of Frito-Lay's® Dips, however, are sold through supermarkets.

Frito-Lay's distribution system is organized around four geographical zones that cover the entire United States. Each zone contains distribution centers that inventory products for the Frito-Lay sales force, which is composed of over 10,000 individuals who make 400,000 sales and delivery calls during an average workday. Each Frito-Lay salesperson follows a specific, assigned route and is responsible for selling company products to present and potential customers on his or her route.

Frito-Lay uses a "front-door store delivery system," in which one person performs the sales and delivery functions. During a visit to a store, the driver/salesperson takes orders, unloads the product, stocks and arranges the shelves, and handles in-store merchandising. This sales and delivery system is particularly suited to the

EXHIBIT 3

Income Statement for Frito-Lay's® Dips, 1985 (in Thousand of Dollars)

	Mexican Dip	Cheese Dip	Total Dip
Net sales	$39,040	$48,296	$87,336
Gross margin	19,146	21,876	41,022
Marketing expense:			
Selling	8,798	11,044	19,842
Freight	1,464	1,825	3,289
Consumer advertising	60	87	147
Consumer and trade promotion	851	1,352	2,203
Total marketing expense	11,173	14,308	25,481
General and administrative overhead	2,781	3,791	6,572
Profit contribution	$5,192	$3,777	$8,969

Note: Selling and freight expenses are variable costs, consumer advertising and consumer and trade promotion are fixed costs budgeted annually, and general and administrative overhead expenses are fixed costs.

270,000 nonchain outlets serviced by Frito-Lay. Experience has indicated, however, that sales calls on chain-store accounts, which include most supermarkets, virtually always require participation by a Frito-Lay Region or Division Manager. Such participation is necessary because chain-store snack buyers purchase for all outlets in the chain and approve in-store merchandising plans as well. Furthermore, the sales task and account servicing are more time-consuming and complex, although no less important, than those required for individual outlets (for example, "mom-and-pop" grocery stores and liquor stores).

Dip Marketing

Prior to 1983, the Frito-Lay's® Dips line was viewed as a nonpromoted profit producer. With the introduction of cheese dips in 1983, Frito-Lay began promoting dips, but virtually all marketing and promotion were directed toward retail-store snack food buyers in the form of trade-oriented promotions. In 1985, the emphasis shifted to consumer promotions such as product sampling and couponing to generate trial

EXHIBIT 4

Frito-Lay's® Dips Advertising and Merchandising Expenditures, 1983–1986

Year	Consumer Advertising[a]	Consumer Promotion[b]	Trade Promotion[c]	Total
1986	$1,170,000	$3,389,220	$169,290	$4,728,510
1985	147,045	1,459,050	744,101	2,350,196
1984	None	535,266	312,180	847,446
1983	None	22,322	425,478	447,800

[a] Television and radio advertising.

[b] Product sampling, cents-off coupons, etc.

[c] Trade discounts, advertising to store buyers, etc.

EXHIBIT 5

Frito-Lay's® Dips Consumer Promotion

of the new products, and television and radio advertising was used for the first time since the 1950s. Frito-Lay's new product effort, coupled with increased competitive activity, resulted in further planned increases in consumer advertising and promotion in 1986. Exhibit 4 summarizes the advertising and merchandising expenditures for dips for the period 1983–1986. Exhibit 5 illustrates a typical consumer promotion, and Exhibit 6 on page 234 shows a typical trade promotion. A Frito-Lay's® Dip television commercial is shown in Exhibit 7 on page 235.

Ann Mirabito provided the following rationale for the change in promotion emphasis:

> The phenomenal success of Frito-Lay's® Dips was due to two factors. First, we had the right products—cheese dips were novel, and our flavors were innovative. Second, we had the right merchandising location next to salty snacks. Prior to 1985, all of our advertising and merchandising spending was trade-oriented because our goal was to gain distribution in supermarkets and shelf space rapidly. Our consumer household penetration increased from 12 percent in 1983 to 20 percent in 1984, driven largely by placing cheese dips near salty snacks. In 1985, penetration flattened, indicating a need for consumer-pull marketing.

For the most part, dips were promoted jointly with Frito-Lay salty snacks, particularly Doritos® tortilla chips. According to Ben Ball, this approach was adopted because "dips are a complementary product." He added, "Growth occurred when our dips were displayed in conjunction with a natural carrier. That's how we built the chip dip business. This association was conveyed in our promotion and in our shelf placement with salty snacks."

E X H I B I T   6

Frito-Lay's® Dips Trade Promotions

4 COLUMN INCHES

6 COLUMN INCHES

EXHIBIT 7

Frito-Lay's® Dips Television Commercial

TRACY-LOCKE
CLIENT: Frito-Lay, Inc.
PRODUCT: Frito Lay's® Dips

TITLE: "Magnetism"
LENGTH: 15 Seconds
COMM'L. NO.: PECD 6193
FIRST AIR DATE: 2/21/86

SFX: LABORATORY SOUNDS
SCIENCE EDITOR: Do you forget Frito-Lay's®
Dip?

Use the theory of magnetism,

so when you pick up the chips you automatically
. . .

SFX: METALLIC CLINK
SCIENCE EDITOR: pick up the Dip.

ANNCR (VO) AND SCIENCE EDITOR EATING:
The best way to remember Frito-Lay's® Dip is to
taste [CRUNCH! Mmmmm!] what it does to our
chips.

SCIENCE EDITOR: What an attractive concept!

■ FUTURE GROWTH OPPORTUNITIES

Two opportunities for the Frito-Lay's® Dips product line were raised at the planning review meeting. Frito-Lay could continue to develop the chip dip market, where it already had a strong foothold, or it could pursue the vegetable dip market as well, using the new sour cream-based dip as a spearhead. The decision would have significant resource allocation consequences, since it was unlikely that funds for dip advertising and merchandising would be increased in 1987 beyond the $4.73 million budgeted for 1986.

Chip Dip Opportunity

One view expressed at the planning meeting was that Frito-Lay should capitalize on its foothold in the chip dip market and attempt to expand the market and build market share. Several arguments were made for this strategy. First, research indicated that only 20 percent of chips were currently eaten with dips; furthermore, only 45 percent of all U.S. households used dips in 1985, whereas 97 percent used salty snacks. "This indicated a major opportunity to build penetration through more aggressive advertising," according to a Frito-Lay executive. Second, research indicated that in 1985 the average number of times shelf-stable dips were purchased by households was four. It was felt that this frequency could be increased through frequency-building promotions such as on-pack coupon offers to encourage repeat sales. In 1985, the purchase frequency of all Frito-Lay's® Dips was 3.6 times per year. A third argument in favor of focusing attention on the chip dip market was the increased competitive activity: 40 new Mexican-style cheese dips had been introduced since 1983. Although many were regional products, each vied for shelf space in or near the salty snack section of supermarkets. At the same time, it was believed that Kraft would be introducing additional products that would compete in the chip dip market. A fourth argument was that historically Frito-Lay had not promoted dips aggressively. It was believed that the typical ratio of advertising and merchandising spending to sales (A/S ratio) for prepared dips was 10 percent.[1] Refrigerated salad dressings had an A/S ratio of 3 percent, and salad dressing dry mixes had an A/S ratio of 13.6 percent. In 1985, Frito-Lay's A/S ratio for its dip product line was 2.7 percent. Therefore, the 1986 advertising and merchandising budget had been more than double 1985 expenditures. (A breakdown of these expenses is shown in Exhibit 8). A fifth argument was that Frito-Lay could spin off other products from its sour cream–based dip.

EXHIBIT 8

Planned Frito-Lay's® Dips Advertising and Merchandising Expenditures by Product Line, 1986

Product Line	Consumer Advertising	Consumer Promotion	Trade Promotion	Total
Mexican and cheese dips[a]	$1,170,000	$2,740,320	$ 56,790	$3,967,110
Sour cream dip	0	648,900	112,500	761,400
Total	$1,170,000	$3,389,220	$169,290	$4,728,510

[a] Total advertising and merchandising expenditures for Mexican and cheese dips were roughly proportional to 1985 sales of the two product lines.

---

[1] The A/S ratio is calculated by dividing total expenditures for consumer advertising and promotion and the trade promotion by total sales for a given year.

Other executives argued that the opportunity in the chip dip category was less promising. They based their argument on three points. First, competitive activity was such that Frito-Lay could only hope to hold, not improve, its position in the chip dip category. The effort and expense necessary to increase penetration and/or increase purchase frequency in the congested chip dip category could be better spent on attacking vegetable dips, where the competition (such as Marie's) was less formidable and more fragmented. Second, Frito-Lay's recent sales growth in dips was due to new products (for example, cheese-based dips), and it was not clear that further product line extensions could produce continued growth. There was also significant potential for cannibalization of existing cheese dips if the line was expanded further. Third, the new sour cream dip represented a break with Mexican-style dips and cheese dips and was probably more suitable for vegetable dipping. To promote and distribute this new dip solely as a chip dip rather than as a vegetable dip could mean a missed opportunity.

Vegetable Dip Opportunity

Executives who voiced concern about focusing on the chip dip category also raised several points in favor of the vegetable dip opportunity. First, they noted that 33 percent of dip sales were linked to vegetables. Moreover, industry research indicated that only one-fourth of the dollar volume associated with vegetable dipping was accounted for by refrigerated salad dressings, such as Marie's. The remainder was accounted for by dip mixes and refrigerated dips, and no major competitors had a strong competitive position in the market. Second, research indicated that sour cream-based dips were more popular than cheese dips for vegetable dipping. Third, trend data indicated that consumers were becoming concerned about the nutritional value and salt content of prepared foods.[2] It was felt that this trend could affect preferences for vegetables and salty snacks and, as a result, dips. Fourth, the Frito-Lay's® Dips line now had a sour cream–based dip that had not yet been promoted and merchandised for vegetable dipping. Fifth, no major competitor had introduced a shelf-stable dip for vegetables. Frito-Lay had pioneered the shelf-stable business for chip dips, and some executives felt that a similar opportunity existed for vegetable dips. Finally, a cost analysis indicated that the gross margins would be largely unaffected. The gross margin on Frito-Lay's sour cream dip was 45 percent.

Other executives expressed the view that pursuing the vegetable dip segment would not be easy, however. These executives cited research indicating that supermarket executives preferred that dips suitable for vegetable dipping be handled by their produce warehouse. This meant that Frito-Lay's front-door delivery system would not be favored. Distribution through the produce warehouse would also involve dealing with supermarket produce buyers and managers. Frito-Lay had never dealt with these individuals in the past, and some company executives believed that a totally new sales approach would be necessary. Even though a complete cost analysis had not been conducted, it was estimated that selling expenses could increase to 25 percent of sales. Current sales expense was 22.7 percent. Freight expense would not be affected. As of 1986, the sour cream dip was not allocated any general and administrative overhead. Furthermore, Frito-Lay driver/salespeople were unfamiliar with merchandising practices in the produce section of supermarkets. This same research indicated that any new vegetable dip should be shelved next to refrigerated salad dressing or near produce.

---

[2] Bob Messenger, "Consumers See the Light . . . and the Lean, with a Touch of Pizzazz," *Prepared Foods* (November 1985): 46–49.

A second concern was that Frito-Lay's® Dips would lose some economies in advertising and merchandizing. Frito-Lay's® Dips had been promoted jointly with the company's chips in the past and thus traded on the "halo effect" of Frito-Lay salty snacks. Mirabito acknowledged that vegetable dips would have to "go it alone" because Frito-Lay's halo effect might not translate to vegetable dips.

A third concern expressed at the meeting was that any foray into vegetable dips would require more than a single item. In addition to the French onion flavor, other flavors (such as ranch style) would be necessary. Such line extensions would require added research and development expenses and promotional support, as had been the case with the successful introduction of cheese dips.

The planning meeting adjourned without resolution of the issue. Ben Ball asked Ann Mirabito to give the "chip dip versus vegetable dip" question further consideration. She was to prepare a recommendation for another meeting to be scheduled within 30 days.

Perpetual Care Hospital
Downtown Health Clinic

In mid-April 1990, Sherri Worth, Assistant Administrator at Perpetual Care Hospital (PCH) in charge of PCH's Downtown Health Clinic (DHC), uncovered an unsettling parcel of news. During a call on the employee benefits director at a downtown department store, she was told that a firm was conducting a study to determine whether sufficient demand existed to establish a clinic five blocks north of PCH's Downtown Health Clinic. The description of the clinic's services sounded similar to those offered by the DHC, and the planned opening date was May 1991.

As Worth walked back to her office, she could not help but think about the possible competition. Upon arriving at her office, Worth called Dr. Roger Mahon, PCH's administrator, to tell him what she had learned. He asked her to contact other employee benefits directors and query patients to see whether they had been surveyed. He expressed concern for two reasons. First, a competitive clinic would attract existing and potential patients of the Downtown Health Clinic. Second, a clinic that provided similar services could hamper the DHC's progress toward achieving its service and profitability objectives. Mahon suggested that Worth summarize the DHC's performance to date so that he could speak to members of the board of trustees' executive committee on what action, if any, the DHC should take to compete for patients. He concluded their discussion by saying, "Who would have thought ten years ago that a hospital administrator would be making decisions not unlike those faced by a retail chain store executive. But I guess it comes with the territory these days."

■ HEALTH CARE AND THE HOSPITAL INDUSTRY

Health care, and specifically the hospital industry, has undergone a dramatic transformation in the past few decades. Until the 1960s, hospitals were largely charitable institutions that prided themselves on their not-for-profit orientation. Hospitals functioned primarily as workshops for physicians and were guided by civic-minded boards of trustees.

Federal legislation introduced in the 1960s created boom times for the hospital industry. The Hill-Burton Act provided billions of dollars for hospital construction, to be repaid by fulfilling quotas for charity care. Additional funds were poured into expansion and construction of medical schools. Medicare and Medicaid subsidized health care for the indigent, disabled, and elderly. These programs reimbursed hospitals for their incurred costs plus an additional return on investment. The 1960s also saw dramatic increases in commercial insurance coverage, offered as employee fringe benefits and purchased in additional quantities by a more affluent public. Ac-

This case was prepared by Professor Roger A. Kerin, of the Edwin L. Cox School of Business, Southern Methodist University, as a basis for class discussion and is not designed to illustrate effective or ineffective handling of an administrative situation. Certain names and data have been disguised.
Copyright © 1995 by Roger A. Kerin. No part of this case may be reproduced without written consent of the copyright holder.

cordingly, health care became accessible to an overwhelming majority of U.S. citizens, regardless of where they lived or their ability to pay. Federal intervention had changed the concept of health-care services from privilege to entitlement.

By the early 1980s, however, skyrocketing health-care costs had forced the federal government to reassess its role in health care. Stringent controls were placed on hospital construction and expansion, and utilization- and physician-review programs were implemented to ensure against too-lengthy inpatient stays. By the end of the decade, hospitals were initiating voluntary cost-cutting programs to stave off additional government intervention. Despite all efforts, however, health-care expenditures continued to outpace the Consumer Price Index. In 1985 Americans spent close to 10 percent of the gross national product on health care, and the government's portion was 43 percent of the $350 billion tab. Only 11 percent of all hospital services were paid for by individuals; the balance was financed by third-party payors, such as insurance companies.

The 1980s ushered in a very different health-care environment, and hospitals particularly were hard hit by the changes. On the one hand, the federal government sought to reduce health-care costs through cutbacks in subsidy programs and cost-control regulations. On the other hand, innovations in health-care delivery severely reduced the number of patients serviced by hospitals.

One such innovation was preventive health-care programs. These fall into two categories: health maintenance organizations (HMOs) and preferred provider organizations (PPOs). HMOs surfaced in the mid-1970s. An HMO encourages preventive health care by providing medical services as needed for a fixed monthly fee. HMOs typically enter into contractual relationships with designated physicians and hospitals and have been successful in reducing hospital inpatient days and health-care expenditures. PPOs, which emerged in the early 1980s, establish contractual arrangements between health-care providers (physicians and/or hospitals) and large employer groups. Unlike HMOs, PPOs generally offer incentives for using preferred providers rather than restricting individuals to specific hospitals or physicians. PPOs are likely to have the same effect on inpatient days and health-care expenditures as HMOs have, and Mahon had planned to design a PPO for Perpetual Care Hospital using the Downtown Health Clinic as a link to large employers in the downtown area.

A second and farther-reaching innovation that had an impact on health-care delivery in the 1980s was ambulatory health-care services and facilities. Ambulatory health-care services consist of treatments and practices that consumers use on an episodic or emergency basis. Examples include physical examinations, treatment of minor emergencies (such as cuts, bruises, and minor surgery), and treatment of common illnesses (such as colds and flu).

Ambulatory health-care facilities are split into two categories: (1) minor emergency centers, known by acronyms such as FEC (Free-Standing Emergency Clinic) and MEC (Medical Emergency Clinic) and (2) clinics that focus on primary or episodic care.[1] Although regulation is nominal, if a clinic positions itself as an emergency-care center, expressing this focus in its name, it generally is required (or pressured by area physicians) to be staffed 24 hours a day by a licensed physician and to have certain basic life-support equipment.

Ambulatory health-care services are the fastest-growing segment of health services. The first no-appointment, walk-in clinic opened in Newark, Delaware, in 1975. By 1990 there were at least 3,500 similar facilities in the United States, not including

---

[1] *Primary care* is the point of entry into the health-care system. It consists of a continuous relationship with a personal physician who takes care of a broad range of medical needs. Primary-care physicians include general practitioners, internal medicine and family practice specialists, gynecologists, and pediatricians.

group-practice physician arrangements and HMOs. Ambulatory health-care services have siphoned away a large portion of the care offered by primary-care physicians and have forced hospitals to deal increasingly with only the most acutely ill and severely injured patients.

Three factors have accounted for the growth of ambulatory health-care services. First, advances in medical technology, miniaturization, and portable medical equipment have made more diagnostic and surgical procedures possible outside the traditional hospital setting. Second, consumers have adopted a more proactive stance on where they will receive their health and medical care. Consumers are choosing the hospital at which they wish to be treated, and the incidence of "doctor shopping" is on the rise. Third, the mystique of medical and health care has been altered with the growth of paramedical professionals and standardized treatment practices.

Most of the early centers emphasized quick, convenient, minor emergency care. Many new centers have positioned themselves as convenient, personalized alternatives to primary-care physicians' practices. These operations typically employ aggressive, sophisticated marketing techniques, including branding, consistent logos and atmospherics, promotional incentives, and mass-media advertising (giving rise to vernacular designations such as "Doc-in-the-Box" and "McMedical"). Although ambulatory-care facilities vary considerably among communities and owners, the following characteristics appear to be universal: (1) branding, (2) extended hours, (3) lower fees than emergency rooms, (4) no appointments necessary, (5) minor emergencies treated, (6) easy access and parking, (7) short waiting times, and (8) credit cards accepted.

Even though these facilities have tapped a market need, not all have been successful. Failure rates are as high as 25 percent in some areas of the country. Many areas were already saturated with many MECs fighting aggressive market-share battles. According to one industry estimate, the average MEC is open 16 hours a day, 7 days a week, with two physicians on each 8-hour shift. The average visit is 15 minutes, and the average break-even volume lies between 30 and 45 visits per day.

■ PERPETUAL CARE HOSPITAL

Perpetual Care Hospital is a 600-bed, independent, not-for-profit, general hospital located on the southern periphery of a major western city. It is one of six general hospitals in the city and twenty in the county. It is financially stronger than most of the metropolitan-based hospitals in the United States. It is debt-free and has the highest overall occupancy rate among the city's six general hospitals. Nevertheless, the hospital's administration and board of trustees have serious concerns about its patient mix, which reflects unfavorable demographic shifts. Most of the population growth in the mid-1980s occurred in the suburban areas to the north, east, and west. These suburban areas attracted young, upwardly mobile families from the city. They also attracted thousands of families from other states—families drawn to the area's dynamic, robust business climate.

As hospitals sprang up to serve the high-growth suburban areas, PCH found itself becoming increasingly dependent on inner-city residents, who have a higher median age and higher incidence of Medicare coverage. Without a stronger stable inflow of short-stay, privately insured patients, the financial health of the hospital would be jeopardized. Accordingly, in the summer of 1988, the board of trustees authorized a study to determine whether to open an ambulatory facility in the downtown area about ten blocks north of the hospital.

■ DOWNTOWN HEALTH CLINIC

The charter for the Downtown Health Clinic contained four objectives:

1. To expand the hospital's referral base
2. To increase referrals of privately insured patients
3. To establish a liaison with the business community by addressing employers' specific health needs
4. To become self-supporting three years after opening

EXHIBIT 1

Present and Planned Locations of Downtown Health Clinics and Service Areas

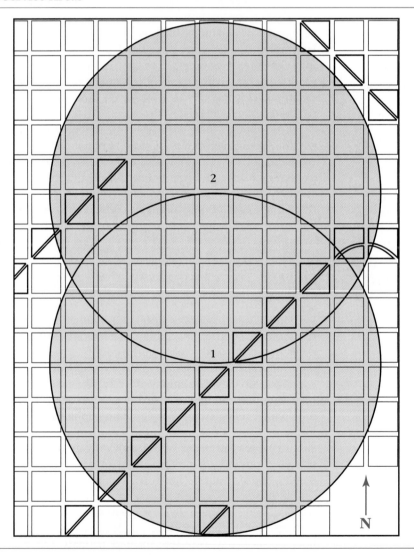

Key:

1. Original DHC and five-block service radius.
2. Planned location of competitor and five-block service radius.

EXHIBIT 2

Downtown Health Clinic: Preliminary 12-Month Expense Budget

Item	Expenditure
Physician coverage: 260 days times 8 hr/day at $33/hr	$68,640
Professional fees	21,360
Lease	38,250
Supplies	23,447
Utilities	3,315
Personnel, including fringe benefits (director, nurse, laboratory assistant, X-ray technician, receptionist)	84,188
Amortization	15,324
Annual expenditure	$254,524

Note: Expenditures were based on the assumption that the DHC would have 4 visits per hour, or 32 visits per day, when operating at full capacity.

The specific services to be offered by the DHC would include (1) preventive health care (for example, physical examinations and immunizations), (2) minor-emergency care, (3) referral for acute and chronic health-care problems, (4) specialized employer services (for example, preemployment examinations and treatment of worker's compensation injuries), (5) primary health-care services (for example, treatment of common illnesses), and (6) basic X-ray and laboratory tests. The DHC would be open 260 days a year (Monday–Friday) from 8:00 A.M. to 5:00 P.M.

The location for the DHC would be in the Greater West Office and Shopping Complex, situated on the corner of Main and West Streets (see Exhibit 1). This location was chosen because a member of the board of trustees owned the Greater West Complex and was willing to share construction, design, and equipment expenses with the hospital.

During the fall of 1988, construction plans for erecting the DHC were well under way, and the expense budget was developed (see Exhibit 2). During the winter months, PCH commissioned a study to determine the service radius of the DHC, estimate the number of potential users of the DHC, assess responsiveness to the services to be offered by the DHC, and review the operations of suburban ambulatory-care clinics. The results indicated that the service area would have a five-block radius, since this was the longest distance office workers would walk. Discussions with city planners indicated the service area contained 11,663 office workers during the 9:00–5:00 Monday–Friday work week. The population in the area was expected to grow 6 percent per year, given new building and renovation activity. Personal interviews with 400 office workers, selected randomly, indicated that 50 percent would use or try the DHC if necessary and that 40 percent of these prospective users would visit the DHC at least once per year (see Exhibit 3 on page 244 for additional findings). Finally, the study of suburban ambulatory-care facilities revealed the data shown in Exhibit 4 on page 245. Given their locations in suburban areas, these facilities were not considered direct competition, but their existence indicated that "the city's populace was attuned to ambulatory health care facilities," remarked Worth.

These results were viewed favorably by the board of trustees and "confirmed our belief that an ambulatory facility was needed downtown," noted Worth. The DHC was formally opened May 1, 1989. Except for the publicity surrounding the opening, however, no advertising or other types of promotion were planned. "Several members of the hospital staff shied away from advertising or solicitation, since it hinted at crass commercialism," said Worth.

E X H I B I T   3

Profile of DHC Service Area, Based on City and Survey Data

1988 Population Estimate (Source: City Planning Department)

Total office worker population in five-block radius	11,663
Expected annual growth, 1988–1993	6.0% yr
Sex breakdown in five-block radius:	
Male	40%
Female	60%

Results from Personal Interviews (January 1988)

Would use/try DHC if necessary for personal illness/exams	50%
Expected frequency of DHC use for personal illness/exams among those saying would use/try if necessary:[a]	
Once every other year	60%
Once per year	25%
Twice per year	10%
Three or more times per year	5%

Selected Cross-Tabulations

	Sex		
	Male	*Female*	*Total*
Would you use or try DHC if necessary?			
Yes	88[b]	168	256
No	72	72	144
Total	160	240	400

	Have Regular Physician (Excluding Gynecologist)		
	Yes	*No*	*Total*
Would you use or try DHC if necessary?			
Yes	58	198	256
No	130	14	144
Total	188	212	400

[a] *No difference between males and females on frequency of use.*

[b] *Of the 160 males interviewed, 88 (55 percent) said they would use the DHC; 88 of the 256 interviewees (34 percent) who said they would use the DHC were male.*

Performance: May 1989–March 1990

A financial summary of DHC performance through March 1990 is shown in Exhibit 5 on page 246. According to Mahon:

> We are pleased with the performance to date and hope the DHC will be self-supporting by April 1991. We are getting favorable word of mouth from satisfied patients that will generate both new and repeat patients. We expect 410 patient visits in April [1990]. In addition, we have taken steps to improve our financial standing. For example, our bad debts have been costing us 4 percent of gross revenue. With a better credit and collection procedure established just last month, we will reduce this figure to 2 percent. We plan to initiate an 8 percent across-the-board increase in charges on May 1 and will experience only a 5 percent increase in personnel and professional services expenses next year.

E X H I B I T 4

Suburban Ambulatory-Care Clinics: Operations Profile

Operations	EmerCenter #1	EmerCenter #2	Adams Industrial Clinic	Health First	Medcenter
Opening	March 1984	November 1986	June 1984	May 1986	June 1987
Patients/year	9,030	6,000	8,400	5,700	8,661
Hours of operation	10:00 A.M.–10:00 P.M. Monday–Friday	10:00 A.M.–10:00 P.M. Monday–Sunday	8:00 A.M.–5:00 P.M. Monday–Friday	5:00 P.M.–11:00 P.M. Monday–Friday; 10:00 A.M.–10:00 P.M. Saturday–Sunday	8:00 A.M.–8:00 P.M. Monday–Sunday
Physicians/8-hr shift	2	2	2	2	2
Estimated patient visits/hour	3.8/hr	3.4/hr	5.0/hr	3.0/hr	3.0/hr
Estimated average charge per visit	$30.00	$31.00	$38.00	$31.00	$32.00
Services provided:					
Preventive health care			✓	✓	✓
Minor emergencies	✓	✓	✓	✓	✓
Employer services			✓		
X-ray/lab tests	✓	✓	✓	✓	✓
Miscellaneous	✓	✓	✓	✓	✓
Use direct-mail advertising	✓	✓		✓	✓

EXHIBIT 5

Downtown Health Clinic Financial Summary

				1989						1990			Total Year to Date
	May	June	July	Aug.	Sept.	Oct.	Nov.	Dec.	Jan.	Feb.	March	
Gross revenue	$ 4,075	$ 8,387	$ 8,844	$ 9,697	$11,206	$ 11,406	$11,672	$11,758	$12,846	$13,879	$14,715	$ 118,485
Variable expenses:												
Bad debt	163	355	354	388	448	456	467	470	513	555	588	4,757
Medical/surgical supplies	6,591	798	935	643	1,063	1,213	1,661	612	976	1,580	1,078	17,150
Drugs	159	54	65	52	305	93	0	56	186	253	76	1,299
Office supplies	647	222	596	718	315	(190)	24	281	467	0	64	3,144
Total variable expense	$ 7,560	$ 1,429	$ 1,950	$ 1,801	$ 2,131	$ 1,572	$ 2,152	$ 1,419	$ 2,142	$ 2,388	$ 1,806	$ 26,350
Contribution	(3,485)	6,958	6,894	7,896	9,075	9,834	9,520	10,339	10,704	11,491	12,909	92,135
Fixed expenses:												
Personnel	7,816	7,459	6,670	5,900	6,816	11,490	7,320	6,249	6,705	8,995	7,644	83,064
Professional services[a]	10,009	6,945	7,732	7,158	7,385	6,800	7,200	7,450	7,242	7,078	7,187	82,186
Facility[b]	3,222	2,537	2,890	2,905	2,622	2,655	2,620	2,613	2,836	2,622	2,719	30,241
Miscellaneous	705	107	133	140	238	45	111	76	106	123	57	1,841
Amortization	1,277	1,277	1,277	1,277	1,277	1,277	1,277	1,277	1,277	1,277	1,277	14,047
Total fixed expense	$ 23,029	$ 18,325	$ 18,702	$17,380	$18,338	$ 22,267	$18,528	$17,665	$18,166	$20,095	$18,884	$ 211,379
Net gain (loss)	$(26,514)	$(11,367)	$(11,808)	$ (9,484)	$ (9,263)	$(12,433)	$ (9,008)	$ (7,326)	$ (7,462)	$ (8,604)	$ (5,975)	$(119,244)
Number of patient visits	109	231	275	277	322	320	321	366	383	463	423	3,490
Number of working days	22	21	21	22	20	23	22	20	22	21	23	237

[a] Includes professional fees paid (see Exhibit 2).
[b] Includes lease payments, utilities, and maintenance.

Records kept by PCH revealed that the DHC was realizing its objectives. For example, the referral objective was being met, since the DHC had made 105 referrals to PCH and produced slightly over $189,000 in revenue and an estimated $15,000 in net profit. Almost all of these patients were privately insured. The service mix, though dominated by treatment of common illnesses and examinations, did indicate that the DHC was being used for a variety of purposes. A breakdown of the reasons for patient visits for the first 11 months of operations is as follows:

Personal illness exams	53%
Worker's compensation exam/treatment	25
Employment/insurance physical exams	19
Emergency	3
Total	100%

Patient records indicated that 97 percent of all visits were by first-time users of the DHC and 113 visits were by repeat patients. Approximately 5 percent of the visits in each month from October 1989 through March 1990 were repeat visits. "We are pleased that we are already getting repeat business because it shows we are doing our job," Worth commented. The average revenue per patient visit during the first 11 months was $33.95.[2] A breakdown of the average charge by type of visit follows. The average charge was to increase 8 percent on May 1, 1990.

Personal illness/exam	$25 per visit
Worker's compensation exam/treatment	$39 per visit
Employment/insurance physical examination	$47 per visit
Emergency	$67 per visit

In an effort to monitor the performance of the DHC, patients were asked to provide selected health-care information as well as demographic information. This information was summarized monthly, and Exhibit 6 on page 248 shows the profile of patients visiting the DHC for the first 11 months of operation. In addition to this information, patients were asked for suggestions on how the DHC could serve the downtown area. Suggestions typically fell into three categories: service hours, services offered, and waiting time. Thirty percent of the patients suggested expanded service hours, with an opening time of 7:00 A.M. and a closing time of 7:00 P.M. One-half of the female patients requested that gynecological services be added.[3] A majority of the patients expressed concern about the waiting time, particularly during the lunch hours (11:00 A.M.–2:00 P.M.). A check of DHC records indicated that 70 percent of patient visits occurred during the 11:00 A.M.–2:00 P.M. period and that one-half of the visits were for personal illnesses.

Worth believed all three suggestions had merit, and she had already explored ways to expand the DHC's hours and reduce waiting time. For example, the reason for her call on the employee benefits director at a local department store was to schedule employee physical examinations in the morning or late afternoon hours to minimize crowding during the lunch hour. Nevertheless, she believed a second licensed physician might be necessary, with one physician working the hours from 7:00 A.M. to 3:00 P.M. and the other working between 11:00 A.M. and 7:00 P.M. The overlap during the lunch period would alleviate waiting times, she thought. Expanding from 9- to 12-hour days would entail a 33 percent increase in personnel costs, however, as well as the cost of another physician.[4]

---

[2] The average charge per patient visit excluded the charge for basic X-ray and laboratory tests.

[3] *Gynecology* is that branch of medicine dealing with the female reproductive tract.

[4] Expanded hours would be staffed by part-time personnel, who would receive the same wages as full-time personnel.

EXHIBIT   6

Profile of Downtown Health Clinic Patients:
Personal Illness/Exam Visits Only

Occupation

Clerical	48%
Professional/technical/managerial	23
Operator	19
Other	10
	100%

Sex

Male	30%
Female	70
	100%

Referral Source

Friend/colleague	35%
Employer	60
Other	5
	100%

Patient Origin

Distance:

One block	25%
Two blocks	28
Three blocks	22
Four blocks	15
Five blocks	8
More than five blocks	2
	100%

Direction:

North of DHC	10%
South of DHC	25
Northeast of DHC	5
Southwest of DHC	15
East of DHC	20
West of DHC	10
Southeast of DHC	10
Northwest of DHC	5
	100%

Have Regular Physician

Yes	18%
No	82
	100%

Worth believed that scheduling was more of a problem than she or the PCH staff had expected. "You just can't schedule the walk-ins," she said, "and pardon me for saying it, but the people coming in with personal care needs have really caused the congestion." She added that the problem would get worse because the mix of patient needs was moving toward personal illnesses and examinations. "If the trend continues, we should have 20 percent more personal illness visits next year than last year."

Worth believed that gynecological services would be a plus, since 70 percent of the visits were made by women and almost all were under 35 years of age. She said:

> Women should see a gynecologist regularly at least once a year and often twice a year. We could add an additional 2,000 visits per year by having a hospital gynecologist work at the DHC two eight-hour days a week by appointment. An average charge per visit would be about $52 including lab work, and the physician cost would be $35 per hour.

Worth had also given some thought to how the DHC could improve its relations with the business community. Currently, business-initiated visits (worker's compensation examinations and treatments and employment/insurance physical examinations) accounted for 44 percent of the visits to the DHC. Construction in the downtown area had stimulated worker's compensation activity, and growth in employment in the five-block service radius had contributed to employment physicals. Worth believed worker's compensation visits would stabilize at about 81 per month and then decline with slowed building activity. Employment physicals accounted for 50 visits per month and were expected to remain at this level with the current operating hours. Insurance physicals were not expected to increase beyond current levels, nor were emergency visits.

Commenting on her calls on businesses, Worth remarked:

> I have actively called on businesses under the guise of community relations because the PCH staff has not sanctioned solicitation. My guess, after talking with businesspeople, is that we could get virtually every new employment physical if we didn't interfere with employment hours and scheduled them before 8:00 A.M. or after 5:00 P.M. Given net new employment in the area and new employees due to turnover, I'd guess we could schedule an additional 65 employment physicals every month—that is, a total of 115 a month.

Worth added that she had also received approval to run an "informational advertisement" in the downtown weekly newspaper each week next year provided that the advertisement did not feature prices or appear to be commercial in its presentation. The weekly advertisement would cost $5,200 per year.

The Possibility of Competition

Worth's calls on local businesses and patient interviews indicated that someone was conducting a survey. She believed that Medcenter, a privately owned suburban ambulatory facility, was the sponsor. Medcenter appeared to be successful in its suburban location (see Exhibit 4) and had a reputation for being an aggressive, marketing-oriented operation. Even though Medcenter did not provide employer services at its suburban location, Worth thought the fact that an employee benefits director had been interviewed suggested that such services might be offered.

The proposed location for the new clinic was five blocks directly north of the DHC. Based on the research for the DHC, Worth estimated that the number of office workers within a five-block radius of the competitive clinic would be 11,652 in 1991 and 13,590 in 1992, and would grow at an annual rate of 7 percent through 1999 because of new construction and building renovation. Worth believed the competitor's service area had the same socioeconomic profile and the same usage and employment characteristics as the DHC's service area.

The overlap in service areas was due to the layout of the downtown area and the availability of high-quality street-level space. According to Worth, "It is possible that a third of our current personal illness/exam patients from the northern portion of our service area will switch to the new clinic and about 40 percent of potential personal illness/exam patients in this area will go to the new location." Worth went on to say that the overlap in service areas would cover 3,424 office workers in 1990.

The effect of the competing clinic on the volume of emergency, worker's compensation, and employment/insurance exam work was more difficult to assess. Worth felt that worker's compensation visits would not be materially affected because most construction was being undertaken in areas south, east, and west of the DHC. Emergency visits were so random that it was not possible to assess what effect the competing clinic would have. The projected volume of employment and insurance physicals could change with the addition of a competing clinic, however. Worth guessed, "At worst, we would see no increase in these types of visits over last year since we have not gotten many visits from this area."

A week after she first heard about the possibility of competition, Worth and Mahon met to review the information on the DHC. Just before Worth finished giving her overview, Mahon's administrative assistant interrupted to tell him he had to leave to catch a plane for a three-day conference dealing with health-care marketing. As he left the room, Mahon asked Worth to draft a concise analysis of the DHC's position. He also asked her to specify and evaluate the alternatives for the DHC assuming Medcenter either did or did not open a facility. "Remember," Mahon said, "we have a lot riding on the DHC. Making it work involves not only dollars and cents, but our image in the community as well."

Citibank

Launching the Credit Card
in Asia Pacific (A)

On a rainy afternoon in 1989, Rana Talwar, head of Citibank's Asia Pacific Consumer Bank, reflected upon the 11 years that had gone by since the Consumer Bank had established its consumer business in Asia. The branch banking business operations in 15 countries throughout Asia Pacific and the Middle East projected Citibank as a prestigious, consumer-oriented international bank and as the undisputed leader in most marketplaces. With earnings of $69.7 million in 1988, and a goal of $100 million in 1990, Talwar considered the launch of a new product (credit cards) as a way of growing future revenues. (See Exhibit 1 on page 252 for 1988 performance.) Cards could prove to be an excellent way to overcome distribution limitations imposed on foreign banks in the Asia-Pacific region: first, by acquiring card members, by targeting customers outside its branch business and, then, by actively cross-selling other Citibank products and services to these customers.

In the past, the credit card idea had met with skepticism from Citibank's New York headquarters as well as its country managers. Many in New York considered it a risky investment. Senior credit managers questioned the wisdom of issuing cards in markets with annual per capita income of $350 and also in markets with little credit experience and hardly any infrastructure. The Citibank management recognized that the economics of most Asia-Pacific countries were relatively underdeveloped compared with the United States and Europe; consumers' attitudes and credit card usage patterns differed country by country. In this context, several country managers were unsure whether the success of Citibank's U.S. card business could be projected onto Asia Pacific. Further, they wondered whether Citibank could adopt a mass-market positioning to acquire enough credit card customers and still maintain its up-market positioning with the current upscale branch banking customers. A premium-priced card product would not sell in the marketplace in a large way, it was argued. Moreover, country managers were not comfortable with an unsecured credit product such as credit cards and did not want to take the large losses of a card business, in the initial years, that their projections seemed to indicate. Weak local infrastructure, limited distribution capabilities, and the experience with loss-making proprietary credit card businesses that some of the countries had, served to underline arguments against a credit card launch.

Pei Chia, who had been appointed in late 1987 to head Citibank's International Consumer businesses, had experience managing Citibank's huge U.S. card businesses and was favorably disposed towards international expansion. Confident of

Professor V. Kasturi Rangan prepared this case with research assistance from Marie Bell and Melanie Alper as the basis for class discussion rather than to illustrate either effective or ineffective handling of an administrative situation.

E X H I B I T   1

Citibank's Asia-Pacific Consumer Bank Performance: 1988

	($ Million)
Net revenue from funds (NRFF)	$209.0
Fees/commissions/insurance	31.3
Customer net revenue	$240.3
Net credit losses/fraud	4.8
Credit/collection	11.7
Total credit cycle	$ 16.5
Delivery expense	$138.3
Other revenues/(expense)	$(15.9)
Net earnings before tax	69.7
Tax	$ 23.5
Profit center earnings (PCE)	$ 46.2
Customer liabilities ($ billion)	4.9
Customer assets ($ billion)	2.3
Average total assets ($ billion)	3.0
Full-time equivalent employees	3,536
Number of accounts (000)	846
Number of branches	56

Note: NRFF for the card business was about $10 million, with a PCE of (−$3) million. Concentrated in Hong Kong, this business was growing rapidly and by the middle of 1989 Citibank had nearly 100,000 customers.

Source: Company documents.

support from his boss if a viable proposition could be structured, Talwar pondered the pros and cons of a credit card product. If he decided to push for the product, he would need to articulate a viable business strategy.

■ CITIBANK'S ASIA-PACIFIC OPERATIONS

Unlike many of its competitors, Citibank operated on a view of the world as one marketplace and had consistently pursued a global strategy for growth. (See Exhibits 2 and 3 on pages 253 and 254 for a summary of Citibank's global operations.)

Citibank's mission in the Asia-Pacific region was to be the most profitable and preeminent provider of a wide array of financial services to an increasingly affluent upper- and middle-income market, and to reach the rapidly growing middle-income households in this region. The bank operated in 15 countries throughout Asia-Pacific and the Middle East: Hong Kong, Taiwan, Australia, the Philippines, Guam, Singapore, India, the Gulf (United Arab Emirates, Bahrain, Oman), Malaysia, Indonesia, Thailand, Pakistan, and Korea.

Rapid economic development (see Exhibit 4 on page 255) had made these countries attractive business propositions for many international banks. However, most Asian governments had a number of regulations designed to protect local

EXHIBIT 2

Citibank Background

With about $228 billion in assets in 1989, Citicorp was the largest banking company in the United States and ranked eleventh in the world. Its operations were broadly diversified across the banking industry in order to serve a variety of individual, institutional, and commercial customers.

Global Finance Citicorp's commercial banking operation served the needs of the world's business community. Recognized as the leader in the foreign exchange market, its wide range of services included commercial lending, real estate, and services to financial organizations, such as insurance companies, securities companies, institutional investors, and other banks.

Global Consumer The Global Consumer business aimed to serve the fullest possible range of financial needs for individual consumers. Its $106 billion in assets constituted 50% of the bank's asset base. The majority of Citibank consumers were in the United States, where one out of six American households had a relationship with the bank. However, its international presence had been growing rapidly, and while other large banks had been scaling back their efforts overseas, Citibank had expanded its services into 9 million households in 15 countries outside the United States.

By 1989 Citibank, which had started as a commercial bank, offered a variety of products for consumers as well, especially in the United States. In the United States alone, Citibank had grown its card membership from a mere 6 million in 1980 to more than 27 million in 1987.

Citibank: Summary of Aggregate Performance

	1986		1987		1988	
	Net Income (Loss) $ Millions	Average Assets $ Billions	Net Income (Loss) % Millions	Average Assets $ Billions	Net Income/ (Loss) $ Millions	Average Assets $ Billions
Global consumer	362	71	556	85	626	106
Global finance						
Developed economies	538	81	513	84	810	88
Developing economies	143	18	195	17	285	17
Corporate initiatives/ information business	(34)	—	(89)	1	(105)	1
Cross-border refinancing portfolio	124	14	(3,288)	13	278	12
Other	(75)	—	931	(2)	(36)	(3)
Total	1,058	184	(1,182)	198	1,858	221

Offices and Branches (1988)

United States		*Overseas (in 89 countries)*	
Citibank, N.A.		Citibank branches and representative offices	291
Branches	293	Banking subsidiaries	653
Subsidiaries	71	Banking affiliates	115
Citibank (New York State)		Other financial affiliates and subsidiaries	1,121
Branches	39		
Subsidiaries	8	**Total overseas**	2,180
Citicorp savings	252		
Other Citicorp subsidiaries	522		
Total Domestic	1,185	**Total**	3,365

Source: Annual Reports.

EXHIBIT 3

Citibank: Global Consumer Bank ($ Millions)

	1986	1987	1988
Net revenue from fund	$5,638	$6,476	$6,899
Credit cycle expense	1,701	1,580	1,746
Delivery expense	3,392	3,952	4,295
Total expense	5,093	5,532	6,041
Other income (expense)	92	65	92
Income before taxes	637	1,009	950
Net Income	362	556	626
Average assets ($ billions)	$71	$85	$97
Return on assets (%)	.51	.65	.64
Return on equity (%)	12.7	16.3	16.1
Assets ($ billions)			
Revolving loans	NA	$17.2	$21.8
Shelter loans		39.7	41.6
Student loans		1.8	2.1
Other loans		21.8	25.5
Other assets		12.0	13.3
		$92.5	$104.3
Liabilities			
Transaction account deposits	NA	$11.6	$13.5
Savings deposits		60.0	65.0
Other		20.9	25.8
		$92.5	$104.3
No. of accounts (millions)	NA	42.0	45.0

*Source:*Annual Reports.

banks and limit the expansion of foreign banks. For instance, foreign banks in Indonesia could operate only two branches; in Malaysia and Singapore, they were limited to three; and in Thailand, each foreign bank was allowed only one branch.

Citibank's senior managers knew that they could not rely only on breakthroughs in the regulatory environment to gain increased access in the local market. Therefore, offering the most innovative and high-quality products, services, and technology was critical to acquiring and retaining customers. For example, Citibank pioneered telephone banking in much of Asia. It developed alternate distribution channels for products such as automobile loans. With the dealers acting as the bank's agents, customers did not ever have to visit the branch. (More details about Citibank's core products and services are provided in Exhibit 5 on page 256.)

Against such a backdrop, it was felt that the introduction of a credit card in Asia would support Citibank's strategy of expanding its customer base from the upper-income segment to include the rapidly growing middle-income households. Supporters of the card product suggested:

> We do not need bricks-and-mortar branches to access the middle market in most of our countries. We can acquire card customers through innovative new channels. When we get card customers, we have the opportunity to cross-sell our entire product line: Auto Loans, Ready Credit, Deposits, and Mortgage Power. This could be a wonderful opportunity for us to add customers.

EXHIBIT 4

Country Profile

	Australia	Hong Kong	India	Indonesia	Malaysia	Philippines	Singapore	Taiwan	Thailand
Population (millions)	16.5	5.6	797.0	167.7	16.9	61.9	2.7	19.8	55.0
Urban population	85%	90%	23%	25%	38%	50%	100%	72%	20%
Economy									
1988 real GNP (US$ billion)	$196.8	$45.7	$222.5	$63.4	$34.1	$32.6	$23.8	$95.8	$51.1
Per capita (US$)	$11,929	$8,158	$279	$338	$2,018	$527	$8,817	$4,837	$930
1988 growth rate	4.0%	7.3%	9.7%	4.8%	8.1%	6.8%	11.0%	7.3%	10.8%
Five-year average growth rate	4.6%	8.4%	6.1%	4.2%	4.2%	0.5%	5.6%	9.3%	7.2%
Savings rate	6.7%	30.0%	19.6%	27.9%	23.8%	NA	NA	31.2%	10.3%
Inflation									
1988	7.6%	7.4%	9.8%	8.0%	2.0%	8.7%	1.5%	1.2%	3.8%
Five-year average	7.1%	5.5%	8.2%	7.6%	1.6%	16.6%	0.7%	0.5%	2.3%
Literacy rate	99%	88%	48%	72%	80%	88%	87%	90%	89%
Ethnic composition	95% Caucasian; 4% Asian; 1% other	98% Chinese; 2% other	80% Hindu; 10% Muslim; 10% Christian, Sikh, Parsi, and others	74% various Malay groups; 26% other (mainly Chinese)	60% Malay; 31% Chinese; 9% Indian	91% Christian Malay; 4% Muslim Malay; 2% Chinese; 3% other	76% Chinese; 15% Malay; 7% Indian; 2% other	84% Taiwanese; 14% Mainland Chinese; 2% other	75% Thai; 14% Chinese; 11% other
No. of passenger cars in use	7,244,000	250,000	1,351,200	1,170,100	1,578,900	352,900	251,400	650,000	770,400
No. of telephones in use	8,727,000	2,461,000	4,409,000	907,000	1,646,000	658,400	1,122,000	7,800,000	1,000,000
No. of televisions in use	7,900,000	1,400,000	6,000,000	7,112,000	2,350,000	2,200,000	570,000	6,386,000	5,600,000
(Some of these data are for 1985, others for 1987)									
Political/Economic Risk Factor	A	B	C	C	B	D	B	A	B
A—Most Stable D—Most Risky	Highly Westernized economy with opportunities for development	1997 return to Mainland China causes political uncertainty	Unstable federal government, political corruption	Large national debt, political corruption, speculation on new political leadership	Low inflation and fast high-tech growth, but political infighting	Political corruption, threats of Communist insurgency	Transition to new leadership after 30-year reign of Lee Kuan Yew	Strong economic and political stability	Strong growth, but heavy reliance on tourism. Political corruption

Source: United Nations Statistical Yearbook for Asia and the Pacific, 1991, and U.S. Central Intelligence Agency, Handbook of the Nations, 1991.

E X H I B I T   5

Citibank Asia-Pacific Consumer Bank: Core Products and Services

CORE PRODUCTS

In offering the *Citi-One* account, Citibank used its advances in technology to provide customers something none of its competitors could reproduce: a consolidated deposit and investment account based on the sum total of all of a customer's accounts with Citibank. By enrolling in Citi-One, customers benefited from

- a consolidated statement showing the status of all their Citibank accounts,
- banking by phone,
- an automatic checking overdraft facility,
- linked savings and checking accounts where funds were swept from checking into savings overnight in order to earn interest, and
- a designated customer service officer to manage their accounts.

In order to fully offer its resources to branch banking customers, Citibank imposed relatively high deposit requirements of its checking/savings customers—usually about $10,000.

Mortage Power, targeted at housing loan customers, allowed those whose homes were worth more than the existing mortgage to obtain a revolving line of credit on top of their existing loan.

Citibank was also one of the largest providers of *auto loans* in Asia. The bank worked to establish and maintain relationships with car dealers as one way to gain access to new customers; auto loans were then sourced and marketed through car dealerships.

Unlike other credit line accounts, Citibank's *Ready Credit*, a revolving credit facility which worked like a checking account, enabled customers to apply for an overdraft line of credit without having to formally apply for a loan. This product was targeted at mid-level professionals and provided them a ready source of funds for unexpected expenditures or emergencies. It offered a number of benefits, including low mandatory repayment of the loan, no collateral or guarantors required, and ready cash withdrawals through ATMs (automated teller machines).

To attract the high net worth segment of the market, Citibank offered its exclusive, personalized *Citigold* service. Its creators likened the Citigold concept to traveling in the first class cabin of an airplane. With Citigold service, customers who met the minimum average deposit requirements (this varied from country to country but was usually around $100,000) did their banking in exclusive, lavishly furnished service areas where they did not have to wait in lines for teller service. Soft music, warm lighting, tastefully selected artwork, and service from immaculately groomed, more experienced representatives all served to differentiate this class of customer. Access to more sophisticated products, investment advisory services, complimentary magazines subscriptions, and updates on currency trends were just some of the additional benefits bestowed upon Citigold customers. The Asia-Pacific division innovated the Citigold idea, and a much larger proportion of its customers in Asia compared with its U.S. operations were Citigold customers.

CitiPhone banking enabled customers to complete routine banking transactions, such as fund transfers and account balance inquiries, via phone, from the privacy of their own homes or offices, or even from mobile phones. Moreover, with CitiPhone Banking, customers could access their accounts 24 hours a day, 7 days a week, and 365 days a year.

Citibank had also revolutionized the banking industry in Asia via *automated teller machines*. Customers could use ATM cards to access their funds from stylishly decorated, highly secured Citicard Banking Centers in the language of their choice, and all ATMs contained phones which automatically connected customers with a Citibank officer in case of a problem. With the International Citibank Citicard, customers could carry out transactions on their accounts virtually anywhere in the world.

BUSINESS SEGMENTS

In addition to its regular branches, Citibank operated separate offices to serve certain strategic customer segments. Each of these offered a portfolio of products designed to meet the unique needs of customers in those segments.

Citibank's *Non-Resident Indian Business (NRI)* was set up to capture the business of Indian customers who did not reside in India. Citibank offered special foreign currency time deposit accounts and rupee (local currency) savings accounts in India which enabled *NRI* customers to invest their overseas earnings in Indian rupees or in foreign currencies. The former earned a significantly higher interest rate. This helped Citibank develop relations with the Indian government by helping the Central Bank to procure foreign currencies. *NRI* had branches in major financial centers all over the world.

EXHIBIT 5 *(continued)*

With 21 banking centers in 15 countries around the world, the *International Personal Banking (IPB)* business was designed to service the growing group of affluent Asian offshore clients with global financial needs. *IPB* provided such innovative products as the International University Plan, which would allow customers to create the funds necessary to send their children to prestigious universities in the United States, Canada, and Europe, while insuring the funding for college against death or disability. It helped them cushion political and economic instability, offering them foreign currency advisory services and access to global investment products, while providing unique local tax benefits. IPB's focus on personalized service (a personal finance manager specially trained in international transactions), confidentiality, and accessibility made Citibank the choice of more than 120,000 customers worldwide.

Country managers, on the other hand, sought to highlight realities of the local marketplace. Bob Thornton, country manager of Citibank Indonesia, argued:

> There is a history of poor consumer payment on installment debt in Indonesia, as has been our experience with the mortgage portfolio, and a high level of fraud in the financial sector. I wonder if credit card customers will perform any differently. The legal infrastructure is inadequate so that we cannot collect legally, if necessary. Also, while there is a small market for a card product, I am not sure that we can get the right kind of staffing and infrastructure to run such a business successfully and profitably. Yet, with a population of 180 million, it is among the few potentially large markets in Asia Pacific.

According to Dave Smith, country manager for Singapore:

> We have a small two-million population and an already saturated card market. Moreover, American Express has the market in its pocket. Entering this market this late will most likely result in us losing money. We can do without this distraction from our main banking business.

Jaitirth Rao, country manager for India, who had, in a matter of two years, made the consumer bank an innovator of products and a catalyst for service orientation in the Indian financial services sector, expressed his concern: "Launching a credit card in a large country like ours with little infrastructure has great potential to be a major headache down the road. It's a dog. Let us delay it."

Card Business Basics

Banks issued Visa or MasterCards, both of which were organized as international franchises. Any bank or financial institution could become a member of these franchises by fulfilling certain eligibility criteria. On becoming a member, they all had to follow a certain common set of practices. An example was Gold Cards; they had to be a gold color, and the issuing bank was obliged to provide travel accident insurance and a 24-hour help line for its cardholders. In general, Visa/MasterCard set common standards for card-logo design and operating rules that its member franchises all had to abide by. It was up to the individual banks, however, to decide on pricing, branding, positioning, and customer acquisition strategies. The franchisers, Visa or MasterCard, provided the banks an extensive information network both within the country and internationally to clear transactions. Member banks and financial institutions paid Visa and MasterCard a fee in proportion to their volume of network usage, and a franchise royalty (a small percentage of sales volume) as well. Banks and financial institutions in addition to issuing cards could also participate in the Visa and MasterCard Merchant Acquisition franchise. The objective here was to enlist retail merchants to clear their credit card transactions through the "acquiring" bank. That is, regardless of which bank issued the card to the customer, the retail merchant would forward transactions to its "acquiring" bank for clearance. Visa and MasterCard provided a worldwide communication flow, via satellite hookups and computer networks, to enable a convenient consummation of the credit card transaction—often involving a merchant, a customer, an acquiring bank, and an issuing bank, all within a matter of seconds.

When a Citibank cardholder approached a Citibank merchant to purchase goods, the following round of transactions would result: say the customer bought $100 worth of goods on her Citibank card. The merchant would present the $100 charge slip to the acquiring bank and receive $97.00 for the same transaction. Hence in this transaction, the acquiring bank would generate a merchant discount revenue of $3.00 (or 3.0%) from which it would have to make franchise payment to Visa or Master-Card, pay the card issuer (Citibank) an interchange fee, and also cover all its expenses related to the acquiring business. Citibank, the card issuer, would bill the cardholder the $100 in full, in the monthly statement. The cardholder would then have the choice of making a part payment or full payment, depending upon the payment terms. (Exhibit 6 provides a graphical representation of a typical transaction cycle.)

The gross discount percentages shown in the above illustrations, though representative, differed from country to country, and even by merchant to merchant, depending on the competitive context.

EXHIBIT 6

Typical Credit Card Purchase Transaction Cycle

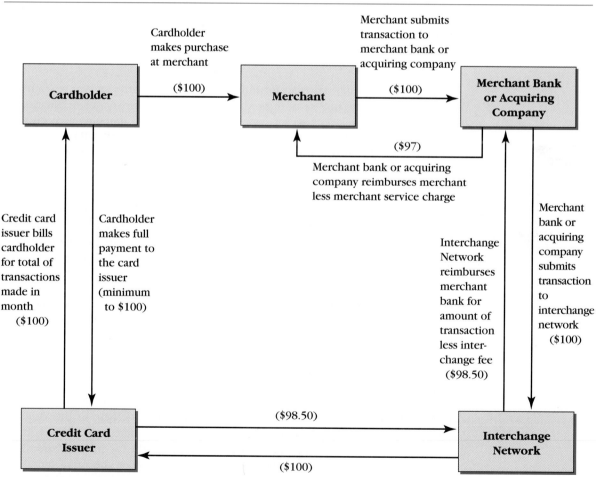

Local banks held back merchant discounts in the 1.5% to 2.0% range—far lower than Citibank's 3.0%. As a result, merchant acquisition was getting to be very tough in developed markets. Citibank had enrolled about 3,000 merchants in Hong Kong. In order to compete effectively with the local banks, it guaranteed merchants a faster transaction settlement time. In most Asia Pacific markets, American Express had the higher-caliber merchants. Even though, like Citibank, it charged a 3% discount rate, most quality hotels, restaurants, and retailers accepted its affiliation in order to attract and retain travel-related international clients.

As part of a strategy to counter American Express's growing international presence, Citibank decided to look for an international proprietary card payment system. In 1981, Citibank acquired Diners Club International (DCI) which managed an international franchise for the Diners Club card. DCI allowed only one franchisee to be signed up in each country. The franchisee would be the sole issuer of Diners Club cards and the sole acquirer of Diners Club merchant business in that country. While Citibank owned the Diners Club franchise in some countries, private companies managed the franchise in most other countries.

Positioned as a travel and entertainment card for senior executives and successful businessmen, the Diners Club card is a charge card, i.e., all outstandings on the card have to be settled in full at the end of every billing month. With no interest revenue, unlike bankcards, the primary revenue sources are fees and merchant discounts.

■ LAUNCHING A CREDIT CARD IN ASIA PACIFIC

While opinion was divided on whether a card launch made sense, Talwar wondered whether a staged, sequential plan could be the basis for any possible consensus and a regional thrust if he chose in favor of the credit card. This way, each subsequent country launch would benefit from the experience of all the countries preceding it. Management debated which country to lead off with, how to enter the market, and how to develop the rest of the region.

Profiles of the target countries in Citibank's Asia Pacific markets are provided in Exhibit 7 on page 260. Exhibit 8 on page 261 provides a quick overview of the distribution of cards by income group for each country, and Exhibit 9 on page 262 provides comparative information on card pricing.

Market Entry Costs

Citibank could enter the market either by acquiring an already existing card portfolio from another company or do greenfield market development to build a customer base or adopt a combination of the two.

Acquiring an existing card portfolio would facilitate a quick entry into the market. Further, the bank could consider leveraging off an already developed operations infrastructure and trained human resources in the acquired company to further consolidate the market share. On the other hand, there were several arguments that questioned market entry through acquisition. Looking back at the Hong Kong entry, one manager reflected:

> We never really started a credit card business in Hong Kong. We simply acquired the existing Bank of America business with all the baggage that usually accompanies such acquisition. Further, the bulk of our branch banking business was aimed at a limited target market, whereas the credit card business was targeted at the mass market. There was a mismatch right there.

If Citibank chose greenfield market development, it would need to invest in a direct marketing program, typically consisting of (1) direct mail, (2) take-ones,

EXHIBIT 7

Citibank Country Profile (1988)

	Australia	Hong Kong	India	Indonesia	Malaysia	Philippines	Singapore	Taiwan	Thailand
No. of branches	9	27	6	2	3	3	3	2	1
No. of bank customers (thousands)	85	130	61	21	29	46	18	16	12
No. of bank accounts (thousands)	150	250	165	25	58	85	67	30	16
No. of Citigold customers	—	7,600	1,000	550	487	2,300	1300	680	—
No. of IPB customers	—	9,900	—	—	—	—	12,800	—	—
No. of auto loan customers (thousands)	36	200	15	13	—	4	10	11	4
No. of mortgage customers (thousands)	27	22	—	2	9	—	3	2	5
No. of card customers	—	102	—	—	—	—	—	—	—
% of bank customers owning Citibank card	—	6	—	—	—	—	—	—	—
Net revenue from funds ($ millions)	59	67	6	12	11	19	16	11	8
Average annual customer income (US$)	$60,000	$36,000	$10,000	$24,000	$14,000	$10,000	$20,000	$25,000	$15,000
Average customer bank balance (US$)	$24,000	$20,000	$3,500	$9,000	$23,000	$4,000	$13,000	$9,000	$5,000

EXHIBIT 8

Estimated Distribution of Population and Cards by Income

	Annual Income					Total
	Above $25,000	$12,500 to $25,000	$6,000 to $12,500	$2,000 to $6,000	Below $2,000	(in millions)
Australia						
% of population	12.5[a]	30	37.5	15	5	16.5
% of cards	30[b]	35	30	5	0	10.5
Hong Kong						
% of population	10	25	50	10	5	5.6
% of cards	15	25	50	10	0	2.0
India						
% of population	1	2	2	5	90	800
% of cards	10	10	10	70	0	.280
Indonesia						
% of population	3	2	2	3	90	168
% of cards	40	10	10	40	0	.120
Malaysia						
% of population	5	10	20	45	20	17
% of cards	10	45	45	0	0	.380
Philippines						
% of population	3	5	22	30	40	62
% of cards	50	45	5	0	0	.240
Singapore						
% of population	5	5	10	25	55	2.7
% of cards	30	70	0	0	0	.630
Taiwan						
% of population	12.5	30	35	10	5	20
% of cards	30	50	20	0	0	.100
Thailand						
% of population	5	10	10	20	55	55
% of cards	12.5	12.5	50	25	0	.210

Note: The minimum age for cardholders was 18 years in Australia and 21 in the other countries. While the card issuers imposed their own income requirements, the government of Malaysia imposed a minimum income of $9,000/year, and Singapore imposed a minimum of $14,000/year.

[a] Of Australia's 16.5 million people, 12.5% were estimated to have an income above $25,000.

[b] Of Australia's 10.5 million credit cards, 30% were owned by individuals with incomes above $25,000.

(3) direct sales force, and (4) bind-ins. Each had its advantages and drawbacks. Direct mail could target applications to the intended audience. However, it was much more expensive than some of the other methods available. "Take-Ones," applications distributed at in-store countertop displays, offered a much broader reach; yet being available to the general public regardless of qualification, more than half of the applicants usually would not qualify. Using direct sales representatives was very expensive, although a competitor had achieved enormous success at a very low per-customer acquisition cost in South Korea. Finally, newspaper and magazine inserts

EXHIBIT 9

Competing Product Profiles: Pricing

	American Express		Diner's Club	Local Banks	
	Green	Gold	Regular	Classic	Gold
Australia					
Joining Fee	$30	$45	$45	Nil	Nil
Annual Membership Fee	$45	$60	$60	Nil	Nil
Payment Terms	Balance due monthly	Balance due monthly	Balance due monthly	Balance due monthly (overdue int. 2% p.m.)	Balance due monthly (overdue int. 2% p.m.)
Hong Kong					
Joining Fee	$32	$50	$32	Nil	Nil
Annual Membership Fee	$50	$83	$54	$28	$61
Payment Terms	Monthly	Monthly	Monthly	Monthly (overdue int. 2%)	Monthly (overdue int. 2%)
India					
Joining Fee	NA	NA	$25	Nil	NA
Annual Membership Fee	NA	$40	$10 to $19	NA	NA
Payment Terms	NA	NA	Monthly	Monthly (overdue int. 2.5%)	NA
Indonesia					
Joining Fee	$60	$60	$40	$15 to $40	$30 to $60
Annual Membership Fee	$50	$60	$35	$20 to $30	$30 to $45
Payment Terms	Monthly	Monthly	Monthly	Monthly (overdue int. 2.5%)	Monthly (overdue int. 2.5%)
Malaysia					
Joining Fee	$31	$38	$40	0 to $30	0 to $50
Annual Membership Fee	$54	$75	$60	$20 to $50	$50 to $75
Payment Terms	Monthly	Monthly	Monthly	Monthly (overdue int. 2.5%)	Monthly (overdue int. 2.5%)
Philippines					
Joining Fee	$35	$50	$40	Nil	$5 to $20
Annual Membership Fee	$50	$60	$50	$20	$50
Payment Terms	Monthly	Monthly	Monthly	Monthly (overdue int. 3%)	Monthly (overdue int. 3%)

Singapore

Joining Fee	$50	$50	$45	Nil	Nil
Annual Membership Fee	$60	$95	$60	0 to $50	0 to $65
Payment Terms	Monthly	Monthly	Monthly	Monthly (overdue int. 2%)	Monthly (overdue int. 2%)

Taiwan

Joining Fee	$60	$40	$45	Nil	Nil
Annual Membership Fee	$120	$72	$80	$48	$96
Payment Terms	Monthly	Monthly	Monthly	Monthly (overdue int. 1.5%)	Monthly (overdue int. 1.5%)

Thailand

Joining Fee	$60	$40	$40	Nil	Nil
Annual Membership Fee	$120	$65	$80	$20	$40
Payment Terms	Monthly	Monthly	Monthly	Monthly (overdue int. 1.5%)	Monthly (overdue int. 1.5%)

Competing Product Profiles: Services

	American Express	Diners Club	Banks
Card replacement	24 hours or next business day at 1,500 locations worldwide	24 to 48 hours at Diners offices	1 to 2 weeks. Written loss report required
Loss/misuse liability	$100 maximum	$100 maximum	Some provide no coverage until loss reported, others provide $100 maximum
Spending limits	None	None	Yes
Emergency check cashing	$1,000 (Green) $5,000 (Gold) at AMEX locations $250 at hotels $100 at airlines	$1,000 at Diners offices and Citibank branches $250 at hotels $100 at airlines	$250 at hotels $100 at airlines
Cash advance	None (except through Express Card ATM)	$1,000 at Diners office and Citibank branches	$1,000 to $10,000 or up to credit limit
Year-end summary	Gold Card only	No	No
Interest-free period	45 days	30 days	25 days
Minimum payment	Full	Full	10% of balance
Replacement card	Free	Free	$20 to $50

(known as bind-ins) were by far the least expensive to circulate but they had a very low response rate.

The Hong Kong launch following the acquisition had used a combination of widespread Take-One displays in more than 4,000 merchant locations and direct mailings as well as cross-selling to existing branch customers. Bursts of thematic television and print advertising were also used to enforce brand positioning to achieve maximum effectiveness in customer acquisition efforts and to promote customers' spending on the card.

A regional market research agency estimated that in order to acquire about 25,000 customers in Singapore (see Table A), Citibank would typically need to invest in a multifaceted direct marketing program consisting of direct mail, take-ones, direct sales force (making about 10 calls a day), and bind-ins. The agency further estimated that of the prospects who had responded through direct mail or direct sales, nearly two-thirds would qualify for a card, and of those who responded to take-ones or bind-ins, nearly one-third would qualify for a card. Over 80% of those who qualified would usually become a card customer. An additional $1.6 million would also have to be invested in TV advertising to complement the direct marketing program. Such a budget would typically support 300 30-second spots during Christmas, New Year, Chinese New Year, and Eid ul Fitri (Muslim New Year). Such image advertising not only helped to bring in prospects, but also converted qualified prospects into firm customers. While a $1.6 million to $2.5 million advertising budget was adequate to reach a broad customer base within a country, a similar expenditure would be needed in each country if Citibank chose to enter several markets.

Table A Customer Acquisition Cost

Channel	*Unit Cost ($)*	*Prospects Reached*	*Response Rate*
Direct Mail	1.5	300,000	2%
Take-Ones	0.25	2,000,000	1.5%
Direct Sales	18,000/sales person	30,000	50%
Bind-Ins	0.15	3,000,000	1%

In addition to the launch costs of the card program, the infrastructural support (that is, computer systems, software development, customer support, merchant liaison, and other such fixed overhead costs) were estimated at about $35 million per year for supporting about 250,000 customers. For every incremental 250,000 customers, an additional $10 million per year to $15 million per year of overhead would result. The direct cost, including that of the card itself, mailing, correspondence, and so on, currently cost about $25 per card in 1989, but was expected to drop to $6 to $8 per card when volume reached about one million cards.

Card Business Operation Economics

Revenues from cards could come on an ongoing basis from several sources: joining/annual fee, interest payment, merchant discounts, and other transaction-related fees. (Exhibit 9 provides some basic information on how the card transaction settlement cycle works.) Setting the proper joining/annual fee was of some concern. Pricing the card too low would conflict with Citibank's stated positioning and would have a major impact on break-even projections. However, pricing it too high might mean low customer acceptance. One proposal was to waive the joining fee to induce more customers to buy the product, and charge a higher annual fee to provide a steady recurring revenue. Conventional wisdom, however, dictated a joining fee to cover the cost of acquisition, and a low annual fee to retain customers. Results from the Hong Kong card operations could be used to estimate revenues based on the in-

Table B Net Revenue Impact of Citibank Hong Kong Credit Card Business, 1989

Annual Income	% of card Owners	Average No. of Cards Owned	No. of Card Owners	No. of Cards	Annual Interest Payment[a] per Customer	Other Annual Revenue[b] per Customer	Total Annual Revenue[c] per Customer
Less than $6,200	—	—	—	—	—	—	—
$6,200–$12,400	67.5%	1.49	67,507	100,633	$102.18	$34.70	$136.88
$12,400–$23,000	20.9%	1.96	20,938	41,118	$134.44	$62.87	$197.31
Greater than $23,000	11.6%	2.43	11,640	28,249	$166.97	$82.84	$249.81
Total	100.0%	1.70	100,985	170,000	$116.46	$46.19	$162.65

[a] *The interest payment reported is net after subtracting the cost of working capital to the bank.*

[b] *This revenue consisted of merchant discounts and annual fee.*

[c] *Though a large proportion of customers usually paid the interest and other charges on time, about 3% to 7% usually defaulted on payments, of whom only about 50% were able to eventually pay.*

come levels of the customer base. As Table B shows, the Hong Kong business projected revenues of $16,279,144, or $162.65 per customer, in 1989.

Options and Controversies

Citibank's management were concerned that consumers' attitudes and credit card usage patterns differed by country. This formed the basis for debate on introducing one card with a single set of features versus developing customized offerings for each market. (Exhibit 10 on pages 266–269 provides a qualitative description of the various customer markets and their competitive environments.)

One of the most controversial ideas was that of premium pricing a card product. One of the proponents explained, "In Asia Pacific, we started business as a commercial bank. Our relationships were with large business houses. As a result, we have had a steady flow of high-status clients. Reaching out to the mass market here would certainly kill our unique positioning in the consumer's mind." Opponents argued that a premium price might mean staying out of the market, since almost all local card issuers were giving away free or low-fee credit cards.

Opinion was divided on whether each country should issue a local-currency credit card or whether the U.S. dollar should be the standard currency for all cards. American Express, which had a dominant market position in terms of market share and image, issued only a U.S.-dollar card in the region, while local players in each market issued local-currency cards. A decision in this matter would have to take into account two aspects. First, local-card spend versus overseas-card spend patterns in each market would help decide which currency type would appeal to customers. Second, asset growth of a local-currency card would hinge upon steady, matching growth of funding through local-currency deposits based on the limited branch network of Citibank.

There was considerable skepticism surrounding the idea of a centralized data processing setup, the Regional Card Center. Country managers feared that centralized processing would slow the speed of response, and system developers would be cut off from local markets. "I don't know how we can call ourselves a service company, if our systems are all centralized in Singapore," queried a country manager. "Also, it does not make cost sense to spend so much money on creating a huge cen-

E X H I B I T   1 0

Asia-Pacific Markets: Country Profiles

From the bustling financial metropolis of Singapore to the rice fields of Indonesia, the eight additional Asian markets Citibank considered for expanding its credit card business represented a broad spectrum of cultural, industrial, and economic diversity. Moreover, the level of credit card penetration and market development differed from one country to the next, as did consumers' attitudes toward card ownership and usage. Detailed descriptions of the market in each country follow.

AUSTRALIA

With its highly developed service sector, high per capita GDP, and predominantly Caucasian population, Australia closely resembled the commercialized, industrialized nations of the West in many ways, including its financial services and banking infrastructure. Compared with other developed economies, Australia ranked second only to France in the number of outlets, such as branch offices and ATMs, offering banking services per capita.

In contrast to other Asia-Pacific markets, Australia's credit card market was already saturated by 1989. With about 10.5 million cards in force, the average Australian carried two cards. Of these, about half were Bankcards, cards issued by 10 local banks for local use only. Bankcards were an introduction to credit cards for many consumers, and most still reported owning at least one. Because they had been in use for so long, and because of their usage limitations outside the country, consumers perceived Bankcards as becoming less popular, if not almost obsolete.

Visa and MasterCard had also developed large franchises in Australia, with 17.6% and 16.8% of the market, respectively. Though both were known for their wide domestic and international retail acceptance and were highly regarded in overall reputation, consumers viewed the Visa card as slightly more prestigious and higher in merchant acceptability. Twenty-three local banks and six foreign banks offered a total of 4.1 million Visas and MasterCards, though the majority were issued by Australia's four largest banks, Westpac, Commonwealth, ANZ, and National Australia Bank.

American Express and Diners Club also operated in Australia; with 600,000 and 180,000 cards in force, respectively, their franchises were much smaller than the other brands. Both cards had been known as symbols of status and had been very strong businesses at one time. However, by 1989 both were experiencing problems, due primarily to decreases in retailer acceptance and consumers' negative attitudes toward AMEX and Diners Club membership fees. Unlike the local banks, both AMEX and Diners Club charged consumers a joining fee as well as an annual membership fee.

In Australia, as in other parts of Asia, consumers recognized credit cards as an important shopping tool that freed them from carrying cash and allowed them to shop whenever and wherever they wanted. Credit card purchases varied, but most of them were related to travel, entertainment, or shopping. However, card usage had become so commonplace in Australia that prestige and image associated with the card or the issuing bank was no longer an important consideration when choosing a credit card. Australian consumers, more concerned with how credit cards could be used in conjunction with other banking services to better manage their finances, viewed credit cards as an extension of an existing relationship with their banks. Therefore, MasterCards and Visas that allowed for easy cash withdrawal through ATMs, provided for payment of monthly bills, linked all of a customer's bank accounts, provided lost wallet protection service, and had no annual fee were the most popular. The MasterCards and Visas offered by the four major national banks offered one or more of these features.

Debit cards were also available; however, penetration was less than 5% and these were primarily seen as a nonbank financial institution product linked to savings accounts.

HONG KONG

Citibank had been in the credit card business in Hong Kong since 1983, when it acquired the Diners Club card business from Hong Kong's Standard Chartered Bank. The business was expanded in 1987 through the acquisition of Bank of America's Visa card portfolio, that had grown to 75,000 customers over the previous 12 years.

With the country's impressive economic growth and rapid industrialization, the relatively affluent population of 5.6 million with an average annual income of $8,158, and a high concentration of people living in urban centers, the people of Hong Kong were no strangers to the use of credit cards. By the late 1980s, consumers were sophisticated in their knowledge and usage of credit cards—using them for a variety of occasions from daily trips to the grocery store to business travel to family vacations. They had a number of credit card options to choose from. Visas and MasterCards issued by the local Hong Kong Bank and Standard Chartered Bank were considered popular. By 1989, Hong Kong had nearly two million cards in force, with cardholders owning an average of 1.7 cards each.

Citibank viewed its Hong Kong card business as a way to grow its customer base by targeting customers outside its branch business; the bank would then deepen its relationships with these customers by actively cross-selling other Citibank products and services. By 1989, Citibank's 140,000 Classic and Gold Visas held an 8.7% share of the credit card market. In addition, it owned 100,000 Diner's Club card customers. This charge card competed directly with American Express, which had issued 175,000 cards in Hong Kong.

EXHIBIT 10 *(continued)*

INDIA

With 80% of the country's population living in rural areas, agriculture formed the foundation of India's economy. Growth in the country's key industries—textiles, food processing, and pharmaceuticals—and in the service sector contributed to India's strong economic development in the late 1980s.

Because the majority of the country's wealth was concentrated among a small group of urban households, credit card penetration in India was extremely low. Credit cards served as status symbols for India's upper-middle-class consumers and provided the convenience of not having to carry lots of cash. Consumers preferred to pay on time and not use the card as a means of revolving credit. Though merchant acceptance was generally not as high in India as in other Asian countries, consumers were able to use their cards for a variety of purchases, more than half of which were related to travel and entertainment.

To this select group of card owners, wide acceptance, brand/bank image, and ease of the application process were a card's most important features. With regard to these preferences, only Diners Club, with about 70,000 members, was strong and presented a distinct positioning. American Express did not issue a local credit card. The other major competitors were bank cards. Two of them with about 100,000 cards had already overtaken Diners Club. The local banks did not charge a joining fee and kept the annual fee at about $15. All foreign-exchange transactions in India were heavily regulated by the central bank. As a result, credit cards issued in India could be used only for local transactions in local currency.

INDONESIA

Despite its 9 billion barrels of proven oil reserves and its wealth of other minerals, Indonesia remained a relatively poor country, with about 80% of the population living in rural areas and earning less than $500 per year. A significant portion of Indonesia's small but rapidly growing wealthy class was the local Chinese business community—part of a larger network of some 27 million mainland Chinese whose growing international business interests had prompted them to settle in foreign places around the world.[1] But many wealthy Indonesian business people shared a similar international outlook as their business travels took them frequently to Malaysia, Singapore, and Australia.

The government did not impose restrictions on card ownership, but because of low income levels many did not qualify for membership, and this severely limited the size of the customer base. Thus, Indonesians perceived card ownership as a measure of high social standing. Among the major competitors were Visa and MasterCard, issued by local banks. American Express and Diners Club also operated there, offering products and services for the small pool of professionals and well-to-do citizens. Three local banks, American Express, and Diners Club shared the market equally. Whereas all charged a joining fee as well as an annual membership fee, the local banks priced their offerings significantly lower.

To those few who were able to use credit cards, a number of features were important in choosing which card to use, especially outstanding service, prestige, billing in rupiahs (local currency), and extra "perks" of membership, such as prizes for joining and purchase protection. Even among those eligible for membership, low credit limits kept consumers from using their cards intensely. Consumers were able to use their cards for a wide variety of purchases, including travel expenses, groceries, and hospital bills.

MALAYSIA

An important world producer of rubber and timber, Malaysia was largely a rural country, with 61% of the population living in rural areas. However, as a growing industrial nation, it was also the world's third-largest producer and largest exporter of semiconductors. As with neighboring Indonesia, Malaysia had a prosperous business population of nearly one million (half of whom were of Chinese origin) whose business interests took them to many countries in the Asia-Pacific region as well as to the United Kingdom.

Convenience and extra credit were important reasons for owning credit cards. Malaysians considered it acceptable to revolve credit, so that though some customers paid their monthly bills in full, many others relied on their cards to finance short-term expenses. Cards were used mostly to pay for personal and family retail purchases, with the exception of a small group of corporate customers who used the cards for business travel and entertainment.

Malaysians had plenty of card options to choose from in 1989. American Express, for instance, with a 15% share of the market, offered a charge card that was recognized internationally for its premium image and superior customer service and that had no preset spending limit. The rest of the market was divided between international banks, which used credit cards as a way of reaching new customers (foreign banks were limited to three branches in Malaysia), and local banks, which tapped into their base of branch customers to develop their card businesses. Established international banking groups, such as Hong Kong Bank and Standard Chartered Bank, offered their cards globally and were particularly attractive to customers with international interests. With its extensive branch and ATM network,

---

[1] *Source:* "The Worldwide Web of Chinese Business," *Harvard Business Review*, March–April 1993: 24-37.

EXHIBIT 10 *(continued)*

MALAYSIA *(continued)*

Malayan Banking Berhad, with a 10% share, was viewed as an established local bank whose cards were a vehicle of convenience. Finally, offering high credit limits but lacking in customer service and prestige, Malayan Borneo Finance offered numerous card types with varied pricing levels in order to be all things to all people and gain the widest possible market share. In general, MasterCard and Visa were known for their flexibility and wide retail acceptance, and the reputations of the banks issuing these cards helped consumers decide which one to choose. Local banks usually did not charge a joining fee for the classic card, but they all charged an annual fee, and they all offered an exclusive Gold card. According to Malaysian law, only consumers with an annual income of $9,000 or more could own a credit card.

PHILIPPINES

After a deep recession from 1984 through 1986, the Philippines during the late 1980s was in the midst of a booming recovery. Jumps in consumer demand helped fuel the economy as more and more jobs became available through new sources of capital and government programs. Food and beverage consumption was rising tremendously, as were sales of "big-ticket" items.

Even in the context of this rapid economic growth, credit card penetration in the Philippines was extremely low.

The credit card market was relatively underdeveloped, with only two major banks issuing MasterCards and Visas. Consumers valued these cards for their wide acceptance and revolving credit facility. American Express, perceived as the card for the international consumer, and Diners Club, known as the prestigious card, were also available. Between the two, they had nearly 50% of the market.

To their owners, credit cards provided value by allowing them to make purchases and pay for services at any time without having to worry about carrying large amounts of cash. Groceries were the most common kinds of card purchases, followed by restaurant meals, clothing, and gasoline. Wide acceptance was therefore by far the most important factor considered in selecting a card, followed by its terms, such as interest rate, repayment terms, and credit limit. The reputation of a card and its issuing bank were also important to consumers, but far less critical than other factors. Credit cards issued in the Philippines could be used only for local transactions in local currency.

SINGAPORE

Thirty years of political stability under the strong-handed rule of Prime Minister Lee Kuan Yew helped Singapore develop into one of the world's largest centers for international trade and services, as well as the site of one of the world's biggest oil refineries. A host of multinational corporations had clamored to set up operations in this "high-tech Mecca." With an average per capita income of $8,800, the standard of living in Singapore was closer to that of industrialized Westernized nations than to that of its neighbors.

By 1989, Singaporeans were quite familiar with credit cards. In fact, with cardholders owning an average of two credit cards each and with nearly 500,000 cards in force, many felt the market was already saturated. In consumers' minds, cards fell into three categories. First, American Express, with about a 15% share, the high-price charge card with no spending limit, was known for its prestige, worldwide acceptance, and outstanding global service. Second, large international banks such as Hong Kong Bank, Chase, and Standard Chartered Bank offered MasterCards and Visas with worldwide acceptance and an international image. Consumers perceived their service and prestige to be lower than that of American Express but greater than that of the local banks. Finally, a number of local banks such as UOB, DBS, OUB, and OCBC offered low-priced MasterCards and Visas with worldwide acceptance but no international image. These cards were considered to have minimum levels of service and prestige, but were seen as patriotic and conservative choices. Consumers attached a lot of importance to the reputation of the issuing bank when choosing a card. American Express was the only card to charge a joining fee. By also waiving annual membership fees, local banks UOB and DBS had each captured a 20% share of the market.

As members of a society that prided itself on introducing the latest technology and service to make things run most efficiently, Singaporean consumers viewed credit cards as vehicles of convenience. At the same time, because government regulations required all cardholders to be at least 21 years old and to earn at least $14,400 per year, credit cards were also considered a status symbol. Because the market was so well developed, cards were used to purchase high-priced and low-priced items alike, from clothing, appliances, and electronics to restaurants, entertainment, and travel.

TAIWAN

As the world's twelfth-largest trading power, Taiwan was a major investor in the Philippines, Thailand, Malaysia, Indonesia, and Mainland China. Once a rural nation, Taiwan had rapidly developed its capital- and technology-intensive industries, making its population one of the wealthiest and best educated in the region.

E X H I B I T   1 0 *(continued)*

TAIWAN *(continued)*

Though heavy government protection and support helped foster this industrial growth, it was a barrier to growth in the credit card business. Prior to 1989, laws prohibited consumers from owning more than one credit card, from revolving credit, and from using their cards to obtain cash advances. Also, international cards could not be issued in Taiwan. Anyone wanting a charge card from Citibank, American Express, or Chase Manhattan had to obtain it in Hong Kong. (The Taiwanese branches of these companies supported the Hong Kong branches in promoting these cards.)

Reforms in banking regulations, passed in July of 1989, lifted the restrictions on international cards, on multiple-card ownership, and on revolving credit. However, the government retained much control over the entire industry through its National Credit Card Center (NCCC), which engaged in developing merchant acceptance, maintained an extensive database on all member cardholders, and settled overseas transactions. Though the government exempted American Express and Diners Club from NCCC control, any bank wanting to issue a MasterCard or Visa had to obtain authority from the NCCC.

Such heavy regulation had kept all but a few players out of the credit card business, making it an industry in relatively early stages of development. Based on their global networks and premium-quality service, American Express and Diners Club developed a prestigious reputation, which they used to attract their target customers: executives, world travelers, and upper-class Taiwanese. Conversely, China Trust and Cathay Trust provided a lower-cost MasterCard and Visa suited for a wider audience. Consumers perceived American Express as the card to use for travel, Diners Club as the highest symbol of prestige, Visa as the most popular, widely accepted card in the world, and MasterCard as the second card to have in the wallet. American Express had about 50% of the market share. Unlike American Express and Diners Club, the local banks did not charge a joining fee.

To the Taiwanese consumer, the charge card was a badge of status. Taiwan was a cash-oriented society in which it was considered unacceptable to owe other people money. Even when it became legal to revolve credit, the majority of Taiwanese refrained from doing so. With an average purchase valued at $80 to $110, most credit cards were used in department stores, supermarkets, nightclubs, restaurants, and, of course, for travel—50% of credit card purchases were made overseas.

THAILAND

With its economy growing at an average of 11.6% from 1986 to 1989, Thailand was one of Asia's most rapidly developing nations; foreign investment was growing faster there than anywhere else in Southeast Asia. Most of the increases came from the country's small but strong industrialized sector and from tourism, Thailand's largest source of foreign exchange. This continued strong economic performance resulted in a growth in consumer affluence and spending.

Compared with the more industrialized nations such as Singapore and Hong Kong, the card market in Thailand had relatively few major players. Card products could be divided into two groupings. First, there was American Express and Diners Club, whose core business was charge cards and which issued about 50% of the cards in the market. Prestige was the key to their positioning, as they focused on acquiring an upscale customer base.

KOREA

Local regulations did not permit banks to issue cards with revolving credit. Further, due to strict foreign exchange control measures, only local currency cards could be issued. As a result, several local banks were issuing Visa/MasterCards as charge and debit cards. For many years, Citibank had been managing the Diners Club business in Korea. Management experience with the Korean card business was far from satisfactory, with financial losses as well as labor problems.

tralized unit, and on leasing unreliable local and overseas communication lines when we can instead piggyback on our local systems, which can be upgraded with less expense." Moreover, if the centralized system broke down, the service platforms in all countries would suffer.

The advocates of a Regional Card Center, however (except Hong Kong, which had its own system capabilities), cited two important benefits:

1. Lower costs because of scale economies, especially with respect to software development. For example, if Citibank introduced a new reporting feature for its card customers, the programming could be done centrally, and simply

downloaded to the countries. There would be no need to customize by country.

2. Capability to do quick card product launches in Asia Pacific, because of the ease of transferring best practices.

Talwar attributed the root cause of his country managers' resistance to Citibank's Asia-Pacific organization structure. Responsibility for launching the card would rest with the country managers who were already handling the branch banking side of the business. In the United States and Europe, the card business was handled by a dedicated team outside the branch banking organization. Few country managers in Asia Pacific wished to take the initial huge losses of a credit card product their projections indicated was a distinct possibility. They argued that Citibank, instead of attempting to dilute its efforts in acquiring mass-market customers, should in fact focus on its upscale customers and reinforce its depth of relationship with Citi-One and Citigold types of products and services. Some of the country managers felt they were already stretched on resources, while aggressively developing the branch banking business. It would be difficult, they said, to fund the people needs in a demanding card business since the market had no trained talent available. Countries could, then, lose focus in branch banking and would not be able to do justice to the new card business either.

The credit card idea was not without its supporters. Rajive Johri, a business manager in Indonesia, expressed his exuberance:

> In a country of 180 million, it should not be difficult to find the right staff and a million customers. We have the expertise in the United States and other markets, and if we can source enthusiastic people, we can train them in the business too. We will not only be building new business in a virgin territory but be a catalyst for changing the cash societies in emerging and rapidly growing economies of Asia Pacific.

If a decision to "go-ahead" was approved, then questions of positioning, pricing, and launch economics would have to be carefully addressed. Jeannine Farhi, who had moved to Asia from Citibank in the United States, cautioned:

> It is useful to remember that poor implementation can often kill great strategy. I am not really sure if the U.S. experience can be directly translated here. For example, I am not sure if the postal service here can handle the kind of direct mail program we often mount in the United States. Post offices here are not accustomed to handling such large masses of mail. Moreover, we have to be creative about how we put together the direct mailing lists to target customers. Ready-made lists, of course, are simply unavailable. The telecom infrastructure of many countries in this region is inadequate. Some countries take several months, or even years, to provide new telephone connections at high costs, and their reliability is poor. I have not heard of any credit bureaus which could help us evaluate potential customers. All these difficult issues should be addressed in any launch plan.

At Singapore's Changi International Airport, as Rana Talwar boarded his flight to Australia, he contemplated the diversity of his markets as well as his management's views on the card product.

> On the one hand, the expedient move would be to stick to our proven upmarket branch banking strategy. This seems to have the support of a large majority of country managers. On the other hand, we cannot be unmindful of the growth opportunities that the card product offers us. It is not clear we have a strategy for the credit card positioning, pricing, or country selection.

We are never going to get a consensus; that's why it is important for me to make a decision soon, one way or the other.

Procter and Gamble, Inc.
Scope

As Gwen Hearst looked at the year-end report she was pleased to see that Scope held a 32 percent share of the Canadian mouthwash market for 1990. She had been concerned about the inroads that Plax, a prebrushing rinse, had made in the market. Since its introduction in 1988, Plax had gained a 10 percent share of the product category and posed a threat to Scope. As Brand Manager, Hearst planned, developed, and directed the total marketing effort for Scope, Procter and Gamble's (P&G) brand in the mouthwash market. She was responsible for maximizing the market share, volume, and profitability of the brand.

Until the entry of Plax, brands in the mouthwash market were positioned around two major benefits: fresh breath and killing germs. Plax was positioned around a new benefit—as a "plaque fighter"—and indications were that other brands, such as Listerine, were going to promote this benefit. The challenge for Hearst was to develop a strategy that would ensure the continued profitability of Scope in the face of these competitive threats. Her specific task was to prepare a marketing plan for P&G's mouthwash business for the next three years. It was early February 1991, and she would be presenting the plan to senior management in March.

COMPANY BACKGROUND

Based on a philosophy of providing products of superior quality and value that best fill the needs of consumers, Procter and Gamble is one of the most successful consumer goods companies in the world. The company markets its brands in more than 140 countries and had net earnings of $1.6 billion in 1990. The Canadian subsidiary contributed $1.4 billion in sales and $100 million in net earnings in 1990. It was recognized as a leader in the Canadian packaged-goods industry, and its consumer brands led in most of the categories in which the company competed.

Between 1987 and 1990, worldwide sales of P&G had increased by $8 billion and net earnings by $1.3 billion. P&G executives attributed the company's success to a variety of factors, including the ability to develop truly innovative products to meet consumers' needs. Exhibit 1 on page 272 contains the statement of purpose and strategy of the Canadian subsidiary.

P&G Canada has five operating divisions, organized by product category. The divisions, and some of the major brands, are:

1. *Paper products*: Royale, Pampers, Luvs, Attends, Always
2. *Food and beverage*: Duncan Hines, Crisco, Pringles, Sunny Delight

This case was prepared by Professors Gordon H. G. McDougall and Franklin Ramsoomair, of the Wilfrid Laurier University, as a basis for class discussion and is not designed to illustrate effective or ineffective handling of an administrative situation. Used with permission.

EXHIBIT 1

A Statement of Purpose and Strategy: Procter and Gamble, Canada

We will provide products of superior quality and value that best fill the needs of consumers.

We will achieve that purpose through an organization and a working environment which attracts the finest people, fully develops and challenges our individual talents; encourages our free and spirited collaboration to drive the business ahead; and maintains the Company's historic principles of integrity, and doing the right thing.

We will build a profitable business in Canada. We will apply P&G worldwide learning and resources to maximize our success rate. We will concentrate our resources on the most profitable categories and on unique, important Canadian market opportunities. We will also contribute to the development of outstanding people and innovative business ideas for worldwide company use.

We will reach our business goals and achieve optimum cost efficiencies through continuing innovation, strategic planning, and the continuous pursuit of excellence in everything we do.

We will continuously stay ahead of competition while aggressively defending our established profitable businesses against major competitive challenges despite short-term profit consequences.

Through the successful pursuit of our commitment, we expect our brands to achieve leadership share and profit positions and that, as a result, our business, our people, our shareholders, and the communities in which we live and work, will prosper.

Source: Company records.

3. *Beauty care*: Head & Shoulders, Pantene, Pert, Vidal Sassoon, Clearasil, Clarion, Cover Girl, Max Factor, Oil of Olay, Noxzema, Secret

4. *Health care*: Crest, Scope, Vicks, Pepto Bismol, Metamucil

5. *Laundry and cleaning*: Tide, Cheer, Bounce, Bold, Oxydol, Joy, Cascade, Comet, Mr. Clean

Each division had its own Brand Management, Sales, Finance, Product Development and Operations line management groups and was evaluated as a profit center. Typically, within each division a Brand Manager was assigned to each brand (for example, Scope). Hearst was in the Health Care division and reported to the Associate Advertising Manager for oral care, who, in turn, reported to the General Manager of the division. After completing her business degree (B.B.A.) at a well-known Ontario business school in 1986, Hearst had joined P&G as a Brand Assistant. In 1987 she became the Assistant Brand Manager for Scope, and in 1988 she was promoted to Brand Manager. Hearst's rapid advancement at P&G reflected the confidence that her managers had in her abilities.

■ THE CANADIAN MOUTHWASH MARKET

Until 1987, on a unit basis the mouthwash market had grown at an average of 3 percent per year for the previous 12 years. In 1987, it experienced a 26 percent increase with the introduction of new flavors such as peppermint. Since then, the growth rate had declined to a level of 5 percent in 1990 (Exhibit 2).

The mouthwash market was initially developed by Warner-Lambert with its pioneer brand Listerine. Positioned as a therapeutic germ-killing mouthwash that eliminated bad breath, it dominated the market until the entry of Scope in 1967. Scope, a green, mint-tasting mouthwash, was positioned as a great-tasting, mouth-refreshing brand that provided bad-breath protection. It was the first brand that offered both effective protection against bad breath and a better taste than other mouthwashes. Its advertising focused, in part, on a perceived weakness of Listerine—a medicine

EXHIBIT 2

Canadian Mouthwash Market

	1986	1987	1988	1989	1990
Total retail sales (millions)	$43.4	$54.6	$60.2	$65.4	$68.6
Total factory sales (millions)	$34.8	$43.5	$48.1	$52.2	$54.4
Total unit sales (thousands)[a]	863	1,088	1,197	1,294	1,358
(% change)	3	26	10	8	5
(% change—"breath only")[b]	3	26	0	3	5
Penetration (%)[c]	65	70	75	73	75
Usage (number of times per week)[d]	2.0	2.2	2.3	2.4	3.0

[a] One unit or statistical case equals 10 liters or 352 fluid ounces of mouthwash.

[b] Excludes Plax and other prebrushing rinses.

[c] Percent of households having at least one brand in home.

[d] For each adult household member.

Source: Company records.

breath (for example, "Scope fights bad breath. Don't let the good taste fool you")—and in 1976, Scope became the market leader in Canada.

In 1977, Warner-Lambert launched Listermint mouthwash as a direct competitor to Scope. Like Scope, it was a green, mint-tasting mouthwash and positioned as a "good tasting mouthwash that fights bad breath." Within a year it had achieved a 12 percent market share, primarily at the expense of Listerine and smaller brands in the market.

In the 1970s Merrell Dow, a large pharmaceutical firm, launched Cepacol, which was positioned very close to Listerine. It achieved and held approximately 14 percent of the market in the early 1980s.

During the 1980s, the major competitive changes in the Canadian mouthwash market were:

- Listerine, which had been marketed primarily on a "bad breath" strategy, began shifting its position and in 1988 introduced the claim "Fights plaque and helps prevent inflamed gums caused by plaque." In the United States, Listerine gained the American Dental Association seal for plaque but, as yet, did not have the seal in Canada.

- Listermint added fluoride during the early 1980s and added the Canadian Dental Association seal for preventing cavities in 1983. More recently, Listermint had downplayed fluoride and removed the seal.

- In early 1987, flavors were introduced by a number of brands including Scope, Listermint, and various store brands. This greatly expanded the market in 1987 but did not significantly change the market shares held by the major brands.

- Colgate Fluoride Rinse was launched in 1988. With the seal from the Canadian Dental Association for cavities, it claimed that "Colgate's new fluoride rinse fights cavities. And, it has a mild taste that encourages children to rinse longer and more often." Colgate's share peaked at 2 percent and then declined. There were rumours that Colgate was planning to discontinue the brand.

- In 1988, Merrell Dow entered a licensing agreement with Strategic Brands to market Cepacol in Canada. Strategic Brands, a Canadian firm that markets a variety of consumer household products, had focused its efforts on gaining greater distribution for Cepacol and promoting it on the basis of price.

- In 1988, Plax was launched on a new and different platform. Its launch and immediate success caught many in the industry by surprise.

■ THE INTRODUCTION OF PLAX

Plax was launched in Canada in late 1988 on a platform quite different from the traditional mouthwashes. First, instead of the usual use occasion of "after brushing," it called itself a "prebrushing" rinse. The user rinses before brushing, and Plax's detergents are supposed to help loosen plaque to make brushing especially effective. Second, the product benefits were not breath-focused. Instead, it claimed that "Rinsing with Plax, then brushing normally, removes up to three times more plaque than just brushing alone."

Pfizer Inc., a pharmaceutical firm, launched Plax in Canada with a promotion campaign that was estimated to be close to $4 million. The campaign, which covered the last three months of 1988 and all of 1989, consisted of advertising estimated at $3 million and extensive sales promotions including (1) trial-size display in three drugstore chains ($60,000), (2) co-op mail couponing to 2.5 million households ($160,000), (3) an instantly redeemable coupon offer ($110,000), (4) a professional mailer to drug and supermarket chains ($30,000), and (5) a number of price reductions ($640,000). Plax continued to support the brand with advertising expenditures of approximately $1.2 million in 1990. In 1990, Plax held a 10 percent share of the total market.

When Plax was launched in the United States, it claimed that using Plax "removed up to 300% more plaque than just brushing." This claim was challenged by mouthwash competitors and led to an investigation by the Better Business Bureau. The investigation found that the study on which Plax based its claim had panelists limit their toothbrushing to just 15 seconds—and didn't let them use toothpaste. A further study, where people were allowed to brush in their "usual manner" and with toothpaste, showed no overall difference in the level of plaque buildup between those using Plax and a control group that did not use Plax. Plax then revised its claim to "three times more plaque than just brushing alone." Information on plaque is contained in Appendix 1.

■ THE CURRENT SITUATION

In preparing for the strategic plan, Gwen Hearst reviewed the available information for the mouthwash market and Scope. As shown in Exhibit 2, in 1990, 75 percent of Canadian households used one or more mouthwash brands, and, on average, usage was three times per week for each adult household member. Company market research revealed that users could be segmented on frequency of use; "heavy" users (once per day or more) comprised 40 percent of all users, "medium" users (two–six times a week) comprised 45 percent, and "light" users (less than once a week) comprised 15 percent. No information was available on the usage habits of prebrushing rinse users. Nonusers currently don't buy mouthwash because they either (1) don't believe they get bad breath, (2) believe that brushing their teeth is adequate, and/or (3) find alternatives like gums and mints more convenient. The most important reasons why consumers use mouthwash are:

Most important reason for using a mouthwash:	%
It is part of my basic oral hygiene	40*
It gets rid of bad breath	40
It kills germs	30
It makes me feel more confident	20
To avoid offending others	25

* Multiple reasons allowed.

During 1990, a survey was conducted of mouthwash users' images of the major brands in the market. Respondents were asked to rate the brands on a number of attributes, and the results show that Plax had achieved a strong image on the "removes plaque/healthier teeth and gums" attributes (Exhibit 3).

Market share data revealed there was a substantial difference in the share held by Scope in food stores, 42 percent (for example, supermarkets) versus drugstores, 27 percent (Exhibit 4 on page 276). Approximately 65 percent of all mouthwash sales went through drugstores, while 35 percent went through food stores. Recently, wholesale clubs, such as Price Club and Costco, were accounting for a greater share of mouthwash sales.[1] Typically, these clubs carried Cepacol, Scope, Listerine, and Plax.

EXHIBIT 3

Consumer Perceptions of Brand Images

	All Users[a]					
Attributes	Cepacol	Colgate	Listerine	Listermint	Plax	Scope
Reduces bad breath	. . .	. . .	. . .	. . .	—	. . .
Kills germs	+	. . .	+	. . .	. . .	—
Removes plaque	. . .	. . .	. . .	. . .	+	—
Healthier teeth and gums	. . .	. . .	. . .	. . .	+	—
Good for preventing colds	. . .	. . .	+	. . .	. . .	. . .
Recommended by doctors/dentists	. . .	—	. . .	. . .	+	. . .
Cleans your mouth well	. . .	. . .	. . .	. . .	. . .	. . .

	Brand Users[b]					
Attributes	Cepacol	Colgate	Listerine	Litermint	Plax	Scope
Reduces bad breath	+	—	+	+	—	+
Kills germs	+	. . .	+	—	—	. . .
Removes plaque	—	+	+	—	+	—
Healthier teeth and gums	. . .	+	+	—	+	—
Good for preventing colds	+	—	+	—	—	—
Recommended by doctors/dentists	+	+	+	—	+	—

[a] Includes anyone who uses mouthwash. Respondents asked to rate all brands (even those they haven't used) on the attributes. A "+" means this brand scores higher than average. A ". . ." means this brand scored about average. A "—" means this brand scored below average. For example, Cepacol is perceived by those who use mouthwash as a brand that is good/better than most at "preventing germs."

[b] Includes only the users of that brand. For example, Cepacal is perceived by those whose "usual brand" is Cepacal as a brand that is good/better than most at "reducing bad breath."

Source: Company records.

---

[1] Wholesale clubs were included in food store sales.

EXHIBIT 4

Canadian Mouthwash Market Shares

	Units			1990 Average	
	1988	*1989*	*1990*	*Food*	*Drug*
Scope	33.0%	33.0%	32.3%	42.0%	27.0%
Listerine	15.2	16.1	16.6	12.0	19.0
Listermint	15.2	9.8	10.6	8.0	12.0
Cepacol	13.6	10.6	10.3	9.0	11.0
Colgate oral rinse	1.4	1.2	0.5	0.4	0.5
Plax	1.0	10.0	10.0	8.0	11.0
Store brands	16.0	15.4	16.0	18.0	15.0
Miscellaneous other	4.6	3.9	3.7	2.6	4.5
Total	100.0%	100.0%	100.0%	100.0%	100.0%
Retail sales (000,000)	$60.2	$65.4	$68.6	$24.0	$44.6

Source: Company records.

Competitive data were also collected for advertising expenditures and retail prices. As shown in Exhibit 5, total media spending of all brands in 1990 was $5 million, with Scope, Listerine, and Plax accounting for 90 percent of all advertising. Retail prices were calculated based on a 750 ml bottle, both Listerine and Plax were priced at a higher level in food stores, and Plax was priced at a premium in drugstores.

Information on the U.S. market for 1989 was also available (Exhibit 6, page 278). In contrast to Canada, Listerine held the dominant share in the U.S. market. Since early 1989, Listerine had been advertised heavily in the United States as "the only nonprescription mouthwash accepted by the American Dental Association for its significant help in preventing and reducing plaque and gingivitis." In clinical tests in the United States, Listerine significantly reduced plaque scores by roughly 20 to 35 percent, with a similar reduction in gingivitis. In Canada, the 1990 advertising campaign included the claim that Listerine has been clinically proven to "help prevent inflamed and irritated gums caused by plaque build-up." Listerine's formula relied on four essential oils—menthol, eucalyptol, thymol, and methyl salicylate—all derivatives of phenol, a powerful antiseptic.

Listerine had not received the consumer product seal given by the Canadian Dental Association (CDA) because the association was not convinced a mouthrinse could be of therapeutic value. The CDA was currently reviewing American tests for several products sold in Canada. In fact, any proposed changes to the formulation of mouthwashes or advertising claims could require approval from various regulatory agencies.

■ THE REGULATORY ENVIRONMENT

1. **Health Protection Branch:** This government body classifies products into "drug status" or "cosmetic status" based on both the product's action on bodily functions and its advertising claims. Drug products are those that affect a bodily function (for example, prevent cavities or prevent plaque buildup). For "drug status" products, all product formulations, packaging, copy, and ad-

EXHIBIT 5

Competitive Market Data, 1990

Advertising Expenditures (000)

Scope	$1,700
Listerine	1,600
Plax	1,200
Listermint	330
Cepacol	170

Media Plans

	Number of Weeks on Air	GRPs[a]
Scope	35	325
Listerine	25	450
Plax	20	325

Retail Price Indices

	Food Stores	Drugstores
Scope	98	84
Listerine	129	97
Listermint	103	84
Colgate	123	119
Plax	170	141
Store brand	58	58
Cepacol	84	81
Total Market[b]	100	100

[a] GRP (Gross Rating Points) is a measurement of advertising impact derived by multiplying the number of persons exposed to an advertisement by the average number of exposures per person. The GRPs reported are monthly.

[b] An average weighted index of the retail prices of all mouthwash brands is calculated and indexed at 100 for both food stores and drugstores. Scope is priced slightly below this index in food stores and about 16 percent below in drugstores.

Source: Company records.

vertising must be pre-cleared by the Health Protection Branch (HPB), with guidelines that are very stringent. Mouthwashes like Scope that claim to only prevent bad breath are considered as "cosmetic status." However, if any claims regarding inhibition of plaque formation are made the product reverts to "drug status," and all advertising is scrutinized.

2. **The Canadian Dental Association:** Will, upon request of the manufacturer, place its seal of recognition on products that have demonstrated efficacy against cavities or against plaque/gingivitis. However, those products with the seal of recognition must submit their packaging and advertising to the CDA for approval. The CDA and the American Dental Association (ADA) are two separate bodies and are independent of each other and don't always agree on issues. The CDA, for example, would not provide a "plaque/gingivitis" seal unless clinical studies demonstrating actual gum health improvements were done.

3. **Saccharin/Cyclamate sweeteners:** All mouthwashes contain an artificial sweetener. In Canada, cyclamate is used as the sweetener, as saccharin is con-

EXHIBIT 6

Canada-U.S. Market Share Comparison, 1989 (% units)

Brands	Canada	United States
Scope	33.0	21.6
Listerine	16.1	28.7
Listermint	9.8	4.5
Cepacol	10.6	3.6
Plax	10.0	9.6

Source: Company records.

sidered a banned substance. In contrast, the United States uses saccharin because cyclamate is prohibited. Thus, despite the fact that many of the same brands compete in both Canada and the United States, the formula in each country is different.

■ THE THREE-YEAR PLAN

In preparing the three-year plan for Scope, a team had been formed within P&G to examine various options. The team included individuals from Product Development (PDD), Manufacturing, Sales, Market Research, Finance, Advertising, and Operations. Over the past year, the team had completed a variety of activities relating to Scope.

The key issue, in Hearst's mind, was how P&G should capitalize on the emerging market segment within the rinse category that focused more on "health-related benefits" than the traditional breath strategy of Scope. Specifically with the launch of Plax, the mouthwash market had segmented itself along the "breath-only" brands (like Scope) and those promising other benefits. Plax, in positioning itself as a pre-brushing rinse, was not seen as, nor did it taste like, a "breath refreshment" mouthwash like Scope.

Gwen Hearst believed that a line extension positioned against Plax, a recent entry into the market, made the most sense. If the mouthwash market became more segmented, and if these other brands grew, her fear was that P&G would be left with a large share of a segment that focused only on "breath" and hence might decline. However, she also knew that there were questions regarding both the strategic and financial implications of such a proposal. In recent meetings, other ideas had been proposed, including "doing nothing" and looking at claims other than "breath" that might be used by Scope instead of adding a new product. Several team members questioned whether there was any real threat, as Plax was positioned very differently from Scope. As she considered the alternatives, Hearst reviewed the activities of the team and the issues that had been raised by various team members.

Product Development

In product tests on Scope, PDD had demonstrated that Scope reduced plaque better than brushing alone because of antibacterial ingredients contained in Scope. However, as yet P&G did not have a clinical database to convince the HPB to allow Scope to extend these claims into the prevention of inflamed gums (as Listerine does).

PDD had recently developed a new prebrushing rinse product that performed as well as Plax but did not work any better than Plax against plaque reduction. In fact, in its testing of Plax itself, PDD was actually unable to replicate the plaque reduction claim made by Pfizer that "rinsing with Plax, then brushing normally removes up to three times more plaque than brushing alone." The key benefit of P&G's prebrushing rinse was that it did taste better than Plax. Other than that, it had similar aesthetic qualities to Plax—qualities that made its "in-mouth" experience quite different from that of Scope.

The Product Development people in particular were concerned about Hearst's idea of launching a line extension because it was a product that was only equal in efficacy to Plax and to placebo rinses for plaque reduction. Traditionally, P&G had only launched products that focused on unmet consumer needs—typically superior performing products. However, Gwen had pointed out, because the new product offered similar efficacy at a better taste, this was similar to the situation when Scope was originally launched. Some PDD members were also concerned that if they couldn't replicate Plax's clinical results with P&G's stringent test methodology, and if the product possibly didn't provide any greater benefit than rinsing with any liquid, then P&G's image and credibility with dental professionals might be impacted. There was debate on this issue, as others felt that as long as the product did encourage better oral hygiene, it did provide a benefit. As further support they noted that many professionals did recommend Plax. Overall, PDD's preference was to not launch a new product but, instead, to add plaque-reduction claims to Scope. The basic argument was that it was better to protect the business that P&G was already in than to launch a completely new entity. If a line extension was pursued, a product test costing $20,000 would be required.

Sales

The sales people had seen the inroads Plax had been making in the marketplace and believed that Scope should respond quickly. They had one key concern. As stock-keeping units (SKUs) had begun to proliferate in many categories, the retail industry had become much more stringent regarding what it would accept. Now, to be listed on store shelves, a brand must be seen as different enough (or unique) from the competition to build incremental purchases—otherwise retailers argued that category sales volume would simply be spread over more units. When this happened, a retail outlet's profitability was reduced because inventory costs were higher, but no additional sales revenue was generated. When a new brand was viewed as not generating more sales, retailers might still list the brand by replacing units within the existing line (for example, drop shelf facings of Scope), or the manufacturer could pay approximately $50,000 per stock-keeping unit in listing fees to add the new brand.

Market Research

Market Research (MR) had worked extensively with Hearst to test the options with consumers. Its work to date had shown:

1. A plaque reassurance on current Scope (that is, "Now Scope fights plaque") did not seem to increase competitive users' desire to purchase Scope. This meant that it was unlikely to generate additional volume, but it could prevent current users from switching.

    MR also cautioned that adding "reassurances" to a product often takes time before the consumer accepts the idea and then acts on it. The issue in Hearst's mind was whether the reassurance would ever be enough. At best it might stabilize the business, she thought, but would it grow behind such a claim?

2. A "Better-Tasting Prebrushing Dental Rinse" product did research well among Plax users, but did not increase purchase intent among people not currently using a dental rinse. MR's estimate was that a brand launched on this posi-

tioning would likely result in approximately a 6.5 percent share of the total mouthwash and "rinse" market on an ongoing basis. Historically, it has taken approximately two years to get to the ongoing level. However, there was no way for them to accurately assess potential Scope cannibalization. "Use your judgment," they had said. However, they cautioned that although it was a product for a different usage occasion, it was unlikely to be 100 percent incremental business. Hearst's best rough guess was that this product might cannibalize somewhere between 2 and 9 percent of Scope's sales. An unresolved issue was the product's name—if it were launched, should it be under the Scope name or not? One fear was that if the Scope name was used it would either "turn off" loyal users who saw Scope as a breath refreshment product or confuse them.

MR had questioned Hearst as to whether she had really looked at all angles to meet her objective. Because much of this work had been done quickly, they wondered whether there weren't some other benefits Scope could talk about that would interest consumers and hence achieve the same objective. They suggested that Hearst look at other alternatives beyond just "a plaque reassurance on Scope" or a "line extension positioned as a 'Better-Tasting Prebrushing Rinse.' "

EXHIBIT 7

Scope Historical Financials

Year	1988		1989		1990	
Total market size (Units) (000)	1,197		1,294		1,358	
Scope market share	33.0%		33.0%		32.4%	
Scope volume (Units) (000)	395		427		440	
	$(000)	$/Unit	$(000)	$/Unit	$(000)	$/Unit
Sales	16,767	42.45	17,847	41.80	18,150	41.25
COGS	10,738	27.18	11,316	26.50	11,409	25.93
Gross margin	6,029	15.27	7,299	15.30	6,741	15.32

Scope Marketing Plan Inputs
Scope "Going" Marketing Spending

Year	1990	1989	1988
Advertising (000)	$1,700	—	—
Promotion (000)	1,460	—	—
Total (000)	3,160	3,733	2,697

Marketing Input Costs

Advertising:		(See previous table)
Promotion:	Samples	(Including Distribution): $0.45/piece
	Mailed couponing	$10.00 per 1,000 for printing distribution
		$0.17 handling per redeemed coupon (beyond face value) redemption rates: 10% to 15%
	In-store promotion	$200/store (fixed)
		$0.17 handling per redeemed coupon (beyond face value) redemption rates: 85%+

Source: Company records.

EXHIBIT 8

Scope 1990 Financials

	$(000)	$/Unit
Net sales[a]	18,150	41.25
Ingredients	3,590	8.16
Packaging	2,244	5.10
Manufacturing[b]	3,080	7.00
Delivery	1,373	3.12
Miscellaneous[c]	1,122	2.55
Cost of goods sold	11,409	25.93
Gross margin	6,741	15.32

[a] Net sales = P&G revenues.

[b] Manufacturing: 50 percent of manufacturing cost is fixed of which $200,000 is depreciation; 20 percent of manufacturing cost is labor.

[c] Miscellaneous: 75 percent of miscellaneous cost is fixed. General office overhead is $1,366,000. Taxes are 40 percent. Currently the plant operates on a five-day one-shift operation. P&G's weighted average cost of capital is 12 percent. Total units sold in 1990 were 440,000.

Source: Company records.

Finance

The point of view from Finance was mixed. On the one hand, Plax commanded a higher dollar price/liter and so it made sense that a new rinse might be a profitable option. On the other hand, they were concerned about the capital costs and the marketing costs that might be involved to launch a line extension. One option would be to source the product from a U.S. plant where the necessary equipment already existed. If the product was obtained from the U.S. delivery costs would increase by $1 per unit. Scope's current marketing and financial picture is shown in Exhibits 7 and 8 and an estimate of Plax's financial picture is provided in Exhibit 9.

EXHIBIT 9

Plax Financial Estimates ($/Unit)

Net Sales	65.09
COGS	
Ingredients	6.50
Packaging	8.30
Manufacturing	6.50
Delivery	3.00
Miscellaneous	1.06
Total	25.36

Notes: General overhead costs estimated at $5.88/unit.

Source: P&G estimates.

Purchasing

The Purchasing Manager had reviewed the formula for the line extension and had estimated that the ingredients cost would increase by $2.55 per unit due to the addition of new ingredients. But, because one of the ingredients was very new, Finance felt that the actual ingredient change might vary by ± 50%. Packaging costs would be $0.30 per unit higher owing to the fact that the setup charges would be spread over a smaller base.

Advertising Agency

The Advertising Agency felt that making any new claims for Scope as a huge strategic shift for the brand. They favored a line extension. Scope's strategy had always been "breath refreshment and good tasting" focused, and they saw the plaque claims as very different, with potentially significant strategic implications. The one time they had focused advertising only on taste and didn't reinforce breath efficacy, share fell. They were concerned that the current Scope consumer could be confused if plaque or any "nonbreath" claims were added and that Scope could actually lose market share if this occurred. They also pointed out that trying to communicate two different ideas in one commercial was very difficult. They believed the line extension was a completely different product from Scope with a different benefit and use occasion. In their minds, a line extension would need to be supported on a going basis separately from Scope.

■ WHAT TO RECOMMEND?

Hearst knew the business team had thought long and hard about the issue. She knew that management was depending on the Scope business team to come up with the right long-term plan for P&G—even if that meant not introducing the new product. However, she felt there was too much risk associated with P&G's long-term position in oral rinses if nothing was done. There was no easy answer—and compounding the exigencies of the situation was the fact that the business team had differing points of view. She was faced with the dilemma of providing recommendations about Scope, but also needed to ensure that there was alignment and commitment from the business team, or Senior Management would be unlikely to agree to the proposal.

■ APPENDIX 1

Plaque

Plaque is a soft, sticky film that coats teeth within hours of brushing and may eventually harden into tartar. To curb gum disease—which over 90 percent of Canadians suffer at some time—plaque must be curbed. Research has shown that, without brushing, within 24 hours a film (plaque) starts to spread over teeth and gums and, over days, becomes a sticky, gelatinous mat, which the plaque bacteria spin from sugars and starches. As the plaque grows it becomes home to yet more bacteria—dozens of strains. A mature plaque is about 75 percent bacteria; the remainder consists of organic solids from saliva, water, and other cells shed from soft oral tissues.

As plaque bacteria digest food, they also manufacture irritating malodorous byproducts, all of which can harm a tooth's supporting tissues as they seep into the crevice below the gum line. Within 10 to 21 days, depending on the person, signs of gingivitis—the mildest gum disease—first appear; gums deepen in color, swell, and lose their normally tight, arching contour around teeth. Such gingivitis is entirely reversible. It can disappear within a week after regular brushing and flossing are resumed. But when plaque isn't kept under control, gingivitis can be the first step down toward periodontitis, the more advanced gum disease in which bone and other structures that support the teeth become damaged. Teeth can loosen and fall out—or require extraction.

The traditional and still best approach to plaque control is careful and thorough brushing and flossing to scrub teeth clean of plaque. Indeed, the antiplaque claims that toothpastes carry are usually based on the product's ability to clean teeth mechanically, with brushing. Toothpastes contain abrasives, detergent, and foaming agents, all of which help the brush do its work.

Swisher Mower and Machine Company

In early 1990, Max Swisher, President of Swisher Mower and Machine Company (SMC), received a certified letter from a major national retail merchandise chain inquiring about a private branding arrangement for his company's line of riding mowers. He thought the inquiry presented an opportunity worth consideration, since unit volume sales of the SMC riding mower had eroded in recent years. However, details concerning the inquiry would have to be studied more closely.

■ COMPANY BACKGROUND

The origins of Swisher Mower and Machine Company can be traced to the mechanical aptitude of its founder, Max Swisher. He received his first patent for a gearbox drive assembly when he was 18 years old. Shortly thereafter, he developed a self-propelled push mower utilizing this drive assembly. He began selling these mowers to neighbors after converting his parents' garage into a small manufacturing operation and formed Swisher Mower and Machine Company in 1949. In the early 1950s, Swisher decided to integrate his drive mechanism into a riding mower and began selling these mowers under the Ride King name in 1956.

In 1966, unit volume for SMC riding mowers peaked at 10,000 units with sales of $2 million. In the early 1970s, sales volume began a downward trend as a result of poor economic conditions in the geographic markets served by SMC. From 1975 to 1989, unit volume remained relatively constant and averaged 4,335 units per year. In 1989, the company sold 4,100 riding mowers and recorded sales of $3.5 million. Exhibit 1 shows the company's unit sales history for riding mowers since 1956.

SMC has 17 employees—3 managers, 1 administrative assistant, and 13 production workers. The company manufactures mowers at its plant in Warrensburg, Missouri, but utilizes outside suppliers for some machine tool work and subassembly. Its facilities have an annual production capacity of 10,000 riding mower units on a single 40-hour-per-week shift. The company's production facility and office space are rented from a related firm.

Max Swisher has always insisted that his company be customer-oriented in recognizing and providing for both dealer and end-user needs. Maintaining a "small company" image has also been an important aspect of Swisher's business philosophy, which in turn has resulted in personal relationships with dealers and customers alike. A special loyalty has been demonstrated to the original SMC dealers and dis-

The cooperation of Swisher Mower and Machine Company in the preparation of this case is gratefully acknowledged. This case was prepared by Professor Roger A. Kerin, of the Edwin L. Cox School of Business, of Southern Methodist University, and Wayne Swisher, Swisher Mower and Machine Company, as a basis for class discussion and is not designed to illustrate effective or ineffective handling of an administrative situation. The case benefited from the assistance of Derek Siewert and Bennet Grayson, graduate students. Certain financial and operating data are disguised and not useful for research purposes. Copyright © 1995 by Roger A. Kerin. No part of this case may be reproduced without written permission of the copyright holder.

EXHIBIT 1

Unit Sales History for SMC Riding Mowers

Thousands

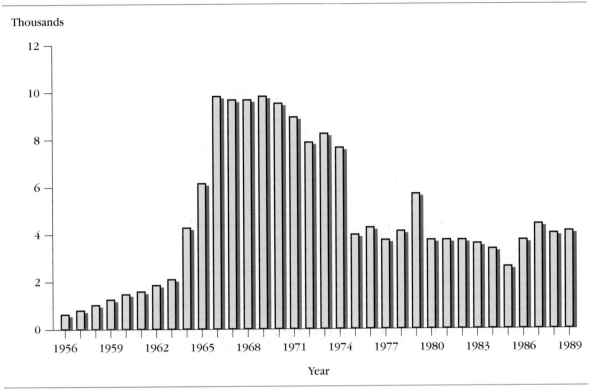

Year

tributors that helped build the sales foundation of the company. SMC continues to guarantee protection of these and other dealers' trade territories whenever possible.

Product Line

SMC produces three types of lawn mower units. Its flagship product, the Ride King, is a three-wheel riding mower that has a zero turning radius. Developed by Swisher in the 1950s, this design is distinct from competitors' in that the single steerable front wheel is also the drive unit. This feature allows the mower to be put in reverse without changing gears and by simply turning the steering wheel 180 degrees. The company is credited with producing the first zero-turning-radius riding mower.

The manufacturer's list price for the standard Ride King model is $550. Manufacturer gross profit margin on this unit is approximately 17 percent. The cost of goods sold for this product is approximately $100 for labor and $356.50 for parts.

SMC has a reputation for producing high-quality riding mowers that have a simple design allowing for ease of customer use and maintenance. These features and benefits are prominently displayed in the product literature for Ride King (see Exhibit 2 on page 286). The reliability and ruggedness of the riding mower are demonstrated by the product's longevity. SMC mowers often run for more than 25 years before having to be replaced. The company provides a one-year warranty on all parts and labor. Riding mowers accounted for 63.6 percent of SMC's total sales and 57.8 percent of total gross profit in 1989.

Most current mowers' parts are interchangeable with the parts of older models that date back to 1956. Even though the patent for the zero-turning-radius drive unit has expired, no competitors have copied this design.

EXHIBIT 2

Ride King Product Literature

SMC also produces a "trailmower" called T-40. This unit consists of a trailer-type mower that has a cutting width of 40 inches. When hitched to any riding lawn mower this unit effectively increases the cutting width by 40 inches. The "trailmower" can also be pulled behind all-terrain vehicles. The T-40 was introduced in

EXHIBIT 2 *(continued)*

THE ORIGINAL ZERO TURNING RADIUS

32" cut
REVERSES WITHOUT CHANGING GEARS OR BELTS

The Ride King pulls by a single, steerable front wheel which pivots 360° for sharp turns or reverse. Turning of the steering wheel gives you reverse without changing gears or belts. This eliminates complicated transmission, differentials, etc.,therefore less maintenance and initial cost.

Ride King trims with 3/8'', turns square corners, makes a clean cut around trees and poles with one pass.

Exclusive patented front wheel drive provides full 360° steering and maximum maneuverability. This front wheel drive prevents tipping over backward. Equipped with automatic brake for stopping on any terrain when clutch is released. Blade stops automatically when blade clutch is released.

Powerful, dependable four cycle engine. ''Stops on a Dime—Turns on a Nickel'' . . . with change to spare!

OUTSTANDING FEATURES

- Zero Turning Radius.
- All Steel Construction.
- Ball Bearings throughout.
- 8 HP Briggs & Stratton Synchro-Balanced.
- Front Wheel Drive—360°Steering reverses by turning the steering wheel.
- Trims close to objects and obstructions.
- 2 Speed Drive, Optional.
- Allows you to shift up or down without disengaging clutch.
- Saf-Lok Clutch, Disengages Blade. Use as tractor.
- Wide Wheelbase. Big Tires. Superior traction, all air.
- Powerful automatic brake prevents coasting.
- Available with recoil, 12V, 110V starter.
- Belt drive blades (means no sprung crankshaft).
- Extra large and well padded seat suspended on springs on both sides for utmost comfort.
- Large one gallon fuel tank separate from engine for greater safety and durability.
- Steering wheel slanted and designed for the greatest comfort and ease of operation.
- Less moving parts than any other riding mower on the market.

SPECIFICATIONS

MODEL A32

Cut	32''
Length	48''
Width	33''
New Weight	210 lbs.
Rear Tires	3.50 x 6 air
Front Tires	3.50 x 6 air
Engine	8 HP Briggs & Stratton Syncro-Balanced Also Available 6 HP Tecumseh
Blade	Austempered twin blades
Clutch	Positive Lok-Over
Wheels	Ball-Bearing
Deck	11 ga. steel
Blade spindle ball bearing lubricated for life.	

SWISHER MOWER AND MACHINE CO., INC.
BOX 67 WARRENSBURG, MISSOURI 64093
PHONE: 816-747-8183
OUTSIDE MISSOURI: 800-222-8183
FAX: 816-747-8650

1985 and accounted for 8.2 percent of SMC's total sales and 13.2 percent of total gross profit in 1989. Exhibit 3 on page 288 shows the product literature for the T-40.

SMC deemphasized the sale of its self-propelled push mower in the early 1960s due to lagging sales and increased demand for the riding mower. When it phased out these units, the company began offering push lawn mower "kits." There are three different push mower kits available, and each consists of all the component parts necessary to assemble push mowers. They do not bear the SMC name and are sold un-

EXHIBIT 3

T-40 Product Literature

THE NEW T-40 TRAILMOWER

- Universal Hitch
- 8 hp Briggs & Stratton or 10 hp Tecumseh
- 40" Cut
- Belt-driven blades (No sprung crankshaft)
- Center mounted wheels to eliminate scalping
- Independent/Quick height adjuster (for fine tuning cut)

- Rear discharge
- 11 gauge All steel construction
- Sealed bearings
- Idler clutch (for easy starting)
- Pneumatic tires 3.50 × 6
- Weight – 225 lbs.

40" cut

The new T-40 Trailmower is a totally universal pull-behind lawnmower. It has a fully adjustable hitch so that it can be pulled behind any make ATV or offset with any lawn tractor for an additional 40" of cutting width.

The T-40 has a well-balanced design and its center mounted wheels give a smooth cut even on the roughest terrain. The Trailmower features belt-driven twin blades and is available with either the 8 hp Briggs & Stratton or 10 hp Tecumseh engine.

This unit provides a perfect way to use your ATV as a lawn tractor or to expand the cutting width of your present tractor.

Offset for mowing around ponds or low hanging trees

SWISH-ERR

SWISHER MOWER AND MACHINE CO., INC.
BOX 67, WARRENSBURG, MO 64093
PHONE: 816-747-8183
TOLL FREE: 800-222-8183

der dealers' labels. Kits are sold only to satisfy dealer demand and do not provide a material contribution to the company's gross profit. Kits accounted for 8.2 percent of SMC's total sales in 1989.

The replacement parts business for mowers accounts for the remainder (20 percent) of SMC sales. Since little standardization exists among mower parts in the industry, SMC must provide customers with replacement parts for its mowers. Replacement parts accounted for 29 percent of the company's total gross profit in 1989.

Distribution and Promotion

SMC distributes its lawn mowers through farm supply stores, lawn and garden stores, home centers, and hardware stores located primarily in nonmetropolitan areas. About 75 percent of company sales are made in nonmetropolitan areas.

SMC sells the Ride King mower through wholesale distributors that supply independent dealers and directly to dealers. Wholesalers that represent SMC are located throughout the country, but they mainly supply dealers situated in the south central and southeastern United States. Wholesalers account for 30 percent of riding mower sales; direct-to-dealer sales account for 25 percent of sales.

Private-label riding mower sales account for 40 percent of SMC sales. Its private-label Big Mow mowers are produced for two buying networks: Midstates (Minneapolis, Minnesota) and Wheat Belt (Kansas City, Missouri). These two organizations represent independent farm supply stores and home centers in the upper and central midwestern United States and provide a central purchasing service. Even though

EXHIBIT 4

Geographic Scope of SMC Distribution

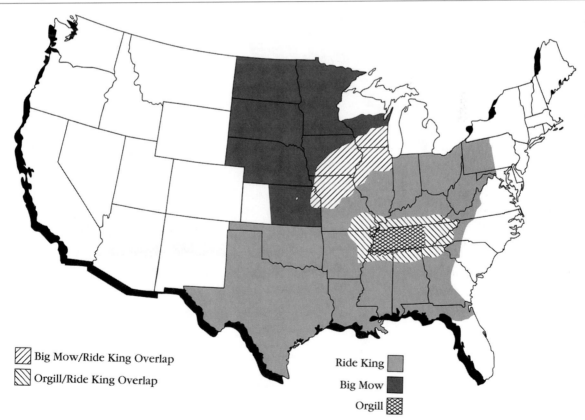

Big Mow/Ride King Overlap
Orgill/Ride King Overlap

Ride King
Big Mow
Orgill

these buying groups operate in roughly the same territory, their stores are not generally located in the same towns.

The company's other private label, Big O, is produced for Orgill Brothers wholesale hardware supply center located in Memphis, Tennessee. Orgill acts as a warehousing distributor for its network of hardware stores throughout the upper southeastern United States. Exhibit 4 on page 289 shows the geographic scope of SMC's distribution in the United States by brand name.

In recent years the company has developed distributor arrangements in parts of Europe and in the South Pacific. These arrangements produce 5 percent of total company sales.

Prior to 1985, SMC advertising focused on trade-oriented promotion to wholesalers and dealers. Since 1985, SMC has used consumer advertising to promote Ride King through a co-op advertising program with its dealers utilizing radio, television, and newspapers. A representative newspaper advertisement is shown in Exhibit 5.

Financial Position

SMC has remained a profitable company despite reduced sales volume. The company has consistently generated a net profit return on sales of 10 percent or more annually. Moreover, SMC has been able to produce cash flow at levels large enough to minimize the need for any major short-term or long-term financing. During 1989, accounts receivable and inventory had turns of 8.1 and 5.8, respectively. Nevertheless, Max Swisher was concerned with the availability and cost of short-term financing. Exhibit 6 on page 291 shows financial statements for 1989.

EXHIBIT 5

Ride King Print Advertisement

EXHIBIT 6

SMC Financial Statements

Income Statement
(Year ended September 30, 1989)

Sales		$3,547,644
Cost of goods sold		2,885,086
Gross profit		$662,558
Expenses		
Administrative salaries	$75,000	
Commissions	13,000	
Advertising	53,000	
Travel	7,500	
Insurance for employees	16,500	
Professional services	17,000	
Office expense	10,500	
Bad debts	9,500	
General taxes	1,600	
Depreciation	2,000	
Other	13,200	
Total expenses		$218,800
Income from continuing operations		$443,758
Other income (expenses)		(6,350)
Net income[a]		$437,408

Balance Sheet
(September 30, 1989)

Current assets	
Cash	$95,000
Accounts receivable	205,434
Notes receivable	612,540
Inventories	612,540
Prepaid insurance	7,055
Total current assets	$936,459
Net property plant and equipment	43,878
Other assets	4,300
Total assets	$984,637
Liabilities and owner's equity	
Current liabilities	
Accounts payable	$165,490
Accrued sales and payroll taxes	10,400
	$175,880
Owner's equity	
Common stock	$100,000
Retained earnings	717,147
	$817,147
Less: Treasury stock	($8,400)
Total owner's equity	$808,747
Total liabilities and owner's equity	$984,637

[a] SMC is an "S" Corporation and therefore pays no federal or state income taxes.

■ RIDING LAWN MOWER INDUSTRY

Riding lawn mowers are classified as lawn and garden equipment. This category is composed of numerous products, including walk-behind rotary mowers, riding mowers and tractors, garden tillers, snow throwers, and other outdoor power equipment designed primarily for the consumer market.

A survey by the Outdoor Power Equipment Institute (OPEI) estimated that the lawn and garden equipment industry produced sales of $4.5 billion in 1989, at manufacturers' prices. Of this amount, $3.3 billion was for finished goods and $1.1 billion was for engines. Components, including parts, accounted for the remainder of industry sales.

Sales Trends

Industry statistics show that riding mower unit volume peaked in 1973, when 1.2 million units were sold. Following the decline in the economy in 1975, volume fell to 790,000 units. By 1979, unit shipments had gradually risen to 1 million, but with the slowed economic conditions in the early 1980s, unit shipments again declined. From 1983 to 1987, shipment volume increased each year by an average of 6.7 percent, but the average increase tapered off to 2 percent from 1987 to 1989. Sluggish unit sales have been attributed to drought conditions prevalent in the midwestern United States. Industry estimates indicated that residential riding mower sales would be flat in 1990 and 1991. Commercial and export sales were expected to exhibit modest growth during this period.

The riding lawn mower industry is highly seasonal and cyclical. About one-third of riding lawn mower retail sales occur in March, April, and May. Over half of manufacturer shipments of these products occur in the four-month period from January to April. Industry sales patterns mirror cyclical patterns in the U.S. economy.

Product Configuration

Riding lawn mowers are usually designed in two basic configurations: (1) front-engine lawn tractors and (2) rear-engine riding mowers. However, there are some mid-engine riding mowers on the market, such as those produced by SMC. Lawn tractors with larger engines (20 horsepower or more) are classified as garden tractors.

Riding lawn mowers are targeted at consumers who have large mowing areas, usually composed of an acre or more. Front-engine lawn tractors are the most popular design, with unit sales of 812,000 in 1988, up 1.5 percent from 1987. Rear-engine riding mower unit sales were unchanged from 1987 to 1988, with sales of 375,000 units. Garden tractors posted a 13 percent increase in unit sales for 1988, with a volume of 170,000 units. Statistics for mid-engine mowers are unavailable but are believed to be included in the above figures.

According to industry surveys, the front-engine configuration (lawn tractors and garden tractors) is perceived to be more powerful than the rear-engine configuration and capable of handling bigger jobs. Since the physical dimensions of the front-engine configuration tend to be larger than the rear-engine configuration, consumers tend to perceive lawn tractors and garden tractors as stronger and more durable.

Competition

Sixteen manufacturers comprise the major competitors in the riding lawn mower market. They are American Yard Products (formerly Roper), Ariens, Honda, John Deere, Kubota, Lawn Boy, Lawn Chief Manufacturing, MTD, Inc. (formerly Modern Tool and Die), Murray of Ohio, Noma, Power King, Snapper, Toro, Troy-Bilt, Wheelhorse, and White.

Ariens, Honda, John Deere, Kubota, Lawn Boy, Power King, Snapper, Toro, Troy-Bilt, Wheelhorse, and White sell their products through lawn and garden stores and specialty retailers. Kubota and Troy-Bilt also sell to national mass-merchandise stores. All of these companies manufacture riding mowers only under a nationally branded name. None engage in private-label production.

MTD, Inc., produces the Cub Cadet brand mower sold exclusively in lawn and garden stores and by specialty retailers. MTD also manufactures mowers for JCPenney and Sears under the GrassHandler and Craftsman names, respectively. Kmart sells an MTD nationally branded lawn mower under the MTD name. Murray of Ohio produces private-label mowers for Sears and JCPenney and also manufactures mowers for Kmart, Wal-Mart, and Home Depot under the Murray brand name. However, each of these retailers has different specifications for its mowers. American Yard Products manufactures a nationally branded mower called the Yard Pro, which is sold through specialty retailers. However, a significant portion of its production (70 percent or more) is sold to Sears under the Craftsman label. Noma produces private-label mowers for Kmart, Western Auto, Lowes (a hardware chain), and TSC (Tractor Supply Company). The TSC mower is named Huskee; the Lowes mower is called Turf-master. Dynamark, the Kmart private label, is produced by Noma. Lawn Chief Manufacturing (a division of Cotter and Company) produces mowers exclusively for True Value Hardware stores and is the only manufacturer that produces a private-label mower for one retail chain.

Private-label riding mowers have captured a growing percentage of unit sales in the industry. It is estimated that private-label mowers currently account for 60–70 percent of total industry sales.

Each of the major competitors produces several riding mowers at different price points. Although retail prices vary by type of retail outlet, representative retail prices for national and private label riding mowers typically range from $700 to $5,000.

Retail Distribution

Outdoor power equipment (OPE), including riding mowers, is distributed through a variety of retail outlets. National retail merchandise chains such as JCPenney and Sears account for the largest percentage of sales. However, the percentage of sales captured by national merchandisers has declined in the past decade from 35 percent

EXHIBIT 7

Retail Distribution of Outdoor Power Equipment

Outlet Type	Percentage of Sales by Year		
	1988	1983	1978
OPE/farm equipment stores	10	19	7
Hardware stores	13	12	16
Lawn/garden stores	16	17	17
Home centers	5	3	1
National merchandisers	24	22	35
Discount stores	7	8	5
Farm supply stores	4	0	0
Department stores	3	1	2
Other	18	18	17
Total	100	100	100

in 1978 to 24 percent in 1988. Lawn and garden stores, hardware stores, and OPE/farm equipment stores represent the three largest retail distributors after national merchandisers. Exhibit 7 on page 293 shows the breakdown of sales by type of retailer for 1978, 1983, and 1988.

■ THE PRIVATE-LABEL PROPOSAL

The inquiry received by SMC concerning a private-label arrangement requested a sample order of 700 standard riding mower units to be delivered in February 1991. The national retail merchandise chain expected to make an annual order of approximately 8,200 units. The proposed arrangement had features that made it quite different from SMC's typical manner of doing business with its other private-label organizations. The chain wanted to purchase the mowers at a price 5 percent lower than SMC's manufacturer's list price for its standard model. They also wished to be a house account without manufacturer's representatives or company sales representatives calling on them. They did not want any seasonal or promotional discounts but only a single guaranteed low price. Reorders would be at the same price. The mowers would be shipped FOB factory (that is, the chain would pay for all freight charges).

The chain wanted to carry inventories in its regional warehouses, but did not want title to transfer to itself until the mowers were shipped to a specific company store. From that point, payment would be made in 45 days. However, the chain agreed to take title to mowers that had been in one of its warehouses for two months. A 45-day payment period would follow the title transfer.

There would be small changes in the appearance of the mower to help differentiate it from SMC's Ride King. The chain requested a different seat and a particular color and type of paint and specified that all parts be American-made or that the mower at least display an "American name" as its producer. The chain would supply all decals displaying its brand name.

The chain did not propose any mechanical specifications for the mower. The letter expressed satisfaction with the design and performance of the machine and noted that only minor cosmetic changes were necessary. SMC's standard warranty would be required for all mower parts. The chain expected SMC to reimburse them for any labor costs resulting from warranty work at $22.00 per hour. Replacement parts would be purchased at present price points and shipped FOB factory.

A two-year contract was offered, which could be automatically extended on a year-to-year basis. Either party could terminate the contract with a six-month notice. A new price would be negotiated at the end of the original two-year period. The contract would be negotiated annually thereafter. The chain also required SMC to assume liability for personal injury that might result from the use and maintenance of the mowers. The chain would supply all advertising related to the product and would not allow SMC to mention its relationship with the chain in any of its advertising or promotion.

■ EVALUATING THE PROPOSAL

The private-label proposal required careful consideration, according to Swisher. The opportunity to expand production, given excess capacity, coupled with the added benefit of broadened distribution in metropolitan areas seemed inviting. Moreover, increased sales of parts were likely, and the potential for selling the "trail-mower" was possible. At the same time, other factors would have to be considered. For example, SMC was self-insured and had not experienced any significant product-liability claims with some 150,000 units having been sold or used since 1956. However, if the private-label proposal was pursued, greater exposure to liability claims was possible. According to industry sources, manufacturer product-liability insurance premiums for riding mowers could cost $150,000 per year for $1 million in coverage. Insurance companies writing these policies generally required a minimum sales volume of 10,000 units.

Furthermore, although increased production could be handled by paying overtime to SMC production workers, the cost of overtime, reflected in the direct labor cost, would represent about 4 percent of the current manufacturer's sales price for riding mowers. Other direct materials costs could represent another 1 percent of the current manufacturer's price. Additional overhead costs were estimated to be another 1 percent, and other related costs, including additional inventory insurance, pilferage and breakage, additional wear and maintenance on machines, and a county property tax based on inventory, would acccount for an additional 1.5 percent.

A production agreement would create some one-time added costs for SMC. These costs would include arranging sources for specified materials that differed from those used in standard production and a rearrangement of production facilities to accommodate the new output levels. These one-time costs would be in the range from $10,000 to $12,000.

The added financing costs were of particular importance. Normally, SMC obtained short-term funds from local banks at 2.5 percentage points above the prime rate (currently 10 percent). These funds were used to finance accounts receivable and riding mower inventories, both of which would increase with the new arrangement. For example, the incremental average inventory carried with this proposal would be 2,100 units.

Sales of SMC mowers by the national merchandiser could cannibalize some existing sales. Although the chain's outlets were located in metropolitan areas, there would be some overlap in trade areas with SMC's current dealers. Swisher felt that, as a result, SMC could initially lose approximately 200 units a year of Ride King sales volume. In addition, dealers directly affected would not welcome the added competition, and Swisher believed that a small percentage of independent dealers would be likely to drop the SMC line.

Swisher felt that some aspects of the proposal might be negotiable, such as the title transfer and payment dates. From his experience, he knew that the unit price in the proposal was probably fixed and that the cosmetic changes were not negotiable. He knew that his bargaining position was limited because the chain would be approaching other manufacturers with the same opportunity. However, he also knew that SMC offered a highly differentiated and proven riding mower. This would be an advantage, since many other manufacturers' mowers were indistinguishable.

Swisher had been concerned for several years about SMC's future prospects. The private-label arrangement might offer numerous benefits to SMC, but he wondered if other actions might be even more attractive. For example, a more aggressive advertising and sales effort to recruit new dealers and assist current dealers was being considered. He leaned back in his chair, which he had purchased when he founded SMC, and pondered the possibilities.

CHAPTER 7

Integrated Marketing Communication Strategy and Management

 Marketing communication is the process by which information about an organization and its offerings is disseminated to selected markets. Given the role communication plays in facilitating mutually beneficial exchange relationships between an organization and prospective buyers, its importance cannot be overstated. The goal of communication is not just to induce initial purchases; it is also to achieve postpurchase satisfaction, thus increasing the probability of repeat sales. Even if prospective buyers possessed a pressing need and an organization possessed an offering that precisely met that need, no exchange would occur without communication. Communication is necessary to inform buyers of the following:

- The availability of an offering
- The unique benefits of the offering
- The where and how of obtaining and using the offering

Exactly how potential buyers are to be informed—the actual message communicated—is one of the most subjective communication decisions. Although message development can be somewhat aided by research, there are no guaranteed message strategies available for all offerings, markets, or organizations. Each individual situation must determine whether the message is to be hard-sell, fearful, humorous, or informational. Whatever message format is chosen, the message communicated should be desirable to those to whom it is directed, exclusive or unique to the offering being described, and believable in terms of the benefit claims made for the offering.

It is the task of the marketing manager to manage the communication process most effectively. Marketing managers have at their disposal specific communication activities, often called *elements, functions, tools,* or *tasks.* These include advertising, personal selling, and sales promotion. Collectively, the activities are termed the *marketing communication mix.*[1] Elements of the communication mix range from very flexible (for example, personal selling) to very inflexible (for example, mass advertising), and each has a unique set of characteristics and capabilities. To a certain extent, however, they are interchangeable and substitutable. It is the responsibility of the marketing manager to find the most effective communication mix at the least possible cost.

Marketing managers should not limit their thinking to which communication activity to use when designing communication strategies. Rare is the organization that employs only one form of communication. Rather, managers should broaden their perspective to think of *integrated marketing communications*—the practice of blending different elements of the communication mix in mutually reinforcing ways. In this context, attention is directed to which activity should be emphasized, how intensely it should be applied, and how communication activities can be most effectively combined and coordinated. For instance, advertising activities might be employed to develop offering awareness and comprehension; sales promotion might be used to increase purchase intention; and personal selling might be utilized to obtain final conviction and purchase.[2]

■ INTEGRATED COMMUNICATION STRATEGY FRAMEWORK

From a managerial perspective, the formulation of an integrated marketing communication strategy requires six major decisions. Once the offering and target markets have been defined, the manager must consider the following decisions:

1. What are the information requirements of target markets as they proceed through the purchase process?

2. What objectives must the communication strategy achieve?

3. How might the mix of communication activities be combined to convey information to target markets?

4. How much should be budgeted for communicating with target markets, and in what manner should resources be allocated among various communication activities?

5. How should the communication be timed and scheduled?

6. How should the communication process be evaluated as to its effectiveness, and how should it be controlled?

Theoretically, these questions are distinct and thus can be approached in a sequential manner. In practice, however, they are likely to be approached simultaneously, since they are closely interrelated.

■ INFORMATION REQUIREMENTS IN PURCHASE DECISIONS

The first step in designing a communication strategy is to determine how buyers purchase a particular offering and to define the role of information in the purchase process. This often requires use of a purchase-process (or adoption-process) model. Usually, such a model treats buyers as though they were moved through a series of sequential stages in their purchase processes, such as

Unawareness → Knowledge → Preference → Purchase

At any point in time, different buyers are in different stages of the model, and each stage requires a different communication strategy.

Most models allow the marketing manager to distinguish between solitary and joint decision making. In any purchase decision, the person or persons involved can play several possible roles—purchaser, influencer, decision maker, and/or consumer. In certain purchase situations, one individual may play more than one role. In other purchase situations, such as a joint purchase decision, the roles may be played by different individuals. Whereas a mother may be the family member who purchases breakfast cereal, her children may influence the brand purchase, and the father may consume the product. A similar situation could exist in an industrial setting. A purchasing agent may be the buyer, an engineer the influencer and decision maker, and a technician the user. Understanding who is playing the roles is a prerequisite for successfully determining what the communication message should be, as well as to whom it should be directed and how it should be communicated.

Similarly, the process used by buyers to purchase an offering influences the role of information, and hence the most effective communication strategy. For example, in industrial settings purchasing procedures are often prescribed. Therefore, understanding when, where, how, and what information is employed in the purchase decision will enable an organization to direct the proper communication to the proper individual at the proper time. These remarks also apply to communication directed toward consumers. Consider the case of consumers making a decision to buy a house. To communicate effectively, an organization must know *what* information these consumers think is necessary (price, location, size), *where* they will seek it (newspapers, brokers, friends), *when* they will seek it (how far in advance, on what days), and *how* they will apply the information once obtained. Advances in database direct marketing, which enable identification of prospective buyers who have a predisposition to purchase certain products and services and who are accessible through mail and telephone solicitation, have made the communication process even more effective. For instance, Kimberly-Clark Corporation, the maker of Huggies diapers, buys mailing lists of new mothers and sends coupons, child-care tips, and new-product information to them during their babies' diaper-wearing stage.[3]

Finally, the way in which buyers perceive an organization and its offering is closely related to their information needs. The perceived importance of the offering and the perceived risk in making an incorrect purchase decision influence the extent to which buyers receive information, as well as their choice of information source(s). The more important or risky an offering is perceived to be (because of large dollar outlays, ego involvement, or health and safety reasons), the more likely it is that buyers will seek information from sources other than the organization providing the offering.

■ REASONABLE COMMUNICATION OBJECTIVES

The objectives set for communication programs will depend on the overall offering-market strategies of the organization and the stage of the product's life cycle. Communication objectives will differ according to whether the strategy being employed is market penetration, market development, or product development. For instance, a market penetration strategy will suggest communication objectives that emphasize more frequent offering usage or that build preference for or loyalty to the offering. On the other hand, a market development strategy will encourage communication that will stimulate awareness and trial of the offering.

Life-cycle stage plays a role in determining whether communication objectives should stimulate primary demand or selective demand. Early in the life cycle, communication efforts focus on stimulating *primary demand*—demand for the product or service class, such as dairy products, personal computers, or financial planning. Typically, the message conveyed focuses on introducing the benefits of a product or service or overcoming objections to the product or service. Later in the life cycle, when substitute products or services exist, communication efforts focus on stimulating *selective demand*—demand for a particular brand or product/service such as

Borden milk, Compaq personal computers, or Merrill Lynch financial planning. Typically, the message conveyed extols the benefits of a particular competitive offering and seeks to differentiate that offering from others.

Objectives must also be delineated for individual communication tools. Both general and specific communication objectives need to relate directly to the tasks that the tools are to accomplish. Communication objectives and the tasks must be reasonable—*consistent* both among themselves and with other marketing elements, *quantifiable* for measurement and control purposes, and *attainable* with an appropriate amount of effort and expenditure and within a specific time frame.

■ INTEGRATED COMMUNICATION MIX

Development of an integrated communication mix requires the assignment of relative weights to particular communication activities, based on communication objectives. Although no established guidelines exist for designing an optimal communication mix, several factors that influence the mix need to be considered. These factors are:

- The information requirements of potential buyers
- The nature of the offering
- The nature of the target markets
- The capacity of the organization

Information Requirements of Buyers

As a starting point in crafting an integrated communication mix, an analysis of the relative value of the communication tools used at various stages in the purchase-decision process ought to be undertaken. Consider the purchase-decision process for a new automobile.[4] Through advertising, manufacturers seek to stimulate awareness of the new models and to indicate where they can be purchased. Sales personnel provide information on specific options available, financing, and delivery. Sales promotion, brochures and catalogs provide descriptions of performance characteristics and other salient features. Which communication tool has the greatest impact on prospective buyers? The answer to this question, while admittedly difficult to arrive at, will lead to a weighing of the importance of the communication tools. The manager will achieve an effective communication mix only by understanding the information requirements of potential buyers and by meeting those requirements with the appropriate communication-mix elements.

Nature of the Offering

A major consideration in developing the communication mix is the organization's offering. A highly technical offering, one with benefits not readily apparent (such as performance or quality), or one that is relatively expensive is likely to require personal selling. On the one hand, advertising is a potent communication tool when the offering is not complex, is frequently purchased, is relatively inexpensive, or has benefits that readily differentiate it from competing offerings. Sales promotion lends itself to nearly every offering type because of the wide variety of forms it can assume. Its main use, however, is to induce immediate action on frequently purchased products.

Target-Market Characteristics

The nature of the target market is another consideration. A target market consisting of a small number of potential buyers, existing in close proximity to one another and each purchasing in large quantities, might suggest a personal selling strategy. In contrast, a mass market that is geographically scattered generally calls for an emphasis on advertising. However, firms are finding that direct marketing also can be used to reach a geographically dispersed target market. This realization has led many firms to substitute mail and telephone solicitations for mass media (radio, print, and television) advertising.[5]

Organizational Capacity

A fourth consideration is the ability or willingness of the organization to undertake certain communication activities. The organization is continually faced with *make-or-buy decisions.* If an organization decides to employ a particular communication activity, should it perform the activity internally (that is, make it) or contract it out (in other words, buy it)?

One such make-or-buy decision is the choice between a company sales force and independent sales representatives.[6] The decision has both economic and behavioral dimensions. The economic dimension relates to the issue of fixed versus variable costs. The cost of independent representatives is variable; they are paid on sales commission only. A company sales force, on the other hand, typically includes a variable-cost element *and* a fixed-cost component. If independent representatives fail to sell, no costs are incurred; however, if a company sales force fails to sell, the fixed costs still have to be paid. These concepts are useful in determining whether independent representatives or company representatives are more cost-effective at different sales levels.

Suppose independent representatives received a 5 percent commission on sales and company sales personnel received a 3 percent commission in addition to incurring a salary and administration cost of $500,000. At what sales level would company representatives become more or less costly than independent representatives? This question can be resolved by setting the cost equations for both types of representatives equal to each other and solving for the sales level amount, as follows:

$$\frac{\text{Cost of company reps}}{0.03(x) + \$500,000} = \frac{\text{Cost of independent reps}}{0.05(x)}$$

where x = sales volume. Solving for x, we get $25 million as the sales volume at which the costs of company and independent reps are equal.

The calculation indicates that if the sales volume were below $25 million, the independent representative would be cheaper; above that amount, the company sales force would be cheaper. Of course, a fundamental issue is the likelihood of achieving a $25 million sales level.

Behavioral dimensions of this decision focus on issues of control, flexibility, effort, and availability of independent and company sales representatives. There is considerable difference of opinion as to the relative advantages and disadvantages of company and independent representatives with respect to each factor. Proponents of a company sales force argue that this strategy offers greater control, since the company selects, trains, and supervises sales personnel. The sales effort is enhanced because sales personnel are representing only one company's product line. Flexibility exists because the firm can change sales-call patterns and customers and can transfer personnel. Finally, availability of sales personnel is superior, since an independent representative might not exist in a geographical area, whereas a company representative can be relocated. Proponents of independent sales representatives argue that selection, training, and supervision of sales personnel can be done equally well by sales agencies and at no cost to the firm. Flexibility is improved, since fixed investment in a sales force is minimal. Effort is increased, since independent representatives live on their commissions. Finally, availability is no problem, since the entrepreneurial spirit of these individuals will take them wherever effective demand exists. These economic and behavioral dimensions were carefully considered when Coca-Cola's Food Division recently decided to eliminate 110 sales positions and sell through independent agents (food brokers).[7]

Another make-or-buy decision relates to advertising. Often it is advantageous to have intermediaries (such as wholesalers, retailers, and dealers) assume advertising costs and placement responsibilities. Cooperative advertising, where a manufacturer shares the costs of advertising or sales promotion, is an example of this type of strategy.

Push versus Pull Communication Strategies

Two approaches that incorporate the topics just discussed are termed push and pull communication strategies.[8] A *push communication strategy* is one in which the offering is pushed through a distribution channel in a sequential fashion, with each channel level representing a distinct target market. A push strategy concentrates on channel intermediaries, building relationships that can have long-term benefits. With such a strategy, advertisements are likely to appear in trade journals and magazines, and sales aids and contests are likely to be used as incentives to gain shelf space and distribution. A principal emphasis, however, is on personal selling to wholesalers and retailers. This strategy is typically used when (1) an organization has easily identifiable buyers, (2) the offering is complex, (3) buyers view the purchase as being risky, (4) a product or service is early in its life cycle, and/or (5) the organization has limited funds for direct-to-consumer advertising.

A *pull communication strategy* seeks to create initial interest among potential buyers, who in turn demand the product from intermediaries, ultimately pulling the offering through a channel. A pull strategy normally employs heavy end-user (consumer) advertising, free samples, and coupons to stimulate end-user awareness and interest. Consumers might be encouraged to ask their favorite retailer for the offering to pressure retailers into carrying the product. Pennzoil Motor Oil's "Ask for Pennzoil" and General Motors' "Ask for Genuine GM parts" advertising campaigns are prime examples of a pull communication strategy in practice.

The conditions favoring a pull strategy are virtually opposite to those favoring a push strategy. A central issue in choosing a push strategy is the ability and willingness of wholesalers and retailers to implement selling and sales promotion programs advocated by manufacturers. An important consideration in using a pull strategy is whether an *advertising opportunity* exists for a product or service. Such an opportunity exists when (1) there is a favorable primary demand for a product or service category, (2) the product or service to be advertised can be significantly differentiated from its competitors, (3) the product or service has hidden qualities or benefits that can be portrayed effectively through advertising, and (4) there are strong emotional buying motives involved, such as buyers' concern for health, beauty, and safety. The value of an advertising opportunity decreases if one or more of these conditions are not met. Nonprescription drugs and cosmetics often satisfy most of these conditions and are frequently advertised. Commodities such as unprocessed foods (for example, corn, oat, and wheat) are rarely advertised; however, when they are processed and dietary supplements and flavors are added to produce cereals, they are advertised effectively.

Nevertheless, push and pull communication strategies are often used together.[9] Investment in end-user advertising stimulates consumer demand and hence product or service sales volume. Investment in efforts to gain display space for products, promote specific services, and educate retail salespeople builds channel relationships that have long-term benefits.

■ COMMUNICATION BUDGETING

As you might expect, the question of how much to spend on communication is difficult to answer. Many factors, including those previously mentioned, must be considered in communication budget determination.[10] In general, the greater the geographical dispersion of a target market, the greater the communication expenditure required; the earlier an offering is in its life cycle, the greater the necessary expenditure, and so forth.

The primary rule in determining a communication budget is to *make the budget commensurate with the tasks required of the communication activities.* The more important communication is in a marketing strategy, the larger the amount of funds that should be allocated to it. Conceptually, budget determination is straightforward—set the budget so that the marginal costs of communication equal the marginal revenues resulting from it. This, though, requires an assessment of the effectiveness of communication.

Because it is difficult to evaluate communication effectiveness, attempts to establish a relationship between budget size and communication effectiveness have generally proven unproductive. For this reason, there is no widely agreed-on criterion for establishing the size of a communication budget. Instead, numerous guidelines have been suggested. These guidelines can be roughly grouped as *formula-based* or *qualitatively based.*

The most widely used formula-based approach is the *percentage-of-sales approach.* Most frequently, past sales are employed, but anticipated sales are also occasionally used. Hence, when sales increase, communication activity increases. Although it creates certain conceptual problems (for example, which should come first—sales or communication?), this approach is commonly used as a starting point because of its simplicity. A second formula-based method is to allocate for communication a fixed dollar amount per offering unit, and then to calculate the communication budget by multiplying this per-unit allocation by the number of units expected to be sold. This method is most often used by durable-goods manufacturers such as automobile companies.

In practice, the formula-based approaches tend to be rather inflexible and not marketing-oriented, so they are often supplemented by qualitatively based approaches. Management may use the *competitive-parity approach,* whereby an organization attempts to maintain a balance between its communication expenditures and those of its competitors. Another approach is to use *all available funds* for communication. This strategy might be employed in introducing a new offering for which maximum exposure is desired; it is also sometimes used by nonprofit organizations.

A final approach is termed the *objective-task* approach. Here an organization budgets communication as a function of the objectives set for a communication program and the costs of the tasks to be performed to accomplish the objectives. The approach involves three steps: (1) define the communication objectives, (2) identify the tasks needed to attain the objectives, and (3) estimate the costs associated with the performance of these tasks.[11]

Although all of these approaches are useful, each has decided limitations. More often than not, managers use these approaches in conjunction with one another.

Communication Budget Allocation

Once a communication budget has been settled on, it must be allocated across the communication activities. This can be accomplished by using guidelines similar to those discussed previously for general communication budget determinations. Advertising and personal selling will be used to illustrate necessary budgetary allocation decisions. As a general rule, marketers of consumer products and services spend more for advertising as a percentage of their communication budget; marketers of industrial products and services spend more for personal selling as a percentage of their communication budget.[12]

Advertising Budget Allocation Decisions about advertising budget allocation revolve around media selection and scheduling considerations. Basically, there are five mass media—television, radio, magazine, newspaper, and outdoor (billboard)—that an organization can use in transmitting its advertising messages to target markets. Each of these media, or *channels*, consists of *vehicles*—specific entities in which advertisements can appear. In magazines, the vehicles include *Newsweek* and *Mechanics Illustrated. Newsweek* can be thought of as a mass-appeal vehicle, whereas *Mechanics Illustrated* might be considered a selective-appeal vehicle. Moreover, media can be *vertical* (reaching more than one level of a distribution channel) or *horizontal* (reaching only one level of a channel).

Media selection is based on numerous factors, the most important of which are cost, reach, frequency, and audience characteristics. Cost frequently acts as a constraint—for example, a 30-second national television commercial (spot) during the Superbowl costs over $1 million, not including associated production costs. *Cost* is usually expressed as cost per thousand (CPM) readers, viewers, and so on, to facilitate cross-vehicle comparisons. *Reach* refers to the number of buyers potentially exposed to an advertisement in a particular vehicle. *Frequency* refers to the number of times buyers are exposed to an advertisement in a given time period; total exposure equals reach multiplied by frequency. The more closely the characteristics of the target market match those of a vehicle's audience, the more appropriate the vehicle.

Other considerations include the purpose of the advertisement (image building, price, and so on), product needs, and the editorial climate of the vehicle. Whereas price advertisements (those emphasizing an immediate purchase) are more likely to be found in newspapers than in magazines, the opposite is true for advertisements of products requiring color illustration and detailed explanation. Finally, audience characteristics determine which advertisements are acceptable, as well as which are appropriate. For example, Van Heusen advertises its men's shirts in *Vogue, Cosmopolitan*, and *Glamour* magazines because 70 percent of men's shirts are purchased by women.[13]

The timing, or scheduling, of advertisements is critical to their success. Purchases of many offerings (such as skis, snowblowers, and swimsuits) are seasonal or are limited to certain geographical areas. Thus, the advertising budgeting must take into account purchasing patterns. For example, advertising snowblowers in Ohio during the month of July is probably not a worthwhile endeavor.

There are numerous timing strategies that a marketing manager can employ when undertaking an advertising campaign. One alternative is to concentrate advertising dollars in a relatively short time period—a *blitz strategy*. This strategy is often used when new products or services are introduced. Another alternative is to spend advertising dollars over the long term to maintain continuity. A *pulse strategy* might be employed, whereby an organization periodically concentrates its advertising but also attempts to maintain some semblance of continuity.

Sales-Force Budget Allocation The sales-force budgeting problem is two-faceted: How many salespeople are needed, and how should they be allocated? A commonly used formula is

$$NS = \frac{NC \times FC \times LC}{TA}$$

where

NS = number of sales people

NC = number of customers (actual or potential)

FC = necessary frequency of customer calls

LC = length of average customer call, including travel time

TA = average available selling time per salesperson (less time spent on administrative duties)

In most instances, the time period is one business year. Although this formula can be used for nearly all types of salespeople, from retail clerks to highly creative salespeople, it is more likely used with the latter.

Assume that the number of potential customers is 2,500 and four calls should be made per customer per year. If the length of the average call and travel time is two hours and there are 1,340 working hours per year available for selling (50 weeks × 40 hours × 67 percent available selling time per week), then

$$NS = \frac{2,500 \times 4 \times 2}{1,340} = 15 \text{ salespeople needed}$$

The formula is flexible. It is possible to create several different strategies simply by varying (1) how the various elements in this formula are defined and (2) the elements themselves, such as the frequency of calls with actual customers and potential customers.

A related decision concerns the allocation of salespeople. Every salesperson must have a territory, whether defined as square feet of selling space, a geographical area, or a delivery route. In determining how large the sales territory should be, decision makers should attempt to equate selling opportunities with the work load associated with each sales territory.

The question of how the sales force should be organized is perhaps more difficult to answer, as it directly relates to organization and marketing objectives, offering characteristics, competitor and industry practices, and the like. The alternatives include having salespeople specialize in certain offerings or in customer types or in a combination of offerings and customer types. For instance, Procter and Gamble and Black & Decker organize their sales forces by customer size with large customers (Wal-Mart and Home Depot) having "customer specialists" who focus on delivering superior customer service. Firestone Tire and Rubber has a sales force that calls on its own dealers and another that calls on independent dealers, such as gasoline stations. Lone Star Steel has a sales force that sells drilling pipe to oil companies and another that sells specialty steel products to manufacturers.

■ EVALUATION AND CONTROL OF THE COMMUNICATION PROCESS

As part of every communication strategy, there must be mechanisms for evaluation and control. Without them, a marketing manager would be hard-pressed to manage the communication process effectively. There would be no way to determine whether a strategy had achieved its objectives, nor would there be a way to make changes in a strategy in response to competitive activities or environmental occurrences, whether fortuitous or not.

Implicit in both mechanisms is the concept of *continuousness*. The marketing manager must continuously monitor the execution of any communication plan or strategy to ensure that the communication objectives are being attained.

Ideally, evaluation and control should incorporate some measure of sales or profits. Although this is possible for certain communication tools (the sales effectiveness of a direct-mail program can be judged in a relatively straightforward way), for others, it is not. It is nearly impossible to isolate the contribution of institutional advertising to any individual sales transaction.

Budgeting is the ultimate form of control because slashing or adding to the budget of a communication activity effectively eliminates or accentuates the activity itself. The budgeting element is illustrated by the decision to add an additional sales representative at a salary of $50,000 or to allocate the same amount to a direct-mail sales promotion program, when the product mix contribution margin is 25 percent. A simple break-even calculation ($50,000 ÷ 0.25) reveals that $200,000 in additional sales must be generated to cover the incremental cost. The issue is therefore whether the new sales representative or the sales promotion is more likely to achieve this break-even sales volume. Incremental analysis of this type is increasingly being viewed as the appropriate approach for evaluating and controlling expenditures for sales promotion, advertising, and personal selling.[14]

NOTES

1. Publicity is a fourth element often included in the communication mix, but it is not considered here for two reasons. First, publicity is often uncontrollable except through the broader public relations function of an organization; hence, it is not typically the responsibility of the marketing manager. Second, even if publicity is the responsibility of the marketing manager, it is often managed as a mixture of advertising and personal selling, and thus does not require separate treatment.

2. For a comprehensive description of integrated marketing communications, see Don E. Schultz, Stanley I. Tannenbaum, and Robert F. Lauterborn, *Integrated Marketing Communications* (Chicago: NTC Business Books, 1993).

3. Gary Levin, "Data Bases Loom Large for '90s," *Advertising Age* (October 21, 1991): 21, 24.

4. "Automotive Marketing," *Advertising Age* (April 3, 1995): 52.

5. "How to Turn Junk Mail into a Goldmine—or Perhaps Not," *The Economist* (April 1, 1995): 51–52.

6. Independent representatives are individuals or firms paid commissions for selling a manufacturer's product. These individuals or companies represent several noncompeting products that are sold to one or several categories of customers. They do not carry product inventories or take legal title to goods. Their functions vary from selling only a firm's products to broader activities including applications engineering, in-store merchandising support (point-of-purchase displays, stocking), and product maintenance. Independent representatives go by a variety of names, including broker, manufacturer's representative, and sales agent.

7. "Coca-Cola Foods' Teasley Focuses Marketing on Minute Maid Juices," *The Wall Street Journal* (June 23, 1988): 32.

8. Debate on push versus pull strategies can be found in Alvin Achenbaum and F. Kent Mitchel, "Pulling Away from Push Marketing," *Harvard Business Review* (May–June 1987): 38–42.

9. Portions of this discussion are based on Robert C. Blattberg and Scott A. Neslin, *Sales Promotion: Concepts, Methods, and Strategies* (Upper Saddle River, NJ: Prentice Hall, 1990): 466–471.

10. For an extensive discussion of promotional budgeting with an emphasis on advertising, see Simon Broadbent, *The Advertiser's Handbook for Budget Determination* (Lexington, MA: Lexington Books, 1988).

11. George E. Belch and Michael A. Belch, *Introduction to Advertising & Promotion: An Integrated Marketing Communications Perspective*, 3rd ed. (Chicago: R. D. Irwin, 1995): 251–253.

12. "Business-to-Business Captures 37.4% of All Marketing Spending," *Advertising Age* (June 3, 1996): 46.

13. "Women Help Van Heusen Collar Arrow," *The Wall Street Journal* (May 22, 1992): B1, B5.

14. Magid Abraham and Leonard Lodish, "Getting the Most Out of Advertising and Promotion," *Harvard Business Review* (May–June 1990): 50–58.

Carrington Furniture, Inc. (A)

Late in the evening of January 10, 1996, Charlton Bates, President of Carrington Furniture, Inc., called Dr. Thomas Berry, a marketing professor at a private university in the Northeast and a consultant to the company. The conversation went as follows:

BATES: Hello, Tom. This is Chuck Bates. I'm sorry to call you this late, but I wanted to get your thoughts on the tentative 1996 advertising program proposed by Mike Hervey of Hervey and Bernham, our ad agency.

BERRY: No problem, Chuck. What did they propose?

BATES: The crux of their proposal is that we should increase our advertising expenditures by $200,000. They suggested that we put the entire amount into our consumer advertising program for ads in several shelter magazines.[1] Hervey noted that the National Home Furnishings Foundation has recommended that furniture manufacturers spend 1 percent of their sales exclusively on consumer advertising.

BERRY: That increase appears to be slightly out of line with your policy of budgeting 5 percent of expected sales for total promotion expenditures, doesn't it? Hasn't John Bott [Vice President of Sales] emphasized the need for more sales representatives?

BATES: Yes, John has requested additional funds. You're right about the 5 percent figure too, and I'm not sure if our sales forecast isn't too optimistic. Your research has shown that our sales historically follow industry sales almost perfectly, and trade economists are predicting about a 4 percent increase for 1996. Yet, I'm not too sure.

BERRY: Well, Chuck, you can't expect forecasts to be always on the button. The money is one thing, but what else can you tell me about Hervey's rationale for putting more dollars into consumer advertising?

BATES: He contends that we can increase our exposure and tell our quality and styling story to the buying public—increase brand awareness, enhance our image, that sort of thing. He also cited industry research data that showed that as baby boomers [consumers between the ages of 33 and 50] age they are becoming more home-oriented and are replacing older, cheaper furniture with more expensive, longer-lasting pieces. All I know is that my contribution margin will fall to 25 percent next year because of increased labor and material cost.

BERRY: I appreciate your concern. Give me a few days to think about the proposal. I'll get back to you soon.

---

[1] Shelter magazines feature home improvement ideas, new ideas in home decorating, and so on. *Better Homes and Gardens* is an example of a shelter magazine.

This case was prepared by Professor Roger A. Kerin, of the Edwin L. Cox School of Business, Southern Methodist University, as a basis for class discussion and is not designed to illustrate effective or ineffective handling of an administrative situation. All names and data have been disguised. Copyright © 1997 by Roger A. Kerin. No part of this case may be reproduced without written permission of the copyright holder.

After hanging up, Berry began to think about Bates' summary of the proposal, Carrington's present position, and the furniture industry in general. He knew that Bates expected a well-thought-out recommendation on such issues and a step-by-step description of the logic used to arrive at that recommendation.

■ THE COMPANY

Carrington Furniture is a manufacturer of medium- to high-priced wood bedroom, living room, and dining room furniture. The company was formed at the turn of the century by Charlton Bates' grandfather. Bates assumed the presidency of the company upon his father's retirement. Year-end net sales in 1995 were $75 million with a before-tax profit of $3.7 million.

Carrington sells its furniture through 1,000 high-quality department stores and independent furniture specialty stores nationwide, but all stores do not carry the company's entire line. The company is very selective in choosing retail outlets. According to Bates, "Our distribution policy, hence our retailers, should mirror the high quality of our products." As a matter of policy, Carrington does not sell to furniture chain stores or discount outlets.

The company employs ten full-time salespeople and two regional sales managers. Sales personnel receive a base salary and a small commission on sales. A company sales force is atypical in the furniture industry; most furniture manufacturers use sales agents or representatives who carry a wide assortment of noncompeting furniture lines and receive a commission on sales. "Having our own sales group is a policy my father established years ago," noted Bates, "and we've been quite successful in having people who are committed to our company. Our people don't just take furniture orders. They are expected to motivate retail salespeople to sell our line, assist in setting up displays in stores, and give advice on a variety of matters to our retailers and their salespeople." He added, "It seems that my father was ahead of his time. I was just reading in the *Standard & Poor's Industry Surveys* for household furniture that the competition for retail floor space will require even more support, including store personnel sales training, innovative merchandising, inventory management, and advertising."

In early 1995, Carrington allocated $3,675,000 for total promotional expenditures for the 1995 operating year, excluding the salary of the Vice President of Sales. Promotion expenditures were categorized into four groups: (1) sales expense and administration, (2) cooperative advertising programs with retailers, (3) trade promotion, and (4) consumer advertising. Sales costs included salaries for sales personnel and sales managers, selling-expense reimbursements, fringe benefits, and clerical/office assistance, but did not include salespersons' commissions. Commissions were deducted from sales in the calculation of gross profit. The cooperative advertising budget is usually spent on newspaper advertising in a retailer's city. Cooperative advertising allowances are matched by funds provided by retailers on a dollar-for-dollar basis. Trade promotion is directed toward retailers and takes the form of catalogs, trade magazine advertisements, booklets for consumers, and point-of-purchase materials, such as displays, for use in retail stores. Also included in this category is the expense of participating in trade shows. Carrington is represented at two shows per year. Consumer advertising is directed at potential consumers through shelter magazines. The typical format used in consumer advertising is to highlight new furniture and different bedroom, living room, and dining room arrangements. The dollar allocation for each of these programs in 1995 is shown in Exhibit 1.

EXHIBIT 1

Allocation of Carrington's Promotion Dollars, 1995

Sales expense and administration	$ 995,500
Cooperative advertising allowance	1,650,000
Trade advertising	467,000
Consumer advertising	562,500
	$3,675,000

Source: Company records.

■ THE HOUSEHOLD FURNITURE INDUSTRY

The household furniture industry is divided into three general categories: wood, upholstered, and other (ready-to-assemble furniture and casual furniture). Total furniture industry sales in 1995 were estimated to be $33 billion at manufacturers' prices.

Household wood furniture sales accounted for 50 percent of total household furniture sales in 1995, according to the American Furniture Manufacturers Association (AFMA). The principal types of wood furniture are dressers, tables, and dining room suites. Bedroom and dining room furniture account for the majority of wood furniture sales.

In recent years, wood furniture manufacturers have increased their emphasis on quality by monitoring the entire production process from the raw materials used to construction, finishes, and packaging. In addition to improving quality controls, companies also stress price points and basic styling features, and are trying to improve shipping schedules. Wood furniture manufacturers' sales rose only 2.0% in 1995 but are expected to rise by 4.0% in 1996, according to the AFMA.

Major well-known U.S. manufacturers of wood furniture include Bassett Furniture Industries, Drexel Heritage, Ethan Allen, Interco Inc.'s Broyhill and Lane divisions, Ladd Industries' Pennsylvania House and Kittinger divisions, Lexington Furniture Co., Masco Inc.'s Henredon, and Thomasville (a division of Armstrong World Industries). Imports are not a factor in the U.S. household wood furniture industry.

The top 25 manufacturers account for 45 percent of industry sales; the top 50 manufacturers capture 60 percent of total industry sales. No one manufacturer accounts for more than 9 percent of U.S. wood furniture sales.

A powerful trend sweeping the furniture industry is shifting ownership. According to *Furniture Today*, an industry trade publication, 9 percent of the U.S. furniture manufacturing base was for sale in 1995. In mid-1995, Masco Corp. announced that it was considering divesting the world's largest furniture manufacturing empire, with $1.9 billion in 1994 sales. Similarly, Ladd Furniture, the fifth-largest U.S. manufacturer, sold four of its furniture units in order to reallocate its resources to its eight remaining, more profitable, divisions. Many analysts also believe that Armstrong World Industries would like to sell its Thomasville unit, due to this division's relatively low margins over the past few years.

Consumer Expenditures for Furniture

Consumer spending for wood furniture is highly cyclical and closely linked to the incidence of new housing starts, consumer confidence, and disposable personal income. Since wood furniture is expensive and often sold in sets, such as a dining room table and chairs, consumers consider these purchases deferrable.

Expenditures for furniture of all kinds have fluctuated as a percentage of consumer disposable personal income since 1979. It has been estimated that about 3

E X H I B I T   2

**Total Retail Furniture Sales in the United States, 1986–1995
(In Billions of Dollars at Retail Prices)**

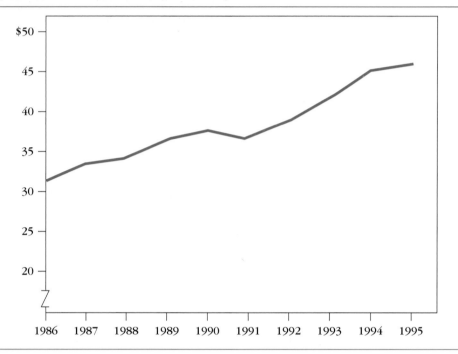

Source: U.S. Department of Commerce.

percent of a U.S. household's disposable income was spent for household furniture and home furnishings in 1995. The expected absolute growth in consumer disposable income has led industry economists to forecast an average annual industry growth in furniture in the range from 3 percent to 5 percent from 1997 through 2000. Exhibit 2 shows annual furniture sales at retail prices for the period 1986 to 1995.

Furniture Buying Behavior

Even though industry research indicates many consumers consider the furniture shopping process to be enjoyable, consumers acknowledge that they lack the confidence to assess furniture construction, make judgments about quality, and accurately evaluate the price of furniture. Consumers also find it difficult to choose among the many styles available, fearing they will not like their choice several years later, or that their selection will not be appropriate for their home and they will be unable to return it. According to a recent summary of furniture buying behavior published in *Standard & Poor's Industry Surveys*:

> Consumers are quite finicky when it comes to buying furniture—a procedure fraught with concerns that are often not associated with buying other consumer durables, such as appliances and cars. With appliances and cars, consumers may have a more limited selection, they can do their own research, and they know what they are buying and what to expect. On the other hand, most consumers know little about evaluating the price or quality of furniture. It is also difficult for consumers to imagine how furniture will look in their homes, or whether they will still like their purchase in several years. Furthermore, there are questions about delivery—as in whether the item will arrive on time and in good condition and whether it can be returned for a full refund.

The furniture industry's efforts to educate consumers over the past years have failed for the most part. These efforts have included in-depth market studies to learn what consumers look for when they buy furniture, improved distribution, and new programs for training sales personnel. Despite these efforts, consumers still find the quality of furniture difficult to discern, and tend to base their furniture choice on price.

Results of a consumer panel sponsored by *Better Homes and Gardens* and composed of its subscribers provide the most comprehensive information available on furniture-buying behavior. Selected findings from the *Better Homes and Gardens* survey are reproduced in the appendix following this case. Other findings arising from this research are as follows:

- 94 percent of the subscribers enjoy buying furniture somewhat or very much.
- 84 percent of the subscribers believe "the higher the price, the higher the quality" when buying home furnishings.
- 72 percent of the subscribers browse or window-shop furniture stores even if they don't need furniture.
- 85 percent read furniture ads before they actually need furniture.
- 99 percent of the subscribers agree with the statement "When shopping for furniture and home furnishings, I like the salesperson to show me what alternatives are available, answer my questions, and let me alone so I can think about it and maybe browse around."
- 95 percent of the subscribers say they get redecorating ideas or guidance from magazines.
- 41 percent of the subscribers have written for a manufacturer's booklet.
- 63 percent of the subscribers say they need decorating advice to "put it all together."

Consumer research data have prompted both furniture retailers and manufacturers to stress the need for well-informed retail sales personnel to work with customers. For example, many manufacturers have established education centers where they train retail salespersons in the qualitative and construction details of the furniture they sell. Some manufacturers also distribute product literature to customers via retailers. Drexel Heritage, for instance, provides a series of books, entitled *Living with Drexel Heritage,* to its authorized retailers, who then give them to customers.

Distribution

Furniture is sold through over 110,000 specialty furniture and home furnishings stores, department stores, and mass-merchandise stores in the United States. Exhibit 3 on page 312 shows the breakdown of furniture sales by type of retail outlet. Industry trends indicate that the number of independently owned furniture stores has declined, while furniture store chains have grown in popularity. Also, mass merchandisers and department stores such as JCPenney and Sears are moving their furniture lines to free-standing furniture stores. The most significant recent trend among independent and chain furniture stores, department stores, and mass merchandisers is the movement toward the "gallery concept"—the practice of dedicating an amount of space and sometimes an entire free-standing retail outlet to one furniture manufacturer. There are currently 9,500 galleries, and it is estimated this number will reach 11,000 by 1997. Commenting on the gallery concept, Charlton Bates said:

> The gallery concept has great appeal for a furniture manufacturer, since product is displayed in a unique and comfortable setting without the lure of competitive

EXHIBIT 3

Retail Distribution of Furniture

	Percent of Sales by Year	
Outlet Type	1994	1990
Furniture stores (chains and sole proprietorships)	45	52
Specialty stores and home centers	28	23
Galleries	5	4
Department stores (e.g., Macy's)	5	4
Mass merchants (e.g., Sears, JCPenney, and Montgomery Ward)	5	6
Interior designers and decorators	4	5
Discount department stores (e.g., Target)	3	3
Warehouse clubs	2	1
Catalogs	2	2
	100	100

Source: Company records.

brands. We have galleries in a small number of our furniture stores. The fact that we are not getting our full line in all of our retailers galls me because the opportunity to even discuss the gallery concept with many of our retailers doesn't exist.

According to a recent study in *Furniture/Today*, the 100 largest furniture retailers in the United States accounted for 38 percent of all furniture sales. The top ten furniture store chains commanded 15 percent of total furniture sales in 1994.

The selling of furniture to retail outlets centers on manufacturers' expositions held at selected times and places around the country. The major expositions occur in High Point, North Carolina, in October and April. Regional expositions are also scheduled during the June–August period in locations such as Dallas, Los Angeles, New York, and Boston. At these *marts*, as they are called in the furniture industry, retail buyers view manufacturers' lines and often make buying commitments for their stores. However, Carrington's experience has shown that sales efforts in the retail store by company representatives account for as much as one-half of the company's sales in any given year.

Advertising Practices

Manufacturers of household furniture spend approximately 4 percent of annual net sales for advertising of all types (consumer, trade, and cooperative advertising). This percentage has remained constant for many years. The typical vehicles used for consumer advertising are shelter magazines such as *Better Homes and Gardens, House Beautiful*, and *Southern Living*. Trade advertising directed primarily toward retailers includes brochures, point-of-purchase materials to be displayed on a retailer's sales floor, and technical booklets describing methods of construction and materials. Cooperative advertising, shared with retailers, usually appears in newspapers, but there are also some television and radio spots featuring the brands carried by retailers.

Since 1990, the Home Furnishings Council has conducted an advertising campaign designed to promote home furnishings in general. This effort was undertaken to stimulate demand and halt the decline in the percentage of consumer disposable income devoted to furniture purchases. The campaign slogan "Home Is Where the Heart Is," focused on the importance of a home to families and their quality of life (see Exhibit 4).

EXHIBIT 4

Home Furnishings Council Print Advertisement

Home Furnishings Tips From Kathie Lee Gifford.

Second In A Series:
"How Do I Start?!" My Answer: Don't Panic, Breathe Easy, And Read This.

Nobody ever said that decorating a room, or a whole house, was a piece of cake. But it's definitely *not* hard, and can actually be fun—especially if you start off right.

You can do that by following the terrific "Getting Started" tips found in Haven. It's the incredibly easy to use, complete decorating guide that's *free* at home furnishings stores everywhere that display the "heart and home" sign of the Home Furnishings Council.

Here are a few of Haven's time-saving, money-saving, sanity-saving ideas on starting off right.

1. For Step One, you don't even have to step out of your home, just go through all the decorating magazines you've been saving to find the rooms, the home furnishings, the colors and styles you like. Then take a grand tour of your own home, to see what you like, and what you'd like to never see again. Put all your thoughts on paper.

2. Next comes my favorite part, visiting home furnishings stores and galleries.

3. Take advantage of all the help and advice that these stores' sales experts have to offer you. Tell them your budget (don't be timid about it!) so they can help you get the best value for your dollar. Show them the pictures you tore out of magazines, bring along your room dimensions, your likes and dislikes—the more they know, the more they can help.

> For the store nearest you offering free copies of Haven, please call 1-800-521-HOME, ext. 345

4. And, most important, work with them to realistically plan your decorating in phases—no one expects you to buy *everything* you want at once.

See, making a beautiful home for the most wonderful family in the world *is* a whole lot easier than you thought.

HOME FURNISHINGS COUNCIL

Home Is Where The Heart Is.

Source: Courtesy of the Home Furnishings Council.

■ THE BUDGET MEETING

At the January 10 meeting attended by Hervey and Bernham executives and Carrington executives, Michael Hervey proposed that the expenditure for consumer advertising be increased by $200,000 for 1996. Cooperative advertising and trade advertising allowances would remain at 1995 levels. Hervey further recommended that shelter magazines account for the bulk of the incremental expenditure for consumer advertising.

John Bott, Carrington's Vice President of Sales, disagreed with the budget allocation and noted that sales expenses and administration costs were expected to rise by $50,000 in 1996. Moreover, Bott believed that an additional sales representative was needed to service Carrington's accounts, since 50 new accounts were being added. He estimated that the cost of the additional representative, including salary and expenses, would be at least $70,000 in 1996. "That's about $120,000 in additional sales expenses that have to be added into our promotional budget for 1996," Bott noted. He continued:

> We recorded sales of $75 million in 1995. If we assume a 4 percent increase in sales in 1996, that means our total budget will be about $3.9 million, if my figures are right—a $225,000 increase over our previous budget. And I need $120,000 of that. In other words, $105,000 is available for other kinds of promotion.

Hervey's reply to Bott noted that the company planned to introduce several new styles of living room and dining room furniture in 1996 and that these new items would require consumer advertising in shelter magazines to be launched successfully. He agreed with Bott that increased funding of the sales effort might be necessary and thought that Carrington might draw funds from cooperative advertising allowances and trade promotion.

Bates interrupted the dialogue between Bott and Hervey to mention that the $200,000 increase in promotion was $25,000 less than the 5 percent percentage-of-sales policy limit. He pointed out, however, that higher material costs plus a recent wage increase were forecasted to squeeze Carrington's gross profit margin and threaten the company objective of achieving a 5 percent net profit margin before taxes. "Perhaps some juggling of the figures is necessary," he concluded. "Both of you have good points. Let me think about what's been said and then let's schedule a meeting for a week from today."

As Bates reviewed his notes from the meeting, he realized that the funds allocated to promotion were only part of the question. How the funds would be allocated within the budget was also crucial. A call to Tom Berry might be helpful in this regard, too.

■ APPENDIX A: SELECTED FINDINGS FROM THE BETTER HOMES AND GARDENS CONSUMER PANEL REPORT—HOME FURNISHINGS[2]

Question: If you were going to buy furniture in the near future, how important would the following factors be in selecting the store to buy furniture? (Respondents: 449)

Factor	Very Important	Somewhat Important	Not too Important	Not at All Important	No Answer
Sells high-quality furnishings	62.6%	31.0%	3.8%	1.1%	1.5%
Has a wide range of different furniture styles	58.8	29.2	8.2	2.9	0.9

[2] Reprinted courtesy of the *Better Homes and Gardens*® Consumer Panel.

Factor	Very Important	Somewhat Important	Not too Important	Not at All Important	No Answer
Gives you personal service	60.1	29.9	7.8	0.9	1.3
Is a highly dependable store	85.1	12.7	1.1	—	1.1
Offers decorating help from experienced home planners	26.5	35.9	25.4	10.9	1.3
Lets you "browse" all you want	77.1	17.8	3.3	0.7	1.1
Sells merchandise that's a good value for the money	82.0	15.6	0.9	0.2	1.3
Displays furniture in individual room settings	36.3	41.2	18.7	2.4	1.3
Has a relaxed no-pressure atmosphere	80.0	17.1	1.6	—	1.3
Has well-informed salespeople	77.5	19.8	1.6	—	1.1
Has a very friendly atmosphere	68.2	28.1	2.4	—	1.3
Carries the style of furniture you like	88.0	10.0	0.9	—	1.1

Question: Please rate the following factors as to their importance to you when you purchase or shop for case-goods furniture, such as a dining room or living room suite, *1* being the most important factor, *2* being second most important, and so on, until all factors have been ranked. (Respondents: 449)

Factor	1	2	3	4	5	6	7	8	9	10	No Answer
Construction of item	24.1%	16.0%	18.5%	13.1%	10.5%	6.9%	4.9%	1.6%	0.2%	1.1%	3.1%
Comfort	13.6	14.7	12.9	12.3	12.7	10.9	8.2	4.5	4.0	2.4	3.8
Styling and design	33.6	19.8	11.1	9.6	4.7	7.3	4.5	1.6	2.9	1.6	3.3
Durability of fabric	2.2	7.6	9.8	14.5	15.1	14.7	12.9	5.6	5.8	7.8	4.0
Type and quality of wood	10.9	17.8	16.3	15.8	14.7	5.8	5.3	3.1	4.9	2.0	3.4
Guarantee or warranty	1.6	3.8	1.6	5.3	8.7	10.0	13.8	25.2	14.5	11.1	4.4
Price	9.4	6.2	8.7	8.5	10.0	12.5	14.2	11.8	6.9	8.0	3.8
Reputation of manufacturer or brand name	6.2	3.6	4.7	5.6	6.2	6.2	12.7	17.1	22.7	11.6	3.4
Reputation of retailer	1.6	1.8	1.6	2.4	4.0	7.3	7.4	13.6	22.0	34.5	3.8
Finish, color of wood	4.7	7.6	10.2	8.0	8.9	13.4	10.7	10.0	10.2	12.7	3.6

Question: Below is a list of 15 criteria that may influence what furniture you buy. Please rate them from *1* as most important to *5* as least important. (Respondents: 449)

Criterion	1	2	3	4	5	No Answer
Guarantee or warranty	11.4%	11.1%	26.3%	16.9%	5.3%	29.0%
Brand name	9.1	6.5	14.3	25.6	11.6	32.9
Comfort	34.7	27.8	14.5	8.5	4.7	9.8

Criterion	1	2	3	4	5	No Answer
Decorator suggestion	4.0	2.4	2.7	8.2	44.8	37.9
Material used	14.9	24.1	14.9	13.4	6.2	26.5
Delivery time	0.7	0.5	1.3	2.9	55.2	39.4
Size	7.6	10.7	13.6	30.9	4.0	33.2
Styling and design	33.4	17.8	21.8	13.6	2.2	11.2
Construction	34.3	23.6	13.1	11.4	2.9	14.7
Fabric	4.0	25.6	24.9	14.0	4.5	27.0
Durability	37.0	19.4	13.6	6.9	4.9	18.2
Finish on wooden parts	5.8	14.7	16.7	10.7	16.7	35.4
Price	19.4	21.8	16.0	10.9	15.4	16.5
Manufacturer's reputation	4.2	9.1	15.4	22.9	14.3	34.1
Retailer's reputation	2.2	4.7	10.5	21.2	26.5	34.9

Question: Listed below are some statements others have made about shopping for furniture. Please indicate how much you agree or disagree with each one. (Respondents: 449)

Statement	Agree Completely	Agree Somewhat	Neither Agree nor Disagree	Disagree Somewhat	Disagree Completely	No Answer
I wish there were some way to be really sure of getting good quality in furniture	61.9%	24.7%	4.7%	4.2%	3.6%	0.9%
I really enjoy shopping for furniture	49.2	28.3	7.6	9.8	4.2	0.9
I would never buy any furniture without my husband's/wife's approval	47.0	23.0	10.9	9.8	7.1	2.2
I like all pieces in the master bedroom to be exactly the same style	35.9	30.7	12.7	11.1	7.6	2.0
Once I find something I like in furniture, I wish it would last forever so I'd never have to buy again	36.8	24.3	10.0	18.9	9.1	0.9
I wish I had more confidence in my ability to decorate my home attractively	23.1	32.3	12.5	11.6	18.7	1.8
I wish I knew more about furniture styles and what looks good	20.0	31.0	17.1	13.4	16.7	1.8
My husband/wife doesn't take much interest in the furniture we buy	6.5	18.0	12.3	17.8	41.4	4.0
I like to collect a number of different styles in the dining room	3.3	10.5	15.2	29.8	38.3	2.9
Shopping for furniture is very distressing to me	2.4	11.6	14.3	18.0	51.9	1.8

Question: Listed below are some factors that may influence your choice of furnishings. Please rate them with *1* being most important, *2* being second most important, and so on, until all factors have been rated. (Respondents: 449)

Factor	1	2	3	4	5	No Answer
Friends and/or neighbors	1.3%	16.9%	15.8%	22.1%	41.7%	2.2%
Family or spouse	62.8	9.4	14.3	9.8	2.0	1.7
Magazine advertising	16.3	30.3	29.6	17.6	4.2	2.0
Television advertising	1.1	6.7	14.7	32.5	42.3	2.7
Store displays	18.9	37.2	22.1	14.0	5.6	2.2

Question: When you go shopping for a *major piece* of furniture or smaller pieces of furniture, who, if anyone, do you usually go with? (Respondents: 449—multiple responses)

Person	Major Pieces	Other Pieces
Husband	82.4%	59.5%
Mother or mother-in-law	6.2	9.1
Friend	12.0	18.9
Decorator	4.2	1.6
Other relative	15.6	15.4
Other person	2.9	3.3
No one else	5.1	22.3
No answer	0.9	3.1

Question: When the time comes to purchase a *major* item of furniture or other smaller pieces of furniture, who, if anyone, helps you make the final decision about which piece to buy? (Respondents: 449—multiple responses)

Person	Major Pieces	Other Pieces
Husband	86.0%	63.5%
Mother or mother-in-law	2.4	4.5
Friend	3.6	8.0
Decorator	3.1	2.7
Other relative	10.0	12.9
Other person	1.6	1.8
No one else	7.1	24.3
No answer	0.9	2.2

Carrington Furniture, Inc. (B)

In April 1996, Carrington Furniture, Inc. merged with Lea-Meadows, Inc., a manufacturer of upholstered furniture for living and family rooms. The merger was not planned in a conventional sense. Charlton Bates' father-in-law died suddenly in early February 1996, leaving his daughter with controlling interest in Lea-Meadows. The merger proceeded smoothly, since the two firms were located on adjacent properties and the general consensus was that the two firms would maintain as much autonomy as was economically justified. Moreover, the upholstery line filled a gap in the Carrington product mix, even though it would retain its own identity and brand names.

The only real issue that continued to plague Bates was merging the selling effort. Carrington had its own sales force, but Lea-Meadows relied on sales agents to represent it. The question was straightforward, in his opinion: "Do we give the upholstery line of chairs and sofas to our sales force, or do we continue using the sales agents?" John Bott, Carrington's Vice President of Sales, said the line should be given to his sales group; Martin Moorman, National Sales Manager at Lea-Meadows, said the upholstery line should remain with sales agents.

■ LEA-MEADOWS, INC.

Lea-Meadows, Inc. is a small, privately owned manufacturer of upholstered furniture for use in living and family rooms. The firm is more than 75 years old. The company uses some of the finest fabrics and frame construction in the industry, according to trade sources. Net sales in 1995 were $5 million. Total industry sales of upholstered furniture manufacturers in 1995 were $11.9 billion. Forecasted 1996 industry sales for upholstered furniture were $12.4 billion. Company sales had increased 7 percent annually over the past five years, and company executives believed this growth rate would continue for the foreseeable future.

Lea-Meadows employed 15 sales agents to represent its products. These sales agents also represented several manufacturers of noncompeting furniture and home furnishings. Often a sales agent found it necessary to deal with several buyers in a store in order to represent all the lines carried. On a typical sales call, a sales agent first visited buyers to discuss new lines, in addition to any promotions being offered by manufacturers. New orders were sought where and when it was appropriate. The sales agent then visited the selling floor to check displays, inspect furniture, and inform salespeople about furniture styles and construction. Lea-Meadows paid an agent commission of 5 percent of net company sales for these services. Moorman thought sales agents spent 10 to 15 percent of their in-store time on Lea-Meadows products.

This case was prepared by Professor Roger A. Kerin, of the Edwin L. Cox School of Business, Southern Methodist University, as a basis for class discussion and is not designed to illustrate appropriate or inappropriate handling of administrative situations. All names and data are disguised. Copyright © 1997 by Roger A. Kerin. No part of this case may be reproduced without written permission from the copyright holder.

The company did not attempt to influence the type of retailers that agents contacted, although it was implicit in the agency agreement that agents would not sell to discount houses. Sales records indicated that agents were calling on specialty furniture and department stores. An estimated 1,000 retail accounts were called on in 1995 and 1996. All agents had established relationships with their retail accounts and worked closely with them.

■ CARRINGTON FURNITURE, INC.

Carrington Furniture, Inc. is a manufacturer of medium- to high-priced wood bedroom, living room, and dining room furniture.[1] Net sales in 1995 were $75 million; before-tax profit was $3.7 million. Industry sales of wood furniture in 1995 were $16.5 billion at manufacturers' prices. Projected industry sales for 1996 were $17.2 billion.

The company employed ten full-time sales representatives, who called on 1,000 retail accounts. These individuals performed the same function as sales agents but were paid a salary plus a small commission. In 1995, the average Carrington sales representative received an annual salary of $70,000 (plus expenses) and a commission of 0.5 percent on net company sales. Total sales administration costs were $130,000.

Carrington's salespeople were highly regarded in the industry. They were known particularly for their knowledge of wood furniture and willingness to work with buyers and retail sales personnel. Despite these advantages, Bates knew that all retail accounts did not carry the complete Carrington furniture line. He had therefore instructed Bott to "push the group a little harder." At present, sales representatives were making ten sales calls per week, with the average sales call running three hours. Salespersons' remaining time was accounted for by administrative activities and travel. Bates recommended that the call frequency be increased to seven calls per account per year, which was consistent with what he thought was the industry norm.

■ MERGING THE SALES EFFORTS

Through separate meetings with Bott and Moorman, Bates was able to piece together a variety of data and perspectives on the question of merging the sales efforts. These meetings also made it clear that Bott and Moorman differed dramatically in their views.

John Bott had no doubts about assigning the line to the Carrington sales force. Among the reasons he gave for this view were the following. First, Carrington had developed one of the most well respected, professional sales forces in the industry. The representatives could easily learn the fabric jargon, and they already knew personally many of the buyers who were responsible for upholstered furniture. Second, selling the Lea-Meadows line would require only about 15 percent of present sales call time. Thus, he thought that the new line would not be a major burden. Third, more control over sales efforts was possible. Bott noted that Charlton Bates's father had created the sales group 30 years earlier because of the commitment it engendered and the service "only our own people are able and willing to give." Moreover, the company salespeople have the Carrington "look" and presentation style, which is

---

[1] Additional background information on the company and industry can be found in the case titled "Carrington Furniture, Inc. (A)."

instilled in every one of them. Fourth, Bott said that it wouldn't look right if both representatives and agents called on the same stores and buyers. He noted that Carrington and Lea-Meadows overlapped on all their accounts. He said, "We'd be paying a commission on sales to these accounts when we would have gotten them anyway. The difference in commission percentages would not be good for morale."

Martin Moorman advocated keeping sales agents for the Lea-Meadows line. His arguments were as follows. First, all sales agents had established contacts and were highly regarded by store buyers, and most had represented the line in a professional manner for many years. He, too, had a good working relationship with all 15 agents. Second, sales agents represented little, if any, cost beyond commissions. Moorman noted, "Agents get paid when we get paid." Third, sales agents were committed to the Lea-Meadows line: "The agents earn a part of their living representing us. They have to service retail accounts to get the repeat business." Fourth, sales agents were calling on buyers not contacted by the Carrington sales force. Moorman noted, "If we let Carrington people handle the line, we might lose these accounts, have to hire more sales personnel, or take away 25 percent of the present selling time given to Carrington product lines."

As Bates reflected on the meetings, he felt that a broader perspective was necessary beyond the views expressed by Bott and Moorman. One factor was profitability. Existing Carrington furniture lines typically had gross margins that were 5 percent higher than those for Lea-Meadows upholstered lines. Another factor was the "us and them" references apparent in the meetings with Bott and Moorman. Would merging the sales effort overcome this, or would it cause more problems? The idea of increasing the sales force to incorporate the Lea-Meadows line did not sit well with him. Adding new salespeople would require restructuring of sales territories, involve potential loss of commissions by existing salespeople, and be "a big headache." Finally, there was the subtle issue of Moorman's future. Moorman, who was 55 years old, had worked for Lea-Meadows for 25 years and was a family friend and godfather to Bates' youngest child. If the Lea-Meadows line was represented by the Carrington sales force, Moorman's position would be eliminated.

Cadbury Beverages, Inc.

CRUSH® Brand

In January 1990, marketing executives at Cadbury Beverages, Inc. began the challenging task of relaunching the CRUSH, HIRES, and SUN-DROP soft drink brands. These brands had been acquired from Procter and Gamble in October 1989.

After considerable discussion, senior marketing executives at Cadbury Beverages, Inc. decided to focus initial attention on the CRUSH brand of fruit-flavored carbonated beverages. Three issues were prominent. First, immediate efforts were needed to rejuvenate the bottling network for the CRUSH soft drink brand. Second, according to one executive, "[we had] to sort through and figure out what the Crush brand equity is, how the brand was built . . . and develop a base positioning."[1] Third, a new advertising and promotion program for CRUSH had to be developed, including setting objectives, developing strategies, and preparing preliminary budgets.

Kim Feil was assigned responsibility for managing the relaunch of the CRUSH soft drink brand. She had joined Cadbury Beverages, Inc. on December 12, 1989, as a Senior Product Manager, after working in various product management positions at a large consumer goods company for five years. Recounting her first day on the job, Feil said, "I arrived early Wednesday morning to find 70 boxes of research reports, print ads, sales and trade promotions and videotapes stacked neatly from the floor to the ceiling." Undaunted, she began to sift through the mountains of material systematically, knowing that her assessment and recommendations would soon be sought.

■ CADBURY BEVERAGES, INC.

Cadbury Beverages, Inc. is the beverage division of Cadbury Schweppes PLC, a major global soft drink and confectionery marketer. In 1989, Cadbury Schweppes PLC had worldwide sales of $4.6 billion, which were produced by product sales in more than 110 countries. Cadbury Schweppes PLC headquarters are located in London, England; Cadbury Beverages, Inc., worldwide headquarters are in Stamford, Connecticut. Exhibit 1 on page 322 shows the product list sold worldwide by Cadbury Beverages, Inc. Exhibit 2 on page 323 details the product list for the United States.

History

Cadbury Schweppes PLC has the distinction of being the world's first soft drink maker. The company can trace its beginnings to 1783 in London, where Swiss na-

---

[1] Patricia Winters, "Fresh Start for Crush," *Advertising Age* (January 6, 1990): 47.

The cooperation of Cadbury Beverages, Inc. in the preparation of this case is gratefully acknowledged. This case was prepared by Professor Roger A. Kerin, of the Edwin L. Cox School of Business, Southern Methodist University, as a basis for class discussion and is not designed to illustrate effective or ineffective handling of an administrative situation. Certain information has been disguised and is not useful for research purposes. Crush is a registered trademark used by permission from Cadbury Beverages, Inc. Copyright © 1995 by Roger A. Kerin. No part of this case may be reproduced without written permission of the copyright holder.

EXHIBIT 1

Worldwide Product List for Cadbury Beverages, Inc.

Carbonates	*Waters*	*Still Drinks/Juices*
Canada Dry	Schweppes	Oasis
Schweppes	Canada Dry	Atoll
Pure Spring	Pure Spring	Bali
Sunkist	Malvern	TriNaranjus
Crush		Vida
'C' Plus		Trina
Hires		Trina Colada
Sussex		Red Cheek
Old Colony		Allen's
Sun-Drop		Mitchell's
Gini		Mott's
		Clamato
		E. D. Smith
		Rose's
		Mr & Mrs "T"
		Holland House

tional Jacob Schweppe first sold his artificial mineral water. Schweppe returned to Switzerland in 1789, but the company continued its British operations, introducing a lemonade in 1835 and tonic water and ginger ale in the 1870s. Beginning in the 1880s, Schweppes expanded worldwide, particularly in countries that would later form the British Commonwealth. In the 1960s, the company diversified into food products.

In 1969, Schweppes merged with Cadbury. Cadbury was a major British candy maker that traced its origins to John Cadbury, who began his business making cocoa in Birmingham, England, in the 1830s. By the middle of this century, Cadbury had achieved market presence throughout the British Commonwealth, as well as other countries.

In 1989, Cadbury Schweppes PLC was one of the world's largest multinational firms and was ranked 457 in *Business Week*'s Global 1000. Beverages accounted for 60 percent of company worldwide sales and 53 percent of operating income in 1989. Confectionery items accounted for 40 percent of worldwide sales and produced 47 percent of operating income.

Soft Drinks

Cadbury Schweppes PLC is the world's third largest soft drink marketer behind Coca-Cola and PepsiCo. The company has achieved this status through consistent marketing investment in the SCHWEPPES brand name and extensions to different beverage products such as tonic, ginger ale, club soda, and seltzer in various flavors. In addition, the company has acquired numerous other brands throughout the world, each with an established customer franchise. For example, Cadbury Schweppes PLC acquired the CANADA DRY soft drink brands and certain rights to SUNKIST soft drinks in 1986. In 1989, the company acquired certain soft drink brands and associated assets (for TriNaranjus, Vida, Trina, and Trina Colada) in Spain and Portugal and purchased the GINI brand, which is the leading bitter lemon brand

EXHIBIT 2

U.S. Product List for Cadbury Beverages, Inc.

Schweppes	Canada Dry	Sunkist	Crush, Hires, Sun-Drop	Mott's, Red Cheek, Holland House, Mr & Mrs "T," Rose's
Tonic Water	Tonic Water	Sunkist Pineapple Soda	Crush Orange	Mott's 100% Pure Apple Juices
Diet Tonic Water	Sugar-Free Tonic Water	Sunkist Grape Soda	Crush Diet Orange	Mott's 100% Pure Juice Blends
Club Soda	Club Soda	Sunkist Fruit Punch	Hires Root Beer	Mott's Juice Drinks
Seltzer Water	Seltzer Waters	Sunkist Strawberry Soda	Hires Diet Root Beer	Mott's Apple Sauce
Sparkling Waters	Sparkling Mineral Waters	Sunkist Orange Soda	Hires Cream Soda	Mott's Apple Sauce Fruit Snacks
Grapefruit Soda	Barrelhead Root Beer	Sunkist Diet Orange Soda	Hires Diet Cream Soda	Mott's Prune Juice
Collins Mix	Barrelhead Sugar-Free	Sunkist Sparkling	Crush Strawberry	Clamato
Grape Soda	Root Beer	Lemonade	Crush Grape	Beefamato
Ginger Ale	Wink	Sunkist Diet Sparkling	Crush Cherry	Grandma's Molasses
Diet Ginger Ale	Ginger Ale	Lemonade	Crush Pineapple	Rose's Lime Juice
Raspberry Ginger Ale	Diet Ginger Ale		Crush Cream Soda	Rose's Grenadine
Diet Raspberry Ginger Ale	Cherry Ginger Ale		Sun-Drop Cherry Citrus	Red Cheek Apple Juice
Bitter Lemon	Diet Cherry Ginger Ale		Sun-Drop Diet Citrus	Red Cheek Juice Blends
Lemon Sour	Bitter Lemon			Mr & Mrs "T" Margarita Salt
Lemon Lime	No-Cal Brand Soft Drinks			Mr & Mrs "T" Bloody Mary Mix
	Cott Brand Soft Drinks			Mr & Mrs "T" Liquid Cocktail Mixers
	Lemon Ginger Ale			Mr & Mrs "T" Rich & Spicy
	Diet Lemon Ginger Ale			Holland House Cooking Wines
				Holland House Dry Mixers
				Holland House Wine Marinades
				Holland House Smooth & Spicy
				Holland House Coca Casa
				Cream of Coconut
				Holland House Liquid Mixers

in France and Belgium. Also, in October 1989, the company acquired all the CRUSH-brand worldwide trademarks from Procter and Gamble for $220 million.

Cadbury Schweppes PLC (Cadbury Beverages, Inc.) was the fourth largest soft drink marketer in the United States in 1989 with a carbonated soft drink market share of 3.4 percent. (The three leading U.S. soft drink companies, in order, were Coca-Cola, PepsiCo, and Dr. Pepper/7Up.) Nonetheless, the company's brands were often the market leader in their specific categories. For example, CANADA DRY is the top-selling ginger ale in the United States, SCHWEPPES is the leading tonic water, and CANADA DRY Seltzers top the club soda/seltzer category. The combined sales of SUNKIST and CRUSH brand orange drinks lead the orange-flavored carbonated soft drink category.

According to industry analysts, the 1989 acquisition of CRUSH meant that CANADA DRY would account for 39 percent of Cadbury Beverages soft drink sales in the United States. SUNKIST, CRUSH, and SCHWEPPES would account for 22 percent, 20 percent, and 17 percent of U.S. sales, respectively. The remaining 2 percent of U.S. sales would come from other soft drink brands.[2]

■ CARBONATED SOFT DRINK INDUSTRY

American consumers drink more soft drinks than tap water. In 1989, the average American consumed 46.7 gallons of carbonated soft drinks, or twice the 23 gallons consumed in 1969. Population growth compounded by rising per capita consumption produced an estimated $43 billion in retail sales in 1989.

Industry Structure

There are three major participants in the production and distribution of carbonated soft drinks in the United States. They are concentrate producers, bottlers, and retail outlets. For regular soft drinks, concentrate producers manufacture the basic flavors (for example, lemon-lime and cola) for sale to bottlers, which add a sweetener to carbonated water and package the beverage in bottles and cans. For diet soft drinks, concentrate producers include an artificial sweetener, such as aspartame, with their flavors.

There are over 40 concentrate producers in the United States. However, about 82 percent of industry sales are accounted for by three producers: Coca-Cola, PepsiCo, and Dr. Pepper/7Up.

Approximately 1,000 bottling plants in the United States convert flavor concentrate into carbonated soft drinks. Bottlers are either owned by concentrate producers or franchised to sell the brands of concentrate producers. For example, roughly one-half of Pepsi-Cola's sales are through company-owned bottlers; the remaining volume is sold through franchised bottlers. Franchised bottlers are typically granted a right to package and distribute a concentrate producer's branded line of soft drinks in a defined territory and not allowed to market a directly competitive major brand. However, franchised bottlers can represent noncompetitive brands and decline to bottle a concentrate producer's secondary lines. These arrangements mean that a franchised bottler of Pepsi-Cola cannot sell Royal Crown (RC) Cola but can bottle and market orange CRUSH rather than PepsiCo's Mandarin Orange Slice.

Concentrate producer pricing to bottlers was similar across competitors within flavor categories. Exhibit 3 shows the approximate price and cost structure for orange concentrate producers and bottlers.

---

[2] Patricia Winters, "Cadbury Schweppes' Plan: Skirt Cola Giants," *Advertising Age* (August 13, 1990): 22–23.

EXHIBIT 3

Approximate Price and Cost Structure for Concentrate Producers and Bottlers

	Concentrate Producers			
	Regular (Sugar)		Diet (Aspartame)	
	$/Case	Percentage	$/Case	Percentage
Net selling price	$0.76	100%	$0.92	100%
Cost of goods sold	0.11	14	0.12	13
Gross profit	$0.65	86%	$0.80	87%
Selling and delivery	0.02	3	0.02	2
Advertising and promotion	0.38	50	0.38	41
General and administrative expense	0.13	17	0.13	14
Pretax cash profit/case	$0.12	16%	$0.27	30%

	Bottlers			
	Regular (Sugar)		Diet (Aspartame)	
	$/Case	Percentage	$/Case	Percentage
Net selling price	$5.85	100%	$5.85	100%
Cost of goods sold	3.16	54	3.35	57
Gross profit	$2.69	46%	$2.50	43%
Selling and delivery	1.35	23	1.35	23
Advertising and promotion	0.40	7	0.40	7
General and administrative expense	0.05	1	0.05	1
Pretax cash profit/case	$0.89	15%	$0.71	12%

The principal retail channels for carbonated soft drinks are supermarkets, convenience stores, vending machines, fountain service, and thousands of small retail outlets. Soft drinks are typically sold in bottles and cans, except for fountain service. In fountain service, syrup is sold to a retail outlet (such as McDonald's), which mixes the syrup with carbonated water for immediate consumption by customers. Supermarkets account for about 40 percent of carbonated soft drink industry sales. Industry analysts consider supermarket sales the key to a successful soft drink marketing effort.

Soft Drink Marketing

Soft drink marketing is characterized by heavy investment in advertising, selling and promotion to and through bottlers to retail outlets, and consumer price discounting. Concentrate producers usually assume responsibility for developing national consumer advertising and promotion programs, product development and planning, and marketing research. Bottlers usually take the lead in developing trade promotions to retail outlets and local consumer promotions. Bottlers are also responsible for selling and servicing retail accounts, including the placement and maintenance of in-store displays and the restocking of supermarket and convenience store shelves with their brands.

Flavor and Brand Competition Colas account for slightly less than two-thirds of total carbonated soft drink sales. Other flavors, such as orange, lemon-lime, cherry, grape, and root beer account for the remaining sales. Estimates of market shares for flavors in 1989 were as follows:

Flavor	Market Share
Cola	65.7%
Lemon-lime	12.9
Orange	3.9
Root beer	3.6
Ginger ale	2.8
Grape	1.1
Others	10.0
	100.0%

Diet soft drinks represented 31 percent of industry sales in 1989. Industry trend data indicate that sales of diet drinks accounted for a large portion of the overall growth of carbonated soft drink sales in the 1980s.

There are more than 900 registered brand names for soft drinks in the United States. Most of these brands are sold only regionally. Exhibit 4 shows the top ten soft drink brands in 1989. Six of these brands were colas, and all ten brands were marketed by Coca-Cola, PepsiCo, or Dr. Pepper/7Up.

Soft Drink Purchase and Consumption Behavior Industry research suggests that the purchase of soft drinks in supermarkets is often unplanned. Accordingly, soft drink purchasers respond favorably to price (coupon) promotions, in-store (particularly end-of-aisle) displays, and other forms of point-of-sale promotions (such as shelf tags). The importance of display is evidenced in the view held by an industry analyst who estimated that a brand is "locked out of 60 percent of the [supermarket soft drink] volume if it can't get end-aisle displays."[3] The typical supermarket purchaser of soft drinks is a married woman with children under 18 years of age living at home.

Soft drink buying is somewhat seasonal, with consumption slightly higher during summer months than winter months. Consumption also varies by region of the country. Per capita consumption in the East South Central states of Kentucky, Ten-

EXHIBIT 4

Market Share of Top Ten Soft Drink Brands in the United States, 1989

Brand	Market Share
1. Coca-Cola Classic	19.8%
2. Pepsi-Cola	17.9
3. Diet coke	8.9
4. Diet Pepsi	5.7
5. Dr Pepper	4.5
6. Sprite	3.7
7. Mountain Dew	3.6
8. 7Up	3.2
9. Caffeine-free Diet Coke	2.5
10. Caffeine-free Diet Pepsi	1.6
Top Ten Brands	71.4
Other Brands	28.6
Total Industry	100.0%

---

[3] Patricia Winters, "Crush Fails to Fit on P&G Shelf," *Advertising Age* (July 10, 1989): 1, 42–43.

nessee, Alabama, and Mississippi was highest in the United States in 1989, with 54.9 gallons compared with the national per capita average of 46.7 gallons. In the Mountain states of Montana, Idaho, Wyoming, Colorado, New Mexico, Arizona, Utah, and Nevada, per capita consumption was 37.1 gallons—the lowest in the nation.

Consumption of diet beverages was more pronounced among consumers over 25 years of age. Teenagers, and younger consumers generally, were heavier consumers of regular soft drinks.

■ ORANGE CATEGORY

Orange-flavored carbonated soft drinks recorded sales of 126 million cases in 1989, or 3.9 percent of total industry sales sold through supermarkets.[4] Prior to 1986, annual case volume had hovered in the range from 100 to 102 million cases. In the mid-1980s, PepsiCo introduced Mandarin Orange Slice, and Coca-Cola introduced Minute Maid Orange. Entry of these two brands, supported by widespread distribution and heavy advertising and promotion, revitalized the category and increased supermarket sales to 126 million cases. Annual supermarket case volume for the period 1984–1989 was as follows:

Year	Annual Supermarket Case Volume of Orange-Flavored Soft Drinks
1984	102,000,000
1985	100,000,000
1986	126,000,000
1987	131,000,000
1988	131,000,000
1989	126,000,000

Major Competitors

Four brands captured the majority of orange-flavored soft drink sales in 1989. Mandarin Orange Slice marketed by PepsiCo was the category leader with a market share of 20.8 percent. SUNKIST, sold by Cadbury Beverages, Inc., and Coca-Cola's Minute Maid Orange had market shares of 14.4 percent and 14 percent, respectively. Orange CRUSH had a market share of 7.5 percent. Other brands accounted for the remaining 43.3 percent of sales of orange-flavored soft drinks. Exhibit 5 on page 328 shows the market shares for the major competitors for the period 1985–1989.

The major competitors sold both regular and diet varieties of orange-flavored drink. As shown in Exhibit 6 on page 328, slightly over 70 percent of sales in this category were regular soft drinks. Orange CRUSH sales mirrored this pattern. SUNKIST, however, exceeded the category average with 82 percent of its case volume sales being the regular form. For Mandarin Orange Slice and Minute Maid Orange, case volume was almost evenly split between regular and diet drinks.

Major competitors also differed in terms of market coverage in 1989. SUNKIST was available in markets that represented 91 percent of total orange category sales. By comparison, orange CRUSH was available in markets that represented only 62

---

[4] *Case author's note*: The soft drink industry uses supermarket sales and market shares as a gauge to assess the competitive position of different brands and flavors, since supermarket volumes affect sales through other retail outlets and fountain service. As an approximation and for analysis purposes, *total case* volume for a brand or flavor can be estimated as 2.5 times supermarket case volume. Therefore, total sales of orange-flavored soft drinks are $2.5 \times 126,000,000 = 315$ million cases.

EXHIBIT 5

Orange Carbonated Soft Drink Brand Market Shares, 1985–1989 (Rounded)

Brand	1985	1986	1987	1988	1989
	Year				
SUNKIST	32%	20%	13%	13%	14%
Mandarin Orange Slice	NA	16	22	21	21
Minute Maid Orange	NA	8	14	13	14
CRUSH	22	18	14	11	8
Total Top Four Brands	54	62	63	58	57
Others	46	38	37	42	43

percent of orange category sales. Mandarin Orange Slice and Minute Maid Orange were available in markets that represented 88 percent of orange category sales. Exhibit 7 shows the market coverage by the four major competitors for the period 1985–1989.

Competitor Positioning and Advertising

Each of the four major competitors attempted to stake out a unique position within the orange category. For example, Minute Maid Orange appeared to emphasize its orange flavor, while SUNKIST focused on the teen lifestyle. Mandarin Orange Slice and Minute Maid Orange appeared to be targeted at young adults and households without children. These brands also appeared to be emphasizing the "better for you" idea. CRUSH and SUNKIST targeted teens and households with children at home. Exhibit 8 summarizes the apparent brand positionings of the major competitors and selected performance data compiled by the CRUSH marketing research staff.

Slightly over $26 million was spent on advertising by the four major brands in 1989. Mandarin Orange Slice and Minute Maid Orange accounted for 84 percent of all advertising expenditures in the orange category. Although both brands were advertised on network and cable television and both used spot television commercials in local markets, their advertising differed in other respects. Minute Maid Orange used outdoor billboards and network radio for advertising, but Mandarin Orange Slice did not. In comparison, Mandarin Orange Slice was advertised in magazines and newspapers, but Minute Maid Orange was not.

CRUSH and SUNKIST spent less on advertising and used fewer advertising vehicles than did Minute Maid Orange and Mandarin Orange Slice. CRUSH was promoted most frequently on spot television and in newspaper and outdoor signage. SUNKIST used newspapers, spot television, outdoor billboards, and some syndicated television.

EXHIBIT 6

Case Volume in 1989 by Type of Drink: Regular versus Diet

Type	Total Soft Drinks	Total Orange	CRUSH	SUNKIST	Mandarin Orange Slice	Minute Maid Orange
Regular	68.9%	73.2%	71.3%	82.1%	49.0%	53.1%
Diet	31.1	26.8	28.7	17.9	51.0	46.9
	100.0%	100.0%	100.0%	100.0%	100.0%	100.0%

EXHIBIT 7

Market Coverage of Orange Category by Major Competitors, 1985–1989

Brand	Year				
	1985	*1986*	*1987*	*1988*	*1989*
CRUSH	81%	81%	78%	78%	62%
SUNKIST	95	83	79	86	91
Mandarin Orange Slice	10	68	87	88	88
Minute Maid Orange	10	60	87	88	88

Two advertising trends were evident in the orange category since 1986. First, total expenditures for measured print and broadcast media declined each year since 1986, when $52.2 million was spent for advertising. In that year, Mandarin Orange Slice and Minute Maid Orange were introduced nationally. Second, competitors increased the variety of media used for advertising. In 1986, spot television and outdoor billboards were used almost exclusively. By 1989, a broader spectrum of vehicles was used, including broadcast media (network, spot, syndicated, and cable television and network radio) and print media (outdoor, magazines, and newspapers). Exhibit 9 on page 330 shows advertising expenditures for the four major brands for the period 1985–1989.

Competitor Pricing and Promotion

Concentrate pricing among the four major competitors differed very little. Typically, no more than a one-cent difference existed. The price differential between regular (with sugar) and diet (with aspartame) concentrate was virtually the same across competitors. The similarity in pricing as well as in raw material costs resulted in similar gross profit margins across competitors in the orange category. However, as noted in Exhibit 3, the gross profit margin differs between regular and diet soft drink concentrate.

EXHIBIT 8

Competitive Positioning and Performance, 1989

	SUNKIST	Mandarin Orange Slice	Minute Maid Orange	CRUSH
Positioning	"Teens on the Beach"; "Drink in the Sun"	"Who's Got the Juice?" Contemporary youth culture	"The orange, orange" orange flavor, taste of real orange	"Don't just quench it, CRUSH it"; bold user imagery with thirst quenching benefit
Target	Teens, 12–24	Young adults, 18–24	Young adults, 18–34	Teens, 13–29
Household size of purchaser	3–4 (children at home)	1–2 (no children)	1–2 (no children)	3–5 (children at home)
Package sales mix	Two-liter 51% Cans 42% Other 9%	Two-liter 54% Cans 42% Other 4%	Two-liter 54% Cans 41% Other 5%	Two-liter 64% Cans 31% Other 5%
Loyalty (percentage of brand buyer's orange volume)	36%	55%	48%	46%

Source: CRUSH Marketing Research Staff Report. Based on trade publications and industry sources.

EXHIBIT 9

Concentrate Producers' Advertising Expenditures for Broadcast and Print Media for Major Orange Soft Drink Brands, 1985–1989 (In Thousands of Dollars)

Brand	1985	1986	1987	1988	1989
Mandarin Orange Slice (Total)	$17,809.4	$32,079.9	$29,555.8	$15,001.3	$11,388.1
Regular	12,739.4	27,704.2	20,123.2	10,247.9	11,199.5
Diet	5,070.0	4,375.7	2,676.4	1,881.9	
Regular and Diet			6,756.2	2,872.5	188.6
SUNKIST (Total)	$ 7,176.2	$ 4,013.0	$ 910.7	$ 1,719.3	$ 2,301.9
Regular	4,816.5	1,340.6	887.2	309.4	281.5
Diet	2,316.0	1,269.5	1.3		
Regular and Diet	43.7	1,402.9	22.2	1,409.9	2,020.4
CRUSH (Total)	$ 4,371.2	$ 7,154.9	$ 4,296.7	$ 6,841.1	$ 1,853.6
Regular	3,282.7	4,712.9	2,729.8	2,561.6	1,382.2
Diet	1,004.6	2,413.1	959.4	1.2	127.7
Regular and Diet	83.9	28.9	607.5	4,278.3	343.7
Minute Maid Orange (Total)	$ 174.4	$ 7,952.3	$ 9,027.2	$12,811.3	$10,463.1
Regular	174.4	7,508.2	7,211.6	9,252.5	10,191.9
Diet			1,745.1	3,450.2	
Regular and Diet		444.1	70.5	108.6	271.2

Advertising and promotion programs were jointly implemented and financed by concentrate producers and bottlers. Concentrate producers and bottlers split advertising costs 50–50. For example, if $1 million were spent for television brand advertising, $500,000 would be paid by the brand's bottlers and $500,000 would be paid by the concentrate producer. Bottlers and concentrate producers split the cost of retail-oriented merchandise promotions and consumer promotions 50–50.

A variety of merchandising promotions are used in the soft drink industry. One kind of promotion, called a "dealer loader," is a premium given to retailers. A common form is a "display loader" such as ice chests, insulated can coolers, T-shirts, or sweatshirts, which are part of an in-store or point-of-purchase display. After the display is taken down, the premium is given to the retailer. End-of-aisle displays and other types of special free-standing displays are also provided, as are shelf banners. Concentrate producers will often allocate 10 cents (for shirts) to 20 cents (for displays) per case sold to bottlers who implement these merchandising promotions. Consumer promotions include sponsorship of local sports and entertainment events, plastic cups and napkins with the brand logo, and stylish baseball caps, T-shirts, or sunglasses featuring the brand name. Assorted other promotions are also used, including coupons, on-package promotions, and sweepstakes. Concentrate producers will offer anywhere from 5 cents (for cups, caps, or glasses) to 25 cents (for local event marketing including cups, caps, or glasses) per case sold to bottlers who use these promotions. Examples of trade and consumer promotions are shown in Exhibits 10 (page 331) and 11 (page 332).

Concentrate producers occasionally offer bottlers price promotions in the form of distribution incentives. These incentives are typically based on case sales and are frequently used to stimulate bottler sales and merchandising activity. These incentives are often in the range from 15 to 25 cents per case depending on the amount of effort desired or needed.

EXHIBIT 10

Example of CRUSH Trade Promotion

HAVE A CRUSH ON US!
DEALER LOADERS

Item

A Crush Adventure Back Pack
B Beach Bag/Blanket
C Neon Cap
D Sony® Walkman
E Dirty Dunk®

EXHIBIT 11

Example of CRUSH Consumer Promotion

■ CRUSH MARKETING PROGRAM

In January 1990, several strategic marketing decisions were made concerning the CRUSH brand. Most notably, a decision was made to focus initial attention on the orange flavor. Even though the CRUSH line featured several flavors, orange (regular and diet) accounted for almost two-thirds of total CRUSH case volume. (Exhibit 12 shows the CRUSH product line.) Second, marketing executives at Cadbury Beverages, Inc. decided to focus immediate attention and effort on reestablishing the bottling network for the CRUSH line, particularly orange CRUSH. Third, it was decided that careful consideration of CRUSH positioning was necessary to build on the existing customer franchise and provide opportunities for further development of the CRUSH brand and its assorted flavors. Finally, the executives agreed to the development of an advertising and promotion program, including the determination of objectives, strategies, and expenditures.

Bottler Network Development

Recognizing the traditional and central role that bottlers play in the soft drink industry, company marketing and sales executives immediately embarked on an aggressive effort to recruit bottlers for the CRUSH line. The CRUSH bottling network had gradually eroded in the 1980s due in part to Procter and Gamble's decision to test a distribution system for selling CRUSH through warehouses rather than through bottlers. This action, which centralized bottling in the hands of a limited number of bottlers that shipped product to warehouses for subsequent delivery to supermarkets and other retail outlets, had led many in the CRUSH bottler network to question their fu-

EXHIBIT 12

CRUSH Product Line

EXHIBIT 13

Positioning of CRUSH, 1954–1989

Year	Positioning	Target	Campaign
1954	Natural flavor from Valencia orange	All-family	"Naturally—it tastes better, Orange CRUSH"
1957–Late 1960s (est.)	Good for you; fresh juice from specially selected oranges	All-family	"Tastes so good . . . so good for you!"
1963–1964 (est.)	Introduced full line of flavors: grape, strawberry, grapefruit, root beer, cherry	All-family	No clear introduction effort: • "Thirsty? CRUSH that thirst with Orange CRUSH" • "Delicious, refreshing, satisfying—Grape CRUSH" • "Clean fruit taste—Grapefruit CRUSH" • "Mellow CRUSH Root Beer"
Early 1970s (est.)	Unique taste, the "change of pace" drink	All-family directed toward purchaser who is female 18–35, promotions targeted children/young adults	"Ask for CRUSH, the taste that's all its own."
1979–1980	Competitive taste superiority	Maintained early 1970s TV but focused on young males with sports	Added "There is no orange like orange CRUSH . . ." to "Ask for CRUSH, the taste that's all its own."
1980	Competitive taste superiority in fruit flavors	Added new radio for 10–19 target	Same as above
1981	100% natural flavors, contemporary wholesome brand	13–39 Teens and young adults	"Orange lovers have a CRUSH on us"
1980–1985	Great, irresistible taste	13–39	"Orange lovers have a CRUSH on us"
1981–1982	Great taste	13–39	Test: "First CRUSH"
1983	More orangery taste	13–39	"Orange lovers"
1984	Sugar-free CRUSH, great taste of Nutrasweet	13–49	"Celebrate"
1986–1987	Taste with 10% real juice	Teens, 12–17	"Peel Me a CRUSH"
1987	The drink that breaks monotony	Teens, 12–17	Test: "Color Me CRUSH"
1987–1989	Bold user imagery with thirst-quenching benefit	Teens, 13–29	"Don't just quench it, CRUSH it"

ture role with CRUSH. An outgrowth of this action was that CRUSH had the lowest market coverage of orange category sales potential among major competitors.

Recruitment efforts in early 1990 broadened the bottler network. By mid-1990, new bottling agreements had been arranged, and trade relations with 136 bottlers were established. The revitalized bottler network meant that CRUSH would be available in markets that represented 75 percent of total orange category sales in time for the CRUSH relaunch. The broadened bottler network would also require promotional support. According to Kim Feil, "We knew that reestablishing trade relations was an important first step. However, we also knew that new and existing bottlers would be gauging the kind and amount of advertising and promotional support we would provide when we relaunched CRUSH."

Positioning Issues

Numerous issues related to positioning were being addressed while the bottler recruitment effort was under way. First, since the company already marketed SUNKIST, questions arose concerning the likely cannibalization of SUNKIST sales if a clearly differentiated position for orange CRUSH in the marketplace was not developed and successfully executed. A second issue concerned the relative emphasis on regular and diet CRUSH with respect to Mandarin Orange Slice and Minute Maid Orange. These two competitors had outpaced CRUSH and SUNKIST in attracting the diet segment of orange drinkers. Third, viable positions had to be considered that did not run contrary to previous positionings and would build on the customer franchise currently held by orange CRUSH. In this regard, a historical review of CRUSH positioning was conducted. The results of this effort are reproduced in Exhibit 13.

Company executives recognized that issues relating to positioning needed to be addressed in a timely manner. Without a clear positioning statement, the creative process underlying the advertising program could not be initiated.

Advertising and Promotion

CRUSH marketing executives were pleasantly surprised to learn that the CRUSH brand had high name awareness in the markets served by existing and new bottlers. According to the company's consumer awareness tracking research, of the four major brands, CRUSH had the highest orange-brand awareness in Seattle, San Francisco, New York, Miami, Los Angeles, Chicago, and Boston. Nevertheless, numerous issues had to be addressed concerning the CRUSH advertising and promotion program.

In particular, objectives for the advertising and promotion had to be established and communicated to the advertising agency that would represent CRUSH. Next, the relative emphasis on consumer advertising and on types of trade and consumer promotion had to be determined. Specifically, this meant setting the budget for advertising expenditures and the amounts to be spent on a per case basis for promotions. Ultimately, a *pro forma* statement of projected revenues and expenses would be necessary for presentation to senior management at Cadbury Beverages, Inc. Implicitly, this required a case volume forecast for orange CRUSH that realistically portrayed market and competitive conditions and "the quality of my marketing program," said Feil.

PepsiCo Restaurants International

In late June 1995, Dwight Riskey, Senior Vice President of Marketing at PepsiCo Restaurants International (PRI), returned to the United States after a 22-hour flight from Shanghai, China. The China trip was the last leg of a 21-country tour of PepsiCo's Pizza Hut, KFC, and Taco Bell international restaurants begun in December 1994.

The "world tour," as Riskey called it, was prompted by developments in Pepsi-Co's international restaurant business, a recent organizational realignment, and his desire to gather first-hand knowledge of international restaurant operations. Pepsi-Co's international restaurant business had recorded two consecutive years of declining profit. To remedy the situation, PepsiCo created PRI to oversee and direct the international expansion of Pizza Hut, KFC, and Taco Bell and find marketing and operations efficiencies that would improve the international restaurant business operating results and returns to PepsiCo. Riskey joined PRI as the Senior Vice President of Marketing, having no previous experience in either the domestic (U.S.) or international restaurant business. The "world tour" gave him a chance to visit restaurants and listen to customers in 21 countries in Europe, Asia, and Central and South America, meet with PepsiCo executives, restaurant franchisees, and joint-venture partners, and develop a sense of the marketing opportunity and challenge facing PRI.

Since joining PRI in December 1994, Riskey and a small marketing staff had been gathering and consolidating a vast amount of consumer, marketing, and competitive information pertaining to PepsiCo's international restaurant business. Riskey was particularly struck by comments from consumer focus group studies conducted in most of the 21 countries he visited. He described what he had observed:

> During each country tour, we looked at our brands . . . Pizza Hut, KFC, and where possible, Taco Bell. In every case we also looked at McDonald's and any other local competitors of interest. We looked at facilities, service, decor . . . just tried to get a broad understanding of how our brands operate compared with those of our competitors.
>
> Probably the most important part of these tours was the focus groups that we conducted in almost all of these countries. These groups tapped the voice of the consumer. The focus groups were set up to be fairly broad consumer discussions of our brands and those of our competitors. We didn't identify ourselves . . . we wanted honest, from-the-heart reactions.
>
> I observed some amazing things . . . some reassuring, some worrisome. The good news is our brands are well known and loved. Almost every consumer talked about our mouthwatering fried chicken, or the Pan Pizza they crave. That's a very strong basis upon which to build a powerful brand.

The cooperation of PepsiCo Restaurants International in the preparation of this case is gratefully acknowledged. This case was prepared by Professor Roger A. Kerin, Edwin L. Cox School of Business, Southern Methodist University, as a basis for class discussion and is not designed to illustrate effective or ineffective handling of an administrative situation. Certain information is disguised and not useful for research purposes. Copyright © 1997 by Roger A. Kerin. No part of this case may be reproduced without written permission of the copyright holder.

Unfortunately, our brands also had some real liabilities. For example, our brand equities were not rich in personality and feeling in the same way, for example, as McDonald's. Consumers could wax eloquent about the personality, environment, and service afforded by McDonald's. But the brand essence of KFC was largely just fried chicken . . . and for Pizza Hut it was great pizza and little more. It struck me that our brands simply did not have the power of an integrated, clear, rich brand equity.

Riskey added:

I also discovered that our marketing programming and advertising are not as impactful as they should be. Virtually nowhere was our marketing the most talked about in the marketplace. This is not the way it's supposed to be for a PepsiCo company. We're used to being the big news. And even in the world of restaurants, our advertising and promotions just did not seem to be breaking through to the degree they should. We have a huge opportunity here to bring the PepsiCo spirit of big idea marketing to every market in the world.

Riskey knew he had little time to put together a PRI marketing and advertising program that managers of company-owned units and restaurant franchisees and joint-venture partners could endorse and implement in 1996. The task would not be easy. None of the international operations of Pizza Hut, KFC, and Taco Bell had ever embraced such a PepsiCo-sponsored program in the past, preferring instead to market and advertise their restaurants on a country-by-country, locality-by-locality, or individual franchise or joint venture basis.

■ PEPSICO, INC.

PepsiCo, Inc. is a *Fortune* 500 company with corporate headquarters located in Purchase, New York. The company recorded a consolidated operating profit of $3.2 billion on consolidated net sales of $28.5 billion in 1994. PepsiCo was the largest food service company in the United States in 1994.

Principal Businesses

PepsiCo operates on a worldwide basis within three industry segments: (1) beverages, (2) snack foods, and (3) restaurants. About 29 percent of PepsiCo's net sales and 19 percent of operating profit were generated outside the United States in 1994. Exhibit 1 on page 338 shows 1994 net sales and operating profit by business segment.

Beverages PepsiCo's beverage business primarily markets its Pepsi, Diet Pepsi, Mountain Dew, and other brands worldwide and 7UP internationally, and manufactures concentrates for its brands for sale to franchised bottlers worldwide. The beverage business also operates bottling plants and distribution facilities located in the United States and in a number of international markets, and manufactures and distributes ready-to-drink Lipton tea products in North America.

With worldwide sales of $9.7 billion and an operating profit of $1.2 billion, PepsiCo's beverage business accounted for 34 percent of total company sales and 38 percent of total company operating profit in 1994. Net sales of the beverage business had grown at a five-year compounded annual growth rate of 10.9 percent through 1994; operating profit grew at a compounded annual growth rate of 13.2 percent during this period. Sales and profit growth in the beverage business has been fueled by the introduction of new products. The company's ready-to-drink Lipton tea became the best selling iced tea in the United States in 1994. All Sport, which the company launched in the United States in 1994, became the nation's number two sports drink behind Gatorade. Pepsi Max, a low-calorie cola containing a sweet-

EXHIBIT 1

PepsiCo, Inc. 1994 Net Sales and Operating Profit by Business Segment (Dollars in Millions)

	Beverages	Snack Foods	Restaurants
Net Sales	$9,687.5	$8,264.4	$10,520.5[1]
Domestic (U.S.)	6,541.2	5,011.3	8,693.9
International	3,146.3	3,253.1	1,826.6
Operating Profit	$1,217.0	$1,376.9	$730.3
Domestic (U.S.)	1,022.3	1,025.1	658.8
International	194.7	351.8	71.5
Net Sales as a Percent			
of Total PepsiCo Sales	34%	29%	37%
Domestic (U.S.)	23%	18%	31%
International	11%	11%	6%
Operating Profit as a Percent			
of Total PepsiCo Profit[2]	38%	43%	23%
Domestic (U.S.)	32%	32%	21%
International	6%	11%	2%

[1] *Franchise arrangements with restaurant franchisees generally provide for initial fees and continuing royalty payments based on a percentage of sales. On a limited basis, franchisees have also entered into leases of restaurant properties leased or owned by PepsiCo. Royalty revenues, initial fees, and rental payments from franchises are included in Net Sales.*

[2] *The operating profit as a percent of total PepsiCo profit does not sum to 100% across the three business segments due to unallocated expenses.*

Source: PepsiCo, Inc. 1994 *Annual Report* and case writer calculations.

ener not yet available in the United States, achieved a sizable market presence in 27 countries in 1994, and 30 more countries were scheduled for market entry in 1995. Pepsi was the second largest-selling cola soft drink in the United States in 1994; Diet Pepsi and Mountain Dew were the fifth and sixth largest-selling soft drink brands in the United States. Pepsi-Cola brands were available in 195 countries and territories outside the United States in 1994. Their sales accounted for about one-fifth of total international soft drink industry sales.

Snack Foods The snack food business manufactures, distributes, and markets chips and other snacks worldwide, with Frito-Lay, Inc. representing the domestic business. The company's most well-known brands are Lays® brand and Ruffles® brand potato chips, Fritos® brand corn chips, Doritos® brand, Tostitos® brand, and Santitas® brand tortilla chips, Chee-tos® brand cheese-flavored snacks, and Rold Gold® brand pretzels. Other well-known Frito-Lay products include Baken-Ets®, brand fried pork skins, Munchos® brand potato crisps, and Funyuns® brand onion-flavored snacks. In addition, the company markets a line of dips, nuts, peanut butter crackers, processed beef sticks, Smartfood® brand ready-to-eat popcorn, and Grandma's® brand cookies.

With worldwide sales of $8.3 billion and an operating profit of $1.4 billion, PepsiCo's snack food business accounted for 29 percent of total company sales and 43 percent of total company operating profit in 1994. Net sales of the snack food business had grown at a five-year compounded annual growth rate of 15.5 percent through 1994; operating profit grew at a compounded annual growth rate of 12.2 percent during this period.

New products and line extensions of existing brands accounted for much of the recent sales growth. The recent introduction of Wavy Lay's® brand and Lay's KC Masterpiece Barbecue Flavor® potato chips added more than $300 million to retail sales of the Lay's® brand potato chip brand. A fat-free version of Rold Gold® brand pretzels and Baked Tostitos® brand tortilla chips also fueled sales growth in the snack food segment. In 1994, PepsiCo snack foods captured an estimated 28 percent of total international retail sales of snack chips. Frito-Lay sales represented more than one-half of the total U.S. retail sales of snack chips and about 12 percent of total U.S. retail sales of snack foods overall (including such snacks as chips, cookies, candy, nuts, and other snack items).

Restaurants The restaurant business consists primarily of the operations of the worldwide Pizza Hut, Taco Bell, and KFC chains. PepsiCo acquired the Pizza Hut chain in 1977, Taco Bell in 1978, and KFC in 1986. PepsiCo operated the largest U.S. restaurant system with almost 19,500 units, and the world's largest restaurant system with almost 27,000 units in 1994. Exhibit 2 provides an overview of the unit growth

EXHIBIT 2

PepsiCo, Inc. Restaurant System Overview

A. Number of System Units Worldwide (Year-end 1989–1994)

Year	Pizza Hut	Taco Bell	KFC	Total
1989	7,502	3,125	7,948	18,575
1990	8,220	3,349	8,187	19,756
1991	8,837	3,670	8,480	20,987
1992	9,454	4,153	8,729	22,336
1993	10,433	4,921	9,033	24,387
1994	11,546	5,846	9,407	26,799

B. Number of System Units Worldwide (Year-end 1994)

	Pizza Hut	Taco Bell	KFC	Total
United States				
Company-owned	5,249	3,232	2,039	10,520
Franchised	2,708	1,523	3,007	7,238
Licensed	661	929	103	1,693
Total U.S.	8,618	5,684	5,149	19,451
International				
Company-owned	1,035	93	1,094	2,222
Joint Venture	466	—	397	863
Franchised/Licensed	1,427	69	2,767	4,263
Total International	2,928	162	4,258	7,348
Total Worldwide	11,546	5,846	9,407	26,799

Unit totals include 900 kiosks (primarily Pizza Hut) and 1,452 other special concepts (mostly carts and express units), as well as the following U.S. chains: D'Angelo Sandwich Shops (Pizza Hut)—148 company and 49 franchised, East Side Mario's (Pizza Hut)—4 company and 21 franchised, Hot 'n Now (Taco Bell)—135 company and 43 franchised, and Chevys (Taco Bell)—53 company. Unit totals do not include California Pizza Kitchen—66 company, 2 joint venture, and 2 franchised, all U.S.

Source: PepsiCo, Inc. 1994 *Annual Report*.

and unit composition for Pizza Hut, Taco Bell, and KFC in the U.S. and in international markets.

With worldwide sales of $10.5 billion and an operating profit of $730 million, PepsiCo's restaurant business accounted for 37 percent of total company sales and 23 percent of total company operating profit in 1994. Net sales of the restaurant business had grown at a five-year compounded annual growth rate of 15.9 percent through 1994; operating profit grew at a compounded annual growth rate of 11.3 percent during this same period.

The sales and profit performance of PepsiCo's restaurant business since 1993 had been a concern to top management. Even though worldwide sales had increased to a record $10.5 billion in 1994, most of the sales growth was due to the addition of new units, and not to increases in sales through existing units. For example, 78 percent of the $1.2 billion increase in sales between 1993 and 1994 came from additional units (units constructed and acquired, principally from franchisees, net of units closed and sold). Similarly, of the $1.1 billion sales increase between 1992 and 1993, 83 percent of the sales growth was due to additional units. Operating profit also had declined in 1994. Operating profit for domestic restaurants had declined from $685.1 million in 1993 to $658.8 million in 1994. International restaurants recorded a second consecutive year of declining profit in 1994 after a record setting operating profit of $120.7 million in 1992 (see Exhibit 3).

In late November 1994, Roger A. Enrico, formerly President and Chief Executive Officer of Frito-Lay, Inc. and presently Vice Chairman of the Board of PepsiCo, Inc., assumed responsibility for PepsiCo's restaurant business. As Chairman and Chief Executive Officer of the newly formed PepsiCo Worldwide Restaurants Division, he assembled a team of senior PepsiCo executives to identify and evaluate options to improve operating results and returns on PepsiCo's U.S. and international restaurant operations.

PepsiCo Restaurants International

Soon after the formation of PepsiCo Worldwide Restaurants as a separate operating division within PepsiCo, Inc., Enrico established PepsiCo Restaurants International (PRI). PRI was created to focus attention on PepsiCo's international operations of Taco Bell, KFC, and Pizza Hut, apart from the U.S. and Canadian operations of these chains. PRI's senior management team included a newly appointed president and chief operating officer (COO) of PRI, the chief executive officers of Taco Bell, KFC, and Pizza Hut, and Dwight Riskey, Senior Vice President of Marketing. Riskey had been the vice president of marketing research and new business at Frito-Lay, Inc., a position he occupied for nine years.

The PRI senior management team was to jointly oversee and direct the international expansion of Taco Bell, KFC, and Pizza Hut, finding marketing and operations

EXHIBIT 3

PepsiCo, Inc. International Restaurant Sales and Operating Profit: 1990–1994

	1994	1993	1992	1991	1990
Net Sales ($ millions)	$1,826.6	$1,330.0	$1,116.9	$868.5	$684.8
Operating Profit ($ millions)	$71.5	$92.9	$120.7	$96.2	$75.2
Operating Profit Margin	3.9%	7.0%	10.8%	11.1%	11.0%

Source: PepsiCo, Inc. 1994 *Annual Report.*

efficiencies where applicable outside the United States and Canada and implementing them in an expeditious and effective manner. Previously, the three separate restaurant concepts had been managed independently and as extensions of their domestic (U.S.) operations. The three restaurant chains would maintain their autonomy in the United States and Canada.

International Restaurants Pizza Hut, Taco Bell, and KFC, collectively, had 7,348 units in 93 countries (including Canada) outside the United States in 1994. Principal international markets included Australia, Canada, Japan, Korea, Mexico, New Zealand, Spain, and the United Kingdom. The geographic distribution of PepsiCo's 7,348 international units is shown below:

Country	Percent
Canada	19%
Japan	15
Australia	11
United Kingdom	10
All other countries	45
	100%

Slightly over 30 percent of Pizza Hut, Taco Bell, and KFC restaurants located outside the United States were company-owned. The majority of restaurants (58 percent) in international markets were franchised or licensed operations owned by independent business people or concerns (franchisees/licensees). Some 365 separate franchisees/licensees operated 4,263 franchise/licensed units outside the United States and Canada. Each franchisee/licensee was governed by a franchise/license agreement with PepsiCo. This agreement typically described the restaurant menu, price structure, trade dress,[1] franchise fees, and other aspects of operations. Pizza Hut and KFC also had engaged in a number of joint ventures, the most significant of which were located in Japan and the United Kingdom. In these joint ventures, PepsiCo exercised significant influence, but not control. In 1994, 863 Pizza Hut and KFC units were operated under 20 separate joint-venture arrangements.

Riskey's tour of PepsiCo's restaurants led him to conclude that there were large differences within and between Pizza Hut, KFC, and Taco Bell company-owned units and non-company-owned units which he believed detracted from a coherent brand positioning around the world. He said:

> It surprised me to find that in different parts of the world our brands have radically different positionings. Different menus, different product recipes, wildly different store designs and decor, even different brand signage . . . it's almost as if we have different brands entirely in different markets. You might ask why this is a problem. If the brands need to evolve differently in different markets to be successful, why not just let them? There's one big, overriding reason. Managing a business with significantly divergent brand positionings eliminates, or at least minimizes, an important potential competitive advantage . . . economies of scale.

International Restaurant Organization Each of PepsiCo's international restaurant concepts was managed on a geographical basis. Depending on the size of markets, country general managers or regional general managers were responsible for company-owned restaurants. For example, Mexico had its own country manager; restaurants in south Asia and the Middle East were under the direction of a regional man-

---

[1] Trade dress refers to interior and exterior signage and colors and other aspects of decor used in restaurants.

ager. These managers also served as the liaison between PepsiCo and franchisees and joint-venture partners in a country or region.

A vice president of marketing for a country or region typically reported to a general manager. This individual had responsibility for PepsiCo restaurant marketing within a geographical area, including advertising, public relations, and promotional programs. In this context, the vice president of marketing developed the "marketing calendar" for the country or region in consultation with company-owned restaurant management and non-company-owned restaurant operators. The "marketing calendar" included the television media schedule, seasonal or special promotions, and new product introductions.

Funding for international restaurant marketing and advertising came from PepsiCo and franchise marketing cooperatives. Marketing cooperatives consisted of coalitions of franchisees in a country or region. These cooperatives, managed by member franchisees, funded advertising, promotion, and marketing programs from pooled monies provided by franchisees. The monetary contributions of individual franchisees was based on a percentage of their sales. Marketing cooperatives and PepsiCo management jointly selected advertising agencies which developed and produced messages for television, radio, and print media. This collaboration also applied to the allocation of media monies and, more generally, the funding of different elements of the "marketing calendar." Marketing cooperatives had considerable influence in determining where and how marketing dollars were spent, valued their autonomy in making such decisions, and had been known to veto proposals made by PepsiCo country/region managers and marketing executives.

■ THE WORLDWIDE QUICK-SERVICE RESTAURANT INDUSTRY

Pizza Hut, KFC, and Taco Bell compete in the worldwide quick-service restaurant industry. The worldwide quick-service restaurant (QSR) industry consists of restaurants that feature fast service and a limited menu of moderately priced, cooked-to-order items. The QSR industry originally divided into on-premises (dine-in) and off-premises (carry-out) consumption occasions. The industry has since expanded its domain to include drive-thru and delivery consumption occasions.

Market Size and Competitors

Worldwide QSR retail sales were estimated to be $146 billion in 1994. The United States accounted for 57 percent of estimated worldwide QSR retail sales, or $84 billion; international QSR retail sales accounted for $62 billion. QSR sales in the United States have grown at a compounded rate of 6 percent since 1989. International QSR sales have grown at a compounded rate of 8 percent over the past five years. QSR retail sales represented about 31 percent of total food service sales in the United States. No comparable figure was available for the international market, although it was believed by industry analysts that QSR international sales represented a very small fraction of total international food service sales.

Ten QSR chains operated on a truly worldwide scale in 1994. All ten chains were based in the United States. Exhibit 4 shows the eight largest QSR chain systems based on total restaurant units. PepsiCo managed the largest worldwide QSR system with almost 27,000 units composed of the Pizza Hut, Taco Bell, and KFC chains. McDonald's was the second largest QSR system measured by the total number of units. However, McDonald's was the world's largest QSR chain operating under a single name with 15,950 units and worldwide revenues of $8.3 billion in

EXHIBIT 4

Ten Largest Worldwide Restaurant Systems in 1994
(Units in Thousands)

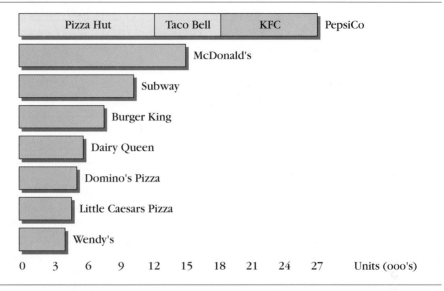

Source: PepsiCo, Inc. 1994 *Annual Report*.

1994. In 1995, McDonald's publicly announced that its vision was to dominate the global food service industry.[2]

PepsiCo restaurants had worldwide retail sales of $18.5 billion in 1994, 70 percent of which were registered in the United States. McDonald's recorded worldwide retail sales of $25.9 billion, 57 percent of which were recorded in the U.S. Exhibit 5 on page 344 shows worldwide QSR system retail sales for PepsiCo (Pizza Hut, Taco Bell, and KFC) and McDonald's in 1994.[3]

Market and Competitive Trends

Six market and competitive trends are apparent in the worldwide QSR industry.[4] First, an increasing amount of a consumer's food dollar is spent for food away from home. For every dollar spent at U.S. food stores, consumers spent 55 cents at restaurants, up from 34 cents for every food dollar in 1970. A similar change is occurring in industrialized nations around the world and in developing countries as well. This trend is being driven in part by the growing internationalization of the QSR industry as more restaurants are being opened in non-U.S. markets.

---

[2] McDonald's 1995 *Annual Report*: 7.

[3] Worldwide QSR system sales for PepsiCo and McDonald's reflect actual retail sales through company-owned, joint-venture, and franchised units and are larger than PepsiCo and McDonald's net sales/revenues. The difference is due to the fact that PepsiCo and McDonald's net sales/revenues reflect sales through company-owned units and franchisee royalty revenues, initial fees and rental payments which are based on a percentage of franchisee sales.

[4] This discussion is based on information contained in "Restaurants: Challenges and Opportunities in the Greying '90s," *Standard & Poor's Industry Surveys* (April 6, 1995): L51; Andrew E. Serwer, "McDonald's Conquers the World," *Fortune* (October 17, 1994): 103–116; "Satellites, No Frills, Tandems Feed Fast Food," *Advertising Age* (September 25, 1995): 36; PepsiCo 1994 and 1995 Annual Reports; and McDonald's 1994 and 1995 Annual Reports.

E X H I B I T 5

Worldwide QSR System Retail Sales of PepsiCo and McDonald's in 1994 (Billions of Dollars)

	Domestic (U.S.)		International		Row Total	
PepsiCo Worldwide Sales	$12.9	(70%)	$5.6	(30%)	$18.5	(100%)
Pizza Hut	5.0	72	1.9	28	6.9	100
Taco Bell	4.4	98	.1	2	4.5	100
KFC	3.5	49	3.6	51	7.1	100
McDonald's Worldwide Sales	$14.9	57	$11.0	43	$25.9	100

Source: PepsiCo, Inc. and McDonald's 1994 *Annual Reports*.

A second trend is the growing emphasis on lowering the development costs of new restaurants and the increasing speed with which new restaurants are built. For example, McDonald's has reduced the cost of building materials and equipment through standardization and global sourcing. It has also pioneered modular building design and construction in England. This practice makes it possible to put in place a fully operational restaurant on a vacant lot in nine hours.

A third trend is the search for new types of locations to reach consumers. For example, Little Caesars Pizza has outlets in Kmart stores, and McDonald's has nearly 750 "satellite" restaurants in zoos, hospitals, airports, and retail stores such as Wal-Mart, Home Depot, and Carrefour (a French retail store chain).

Co-branding is a fourth trend. McDonald's has implemented this approach through alliances with Chevron and AMOCO whereby the restaurant and oil company jointly utilize and promote a site. PepsiCo has used this approach by locating two or more of its restaurant chains on the same site, such as a Taco Bell and KFC. In Warsaw, Poland, for example, PepsiCo operates Pizza Hut, Taco Bell, and KFC restaurants on a single site.

A fifth trend is the growing emphasis on delivery service and drive/walk-by service. For example, 47 percent of Pizza Hut U.S. sales arise from delivery service; in Germany, 40 percent of Pizza Hut sales arise from walk-by windows where pedestrians purchase pizza by the slice.

A sixth trend is the increasing use of franchising as a means for market penetration in the United States and market development abroad. McDonald's, for example, has expanded its international business mostly through franchising. Ten years ago, the ratio of franchised units to company-owned units in non-U.S. markets was 1.2 to 1.0. This ratio was 1.7 to 1.0 in 1994. In the United States, this ratio was 3.5 to 1.0 ten years ago; in 1994 this ratio was 5.1 to 1.0. PepsiCo has begun to "refranchise" (sell company-owned restaurants to franchisees) many of its restaurants and pursue new franchising opportunities in international markets.

■ STRATEGY INITIATIVES AT PEPSICO RESTAURANTS INTERNATIONAL

Strategy development at PRI began shortly after its formation in December 1994. By early 1995, PRI's strategy initiatives crystallized and focused on three areas: (1) leverage PepsiCo's business systems and restaurant development activities, (2) achieve operational excellence, and (3) leverage the collective strength of PepsiCo's three restaurant concepts by strengthening the brand leadership of each.

Business Systems and Restaurant Operations

By mid-1995, progress in all three areas was evident. With respect to business systems, consolidation of international headquarters administration of Pizza Hut, KFC, and Taco Bell was completed and located in Dallas, Texas. Consolidation of international regional and country administration was underway. Also, consolidation of restaurant procurement on a worldwide basis was substantially completed. Finally, the co-branding of PepsiCo restaurants continued, but at a faster pace, as did the refranchising initiative begun in 1994.

With respect to building operational excellence, PRI made investments targeted at consistently providing restaurant customers with consistently high-quality products, courteous and timely service, and clean and attractive restaurants. In addition, customer satisfaction measures were put in place to track the success of these efforts.

Marketing Initiatives

The third pillar in PRI's strategy initiative focused on leveraging the collective strength of PepsiCo's three restaurant concepts by strengthening the brand leadership of each. Riskey knew this initiative would require careful study before any action was taken. Accordingly, initial attention focused on conducting a number of large-scale consumer studies and evaluating advertising and promotion for PepsiCo's international restaurants.

Country Market Studies Riskey commissioned 15 large-scale country market studies designed to identify consumer perceptions of PepsiCo's two major international restaurant operations: Pizza Hut and KFC. Six of these studies were conducted in the principal markets served by Pizza Hut and KFC—Australia, Japan, Korea, Mexico, New Zealand, and Great Britain—and in other representative countries such as Brazil, Indonesia, the Philippines, and Puerto Rico, where these restaurant chains had a significant market presence. The studies were conducted during the winter and spring of 1995.

Each of the country market studies surveyed patrons of KFC, Pizza Hut, and McDonald's. A central component of these studies was the rating of each restaurant by consumers on 21 attributes such as food quality, restaurant cleanliness, and value for the money spent. Consumer comments were also solicited. McDonald's was chosen as a benchmark restaurant given its strong international market presence with 5,712 units in 78 countries outside the United States in 1994. By mid-summer, 1995, data from the country market studies had become available and were analyzed by the PRI marketing team. Its analysis uncovered a remarkable similarity in consumer ratings of KFC and Pizza Hut, relative to McDonald's, across the 15 countries. While the magnitude in mean differences for restaurant attributes differed across countries, the pattern was generally the same.

More in-depth quantitative analysis of the market study data yielded another surprising finding. About 31 percent of overall consumer appeal of a restaurant could be attributed to food. Experiential aspects of buying and consuming food accounted for 56 percent of consumer appeal; aspects of "value for the money" accounted for 13 percent of consumer appeal. These quantitative results demonstrated that KFC and Pizza Hut food compared favorably with McDonald's food and actually exceeded McDonald's on every food-related attribute (e.g., quality, taste, nutrition), except food consistency. However, KFC and Pizza Hut fared less favorably on restaurant-related attributes (e.g., speed, interior/exterior, atmosphere, ample seating) and "value" attributes (e.g., inexpensive, special offers). "Clearly, 'owning food' is not enough to win in this business. Even if we win on food but lose on experience and value, we'll lose the war," concluded Riskey. He added:

It was also apparent from our research that while we have focused on food, we have largely ignored another important part of the consumer event . . . consumers call it "the experience"—some combination of the service they receive, and the restaurant in which they receive it. They described McDonald's, for example, as being in a class by itself in hospitality, cleanliness, comfort . . . in fact, one consumer (I think it was in Brazil) described McDonald's as having "it's own special culture. Everyone feels comfortable there." Another particularly articulate consumer said McDonald's was "like . . . an embassy." An embassy! You get the point. These guys are doing something special—something that we apparently aren't—to make consumers feel comfortable, safe, happy, while they visit.

A PRI marketing team member echoed this view citing a passage from a recent McDonald's *Annual Report.* Opening the report, he said, "Listen to what McDonald's has to say about experience":

> Price brings customers in the door. But the value of the entire experience—tasty food . . . fast and accurate service . . . friendly people . . . clean restaurants . . . and the comfort of the entire experience—that's what brings customers back.[5]

Review of International Restaurant Advertising The PRI marketing team also examined the advertising and promotion efforts and expenditures that supported PepsiCo's international restaurants. This task proved to be very time-consuming since PepsiCo's international restaurants were using 12 different advertising agencies around the world.

Further inquiry into international restaurant advertising indicated that a majority of the agencies used were foreign local or national agencies hired by marketing cooperatives which represented a coalition of franchises in a country or region. A small percentage of advertising agencies were affiliates of the U.S. advertising agency responsible for domestic (U.S.) advertising and promotion. Television, radio, and print advertising were used by PepsiCo's international restaurants.

As part of the data collection process undertaken by the PRI marketing team, it was determined that 200 different Pizza Hut, KFC, and Taco Bell television commercials were being shown around the world in 1995. The media cost for these commercials was roughly $180 million; another $25 million was spent for producing these commercials. For comparison, industry sources reported that McDonald's spent an estimated $358.8 million outside the United States for television, radio, and print media in 1994.[6] McDonald's advertising production costs were unknown.

A content analysis of TV commercials shown by PepsiCo's international restaurants indicated that a vast majority were promotional in nature. They typically featured "two-for-the-price-of-one" pizzas, various "Meal Deals" emphasizing discount pricing, and consumer promotions for a free dessert or a free toy. Exhibits 6 (on facing page) and 7 (on page 348) show print advertisements in Hong Kong and Mexico illustrating promotional appeals for KFC. Riskey acknowledged that such appeals, and the temporary value they bestowed on consumers, probably did have quick and possibly noticeable short-term effects on sales volume. However, he expressed his concerns with the apparent disproportional use of promotional advertising. In a meeting with senior PepsiCo restaurant executives, he said:

> I find this (the heavy use of promotional advertising) ironic. That a division of PepsiCo . . . a company more famous than any on earth for the quality of its brand advertising . . . chooses to advertise its *prices* with higher priority than its *brands.*

---

[5] McDonald's 1995 *Annual Report*: 9.

[6] "Top 50 Non-U.S. Spenders," *Advertising Age* (November 20, 1995): I–20.

EXHIBIT 6

KFC Advertisement in Hong Kong

Source: Courtesy of PepsiCo Restaurants International.

Now don't misunderstand me. I would be the last one to suggest that we should walk away from promotional advertising. It is the most important tool we have for driving short-term sales volumes, and for offsetting competitive marketing actions. But by itself, promotional advertising cannot and will not *sustain* a great brand. Certainly it cannot *build* one.

The reason? It's not intended to. Promotional advertising is a quick surge of adrenaline, meant to stimulate a consumer reaction now. But it can only work well as part of a larger plan, a bigger picture—where the brand's DNA has already been expressed. That DNA carries all the information about the brand's essence. It shapes the brand's image, its personality, its entire identity in the consumer's mind . . . so

EXHIBIT 7

KFC Advertisement in Mexico

Source: Courtesy of PepsiCo Restaurants International.

that the consumer relates to the brand . . . sees value in it . . . and attaches a sense of quality and worth. This brand DNA then gives our promotional ads a context . . . and signals the consumer that "KFC, which is always good, right now, is even better." Or "Here's an even better reason to get to Pizza Hut this weekend."

The point is, promotion works best when it starts with a preconceived belief— that brands are superior and meaningful to begin with. That way—and only that way—can a promotion work as it should. As a value added on top of an already existing valued brand.

Riskey went on to say how he thought PepsiCo might go about building its Pizza Hut, KFC, and Taco Bell brands in international markets:

So, how do we go about building that belief? How do we go about establishing the brand DNA? Well, of course, it's done in a lot of ways. Great service, great food, great restaurants . . . and importantly, advertising that, quite simply, will encourage consumers to develop regard, friendship, warmth, a strong personal relationship with our brands. The kind of advertising I'm describing has a greater focus on building the long-term strength of the brand rather than such a heavy focus on short-term spikes in sales volumes. The intention is to build the "worth" or "equity" value of the brand. As we continue to get the sales, to also get the profits that come with those sales . . . and finally, very importantly, to make the brand a better, stronger, more meaningful and loved entity. The goal is to "build" our brands across time, as we also "use" them promotionally to generate weekly sales.

You might say we're putting way more of our energy against how we "use" our brands to get sales . . . than against how we *"build"* them to make them stronger. We're selling our price harder than we're selling the benefit of our brand. I heard a famous marketing guy once say, "The easiest thing on earth is to make a sales or profit plan by selling off the brand." There's possibly a little of that business strategy in the purely promotion approach we sometimes take in our (international restaurant) marketing.

At the end of the day, we want to achieve our sales and profit numbers, of course . . . *but we also* want a stronger, healthier brand over the long haul.

Proposed PRI Marketing University A third marketing initiative was a proposal for a PRI "Marketing University." This proposal resulted from the experience Riskey and the PRI marketing team had with gathering and consolidating consumer, marketing, and competitive information and the findings from their efforts. It had become clear that PepsiCo had no central repository for information pertaining to its international restaurant business, no mechanism for information transfer and shared learning among and between Pizza Hut, KFC, and Taco Bell operations, and no means to build a systemic marketing capability. "If we were going to leverage the collective strength of PepsiCo's three restaurant concepts, we needed a PRI Marketing University," said Riskey.

While still in the concept stage in mid-1995, the PRI Marketing University was envisioned as a one- to two-week course for PepsiCo restaurant marketing personnel worldwide. The curriculum would focus on training, including aligning restaurant objectives, assessing "best practices" across restaurants, and the use of marketing intelligence systems, including the application of analytical tools for making marketing decisions. When appropriate, advertising agency personnel and restaurant suppliers would be invited to attend sessions as part of a system-wide effort to build a global marketing capability.

■ MARKETING AND ADVERTISING DECISIONS AT PEPSICO RESTAURANTS INTERNATIONAL

Riskey assembled the PRI marketing team in the morning of July 14, 1995. The purpose of the gathering was to move forward the planning effort behind a PepsiCo-sponsored marketing and advertising program for its international restaurant business. Riskey was scheduled to depart that afternoon for two weeks of business meetings in Australia, Malaysia, and Indonesia.

The agenda for the meeting was short. It consisted of three tasks he wanted the PRI marketing team to address in his absence. First, the team was asked to prepare a concise description of the competitive and marketing situation faced by PepsiCo's international restaurant business. Second, he wanted the team to draft a position paper that outlined the pros and cons of a worldwide thematic advertising effort. Finally, the team was asked to consider the merits of placing PRI's advertising program under the creative and execution direction of a single advertising agency for Pizza Hut and another single agency for KFC.

The three tasks were not simply exercises. Riskey and the PRI marketing team were scheduled to make a presentation including recommendations to PRI's senior management group in three weeks. This group consisted of PRI's President and COO and the chief executive officers of Pizza Hut, KFC, and Taco Bell. Roger A. Enrico, Vice Chairman of the Board of PepsiCo, Inc. and Chairman and CEO of PepsiCo Worldwide Restaurants, would be in attendance as well as other senior PepsiCo executives.

Competitive and Marketing Situation Analysis

Riskey began the meeting by reiterating the PRI mission: To find marketing and operations efficiencies that would improve the international restaurant business operating results and returns to PepsiCo and leverage PepsiCo's three restaurant concepts by strengthening the brand leadership of each. He reminded the PRI marketing team that an assessment of the competitive and marketing situation should not lose sight of this mission and said:

> We all have been studying the same consumer, marketing, and competitive information for some time. You know my interpretation of the data and views on the situation. What I want you to do is prepare a concise description of the competitive situation including an assessment of our marketing strengths, shortcomings, and possible opportunities, while acknowledging the marketing challenges we face.

He added that the effectiveness of marketing and advertising efforts should not be compromised in pursuit of efficiency, however.

Thematic Advertising and the Agency Decision

Riskey then addressed the second and third tasks. He wanted the marketing team to assess the merits of (1) a worldwide thematic advertising program and (2) putting PRI's advertising program under the direction of a single advertising agency for Pizza Hut and another agency for KFC. Neither of these approaches had been used previously by PepsiCo's international restaurants.

Thematic Advertising The notion of thematic advertising surfaced after the PRI marketing team completed its content analysis of television commercials for PepsiCo's international restaurants. The results of this analysis, which documented the presence of mostly promotional advertising, ran contrary to PepsiCo's marketing and advertising philosophy. According to Riskey:

> At PepsiCo and Frito-Lay, we think one of the things we do best of all is "big idea marketing." We believe that one big idea, marketed well, communicated with power and surprise and entertainment value and fun, is worth an infinite number of small, incremental ideas. Why? Because big ideas communicated with power and surprise, and entertainment value and fun—make magic. We take pride in being able to identify big ideas . . . and when we identify one, we put big resources, and big money behind it.

Riskey encouraged the PRI marketing team to give consideration to "big idea marketing" for Pizza Hut and KFC. He also asked them to consider how the concept of "big idea marketing" might be translated into a thematic advertising program that could be conveyed worldwide. As a practical matter, this would mean changing the mix of television commercials in international markets and the allocation of media expenditures. Presently, almost 100 percent of media spending was devoted exclusively to promotional advertising; virtually no media expenditures were spent on thematic advertising. Pizza Hut and KFC marketing cooperatives would have a lot to say about this approach since they would be funding much of the endeavor. Riskey asked the PRI marketing team to also consider what percentage of total media expenditures might be allocated to such an approach.

"Big idea marketing means big money," said Riskey. Pizza Hut and KFC international restaurants were spending an average of about $130,000 to produce a single promotional television commercial. Riskey believed the cost to develop and produce a high-quality television commercial with exceptional production values could cost as much as $2 million. This cost, too, would be partially funded by marketing cooperatives. Accordingly, he asked the PRI marketing team to consider how many of such commercials might be produced.

The Agency Decision Finally, Riskey asked the PRI marketing team to consider the merits of placing PRI's advertising program under the creative and execution direction of a single advertising agency for Pizza Hut and another agency for KFC. Like the notion of thematic advertising, this idea emerged during the review of PepsiCo's international restaurant advertising. Some 12 different agencies were involved in producing and scheduling PepsiCo's international restaurant advertising in 1994. Most had long-term relationships with Pizza Hut and KFC international restaurants, marketing cooperatives, and PepsiCo's country/regional management.

Riskey noted that this matter would involve careful consideration of implementation issues. "No one advertising agency is truly global in its market presence. Most large agencies operate through networks of independent agency affiliates," Riskey said. Nevertheless, a number of large advertising agencies did have offices or affiliates in the largest international markets served by Pizza Hut and KFC.

Price Waterhouse

The 1980s witnessed widespread innovation in the public accounting industry in the United States. To better serve client needs, public accounting firms expanded their client services to include management consulting and industry-based specialties in addition to their traditional auditing and tax services, and they also broadened the international scope of their operations. Another innovation has been the addition of investment banking-related capabilities to further position public accounting firms as full-service financial counselors for their clients. Specifically, some public accounting firms have begun to assist their clients in assessing the merits of using and pursuing different forms of debt and/or equity financing and to conduct merger, acquisition, and divestiture analyses and negotiations. The latter function consists of bringing a potential seller and buyer together and helping them negotiate an agreement relating to the sale or purchase of securities or sometimes firms or divisions of companies.

The inclusion of investment banking-related services represents a significant change in the role public accounting firms have played. Historically, when it came to the buying and selling of companies, public accounting firms provided due diligence services, assisted their clients in assessing the accounting and tax implications of sale and purchase decisions, and provided postacquisition services including postmerger integration of accounting and management systems.[1] By offering direction and assistance in the strategy and negotiation phase that precedes the actual sale and purchase decision and on subsequent integration issues, public accounting firms have entered territory traditionally occupied by investment bankers.

Interest in providing investment banking-related services to its clients emerged at Price Waterhouse in the late 1980s. After considerable study, the firm decided in mid-1989 to offer these services and formed the Corporate Finance Group in early 1990. In early 1991, senior management was focusing attention on making these services achieve their potential and relating them to existing services offered by Price Waterhouse.

■ THE PUBLIC ACCOUNTING INDUSTRY

The public accounting industry in the United States can trace its roots to the early nineteenth century. At that time, British industrialists hired accountants who were given responsibility for overseeing their commercial interests in America. This responsibility for establishing checks and balances and assessing the accuracy of financial statements has remained an important function performed by the accounting profession.

---

[1] *Due diligence* refers to the practice of examining a company's records, financial statements, and other aspects of its operation prior to a sale or purchase decision.

The assistance of Price Waterhouse in the preparation of this case is gratefully acknowledged. This case was prepared by Angela Bullard and Lawrence Cervetti, graduate students, under the supervision of Professor Roger A. Kerin, of the Edwin L. Cox School of Business, Southern Methodist University, as a basis for class discussion and is not designed to illustrate effective or ineffective handling of an administrative situation. Selected information has been disguised and is not useful for research purposes.

Nature of Public Accounting

The purpose of accounting is to provide quantitative information, primarily financial in nature, that concerns economic entities and is intended to be useful in making economic decisions. Public accounting is an aspect of accounting that primarily focuses on the rendering of an opinion by an independent auditor as to whether an entity's financial statements are fairly presented. That is, the auditor attests that the accounting practices used in the preparation of financial statements are (or are not) in accordance with generally accepted accounting principles proposed by the Financial Accounting Standards Board.

The public accounting profession is composed of certified public accountants (CPAs), who have met certain educational requirements and have satisfied the statutory and administrative requirements to be registered or licensed as a public accountant. In addition, these individuals have successfully completed the Uniform CPA Examination administered by the American Institute of Certified Public Accountants. There are approximately 307,000 practicing certified public accountants in the United States.

Public Accounting Firms and Services

There are thousands of public accounting firms in the United States. Many of these firms are small professional corporations whose certified public accountants provide a variety of services (bookkeeping, tax preparation, and so forth) for small businesses and individuals. However, public accounting is typically associated with what is termed the "Big Six." The six largest public accounting firms in the United States are Arthur Andersen and Company, Ernst and Young, Deloitte and Touche, KPMG Peat Marwick, Coopers and Lybrand, and Price Waterhouse. These six firms combined produced U.S. revenues of approximately $10.9 billion and worldwide revenues in excess of $25 billion in 1990. Exhibit 1 profiles the Big Six accounting firms.

Public accounting firms, and particularly the Big Six, provide their clients with a wide range of services. Even though these firms still perform their traditional role of

EXHIBIT 1

Overview of the Big Six Accounting Firms: 1990

	Arthur Andersen & Co.	Coopers & Lybrand	Deloitte Touche	Ernst & Young	KPMG Peat Marwick	Price Waterhouse
Revenues (billions)						
U.S. revenues	$2.28	$1.40	$1.92	$2.24	$1.83	$1.20
Worldwide revenues	$4.16	$4.10	$4.20	$5.01	$5.40	$2.90
U.S. professional staff						
(including partners)	19,992	10,898	18,800	16,911	15,000	9,560
Total number of partners	1,344	1,301	1,670	2,025	1,876	920
Number of U.S. offices	87	99	110	125	135	100
Percentages of revenue by function						
Auditing/advisory	35%	60%	57%	53%	53%	47%
Tax	23	20	23	25	27	29
Management consulting	42	20	20	22	20	24

Source: Based on company publications and Public Accounting Report (February 15, 1991). Information on Arthur Andersen and Company is both Arthur Andersen and Company public accounting and Arthur Andersen Consulting. Coopers and Lybrand revenue estimates are from Public Accounting Report, since the company does not disclose revenues.

attesting to the fairness of financial statements through the auditing function, they have expanded their services to include a variety of other activities, such as management consulting of various kinds, tax consulting and preparation, employee compensation and benefit studies, and various types of litigation support work. The expanded mix of services has broadened the appeal of public accounting firms by making many firms a "one-stop" source of business expertise. In 1990, almost one-half of the revenues generated by the Big Six firms arose from services other than auditing.

Several factors have fueled the addition of new services. First, the audit business, which had been the mainstay of public accounting firms and a continuing source of revenue and profit, has become an undifferentiated service in the eyes of many clients. This perception has resulted in the practice of competitive bidding, whereby the lowest bid for auditing services generally wins a proposal. While still a valued service and profit center in 1990, auditing services were no longer generating the same profit margins as existed as recently as the mid-1980s. Second, the incidence of mergers and acquisitions in the 1980s shrank the client base for larger public accounting firms. Third, public accounting firms began to recognize that their clients needed assistance in a variety of areas and that many of these areas were allied with the skill and technical competence presently available within public accounting firms.

■ PRICE WATERHOUSE

Price Waterhouse was formed in 1860 in England by two chartered accountants, Samuel Lowell Price and Edwin Waterhouse. The firm opened its first office in the United States in 1890 under the name Jones, Caesar and Company. By 1990, Price Waterhouse operated 100 offices in the United States and had a total of 400 offices in 103 countries and territories worldwide. The U.S. firm reported fiscal 1990 net revenues of $1.2 billion.

Price Waterhouse is considered by many in the public accounting industry to be the most prestigious of the Big Six firms and lists more *Fortune* 500 firms among its clients than any other firm. In fiscal 1990, the U.S. firm was the auditor for 93 of the *Fortune* 500 companies. Current major clients include such well-known companies as IBM, Exxon, USX, DuPont, W.R. Grace, Borden, Walt Disney, Hewlett-Packard, Bristol-Myers, and Shell Oil. The firm also had a sizable client base among companies with annual sales under $150 million.

Client Services

The emphasis Price Waterhouse places on delivering exceptional client service is evident in the firm's "Client Bill of Rights," which encapsulates the client credo for all Price Waterhouse employees (see Exhibit 2). This credo applies to every service provided. Exhibit 3 on page 356 lists and briefly describes the 16 prime service categories provided by Price Waterhouse.

Even though Price Waterhouse offers a wide variety of professional services, the firm in fiscal 1990 dedicated professional and financial resources to specific markets and services that offered the greatest potential for profitable growth. These included multinational corporations, the financial services industry, information technology consulting, specialized tax services, and services for rapidly growing and middle-market companies (those with annual revenues in the range from $10 million to $150 million). Special emphasis was placed on services for which business conditions created demand. These included services related to litigation consulting, reorganization and bankruptcy, and corporate finance.

EXHIBIT 2

Price Waterhouse's Client Bill of Rights

1. The Right to Professional Excellence

We will be technically proficient in all areas in which we provide advice. We will stay current on business and technical developments and seek counsel from appropriate firm professionals when in doubt about a course of action. We will keep abreast of all issues affecting our client so we can anticipate challenges and provide appropriate advice.

2. The Right to Be Served by Professionals Who Understand Our Business

We will learn all we can about our client's industry and business. We will get to know people within the client organization and outside it who have in-depth knowledge of the client's business, its culture, and its strategic objectives, and we will listen to our client to understand its needs. Being in the thick of our client's business—not on the sidelines—will allow us to identify and anticipate issues of concern to our client. While others may learn on the job, we will strive to know as much as possible about the client and its industry before we ever begin working with a client.

3. The Right to Proactive Advice and Creative Business Ideas

We will take the initiative in proposing actions to enhance our client's success, striving always to offer the innovative recommendations our client expects from its business advisers. We will demonstrate to our client that we expect to be and are qualified to be among those who are consulted about significant client events at the planning stage. We will be thought of as the "idea people." When asked for creative ways to help our client achieve its objectives, we will be the firm that says "Yes, can do. . . ."

4. The Right to Independent Viewpoints and Perspectives

We will advise our client about actions that are in its best long-term interests. Although we will keep client objectives clearly in mind as we aid in decision-making, we will not be sycophants. We will have the independence of spirit, the courage, and the confidence to discourage the client from pursuing a course of action that we believe to be ill-advised.

5. The Right to Effective Communication

We will keep our client contacts informed about the progress of our work and any issues that require their attention. Our written communication will be literate and clear, and our oral communication equally articulate. We will treat our client contacts as professional equals, extending to them and their staffs the same courtesy and respect we ourselves expect. In our communications with client executives and staff, we will demonstrate that we are well-rounded people they can relate to on levels other than the professional one; clients like to do business with people who are interesting and personable, just as we do.

6. The Right to a Wide Range of Professional Resources

We will tap the extensive resources of Price Waterhouse to provide our client with the most experienced and savvy business advice available. We will introduce our colleagues to our client contacts and, when relevant, involve them in client service planning and delivery. To promote well-coordinated services, we will ensure that all appropriate PW professionals are kept informed about services proposed and provided to a client.

7. The Right to Dependable Service

We will never miss a deadline or renege on a commitment. We will do it right the first time and complete the assignment better and faster than the client expects. We will avoid surprises about technical and reporting issues, fees, and staff turnover. When we are the best, we will let the client know; if we do not have the required depth in a particular area, we will have the confidence to direct the client elsewhere.

8. The Right to Service Anytime and Anyplace

We will always be available to our client, anytime and anyplace we are needed. That means spending more time in our client's office than in our own, being "on call" for our client at all times, and keeping in close touch with client contacts when we are not on the premises. And it means bringing the worldwide resources of the firm to bear on client issues, providing the services needed across town or across the globe.

EXHIBIT 2 *(continued)*

9. The Right to State-of-the-Art Technology

We will take advantage of the vast technological resources the firm has created to benefit PW professionals and clients. We will use internal tools to enhance the efficiency and cost-effectiveness of our services. And we will implement PW proprietary software and customize other products that will help our client attain better management information and more effective operations.

10. The Right to Value-added Service

We will always be thinking about how our client can be more successful and of ways we can help it achieve its business goals. We will make our client's concerns our concerns and put its needs ahead of our own. We will challenge ourselves and our client, asking the tough questions, not being afraid to be wrong. We will be ever vigilant in identifying additional ways we can strengthen our client's competitive edge, ways in which we can offer even more than the client expects.

A central figure in rendering client service is the "engagement partner." This person is typically the senior professional who, along with a team of professionals, is assigned to a client to deliver the services desired. Engagement partners have other responsibilities beyond providing their technical knowledge. Increasingly, these individuals are responsible for identifying new clients and uncovering opportunities to match client needs with other Price Waterhouse services. For example, in fiscal 1990, Price Waterhouse was engaged to assist a long-term client, a commercial bank, in laying the groundwork for successful management of a troubled bank it had acquired in a neighboring state. The firm helped to establish management and control

EXHIBIT 3

Price Waterhouse Services

Audit and Business Advisory Services

Assist companies by enhancing management, strengthening financial controls, and improving competitiveness. In order to accomplish these goals, Price Waterhouse takes an approach based on an in-depth study of a business, its management philosophy and goals, and the environment in which it operates.

Middle-market and Growing Companies (MMG)

Assist small and middle-market companies in all aspects of their operations. A group of specially trained business advisers provide services including tax assistance, compensation planning, audit procedures, and management training.

Employee Benefit Services

Assist companies in designing and implementing compensation and benefits programs that are both cost-effective and competitive, as well as fair. These programs include retirement plans, executive compensation programs, and employee benefit plans.

Government Services

Provide foreign, federal, state, and local governments and their respective quasi-governmental agencies with assistance in meeting their goals of reducing costs, increasing productivity, and improving services. Services include statistical and economic analyses, rate structures and strategies, and design and implementation of productivity improvement programs.

Industry Services

Monitor industry developments and participate in industry association activities in several industries in order to produce publications that explore business trends and conduct seminars and inform industry members of emerging issues.

EXHIBIT 3 (*continued*)

International Business Development Services

Assist U.S. companies with operations abroad and foreign companies with operations in the United States. Services include trade and customs consulting, tax planning, and marketing and strategic planning.

International Trade Services

Help improve the profitability and efficiency of an organization's international operations in areas that are directly related to trade at international levels. The focus lies in two areas, trade and investment development and trade information.

Inventory Services

Assist companies in managing inventory size, mix, pricing, cost, and value. Services include accounting and tax advisory and internal planning and implementation of systems.

Investment Management and Securities Operations Consulting

Work with organizations that sponsor, manage, and support securities and investment companies to provide assistance with systems development and implementation, operational efficiency evaluations, and business feasibility studies for new products and services. Also work closely with the accounting and tax services arms of PW to provide a comprehensive range of investment management services.

Management Consulting Services

Attempt to take advantage of new business technologies, implement innovative business strategies to improve operating efficiency, identify cost-effective solutions to business problems, and successfully implement changes that will solve these problems. PW operates the Technology Center to help identify and promote new technologies and develop strategies that can effectively take advantage of these technologies.

Corporate Finance Services

Assist middle-market clients in the sale of their business or the purchase of an additional business. Services include identification of buyers or acquisition candidates, financial analyses and projections, development of a negotiating strategy, private placement assistance, and acting as an agent in placing debt and/or equity securities with institutional investors.

Partnership Services

Offer experienced assistance in systems and tax accounting as well as determine the appropriateness of a Master Limited Partnership or syndication for a company and assist in developing and operating this type of partnership.

Personal Financial Services

Help executives with personal financial planning decisions and provide similar assistance to large populations of employee groups in order to help meet company objectives while offering employees financial peace of mind through financial and retirement planning, flexible benefits development, and benefits communication.

Litigation and Reorganization Consulting

Assist debtors, creditors, and other parties in Chapter 11 bankruptcy proceedings in order to successfully rehabilitate debtors and protect creditors' rights by evaluating debtor operations and developing solutions to their operating problems.

Tax Services

Attempt to minimize taxes and increase profitability by alerting clients to the tax consequences of their business decisions, informing them of legislative developments affecting their taxes, and advising them as to their best tax strategies.

Valuation Services

Determine the current value of assets, stock, and business interests for corporations and individuals for use in tax and business planning, mergers and acquisitions, financing, recapitalization, insurance, and litigation purposes.

systems, including employee training, for a multibillion-dollar portfolio of loans. In addition, the engagement partner recognized other opportunities, and Price Waterhouse was contracted to provide personal financial planning services to the senior executives of the acquired bank.

Corporate Finance Services

Price Waterhouse has provided numerous services related to the merger and acquisition (M&A) activities of its clients since the early 1900s. Early on, the firm typically became involved in the M&A process only after a client decided to purchase or sell its business or a division. According to a senior Price Waterhouse official, the M&A process can be distilled into three sequenced phases: (1) strategy, (2) execution, and (3) finalization and integration (see Exhibit 4). This official noted:

> We were often engaged to offer assistance in the execution and finalization and integration phase of the M&A process. We were rarely engaged to participate in the earlier strategy phase. Investment bankers were usually involved there, almost as a matter of tradition.

He added:

> The strategy phase is not only the starting point, but also lucrative in financial terms. In addition, it is a service that should have naturally occurred as a result of our auditing and management consulting business. Too often an engagement partner did not pursue this business, while investment bankers did.

The process of mergers and acquisitions is very complex and frequently conducted over a lengthy time period. It also often involves a great deal of personal and professional attention by the parties involved. "Deals aren't made easily," said a Price Waterhouse M&A specialist, "and companies require a significant amount of counseling not only in terms of technicalities, but in terms of strategic implications as well. A CEO wants to know and have confidence in the people giving the advice on whether to buy or sell and how best to do it."

Recognizing that the nature of corporate finance and the nuances of investment banking-related services require unique skills and abilities, particularly in the strategy phase of the M&A process, Price Waterhouse elected to recruit professionals with

EXHIBIT 4

Anatomy of the Merger and Acquisition Process

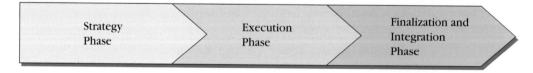

Strategy Phase	Execution Phase	Finalization and Integration Phase
• Identify objectives • Strategy development • Valuation analysis • Candidate identification • Financing strategy	• Descriptive memorandum • Strategy implementation • Alternatives evaluation • Negotiation assistance • Due diligence • Technical accounting and tax • Operations and systems evaluation	• Purchase price adjustments • Post-completion integration: operational, organizational, systems, financial • Asset disposal planning

such qualities and experience in early 1990 and to form the Corporate Finance Group, which also included accounting, tax, and consulting professionals who had experience with mergers and acquisitions. The decision to recruit corporate finance professionals, many of whom held MBA degrees with a corporate finance specialization and had extensive experience in the investment banking industry, was a departure from what other Big Six accounting firms had done. Other Big Six firms had tended to reassign accounting professionals to advance their corporate finance initiatives. According to some industry observers, these two different approaches regarding corporate finance initiatives resulted in an interesting situation in public accounting firms. One such observer commented:

> Both approaches have merit and will probably work, but the subtleties of how they will work present some fascinating professional and interpersonal dynamics. First, accounting and finance people are different in both their training and orientation. Surprisingly, few accountants have extensive formal training in finance, and few financial people are well-versed in accounting. This means that accountants in those firms that reassign them will have to learn the techniques and terminology of finance. On the other hand, firms that recruit corporate finance people will benefit quickly from the expertise and experience they bring. However, these corporate finance professionals may be looked at as outsiders and not be easily accepted into the public accounting culture. It is still the case in many public accounting firms that the non-CPA professionals often employed as management consultants are looked upon differently by their accountant colleagues.

■ INVESTMENT BANKING INDUSTRY

The movement by public accounting firms into the domain of investment banking-related services represented a significant departure from past practices. According to one industry observer,

> By moving "upstream" and becoming involved in decisions previously considered sacred territory by investment bankers, public accounting firms will have to develop or acquire new competencies. Advising on matters of capital structure, managing sensitive negotiations related to acquisitions, divestitures, and financing, assessing strategies for creating shareholder value, and a host of traditional activities upon which investment bankers have built reputations for many years will require new skills and possibly a new cultural orientation for accountants and public accounting firms. Investment banking is transaction-oriented, and investment bankers pride themselves on structuring deals. Many are effective salespeople, some view themselves as marriage brokers, and still others see their function as building relationships and becoming confidants of their clients. Some accountants will feel comfortable performing these roles and tasks, but many will not. For example, a partner with a long-term auditing client isn't likely to actively promote the notion that the client sell its business, since that would be running the risk of losing the client to the buyer's auditing firm.

Scope of Investment Banking

Simply put, an investment banker is an agent who joins buyers and sellers of money. Many investment bankers view themselves as facilitators of the flow of financial capital. Investment bankers are usually experts in financial markets and essentially provide their expertise to firms that wish to raise funds. For example, most of them have specific knowledge of potential buyers of financial securities. Since the role of investment bankers is primarily advisory in nature, building and sustaining relationships play a large part in their day-to-day activities.

Investment bankers perform several important services for their client firms. Specific services fall into three general categories:

1. *Assistance in raising capital.* Investment bankers are engaged to assist companies in raising capital to fund growth. These efforts divide into two categories: public security issues and private placements. *Public security issues* represent the most well-known investment banking function. Initial and secondary public offerings, as they are commonly known, consist of public offerings of debt or equity. Investment bankers may underwrite an issue and assume the risk of selling it in the open market. *Private placements* involve sales of new issues of debt (and occasionally equity) to a limited number of firms such as banks or insurance companies without a public offering. The issuing firm can be public or private.

2. *Merger and acquisition services.* When two firms want to merge their operations or when one firm acquires another, investment bankers are customarily asked to consult for the parties to the transaction. Their function often entails issuing opinions regarding the value of the acquired company or the fairness of the negotiated contract. Some larger investment banking firms often take a more active role and commit capital to help finance a merger or acquisition.

3. *General financial advisory services.* Investment bankers are paid for their knowledge of and access to capital markets. While they are predominantly involved directly in the capital-raising process, they may be engaged to assist in the valuation of a particular issue of securities or a company. Their advice is also sought in areas concerning the use of equity (for example, stock) and debt to fund company growth.

Investment Banking Firms

There are over 200 investment banking firms in the United States. However, industry observers typically recognize six firms as being industry leaders: Merrill Lynch, Pierce, Fenner and Smith; Lehman Brothers; Goldman Sachs; Morgan Stanley; First Boston; and Salomon Brothers. Other well-known firms are Dean Witter Reynolds; Alex Brown and Sons; Prudential Securities; and Smith Barney, Harris Upham and Company. Some firms are primarily regional. For example, Rauscher Pierce Refsnes, Inc. is prominent in the southwestern United States, William Blair in the upper Midwest, and Robinson Humphrey in the southeastern states. Even though investment banking firms provide a variety of services for their clients, they often differ in the extent to which they provide specific services. For example, in 1990, Alex Brown and Sons led the industry in initial public offerings; that is, securities issued for the first time to the public. Merrill Lynch and Goldman Sachs were industry leaders in the issuance of overall corporate debt and equity.[2] Morgan Stanley, First Boston, Lehman Brothers, and Goldman Sachs are typically viewed as leaders in the area of mergers and acquisitions. In addition, larger, national investment-banking firms tend to work with larger clients, while smaller or regional investment-banking firms work with smaller clients.

Credibility, reliability, and a history of past successes benefit established investment banking firms. For these reasons and others, established firms typically experience a high incidence of repeat business from existing clients. Nevertheless, these firms are constantly seeking new clients through referrals and missionary efforts (for example, "cold calling"). Referrals often arise from existing clients and from other

---

[2] *Institutional Investor* (February 1991).

professionals (law firms and public accounting firms), financial institutions, and private investors.

Many larger banks in the United States are also involved in some investment banking-related activities. Although these banks are prohibited from issuing new securities by the Glass-Steagall Act of 1933, some of them have circumvented this prohibition by establishing foreign subsidiaries that operate in countries that allow banks to enter the securities field.[3] Moreover, there is evidence that the regulatory prohibitions on issuing new securities are being relaxed.

■ CORPORATE FINANCE INITIATIVE AT PRICE WATERHOUSE

The corporate finance initiative at Price Waterhouse prompted an extensive recruiting effort during much of 1990. By early 1991, about 35 corporate finance professionals were working out of six Price Waterhouse offices in the United States. These offices were located in New York, Chicago, Dallas, Los Angeles, San Francisco, and Atlanta.

Client Focus

The Corporate Finance Group was to focus primarily on what Price Waterhouse considered "middle-market" companies, or those companies with annual sales revenue between $10 million and $150 million. Companies in this category could already be clients of Price Waterhouse or not currently availing themselves of Price Waterhouse services. The decision to focus on "middle-market" companies was based on the view that larger, national investment banking firms typically directed their efforts toward larger companies, many of which were *Fortune* 1000 corporations. Furthermore, statistics on merger and acquisition activity indicated that approximately 45 percent of all such transactions were undertaken by "middle-market" companies.[4] However, Price Waterhouse officials acknowledged that by targeting such companies, they would be in direct competition with smaller, regional investment banking firms.

Service Focus

The Corporate Finance Group would provide a variety of services for new and prospective Price Waterhouse clients, including merger and acquisition advisory services, private placement advisory services, and general financial advisory services. According to a presentation made by one corporate finance professional, a sampling of services that could be provided included (1) exclusive sale assignments, (2) development and implementation of acquisition strategies, (3) structuring and financing of corporate recapitalizations, and (4) advice on financial restructuring options. Exhibit 5 on page 362 details aspects of these four types of services. The mix of services provided by the Corporate Finance Group was intended to complement and expand the currently available expertise and services provided by Price Waterhouse.

Global Reach

The Corporate Finance Group would also benefit from the worldwide presence of Price Waterhouse in 103 countries and territories. This presence, involving thousands of clients, access to financing sources, and knowledge of foreign and domestic

---

[3] "Glass-Steagall Act Repeal: An Issue for 'Everybank,'" *American Banker* (July 6, 1990): 4.

[4] *Mergers & Acquisitions* (March–April, 1991): 40.

EXHIBIT 5

Representative Sampling of Service Opportunities for Corporate Finance Group

Opportunity	Services Provided by CFG

Exclusive sale assignment: Client wishes to sell all or a portion of its business.	1. Identify and evaluate financial alternatives, including
	  • selling off the entire business
	  • divestiture of operating unit(s) or significant assets
	2. Assess likely range of value for business, operating unit, or assets
	3. Identify interested buyers
	4. Prepare descriptive memorandum
	5. Evaluate proposals and negotiate with qualified buyers

Acquisition: Client believes the value of its business can be enhanced with a strategic acquisition.	1. Identify acquisition candidates 2. Perform a valuation analysis 3. Advise on bidding strategies 4. Approach target acquisition on behalf of client 5. Negotiate on behalf of client 6. Assist in financing if necessary

Recapitalization: Client wishes to realize a portion of the values of its business.	1. Identify and evaluate alternatives, including
	  • leveraged recapitalization
	  • leveraged employee stock ownership plan (ESOP)
	  • strategic alliance
	2. Assess debt capacity
	3. Identify appropriate financing sources
	4. Prepare descriptive memorandum
	5. Evaluate proposals and negotiate with lenders or investors

Financial restructuring: Client has a sound business but has inappropriate capitalization.	1. Identify and evaluate the strategic and financial alternatives to improve the client's financial strength and capital structure 2. Prepare descriptive memorandum for use in negotiations with lenders or investors

firms, affords information and technical resources that could strengthen the corporate finance initiative. A recent example involving an acquisition illustrates the benefits of Price Waterhouse's global reach:

> Learning that a major U.S. firm planned overseas acquisitions, a corporate finance specialist proposed to qualify an acquisition candidate in Western Europe. Given the mandate to act, the specialist drew on Price Waterhouse Europe's network to develop a list of targets with the right characteristics. Eventually, this search resulted in a successful offer for a company that happened to be audited by Price Waterhouse Europe.

Implementation

Field implementation of the corporate finance initiative at Price Waterhouse began in earnest in mid-1990 as the Corporate Finance Group began to take shape. According to a corporate finance specialist, "much of the first few months were devoted to making our presence and purpose known at Price Waterhouse." In this regard, corporate finance specialists often made presentations to the Price Waterhouse staff to introduce themselves and the services they could offer to present and prospective clients. Corporate finance specialists also spent time with auditing and management-consulting engagement partners to discuss opportunities for joint work on behalf of existing clients and opportunities for reaching new clients. During this period, corporate finance specialists occasionally accompanied an engagement partner on a visit to an existing client. Firms that were not Price Waterhouse clients were typically called on exclusively by corporate finance specialists. No advertising was employed. However, the Corporate Finance Group used brochures and formal presentation materials to communicate the nature and scope of its services. "These initial efforts were very useful in introducing our capabilities," said a corporate finance specialist. "However, interest in our services was dealt a blow in August [1990] by the invasion of Kuwait by Iraq and the subsequent threat of international turmoil. Companies were not disposed toward buying and selling businesses and pursuing private placements given the economic and political uncertainty during the fourth quarter of 1990."

Integration of the Corporate Finance Group

Even though potential demand for corporate finance services was negatively affected by the Persian Gulf conflict, efforts to build internal linkages within Price Waterhouse continued. A corporate finance specialist estimated that about 20 percent of the Price Waterhouse partners had embraced the Corporate Finance Group and its services by early 1991 and had actively communicated its capabilities to prospective clients. An engagement partner in the auditing area noted that this new service area was a "real plus" but added:

> Very often you have little time to describe the many services that Price Waterhouse provides. Most of a typical one-hour client meeting is spent listening to the client. If corporate finance service opportunities are not indicated by something the client says, they, like some other services, are put on a "second priority list" to be raised at a later time.

Another engagement partner, also in the auditing function, recounted an experience related to the Corporate Finance Group. He said:

> People in the CFG had been talking to my client about its business and had recommended that my client buy another company. However, our auditors had identified an underperforming division and recommended to the company president that it be sold. What started out as acquisition mindset ended up as a program for a divestiture.

A corporate finance specialist noted a missed opportunity for the Corporate Finance Group's private placement services:

> A few weeks ago our group read about a private placement by one of our blue chip clients after the placement happened. It seemed that the engagement partner was either not aware of the opportunity or did not bring it to our attention.

Some members of the Corporate Finance Group acknowledge that integration of their capabilities will take time, given the nature of their services. "What will be needed are a few large engagements," said a corporate finance specialist. "However," he added, "since acquisitions, divestitures, and private placements take months and sometimes a year or more to plan and execute, results are not immediately seen. And sometimes the effort does not produce tangible financial results if the deal fails."

Service Mix

One member of the Corporate Finance Group believed that the efforts of the group were "moderately successful" in that both external and internal relationships were being built and service proposals and engagements were being produced. No discernible pattern of service engagements had yet emerged, however.

Business conditions in early 1991 continued to indicate that corporate finance services were in demand and that these services offered significant potential for profitable growth. Given the nature of the services, exclusive sale assignments appeared to provide the greatest profit potential for Price Waterhouse, followed by private placements (including aspects of financial restructuring and recapitalization of companies). Private placements also had the potential for continuing repeat business. Acquisition assignments and engagements and general financial advisory services were next in order of profitability. However, as one engagement partner noted, "A client can buy and buy again, but it can only sell itself once."

Godiva Europe

In July 1991, Charles van der Veken, President of Godiva Europe, examined with satisfaction the financial results of Godiva Belgium for the last period, which showed an operating profit of 13 million Belgian francs. "We've come a long way," he thought to himself, remembering the financial situation he inherited just one year ago, which showed a loss of 10 million francs.[1] Over the course of the past year van der Veken had completely restructured the company. He started by firing the Marketing and Sales staff and then changed the retail distribution network by removing Godiva's representation from numerous stores. He then completely rethought the decoration and design of the remaining stores, and established precise rules of organization and functioning applicable to those stores. These changes made the Godiva-Belgium network of franchises comparable to those in the United States and Japan. For, while in all other countries Godiva stores conveyed an image of luxury and of high scale products, in Belgium, where the Godiva concept was originally conceived, this image was scarcely maintained. Fearing what he called the "boomerang effect," van der Veken had first focused on restructuring the Godiva retail network, an objective that was today on the road to realization. "It is time," thought van der Veken, "to communicate the desired image of Godiva more widely, now that we have a retail network capable of maintaining that image on the level of the Triad Countries."[2]

■ THE GODIVA EUROPE COMPANY

Godiva has its roots in Belgium, where the hand crafting of chocolates stems from a long tradition. Joseph Draps, founder of Godiva in the 1920s, took control of the family business upon the death of his father and created an assortment of prestigious chocolates for which he lacked a name. He finally chose the name "Godiva" because it had an international sound and a history, that of Lady Godiva:

> Lady Godiva is the heroine of an English legend. She was the wife of Leofric, Count of Chester in the 11th century, whom she married around 1050. Roger de Wendower (13th century) tells that Godiva implored Leofric to lower the taxes that were crushing Coventry. The Count would not consent unless his wife would walk through the town completely naked, which she did, covered only by her long hair. John Brompton (16th century) added that nobody saw her. According to a ballad from the 17th century, Godiva ordered all the inhabitants to remain at home. The only one to see her was an indiscreet Peeping Tom. Since 1678, every three years in Coventry, a Godiva Procession is held. (Grand Larousse, Vol. 5, p. 522).

Godiva was purchased in 1974 by the multinational Campbell Soup Company. Godiva International is made up of three decision centers: Godiva Europe, Godiva

---

[1] In 1991, 34 Belgian franc (bf) = $1.00 U.S.

[2] The Triad Countries include the United States, Japan, and countries in Western Europe.

This case study has been prepared by Professor Jean-Jacques Lambin, of Louvain University, Louvain-la-Neuve, Belgium, with the cooperation of Jean-Francois Buslain and Sophie Lambin. Certain names and data have been disguised, and the case cannot be used as a source of information for market research. Used with permission.

EXHIBIT 1

Campbell Soup Organizational Structure

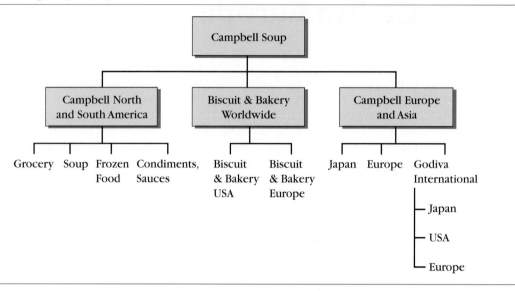

USA, and Godiva Japan, as shown in Exhibit 1. An essentially Belgian company in the beginning, Godiva has become an almost entirely triadic enterprise with a presence in the United States, Japan, and Western Europe.

Godiva Europe is headquartered in Brussels, Belgium. The company's factory, which has 3,000 tons of annual production capacity, is also situated in Brussels, from where products are exported to more than 20 countries throughout the world, including Japan. There is another production unit in the United States, which can provide about 90 percent of the needs of the U.S. market, with the remainder being imported from Belgium.

In 1990, Godiva Europe had annual sales of 926 million Belgian francs. The company is well placed to serve Belgium, its largest market. After Belgium, the principal European markets are France, Great Britain, Germany, Spain, and Portugal. Godiva USA and Godiva Japan distribute Godiva products to their respective markets and constitute the two other most important markets.

The largest part of European production volume (55 percent) is sold under the Godiva brand name, about 10 percent is sold through private labels arrangements, and another 10 percent is sold under the brand Corné Toison d'Or; 25 percent of Godiva Europe's production is sold directly to Godiva Japan and Godiva USA at a company transfer price. Thus, only 65 percent of the total sales are made in Europe under the brand name Godiva. A significant share of Godiva Europe's sales are made through more than 20 airport duty-free shops throughout the world. Those sales, free of a value-added tax (VAT), are made at the expense of local country sales, but they help to establish the international image of Godiva.[3]

Godiva Europe also owns the Corné Toison d'Or brand, which is distributed through 40 stores in Belgium, which are mostly located in the Brussels area. This brand has an image very similar to Godiva: a refined, hand-made, luxury product. The acquisition of Corné Toison d'Or was made in 1989 to fully exploit the production

---

[3] A value-added tax is a government tax levied upon the value that is added to products as they progress from raw material to consumer goods.

capacity of the Brussels plant modernized two years earlier. The original objective was to differentiate the positioning of the brand Corné Toison d'Or from Godiva, but this objective was never pursued by management. A further complication stemmed from the fact that another Corné brand, Corné Port Royal, also exists in the Belgian market with a retail network of 18 stores.

Godiva USA has a factory in Pennsylvania that serves the U.S. market. Godiva Japan, which is solely concerned with marketing, distribution, and sales of Godiva chocolates, imports the product from Belgium. The Japanese market is very important for Godiva International because of the price level, 4,000 bf per kilogram compared to 2,000 bf in the United States, and 1,000 bf in Belgium.[4]

The reference market of Godiva International consists of the Triad Nations. As a branch of Campbell Soup Company, Godiva benefits from a privileged position. Godiva International is directly attached to the Campbell Soup Company Vice President Europe-Asia without an intermediary.

■ THE WORLD CHOCOLATE MARKET

Unlike coffee or tea, chocolate lends itself to multiple preparations. It can be eaten or drunk, munched, or savored. The official journal of the European Community divides chocolate into four categories: bars of chocolate that are filled or not filled, chocolate candies or chocolates (called "pralines" in Belgium) such as Godiva's chocolates, and other chocolate preparations.

Chocolate consumption stabilized in the mid-1980s as a result of increasing raw material costs and an ensuing price rise of finished products. As depicted in Exhibit 2, the past three years have shown very good performances with worldwide consumption of confectionery chocolate (all categories included) of just over 3 million tons in 1989, or an increase of 30.7 percent compared with 1980 consumption. Overproportional consumption was observed in Japan (+54.2 percent), Italy (+102.1 percent), Australia (+45.1 percent), and the United States since 1980.

A distinction is made between industrial and chocolate pralines within the chocolate candies category. Industrial chocolates are sold in prewrapped boxes with or without brand names. The generic boxes are mostly sold through large retail chains at Christmas or Easter; brand boxes are luxurious, offer a high-quality assortment of chocolates, and emphasize the brand name on the package and through mass-media advertising. Typical of this subcategory is the brand Mon Chéri from Ferrero. The sales of generic boxes are stable in Europe, while sales of brand boxes are increasing. This suggests that consumers pay attention to brand names and to the quality image communicated by chocolate packaging and advertising.

EXHIBIT 2

Chocolate Confectionery World Consumption (In Thousands of tons)

Year	1980	1985	1986	1987	1988	1989
Tons	2,359.6	2,778.1	2,780.2	2,862.0	2,990.8	3.083.6
Index	100	118	118	121	127	131

Source: IOCCC, December 1990, p. 45.

---

[4] 1 kilogram = 2.205 pounds.

Chocolate pralines, on the other hand, designate chocolate products that are hand-made or decorated by hand. The distinctive characteristics of pralines are their delicate flavor and luxurious packaging. They are also highly perishable and fragile with regard to conservation and transport. Typically, Godiva chocolates belong to this last product category.

Chocolate Consumption per Country

The per capita consumption of chocolate varies among countries as shown in Exhibit 3. Chocolate consumption is higher in the northern part of Europe and lower in the Mediterranean region. In 1990, Switzerland had the highest per capita consumption with 9.4 kilograms per person. The lowest per capita consumption rate is observed in Spain with 1.2 kilograms per person.

Exhibit 3 also shows that the share of chocolate candies (namely, pralines) with respect to total chocolate confectionery consumption, is strongest in Belgium with 44 percent against 41 percent in Great Britain, 37 percent in France, 35 percent in Italy, and 34 percent in Switzerland. Switzerland is the largest consumer of chocolate candies, followed closely by the United Kingdom and Belgium, while the other countries are found far behind these three leaders.

In examining the level of consumption reached in countries such as Switzerland, the United Kingdom, and Belgium, it is possible to get an idea of the enormous potential that the world chocolates market holds. In fact, countries like Spain, Italy, and Japan are susceptible to one day reaching such a level of consumption roughly comparable to Switzerland, the United Kingdom, and Belgium provided effective marketing programs are implemented. Available industry statistics do not allow more precise estimates of the share of "chocolate pralines" in the category of chocolate candies.

Evolution of Consumption

Growth rates of chocolate confectionery are also very different among countries as shown in Exhibit 4. Countries experiencing the highest growth rates are Italy, Japan, the United Kingdom, and the United States. With the exception of the United Kingdom, these are the countries where the per capita consumption are the lowest. The

EXHIBIT 3

Chocolate Confectionery Consumption per Country

Country	Per Capita Consumption in Kilograms in 1989		Share of Chocolates in Confectionery Chocolate
	Chocolate Candies	Chocolate Confectionery	
Belgium	2.65	6.09	43.5%
Denmark	1.17	5.61	20.9%
France	1.69	4.59	36.8%
Spain	0.14	1.21	11.6%
Italy	0.65	1.84	35.3%
Japan	0.44	1.59	27.8%
Germany, Federal Republic	1.64	6.81	24.1%
Switzerland	3.17	9.41	33.9%
United Kingdom	2.96	7.15	41.4%
United States	1.14	4.77	23.9%

Source: IOCCC, Statistical bulletin, Brussels, December 1990. Chocolate candies: candy bars, pralines, and other chocolate products. Solid and filled bars and chocolate products.

EXHIBIT 4

Evolution of Chocolate Confectionery Consumption: Average Yearly Growth Rates, 1980–1989

Country	Consumption (Kilograms per Person)		Average Growth	
	1980	*1989*	*1980 = 100*	*Average Growth Rate*
Belgium	6.04	6.09	100.8	1.76%
Denmark	4.80	5.61	116.9	1.79%
France	3.96	4.59	115.9	1.65%
Spain	nd	1.21	nd	—
Italy	0.92	1.84	200.0	8.00%
Japan	1.09	1.59	145.9	4.28%
German Federal Republic	6.56	6.81	103.8	0.42%
Switzerland	8.44	9.41	111.5	1.22%
United Kingdom	5.48	7.15	130.5	3.00%
United States	3.69	4.77	129.3	2.89%

nd = no data.

Source: IOCCC, December 1990, p. 49.

largest consumer countries like Belgium, Germany, and Switzerland have probably reached a plateau in terms of per capita consumption.

Purchase Behavior of the Chocolate Consumer

Chocolate was imported to Europe by the Spanish at the time of the exploration of the New World. At that time, only the wealthy ate chocolate.

Today, chocolate is a mass-consumption product, accessible to everyone. Consumers are demanding and desire variety. In making chocolate a luxury product, chocolatiers have given chocolates a certain nobleness. The hand-worked character of production and refined decoration give chocolates their status. Chocolates are offered at holidays and other special occasions, and are eaten among friends in an atmosphere of warmth. They are not purchased like bars of chocolate; the behavior of the consumer of chocolate pralines is much more deliberate and involved. The higher prices of chocolate pralines with respect to the other categories of chocolate do not inhibit the consumer but limit more impulsive purchases.

The consumption of chocolate of all categories is associated with pleasure. A qualitative study of the Belgian market shows that this pleasure is associated with the ideas of refinement, taste pleasure and gift: ". . . chocolate pralines are offered as a gift while chocolate bars are purchased for self-consumption. A praline would be mainly feminine, . . . women seem to appreciate them more and pralines are described by them as refined and fine." In addition, the strong and powerful taste, a particular form, the consistency of chocolate that melts in the mouth, and the feel of the chocolate to the touch are also factors to which the consumer is sensitive. Finally, the idea of health, of a pure product devoid of chemicals, is also in the consumer's mind.

■ GODIVA CHOCOLATES IN THE WORLD

The ancestry of chocolates can be traced to the chef of the Duke of Choiseul de Plessis-Praslin, an ambassador of Louis XIII of France, when he prepared almonds browned in caramelized sugar. However, chocolates as we know them today, a filling surrounded by chocolate, were born in Belgium. It was at the end of the nineteenth century that Jean Neuhaus, son of a confectioner from Neuchatel living in Brussels, created the first chocolates that he named "pralines."

The current concern of Godiva International is to convey a similar image of Godiva chocolates across the world: the image of a luxury chocolate that is typically Belgian. In what follows, the main characteristics of consumers in each country where Godiva is distributed will be briefly presented.

Belgium

Belgium is the birthplace of chocolates and where their consumption is strongest. While there are no significant differences in the consumption rate among the different Belgian regions, differences do exist among the four main socioprofessional categories, as shown in Exhibit 5.

In 60 percent of purchases, chocolates are offered as gifts and consumers make a clear distinction between a purchase for self-consumption and for a gift. The customer prefers a package where he or she may select the assortment. However, the image of chocolate pralines has aged; chocolates have become a product more comparable to flowers than to a luxury product. The results of a brand image study conducted in the Brussels area (see Appendix A) shows that, while Godiva is strongly associated with the items "most expensive," "nicest packaging," and "most beautiful stores," it is not clearly perceived as very different from its main competitors, Neuhaus namely, on items associated with superior quality or a significant quality differential. Neuhaus and Corné, two directly competing brands, are perceived in a very similar way as shown in the perceptual map presented in Exhibit 6.

In Belgium, Godiva holds a 10 percent market share and Léonidas 43 percent. Léonidas also has a large international coverage with more than 1,500 outlets throughout the world and a production capacity of 10,000 tons, or three times that of Godiva Europe. In 1991, the size of the total Belgian market for chocolate pralines is estimated to be 3.6 billion Belgian francs (VAT included) or about 8,800 tons. This estimate is based on the data presented in Exhibit 5.

France

French chocolate is darker, dryer, and more bitter than Belgian chocolates. Belgian chocolates are, however, well-known and appreciated due to Léonidas, which introduced chocolates in France and today holds the largest market share and sells through 250 boutiques. Belgian chocolates are represented as well by Jeff de Bruges, which belongs to Neuhaus. Godiva has a share in a small niche, which is also occupied by several French chocolatiers, none of whom have national market coverage. In France, chocolates are above all regarded as a gift that is offered on certain special occasions, and their purchase is very seasonal (60 percent of all purchases are made at Christmas), which poses problems of profitability during periods of lower sales. Estimates of market size are presented in Exhibit 7.

EXHIBIT 5

The Demand for Pralines in Belgium: Average Expenditures per Household in 1988 (bf)

Regions	Belgium	Brussels	Wallonie	Flanders
	814	884	812	793
Households	Independent	White Collar	Blue Collar	Inactive
	1,239	800	567	755

Source: INS, *Enquête sur less budgets des ménages* (1988). The total population includes 3,876,549 households.

EXHIBIT 6

Brand Image Study: Chocolate Pralines in Belgium (Bubble Area = Awareness)

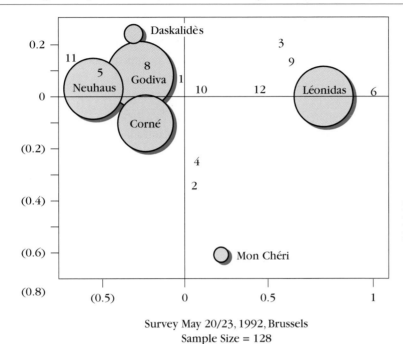

1. Queen of chocolate
2. Ideal for gift
3. For self-indulgence
4. Special occasions
5. Beautiful boutique
6. Attractive price
7. Nice packaging
8. Refined chocolate
9. Belgian chocolate
10. Taste I like best
11. Expensive chocolate
12. Worldly known brand

Survey May 20/23, 1992, Brussels
Sample Size = 128

United Kingdom

An assortment of confectionery products, in which different types of chocolate are mixed, is most appreciated in the United Kingdom. Godiva is currently being introduced to the British market and seeks to create the concept of high-quality and more refined Belgian chocolates. The change in mentality is progressing, but the British are viewed as rather conservative and the economic climate is not very favorable for a luxury product. Marks and Spencer, an upscale British retailer, is selling Belgian chocolates under the private brand name Saint Michael. The Belgian origin of the chocolates is clearly indicated in the packaging, however.

EXHIBIT 7

Estimated Consumption of Chocolates in France, 1988–1990 (In Tons)

Year	1988	1989	1990
Production	44,302	47,660	50,720
Imports (+)	9,677	10,478	11,546
Exports (−)	3,788	5,739	7,970
Total consumption	50,191	52,399	54,365
Per capita consumption	0.900 kg	0.935 kg	0.965 kg

Source: "Production des IAA," SCEES (Décembre 1991): 61 (bonbons de chocolat); Eurostat "Foreign Trade"—Categories; 1806.90.11 and 1806.90.19. The category "bonbons de chocolat" includes other products than chocolate pralines. Thus, total consumption is overestimated.

Spain and Portugal

In Spain and Portugal, chocolate pralines are a completely new concept. Godiva was the first to introduce chocolates a few years ago, and the reception was excellent. Godiva chocolates immediately acquired the image of a refined, luxury product. In Spain, Godiva is sold through the upscale department store Corte Inglese and by several franchises. Consumers' attitudes toward chocolate is very positive. Chocolates are principally offered as gifts and most often in luxurious boxes.

Germany

In Germany, a "chocolates culture" does not really exist. Germans appear to be satisfied with a classic chocolate bar and do not yet place much importance on the distinctive qualities of fine chocolates. Godiva pralines are distributed through five franchised dealers.

Other European Countries

In Holland, chocolate pralines are perceived as too expensive. In Italy and in the Nordic countries, chocolate pralines consumption is still a very marginal phenomenon.

United States

Chocolates are very popular in the United States. Chocolates are given as presents on special occasions such as birthdays, Valentine's Day, and Christmas. Chocolates are typically offered in prewrapped packages, with an interior form to house them. The output of the Godiva facility in Pennsylvania almost suffices to cover the needs of present domestic consumption. A small proportion of the Brussels plant output is exported to the United States. The Belgian factory delivers only new products or some products that cannot be produced by the Pennsylvania plant, such as the Godiva golf balls and the chocolate cartridges. In addition to 95 company-owned stores, 800 outlets carry Godiva chocolates in the United States. These outlets are generally located in upscale department stores situated in suburban shopping malls, like Lord & Taylor, Neiman Marcus, Saks Fifth Avenue, Filenes, and I Magnin.

Japan

In Japan, the Godiva chocolate is perceived foremost as European (60 percent as Belgian and 40 percent as Swiss or French). Chocolates are a prestigious and luxury gift. A large problem of seasonality exists in Japan as 75 percent of purchases take place near Valentine's Day. A unique feature of this market is that Japanese women give Japanese men chocolates on Valentine's Day. The Japanese market is a very attractive market for Godiva International and is still expanding.

The Duty-Free Market

In addition to these countries, one must also include the duty-free market, which represents a very significant market segment in terms of output. The number of duty-free stores is still increasing, and sales are closely linked to the development of passenger traffic. Godiva holds a very strong position in this market where Léonidas is not present.

Generally speaking, the annual growth potential in Europe is very different and varies from country to country. In the United States, growth varies between 5 and 10 percent annually, while in Japan growth is very strong, varying between 20 to 25 percent annually.

■ GODIVA'S MARKETING STRATEGY

Godiva pralines are produced by four means of fabrication: those that are formed in a mold, those that are hollowed then filled, those where a solid filling is coated with chocolate, and finally those that are produced entirely by hand: hand-made chocolates. Seventy percent of Godiva pralines are machine-made, and 30 percent are hand-made. However, 60 percent of the 70 percent machine-made chocolates must be decorated by hand. Hand decoration is necessary to assure the quality level and the look of the praline.

Godiva strives to find an optimal compromise between automation and hand-work, hoping both to ensure the profitability and to perpetuate the name of Godiva as a producer of hand-made luxury chocolates. However, the difference in production costs between machine-made and hand-made chocolates is considerable (hand-made chocolates can cost up to seven times more than machine-made). Charles van der Veken often had second thoughts about the wisdom of maintaining this product policy. He thought:

> Isn't the investment in making hand-made chocolates disproportional to the expectations of our customers? Do they really perceive the added value of these hand-made chocolates? Aren't these chocolates just a bit too sophisticated?

Whatever the case, the objective pursued by Godiva is to convert the European market to the quality level of the Godiva praline. The Belgium consumer is the reference point: "Shouldn't a product that has passed the test of the Belgian consumer, a fine connoisseur of chocolate and a demanding customer, be assured of success throughout the world?"

The Godiva facility in Belgium produces chocolates for the entire world, with the exception of the United States. Products exported from Belgium are identical for all countries, but sales by item are different. For example, in France the demand for drier and more bitter chocolates is stronger, while in the United Kingdom cream and white chocolates are more popular. The production capacity of the Belgian factory is not fully utilized, and there is a significant available capacity. Today, the U.S. factory still produces a slightly different and more limited assortment of chocolate pralines. These differences will progressively vanish, and the trend is toward similar production. The planning of production is particularly complex, however, because of the high seasonality of consumption combined with the emphasis on chocolate freshness.

Packaging Policy

Only packaging will distinguish one country from another in order to better meet national and local chocolate consumption habits. In the United States, the tradition is to purchase chocolates prewrapped, while in Europe and Japan the custom-made assortment dominates. What's more, in Japan, chocolates are purchased in very small quantities (given the price); thus the beauty of the packaging becomes predominant, whereas in Europe and more precisely in Belgium, the value of the gift is more often related to the judicious assortment of chocolates that was chosen. As stated by a Godiva dealer, "Customers have very precise ideas on the type of assortment they want, even for gifts, and they don't like to buy prewrapped standard assortments."

Currently, the trend in packaging at Godiva is packaging by themes called "collections." With these "collections," Godiva leaves the food industry for the luxury products sector. These hand-made creations constitute a research and development activity that ensures continuous innovation and provides renewed promotional displays in the Godiva boutiques. In these "collections," beautiful fabric boxes, hand-crafted according to the principles of "haute couture," will illustrate through the calendar Valentine's Day, Spring, Easter, Mother's Day, Christmas, etc. In Belgium, the price of such a box (1,000 bf) is exorbitant with respect to the price of the chocolates; thus these boxes serve more often for in-store decoration than for sales.

For several years, Godiva has also tried to develop tea rooms attached to Godiva boutiques where customers can eat fine pastries or ice cream. The people who stop here see these rooms as havens of peace where they can rest between purchases while shopping and buy a few chocolates or even a box of chocolates.

Pricing Policy

Making a Godiva chocolate requires an enormous amount of manual labor and the gross margins are modest (35 to 40 percent on average). Top management of Campbell Soup requires a 15 percent rate of return on capital invested for Godiva, a normal rate of return for a luxury product.

From one country to another, the price differences are great as shown in Exhibit 8. One of the main preoccupations of Godiva Europe is to standardize retail prices at the European level, in view of the unified European Union in 1993.

Previously, Godiva franchisees were held to a contract with the Godiva national and had to be supplied within that country. From 1993 on, it will no longer be possible to keep French franchisees from getting their supplies directly from the Belgian factory, which sells its chocolates at a much lower price. This is why prices must be modified. This adaptation has been started in Belgium, with a 10 percent increase in prices effective August 1, 1991. The price of one kilo of Godiva chocolates is 1,080 bf, whereas the average market price for chocolates in Belgium is 450 bf per kilo.

This price policy, however, has not been easily accepted by the market, particularly in Belgium, where the price gap between the high and the low end of the market is already very large (see Exhibit 9). Charles van der Veken observed that, in Belgium, a 10 percent price increase has generated a loss in volume of about 7 percent. He is also aware that this lost volume goes to Léonidas for the most part.

Distribution Policy

The ultimate goal that Godiva is pursuing in its distribution policy is to obtain across the world something akin to the Benetton model: boutiques with a uniform look. This "look" includes a logo with golden letters on a black background, a facade incorporating these same colors, interior fixtures in pink marble, glass counters, and so forth.

EXHIBIT 8

Price of One Kilo of Godiva Pralines (bf)

Country	Price to Franchisees	Retail Price (VAT Included)	VAT (%)
Belgium	640	1,080	6.0
France	763	1,920	18.6
Spain	640	2,145	6.0
United Kingdom	757	1,782	17.5
Italy	640	2,009	9.0
Holland	640	1,261	6.0
Germany	640	1,641	7.0
Portugal	640	2,408	16.0
United States	n.a.	2,040	—
Japan	n.a.	4,000	—

Source: Trade publications.

EXHIBIT 9

Retail Price Comparison Among Brands

Belgium		France		United Kingdom	
Brands (bf/kg)	Price	Brands (ff/kg)	Price	Brands (£/lb)	Price
Godiva	1,080	Godiva	320	Godiva	13.50
Neuhaus	980	Hédiard	640	Gérard Ronay	20.00
Corné PR	880	Fauchon	430	Valrhona	16.80
Corné TO	870	Maison ch.	390	Charbonel	14.00
Daskalidès	680	Le Notre	345	Neuhaus	12.00
Jeff de Bruges	595	Fontaine ch.	327	Léonidas	6.75
Léonidas	360	Léonidas	120	Thorton's	5.80

Source: Trade publications.

The current retail distribution problem lies in the great disparity between the Godiva boutiques in different countries, mainly in Europe and even more particularly in Belgium (Exhibit 10 shows the Godiva distribution network). Through the years the boutiques in Belgium have become less and less attractive. As a consequence, the Godiva brand image has aged. Abroad, however, Godiva benefits from an extremely prestigious image, and the boutiques merit their name. Nevertheless, Charles van der Veken fears the worst:

> If we don't react quickly, we could compromise the world brand image of Godiva. What would a Spanish tourist think in comparing the boutique of a local distributor in Brussels to the refined boutiques that he finds in Spain, although Belgium is the birthplace of chocolates?

EXHIBIT 10

The Godiva Distribution Network

Country	Company-owned Stores	Franchised Dealers	Department Stores and Others	Total Outlets
Belgium	3	54	—	57
France	1	19	—	20
Spain	—	6	18	24
United Kingdom	2	—	15	17
Italy	—	2	—	2
Holland	—	2	—	2
Germany	—	4	1	5
Portugal	—	3	7	10
Total Europe	**6**	**90**	**41**	**137**
United States	95	—	800	895
Japan	—	22	67	89

Source: Trade publications and yellow pages.

Godiva's retail distribution action plan for Belgium covers a period of 18 months. A contract has been made with the franchises in which Godiva imposes both exclusivity and design; all the boutiques must have completed renovation. Once the movement is well established in Belgium, Godiva hopes this will create a spillover effect to all of Europe, because the new boutiques will constitute a reference for the recruitment of new franchises or for spontaneous requests for renovations.

This renovation movement has already begun and every two weeks a "new" boutique is inaugurated. The renovated boutiques have been transformed so that everything is in black and gold, and the entire interior decoration is redone according to the same single standard of luxury.

Generally, consumer reactions in Belgium seem favorable, although in certain respects consumers find the stores almost too beautiful. As for the franchisees, they feel as though they have a new business, and appear to be changing some of their former bad habits. If the effects remain favorable in the medium term, van der Veken said he will increase the margin provided to franchises, which is still different from one country to the other (see Exhibit 8).

The Chairman of Godiva International, Mr. Partridge, has frequently questioned the wisdom of this costly exclusive distribution system because he believes chocolate is not really a destination purchase. In Europe, the adoption of a broader distribution system is difficult, however, because of the reluctance of consumers vis-à-vis prewrapped assortments of chocolates. Van der Veken is convinced, however, that the Godiva boutique is a key component of the Godiva image of a luxury good.

The Competitive Environment

The hand-made luxury chocolate segment is occupied by many other brands. Exhibit 11 presents a ranking of the specialty brands for Belgium, France, and the United Kingdom, in descending order of market share. The strength of the Léonidas competitive position in Europe is clearly shown by this comparison. Léonidas was created in 1910. It did for chocolate pralines what Henry Ford did for the car: a mass-consumption product sold at a low price. Their recipe is simple: a price of 360

EXHIBIT 11

Main European Competitors

Belgium		France		United Kingdom	
Brands	*Share*	*Brands*	*Share*	*Brands*	*Tons*
Léonidas	42.8%	Léonidas	62.0%	Thornton's	1,200
Godiva	10.3	Thornton's	18.0	Léonidas	300
Neuhaus	7.1	Jeff de Bruges	14.0	Godiva	40
Mondose	5.4	Godiva	3.0		
Corné TO	2.7	Le Notre	1.0		
Others	31.7	Others	2.0		

Source: Industry trade publications (market shares are calculated on sales revenues).

bf per kilogram, 8,600 square meters of industrial space, a production capacity of 10,000 tons. Léonidas is a very important competitor for Godiva. With total sales of over 2.6 billion Belgian francs, and a 32 percent operating profit margin, Léonidas has 1,500 stores worldwide, and is now expanding rapidly in the international market. The next major competitor is Neuhaus, which recently merged with Mondose and Corné Port Royal and which is also pursuing an international development strategy. The "others" include the many small confectionery-chocolatiers who nibble at the market share of the larger companies in offering fresh, original products made from pure cocoa.

However, given its broad market coverage, Charles van der Veken believes that Godiva has a significant competitive advantage due to its integration into Campbell Soup 13 years ago, which provided Godiva with an opportunity for global expansion much more quickly than its competitors. Thus, Godiva is present everywhere, and even if it often skirts a competitor in a particular market, it is rarely the same one across the world. Godiva can thus currently be considered the global leader in the luxury chocolate segment.

Only in Belgium is Godiva having difficulties making use of its competitive advantage. The volume growth has proven important everywhere, except in Belgium. According to Charles van der Veken, the market is already too saturated, and it is up to the best to make the difference.

Advertising Strategy

Today Godiva does not need to make itself known on the international level: Its brand name is already globally recognized. Its current concern, in line with the policy that has been pursued for the past several months, is to create a common advertising message for the entire world. However, this will not be an easy task as evidenced by a comparison of the situation in Belgium, the United States, and Japan. In the United States and Japan the product is relatively new and has a strong image inasmuch as there is no direct competitor. In Belgium the consumer has followed the evolution of Godiva chocolates, and the progressive commoditization of the brand. It is therefore more difficult to impress Belgians with a product that is already well-known. What's more, Belgians are in daily contact with other brands of chocolates, with which they can easily compare Godiva.

Thus, as van der Veken pointed out, Godiva finds itself faced with very different worlds. Until now, in the United States advertising was focused on prestige, luxury, and refinement, with a communication style similar to the one adopted by Cartier, Gucci, or Ferrari. These advertisements were presented in magazines well adapted to the desired positioning: gourmet, fashion, or business magazines that cater to higher-income echelons (see Exhibit 12).

In Belgium, however, this type of advertising tended only to reinforce the aged, grandmotherish image of Godiva chocolates. What's more, the gap between the "perceived image" (a food item interchangeable with others of the same type) and the "desired image" (an exceptional luxury product) was so large that spectacular results could not be expected.

A study performed by Godiva seems to show that nobody could remember these advertisements, nor the promises that were made. In Belgium, Godiva had also made use of event marketing: being represented at events at which the target population had a large chance of being present. Thus two years ago, Godiva was the sponsor of a golf competition in Belgium that held its name (Godiva European Master). Such actions are however extremely costly, and their effectiveness is difficult to measure. The total advertising budget of Godiva Europe is 31 million Belgian francs per year.

EXHIBIT 12

Typical Godiva Print Advertisement in the United States

EXHIBIT 13

The Briefing from Godiva International

1. **Current Positioning**
   - To adults who want a quality product for special moments, Godiva is an accessible luxury branded by Godiva Chocolatier and distinguished by superior craftsmanship.

2. **Consumer Benefit**
   - Whether you give Godiva or consume it yourself, you will relish its uniquely sensual pleasures: taste and presentation.

3. **Promise**
   - Using the finest ingredients and Belgian recipes for a remarkable taste experience.
   - Godiva heritage of fine chocolate making.
   - Beautifully crafted packaging.
   - Handcrafted in fine European heritage/style.
   - Created by an expert chocolatier.

4. **Psychographic Characteristics**
   - Godiva purchasers are discerning and driven by quality expectations. While they are value-oriented, they will pay a higher price if a significant quality differential exists, since they aspire to have or share the best.
   - Godiva men and women are sensual individuals, enjoying the pleasures that things of exceptional look, feel, taste, sound, and smell can offer them.

5. **Competitive Frame**
   - Gift: flowers, perfume, wine, other fine chocolates, giftables of the same price range.
   - Self-consumption: any item meant to provide a range of self-indulgences at Godiva's basic price-points.

6. **Target Audience**
   - The Godiva target covers a range of demographic characteristics:
     - Broad age range (25–54 primarily)
     - Women and men
     - Across breadth of income levels, but with reasonable to high disposable incomes.

7. **Advertising Objectives**
   - To revitalize Godiva's worldwide premium position most specifically as it pertains to the superior quality of the chocolate product.
   - To motivate our current Godiva franchise to purchase on more frequent occasions (gifting and self-consumption).
   - To motivate current purchasers of competitive chocolates and nonchocolate giftables to convert to the Godiva franchise.

8. **Message**
   - Godiva chocolates are expertly crafted to provide an unparalleled sensory experience.

9. **Tone and Manner**
   - Luxurious—Energetic—Modern—Upscale—Emotionally involving.

■ THE ADVERTISING DECISION

Aware of this problem, Godiva Europe is in the process of evaluating its advertising strategy. The following situation had to be solved: creating a common advertising message targeted at the three main markets while taking into consideration the inevitable cultural differences among countries.

Godiva USA had just sent Charles van der Veken the briefing of an international advertising campaign, which is summarized in Exhibit 13. He said that adopting this advertising style on the European market worried him to a certain degree:

> The least one can say is that differences of mentality exist between our two continents. We certainly need to wake up our old-fashioned Godiva, but we should also be careful of overly radical changes.

Reflecting with his marketing staff, van der Veken tended to define the advertising objective in the following manner.

> The objective of Godiva USA is to increase the frequency of the purchase of chocolates for gifts as well as for self consumption, whereas Belgium wants to make its brand image more youthful. Thus, the United States should adjust its advertising slightly "downward," in making the product more accessible through convivial advertising and less "plastic beauty." While Belgium should strive, jointly with other marketing efforts (redesign of boutiques, increased quality of service, creation of "collections"), to adjust its advertising slightly "upward," in affirming itself as a prestigious luxury product, only younger.

The upward adjustment for Belgium was a daring challenge. Charles van der Veken wondered if it would not be preferable to pass through a transitory period before beginning a global marketing campaign, which would take into consideration the historical and cultural context of Belgium.

Just then, Mrs. Bogaert, van der Veken's assistant, entered his office holding a fax from Godiva International:

> The campaign cannot be launched in time for Christmas; prepare as quickly as possible your advertising campaign for Belgium and contact your agencies. Meeting in five weeks in New York for the confirmation of our projects.

Charles van der Veken immediately called his Director of Marketing, informed her of the freshly arrived news, and asked her to submit for the Belgian market a campaign project based on the American model, targeted in a first step to the Belgian market, but which could be extended to the other European markets, if not to the entire world. Together they agreed on objectives in three main categories:

1. Qualitative objectives:
   - Rapidly reinforce the luxury image of Godiva
   - Make visibility a priority
2. Quantitative objectives:
   - Increase the frequency of purchase
3. Other objectives:
   - Concentrate all efforts on Belgium during several months (months of peak sales)
   - Synergy of all other methods of promotion and advertising

An additional 13 million (bf) advertising budget would be allocated to the campaign. After some thought, it seemed possible to Mr. van der Veken that a triad campaign would, on a long-term basis, be feasible in spite of cultural differences. He did not believe, however, that business generated in the other European countries would be high enough today to justify the same advertising budget as for Belgium. This became even more obvious when one considered that, in terms of media costs and for a same impact, 1 bf in Belgium is equivalent to 1.6 bf in France and 1.9 bf in the United Kingdom.

Charles van der Veken was also convinced that a European advertising campaign is useless without having first improved and reinforced the Godiva European distribution.

■ APPENDIX A: RESULTS OF THE BRAND IMAGE STUDY IN THE BRUSSELS MARKET AREA

Aided Brand Awareness (%)

Brand name	Not at All	Only by Name	By Experience	Total
Corné	24.2%	28.9%	46.9	100%
Corné Toison d'Or	31.3	25.8	43.0	100
Corné Port Royal	69.3	16.5	14.2	100
Daskalidès	54.3	26.0	19.7	100
Godiva	2.3	19.5	78.1	100
Léonidas	2.3	10.9	86.7	100
Mon Chéri	4.7	23.6	71.7	100
Neuhaus	13.3	25.0	61.7	100

Don't know any of brands Corné, Corné Toison d'Or, Corné Port Royal: 22.7%. Known "by name" or "by experience" at least one of the following brands: Corné, Corné Toison d'Or, Corné Port Royal: 77.3%

Brand Image Analysis

| Attribute | Brand Associated Most with Each Attribute (%) | | | | | | | | | |
	Corné (1)	Corné Toison d'Or (2)	Corné Port Royal (3)	Corné Total (1+2+3)	Daska-lidès	Godiva	Léoni-Das	Mon Chéri	Neu-haus	Total
The queen of chocolates	7.1%	5.5%	0.8%	(13.4%)		37.8%	27.6%	1.6%	19.7%	100%
Ideal for gift	11.0%	3.1%		(14.1)		29.1%	26.8%	10.2%	19.7%	100%
For self-indulgence	4.8%	3.2%	0.8%	(8.8)	0.8%	26.4%	48.0%	1.6%	14.4%	100%
For special occasions	6.5%	8.9%	0.8%	(16.2)	0.8%	26.8%	28.5%	8.1%	19.5%	100%
The most beautiful boutique	6.0%	9.4%		(15.4)		40.2%	12.0%	0.9%	31.6%	100%
The most attractive price	3.3%	2.5%		(5.8)	0.8%	5.7%	81.1%	4.9%	1.6%	100%
The nicest packaging	7.2%	7.2%	0.8%	(15.2)	0.8%	49.6%	6.4%	3.2%	24.8%	100%
The most refined chocolate	8.8%	7.2%	1.6%	(17.6)	0.8%	35.2%	18.4%	0.8%	27.2%	100%
Typically Belgian chocolate	6.5%	2.4%		(8.9)		30.1%	48.1%	2.4%	10.6%	100%
Taste I like best	5.6%	4.0%	1.6%	(11.2)		32.3%	37.9%	3.2%	15.3%	100%
The most expensive chocolate	6.7%	8.4%		(15.1)	2.5%	40.3%	5.9%	0.8%	35.3%	100%
Worldly known brand	4.0%	0.8%		(4.8)	0.8%	42.7%	39.5%	4.8%	7.3%	100%

Brand Preferences by Situation

For Self-consumption		For Gift	
Corné:	2.4%	Corné:	3.9%
Corné Toiuson d'Or:	4.1	Corné Toison d'Or:	3.9
Corné Port Royal:	0.8	Corné Port Royal:	0.8
Daskalidès:	—	Daskalidès:	0.8
Godiva:	24.4	Godiva:	29.1
Léonidas:	48.0	Léonidas:	27.6
Mon Chéri:	2.4	Mon Chéri:	5.5
Neuhaus:	12.2	Neuhaus:	25.2
Other:	5.7	Other:	3.2
	100%		100%

CHAPTER 8

Marketing Channel Strategy and Management

Marketing channels play an integral role in an organization's marketing strategy. Channels not only link a producer of goods to the goods' buyers, but also provide the means through which an organization implements its marketing strategy. Marketing channels determine whether the target markets sought by an organization are reached. The effectiveness of a promotional strategy is determined, in part, by the number of channel intermediaries, their geographical concentration, and their ability and willingness to perform promotion-related functions. Moreover, an organization's price strategy is influenced by the markup and discount policies of intermediaries. Finally, product strategy is affected by intermediaries' branding policies, willingness to stock a variety of offerings, and ability to augment offerings through installation or maintenance services, the extension of credit, and so forth.

To the extent that a marketing manager has alternative channels available for reaching chosen target markets, the task facing the manager is to select those channels that meet three objectives. First, of all channel options, the chosen channel should provide the best coverage of the target markets sought. This means that the channel will place the organization's offerings in the right location, in the right quantity, at the right price, and at a time when buyers wish to purchase them. Second, the channel should satisfy the buying requirements of the target markets sought. Buying requirements refer to buyers' needs for information about the offering, convenience of purchase, and services such as delivery that are incidental to purchasing. Finally, the chosen channel should maximize potential revenues returned to the organization while minimizing the costs of achieving adequate market coverage and satisfying buyer requirements. Channel profitability is determined by the profit margins earned (revenues minus costs) for each channel member and for the channel as a whole.

■ THE CHANNEL-SELECTION DECISION

Making the channel-selection decision is not so much a single act as it is a process of making various component decisions. The process of channel selection involves specifying the type, location, density, and functions of intermediaries, if any, in a marketing channel. However, before addressing these decisions, the marketing manager must conduct a thorough market analysis in order to identify the target markets that will be served by a prospective marketing channel. The target markets sought and their buying requirements form the basis for all channel decisions. In other words, the marketing manager needs answers to fundamental questions such as these: Who are potential customers? Where do they buy? When do they buy? How do they buy? What do they buy? By working backward from the ultimate buyer or user of an offering, the manager can develop a framework for specific channel decisions and can identify alternative channel designs.[1] For example, managers of Ricoh Company Ltd. studied its market, the serious (as opposed to recreational) camera user, and concluded that a change in marketing channels was necessary. The company terminated its contract with a wholesaler who sold to mass-merchandise stores and began using manufacturer's agents who sold to photo specialty stores. These stores agreed to stock and display Ricoh's full line and promote it prominently, and sales volume tripled within 18 months.[2]

Direct versus Indirect Distribution

Exhibit 8.1 illustrates common channel designs for consumer and industrial offerings. Also indicated is the number of levels in a marketing channel, which is determined by the number of intermediaries between the producer and the ultimate buyers or users. As the number of intermediaries between the producer and the ultimate buyer increases, the channel increases in length.

The first decision facing a manager is whether the organization should use intermediaries to reach target markets or contact ultimate buyers directly through its own sales forces or distribution outlets.[3] If the manager elects to use intermediaries, then the type, location, density, and number of channel levels must be determined.

Organizations usually elect to contact ultimate buyers directly rather than through intermediaries when the following conditions exist. Direct distribution is usually employed when target markets are composed of a limited number of buyers who are easily identifiable and are geographically concentrated, when personal sell-

EXHIBIT 8.1

Common Marketing Channel Designs

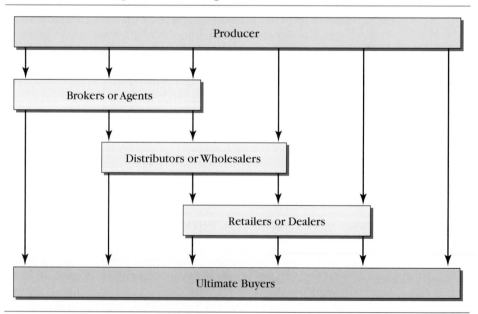

ing is a major component of the organization's communication program, when the organization has a wide variety of offerings for the target market, and when sufficient resources are available to satisfy target market requirements that would normally be handled by intermediaries (such as credit, technical assistance, delivery, and post-sale service). Direct distribution must be considered when intermediaries are not available for reaching target markets, or when intermediaries do not possess the capacity to service the requirements of target markets. For example, Procter and Gamble sells its soap and laundry detergents direct, door to door in the Philippines because there are no other alternatives in many parts of the country. Also, when Ingersoll-Rand first introduced pneumatic tools, a direct channel was used because considerable buyer education and service was necessary. As buyers became more familiar with these products, the company switched to using industrial distributors. Certain characteristics of offerings also favor direct distribution. Typically, sophisticated technical offerings such as mainframe computers, unstandardized offerings such as custom-built machinery, and offerings of high unit value are distributed directly to buyers. Finally, the overall marketing strategy might favor direct distribution. An organization might seek a certain aura of exclusivity not generated by using intermediaries, or an organization might want to emphasize the appeal of "buying direct," presumably important to certain target markets. Direct distribution may also be appropriate if the organization seeks to differentiate its offering from others distributed through intermediaries. A part of the successful differentiation strategy used by Dell Computer Corporation and Gateway 2000, Inc. is their emphasis on mail-order purchases of personal computers.[4]

Even though a variety of conditions favor direct distribution, an important caveat must be noted. The decision to market directly to ultimate buyers involves the absorption of all functions (contacting buyers, storage, delivery, and credit) typically performed by intermediaries. The marketing principle "You can eliminate intermediaries, but not their functions" is particularly relevant to the manager considering direct distribution. This point is occasionally overlooked by marketing managers when they elect to distribute directly. The costs of performing these functions can be prohibitive, depending on the organization's financial resources and the opportunity cost of diverting financial resources from other endeavors. Therefore, even though all signs favor direct distribution, the capacity of the organization to perform tasks normally assigned to intermediaries may eliminate this alternative from final consideration. A similar caveat must be noted with respect to intermediaries who consider acquiring functions typically performed by channel members above or below them in the channel (for example, a retailer who wishes to perform wholesaling functions). Recently, Southland Corporation (7-Eleven) eliminated its warehousing of merchandise in favor of using independent wholesalers. The reasons cited for this decision were that independent wholesalers could perform these functions more efficiently and at a lower cost than Southland.[5]

Channel Selection at the Retail Level

In the event that intermediaries are chosen as the means for reaching target markets, the channel-selection decision then focuses on the type and location of intermediaries at each level of the marketing channel, beginning with the retail level.

Consider the case of a manufacturer of sporting goods. If retail outlets are chosen, the question becomes, What type of retail outlet? Should hardware stores, department stores, sporting goods stores, or some combination be selected to carry the line of sporting goods? Also, where should these retail outlets be located? Should they be in urban, suburban, or rural areas, and in what parts of the country?

Type and location decisions depend on the buying requirements of the target markets and the potential profitability of the outlets to the manufacturer. If retail outlets are to play a role in providing information about the offering to potential buyers, which of the retail outlets will most actively promote the line through point-of-purchase displays, store-sponsored advertising (including cooperative advertising), and/or knowledgeable sales personnel? Which of the stores will carry a reasonable inventory to attract buyers interested in selection and variety? Which outlets carry competing or complementary products? Which outlets are conveniently located for buyers? The profitability of a retail outlet relates to the potential volume in the trade area served by the outlet, the merchandising skill of store management, and the store's competitive environment. Each of these factors must be evaluated before a decision on the type and location of retail outlets is finalized. Consideration of these factors prompted IBM and Apple Computer to broaden their distribution of personal computers beyond traditional dealers to include mass merchandisers and ware-house-like computer superstores.[6]

Next, the density of intermediaries at the retail level of distribution must be determined. *Density* refers to the number of intermediaries carrying the organization's offering in a particular geographical area. Three degrees of density at the retail level are intensive distribution, exclusive distribution, and selective distribution.

1. *Intensive distribution* at the retail level means that a manager attempts to distribute the organization's offerings through as many retail outlets as possible. More specifically, a manager may seek to gain distribution through as many outlets of a specific type (such as drugstores) as possible. In its extreme form, intensive distribution refers to gaining distribution through almost all types of retail outlets, as soft drink and candy manufacturers do.

2. *Exclusive distribution* is the opposite of intensive distribution in that typically *one* retail outlet in a geographical area carries the manufacturer's line. Usually, the geographical area constitutes the defined trade area of the retailer. Magnavox Corporation used this approach for some of its products when it utilized only 3,000 dealers among the several thousand retail outlets available. Mark Cross wallets and Regal shoes are distributed under an exclusive distribution arrangement.

   Occasionally, the exclusive-distribution strategy involves a contractual arrangement between a retailer and manufacturer that gives the retailer exclusive rights to sell a line of products or product in a defined area in return for performing specific marketing functions. A common form of an exclusive agreement is a franchise agreement. Automobile distribution is an example of exclusive distribution with a franchise agreement.

3. *Selective distribution* is between these two extremes. This strategy calls for a manufacturer to select a few retail outlets in a specific area to carry its offering. This approach is often used for marketing furniture, some brands of men's clothing, and quality women's apparel. Selective distribution weds some of the market coverage benefits of intensive distribution to the control over resale evident with the exclusive distribution strategy. For this reason, selective distribution has become increasingly popular in recent years among marketers.

The popularity of selective distribution has come about also because of a phenomenon called effective distribution. *Effective distribution* means that a limited number of outlets at the retail level account for a significant fraction of the market potential. An example of effective distribution is a situation in which a marketer of expensive men's wristwatches distributes through only 40 percent of available outlets, but these outlets account for 80 percent of the volume of the wristwatch market. Increasing the density of retail outlets to perhaps 50 percent would probably increase the percentage of potential volume to 85 percent; however, the attendant costs of this action might lead to only a marginal profit contribution at best.

The decision as to which of the three degrees of density to select rests on how buyers purchase the manufacturer's offering, the amount of control over resale desired by the manufacturer, the degree of exclusivity sought by intermediaries, and the contribution of intermediaries to the manufacturer's marketing effort. General Motors considered these factors when it announced plans to pare its franchised Oldsmobile dealerships by almost 20 percent by 2000.[7]

Intensive distribution is often chosen when the offering is purchased frequently and when buyers wish to expend minimum effort in its acquisition. Almost by definition, convenience goods such as confectionery products, personal-care products, and gasoline fall into this category. Limited-distribution strategies (exclusive and selective) are chosen when the offering requires personal selling at the point of purchase. Major appliances and industrial goods are typically distributed exclusively or selectively.

The density of retail distribution varies inversely with the amount of control over resale desired by the manufacturer. As the density of retail outlets increases, the number of intermediary levels increases, further removing the manufacturer from the ultimate consumer. A manufacturer's control over resale declines sharply in these cases. If control over resale is important, then a strategy of more limited distribution is used. Interests of intermediaries in improving their own competitive advantage also limit distribution. If the nature of the offering demands considerable investment by an intermediary in terms of service capabilities, specialized selling at the point of sale, or unique display methods, limited distribution in the retailer's trade area may be required.

Channel Selection at Other Levels of Distribution

After having determined the nature of retail distribution, the marketing manager must then specify the type, location, and density (if any) of intermediaries that will be used to reach retail outlets. These specific selection decisions closely parallel the retail network decisions made earlier.

If a second-level intermediary (wholesaler, broker, or industrial distributor) is decided on, the question becomes, What type of wholesaler? Should the manager select a specialty wholesaler, which carries a limited line of items within a product line; a general-merchandise wholesaler, which carries a wide assortment of products; a general-line wholesaler, which carries a complete assortment of items in a single retailing field; or a combination of wholesalers? Obviously, an important consideration is what types of wholesalers sell to the retail outlets desired. When Mr. Coffee decided to use supermarkets to sell its replacement coffee filters, it had to recruit food brokers to call on these retailers. Often, the decision is based on what is available. If the available wholesalers do not meet the requirements of the manufacturer in terms of satisfying retailers' requirements for delivery, inventory assortment and volume, credit, and so forth, then direct distribution to retailers becomes the only viable alternative. However, careful study of a wholesaler's role in distribution should precede any decision to bypass them, particularly in countries outside the United States. The Gillette Company's experience in Japan is a case in point.[8] Gillette attempted to sell its razors and blades through company salespeople in Japan as it does in the United States, thus eliminating wholesalers traditionally involved in marketing toiletries. Warner-Lambert Company sold its Schick razors and blades through the traditional Japanese channel involving wholesalers. The result? Gillette captured 10 percent of the Japanese razor and blade market and Schick captured 62 percent.

The location of wholesalers is determined by the location of retail outlets to the extent that geographical proximity affects logistical considerations such as transportation costs and fast delivery service. The density of wholesalers is influenced by the density of the retail network and wholesaler service capabilities. Generally, as the density of retail outlets increases, the density of wholesalers necessary to service them also increases.

Similar kinds of decisions are required for each level of distribution in a particular marketing channel; their determination will depend on the extent of market coverage sought and the availability of intermediaries. Suffice it to say that the number of levels in a marketing channel varies directly with the breadth of the market sought.

■ DUAL DISTRIBUTION

The discussion thus far has focused on the selection of a single marketing channel. However, many organizations use multiple channels simultaneously, a practice called dual distribution.[9] *Dual distribution* occurs when an organization distributes its offering through two or more different marketing channels that may or may not compete for similar buyers. For example, General Electric sells its appliances directly to house and apartment builders but uses retailers to reach consumers.

Dual distribution is adopted for a variety of reasons. If a manufacturer produces its own brand as well as a private store brand, the store brand might be distributed directly to that particular retailer, whereas the manufacturer's brand might be handled by wholesalers. Or a manufacturer may distribute directly to major large-volume retailers, whose service and volume requirements set them apart from other retailers, and may use wholesalers to reach smaller retailer outlets. Finally, geography itself may affect whether direct or indirect methods of distribution are used. The organization might use its own sales group in high-volume and geographically concentrated markets but use intermediaries elsewhere. In some instances, companies use multiple channels when a multibrand strategy is used (see Chapter 6). Hallmark sells its Hallmark brand greeting cards through its franchised Hallmark stores and select department stores, and its Ambassador brand of cards through discount and drugstore chains.

The viability of the dual-distribution approach is highly situational and will depend on the relative strengths of the manufacturer and retailers. If a manufacturer decides to distribute directly to ultimate buyers in a retailer's territory, the retailer may drop the manufacturer's line. The likelihood of this depends on the importance of the manufacturer's line to the retailer and the availability of competitive offerings. If a retailer accounts for a sufficiently large portion of the manufacturer's volume in a market, elimination of the line could have a negative effect on the manufacturer's sales volume.

■ SATISFYING INTERMEDIARY REQUIREMENTS AND TRADE RELATIONS

The role of intermediaries in channel selection has been cited several times; however, a number of specific points require elaboration. The impression given so far may be that intermediaries are relatively docile elements in a marketing channel. Nothing could be further from the truth!

Even though reference has been made to "selecting" intermediaries, selection in actual practice is a two-way street. Intermediaries often choose those suppliers with whom they wish to deal. For instance, Goodyear Tire & Rubber Company was recently selected as the exclusive supplier to Penske Auto Center, Inc.[10] This action meant that competing brands such as Uniroyal, Michelin, and BF Goodrich from

France's Groupe Michelin and Firestone from Japan's Bridgestone Corporation would no longer be sold through 860 Penske automobile service centers. Similarly, the largest soft-drink bottler in Venezuela dropped Pepsi-Cola and began bottling Coca-Cola in an overnight conversion. The result was that Pepsi-Cola lost its distribution in its sixth-largest market in the world.[11]

Intermediary Requirements

Experienced marketing managers know that they must be sensitive to possible requirements of intermediaries that must be met in order to establish profitable exchange relationships. Intermediaries are concerned with the adequacy of the manufacturer's offering in improving its product assortment for its own target markets. If the product line or individual offering is inadequate, then the intermediary must look elsewhere. Intermediaries also seek marketing support from manufacturers. For wholesalers, support often involves promotional assistance; for industrial distributors, it includes technical assistance. As noted previously, intermediaries concerned with competition usually seek a degree of exclusivity in handling the manufacturer's offering. The ability of the intermediary to provide adequate market coverage, given an exclusive agreement, will determine whether this interest can be satisfied by the manufacturer. Finally, intermediaries expect a profit margin on sales consistent with the functions they are expected to perform. In short, trade discounts, fill-rate standards (that is, the ability of the manufacturer to supply quantities requested by intermediaries), cooperative advertising and other promotional support, lead-time requirements (that is, the number of working days from order placement to receipt), and product-service exclusivity agreements each contribute to the likelihood of long-term exchange relationships. A manager who fails to recognize these facts of life often finds that the functions necessary to satisfy buyer requirements, such as sales contacts, display, adequate inventory, service, and delivery, are not being performed.

Trade Relations

Trade relations also are an important consideration in marketing channel management and strategy. Marketing managers recognize that conflicts often arise in trade relations. *Channel conflict* arises when one channel member (such as a manufacturer or an intermediary) believes another channel member is engaged in behavior that is preventing it from achieving its goals. Four sources of conflict are most common.[12] First, conflict arises when a channel member bypasses another member and sells or buys direct. When Wal-Mart elected to purchase products direct from manufacturers rather than through manufacturers' agents, these agents picketed Wal-Mart stores and placed ads in *The Wall Street Journal* critical of the company. Second, there can be conflict over how profit margins are distributed among channel members. This happened when Businessland and Compaq Computer Corporation disagreed over how price discounts were applied in the sale of Compaq's products. Compaq stopped selling to Businessland for 13 months, and sales of both companies suffered. A third source of conflict arises when manufacturers believe wholesalers or retailers are not giving their products adequate attention. For example, H. J. Heinz Company became embroiled in a conflict with supermarkets in Great Britain because the supermarkets were promoting and displaying private brands at the expense of Heinz brands. The fourth source of conflict occurs when a manufacturer engages in dual distribution, and particularly when different retailers or dealers carry the same brands. For instance, the launch of Elizabeth Taylor's Black Pearls fragrance by Elizabeth Arden was put on hold when department store chains such as May and Dillard refused to stock the item once they learned that mass merchants Sears and JCPenney would also carry the brand. Elizabeth Arden subsequently introduced the brand only through department stores.

Conflict can have destructive effects on the workings of a marketing channel. To reduce the likelihood of conflict, one member of the channel sometimes seeks to co-ordinate, direct, and support other channel members. This channel member assumes the role of a *channel captain* because of its power to influence the behavior of other channel members.

This type of power can take four forms. First, economic power arises from the ability of a firm to reward or coerce other members, given its strong financial position or customer franchise. Microsoft Corporation and Toys "R" Us have economic power. Expertness is a second source of power. For example, American Hospital Supply helps its customers—hospitals—manage order processing for hundreds of medical supplies. Identification with a particular channel member may also bestow power on a firm. For instance, retailers may compete to carry Ralph Lauren, or clothing manu-facturers may compete to be carried by Neiman-Marcus or Bloomingdale's. Finally, power can arise from the legitimate right of one channel member to dictate the be-havior of other members. This would occur under contractual arrangements (such as franchising) that allow one channel member to legally direct how another behaves.

■ CHANNEL-MODIFICATION DECISIONS

An organization's marketing channels are subject to modification, but less so than product, price, and promotion. Shifts in the geographical concentration of buyers, the inability of existing intermediaries to meet the needs of buyers, and the costs of distribution represent external reasons for modifying existing marketing channels. Sanyo Electric, Inc., eliminated many of its distributors when managers observed that 20 distributors could cover the same market that 90 had in previous years.[13] An orga-nization might initiate a channel-modification program if the product-market strategy changed with the adoption of a market development or diversification strategy. Gen-eral Motors (Saturn), Honda (Acura), Toyota (Lexus), and Nissan (Infiniti) created separate dealer networks to sell their new luxury models designed for upscale con-sumer markets. Whatever the reason for modifying an organization's marketing chan-nels, at the base of the channel-modification decision should lie the marketing manager's intent to better achieve the three channel objectives cited earlier. The approach taken in making these decisions involves an assessment of both the bene-fits and the costs of making a change.

Qualitative Consideration in Modification Decisions

The qualitative assessment of a modification decision can be based on a series of questions. These questions imply that the modification decision involves a compara-tive analysis of the existing and new channels.

1. Will the change improve the effective coverage of the target markets sought? How?

2. Will the change improve the satisfaction of buyer needs? How?

3. Which marketing functions, if any, must be absorbed in order to make the change?

4. Does the organization have the resources to perform the new functions?

5. What effect will the change have on other channel participants?

6. What will be the effect of the change on the achievement of long-range orga-nizational objectives?

Quantitative Assessment of Modification Decisions

A quantitative assessment of the modification decision considers the financial impact of the change in terms of revenues and expenses. Suppose an organization is considering replacing its wholesalers with its own distribution centers. Wholesalers receive $5 million annually from the margin on sales of the organization's offering. The organization's cost of servicing the wholesalers is $500,000 annually. Therefore, the cost of using wholesalers in this instance is the margin received by wholesalers plus the $500,000 devoted to servicing them, for a total of $5.5 million. Stated differently, the organization would save this amount if the wholesalers were eliminated.

If it eliminated the wholesalers, however, the organization would have to assume their functions, including the costs of sales to retail accounts formerly assumed by the wholesalers. Sales administration costs would be incurred also. In addition, since the wholesalers carry inventories to service retail accounts, the cost of carrying the inventory would have to be assumed, as well as the expenses of delivery and storage. Finally, since wholesalers extend credit to retailers, the cost of carrying the accounts receivable must be included.

Once the costs incurred by eliminating the wholesaler have been estimated, an evaluation of the modification decision from a financial perspective is possible. Such an evaluation is shown below with illustrative dollar values.

Cost of Wholesalers		*Cost of Distribution Centers*	
Margin to wholesalers	$5,000,000	Sales to retailers	$1,500,000
Service expense	500,000	Sales administration	250,000
Total cost	$5,500,000	Inventory cost	935,000
		Delivery and storage	1,877,000
		Accounts receivable	438,000
		Total cost	$5,000,000

Since using wholesalers costs $5.5 million and the cost of distribution centers would be $5 million, a cost perspective suggests selection of the latter option. However, the effect on revenues must be considered. This effect can be determined by first addressing the questions noted earlier and then translating market coverage, the satisfaction of buyer needs, and channel-participant response into dollar values.

NOTES

1. Louis W. Stern and Frederick D. Sturdivant, "Customer-Driven Distribution Systems", *Harvard Business Review* (July–August 1987): 34–41.

2. "Distributors: No Endangered Species," *Industry Week* (January 24, 1983): 47–52.

3. For a comprehensive review of direct versus indirect distribution, see V. Kasturi Rangun, Melvyn A. J. Menezes, and E. P. Mair, "Channel Selection for New Industrial Products: A Framework, Method, and Application," *Journal of Marketing* (July 1992): 69–82.

4. "The Computer is in the Mail (Really)," *Business Week* (January 23, 1995): 76–77.

5. "Southland Loses $39 Million after Charge for Closures," *Dallas Morning News* (February 20, 1993): C3.

6. "A Surprise Lift for Computer Retailers," *Business Week* (October 4, 1992): 63–64.

7. "GM Plans to Cut Number of Olds Dealers," *Dallas Morning News* (January 23, 1996): 6D. See also, "GM Takes Step to Overhaul Its Auto Dealership System," *The Wall Street Journal* (June 26, 1995): A3.

8. "Gillette Tries to Nick Schick in Japan," *The Wall Street Journal* (February 4, 1991): B3, B4.

9. For an extended discussion of dual distribution, see John A. Quelch, "Why Not Exploit Dual Marketing?" *Business Horizons* (January–February 1987): 52–60.

10. "Penske Auto Center Gives Goodyear Exclusive Tire Pact," *The Wall Street Journal* (October 10, 1995): B9.

11. "Pepsi Seeing Red Over Coke's Venezuela Coup," *Dallas Morning News* (August 22, 1996): D1, D10.

12. These examples of channel conflict are found in "Bloody, Bowed, Back Together," *Business Week* (March 19, 1990): 42–43; "Sales Representatives Group to Stage Protest at Wal-Mart," *Dallas Times Herald* (July 2, 1987): C2; "Heinz Struggles to Stay at the Top of the Stack," *Business Week* (March 11, 1985): 49; and "Arden Cancels Fall Launch of Liz Taylor's Fragrance," *The Wall Street Journal* (August 30, 1995): B1.

13. "Sanyo Sales Strategy Illustrates Problems of Little Distributors," *The Wall Street Journal* (September 10, 1985): 31.

Dell Computer Corporation
The Higher Education Market

Diane Jeni hung up the phone slowly. "This could be interesting," she thought to herself. Turning around, she took another look at the whiteboard in her office.

Goals for Planning Year 96/97

Revenue	$150 MM
Units	69,000

Those were the financial goals she'd been given by Matthew Roberts, Vice President of Dell's Education, State & Local Government (ESL) Business Unit. It was early 1996, and Jeni was the marketing manager responsible for the higher education portion of ESL's business. She was concerned because for the past two quarters business had seemed soft. Reflecting on the current uncertainty in the higher education market, she wondered whether this uncertainty offered a window of opportunity for Dell. Although the number of students expected to enroll in higher education institutions was projected to increase steadily over the next few years, the competitive environment was in flux. Until recently the education market, kindergarten through higher education, had been dominated by Apple Computer. But now, at least according to articles just published in *Business Week* and the *Los Angeles Times*, Apple seemed to be leaderless and in financial disarray, and the phone call she had just received led her to believe that other competitors might also be scaling back their efforts to capture the higher education market.

Glancing at her watch, Jeni realized that she was late for a meeting with other members of the Higher Education Planning Team. She hurried off to join them.

■ THE COMPANY

Dell Computer Corporation designs, manufactures, markets, services, and supports a wide range of computer systems, including desktop personal computers, notebook computers, and network servers. It also markets peripheral computer hardware and software, as well as service and support programs. According to most industry observers, Dell Computer is the world's leading direct marketer of personal computer systems.

The story of Dell Computer Corporation is the story of Michael Dell and his strategic vision. As a college freshman in 1983, Michael Dell began selling personal computer disk drive kits and related parts to personal computer (PC) enthusiasts at local meetings of PC users. Within a few months, he was selling "gray market" IBM PCs out of his dormitory room. By April 1984, Dell had dropped out of college and

This case was prepared by Professor Robert A. Peterson, The University of Texas at Austin, as a basis for class discussion and is not designed to illustrate effective or ineffective handling of an administrative situation. Certain corporate information is disguised. Consequently, the case is not useful for research purposes. Copyright © 1997 Robert A. Peterson.

EXHIBIT 1

Dell Computer Corporation's Net Sales, Fiscal Years 1991–1996ᵃ (Thousands of Dollars)

	1991	1992	1993	1994	1995	1996
Americasᵇ	$397,000	$648,000	$1,459,000	$2,037,000	$2,40 0,000	$3,474,000
Other	149,000	241,000	554,000	836,000	1,075,000	1,822,000
Total	$546,000	$889,000	$2,013,000	$2,873,000	$3,475,000	$ 5,296,000

ᵃ *Fiscal years generally run from February through January.*

ᵇ *Includes North and South America.*

Source: Annual reports of the company.

was devoting all of his energies to his burgeoning business. Operating out of a small storefront, he began to assemble and market some of the first IBM clones under the brand name PC's Limited. By 1986, PC's Limited had grown to 400 employees and reached $69.5 million in annual revenues.

In 1988, at the age of 23, Dell took his company public. By the end of January 1990, annual sales had reached $388.6 million, and Michael Dell was named *Inc.* magazine's Entrepreneur of the Year. The following year *Fortune* listed Dell Computer Corporation as one of the 100 fastest growing companies in the United States. During the next few years the company continued to expand rapidly, both in the United States and internationally. By the end of 1995, Dell Computer employed approximately 8,400 people in more than 130 countries worldwide. (See Exhibits 1 and 2 for pertinent sales and operating information.) At the beginning of 1996, Dell Computer was ranked 250th on the *Fortune* 500 list.

Oversimplifying a bit, Dell Computer is organized around three distinct customer groups: major accounts (large corporations, government agencies, and educational and medical institutions), individuals, and small and medium-sized businesses. The former are reached through Dell's Major Accounts Division, the latter two through the Dell Direct Division. As suggested by the sources of its revenues in the boxed insert, nearly two-thirds of Dell Computer's sales are derived from its major accounts. Among Dell Computer's major account customers are seven of the world's eight largest automobile manufacturers, seven of the nine largest airlines, and nine of the ten largest telecommunications companies. Dell itself is among the seven largest computer vendors in the world. Sales to consumers constitute less than 10 percent of Dell Computer's revenues.

Dell Computer Revenues (in Billions)

Customer Group	FY 1995	FY 1996
Major corporate, government, medical, and education accounts	$2.31	$3.36
Individuals, small and medium-sized businesses	1.16	1.93
Total	$3.47	$5.29

Source: 1996 Annual Report.

The Strategic Vision

According to analysts who follow the company, the success of Dell Computer Corporation can be traced to Michael Dell's strategic vision of a high-performance/low-price personal computer marketed directly to end users. Dell computers, although not designed to be the most powerful or the most technically advanced computers, were of higher-than-average quality and very reliable. Dell computers were also not

EXHIBIT 2

Dell Computer Corporation Operating Results, Fiscal Years 1991–1996[a]

| | Percentage of Net Sales | | | | | |
	1991	1992	1993	1994	1995	1996
Net sales	100.0%	100.0%	100.0%	100.0%	100.0%	100.0%
Cost of sales	66.7	68.3	77.7	84.9	78.8	79.8
Gross profit	33.3	31.7	22.3	15.1	21.2	20.2
Operating expenses						
Selling, general and administrative	21.0	20.5	13.3	14.7	12.2	11.3
Research, development, and engineering	4.1	3.7	2.1	1.7	1.9	1.8
Total operating expenses	25.1	24.2	15.4	16.4	14.1	13.1
Operating income (loss)	8.2	7.5	6.9	(1.3)	7.1	7.1
Other income (expense)	(3.2)	(1.8)	.2	—	(1.0)	.1
Income (loss) before taxes	5.0	5.7	7.1	(1.3)	6.1	7.2

[a] *Fiscal years generally run from February through January.*

Source: Annual reports of company.

designed to be the lowest cost PCs available. The key strategic concept of Michael Dell can be described as a combination of "relatively high performance" and "relatively low price" that provides exceptionally high value for buyers.

However, perhaps more important than the high-performance-to-price ratio was the manner in which Dell Computer marketed its products. Rather than marketing its computers through one of the currently existing (indirect) distribution channels—traditional dealers, mass merchandisers, value-added resellers (VARs), and so forth—or by means of a sales force, Dell Computer initially marketed its computers directly to end users by means of direct response advertising in selected computer magazines. Later it added telemarketing activities, an indirect sales force, and field sales representatives. During the first few years of its existence, all products were distributed directly from the Dell factory to the end user by UPS or Airborne Express. This type of marketing provided a single source for complete computing solutions, as well as total accountability to customers. No intermediaries, wholesalers, or retailers were used in the initial distribution channel. The industry recognized Dell as the pioneer of a unique form of direct-relationship marketing.

Interestingly enough, Michael Dell's direct marketing approach did not spring full-grown from his imagination. By age 13 he had already created a successful mail-order stamp-trading business.

As Dell Computer grew rapidly through its manufacturer–direct marketing strategy, its strategic vision evolved to include three key elements: maintaining a direct relationship with the end users of its products, developing high-quality products that are custom-configured and sold at reasonable prices, and providing industry-leading service and support.

The first key element, maintaining direct relationships with end users of its products, has always been standard practice in all distribution channels used by Dell. For example, even when Dell attempted to market its products through mass merchandisers such as CompUSA, Sam's Club, and Best Buy (a practice stopped in 1994), it required all end-user buyers to register their computers with Dell at the time of purchase. This process enabled the company to enter the new buyer into its catalog/mail-out database and immediately begin a direct relationship with the buyer.

The second key element of Dell Computer's success is its commitment to developing high-quality products that are custom-configured and sold at reasonable prices. The company prides itself on providing the highest-quality components and testing standards in the industry, and through innovative market segmentation it offers a combination of competitively priced products and promotional bundles targeting specific market segments.

The third key element of Michael Dell's strategic vision that contributed to the success of Dell Computer Corporation is the unrelenting emphasis on the customer. Since customer satisfaction is dogma at Dell Computer, industry-leading warranty packages, installation, maintenance, repair services, and user support have always been first priority. Dell Computer was the first company in the industry to offer manufacturer-direct, toll-free, 24-hour technical support service and next-day, on-site service programs that have become standard in the industry.

Distinctive Competency

The distinctive competency of Dell Computer in its early years resided in its innovative direct selling model more than anything else. Indeed, in several interviews in the 1980s, Michael Dell stressed his belief that the company's distribution channel was *the* most efficient way to market personal computers. Even the company's advertising reflected Dell's belief. For example, in the mid-1980s, company print advertisements contained a picture of a computer store with a red X drawn through it and featured the line "and you don't have to go there to buy it."

The success of the Dell selling model opened the door to literally hundreds of small PC manufacturers who found that they only needed a telephone number and/or a post-office box to enter the marketplace. Ultimately, Dell Computer's success prompted even its largest competitors to expand into the direct channel. In 1992 both IBM and Compaq began offering new PC lines through direct distribution channels. IBM created a direct sales operation in late 1992 called Ambra, and Compaq created Compaq Direct in attempts to "Dell-ize" their selling methods.

What currently keeps Dell Computer competitive in the PC market is its ability to efficiently deliver new value-added services. It is becoming more and more difficult to distinguish among personal computers on the basis of technology alone, and customers expect more value at lower prices. Therefore, Dell approaches the PC market (which has effectively become a commodity market because of the industry's adoption of open standards) with an array of custom-made products and services. These products and services clearly set the company apart from its competitors.

In addition to its direct selling model, Dell Computer Corporation possesses a second distinction that sets the company apart from its competitors. The computers it sells are "built to order" in that virtually all of its computers are assembled and shipped within three to five days of payment receipt. One implication of this built-to-order production and marketing strategy is that each buyer can have a computer that has been configured specifically to fit its exact needs (including a unique suite of preloaded software). It also means that the company has a minimal finished product inventory (and thus minimal inventory carrying costs) and can take advantage of the constantly decreasing component prices that have characterized the industry in recent years. Simultaneously, the company has minimized the risk of having too many obsolete components in inventory.

Michael Dell's strategic vision has been very successful in part because the company focuses on sophisticated buyers and users (such as those typically found in large corporations). These are not first-time buyers or users but individuals who are very knowledgeable about their computer needs and are comfortable in ordering a computer system from a catalog or over the telephone. They also tend to want higher performance systems than first-time buyers and to be less price sensitive.

Product Offering

Dell Computer's product offering consists of desktop computers, notebook computers, and network servers. With respect to desktop computers, Dell offers two product lines, the OptiPlex and the Dimension. The OptiPlex line was developed for major account customers that need advanced features, high performance, and the ability to network with other computers. OptiPlex computers use industry-standard architecture and components and support a wide range of industry-compatible operating and network systems; they are designed to be easily upgradable as new technology becomes available. At the present time, the OptiPlex line offers a three-year warranty and extensive service and support programs. In general, OptiPlex computers are slightly more expensive than Dimension computers. Major competitors are Compaq, IBM, and Hewlett-Packard.

The Dimension line of desktop computers was developed for smaller, independent users, such as small businesses and self-sufficient home users. Although designed for technologically sophisticated users, the Dimension line is intended to be a more aggressively priced computer line than the OptiPlex. As such, it competes head-to-head with Gateway. The Dimension line has a one-year warranty and is sold primarily through the Dell Direct Division.

The company also offers a notebook computer product line called the Dell Latitude line. This product line is designed for the high-end notebook customer looking for a desktop alternative or a powerful multimedia system. In addition, Dell Computer offers the PowerEdge line of network servers that can be configured for various uses. Finally, in addition to its computer products, Dell Computer offers a wide range of peripheral hardware and software products through its Dellware Catalog. This catalog, which is distributed quarterly to more than a million owners of Dell computers, offers more than 6,500 popular software and hardware add-ons.

Company Sales Organization

At the beginning of 1996, Dell Computer Corporation's worldwide operations were organized according to four geographical regions. Dell Americas focuses on the United States, Canada, and Latin America. Dell Europe focuses on Western European countries. All products sold in this region are assembled at Dell's plant in Limerick, Ireland. Dell Japan focuses only on that country; it was created to focus on what was thought to be (and has turned out to be) a major marketing opportunity. Dell Asia Pacific focuses on Pacific Rim countries (except for Japan) and countries such as Australia. In 1995 Dell opened an assembly plant in Penang, Malaysia, to service this region.

Over time, the company evolved from (1) relying solely on direct marketing to (2) utilizing direct-response ads and telemarketing to (3) employing field account teams. These teams consist of sales representatives, customer service specialists, and systems engineers that are charged with (1) developing comprehensive relationships with large businesses and institutions and (2) building repeat sales through focused customer management. In general, smaller businesses and individuals tend to purchase from Dell because of its low prices (but typically purchase only a small number of low-margin computers). Larger corporations, government agencies, and medical and educational institutions are much larger markets for large numbers of higher priced (and higher margin) computers.

The Education, State & Local Government Business Unit is one of five business units in Dell Americas. The others focus respectively on the federal government (FED), large corporations (LCA), medium-sized businesses (PAD), and individuals and

EXHIBIT 3

ESL Sales Organization

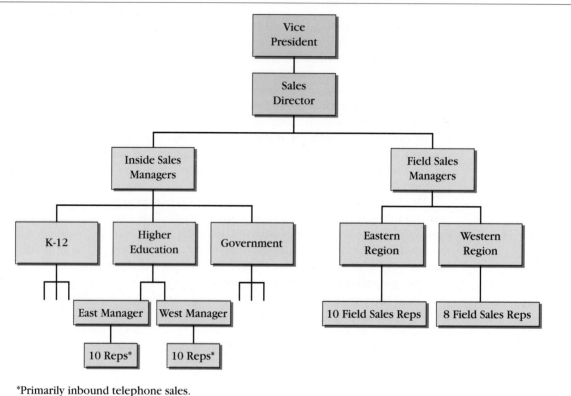

*Primarily inbound telephone sales.

Source: Company records.

small businesses (Dell Direct). ESL possesses the general sales structure set forth in Exhibit 3. Inside sales managers concentrate most of their attention on inbound telephone ordering; typically, telephone sales representatives report to a sales manager. ESL field sales managers are tasked with originating and servicing major accounts on a face-to-face basis and in turn supervise field sales representatives. In addition, the unit has a marketing program manager dedicated to the higher education market, as well as several marketing-related support positions.

Regardless of how a sales lead is generated in the United States, the typical way to purchase a Dell Computer is to telephone the company. This is so even if the buyer is a major corporate customer making a large repeat purchase and a Dell sales team and Dell field engineers currently interact with the corporation's employees. Although provisions are being made for electronic data interchanges with major accounts and a World Wide Web site on the Internet is being expanded, the telephone remains the primary means of communicating.

When a telephone call is made to Dell (1-800-BUY-DELL), a computer voice answers and directs the caller to choose one of the following options:

- Dial the extension number, if known, to reach an individual;
- Dial "2" to make an institution, education, or large business purchase;
- Dial "3" to make a small business or personal purchase;
- Dial "4" to report problems with an order;

- Dial "5" if technical support is required; or
- Stay on the line for an operator if none of these options is appropriate.

By answering a series of queries, the caller is channeled to the appropriate source for taking computer orders, responding to inquiries, or resolving problems. Dial-in options 2 and 3 correspond to Dell's two major business segments in the United States.

■ THE HIGHER EDUCATION MARKET

The higher education market in the United States consists of more than 3,600 institutions of higher learning. These institutions, though, are far from uniform and are widely scattered geographically. Less than half (about 1,500) are two-year junior colleges or community colleges. There are 92 large state-supported universities, as well as some six dozen elite private universities, that offer bachelor's degrees, master's degrees, and doctoral degrees. In addition, there are both public (500+) and private four-year colleges (1,500+). The educational missions of these various institutions differ considerably, as do enrollments; enrollments vary from 200 or so undergraduate students to more than 52,000 undergraduate and graduate students.

In academic year 1995–1996, nearly 14.4 million students enrolled in higher education institutions, and by the year 2000 about 15.5 million students should be enrolled. Slightly less than 40 percent of these students attended a junior college or community college. About 12 percent were graduate students; foreign students comprised 3 percent of all college students. Exhibit 4 shows the number of high school graduates in the United States from 1980 through 1995, together with the projected number of graduates each year through 2004. According to federal government estimates, approximately 62 percent of all high school graduates enroll in an institution

E X H I B I T   4

High School Graduates (Millions)

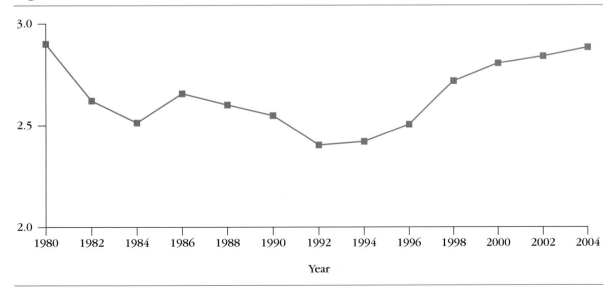

Source: Kenneth C. Green, "Campus Computing, 1995," Sixth National Survey of Desktop Computing in Higher Education, November 1995.

EXHIBIT 5

Ownership of Personal Computers

Type of Institution	1991		1993		1995	
	Students	Faculty	Students	Faculty	Students	Faculty
Public university	19%	42%	27%	50%	33%	62%
Private university	32%	54%	39%	63%	40%	68%
Public 4-year college	17%	43%	21%	45%	28%	54%
Private 4-year college	18%	43%	23%	50%	32%	58%
Community college	15%	31%	18%	39%	26%	46%

Source: Kenneth C. Green, "Campus Computing, 1995," Sixth National Survey of Desktop Computing in Higher Education, November 1995.

of higher learning. Of those who were to enroll in a college or university in the fall of 1996, nearly half were expected to have their own computer.

Of the approximately 1.4 million full-time college and university administrators, faculty, and staff members in the United States, more than 800,000 are faculty members. Many of these faculty members use computers provided by their institutions. Even so, a sizable number have purchased their own computers. Exhibit 5 shows the percentage of college and university faculty members who have their own computers. For comparison, student ownership is also provided. Ownership within both groups has steadily increased since 1991.

The higher education market for computers, estimated to be $5 to $6 billion annually, is divided into two distinct segments. One segment consists of the higher education institutions themselves, primarily departments or specific organizational units. The second segment consists of faculty, staff, and students (FSS). This segment is estimated to account for 75 to 80 percent of the total market potential. The two segments differ with respect to their computing needs and purchasing behaviors. The department segment is essentially a type of major account that requires many computers, large-scale computing capacity, and networking capabilities. Purchases are frequently made through long-term contracts. The FSS segment is very "consumer-like" in that segment members tend to be relatively price conscious and to purchase low volumes of equipment (typically single units), often by personal check or credit card.

In 1995, the higher education market accounted for about 40 percent of ESL unit sales. One analyst in the ESL unit estimated that unit sales were split 80–20 between the department and FSS segments in 1995.

Microcenters

Eighty-one college or university microcomputer centers, or "microcenters," exist in the United States. These microcenters, which are usually owned by larger colleges or universities and are frequently part of a campus bookstore, coordinate the computer purchases of the respective colleges and universities and serve as computer resellers for their faculties, staffs, and students. For the FSS segment, microcenters effectively act as full-service (sales, service) retail stores. Only individuals associated with a college or university that has a microcenter are allowed to buy a computer and software from the center at a price that has traditionally been less than that available from retail stores. What differentiates microcenters from other higher education retailing operations selling computers is that microcenters carry an inventory of computers. Apple Computer, which has the largest share of the higher education market (estimated to be in the neighborhood of 56 percent), requires a microcenter to stock inventory before it will enter into a higher education contract.

Microcenters carry the computers of companies that have specific higher education programs (e.g., Apple and Dell). They cannot sell or advertise the computers to the general public. Generally, microcenters stock computers that provide the best quality and price values. Lower quality computers are not stocked because of the higher warranty costs incurred over the lifetime of the computer.

Microcenters are essentially customer driven because they always try to find the best value for their customers. The type of computers they offer depends largely on customer demand. Microcenters want to meet the needs of their customers and as a policy will not recommend one computer over another. Their customers are primarily students because the institutions themselves do not necessarily purchase their computers through them.

Because students are microcenters' main customers, the choice of computer carried is largely dependent on price. Historically, Apple gave the highest discounts to higher education, relative to other channels, although in the past year other PC manufacturers have increased their discounts to become more competitive. Microcenters make money primarily through the sale of computers, not hardware peripherals or software.

Because of its focus on education, Apple Computer has traditionally supported campus microcenters by its generous pricing and promotional programs. In effect, Apple Computer has covered the overhead of the microcenters in return for being allowed to dominate shelf space and advertising programs. Most microcenters also offer one or two other brands of computers so that the institution and the FSS segment have a non-Macintosh choice.

In 1991, Dell Computer launched a microcenter-focused program to leverage its relationship with those colleges and universities having campus microcenters. This program represented a departure from Dell's direct selling approach and created a new retail distribution channel as part of Dell Computer's higher education strategy. At the end of 1995, Dell Computer offered its products through numerous university microcenters. Collectively, the combined enrollment of these universities was about 1.3 million students. Microcenter sales accounted for 35 to 40 percent of Dell's revenues in the higher education market in FY 1996. The rest of Dell Computer's higher education market revenues resulted from purchases made directly from educational institutions calling Dell's 1-800 number.

Although large higher education institutions tend to be characterized by decentralized computer buying (thus fragmenting the market), recent computer networking requirements have resulted in more centralized network support and maintenance functions. Smaller colleges, though, tend to be characterized by both centralized purchasing and centralized support. In general, there is little consistency across colleges and universities in terms of purchasing institutional computers.

Most Dell computers sold in the higher education market are bundled with software and peripheral products into a system. The average higher education system price for the OptiPlex line in 1995 was $2,381. This compares with an average higher education system price of $2,423 for the Dimension line and an average system price of $3,060 for the Latitude notebook line. In 1995, the average gross margin of an OptiPlex computer in the higher education market was 24 percent. The average gross margin of a Dimension computer was 15 percent in the higher education market, whereas that for a Latitude notebook was 21 percent. Exhibit 6 on page 402 contains a typical Dell advertisement for the education market.

Because of Apple Computer's financial problems, considerable uncertainty existed in the higher education marketplace. Apple was expected to restructure its campus reseller program, probably by reducing its financial support of that channel. Simultaneously, rumors circulated that Compaq Computer, the largest manufacturer

EXHIBIT 6

Typical Dell Computer Corporation Advertisement for Education Market

Source: Company records.

and marketer of personal computers, would also be entering the higher education market. The difficulty that the uncertainty presented for companies like Dell was compounded by stagnant or even declining higher education budgets, especially for infrastructure equipment such as computers.

Moreover, the PC market in general had recently been barraged by the aggressive pricing policies of mass merchandisers such as CompUSA and Best Buy. One consequence was that margins available to microcenters were under increasing pressure. To keep in touch with the microcenters that Dell used, Jeni, along with the higher education sales team, established an advisory council of microcenter managers from which it obtained periodic input. On the basis of a recent survey of its council, one ESL analyst concluded that Dell

- could do a better job providing and coordinating product information to microcenters;
- had potential pricing problems both across Dell divisions and between product lines; and
- needed improvement in its service and support activities for microcenter purchases.

Apparently, however, Dell was not the only company doing a less than satisfactory job with the microcenter business.

■ THE PHONE CALL

Jeni's phone call was from one of the more influential members of the College Reseller Association, a national group of microcenter managers that worked to promote the microcenter channel. Apparently concerned about ensuring the financial well-being and competitiveness of its members, the Association wanted to meet with each of the leading computer hardware manufacturers to discuss how it might be able to negotiate more aggressive prices or discounts for its members. The meetings were to be held over the next two weeks, and it was the Association's intention to select one vendor whose program it would endorse over the coming academic year. Although the Association was clear that its endorsement would by no means be a mandate to its members to buy from that vendor, it would certainly encourage all of its members to at least consider the endorsed vendor. This posed yet another challenge in Jeni's development of a higher education plan. Should Dell aggressively try to become the vendor of choice in this market or, given the uncertainty surrounding the future of the channel, should the company back off from this strategy?

■ THE HIGHER EDUCATION PLANNING TEAM

Dell Computer's Higher Education Planning Team was created early in 1996. Knowing that she would be asked to construct a plan to meet the financial objectives for higher education next year, Jeni pulled together a team of people within ESL to analyze the situation and provide input. This team included several sales managers, a financial analyst, a research analyst, and some of the account executives who worked with higher education customers on a daily basis. After collecting and summarizing information for nearly a month, Jeni condensed it into several reports. Some of the information is presented in Exhibits 7 through 9 (pages 404 and 405).

E X H I B I T   7

Selected Responses to a Survey of the Readership of a Higher Education Publication (Part 1)

Response	Subgroup				
	Senior Administrators	Department Directors/ Managers	Academic Officers	Faculty Members	Information Technology Administrators
Use of PC					
Research	37%	44%	65%	78%	61%
Instruction	29%	44%	70%	90%	52%
Reports	93%	94%	94%	76%	94%
Communication	91%	93%	90%	86%	95%
Access records	58%	66%	65%	46%	69%
Internet	83%	85%	84%	79%	93%
Involved in purchasing or selecting institution's computers in past 12 months	70%	70%	74%	49%	90%
Mean number of computers purchased	59	26	37	30	160
Will be involved in purchasing or selecting institution's computers in next 12 months	71%	60%	70%	42%	86%

Source: Adapted from a 1996 *Chronicle of Higher Education* report titled "Information Technology and Higher Education."

From the reports, Jeni and the planning team knew that enrollment in higher education institutions was likely to increase over the next decade because of the projected number of high school graduates. They noted that the average age of college and university students was likely to increase, as were the number and percentage of minority students. They further noted that both student and faculty ownership of computers continued to grow (even though Dell did not currently have programs specifically targeted to individuals).

From other sources the planning team knew that institutions of higher education were somewhat behind business and government in the use of personal computers, and that some faculty members were even less knowledgeable about computers than were their students (an estimated two-thirds of the freshmen projected to enter in the fall of 1996 would have received computer instruction in high school). Given the increased emphasis on the computer as a learning tool, and on the need to be computer literate in both educational and work environments, the team wondered whether the market for computers was likely to grow in higher education through the remainder of the decade. This question was again raised by one research finding that indicated that about 34 percent of colleges and universities currently recommended or required students to have their own computers (the range was from 11 percent for community colleges to 48 percent for private colleges and universities). Of those institutions recommending or requiring a computer, one in seven specified that a particular brand, configuration, or type of computer be owned.

EXHIBIT 8

Selected Responses to a Survey of the Readership of a Higher Education Publication (Part 2)

Response	Subgroup				
	Senior Administrators	Department Directors/ Managers	Academic Officers	Faculty Members	Information Technology Administrators
Desktop computer brands considered for institutional purchases					
Apple Macintosh	49%	47%	52%	51%	62%
IBM	57%	43%	47%	47%	43%
Compaq	23%	16%	20%	20%	33%
Dell	21%	18%	19%	19%	41%
Hewlett-Packard	21%	14%	17%	19%	33%
Digital	16%	9%	12%	10%	25%
Other	40%	32%	38%	31%	48%

Source: Adapted from a 1996 *Chronicle of Higher Education* report titled "Information Technology and Higher Education."

The Meeting

The meeting Jeni called was a brainstorming session. Now that everyone on the team had a chance to review the data, it was time to throw some ideas out on the table for discussion. Jeni had asked Sylvia Drum, ESL's director of marketing, to facilitate the meeting. Drum began by thanking the team for all the background work that had been done thus far, and then said she would like to open the floor to get the team's initial impressions on what the options were for addressing the higher educa-

EXHIBIT 9

Selected Responses to a Survey of the Readership of a Higher Education Publication (Part 3)

Response	Subgroup				
	Senior Administrators	Department Directors/ Managers	Academic Officers	Faculty Members	Information Technology Administrators
Source of institutional computer purchases in past 12 months[a]					
Direct from manufacturer	4%	29%	35%	20%	52%
Campus computer center	18%	25%	21%	14%	22%
Computer-only reseller	23%	16%	17%	9%	47%
Bookstore	10%	9%	8%	4%	15%
None purchased	28%	33%	31%	58%	8%
Preferred source of institutional computer purchases					
Direct from manufacturer	50%	43%	50%	42%	43%
Campus computer center	16%	28%	21%	23%	18%
Computer-only reseller	22%	21%	18%	22%	26%
Bookstore	12%	8%	11%	13%	13%

[a] *Percentages reflect the use of multiple sources.*

Source: Adapted from a 1996 *Chronicle of Higher Education* report titled "Information Technology and Higher Education."

tion market in the upcoming year. As the team members spoke, Drum documented their thoughts and comments on the whiteboard:

> Do nothing—the uncertainty in the market will cause people to look for alternatives—we're already one of the top PC companies in the country, we'll get the business—invest in other segments where there seems to be great growth opportunity, such as K–12 or state government.
>
> Go all out with the microcenters—a window of opportunity—we could own this channel with all the uncertainty in the market.
>
> Develop a student purchase program—huge market—renewable every year—but what do we sell them (Dimension or Optiplex?)—what about notebooks?
>
> Scale back on microcenters—their future is too risky—too many eggs in one basket—go after direct business from universities instead of relying on microcenters.

Interesting, thought Drum. They all seem to have very strong opinions as to the "correct answer." "OK," she said to the team, "it appears that all of you have been doing a lot of thinking about this. Now comes the hard part. We need to choose. And choosing is difficult because it means focusing on the one or two areas where we believe we can be successful next year and letting some of the other options and ideas sit on the shelf for a while. So let me give you a little more information, and then I'm going to turn the meeting back to Diane."

"First, assume that our total marcom [marketing/communications] budget for higher education is going to be $1 million next year. That needs to cover advertising, direct mail, trade shows, computer fairs, and any other marketing communications activities, including the Internet. Second, let's assume that four of the people in the field organization can be dedicated to higher education beginning October 1. Further assume that we will have the ability to hire eight additional sales reps for this business unit by the end of December. Finally, should you come up with a plan that can deliver substantial upside to the revenue target, don't be afraid to ask for additional resources—people or dollars—to attain it. Of course, you need to be reasonable.

"I know that Matthew Roberts is looking for a first-pass recommendation by the end of next week—so we don't have much time. I would like to see a preliminary recommendation by the beginning of next week, and the financials to support it." She then asked Jeni to take over, and left as the team began debating the various pros and cons of the options listed on the whiteboard.

Konark Television India

On December 1, 1990, Mr. Ashok Bhalla began to prepare for a meeting scheduled for the next week with his boss, Mr. Atul Singh. The meeting would focus on the distribution strategy for Konark Television Ltd., a medium-sized manufacturer of television sets in India. At issue was the nature of immediate actions to be taken as well as long-range planning. Bhalla was Managing Director of Konark, responsible for a variety of activities, including marketing; Singh was President.

■ THE TELEVISION INDUSTRY IN INDIA

The television industry in India started in late 1959 when the Indian Government used a UNESCO grant to build a small transmitter in New Delhi. The station soon began to broadcast short programs promoting education, health, and family planning. Daily transmissions were limited to 20 minutes. In 1965, the station began broadcasting variety and entertainment programs and expanded its programming to one hour per day. Programming increased to three hours per day in 1970 and to four hours per day by 1976, when commercials were first permitted. The number of transmission centers in the country grew slowly but steadily during this period as well.

In July 1982, the Indian government announced a special expansion plan, providing Rs. 680 million for extending the television network to cover about 70 percent of India's population. By early 1988, the 245 TV transmitters in operation were estimated to have met this goal. The government then authorized construction of 417 new transmitters, which would extend network coverage to over 80 percent of India's population. By late 1990, daily programming averaged almost 11 hours per day, and television was the most popular medium for information, entertainment, and education in India. The network itself consisted of one channel except in large metropolitan areas, where a second channel was also available. Both television channels were owned and operated by the government.

Despite the huge increase in network coverage, many in the TV industry still described the Indian government's attitude toward television as conservative. In fact, some said that it was only the pressure of TV broadcasts from neighboring Sri Lanka and Pakistan that forced India's rapid expansion. Current policy was to view the industry as a luxury industry capable of bearing heavy taxes. Thus, the government charged Indian manufacturers high import duties on foreign manufactured components that they purchased plus heavy excise duties on sets that they assembled; in addition, state governments charged consumers sales taxes that ranged from 1 percent to 17 percent. The result was that duties and taxes accounted for almost one-half of the retail price of a color TV set and about one-third of the retail price of a

This case was written by Fullbright Lecturer and Associate Professor James E. Nelson of the University of Colorado at Boulder, and Dr. Piyush K. Sinha, Associate Professor, Xavier Institute of Management, Bhubaneswar, India. The authors thank Professor Roger A. Kerin of the Edwin L. Cox School of Business, Southern Methodist University, for his helpful comments in writing this case. The case is intended for educational purposes rather than to illustrate either effective or ineffective decision making. Some data in the case are disguised. Copyright © 1991 by James E. Nelson.

EXHIBIT 1

Production of TV Sets in India (in Thousands)

| | Black and White | | | |
Year	36 cm	51 cm	Color	Total
1980	—	310	—	310
1981	—	370	—	370
1982	—	440	—	40
1983	—	570	70	640
1984	180	660	280	1,120
1985	440	1,360	690	2,490
1986	820	1,330	900	3,050
1987	1,700	1,400	1,200	4,300
1988	2,800	1,600	1,300	5,700
1989[a]	3,200	1,800	1,300	6,300

[a] *Figures for 1989 are estimated.*

black-and-white set. Retail prices of TV sets in India were estimated to be almost double the prevalent world prices.

Such high prices limited demand. The number of sets in use in 1990 was estimated to be only about 25 million. This number provided coverage to about 15 percent of the country's population, assuming five viewers per set. Increasing coverage to 80 percent of the population would require over 100 million additional TV sets, again assuming five viewers per set. This figure represented a huge latent demand, equal to several years of production at 1989 levels (see Exhibit 1). Many in the industry expected production and sales of TV sets to grow rapidly, if only prices were reduced. Presently, production exceeded demand.

■ INDIAN CONSUMERS

The population of India was estimated at approximately 850 million people in 1990. The majority lived in rural areas and small villages. The gross domestic product per capita was estimated at only $450.

In sharp contrast to the masses was the television market, which was concentrated among the affluent middle and upper social classes, variously estimated at some 12 to 25 percent of the total population. Members of this segment exhibited a distinctly urban lifestyle. They owned video cassette recorders, portable radio/cassette players, motor scooters, and compact cars. They earned MBA degrees, exercised in health spas, and traveled abroad. They lived in dual-income households, sent their children to private schools, and practiced family planning. In short, members of this segment exhibited tastes and purchasing behaviors much like their middle-class, professional counterparts in the United States and Europe.

Although there was no formal marketing research available, Ashok Bhalla thought he knew the consumer fairly well. "The typical purchase probably represents a joint decision by the husband and wife. After all, they will be spending over one month's salary for our most popular color model." That model was now priced at retail at Rs. 11,300, slightly less than retail prices of many national brands. However, a majority in the target segment probably did not perceive a price advantage for Konark. Indeed, those in the segment seemed somewhat insensitive to differentials in the range from Rs. 10,000 to Rs. 14,000, considering their TV sets to be valued possessions that added to the furnishing of their drawing rooms. Rather than price, most consumers seemed influenced by promotions and dealer activities.

■ TELEVISION MANUFACTURERS IN INDIA

Approximately 140 different companies manufactured TV sets in India in 1989. However, many produced fewer than 1,000 sets per year and could not be considered major competitors. Further, Bhalla expected that many would not survive 1990—the trend definitely was toward consolidation to 20 or 30 large firms. Most manufacturers sold in India only, although a few had begun to export sets (mostly black and white) to nearby countries.

Most competitors were private companies whose actions ultimately were evaluated by a board of directors and shareholders. Typical of this group was Videocon. The company was formed only in 1983, yet it was thought to be India's largest producer of color TV sets. A recent trade journal article had attributed Videocon's success to a strategy that combined higher dealer margins (2 percent higher than industry norms), attractive dealer incentives (Singapore trips, etc.), a reasonably good dealer network (about 200 dealers in 18 of India's 25 states), an excellent price range (from Rs. 7,000 to Rs. 18,000), and an advertising campaign that featured a popular Indian film star dressed in a Japanese kimono. Onida, the other leader in color sets, took a different approach. Its margins were slightly below industry standards; its prices were higher (Rs. 13,000 to Rs. 15,000); and its advertising strategy was the most aggressive in the industry. Many consumers seemed sold on Onida before they ever visited a retailer.

Major competitors in the black-and-white market were considered by Bhalla to be Crown, Salora, Bush, and Dyanora. These four companies distributed black-and-white sets to most major markets in the country. (Crown and Bush manufactured color sets as well.) The strengths of these competitors were considered to be high brand recognition and strong dealer networks. In addition, several Indian states had one or two brands, such as Konark and Uptron, whose local success depended greatly on tax shelters provided by state governments.

All TV sets produced by the different manufacturers could be classified into two basic sizes, 51 centimeters and 36 centimeters. The larger size was a console model, while the smaller was designed as a portable. Black-and-white sets differed little in styling. There were differences in picture quality and chassis reliability; however, these differences tended to be difficult for most consumers to distinguish and evaluate. In contrast, differences in product features were more noticeable. Black-and-white sets came with and without handles, built-in voltage regulators, built-in antennas, electronic tuners, audio and video tape sockets, and on-screen displays of channel and time. Warranties differed in terms of coverage and time period. Retail prices for black-and-white sets across India ranged from about Rs. 2,000 to Rs. 3,500, with the average thought by Bhalla to be around Rs. 2,600.

Differences among competing color sets seemed more pronounced. Styling was more distinctive, with manufacturers supplying a variety of cabinet designs, cabinet finishes, and control arrangements. Konark and a few other manufacturers had recently introduced a portable color set in hopes of stimulating demand. Quality and performance variations were again difficult for most consumers to recognize. Differences in features were substantial. Some color sets featured automatic contrast and brightness controls, on-screen displays of channel and time, sockets for video recorders and external computers, remote control devices, high-fidelity speakers, cable TV capabilities, and flat-screen picture tubes. Retail prices were estimated to range from about Rs. 7,000 (for a small-screen portable) to Rs. 19,000 (for a large-screen console), with an average around Rs. 12,000.

Advertising practices varied considerably among manufacturers. Many smaller manufacturers used only newspaper advertisements that tended to be small in size. Larger manufacturers, including Konark, also advertised in newspapers, but used quarter-page or larger advertisements. Larger manufacturers also spent substantial amounts on magazine, outdoor, and television advertising. Videocon, for example, was thought to have spent about Rs. 25 million, or about 4 percent of its sales revenue, on advertising in 1989. Onida's percentage might be as much as twice that. Most advertisements for TV sets tended to stress product features and product quality, although a few were based primarily on whimsy or fantasy. Most ads did not mention price. Perhaps 10 percent of the newspaper advertising was in the form of cooperative advertising, featuring the product prominently in the ad and listing local dealers. Manufacturers would design and place cooperative ads and pay at least 80 percent of media costs.

■ KONARK TV LTD.

Konark TV Ltd. began operations in 1973 with the objective of manufacturing and marketing small black-and-white TV sets for the Orissa state market. Orissa is located on the east coast of India, directly below the state of West Bengal and Calcutta. Early years of operation found production leveling at about 5,000 sets per year. However, in 1982 the company adopted a more aggressive strategy when it became clear that the national market for TV sets was going to grow rapidly. At the same time, the state government invested Rs. 1.5 million in Konark in order to enable it to produce color sets. Konark also began expanding its dealer network to nearby states and to more distant, large metropolitan areas. Sales revenues in 1982 were approximately Rs. 80 million.

The number of Konark models produced grew rapidly to ten, evenly divided between color and black-and-white sets. (Exhibits 2 and 3 on pages 411–414 present sales literature describing two Konark models.) Sales revenues increased as well, to Rs. 640 million for 1989, based on sales of 290,000 units. For 1990, sales revenues and unit volume were expected to increase by 25 percent and 15 percent, respectively, while gross margin was expected to remain at 20 percent of revenues. In early 1990, the state government invested another Rs. 2.5 million to strengthen Konark's equity base, despite an expectation that the company would barely break even for 1990. Employment in late 1990 was almost 700 people. Company headquarters remained in Bhubaneswar, the state capital of Orissa.

Manufacturing facilities were also located in Bhubaneswar, although some assembly was performed by three independent distributors. Assembly was done out of state to save state sales taxes and to lower the prices paid by consumers. Many Indian states charged two levels of sales taxes depending upon whether or not the set was produced within the state. The state of Maharashtra (containing Bombay), for example, charged a sales tax of 4 percent for TV sets produced within the state and 16.5 percent for sets produced outside the state. Sales taxes charged by West Bengal (Calcutta) were 6 percent and 16.5 percent, while rates in Uttar Pradesh (New Delhi) were 0 percent and 12.5 percent. State governments were indifferent as to whether assembly was performed by an independent distributor or by Konark, as long as the activity took place inside state borders. Present manufacturing capacity at Konark was around 400,000 units per year. Capacity could easily be expanded by 80 percent with the addition of a second shift.

EXHIBIT 2 *(continued)*

The New Colour TV from Konark. 'Galaxy Plus.'
Incorporating all the sophisticated features likely to be introduced in the next few years.

Superior German technology. That's what sets the new 'Galaxy Plus' apart from all other colour TVs.

One of the latest models of GRUNDIG (W. Germany), world leaders in entertainment electronics. Brought to you by Konark Television Limited.

A symbol of German perfection

The Galaxy Plus combines the best of everything: World-famous German circuitry and components. The latest international TV technology. And the most demanding standards of picture and sound quality.

All of which make it more sophisticated. More dependable.

Features that are a connoisseur's delight.

The Galaxy Plus has several advanced features which offer you an extraordinary audio-visual experience, the like of which you will probably not feel with any other make.

What the Galaxy Plus offers you that other TVs don't

Never-before picture quality

Through the world's latest Colour Transient Improvement (CTI) technology. Which reduces picture distortion. And improves colour sharpness. Giving you a crystal-clear picture and more natural colours.

Programmes from all over the world

The Galaxy Plus is capable of bringing you the best of international TV networks. Thanks to a satellite dish antenna, a unique 7-system versatility, and 99 channels with memory.

These features of the Galaxy Plus also help it play all types of Video Cassettes. Without any picture or sound distortion.

Simultaneous connection with external devices

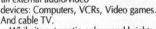

An exclusive 20 pin Euro AV socket helps you connect the Galaxy Plus simultaneously with all external audio/video devices: Computers, VCRs, Video games. And cable TV.

While its automatic colour and brightness tuning save you the bother of frequent knob-fiddling.

Catch all your favourite programmes. Always.

You can preset the Galaxy Plus to switch itself on and off for your favourite programmes. Or, for worry-free operation by your children, in your absence.

Your own musical alarm clock

An on-screen time display reminds you of an important programme or appointment. While a built-in chimer wakes you up every day. Pleasantly.

Automatic pre-selection and operation

Select specific stations or external functions, code them in the 39 + AV programme memory of the Galaxy Plus. And then, get them at the touch of a button. On the full-function Remote Control.

Handles wide voltage fluctuation

From a heart-stopping low of 140V. To a shocking high of 260V. The Galaxy Plus performs merrily through such a large range.

Richer, better TV sound

A higher audio output (8W) brings you all the beauty and power of full-bodied sound and clarity.

Saves power and money

Unlike other TVs, the Galaxy Plus uses only 60W. Besides, it also switches to the stand-by-mode automatically, when there is no TV signal for over 10 minutes.

Both features help you save precious electricity and money.

From Konark Television Limited

The futuristic Galaxy Plus is brought to you by Konark Television Limited. Through its nationwide network of over 500 sales outlets. Each of which also provide you prompt after-sales service. Should you ever need it.

The revolutionary new Galaxy Plus. See it in action at your nearest dealer. Compare it with every other make available in the local market.

And see how, feature by advanced feature, the Galaxy Plus is truly years ahead of its time. And the competition.

A marvel of German Technology

Konark Television Limited
(A Government of Orissa Enterprise)
Electronic Bhawan, Bhubaneswar 751 010. Phone: 53441 Telex: 0675-271

EXHIBIT 3

Sales Literature for a Konark Black-and-White Television

PERFECT CONTRASTS IN B/W

KONARK TV

Rohini Core (51 cm) B&W
The vertical wonder

- Double speakers with 4W output and tape-out facility
- High contrast and brightness ratios
- Better picture resolution (more than 320 lines)
- Built-in voltage stabiliser (150-280V)

EXHIBIT 3 *(continued)*

Rohini Premier
(51 cm) B&W

Elegant excitement

- Exquisitely laminated double-shutter cabinet
- Double speakers with 4W output and tape-in and tape-out facility
- High contrast and brightness ratios
- Superior picture resolution (over 320 lines)
- Built-in voltage protection (150-280V)

Rohini Deluxe
(51 cm) B&W

The classic look

- Exquisitely polished sliding-shutter cabinet
- 4W audio output with 7" speaker
- Audio tape-in and tape-out facility
- Better picture resolution (more than 320 lines)
- Built-in voltage regulator (150-280V)

(A Govt. of Orissa Enterprise)

Konark Television Ltd.
Electronics Bhavan, Rasulgarh,
Bhubaneswar 751 010.

The Konark line of TV sets was designed by engineers at Grundig, Gmbh., a German manufacturer known for quality electronic products. This technical collaboration saved Konark a great deal of effort each year in designing and developing new products. Also, the resulting product line was considered by many in the industry to be of higher quality than the lines of many competitors. Circuitry was well designed, and production engineers at the factory paid close attention to quality control. In addition, each Konark set was operated for 24 hours as a test of reliability before being shipped. The entire line reflected Konark's strategy of attempting to provide the market with a quality product at prices below those of the competition. In retail stores in Orissa, the lowest-priced black-and-white model marketed by Konark sold to consumers for about Rs. 2,200, whereas its most expensive color set sold for about Rs. 15,000. Sales of the latter model had been disappointing to date. The premium market for color sets was quite small and seemed dominated by three national manufacturers.

Konark had a well-established network of more than 500 dealers located in 12 Indian states. In nine states, Konark assembled and sold its products directly to dealers through branch offices (Exhibit 4 on page 416) operated by a Konark area manager. Each branch office also contained two or three salespersons, who were assigned specific sales territories. All together, branch offices were expected to account for about 30 percent of Konark's sales revenues and cost Konark about Rs. 10 million in fixed and variable expenses for 1990. In three states, Konark instead used the services of independent distributors to sell to dealers. The three distributors carried only Konark TV sets and earned a margin of 3 percent (based on cost) on all their activities, including assembly. All dealers and distributors were authorized to service Konark sets. The branch offices monitored all service activities.

In the state of Orissa, Konark used a large branch office to sell to approximately 250 dealers. In addition, Konark used company-owned showrooms displaying the complete line as a second channel of distribution. For these showrooms, Konark leased space at one or two locations in larger cities. The total cost of operating a showroom was estimated at about Rs. 100,000 per year. Prospective customers often preferred to visit a showroom because they could easily compare different models and talk directly to a Konark employee. However, they seldom purchased—only about 5 percent of Orissa's unit sales came from the ten showrooms in the state. Buyers preferred instead to purchase from dealers because dealers were known to bargain and sell at a discount off the list price. In contrast, Konark showrooms were under strict orders to sell all units at list price. About half of Konark's 1990 revenues would come from Orissa.

The appointment of dealers either by Konark or its distributors depended on certain conditions (Exhibit 5 on page 417). Chief among them was the dealer's possession of a suitable showroom for the display and sale of TV sets. Dealers also had to agree to sell Konark TV sets to the best of their ability, at fixed prices, and in specified market areas. Dealers were not permitted to sell sets made by other manufacturers. Dealers earned a margin on every TV set they sold, ranging from Rs. 100 (on a small black-and-white model) to Rs. 900 (on a larger color model). Bhalla estimated that the average margin for 1990 would be about Rs. 320 per set.

■ THE CRISIS

The year 1990 seemed to represent a turning point for the Indian TV industry. Unit demand for TV sets was expected to have grown only 10 percent, compared to almost 40 percent in 1989 and 1988. Industry experts attributed the slowing growth rate to a substantial hike in consumer prices. The blame was laid almost entirely on

EXHIBIT 4

Konark's Branch Office Locations and Proposed Distribution

Branch office locations
Proposed distribution

EXHIBIT 5

Terms and Conditions for Dealers of Konark Products

1. The Dealer shall canvass for, secure orders, and affect sales of Konark Television sets to the best of its ability and experience and will guarantee sale of a minimum of sets during a calendar month.

2. The Company shall arrange for proper advertisements in the said area and shall give publicity of its products through newspapers, magazines, cinema slides, or by any other media and shall indicate, wherever feasible, the Dealer's name as its Selling Agent. The cost of such advertisements may be shared by the Company and the Dealer as may be mutually agreed to.

3. The appointment shall be confirmed after 3 months and initially be in force for a period of 1 year and can be renewed every year by mutual consent.

4. The Company reserves the right to evaluate the performance of a Dealer.

5. This appointment may be terminated with a notice of 1 month on either side.

6. The Company shall deliver the Konark Television sets to the Dealer at the price agreed upon on cash payment at the factory at Bhubaneswar. On such delivery, the title to the goods will pass to the Dealer and it will be the responsibility of the Dealer to transport the sets to [its] place at [its] cost and expenses.

7. The Company may, however, at its discretion allow a credit of 30 (thirty) days subject to the Dealer furnishing a Bank Guarantee or letter of credit or security deposit toward the price of Konark Television sets to be lifted by the Dealer at any time.

8. The Company shall not be responsible for any damage or defect occurring to the sets after delivery of the same to the Dealer or during transit.

9. The Dealer shall undertake to sell the sets to customers at prices fixed by the Company for different models. Dealer margins will be added to wholesale prices while fixing the customer's price of the television sets.

10. The Dealer will not deal with similar products of any other company so long as its appointment with Konark Television continues.

11. The Dealer shall not encroach into areas allocated to any other Dealer.

12. Any dispute or difference arising from or related to the appointment of Dealership shall be settled mutually and, failing amicable settlement, shall be settled by an Arbitrator to be appointed by the Chairman of the Company, whose decision shall be final and binding upon the parties. The place of arbitration shall be within the State of Orissa, and the Court in Bhubaneswar (Orissa) only shall have jurisdiction to entertain any application, suit, or claim arising out of the appointment. All disputes shall be deemed to have arisen within the jurisdiction of the Court of Bhubaneswar.

13. Essential requirements to be fulfilled before getting a Dealership.

    a. The Dealer must have a good showroom for display and sale of television sets.

    b. The Dealer should have sufficient experience in dealing with electronics products (consumer goods).

increases in import duties, excise taxes, and sales taxes, plus devaluation of the rupee—despite election-year promises by government officials to offer TV sets at affordable prices! In addition, Konark was about to be affected by the Orissa state government's decision to revoke the company's sales tax exemption beginning January 1, 1991. "Right now we are the clear choice, as Konark is the cheapest brand with superior quality. But with the withdrawal of the exemption, we will be in the same price range as the 'big boys' and it will be a real run for the money to sell our brand," remarked Ashok Bhalla.

Bhalla was also concerned about some dealer activities that he thought were damaging to Konark. He knew that many dealers played with the assigned margin and offered the same Konark product at differing prices to different customers. Or, equally damaging, different dealers sometimes quoted different prices for the same product to a single customer. Some dealers recently had gone so far as to buy large quantities of TV sets from Konark and sell them to unauthorized dealers in Bhubaneswar or in neighboring districts. This problem was particularly vexing because the offending dealers—while few in number—often were quite large and important to Konark's overall performance. Perhaps as much as 40 percent of Konark's sales revenues came from "problem" dealers.

Early in 1990, Bhalla thought that an increase in the margins that Konark allowed its dealers was all that was needed to solve the problem. However, a modest change in dealer compensation had resulted in several national competitors raising their dealer margins even higher—without an increase in their retail prices. The result was that prices of Konark's models became even closer to those of national competitors and Konark's decline in market share actually steepened. By late 1990, Konark's unit share of the Orissa market had fallen from 80 percent to just over 60 percent. "Unless something is done soon," Bhalla thought, "we'll soon be below 50 percent."

■ THE DECISION

Some immediate actions were needed to improve dealer relations and stimulate greater sales activity. An example was Konark's quarterly "Incentive Scheme," which had begun in April 1989. The program was a rebate arrangement based on points earned for a dealer's purchases of Konark TV sets. Reaction was lukewarm when the program was first announced. However, a revision in August 1989 greatly increased participation. Other actions yet to be formulated could be announced at a dealers' conference that Bhalla had scheduled for next month.

All such actions would have to be consistent with Konark's long-term distribution strategy. The problem was that this strategy had not yet been formulated. Bhalla saw filling this void as his most pressing responsibility, as well as of great interest to Atul Singh. Bhalla hoped to have major aspects of a distribution strategy ready for discussion at next week's meeting. Elements of the strategy would include recommendations on channel structure (branch offices or independent distributors, company showrooms or independent dealers) in existing markets as well as in markets identified for expansion. The latter markets included Bombay, Jaipur, and Trivandrum, areas that contained some 2 million consumers in the target segment. Most importantly, the strategy would have to address actions to combat the loss of the sales tax exemption in Orissa.

Goodyear Tire and Rubber Company

In early 1992, Goodyear Tire and Rubber Company executives were reconsidering a proposal made by Sears, Roebuck and Company. Sears management had approached Goodyear about selling the company's popular Eagle brand tire in 1989. The proposal was declined. At the time, Goodyear's top management believed that such an action would undermine the tire sales of company-owned Goodyear Auto Service Centers and franchised Goodyear Tire Dealers, which were the principal retail sources for Goodyear brand tires. However, following a $38 million loss in 1990 and a change in Goodyear top management in 1991, the Sears proposal resurfaced for consideration.

Two factors contributed to the renewed interest in the Sears proposal.[1] First, between 1987 and 1991, Goodyear brand tires recorded a 3.2 percent decline in market share for passenger car replacement tires in the United States. This share decline represented a loss of about 4.9 million tire units. It was believed that the growth of warehouse membership club stores and discount tire retail claims coupled with multibranding among mass merchandisers contributed to the market share erosion (see Exhibit 1 on page 420). Second, it was believed that nearly 2 million worn-out Goodyear brand tires were being replaced annually at some 850 Sears Auto Centers in the United States. According to a Goodyear executive, the failure to repurchase Goodyear brand tires happened by default "because the remarkable loyalty of Sears customers led them to buy the best tire available from those offered by Sears," which did not include Goodyear brand tires.

The Sears proposal raised several strategic considerations for Goodyear. First, as a matter of distribution policy, Goodyear had not sold the Goodyear tire brand through a mass merchandiser since the 1920s, when it sold tires through Sears. A decision to sell Goodyear brand passenger car tires again through Sears would represent a significant change in distribution policy and could create conflict with its franchised dealers. Second, if the Sears proposal was accepted, several product policy questions loomed. Specifically, should the arrangement with Sears include (1) only the Goodyear Eagle brand or (2) all of its Goodyear brands? Relatedly, should Goodyear allow Sears to carry one or more brands exclusively and have its own dealers carry certain brands on an exclusive basis? Goodyear presently has 12 brands of passenger and light-truck tires sold under the Goodyear name ranging from lower-priced tire brands to a very expensive special high-speed tire for a Corvette that bears the Goodyear name.

---

[1] Modern Tire Dealer, "Newsfocus," March 1992, p. 13.

This case was prepared by Professor Roger A. Kerin, of Edwin L. Cox School of Business, Southern Methodist University, as a basis for class discussion and is not designed to illustrate effective or ineffective handling of an administrative situation. The case is based on published sources. The author wishes to thank Professor Arthur A. Thompson, Jr., of the University of Alabama, for kindly granting permission to extract information from his industry note, "Competition in the World Tire Industry, 1992," for use in this case, the Goodyear Tire and Rubber Company for comments on a previous draft of the case and permission to reproduce its advertising copy, and Michelin Tire Corporation for permission to reproduce its advertising copy. Copyright © 1995 by Roger A. Kerin. No part of this case may be reproduced without written permission of the copyright holder.

EXHIBIT 1

U.S. Market Share of Replacement Tire Sales by Type of Retail Outlet, 1982 and 1992

Type of Retail Outlet	1982	1992*
Traditional multibrand independent dealers	44%	44%
Discount multibrand independent dealers	7	15
Chain stores, department stores	20	14
Tire company stores	10	9
Service stations	11	8
Warehouse clubs	—	6
Other	8	4
	100%	100%

Estimate.

Source: Goodyear Tire and Rubber Company.

■ THE TIRE INDUSTRY

The tire industry is global in scope, and competitors originate, produce, and market their products worldwide.[2] World tire production in 1991 was approximately 850 million tires, of which 29 percent were produced in North America, 28 percent in Asia, and 23 percent in Western Europe. Ten tire manufacturers account for 75 percent of worldwide production. Groupe Michelin, with headquarters in France, is the world's largest producer and markets the Michelin, Uniroyal, and BF Goodrich brands. Goodyear is the second largest producer, with Goodyear, Kelly-Springfield, Lee, and Douglas being its most well-known brands. Bridgestone Corporation, a Japanese firm, is the third largest tire producer. Its major brands are Bridgestone and Firestone. These three firms account for almost 60 percent of all tires sold worldwide.

The Original Equipment Tire Market

The tire industry divides into two end-use markets: (1) the original equipment tire market and (2) the replacement tire market. Original equipment tires are sold by tire manufacturers directly to automobile and truck manufacturers. Original equipment tires represent 25 to 30 percent of tire unit production volume each year. Goodyear is the perennial market share leader for original equipment tires capturing 38 percent of this segment in 1991. Exhibit 2 shows the original equipment tire market shares for major tire suppliers.

Demand for original equipment tires is derived; that is, tire volume is directly related to automobile and truck production. Overall original equipment tire demand is highly price inelastic given the derived demand situation. However, the price elasticity of demand for individual tire manufacturers (brands) was considered highly price elastic, since car and truck manufacturers could easily switch to a competitor's brands. Accordingly, price competition among tire manufacturers was fierce and motor vehicle manufacturers commonly relied upon two sources of tires. For example, General Motors split its tire purchases among Goodyear, Uniroyal/Goodrich, General Tire, Michelin, and Firestone brands in the early 1990s. Even though the original

[2] Portions of the tire industry overview are based on "Competition in the World Tire Industry, 1992," in Arthur A. Thompson, Jr., and A. J. Strickland III, *Strategic Management: Concepts & Cases*, 7th ed. (Homewood, IL, 1993), pp. 581–614.

EXHIBIT 2

Manufacturer Brand U.S. Market Share for Original Equipment Passenger Car Tires

Original Equipment (OE) Buyer	Tire Manufacturer (Brand)						
	Goodyear	Firestone	Michelin	Uniroyal Goodrich	General Tire	Dunlop	Bridgestone
General Motors	33.5%	1.5%	14.5%	32.5%	18.0%	0.0%	0.0%
Ford	26.0	39.0	23.5	0.0	11.5	0.0	0.0
Chrysler	83.0	0.0	0.0	0.0	17.0	0.0	0.0
Mazda	15.0	50.0	0.0	0.0	0.0	0.0	35.0
Honda of U.S.	30.0	0.0	47.0	0.0	0.0	16.0	7.0
Toyota	15.0	40.0	0.0	0.0	3.0	42.0	0.0
Diamond Star	100.0	0.0	0.0	0.0	0.0	0.0	0.0
Nissan	0.0	35.0	22.0	0.0	35.0	8.0	0.0
Nummi (GM-Toyota)	50.0	50.0	0.0	0.0	0.0	0.0	0.0
Volvo	0.0	0.0	100.0	0.0	0.0	0.0	0.0
Saturn	0.0	100.0	0.0	0.0	0.0	0.0	0.0
Isuzu	15.0	35.0	0.0	50.0	0.0	0.0	0.0
Subaru	0.0	0.0	100.0	0.0	0.0	0.0	0.0
Hyundai	35.0	0.0	65.0	0.0	0.0	0.0	0.0
Overall OE market share	38.0%	16.0%	16.0%	14.0%	11.5%	2.75%	1.25%

Source: *Modern Tire Dealer*, January 1991, p. 27.

equipment market was less profitable than the replacement tire market, tire manufacturers considered this market strategically important. Tire manufacturers benefited from volume-related scale economics in manufacturing for this market. Furthermore, it was believed that car and truck owners who were satisfied with their original equipment tires would buy the same brand when they replaced them.

The Replacement Tire Market

The replacement tire market accounts for 70 to 75 percent of tires sold annually. Passenger car tires account for 75 percent of annual sales. Primary demand in this market is affected by the average mileage driven per vehicle. Every 100-mile change in the average number of miles traveled per vehicle produces a 1 million unit change in the unit sales of the replacement market, assuming an average treadwear life of 25,000 to 30,000 miles per tire.[3] Worldwide unit shipments in this segment have been "flat" due in part to the longer treadlife of new tires. Exhibit 3 on page 422 shows original equipment and replacement unit sales in the United States for the period 1987 to 1991.

Tire manufacturers produce a large variety of grades and lines of tires for the replacement tire market under both manufacturers' brand names and private labels. Branded replacement tires are made to the tiremaker's own specifications. Some private-label tires supplied to wholesale distributors and large chain retailers are made to the buyer's specifications rather than to the manufacturer's standards.

The major tire producers often used network TV campaigns to promote their brands, introduce new types of tires, and pull customers to their retail dealer outlets. Their network TV ad budgets commonly ran from $10 million to $30 million, and their budgets for cooperative ads with dealers were from $20 million to $100 mil-

---

[3] "Competition in the World Tire Industry, 1992," p. 587.

EXHIBIT 3

Unit Tire Sales in the United States, 1987–1991

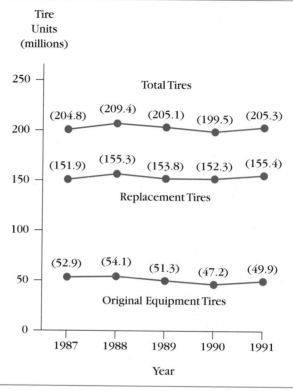

Source: *Modern Tire Dealer,* 1993 Facts/Directory.

lion. Print media were also used extensively. As an illustration, a Michelin print ad featuring the slogan "Michelin, Because So Much Is Riding on Your Tires" is shown in Exhibit 4. Several tire companies also sponsored auto racing events to promote the performance capabilities of their tires.

Goodyear is the perennial market-share leader in the U.S. replacement tire market. The company holds a leadership position in the passenger car, light-truck, and highway truck product categories (see Exhibit 5 on page 424).

Retail Distribution Major brand-name tire manufacturers capitalized on their reputation and experience as producers of original equipment tires by building strong wholesale and retail dealer relationships and networks through which to sell their brand-name replacement tires to vehicle owners. The tire industry uses "retail points of sale" to gauge the retail coverage of tire manufacturers and their brands. Goodyear brand tires have the broadest retail coverage with almost 8,000 "retail points of sale," most of which are company-owned Goodyear Auto Service Centers or franchised Goodyear Tire Store dealers with multiple locations. Groupe Michelin is estimated to have almost 14,000 "points of sale" for its three major brands—Michelin, Goodrich, and Uniroyal. The number of "retail points of sale" for major tire brands is shown in Exhibit 6 on page 424.

Retail Marketing[4] Independent tire dealers usually carried the brands of several different major manufacturers and a discount-priced private-label brand so as to give re-

---

[4] This material is extracted from "Competition in the World Tire Industry, 1992," pp. 588–591.

EXHIBIT 4

Michelin Print Advertisement

placement buyers a full assortment of qualities, brands, and price ranges to choose from. Service stations affiliated with Exxon, Chevron, and Amoco marketed Atlas brand tires produced by Firestone (Bridgestone). Other service stations, especially those that emphasized tire sales, stocked one or two manufacturers' brand tires and a private-label brand. Retail tire outlets that were owned or franchised by the manufacturers (that is, Goodyear Tire Stores and Firestone Auto Master Care Centers) carried only the manufacturer's name brands and perhaps a private-label or lesser-known, discount-priced line made by the manufacturer. Department stores and the major retail chains such as Montgomery Ward and Sears Roebuck and Company occasionally carried manufacturers' label tires but usually marketed only their own private-label brands.

Manufacturers found it advantageous to have a broad product line to appeal to most buyer segments to provide tires suitable for many different types of vehicles driven under a variety of road and weather conditions. When vehicle owners went to a tire dealer to shop for replacement tires, they had a variety of tread designs, tread widths, tread durabilities, performance characteristics, and price categories to

EXHIBIT 5

Estimated U.S. Market Shares of the Top Ten Brands in the Replacement Tire Market, 1991

Passenger Car Tires		Light-Truck Tires		Highway Truck Tires	
Brand	Share	Brand	Share	Brand	Share
Goodyear	15.0%	Goodyear	11.0%	Goodyear	23.0%
Michelin	8.5	BF Goodrich	10.0	Michelin	15.0
Firestone	7.5	Firestone	5.0	Bridgestone	11.0
Sears	5.5	Michelin	6.0	General Tire	7.0
General	4.5	Cooper/Falls	5.0	Firestone	6.0
BF Goodrich	3.5	Kelly-Springfield	5.0	Kelly-Springfield	6.0
Bridgestone	3.5	Armstrong	4.0	Dunlop	6.0
Cooper	3.5	General Tire	4.0	Yokohama	5.0
Kelly-Springfield	3.0	Bridgestone	3.0	Cooper	4.0
Multi-Mile	3.0	Dunlop	2.0	Toyo	3.0
Others	42.5%	Others	44.0	Others	14.0
	100.0%		100.0%		100.0%

Source: *Modern Tire Dealer*, January 1991, p. 27; *Market Data Book*, 1991; *Tire Business*, January 1992, p. 13.

choose from. Car and light-truck owners were often confused by the number of choices they had; few buyers were really knowledgeable about tires. Many buyers ended up choosing a tire on the basis of price, while others followed the recommendation of the local dealer whom they regularly patronized. The retail prices of replacement tires ranged from retreaded (or recapped) tires selling for under $20 to $35 each to top-of-the-line tires going for $125 to $175 each. Tire dealers ran fre-

EXHIBIT 6

Estimated Number of Retail Points of Sale for Major Tire Brands in the United States, 1991

Tire Brand (Parent Company)	Number of Retail Points of Sale
Armstrong (Pirelli)	978
Bridgestone (Bridgestone Corp.)	5,960
Cooper (Cooper Tire and Rubber)	1,518
Dunlop (Sumitomo)	2,046
Firestone (Bridgestone Corp.)	4,208
General (Continental A.G.)	2,107
Goodrich (Groupe Michelin)	4,215
Goodyear (Goodyear Tire and Rubber)	7,964
Kelly-Springfield (Goodyear Tire and Rubber)	2,421
Michelin (Groupe Michelin)	7,159
Pirelli (Pirelli Group)	2,133
Uniroyal (Groupe Michelin)	2,321

Source: *Market Data Book*, 1991; *Tire Business*, January 1992, p. 14.

quent price promotion ads in the local newspapers, making it easy for price-sensitive buyers to watch for sales and buy at off-list prices. In recent years, consumers had become more price conscious and less brand loyal (thus eroding the importance of securing replacement sales through original equipment sales to vehicle manufacturers). However, it was often difficult for car owners to comparison shop on the basis of tire quality and tread durability because of the proliferation of brands, lines, grades, and performance features. Manufacturers had resisted the development of standardized specifications for replacement tires, and there was a general lack of common terminology in describing tire grades and construction features.

In most communities, the retail tire market was intensely competitive. Retailers advertised extensively in newspapers, on outdoor billboards, and occasionally on local TV to establish and maintain their market shares. Price was the dominant competitive appeal. Many dealers featured and pushed their private-label "off-brand" tires because they could obtain higher margins on them than they could selling the name-brand tires of major manufacturers. Dealer-sponsored private-label tires accounted for 15 to 20 percent of total replacement tire sales in the United States in 1991. Surveys showed dealers were able to influence a car owner's choice of replacement tires, both as to brand and type of tire. Most replacement car tire buyers did not have strong tire brand preferences, making it fairly easy for tire salespeople to switch customers to tire brands and grades with the highest dealer margins. Normal dealer margins on replacement tires were in the 35 to 40 percent range, but many dealers shaved margins to win incremental sales.

Retailer Profitability Since the mid-1970s, tire retailers' profit margins had been under competitive pressure, partly because of stagnant growth in tire sales and partly because of declining retail prices since 1980. To bolster profitability, tire dealers had expanded into auto repair services (engine tune-ups, shock-absorber and muffler replacement, and brake repair), retreading, and automobile accessories. Some tire retailers were experimenting with becoming "total car care centers." Auto service work was very attractive because gross profit margins were bigger than the margins earned on replacement tire sales. A recent survey of independent tire dealers indicated that 38.2 percent of their sales and 45.8 percent of their earnings came from automobile service.[5]

■ GOODYEAR TIRE AND RUBBER COMPANY

Goodyear Tire and Rubber Company, headquartered in Akron, Ohio, was founded in 1898 by Frank and Charles Seiberling. The company began as a supplier of bicycle and carriage tires, but soon targeted the fledgling automotive industry. The introduction of the Quick Detachable tire and the Universal Rim (1903) helped make Goodyear the world's largest tire manufacturer by 1916, the same year the company introduced the pneumatic truck tire. Goodyear held the distinction as the world leader in tire production until November 1990, when Groupe Michelin acquired the Uniroyal Goodrich Tire Company (then the second largest U.S. tire manufacturer) for a purchase price of $1.5 billion.

Goodyear's principal business is the development, manufacture, distribution, and sale of tires throughout the world. Tires and tire tubes represented 83 percent of Goodyear's corporate sales of $10.9 billion in 1991. Corporate-wide earnings in 1991 were $96.6 million. In addition to Goodyear brand tires, the company owns the

---

[5] "Dealer Attitude Survey Concerning Automotive Service," *Modern Tire Dealer* (Spring 1992), p. 1.

Kelly-Springfield Tire Company, Lee Tire and Rubber Company, and Delta Tire. The company also manufactures private-label tires.

Goodyear controls 20 to 25 percent of the world's tire manufacturing capacity and about 37 percent of U.S. tire-making capacity. Sales outside of the United States accounted for about 42 percent of company revenues.

Market Presence

Approximately 60 percent of Goodyear worldwide sales were in the tire replacement market and 40 percent were to the original equipment market. The Goodyear brand is the market share leader in North America and in Latin America and number two throughout Asia outside of Japan (behind Bridgestone). The Goodyear brand is third in market share in Europe behind Michelin and Pirelli. Goodyear is second to Groupe Michelin (Michelin, Uniroyal-Goodrich) in terms of worldwide market share for auto, truck, and farm tires (see Exhibit 7). The company operates 44 tire products plants in 28 countries and seven rubber plantations.

Tire Product Line and Pricing

Goodyear produces tires for virtually every type of vehicle. It has the broadest line of tire products of any tire manufacturer. The broad market brand names sold under the Goodyear umbrella include the Arriva, Corsa, Eagle, Invicta, Tiempo, Decathlon, Regatta, S4S, T-Metric, Wrangler (light-truck tire), and Aquatred. The Aquatred brand was the most recent introduction and featured a new tread design that prevented hydroplaning (see Exhibit 8). Sales of this brand were expected to reach 1 million units in 1992 based on initial sales figures.

The Goodyear name is one of the best known brand names in the world. Goodyear brand tires have been traditionally positioned and priced as premium quality brands. Nevertheless, the company has recently introduced mid-priced tire brands. These include the Decathlon and T-Metric brands with lower treadwear and traction performance characteristics than its other brands (see Exhibit 9 on page 428).

Kelly-Springfield Tire Company and Lee Tire and Rubber Company, two Goodyear subsidiaries, also sell some 16 tire brands and engage in private-label manufacturing. For example, Wal-Mart sells the Douglas brand made by the Kelly-Springfield unit.

Goodyear Advertising and Distribution

Goodyear is one of the leading national advertisers in the United States. The company also has maintained a high profile in auto racing to emphasize the high-

EXHIBIT 7

Worldwide Market Shares of Tire Makers, 1990

Tire Manufacturer (Brands)	Market Share
Michelin/Uniroyal-Goodrich	21.5%
Goodyear	20.0
Bridgestone/Firestone	17.0
Continental/General	7.5
Pirelli/Armstong	7.0
Sumitomo/Dunlop	7.0
Others	20.0
	100.0%

Source: Goodyear Tire and Rubber Company, 1991 *Annual Report*, p. 5.

EXHIBIT 8

Aquatred Print Adverisement

ONE GALLON PER SECOND.

POURING BUCKETS? GOODYEAR AQUATRED® PUMPS UP TO A GALLON OF WATER AWAY AS YOU DRIVE.

The award-winning* Aquatred, with its deep-groove AquaChannel,™ moves up to one gallon of water away per second at highway speeds. This keeps more of the tire's tread area in contact with the road for superb wet traction. **ONLY FROM GOODYEAR.** For your nearest Goodyear retailer call 1-800-GOODYEAR.

Aquatred features a 60,000-mile treadlife limited warranty. Ask your retailer for details.

*Which awards? Popular Science, 1991 Best of What's New. Popular Mechanics, 1992 Design & Engineering Award. Fortune, a 1992 "Product of the Year." Industrial Designers Society of America, Gold Industrial Design Excellence IDEA Award. Discover, Discover Award for Technological Innovation.

THE BEST TIRES IN THE WORLD HAVE GOODYEAR WRITTEN ALL OVER THEM.

Experience Goodyear traction for your high-performance, passenger and multi-purpose vehicles.

EAGLE GS-C.®
Dual tread zone for high-performance traction.

AQUATRED.®
Deep-groove design for outstanding wet traction.

WRANGLER GS-A.®
"Triple Traction" tread for all-surface traction.

GOOD YEAR
#1 in Tires

Source: Courtesy of the Goodyear Tire and Rubber Company.

EXHIBIT 9

Goodyear Brand Passenger-car Tires (Including Minimum Assigned Grades for Treadwear, Traction, and Temperature)

| | Treadwear[a] | | | |
| | Rim Diameter 13" | All Others | | |
Brand			Traction[b]	Temperature[c]
Aquatred	320	340	A	B
Arriva	260	310	A	B
Corsa GT	280	280	A	B
Decathlon	220	240	B	C
Eagle GA	280	300	A	B
Eagle GA (HNIZ)	280	300	A	A
Eagle GS-C	—	220	A	A
Eagle GS-D	—	180	A	A
Eagle GT (H)	—	200	A	A
Eagle GT II	—	320	A	B
Eagle GT + 4	—	240	A	B
Eagle GT + 4 (HNIZ)	—	240	A	A
Eagle ST IV	280	300	A	B
Eagle VL	—	220	A	A
Eagle VR	—	220	A	A
Eagle ZR	—	220	A	A
Invicta	—	280	A	B
Invicta GA	—	280	A	B
Invicta GA (HN)	—	280	A	A
Invicta GA (L)	—	300	A	B
Invicta GA (L) (HN)	—	220	A	A
Invicta GFE	280	300	A	B
Invicta GL	260	280	A	B
Invicta GL (H)	—	280	A	A
Invicta GLR	260	280	A	B
Invicta GS	320	340	A	B
Regatta	300	320	A	B
S4S	240	280	A	B
Tiempo	240	280	A	B
T-Metric	240	240	B	C

Note: The U.S. Department of Transportation (DOT) requires tire manufacturers to state the size, load and pressure, treadwear, traction, and temperature on their tires. This information is provided by manufacturers based on their own tests and not provided by the DOT. Treadwear, traction, and temperature are all useful quality indicators and appear on the tire sidewall.

[a] Treadwear. This is an index based on how quickly the tire tread wears under conditions specified by the U.S. Government, relative to a "standard tire." The index does not specify how long a tire tread will last on a car because driving conditions vary. However, a tire with a treadwear index of 200 should wear about twice as long as a tire with an index of 100 under similar conditions.

[b] Traction. This is a measure of a tire's ability to stop on wet pavement under specific conditions. Grades range from A (highest) to C (lowest).

[c] Temperature. This is a measure of a tire's resistance to heat buildup under simulated high-speed driving. Grades range from A (highest) to C (lowest).

Source: "How to 'Read' a Tire," Consumer Reports (February 1992): 78.

performance capabilities of its tires and the company's commitment to product innovation. The Goodyear name is prominently featured on the company's well-known blimps frequently seen at special events in communities throughout the United States. The company's advertising slogan, "The best tires in the world have Goodyear written all over them," communicates the Goodyear positioning as a high-quality, worldwide tire manufacturer and marketer.

Goodyear distributes its tire products through almost 8,000 retail points of sale in the United States and some 25,000 retail outlets worldwide. The company operates about 1,000 company-owned Goodyear Auto Service Centers and sells through 2,500 franchised Goodyear Tire Dealers in the United States, many of which are multisite operators. These retail outlets account for a major portion of Goodyear brand annual tire sales. In addition, the company sells its tires through some multibrand dealers. As of early 1992, the company did not typically sell Goodyear brand tires through discount multibrand dealers, mass-merchandise chain stores, or warehouse clubs.[6]

■ STRATEGIC CONSIDERATIONS IN BROADENING DISTRIBUTION

Interest in reconsidering Sears Auto Centers for selling Goodyear brand tires meant that Goodyear executives would have to revisit the company's long-standing distribution policy. Furthermore, a product policy question relating to which brands might be sold through Sears had to be considered. Decisions on these policy issues were further complicated by Goodyear Tire dealer franchisee reaction to broadened distribution and estimates of incremental sales possible through expanded distribution.

An immediate reaction was forthcoming from franchised Goodyear tire dealers who heard about the Sears proposal. According to comments appearing in *The Wall Street Journal*, one dealer said, "We went with them through thick and thin, and now they're going to drown us."[7] Other dealers indicated they would add private-label brands to their product line. One dealer said: "We [will] sell what we think will give the customer the best value, and that's not necessarily Goodyear." While it was clear that some franchise dealers were critical of broadened distribution of any kind, the pervasiveness of this view was unknown. Furthermore, it was not readily apparent how many dealers would actually carry competitive brands.

Tire industry analysts expected Sears to benefit from carrying Goodyear brand tires. According to market share estimates made by *Modern Tire Dealer*, an industry trade publication, Sears' share of the U.S. replacement passenger car tire market had declined from 6.5 percent in 1989 to 5.5 percent in 1991.[8] Goodyear brand tires would certainly enhance the company's product mix and draw tire buyers who were already Sears customers. The extent of the draw, however, would depend on how many or which Goodyear brands were sold through Sears Auto Centers.

Cannibalization of company-owned Goodyear Auto Service Center and franchised Goodyear Tire Dealers tire sales also meant that Goodyear executives had to consider the incremental replacement passenger car tire sales from broadened distri-

---

[6] Goodyear brand tires could sometimes be purchased at discount multibrand dealers because of "diverting." Diverting is the practice whereby a manufacturer's authorized distributors/dealers sell the manufacturer's products to unauthorized distributors/dealers who, in turn, distribute the manufacturer's products to customers. This practice is common for many consumer products. See W. Bishop, Jr., "Trade Buying Squeezes Marketers," *Marketing Communications* (May 1988): pp 52–53.

[7] "Independent Goodyear Dealers Rebel," *The Wall Street Journal* (July 8, 1992): p B2.

[8] Statistics reported in *Modern Tire Dealer* (January 1991): 27; "Tire Makers Are Traveling Bumpy Road as Car Sales Fall, Foreign Firms Expand," *The Wall Street Journal* (October 19, 1990): B1.

bution. In other words, even though distribution through Sears could increase sales of Goodyear brand tires from the manufacturer's perspective, the danger would be that company-owned and franchised Goodyear Tire Dealers might incur a loss in unit sales. This could be particularly evident in communities where Sears had a strong market presence.

Apex Life Canada

Mark Silver, President and Chief Executive Officer of Apex Life Canada, smiled as he sipped his morning coffee and read the headline of an August 24, 1993, article in the *Toronto Star*: "Universities tell provincial gov't . . . HIKE TUITION 30% . . . and students are outraged." In fact, over the last few months, Mark had encountered several articles regarding this issue and with each one he read, his excitement had grown. Apex Life was about to introduce the Seed Endowment, a new form of educational savings plan. While the finishing touches on the product had almost been completed, several key aspects of the marketing plan had yet to be finalized.

While other educational savings plans already existed in the market, the insurance industry had not introduced a product similar to the Seed Endowment. Mark was excited about the potential of his product and the opportunity it created for Apex Life to enter a new segment of the industry. Mr. Silver did not want to waste any time bringing this new innovation to market. It would not be long before Apex Life's competitors recognized the same potential in this segment of the industry.

■ BACKGROUND

Post-secondary institutions have had no choice but to increase the cost to students in order to compensate for reductions in government funding. A report by the Council of Ontario Universities concerning tuition fee reform was mentioned in the August 24, 1993, article in the *Toronto Star* and included comments such as, "The proposals in this paper require university students to assume a greater share of the cost of providing for their own higher education" (refer to Exhibit 1 on page 432). Over a six-year period, through the late '80s and early '90s, university students witnessed an alarming rise in tuition fees from less than $1,000 to over $2,000 per year. With these fees expected to increase at twice the rate of inflation over the following twenty years, it was easy to understand the increasing difficulties in funding a post-secondary education.

In the early nineties, three major demographic trends had developed:

1. A large portion of the population had moved into retirement years and this group would continue to grow as medical advances increased life expectancy.

This case was prepared by Michael J. Carter, Instructor, under the supervision of Elizabeth M.A. Grasby, Pre-Business Program Director, of the Richard Ivey School of Business, The University of Western Ontario, solely to provide material for class discussion. The case is not intended to illustrate either effective or ineffective handling of a managerial situation. Certain names and other identifying information may have been disguised to protect confidentiality. Copyright © 1994.

EXHIBIT 1

VOL. 22 NO. 210   TORONTO, ONT., TUESDAY, AUG. 24, 1993   104 PAGES   50 CENTS

Universities tell provincial gov't . . .

HIKE TUITION 30%

. . . and students are outraged: Page 5

NEWS 5

Bump tuition by 30%: Report

BY ANNE DAWSON

Queen's Park Bureau

Ontario's 325,000 university students should have their tuition fees hiked 30%—about $1,000 a year—by 1995, says a report forwarded to the government.

The Council of Ontario Universities, representing 22 universities and other institutions across the province, has sent Education Minister Dave Cooke a "Discussion Paper on Tuition Fee Reform" that further recommends a doubling of tuition fees for post-graduate students in high-paying fields such as law and medicine.

"The proposals in this paper require university students to assume a greater share of the cost of providing for their own higher education," states the report.

"These increases would yield maximum tuition fees for undergraduate arts and science students of $3,030 in the second year . . . well below the current level of fees charged at many public universities in the US."

Students only pay 20%

The report says on average, students pay less than 20% of their total education costs once student aid and the income tax system are taken into account." And in some high-cost programs like medicine and dentistry, tuition fees contribute less than 5% of the total cost.

"At the same time, it is important to note that graduates of programs such as medicine and dentistry earn significantly more than others," said the report.

Canadian Federation of Students—Ontario vice-chair Scott Humphrey strongly condemned the report saying many students will no longer be able to afford education if these fee hikes are approved.

"It's completely unacceptable calling for tuition increases on students who already have trouble paying for tuition," said Humphrey, 23, a McMaster University honor history student.

Humphrey pointed out the COU was unfairly "selective" in its statistics. He said Ontario, compared to the other provinces, provides the least funding per student.

A spokesman in Cooke's office said the minister has not yet seen the report.

---

2. The Baby-Boomer generation continued to dominate financial and cultural aspects of society. Because they were now moving towards middle age, insurance needs were changing from protection to protection and accumulation.

3. An increase in the birth rate. As Baby-Boomers matured and continued to have children, they were creating an *Echo-boom*. Older members of the echo-boom were also moving into their child-bearing years.

Coupled with projected cutbacks in government spending, this new "echo-boom" had created an opportunity to sell educational savings products to parents of this new generation, who were increasingly concerned about their ability to pay for their children's future education.

■ THE LIFE INSURANCE INDUSTRY

Like many industries, the Canadian Life and Health Insurance industry suffered from overcapacity. While the bulk of the market was held by a small number of companies, there were over 200 licensed insurers pursuing 28 million Canadians. In fact, the top 10 companies controlled over 80% of the market, while the remaining players competed fiercely to expand their portion of what was left.

The competitive situation was further aggravated by the federal government's recent removal of restrictions on the ownership of companies offering life insurance products. As a result of these changes to the Insurance Companies Act and the Bank Act, heavy competition from large banks and trust companies developed. These organizations already had very large distribution networks through which to sell products. Considering all financial institutions, the 6 Canadian-owned chartered banks represented over 56% of all assets in the market. The largest life insurance company ranked tenth in terms of total assets. These massive new players would only accelerate the already excessive competition in the insurance market.

When questioned about the competitive environment, Mark suggested that:

> In the long run, competition in the market place will continue to drive prices down and depress earnings. It will become increasingly important to carefully target areas which have conditions that offer the opportunity to develop profitable business. Our biggest challenge is being able to create products with features and benefits that enable one to escape the commodity pricing trap—in either current or new segments of the industry.

■ APEX LIFE CANADA

Mark stated:

> Our business objective is to provide quality insurance products and services to meet the evolving financial security of individuals and businesses, allowing us to prosper, attain long-term growth, and provide a fair return to our stockholders.

On the basis of pure fundamentals, Apex Life was in an excellent competitive position. The company was founded in 1964 and purchased in 1966 by a large multinational corporation. Apex Life found a niche in the life insurance market and grew to offer the highest return to shareholders in the industry. Ranked as 29th in the industry in terms of premiums collected last year, and 60th in total assets, Apex Life had still boasted the highest average return on equity in the industry in the previous 4 years. In addition, the company had reported a profit for 15 consecutive years, a feat virtually unheard of for a smaller insurance company.

Apex Life's affiliation with its multinational parent, and consistent profitability, translated into a strong capital base and provided secure funding for future growth. It also suggested stability to potential shareholders and customers. This was an important asset considering the changes that were taking place in the market.

As a result of fierce competition over the last decade, many shareholders were leaving the industry. Years of below average returns had prompted the beginning of a major restructuring in the life insurance industry. Mark saw Apex Life as one of the few companies whose balance sheet was of "uniform high quality." With virtually no debt and the possession of a large pool of capital for investment, the company was well positioned to take advantage of others' misfortunes. It was able to obtain portfolios of other insurance companies who were undergoing their own internal restructuring or leaving the business altogether. This enabled Apex Life to grow at a rate far exceeding that which was available through new business activities alone.

EXHIBIT 2

Selected Financial Data for Apex Life (in $ Millions)[1]

	1992	*1993*	*Est. 1994*
Revenue from Premiums			
New Business[2]	1.2	12.4	12.0
Old Business[3]	14.6	14.8	27.0
Acquisitions[4]	0.0	1.8	2.5
Total	15.8	29.0	41.5
Investment Income Revenue	4.9	7.0	12.0
Total Revenue	20.7	36.0	53.5
Net Income	.2	4.3	5.0
Total Assets	69.0	120.0	150.0

---

[1] *From company reports.*

[2] *Premiums generated through the development of new products.*

[3] *Premiums generated through existing products.*

[4] *Premiums generated through portfolios acquired from other companies.*

While Apex Life was one of the few successful companies in the industry, its size did create some challenges. One such challenge was achieving economies of scale. While its base of operations was small and low cost compared to competitors, Mark indicated that Apex Life was not willing to sacrifice profitability by writing large volumes of new business in a market suffering from "over-capacity, under-performance and excessive price-cutting." Mark realized that the key to success under these conditions was to develop exclusive distribution systems which would enable Apex Life to charge slightly more for its products. As a result, Apex Life turned its efforts towards niche marketing and focused on "aggressive, managed, profitable growth" by taking advantage of these smaller opportunities and pushing its distribution systems to maximum capacity.

Currently, Apex Life was sufficiently staffed to handle significant growth in its existing market segments and to add complementary lines over the next few years. Its modest size and focus on niche markets enabled Apex Life to find opportunities to produce profitable business in segments of the market which would be considered too small by many of its major competitors. By following this strategy, Apex Life had achieved tremendous success (refer to Exhibit 2 for selected financial data).

■ CONSUMER ANALYSIS

With this in mind, Mark spent considerable time deciding who to target with Apex Life's Seed Endowment. In Canada, there were more than 400,000 babies born each year in the early 1990s. Educational savings plans had penetrated only 10% of this market. Mark had broken down the potential consumer into parents and grandparents. This market grew with the population over the years.

Parents could be further subdivided into Baby-Boomers, who had delayed having children, and Echo-Boomers, who were now entering their child-bearing years. Mark was considering two types of parents in these segments. The first were individuals who had attended a university themselves. They knew how important a university was to them and wanted to make sure that their children would have the same opportunity. The second type of parents were thought to be immigrant families. They had come to Canada with nothing and had worked very hard to be successful. They wanted their children to have more advantages than they had. More than likely lacking any formal education themselves, these parents recognized its value and wanted to make sure that their children had the best opportunities possible.

Regardless of their background, Mark felt that these families would require a reasonable income, at least $50,000 a year, in order to afford the annual premiums of an educational savings plan. As costs continued to grow, many parents were worried that they would not be able to afford their children's education when the time came. An educational savings plan forced parents to save now, so that the financial burden down the road would be tremendously reduced.

The second major segment Mark considered was grandparents, between the ages of 55 and 70. They were expected to have the largest disposable income of any segment as they had accumulated a significant amount of capital over the years. This was especially true for the parents of Baby-Boomers. Generally affluent, with large disposable incomes, they paid a considerable amount of taxes. No longer looking for opportunities to help their adult children, grandparents instead looked to their grandchildren. They wanted to make sure that their grandchildren had every opportunity possible. According to Mark, what better gift to give your grandchild than a paid-for education? Mark expected this segment to represent between 25–30% of the market, but he also felt there was a great opportunity here and grandparents could reach as high as 50% of his sales.

There was another issue affecting the educational savings plan industry. This was the idea of *"socially responsible giving,"* which had become an important issue for both parents and grandparents. As opposed to gifts that would be wasted, broken, or even stolen within a short period of time, educational savings plans provided them with a gift that could only help the child's future.

■ EDUCATIONAL SAVINGS PLANS

Unlike traditional life insurance products that were bought in response to the fear of loss through personal life changes or crises, the purchasers of educational planning products were motivated instead by parents' hopes and dreams for their children. Yet Mark noted, "a family's financial plan that does not specifically include educational planning as one of the overall objectives can have future catastrophic financial and personal effects for all concerned."

In addition to the enormous costs for a young family with children, the career costs for a child without a post-secondary education were equally frightening. The relationship between education and unemployment was quite clear (refer to Exhibit 3 for statistics). For these reasons, and others mentioned earlier, specialist companies had been formed to offer educational savings plans.

EXHIBIT 3

Statistics Canada 1986 Unemployment Figures

Level of Education	*Unemployment Rate (%)*
Public School	13.6
High School	12.2
Post-Secondary Diploma	7.2
University Degree	4.3

Educational savings plans were designed to allow a "subscriber" (normally a parent or grandparent) to accumulate funds, over a limited period of time, to help finance the post-secondary education of a designated "beneficiary" (the child). The subscriber would normally contribute to the plan from the time the child was born, until he/she was ready to begin a post-secondary education. Most plans included a limited lifetime. Generally, subscribers could only make contributions to the plan for 18 consecutive years. When the beneficiary began his/her post-secondary education, he/she received the proceeds from the plan in the amount agreed upon by the subscriber and the insurance company when the plan was initiated. As a result, the financial burden was tremendously reduced at the time the individual entered a post-secondary educational institution.

Although not seasonal, economic fluctuations did affect the educational savings plan market. During recessionary times, more people worried about being able to afford a post-secondary education for their children. In addition, rising interest rates also improved the marketability of these plans. As interest rates rose, insurance companies could offer better returns on educational savings plans, since it was easier for them to earn a higher return on their pool of invested funds. Recovering from a lengthy recession, the government had focused heavily on economic issues in the past year. This had resulted in cutbacks in all areas, including education.

■ COMPETITIVE PRODUCTS

While new to Apex Life's portfolio of products, educational savings plans had been on the market for years. Although many companies offered different products, all plans on the market could be grouped into one of two general categories: a "Registered Education Savings Plan" or a "Universal Life" product.

Registered Education Savings Plans (RESP)

RESPs were known as "pooled" funds, since all plans eligible to be cashed in the same year were pooled together. In the first year of post-secondary education, the beneficiary received back almost all of the contributions made by the subscriber during the life of the plan. The amount of money that a beneficiary was entitled to in the second, third, and fourth year was determined by the amount of interest that had accumulated in the pool up to that point. If a subscriber stopped contributing to the fund before the life of the plan was up, or if the beneficiary decided not to continue an academic career, they could collect all contributions made up to that point. However, the interest they had earned stayed in the pool and was divided among the remaining beneficiaries.

Besides the requirement that a child attend an approved post-secondary institution in order to receive his or her fair share of the fund, other restrictions also applied. The child had to attend a school by a certain age (usually 19), and once they had started, they were not allowed to take a break (such as a year off to travel in Europe), until they had completed the term of the policy, normally four years. The only way a beneficiary could break these two rules, and remain eligible, was to obtain special permission from the company managing the fund. This pardon could be difficult to obtain.

Due to their legislation by the federal government, RESPs had some other notable restrictions. For tax shelter purposes, the federal government limited how much the subscriber could contribute to the plan each year ($1,500 annually or $31,500 lifetime). The fund's manager was also restricted as to where the contributions could be invested. This generally resulted in a much more conservative portfolio and, as a result, a smaller return to the beneficiary.

The main attraction of RESP products was the interest income shielding. Through government legislation, subscribers did not have to pay taxes on interest earned during the life of the plan. The interest was taxed only when the plan was cashed in, and the tax was paid by the child, rather than the subscriber. Keeping in mind that the beneficiary would more than likely be in a much lower tax bracket, taxes paid would be much smaller.

"Universal Life" Products

These products were similar to RESPs in that they were also "pooled" funds. However, this pool worked differently in terms of its restrictions and penalties. If subscribers cancelled their policy within the first 7 years, they would lose everything including their contributions. After that, there was something called a surrender clause. Between years 7 and 15 of the policy, the amount of contributions and interest the subscriber would lose, if they forfeited, would decrease from everything to nothing. After the 15th year of the policy, the subscriber could pull out and receive everything contributed up to that point, including the interest those contributions had earned. While it seemed like a larger risk, if one stayed in the program he/she was likely to benefit more from the pool, since those that pulled out early lost either all or most of both their contributions and interest. This left a larger pool to be divided among the remaining eligible beneficiaries. There was also greater potential in the "Universal Life" products, since there were no restrictions on where the contributions could be invested. The funds could be better diversified, and as a result, earn a better return.

Although not registered with the government, the interest earned on these policies was also tax-sheltered. This was only made possible because the subscriber had to buy life insurance on the beneficiary and contribute to the educational savings plan. Keeping in mind that the focus of the customer was not life insurance but rather forced savings for the beneficiary's future education, the insurance portion didn't really make a lot of sense as far as Mark was concerned. As Mark put it, "you can get what you want out of it, but you have to take on some extra baggage." Similar to the RESP, the beneficiary was taxed on the interest rather than the subscriber, provided the policy was gifted to the beneficiary.

The Seed Endowment

When considering what was available, Mark believed that there was a significant opportunity for his company. In his words, there were "no products out there sufficiently satisfying the needs of consumers." As a result, Apex Life developed the "Seed Endowment."

Similar to the Universal Life products, there were no restrictions on how much one could contribute to the plan or where the contributions were invested. Upon maturity the endowment could be utilized for either a "traditional" education or for a "life" experience as Mark indicated. For example, the beneficiary might decide that touring the museums in Europe or opening a small business was the route to pursue. The "Seed Endowment" allowed for alternative "life" choices without penalizing the subscriber.

With the "Seed Endowment," there was only a small portion of life insurance involved. This was minimal compared to the "Universal Life" products. It was just enough that if the child were to die before the policy matured *(18 years)*, the subscriber was insured for the maturity value of the policy. Unlike the other products on the market, the beneficiary was guaranteed a certain portion of the expected pay out each year *(maturity value)*. The beneficiary was not guaranteed everything because of the uncertainty of the return Apex Life would earn on the contributions. However, it was still much better than the pooled funds where nothing was guaranteed.

EXHIBIT 4

Benefit Comparison of Competitive Products at Different Premium Levels[1]

Product	1st Year Payout	Payout for Next 3 Years	Total Payout
@ $250 per year for 18 years[2]			
RESP	$4,300	$1,456/year	$8,668
Universal Life	3,000	1,540/year	7,620
Seed Endowment—Direct Mail	**3,255**	**2,440/year**	**10,575**
—MGA	**2,120**	**1,590/year**	**6,890**
@ $500 per year for 18 years			
RESP	$8,800	$2,912/year	$17,536
Universal Life	6,000	3,080/year	15,240
Seed Endowment—Direct Mail	**6,510**	**4,880/year**	**21,150**
—MGA	**4,420**	**3,180/year**	**13,780**
@ $1,000 per year for 18 years			
RESP	$17,800	$5,824/year	$35,272
Universal Life	12,000	6,160/year	30,480
Seed Endowment—Direct Mail	**13,020**	**9,760/year**	**42,300**
—MGA	**8,480**	**6,360/year**	**27,560**

[1] Numbers based on an estimated return of 6% on all contributions invested in the fund.

[2] Life insurance portion of the premium included.

There was also no forfeiture of interest if the subscriber decided to stop the policy. Only a small surrender clause existed, so that a high proportion of the contributions and interest earned would be returned to the subscriber in the event that he/she decided to cancel the policy. This penalty was considerably smaller than that involved with either the "Universal Life" products or the RESPs. Unfortunately up to this point, Apex Life had not found a way to shield the interest earned from being taxed immediately (the life insurance portion of the premium was too small). However, once the product was gifted to a child, the interest would be taxable on the child's earnings rather than the subscriber's. (For a comparison of the benefits provided by each of the products on the market, refer to Exhibit 4.)

■ DISTRIBUTION ANALYSIS

One of the most important decisions was how to get the product into the hands of the consumer. At the time, Mark was considering two different ways to distribute the Seed Endowment.

1. Managing General Agency

   The first option was to distribute the product through a Managing General Agency (MGA). This was the traditional approach for companies in this market. While the primary role of this company would be to act as a national sales arm, it would also assist Apex Life with further development of the product. This assistance would provide Mark with an understanding of what the agents would sell and what the market needed. As Apex Life's national distributor, the MGA would assume most of the responsibilities in bringing the Seed Endowment to market.

The MGA would recruit regional sales management organizations (or General Agents as they are called in the industry), who in turn would hire individual agents to distribute the product to the end consumer. The MGA, responsible for the management of the entire chain, would have to train, motivate, and offer support to the General Agents. It would have to monitor the completion of application forms, maintain all relationships, and respond to all inquiries from both Apex Life and the agents selling the product to the end consumer. This would allow Apex Life to concentrate on the administration and actual marketing of the product.

Due to the MGA's involvement, Apex Life's marketing costs would be greatly reduced. No direct mail package or significant marketing campaign would be needed since the agents themselves would establish credibility with the end consumer. Aside from the cost of developing the product, Apex Life would also have to assist in training seminars for General Agents regarding both Apex Life and the "Seed Endowment," and cover all relative printing costs. Mark estimated that he would have to spend close to $40,000 to cover everything under this distribution option.

This alternative did have its drawbacks. While the "Seed Endowment" would be the only educational product sold by the MGA, this was not the case for the agents they recruited to sell the product to the end consumer. Both General Agents and the individual agents would carry a variety of life insurance products from several different companies, including other competitive educational savings plans. It was really out of Apex Life's hands when it came to how, and if, the product would actually be presented to the end consumer. It all depended upon the products that the agents felt would best meet the needs of the consumers they were dealing with, their compensation, and the products' projected returns. This placed tremendous importance on not just the seminars, but also on the competitiveness of Apex Life's product.

Like other companies in the industry offering educational savings plans, Mark was concerned about the high commission fees demanded by this distribution alternative. Commissions could run as high as 116% in the first year and then drop down to 5% in the following years. This additional cost would be reflected in the benefits the customer received when cashing in the policy. Apex Life could not adjust the annual premium to compensate for this if it was to remain competitive on price and meet the company's policy of no less than a 17% return on any product sold. While it was not perfect, Mark did realize that on the whole this distribution route provided the opportunity for wider exposure and the greatest potential for rapid sales growth.

2. Direct Mail

The second option was *direct mail.* This required that Apex Life be responsible for all aspects of the marketing plan, including development costs, printing, mailing, advertising, and support staff to handle the end consumer. Rather than dealing with an agent, interested consumers would now phone Apex Life directly to inquire about and purchase the product.

One of Mark's questions with this route was to whom he should mail his packages. He knew who the end consumers would likely be, but how could he find them? One option available was to purchase lists of people from different companies, such as publishers or market research organizations. At the time, Mark was considering nine different lists, yet he was unsure which ones would be the most effective in reaching his end consumer. Two different groups of lists were being considered. The first included magazines and national surveys aimed at young parents, while the second contained similar lists targeting seniors (refer to Exhibit 5 on the following page for a descrip-

EXHIBIT 5

Potential Lists for Direct Mail Distribution

PARENTS

New Parents—Family Communication

This is a list of respondents to bind-ins in *Expecting* and *Best Wishes* magazines. These direct-responsive new mothers are highly targetable through the selections offered, and want the best of everything for their children (birth to 4 years). 73% are female; 99.4% at home address.

Target Families

This is a list of responders to a national survey that promises high-value coupons for completed questionnaires. Survey responders have requested further mailings of interest that match their behaviors, interests, and demographics.

Prospects Unlimited—Kids Base

This is a list of consumers who have recently purchased children's goods, from newborn to teenage items. Information is gathered from subscription files, surveys, retail purchases, and warranty cards.

***Parenting* Magazine**

This is a list of active subscribers to a publication written especially for contemporary parents. The magazine features articles on Health and Fitness, Education, Personal Appearance and Fashion as well as Travel, Investments, and Home Design. Subscribers are upscale, well-educated professionals, with average income in excess of $50,000.

***Parents* Magazine**

This is a list of subscribers to *Parents* magazine. It is edited for young women 18–34 with growing children. Editorial coverage emphasizes family formation and growth, focusing on day-to-day needs and concerns of today's woman as a mother and a woman. Eighty-two percent are female, and 62% of these women are employed; their median age is 31.

***Sesame Street* Magazine**

This is a list of children, ages 2–6, whose parents have subscribed to *Sesame Street*, one of America's leading educational magazines. Eighty-eight percent are between the ages of 25–39; 72% of mothers attended/graduated from college or completed post-graduate work.

Highlights for Children

This is a list of subscribers to *Highlights for Children*. These subscribers are young Canadian families with an above average interest in their children's education and development. They are discriminating parents who demand quality for their children.
Issue: Small quantity (12,000 only) of the total is sold directly to the parents. The majority is sold at schools and delivered to the home.

***Wonders* Catalogue Buyers**

This is a list of buyers and inquirers of clothing from an upscale catalogue. Products are colorful and contemporary clothing for today's best-dressed children and parents.

GRANDPARENTS

Target Mail—Seniors

This is a list of responders to a national survey that promises high-value coupons for completed questionnaires. Survey responders have requested further mailings of interest that match their behaviors, interests, and demographics.

Information obtained from report submitted by *Flair Communications* for Apex Life.

tion of each list). Unfortunately, these lists did not cover everyone Mark wished to target. He was having difficulty in deciding how to reach both lower income parents and families with a strong ethnic background.

Compared to dealing directly with an agent, Mark felt that direct mail involved less pressure from the consumer's perspective. However, with no direct contact between the agent and the end consumer, Apex Life would have

EXHIBIT 6

Circulation and Cost of Potential Magazines

	Circulation		National Costs		Ontario Costs	
	National	*Ontario*	*1 p/4 c*	*1/2 p/4 c*	*1 p/4 c*	*1/2 p/4 c*
Today's Parent	132,732	72,753	$ 8,680	$ 6,570	$ 6,085	—
Chatelaine	904,454	489,667	$30,530	$19,845	$18,015	$11,710
Canadian Living	592,570	319,929	$23,155	$15,050	$14,790	$10,385
Homemakers	1,289,000	675,000	$24,800	—	$16,690	—

Information obtained from report submitted by *Flair Communications* for Apex Life.

to establish its credibility in other ways. This would require a very strong marketing campaign. Mark considered a variety of media channels including local television, daily newspapers, radio and consumer magazines, as well as some co-operative advertising opportunities (refer to Exhibit 6 for potential magazines and relevant costs). There were an unlimited number of companies that could be approached for co-operative activity. However, Mark suggested that "only companies with educational value, commitment to customer service and the environment, and an untarnished reputation should be considered" (refer to Exhibit 7 on page 442 for potential co-operative partners). Although from a financial and exposure standpoint this option looked solid, Mark felt there were some risks. Mark was also concerned about the cost and timing of the direct mail campaign and advertising.

Mark estimated that he would mail approximately 200,000 packages to households across Canada, with an expected net response rate of about 1%. Estimating that the average size of a policy would be around $500, this meant total premiums for the first year would come in around $1,000,000.

In terms of marketing costs, this option was considerably more expensive. Mark estimated that his total budget for marketing this product via the direct mail route would be close to $270,000. This included all printing, mailing, creative development, lists, lettershop, postage, public relations, and about $50,000 for advertising. While these fixed costs would be significantly higher, Mark knew that he would benefit a great deal since there were no commissions to be paid under this distribution route. Although heavily lopsided in the first year, Mark estimated that if he averaged this over the 18 years of the policy, he would be saving about 20.8% of the premium each year. A large portion of these savings would be passed on to the end consumer in terms of a larger payback when the policy was cashed in.

Other costs Mark had to consider, under either distribution option, included a $36 annual administration fee per policy, a 2 percent tax on premiums, and guaranteed fund insurance estimated at .5 percent per policy. In addition, there was a benefit cost to every policy. This was the portion of the annual premium that would have to be paid to the beneficiary when the policy was cashed in, 18 years down the road. (For a breakdown of variable costs under both distribution alternatives, refer to Exhibit 8 on page 443.)[1]

---

[1] Because of the economic reality that a dollar today is more valuable than a dollar a year from now, it is necessary to adjust the future cash flows of Apex Life to reflect this. Subscribers of Apex Life's "Seed Endowment" will be contributing to the plan for up to 18 years. In order to compare these contributions and the related costs to the marketing expenses incurred in the first year of the plan, the future cash flows must be adjusted in order to reflect their value in today's dollars. This adjustment process is referred to as present valuing.

E X H I B I T   7

Potential Co-operative Partners

PACKAGED GOODS
- General Mills—Cheerios
- Kraft/General Foods
- Thomas J. Lipton
- Gerber
- Popsicle
- Campbell Soup
- Nestlé Enterprises
- Kelloggs
- Johnson & Johnson
- Quaker Oats

LEISURE
- Collegiate Sports
- Jumbo Video
- Toys "R" Us
- W. H. Smith
- Moyers
- Double Day
- Pizza Hut
- The Gap
- Grolier
- *Sesame Street* Magazine

MANUFACTURERS
- Reebok
- IBM
- Sony
- Crayola
- Lego
- Roots
- V-Tech
- Little Tikes
- Kodak
- Avon

TRAVEL
- Club Med
- American Express Travel
- Sheraton
- Air Canada

EXHIBIT 8

Cost Structure Under Different Distribution Alternatives

Seed Endowment—Direct Mail				Seed Endowment—MGA		
Annual Cash Flows	Total Cash Flows for 18 Years	18 Years of Cash Flows Present Valued[2]		Annual Cash Flows	Total Cash Flows for 18 Years	18 Years of Cash Flows Present Valued[1]
$250	$4,500	$1,812	**Premiums**	$250	$4,500	$1,812
			Costs:			
$36	$648	$261	• Admin. & Overhead	$46	$828	$333
5	90	36	• Premium tax (2%)	5	90	36
1	18	7	• Guaranteed Fund (.5%) Insurance	1	18	7
0	0	0	• Commission (20.8%)	52	936	377
171	3,078	1,240	• Benefit Cost[3]	112	2,016	812

[1] Figures reflect the cash flows of one unit.

[2] These figures have been actuarially adjusted to reflect the notion that $1 a year for 18 consecutive years is actually worth much less than $18 today, due to present valuing. For example, $1 a year from now, discounted at a rate of 8% is really only worth $.92 today. Similarly $1 two years from now is only worth $.85 today.

[3] Refers to portion of premium paid to beneficiary when plan cashed in.

■ CONCLUSION

Before Apex Life could launch the "Seed Endowment," Mark Silver knew there were several decisions to be made. Although he was unsure when to introduce his product into the market, he realized that a solid marketing plan was an absolute necessity if the "Seed Endowment" was going to have the impact that he felt was possible.

Masterton Mills, Inc.

In September 1996, Suzanne Goldman was scheduled to meet with Robert Meadows, President of Masterton Mills, Inc. Goldman knew that the meeting would relate to the recent board of directors meeting. In her position as Special Assistant to the President, or "troubleshooter," as she called herself, Goldman had noticed that such meetings often led to a project of some type. Her expectations were met, as Meadows began to describe what had happened at the board meeting.

> The directors are not pleased with the present state of affairs even though we were one of a very few carpet mills to make money last year with a decline in sales. As you know, our bread-and-butter residential carpet and rug business is again in the doldrums and our distribution system is feeling the pinch. Our wholesalers are complaining about slow payments from retailers. In many cases, their receivables are taking 90 days to collect, and we are extending our receivables to satisfy them at a 10 percent annual carrying cost. Wholesalers are cutting back on inventory as costs of carrying inventory approach 10 percent annually. Our inventories have increased, and our delivery costs have risen as we attempt to service our wholesalers. Costs of servicing our wholesalers are running about 6 percent of sales and we are getting repeated requests to shave our prices to meet the competition. I could go on, but you get the picture. The possibility of establishing our own distribution centers or wholesale operation was raised, given the recent developments in the industry. We looked at this issue ten years ago and concluded it wasn't strategically in our interest to do so. Besides, we couldn't afford it. Would you examine such a program for me and prepare a position paper for the December board meeting? Focus only on the residential business, since we handle contract sales on a direct basis, assume the same sales level as in fiscal 1996, and address both the strategic and economic aspects of a change in distribution practices. Remember that our policy is to finance programs from internal funds except for capital expansion. I'd like to see you do the same comprehensive job that you did on the advertising and sales program last November.

■ THE U.S. CARPET AND RUG INDUSTRY

U.S. consumers and businesses spend about $25 billion annually for floorcoverings. The largest category of floorcoverings is carpet and rugs, followed by resilient coverings (vinyl and linoleum), hardwood, and ceramic tile.

This case was prepared by Professor Roger A. Kerin, of the Edwin L. Cox School of Business, Southern Methodist University, as a basis for class discussion and is not designed to illustrate effective or ineffective handling of an administrative situation. Certain names and data have been disguised. Copyright © 1997 by Roger A. Kerin. No part of this case may be reproduced without the written consent of the copyright holder.

Carpet and Rug Sales and Trends

The U.S. carpet and rug industry recorded sales of $9.8 billion at manufacturer's prices in 1995.[1] Carpet and rug retail sales were estimated to be $15 billion. These figures represented about a 1.5 percent decline in sales from 1994. Little or no dollar sales growth was projected for 1996.

Industry sales are divided between "contract," or commercial, sales for institutions and businesses, and residential sales for household replacement carpets. The residential segment accounted for about 62 percent of sales based on yards of carpet sold; the contract segment accounted for 38 percent of sales in 1995. These percentages reflected a 6 percent decline in residential sales from 1994 and a 10 percent increase in commercial sales.

It is estimated that carpets and rugs commanded 73.4 percent of total U.S. floorcovering sales in 1995, down from 82 percent in 1985. By comparison, the market share for hardwood and ceramic floorcoverings grew during this period while the resilient floorcovering market share was relatively unchanged (see Exhibit 1). Floorcovering's share of total U.S. retail sales declined from 0.57 percent of the total in 1985 to 0.52 percent in 1995 in spite of the fact that the average price of floorcoverings (including carpet and rugs) has not changed in the past decade. In the late 1980s, carpet and rug's share of U.S. consumers' disposable personal income shrunk to an all-time low and has only recently increased. In addition, U.S. carpet and rug manufacturers have experienced a decline in sales outside the United States. Since 1980, the export market for U.S.-made carpet and rugs has become highly competitive. As recently as 1970, U.S. companies supplied 51 percent of the world's carpet; by 1995, this percentage had declined to 44 percent.

Some industry analysts claim that the carpet and rug industry itself is partially to blame for the present situation. Lack of marketing, particularly in the residential carpet and rug replacement segment, is an often-cited problem area. Even though manufacturers continue to improve the quality of their products and develop new patterns, critics say the industry has not communicated these value-added dimensions to consumers and differentiated carpet and rugs from other floorcoverings. They note that the industry as a whole spends 2.4 percent of its sales on consumer advertising. For comparison, other manufacturers of consumer durable products such as

EXHIBIT 1

U.S. Floorcovering Market Shares

Floorcovering Type	Market Share in . . .		
	1995	1994	1985
Carpet	73.4%	73.6%	82.0%
Resilient	14.4	14.5	14.0
Hardwood	6.5	6.1	1.5
Ceramic	5.7	5.8	2.5
	100.0%	100.0%	100.0%
Total sales ($ millions)	$13,344	$13,509	NA

---

[1] This discussion is based on interviews with individuals knowledgeable about the carpet and rug industry and information contained in *A Profile of the United States Carpet and Rug Industry* (Dalton, GA: The Carpet and Rug Institute, 1996); "The Focus 100," *FOCUS* (May 1996): 15–30; and "The North American Top 50 Carpet & Rug Manufacturers," *Carpet & Rug Industry* (April 1996): 12–56.

household furniture and household appliances spend 4.6 percent and 3.0 percent of sales, respectively, for advertising. Instead, price had become the dominant marketing tool for much of the past decade, and manufacturers focused attention on cost reduction and achieving economies of scale. A result of these efforts was an erratic upward trend in dollar sales over the past decade, but marginal profitability for the industry as a whole.

Competitors

The U.S. carpet and rug industry is undergoing a period of consolidation begun in the mid-1980s. Mergers, acquisitions, and bankruptcies among manufacturers brought about by declining demand for carpet and rugs, excess manufacturing capacity, and dwindling profit margins reduced the number of carpet and rug manufacturers from 300 in the mid-1980s to 100 companies in 1995. This number includes 95 U.S.-based companies and 5 Canadian-based companies, most of which are privately held companies. Some industry analysts predicted that two or possibly three of these companies would close or be acquired in 1996 or 1997.

By 1995, it was estimated that 25 companies in the industry produced 94 percent of carpet and rugs sold in the U.S.; the top 20 companies produced 90 percent; and the top 10 companies manufactured 75 percent of all carpet and rugs. When viewed from a dollar sales perspective, the U.S. carpet and rug industry had an even more skewed distribution. Five companies—Shaw Industries, Mohawk Industries, Beaulieu of America Group, Queen Carpet, and Interface, Inc.—were responsible for 70 percent of industry sales. The top 10 manufacturers alone accounted for 87 per-

EXHIBIT 2

Sales of the Top 15 North American Carpet and Rug Manufacturers in 1994 and 1995

| | Sales (in $ Millions, U.S. only) | |
Manufacturer	1995	1994
1. Shaw Industries	$2,869.8	$2,788.5
2. Mohawk Industries	1,648.5	1,432.4
3. Beaulieu of America Group	920.0	903.0
4. Queen Carpet	720.0	675.0
5. Interface, Inc.	655.0	536.0
6. Collins & Aikman	550.0	428.0
7. Burlington Industries	395.0	380.0
8. Masland Industries	369.0	375.0
9. Dixie Yarns/Carpet Group	360.9	353.9
10. World Carpets, Inc.	315.0	305.0
11. Diamond Rug & Carpet	240.0	260.0
12. Milliken	235.0	305.0
13. Peerless	195.6	396.0
14. Columbus Mills	183.0	168.0
15. Kraus Carpets	173.0	127.2

Source: "The North American Top 50 Carpet & Rug Manufacturers," *Carpet & Rug Industry* (April 1996): 12-56.

cent of industry sales. The remaining 90 manufacturers accounted for 13 percent of sales. These companies were all medium-sized and smaller niche manufacturers; 26 of them specialized in rugs.

The industry sales leader is Shaw Industries with 1995 sales of $2.9 billion. The company also has the distinction of being the largest carpet and rug manufacturer in the world. Exhibit 2 lists the top 15 carpet and rug manufacturers based on annual sales in 1994 and 1995.

Wholesale and Retail Distribution

Wholesale and retail distribution in the U.S. carpet and rug industry has undergone three distinct changes since the mid-1980s.

Mid-1980s: Direct Distribution

In the mid-1980s, the largest carpet and rug manufacturers began to bypass floorcovering wholesalers (distributors) and sell directly to retailers in greater numbers. In many instances, direct distribution involved establishing sales offices located in manufacturer-operated distribution centers. The intent was to capture the margins paid to floorcovering wholesalers and offset declining and often negative manufacturer profit margins at the time. Lacking the capital to invest in distribution centers, smaller manufacturers continued to rely on floorcovering wholesalers that were increasingly expanding their product line to include ceramic, hardwood, and resilient floorcoverings. Although no statistics were available, it was believed that the majority of carpet and rug sales for residential use were distributed through company distribution centers to retailers by 1990. However, the majority of carpet and rug manufacturers still used floorcovering wholesalers.

Distribution through floorcovering wholesalers remained popular with the majority of carpet and rug manufacturers because of the retail distribution of residential carpet and rugs. In the mid-1980s, independent (and often small) floorcovering specialty stores were responsible for 58 percent of residential carpet and rug sales volume. Department stores and furniture stores accounted for 21 percent and 19 percent, respectively, of residential sales volume. Mass merchandisers, chain stores, and discount stores were relatively minor retail outlets for carpet and rugs until the early 1990s.

Early 1990s: Wholesale and Retail Consolidation

The early 1990s was marked by a second significant change in wholesale and retail distribution for residential carpet and rugs in the United States. Department stores, furniture outlets, and independent retail stores were being replaced by large mass merchandise and discount stores (Kmart and Wal-Mart) and later by home centers such as Home Depot. The growing number of large retailers that was capturing an increasing share of residential carpet and rug sales spawned a new phenomenon in the retail floorcovering industry among specialty outlets: the buying group.[2] A retail buying group is an organization of similar retailers that combine their purchases to obtain price (quantity) discounts from manufacturers. These pooled purchases allowed independent specialty floorcovering retailers to buy less inventory per order

---

[2] For an overview of buying groups and how they operate, see Kenneth G. Hardy and Allan J. Magrath, "Buying Groups: Clout for Small Businesses," *Harvard Business Review* (September–October 1987): 16–24.

while still getting a lower price, which reduced their costs and pressure for mark-downs caused by overordering. Lower carpet and rug cost plus an emphasis on service gave independent specialty floorcovering retailers a basis with which they could compete against their larger competitors. Logistical aspects of shipping and storing inventory varied from group to group. Some buying groups took physical custody of goods through a central warehouse that often replaced floorcovering wholesalers. Others simply requested manufacturers to deliver the goods directly to buying-group members from the manufacturer's mill or distribution center.

By 1995, three retail buying groups—CarpetMax, Carpet One, and Abby Carpets—registered $3 billion in floorcovering purchases. Another 10 smaller buying groups made another $1 billion in purchases. According to one industry observer, almost one-half of all U.S. residential carpet and rug sales volume was accounted for when buying-group purchases were combined with those of large to medium-sized carpet store chains (e.g., Carpet Exchange), mass merchandisers and discount stores, and home centers. Although estimates varied, about 40 percent of the roughly 23,000 retail outlets that carried carpet and rugs were members of buying groups or large mass-merchandise, discount, or home center chains.

Increased consolidation of retail purchasing evident in buying groups, chain stores, and large mass-merchandise, discount, and home center stores, had either a positive or negative effect on manufacturers. Even with price discounting, and assuming the retail buying organization operated a central warehouse, it was easier and less expensive for a manufacturer to supply one location with large orders than to supply several separate retailers with smaller orders. On the other hand, if a buying organization flexed its buying power and persuaded manufacturers to take lower-than-normal margins (prices) and ship to diverse locations, a manufacturer risked seeing a lower dollar volume and profit.

Direct distribution by manufacturers in the mid-1980s followed by consolidated purchasing and warehousing by retailers in the early 1990s put many floorcovering wholesalers in a precarious position in the residential segment of the carpet and rug industry. Wholesalers that typically served small and medium-sized independent floorcovering specialty stores were particularly vulnerable to the ascension of retail buying groups that operated their own warehouse facility. These wholesalers advocated their role in distribution to both manufacturers and retailers. They argued that working with a buying group was worthwhile to a manufacturer only if the functions performed by the buying group were not only better than those offered by a floorcovering wholesaler, but significant enough to justify the price discounts demanded by a buying group. Similarly, they argued that retailers benefited from wholesaling functions above and beyond the warehousing function. Nevertheless, the absolute number of floorcovering wholesalers had declined in recent years and was expected to decline further over the next five years. The share of wholesaler floorcovering sales was projected to decline from 26 percent in 1995 to less than 23 percent in 2000.

Mid-1990s: Forward Integration into Retailing

In late 1995, the carpet and rug industry watched as yet another change in distribution practices unfolded. On December 12, 1995, Shaw Industries, the largest carpet and rug manufacturer and sales leader, announced plans to engage itself directly in the residential and contract segments of the floorcovering industry. It would do this by operating its own retail stores and commercial dealer network. In announcing this initiative, Robert E. Shaw, the President and CEO of Shaw Industries said:

> We have realized for some time that the manufacturer must become significantly involved in the retail environment to enhance the viability of our industry. Today, our industry offers products of exceptional quality and unsurpassed value, yet we con-

tinue to lose consumer dollars to other product groups. Moreover, because consumers have traditionally price-shopped our products, profits have stagnated for years, from fiber producer to manufacturer to retailer.

Although our industry has matured considerably in recent years, the current structure cannot address many fundamental problems the industry is facing. A manufacturer-dealer affiliation was inevitable, since the only practical way to improve these adverse conditions is by consolidating the combined resources of the two.[3]

Shortly afterward, Shaw Industries announced that it had purchased a number of commercial carpet dealers and contractors and Carpetland USA, a retail chain of 55 stores. Other acquisitions were still pending and the company planned to have 200 retail outlets nationwide by the end of 1996.

In response to this initiative, Home Depot dropped Shaw Industries as a carpet and rug supplier and switched to Mohawk Industries. Carpet One and Abbey Carpets, two buying groups, asked their members not to do business with Shaw. Shaw Industries countered these actions by creating its own retail buying group—the Shaw Alignment Incentive Program. By mid-1996, other carpet manufacturers began courting floorcovering specialty stores with promises to support them with product and not to enter the retail market as competitors.

■ THE COMPANY

Masterton Mills, Inc., is a privately held manufacturer of a full line of medium- to high-priced carpets primarily for the residential segment. The company markets its products under the Masterton and Chesterton brand names. Contract sales to institutions and businesses are also made but account for only 10 percent of company sales. The company has no export sales. Total company sales in fiscal 1996 were $60 million, with a net profit before tax of $2.4 million. Exhibit 3 on page 450 shows abbreviated company financial statements.

Masterton Mills currently distributes its line through seven floorcovering wholesalers located throughout the United States. These wholesalers, in turn, supplied 4,000 retail accounts, including department stores, furniture stores, and floorcovering specialty stores. Inspection of distribution records revealed that 80 percent of residential segment sales were made through 50 percent of its retail accounts. This relationship exists within all market areas served by Masterton Mills. Meadows believed these sales-per-account percentages indicated that at the retail level the company was gaining adequate coverage, if not over coverage.

Advertising by Masterton Mills appeared primarily in shelter magazines and newspapers. The emphasis in advertisements was on fiber type, colors, durability, and soil resistance. A cooperative advertising program with retailers had been expanded on the basis of Goldman's recommendation. According to Goldman, "The co-op program is being well received and has brought us into closer contact with retail accounts." The company employed two regional sales coordinators, who acted as a liaison with wholesalers, assisted in managing the cooperative advertising program, and made periodic visits to large retail accounts. In addition, they were responsible for handling contract sales.

Floorcovering wholesalers played a major role in Masterton Mills' marketing strategy. Its seven wholesalers had long-term relationships with Masterton Mills. Two

---

[3] Quoted in "The North American Top 50 Carpet & Rug Manufacturers," *Carpet & Rug Industry* (April 1996): 12–13.

EXHIBIT 3

Masterton Mills, Inc. Financial Statements (For the Year Ending June 30, 1996)

Income Statement

Net sales	$60,000,000
Less: Cost of goods sold	45,000,000
Gross margin	$15,000,000
Distribution expenses	$ 1,800,000
Selling and administrative expenses	9,000,000
Other expenses	1,800,000
Net income before tax	$ 2,400,000

Balance Sheet

Current assets	$21,550,000
Fixed assets	19,200,000
Total assets	$40,750,000
Current liabilities	$8,250,000
Long-term debt and net worth	32,500,000
Total liabilities and net worth	$40,750,000

Source: Company records.

had represented Masterton Mills products for over 30 years, four had been with the company for 20–25 years, and one had been with the company for 10 years. Masterton Mills' wholesalers maintained extensive sales organizations, with the average wholesaler employing ten salespeople. On average, retail accounts received at least one sales call per month. Goldman's earlier evaluation of the sales program revealed that wholesaler sales representatives performed a variety of tasks, including checking inventory and carpet samples, arranging point-of-purchase displays, handling retailer questions and complaints, and taking orders. About 25 percent of an average salesperson's time was spent on nonselling activities (preparing call reports, acting as a liaison with manufacturers, traveling, and so forth). About 40 percent of each one-hour sales call was devoted to selling Masterton Mills carpeting; 60 percent was devoted to selling noncompeting products. This finding disturbed company management, who felt that a full hour was necessary to represent them. In addition to making sales, wholesalers also stocked carpet inventory. Masterton Mills' wholesalers typically carried sufficient stock to keep the number of their inventory turnovers at five per year. Masterton Mills' executives felt that inventory levels sufficient for four turns per year were necessary to service retailers properly, however. Finally, wholesalers extended credit to retail accounts. In return for these services, wholesalers received a 20 percent margin on sales billed, at the price to retailers.

At an August 1996 meeting with its wholesalers, Masterton Mills executives were informed that several wholesalers were feeling increased pressure to shave their profit margins to accommodate retailer pricing demands. It seemed that an increasing number of their retail accounts had joined regional retail buying groups and were seeking price breaks comparable to those made possible through their group purchases. Subsequent probing on this topic led Masterton Mills executives to conclude that about 1,200 of Masterton Mills' current retailers were members of buying groups; they represented about a third of Masterton Mills' residential sales. The meeting concluded with Masterton Mills executives agreeing to consider a reduction in its price to wholesalers, which could be passed on to retailers. At the same time, wholesalers agreed to consider a modest reduction in their margins as well. The "Margin Sharing" proposal, so named by a wholesaler, would be given top billing at the next meeting in January 1997. In the meantime, price accommodations would be made where and when it was necessary to meet the competition.

■ DIRECT DISTRIBUTION EXPERIENCE OF COMPETITORS

Following her meeting with Meadows, Goldman sought out information on competitors' experience with direct distribution. Despite conflicting information from trade publications and knowledgeable industry observers, she was able to arrive at several important conclusions. First, competitors with their own warehousing or direct distribution operations located them in or near seven metropolitan areas: Atlanta, Chicago, Dallas–Fort Worth, Denver, Los Angeles, New York City, and Philadelphia. Masterton Mills had wholesalers already operating in these metropolitan areas, except for Dallas–Fort Worth and Atlanta. The company serviced these two areas from wholesalers located in Houston, Texas, and Richmond, Virginia, respectively. Second, approximately $5 million in wholesale sales was necessary to operate a warehouse operation economically. The average warehouse operation could be operated at an annual fixed cost (including rent, personnel, operations) of $700,000. Goldman was informed that suitable warehouse space was available in the metropolitan areas under consideration; therefore, the company would not have to embark on a building program. Third, salaries, expenses, and fringe benefits of highly qualified sales representatives would be about $70,000 each annually. One field sales manager would be needed to manage eight sales representatives. Salary, expenses, and fringe benefits would be approximately $80,000 per field sales manager per year. Sales administration costs were typically 40 percent of the total sales force and management costs per year. Delivery and related transportation costs to retail accounts were estimated to be about 4 percent of sales. Though these figures represented rough approximations, in Goldman's opinion and in the opinion of others with whom she conferred, they were the best estimates available.

In early December 1996, just as Goldman was about to draft her position paper for Robert Meadows, she received a disturbing telephone call from a long-time successful wholesaler of the company's products. The wholesaler told her that he and others were disappointed to hear of her inquiries about direct distribution possibilities given what transpired at the August meeting. Through innuendo, the wholesaler threatened a mass exodus from Masterton Mills once the first company warehouse operation was opened. He implied that plans were already under way to establish a trade agreement with a competitor. This conversation would have significant impact on her recommendation if direct distribution was deemed feasible. In short, a roll-out by market area looked less likely. A rapid transition would be necessary, which would require sizable cash outlays, and an aggressive sales force recruiting program.

CHAPTER 9

Pricing Strategy and Management

 Whether or not it is so recognized, pricing is one of the most crucial decision functions of a marketing manager. To a large extent, pricing decisions determine the types of customers and competitors an organization will attract. Likewise, a single pricing error can effectively nullify all other marketing-mix activities. Despite its importance, price rarely serves as the focus of marketing strategy, in part because it is the easiest marketing-mix activity for the competition to imitate.

It can be easily demonstrated that price is a direct determinant of profits (or losses). This fact is apparent from the fundamental relationship

Profit = total revenue − total cost

Revenue is a direct result of unit price times quantity sold, and costs are indirectly influenced by quantity sold, which in turn is partially dependent on unit price. Hence, price simultaneously influences both revenues and costs.

Despite its importance, pricing remains one of the least understood marketing-mix activities. Both its effects on buying behavior and its determination continue to be the focus of intensive study.[1]

■ PRICING CONSIDERATIONS

Although the respective structures of demand and cost obviously cannot be neglected, other factors must be considered in determining pricing objectives and strategies. Most important, the pricing objectives have to be consistent with an organization's overall marketing objectives. Treating the maximization of profits as the sole pricing objective not only is a gross oversimplification, but may undermine the broader objectives of an organization. Other pricing objectives include enhancing product or brand image, providing customer value, obtaining an adequate return on investment or cash flow, and maintaining price stability in an industry or market.

Exhibit 9.1 on page 454 shows how numerous factors affect a marketing manager's pricing discretion. Demand for a product or service sets the price ceiling. Costs, particularly direct (variable) costs, determine the price floor. More broadly, consumer value perceptions and buyer price sensitivity will determine the maximum price(s)

EXHIBIT 9.1

Conceptual Orientation to Pricing

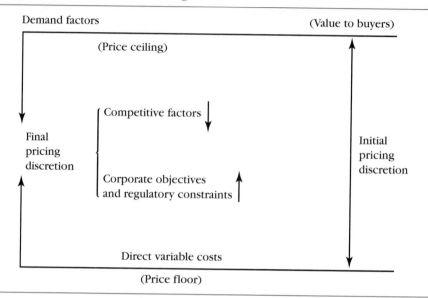

Source: Kent B. Monroe, *Pricing: Making Profitable Decisions*, 2nd ed. (New York: McGraw-Hill, 1990). Reproduced with permission of McGraw-Hill, Inc.

that can be charged. On the other hand, the price(s) chosen must at least cover unit variable cost; otherwise, for each product sold or service provided, a loss will result.

Although demand and cost structures set the upper and lower limit of prices, government regulations, the price of competitive offerings, and organizational objectives and policies narrow a manager's pricing discretion. Regulations prohibiting predatory pricing, the level of differentiation among competitive offerings, and the financial goals set by the organization are all factors that may affect the price range within broad demand and cost boundaries.

There are still other factors that must be considered in pricing a product or service. The life-cycle stage of the product or service is one factor—greater price discretion exists early in the life cycle than later. The effect of pricing decisions on profit margins of marketing channel members must be assessed. The prices of other products and services provided by the organization must be considered as well; that is, price differentials should exist among offerings such that buyers perceive distinct value differences.

Price as an Indicator of Value

In determining value, consumers often pair price with the perceived benefits derived from a product or service. Specifically, *value* can be defined as the ratio of perceived benefits to price:[2]

$$\text{Value} = \frac{\text{perceived benefits}}{\text{price}}$$

This relationship shows that for a given price, value increases as perceived benefits increase. Also, for a given price, value decreases as perceived benefits decrease. Seasoned marketers know that value is more than a low price. According to a Procter and Gamble executive, "Value is not just price, but is linked to the performance and meeting expectations of consumers."[3]

For some products, price alone influences consumers' perception of quality—and ultimately value. For example, in a *Better Homes and Gardens* survey of home furnishing buyers, 84 percent agreed with the statement "The higher the price, the higher the quality." For computer software, it has also been shown that consumers believe a low price implies poor quality.

Price also affects consumer perceptions of prestige so that as price increases, demand for the item may actually rise. Rolls-Royce automobiles, diamonds, French perfumes, fine china, Swiss watches, and crystal may sell worse at lower prices than at higher ones. The recent success of Swiss watchmaker TAG Heuer is an example. The company raised the average price of its watches from $250 to $1,000, and its sales volume increased sevenfold.[4]

Consumer value assessments are often comparative. In such cases, determining value involves a judgment by a consumer as to the worth and desirability of a product or service relative to substitutes that satisfy the same need. A consumer's comparison of the costs and benefits of substitute items gives rise to a "reference value." Although Equal, a sugar substitute containing Nutrasweet, might be more expensive than sugar, some consumers value it more highly than sugar because it has no calories. Retailers have found that they should not price their store brands more than 20 to 25 percent below manufacturers' brands. When they do, consumers often view the lower price as signaling lower quality.[5]

Price Elasticity of Demand

An important concept used to characterize the nature of the price-quantity relationship is that of *price elasticity of demand*. The coefficient of price elasticity, *E*, is a measure of the relative responsiveness of the *quantity* of a product or service demanded to a change in the *price* of that product or service. In other words, the coefficient of price elasticity measures the ratio of the percentage change in the quantity purchased of a product or service to the underlying percentage change in the price of the product or service. This relationship can be expressed as follows:

$$E = \frac{\text{percentage change in quantity demanded}}{\text{percentage change in price}}$$

If the percentage change in quantity demanded is greater than the percentage change in price, demand is said to be *elastic*. In such cases, a small reduction in price will result in a large increase in the quantity purchased; thus, total revenue will rise. Conversely, if the percentage change in quantity demanded is less than the percentage change in price, demand is *inelastic*, and a price reduction will have less of an impact on revenues. Price elasticity of demand is an important factor, for example, in the setting of airline prices for business and leisure fares.[6] Business fares are less price elastic than leisure fares.

A number of factors influence the price elasticity of demand for a product or service. In general,

- The more *substitutes* a product or service has, the greater its price elasticity.
- The more *uses* a product or service has, the greater its price elasticity.
- The higher the *ratio* of the price of the product or service to the income of the buyer, the greater the product's price elasticity.

Product-Line Pricing

In practice, it is common to apply the concept of price elasticity simultaneously to more than one product or service. By computing the *cross-elasticity of demand* for product A and product B, it is possible to measure the responsiveness of the quantity demanded of product A to a price change in product B. A negative *cross-elasticity co-*

efficient indicates that the products are complementary; a positive coefficient indicates that they are substitutes. An understanding of the implications of cross-elasticity is especially important for successful implementation of product-line pricing, in which product demand is interrelated and the goal is to maximize revenue for the entire line and not just for individual products or services.

Consider a marketer of cameras and films (or of copying machines and paper, or of video-game machines and video games). Should the marketer price cameras very low, perhaps close to or even below cost, in order to promote film sales? Film could then be marketed at relatively high prices. Or should an opposite strategy be employed—selling high-priced cameras but low-priced film? Examples of these alternative tie-in pricing strategies are readily available. For instance, Nintendo, a leader in video games, has traditionally priced its hardware at or near cost and made its profit on its software.[7] The important point is that in most organizations, products are not priced in isolation. In certain instances, individual products may be sold at a loss merely to entice buyers or to ensure that the organization can offer potential buyers complete product lines. In such situations, the price may bear little relationship to the actual cost of a product.

In addition, product-line pricing involves determining (1) the lowest-priced product price, (2) the highest-priced product and price, and (3) price differentials for all other products in the line. The lowest- and highest-priced items in the product line play important roles. The highest-priced item is typically positioned as the premium item in quality and features. The lowest-priced item is the traffic builder designed to capture the attention of the hesitant or first-time buyer. Price differentials between items in the line should make sense to customers and reflect differences in their perceived value of the products offered. Behavioral research also suggests that the price differentials should get larger as one moves up the product line to more expensive items.

Estimating the Profit Impact from Price Changes

In Chapter 2, the basic principles of break-even analysis and leverage were described. These same principles can be applied to assessing the effect of price changes on volume.

The impact of price changes on profit can be determined by looking at cost, price, and volume data for individual products and services. Consider the data shown in the top half of Exhibit 9.2 for two products, alpha and beta. These products have identical prices ($10), unit volumes (1,000 units), and net profits ($2,000), but their cost structures differ. Product alpha has a unit variable cost of $7 and assignable fixed costs of $1,000. Product beta has a unit variable cost of $2 and assignable fixed costs of $6,000. The unit break-even volume for product alpha is 333.3 units ($1,000/$3). Product beta's unit break-even volume is 750 units ($6,000/$8).

The lower half of Exhibit 9.2 illustrates the potential profit impact of price changes for the two products. For product alpha to profit from a 10 percent price cut, its sales volume would have to increase by more than 50 percent. In contrast, sales of product beta, with its larger unit contribution, would only have to increase by slightly more than 14 percent for a profit to be realized.

The same type of analysis can be applied to price increases. For example, if product alpha's price were increased 10 percent, its sales volume could decrease by 25 percent before profits would decline. On the other hand, product beta, with its higher unit contribution, could absorb only an 11 percent sales decline with a 10 percent price increase. Other price change effects are shown in Exhibit 9.2 for illustrative purposes.

The procedure for estimating the profit impact from price changes involves three steps:

EXHIBIT 9.2

Estimating the Effect of Price Changes

	Product Alpha	Product Beta
Cost, Volume, and Profit Data		
Unit sales volume	1,000	1,000
Unit selling price	$10	$10
Unit variable cost	$7	$2
Unit contribution	$3 (30%)	$8 (80%)
Fixed costs	$1,000	$6,000
Net profit	$2,000	$2,000
Break-Even Sales Change		
For a 5% price reduction	+20.3%	+6.6%
For a 10% price reduction	+50.0%	+14.3%
For a 20% price reduction	+200.0%	+33.4%
For a 5% price increase	−14.3%	−5.9%
For a 10% price increase	−25.0%	−11.1%
For a 20% price increase	−40.0%	−20.0%

1. Calculate the break-even volume at the original price.
2. Calculate the break-even volume at the new price.
3. Calculate the change in sales before profits are affected.

$$\text{Sales change (\%)} = \frac{\text{new price break-even} - \text{old price break-even}}{\text{old price break-even}} \times 100$$

■ PRICING STRATEGIES

Because of the difficulty of estimating demand, most pricing strategies have a decided reliance on cost as a basic foundation.[8] To a great extent, price strategies can be termed either full-cost or variable-cost strategies. *Full-cost price strategies* are those that consider both variable and fixed costs (sometimes termed *direct* and *indirect costs*). *Variable-cost price strategies* take into account only the direct variable costs associated with offering a product or service.

Full-Cost Pricing

Full-cost pricing strategies generally take one of three forms: markup pricing, break-even pricing, and rate-of-return pricing. *Markup pricing* is a strategy in which the selling price of a product or service is determined simply by adding a fixed amount to the (total) cost of the product. The fixed amount is usually expressed as a percentage of either the cost or the price of the product. If it costs $4.60 to produce a product and the selling price is $6.35, the markup on *cost* would be 38 percent, and the markup on *price* would be 28 percent.

Markup pricing is frequently used in routine pricing situations, such as with grocery or clothing items, but it is also sometimes employed in pricing unique products or services—for example, military equipment or construction projects. Markup pricing may well be the most common type of pricing strategy. Although it possesses decided drawbacks (especially if a single percentage is applied across products without regard to their elasticities or competition), its simplicity, flexibility, and controllability make it highly popular.

As noted in Chapter 2 when discussing the financial aspects of marketing management, break-even analysis is a useful tool for determining how many units of a product or service must be sold at a specific price for an organization to cover its total costs (fixed plus variable costs). Through judicious use of break-even analysis, it is also possible to calculate the break-even price for a product or service. Specifically, the break-even price of a product or service equals the per-unit fixed costs plus the per-unit variable costs.

Rate-of-return pricing is slightly more sophisticated than either markup or break-even pricing. Still, it contains the basic ingredients of both of these strategies and can be viewed as an extension of them. In a *rate-of-return pricing strategy*, price is set so as to obtain a prespecified rate of return on investment (capital) for the organization. Since rate of return on investment (ROI) equals profit (Pr) divided by investment (I),

$$\text{ROI} = \text{Pr}/I = \frac{\text{revenues} - \text{cost}}{\text{investment}} = \frac{P \cdot Q - C \cdot Q}{I}$$

where P and C are, respectively, unit selling price and unit cost, and Q represents the quantity sold.

By working backward from a predetermined rate of return, it is possible to derive a selling price that will obtain that return rate. If an organization desires an ROI of 15 percent on an investment of $80,000, total costs per unit are estimated to be $0.175, and a demand of 20,000 units is forecast, then the necessary price will be

$$\frac{(\text{ROI}) \times I + CQ}{Q} = P = \frac{(0.15)\ \$80,000 + \$0.175 \times 20,000}{20,000} = 0.775$$

or roughly $0.78.

This pricing strategy, popularized by General Motors, is most commonly used by large firms and public utilities whose return rates are closely watched or are regulated by government agencies or commissions. Like other types of full-cost pricing strategies, rate-of-return pricing assumes a standard (linear) demand function and insensitivity of buyers to price. This assumption often holds true only for certain price ranges, however.

Variable-Cost Pricing

An alternative to full-cost pricing strategies is a variable-cost, or contribution pricing, strategy. This type of strategy is sometimes used when an organization is operating at less than full capacity and fixed costs constitute a great proportion of total unit costs. The basic idea underlying *variable-cost pricing* is that, in certain short-run pricing situations, the relevant costs to consider are the variable costs, not the total costs. Specifically, in this strategy, variable unit cost represents the minimum selling price at which the product or service can be marketed. Any price above this minimum represents a contribution to fixed costs and profits.

Variable-cost pricing is a form of demand-oriented pricing. As such, it can serve two different purposes: (1) stimulate demand and (2) shift demand. Since variable-cost prices are lower than full-cost prices, the assumption is that they will *stimulate demand* and increase revenues, and hence will lead to economies of scale, lower unit costs, and greater profits. This is why airlines offer different classes of fares, hotels offer special weekend rates, and movie theaters have discounts for senior citizens. Variable-cost pricing also makes sense because fixed costs must be met no matter whether a product or service is sold—the airline must maintain its flight schedule whether or not there are any passengers; the hotel or movie theater has to remain open even if it is only partially filled—and the incremental (variable) costs of serving one more customer are minimal.

Consider a bus line making a daily run from Duluth to Minneapolis, Minnesota. The price of a one-way ticket is $30.00, and on an average trip the bus is 60 percent full. If unit fixed and variable costs are, respectively, $7.50 and $2.00, should the bus line offer a half-price fare for children under five years of age? Ignoring price elasticity and the like for the moment, the answer is yes, the reduced fare should be offered. The reduced fare ($15.00) covers the variable costs ($2.00) and makes a contribution of $13.00 to fixed costs. Since the bus line will make the trip regardless of how many passengers there are, in the short run every reduced-fare ticket sold contributes $13.00 to fixed expenses. Such a pricing approach always assumes that no more profitable use may be made of the revenue-generating activity.

In addition to stimulating demand, variable-cost pricing can be used to *shift demand* from one time period to another. Movie theaters sometimes have lower matinee ticket prices to encourage customers to switch from evening to afternoon attendance. Likewise, certain utilities (such as telephone companies) have different price schedules to shift demand away from peak load times and smooth it out over extended time periods.

New-Offering Pricing Strategies

Full- and variable-cost pricing strategies are *technical strategies* that can be used when an organization initially sets its prices or when it changes them. When pricing a new product or service, however, a manager also has to consider other, more *conceptual* strategies.

When introducing a new product or service to the marketplace, an organization can employ one of three alternative pricing strategies. With a *skimming pricing strategy*, the price is set very high initially and is typically reduced over time.[9] A skimming strategy may be appropriate for a new product or service if any of the following conditions hold:

1. Demand is likely to be price inelastic.
2. There are different price-market segments, thereby appealing first to buyers who have a higher range of acceptable prices.
3. The offering is unique enough to be protected from competition by patent, copyright, or trade secret.
4. Production or marketing costs are unknown.
5. A capacity constraint in producing the product or providing the service exists.
6. An organization wants to generate funds quickly to recover its investment or finance other developmental efforts.
7. There is a realistic perceived value in the product or service.

Many of these conditions were present when StarSignal, a small California firm, introduced a $26,000 facsimile machine that prints color documents.[10]

At the other extreme, an organization may use a *penetration pricing strategy*, whereby a product or service is introduced at a low price. This strategy may be appropriate if any of the following conditions exist:

1. Demand is likely to be price elastic in the target market segments at which the product or service is aimed.
2. The offering is not unique or protected by patents, copyrights, or trade secrets.
3. Competitors are expected to enter the market quickly.

4. There are no distinct and separate price-market segments.

5. There is a possibility of large savings in production and marketing costs if a large sales volume can be generated.

6. The organization's major objective is to obtain a large market share.

Sony Corporation most likely considered several of these factors and consciously chose a penetration strategy when it introduced its PlayStation video game in 1995. Priced 25 percent lower than competitor video games, Sony's penetration strategy was implemented to quickly capture market share, attract price-sensitive consumers, discourage new competitors from entering the market, and according to a company executive, "achieve a mass market." The strategy accomplished its objective. Sony's PlayStation captured 24 percent of the U.S. video-game market and worldwide sales topped $525 million in its first year of introduction.[11]

Between these two extremes is an *intermediate pricing strategy*. As might be expected, this type of strategy is the most prevalent in practice. The other two types of introductory pricing strategies are, so to speak, more flamboyant; given the vagaries of the marketplace, however, intermediate pricing is more likely to be used in the vast majority of initial pricing decisions.

Competitive Bidding

Although this discussion has centered on administered pricing strategies, one additional form of pricing deserves brief mention. In certain situations, buyers prespecify in contract proposals characteristics of the products or services that they desire to purchase. Potential sellers then bid to obtain the contract. This proposal-bidding procedure, commonly known as *competitive bidding*, is especially prevalent when an organization is marketing to the government or to large industrial concerns.

Competitive bidding requires a highly specialized type of pricing strategy, since (1) demand is known and constant and (2) other marketing-mix elements are virtually uncontrollable or are inconsequential. For this reason, sophisticated mathematical bidding models have been developed to assist organizations in developing winning bids. Most of these models attempt to compute expected profits resulting from different bid prices by associating each price with a probability of winning.

Determination of costs is a vital part of preparing any competitive bidding proposal; depending on organizational goals, either full or variable costs may be used. Still, the most crucial aspect of competitive bidding is undoubtedly estimating the probabilities of award. Not only must these probabilities take into account the needs of the organization, but they must also reflect what the likely bids of the competitors will be.

NOTES

1. For extensive treatments of pricing, see Kent B. Monroe, *Pricing: Making Profitable Decisions*, 2nd ed. (New York: McGraw-Hill, 1990); and Thomas T. Nagle and Reed K. Holden, *The Strategy and Tactics of Pricing*, 2nd ed. (Upper Saddle River, NJ: Prentice Hall, 1995).

2. For a comprehensive review of the price-quality-value relationship, see Valarie A. Zeithaml, "Consumer Perceptions of Price, Quality, and Value," *Journal of Marketing* (July 1988): 2–22.

3. "Laundry Soap Marketers See the Value of 'Value'!" *Advertising Age* (September 21, 1992): 3, 56.

4. "Luxury Steals Back," *Fortune* (January 16, 1995): 112–119.

5. "Store-Brand Pricing Has to Be Just Right," *The Wall Street Journal* (February 14, 1992): B1.

6. Robert A. Crandall, "Different Products, Different Prices," *American Way Magazine* (November 1, 1991): 12.

7. "Giants of Video-Game Industry Rallying for Rebound," *The Wall Street Journal* (May 31, 1996): B3.

8. "The Price Is Wrong, and Economists Are in an Uproar," *The Wall Street Journal* (January 2, 1991): B1.

9. The classic discussion of skimming and penetration pricing is found in Joel Dean, "Pricing Policies for New Products," *Harvard Business Review* (November-December 1976): 141-153.

10. "U.S. Invents Japan Profits (Again)," *Fortune* (March 12, 1990): 14-15.

11. "Nintendo Wakes Up," *The Economist* (August 3, 1996): 55-56.

Southwest Airlines

In late January 1995, Dave Ridley, Vice President–Marketing and Sales at Southwest Airlines, was preparing to join Joyce Rogge, Vice President–Advertising and Promotion, Keith Taylor, Vice President–Revenue Management, and Pete McGlade, Vice President–Schedule Planning, for their weekly "Tuesday meeting." The purpose of this regularly scheduled meeting was to exchange ideas, keep one another informed about external and internal developments pertaining to their areas of responsibility, and coordinate pricing and marketing activities. This informal gathering promoted communication among functional areas and fostered the team spirit that is an integral part of the Southwest corporate culture.

A recurrent "Tuesday meeting" topic during the past six months had been the changing competitive landscape for Southwest evident in the "Continental Lite" and "Shuttle By United" initiatives undertaken by Continental Airlines and United Airlines, respectively. Both initiatives represented targeted efforts by major carriers to match Southwest's price *and* service offering—a strategy that no major carrier had successfully implemented in the past. In early January 1995, Continental's effort was being scaled back due to operational difficulties and resulting financial losses.[1] However, United's initiative remained in effect. Launched on October 1, 1994, "Shuttle By United" was serving 14 routes in California and adjacent states by mid-January 1995, nine of which were in direct competition with Southwest. When "Shuttle By United" was announced, United's CEO predicted: "We're going to match them (Southwest) on price and exceed them on service."[2] In response to United's initiative, Southwest's Chairman Herb Kelleher said, the "United Shuttle is like an intercontinental ballistic missile targeted directly at Southwest."

Just as the meeting began, a staff member rushed in to tell the group that United had just made two changes in its "Shuttle By United" service and pricing. First, its service for the Oakland-Ontario, California market would be discontinued effective April 2, 1995. This market had been among the most hotly contested routes among the nine where United and Southwest competed head-to-head and Southwest had lost market share on this route since October 1994. Second, the one-way walk-up first class and coach fare on all 14 "Shuttle By United" routes had just been increased by $10.00. "Shuttle By United" had previously matched Southwest's fare on the nine competitive routes and, as of mid-January 1995, had been increasing the number of flights on these routes and the five routes where they did not compete.

Changes in United's pricing and service for its shuttle operation caught Southwest executives by surprise. The original agenda for the "Tuesday meeting" was im-

[1] Bridget O'Brian, "Continental's CALite Hits Some Turbulence in Battling Southwest," *The Wall Street Journal* (January 10, 1995):A1, A5.

[2] Quoted in Jon Proctor, "Everyone Versus Southwest," *AIRWAYS Magazine* (November/December 1994): 6-13.

The cooperation of Southwest Airlines in the preparation of this case is gratefully acknowledged. This case was prepared by Professor Roger A. Kerin, of the Edwin L. Cox School of Business, Southern Methodist University, as a basis for class discussion and is not designed to illustrate effective or ineffective handling of an administrative situation. Certain information is disguised and not useful for research purposes. Copyright © 1996 by Roger A. Kerin. No part of this case may be reproduced without written permission of the copyright holder.

mediately set aside. Attention focused on (1) what to make of these unexpected developments and (2) how Southwest might respond, if at all, to the new "Shuttle By United" initiatives.

■ THE U.S. PASSENGER AIRLINE INDUSTRY

The U.S. Department of Transportation classified U.S. passenger airlines into three categories on the basis of annual revenue.[3] A "major carrier" was an airline with more than $1 billion in annual revenue. A "national carrier" had annual revenues between $100 million and $1 billion, and a "regional and commuter airline" had annual revenues less than $100 million. Major carriers accounted for more than 95 percent of domestic passengers carried in 1994. Five carriers—American Airlines, Continental Airlines, Delta Airlines, Northwest Airlines, and United Airlines—accounted for over 80 percent of all major carrier domestic passenger traffic. Exhibit 1 shows major air carrier estimated market shares for 1994 in the United States.

Industry Background

The status of the U.S. passenger airline industry in early 1995 could be traced to 1978. Prior to 1978, and for 40 years, the U.S. airline industry was regulated by the federal government through the Civil Aeronautics Board (CAB). The CAB regulated airline fares, routes, and company mergers, and CAB approval was required before any changes in fares or route systems could be made. In this capacity, the CAB assured that individual airlines were awarded highly profitable and semi-exclusive routes necessary to subsidize less profitable routes which they were also assigned in the public interest. Price competition was suppressed, airline cost increases were routinely passed along to passengers, and the CAB allowed airlines to earn a reasonable rate of return on their investments. In 1978, the Airline Deregulation Act was passed. This Act allowed airlines to set their own fares and enter or exit routes without CAB approvals. Jurisdiction for mergers was first transferred to the U.S. Department of Transportation and subsequently assigned to the U.S. Justice Department in 1988. The CAB was dissolved in 1985.

EXHIBIT 1

Estimated Market Shares for Major U.S. Carriers in 1994 Based on Revenue Passenger Miles Flown

Carrier	Market Share (%)	Carrier	Market Share (%)
1. United Airlines	22.1	6. USAir	7.8
2. American Airlines	20.2	7. Trans World Airlines	5.1
3. Delta Airlines	17.6	8. Southwest Airlines	4.4
4. Northwest Airlines	11.8	9. America West Airlines	2.5
5. Continental Airlines	8.5		

Source: Southwest Airlines company records. Figures rounded.

[3] This section is based on information provided in *FAA Aviation Forecasts* (Washington, D.C.: U.S. Department of Transportation, March 1995); Standard & Poor's *Industry Surveys* (New York: Standard & Poor's, January 1995); *U.S. Industrial Outlook* 1995 (Washington, D.C.: U.S. Department of Commerce, January 1995); Timothy K. Smith, "Why Air Travel Doesn't Work," *Fortune* (April 3, 1995): 42–56; and Jon Proctor, "Everyone Versus Southwest," *AIRWAYS Magazine* (November/December 1994): 6–13.

Deregulation and a Decade of Transition Public policy makers and industry analysts expected that deregulation would proceed in an orderly manner with multiple existing major carriers serving previously semi-exclusive routes, bringing about healthy price competition. However, the carriers responded to deregulation with unexpected changes in their operations that would have long-term effects on the industry.

Two changes in particular were noteworthy. First, major carriers turned their attention to serving non-stop "long-haul" routes anchored by densely populated metropolitan areas or city-pairs which had been highly profitable in a regulated environment. This meant that longer routes such as New York to Los Angeles and Chicago to Dallas were favored over "short-haul" routes between smaller city-pairs such as Baltimore and Newark, New Jersey. As major carriers pruned or reduced service on these short-haul routes, existing regional carriers and new airlines filled the void. In 1978, the United States had 36 domestic carriers; by 1985 the number had grown to 100. Second, major carriers almost uniformly abandoned point-to-point route systems and adopted the hub-and-spoke route system. Point-to-point systems involved non-stop flights between city-pairs and often "shuttle" flights back and forth between city-pairs. The hub-and-spoke system featured "feeder flights" from outlying cities to a central hub city, where passengers would either continue their trip on the same plane or transfer to another plane operated by the same carrier to continue to their final destination. The key to this route system was to schedule numerous feeder flights into the hub airport to coincide with the more profitable long-hauls, with each spoke adding passengers to the larger aircraft flying these longer distances. Potential increased revenue and some cost economies from flying more passengers longer distances, however, were offset by increased costs resulting from reduced utilization of aircraft as they waited to collect passengers, the capital investment in hub facilities, and the need for a larger ground staff.

Competition to survive and succeed intensified in the airline industry immediately following deregulation. Newly formed airlines and regional carriers, which had been permitted to serve only regional markets in a regulated environment, expanded both the number and length of their routes. These carriers typically retained the point-to-point route system which was more economical to operate than hubs. Absent the higher costs associated with the hub-and-spoke system and lower debt than older major carriers had assumed during the regulation era, these carriers had an immediate cost advantage. This advantage resulted in lower fares on both short- and long-haul routes. Price competition quickly erupted as all airlines scrambled to fill their seats. Price competition lowered the average fares paid on the formerly profitable long-haul routes serviced by major carriers while their operating costs remained high. The profit squeeze caused major carriers to cut their schedules and further reduce the number of short-haul routes.

Within five years after deregulation, the major carriers found themselves in a price-cost predicament best described by a senior airline executive: "Either we don't match (fares) and we lose customers, or we match and then because our costs are so high, we lose buckets of money."[4] This situation continued through the remainder of the 1980s as a price war of attrition was waged, ultimately resulting in a flurry of acquisitions by major carriers. Noteworthy acquisitions included Ozark Airlines by Trans World Airlines (TWA), Western Airlines by Delta, and Republic Airlines by Northwest in 1986. In 1987, AMR (American Airlines' parent company), acquired Air California and USAir acquired Pacific Southwest Airlines.

[4] William M. Carley, "Rough Flying: Some Major Airlines Are Being Threatened by Low-Cost Carriers," *The Wall Street Journal* (October 12, 1983): 23.

Financial Calamity in the Early 1990s Acquisition activity in the mid-1980s led industry analysts to believe the U.S. airline industry would soon evolve into an oligopoly with a few carriers capturing a disproportionate share of domestic traffic. By the late 1980s, eight airlines controlled 91 percent of U.S. traffic, but their financial condition was fragile due to a decade of marginal profitability.

Carrier bankruptcy and collapse marked the early 1990s due to a recession, a doubling of fuel prices during the Gulf War in 1991, and excess capacity in the industry. The U.S. airline industry recorded a cumulative deficit of $12 billion from 1990 through 1993. (See Exhibit 2, which plots U.S. air carrier operating revenues and expenses for fiscal year 1979 to 1994.) Between 1989 and 1992, Pan American Airlines (Pan Am), Continental Airlines, America West Airlines, Midway Airlines (a national carrier), Eastern Airlines, and TWA all filed for protection under Chapter 11 of the U.S. Bankruptcy Code. Eastern, Pan Am, and Midway ceased operations in 1991. Continental and TWA emerged from bankruptcy in 1993 as did America West in late 1994, and the industry as a whole recorded a modest operating profit in the 1994 fiscal year. Exhibit 3 on page 466 shows 1994 financial and operating statistics for major U.S. carriers.

As existing airlines collapsed, new airlines were formed. The majority of new carriers, such as ValuJet, Reno Air, and Kiwi International Airlines, positioned themselves as "low-fare, low-frill" airlines. Benefiting from a cheap supply of aircraft grounded by major carriers from 1989 to 1993, the availability of furloughed airline personnel, and cost economies of point-to-point route systems, these new entrants had cost structures that were again significantly below most major carriers. For example, Kiwi was started by former Eastern and Pan Am personnel and was largely

E X H I B I T   2

U.S. Air Carrier Operating Revenues and Expenses, 1979–1994

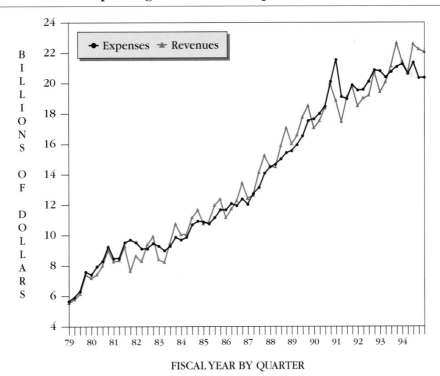

FISCAL YEAR BY QUARTER

Source: U.S. Department of Transportation.

EXHIBIT 3

1994 Financial and Operating Statistics for Major Carriers in the United States

	American Airlines (AMR)	America West Airlines	Continental Airlines	Delta Airlines	Northwest Airlines	Southwest Airlines	Trans World Airlines	United Airlines (UAL)	USAir
Financial Data ($ millions)									
Operating revenue	$14,895	$1,409	$5,670	$12,062	$8,343	$2,592	$3,408	$13,950	$6,997
Passenger	13,616	1,320	5,036	11,197	7,028	2,498	2,876	12,295	6,358
Freight/other	1,279	89	634	865	1,315	94	532	1,655	639
Operating expenses[1]	$14,309	$1,319	$5,921	$12,151	$7,879	$2,275	$3,883	$13,801	$7,773
Operating income	$586	$90	$(251)	$(89)	$464	$317	$(475)	$149	$(776)
Other income (expense)	$(593)	$2	$(399)	$(325)	$52	$(17)	$39	$22	$91
Net income before tax	$(7)	$92	$(650)	$(414)	$516	$300	$(436)	$171	$(685)
Operating Statistics									
Available seat miles (millions)	157,047[5]	18,060	65,861[6]	130,198	85,016	32,124	39,191	152,193	61,540
Revenue passenger miles (millions)	101,382	12,233	31,588	86,296	57,872	21,611	24,906	108,299	37,941
Load factor (%)	64.6	67.7	63.1	66.3	68.1	67.3	63.5	71.2	61.3
Yield (¢)[2]	13.40	10.79	11.44	12.97	12.14	11.56	11.31	11.35	16.76
Cost per available seat-mile (¢)[3]	9.11	7.30	7.86	9.33	9.26	7.08	9.91	9.06	12.63
Labor productivity[4]	1,739	1,695	1,668	1,915	1,968	2,019	1,502	2,125	1,451

[1] Operating expenses include interest expense.

[2] Passenger revenue per revenue passenger mile.

[3] Operating expenses including interest expense per available seat mile.

[4] Thousands of available seat miles per employee.

[5] Includes the American Eagle commuter airline and transportation business only.

[6] Continental Airlines operating statistics are for jet operations only.

Source: Company annual reports. Data and calculations (all rounded) are useful for case analysis, but not for research purposes. Revenue, expense, and operating statistics also include international operations.

funded by its employees (pilots paid $50,000 each to get jobs; other employees paid $5,000). These new "low-fare, low-frill" carriers reported combined revenues of about $1.4 billion in 1994 compared with $450 million in 1992. Although accounting for a small percentage of industry revenue, their pricing practices depressed fares on a growing number of routes also served by major carriers. In 1994, 92 percent of airline passengers bought their tickets at a discount, paying on average just 35 percent of the posted full fare.

Industry Economics and Carrier Performance

The financial performance of individual carriers and the U.S. airline industry as a whole could be attributed, in part, to the underlying economics of air travel. The majority of a carrier's costs (e.g., labor, fuel, facilities, planes) were fixed, regardless of the numbers of passengers served. The largest single cost to a carrier was people (salaries, wages, and benefits) followed by fuel. These two cost sources represented almost one-half of an airline's costs and were relatively fixed at a particular level of operating capacity. Fuel costs were uncontrollable and the industry had been periodically buffeted with skyrocketing fuel prices, most recently during the Gulf War in 1991. Fuel cost was expected to increase by 4.3 cents per gallon in late 1995 based on a tax imposed by the Revenue Reconciliation Act of 1993. Industry observers estimated that this tax would cost the U.S. airline industry an additional $500 million annually in fuel expense.

Labor cost, by comparison, was a controllable expense within limits, and more than 100,000 airline workers lost their jobs between 1989 and 1994. Recent efforts by major carriers to reduce labor cost included United Airlines, which completed an employee buyout of 55 percent of the company in exchange for $4.9 billion in labor concessions in the summer of 1994. In the spring of 1994, Delta Airlines announced a three-year plan to reduce operating expenses by $2 billion, which would involve 12,000 to 15,000 jobs being eliminated.

Carrier Operating Performance Whereas the majority of a carrier's costs were fixed at a particular capacity level regardless of the number of passengers carried, a carrier's passenger revenues were linked to the number of passengers carried and the fare paid for a seat at a particular passenger capacity level. A carrier's passenger capacity is measured by the available seat miles (ASMs) it can transport given its airplane fleet, flight scheduling, and route length. An ASM is defined as one seat flown one mile whether the seat is occupied by a passenger or is empty. Carrier productivity is typically tracked by dividing a carrier's total operating cost by available seat miles. Carrier utilization is measured by what is termed a load factor. Load factor is computed by dividing a carrier's revenue passenger miles (RPMs) by its available seat miles. An RPM is defined as one seat flown one mile with a passenger in it and is a measure of a carrier's traffic. Yield is the measure of a carrier's passenger revenue-producing ability and is expressed as an average dollar amount received for flying one passenger one mile. Yield is calculated by dividing passenger revenue by revenue passenger miles.

The following expression shows how yield, load factor, and cost combine to determine the profitability of passenger operations for individual carriers, routes, and the industry:

Operating Income = (Yield × Load factor) − Cost, or

$$\frac{\text{Operating Income}}{\text{ASM}} = \left(\frac{\text{Passenger Revenue}}{\text{RPM}} \times \frac{\text{RPM}}{\text{ASM}}\right) - \frac{\text{Operating Cost}}{\text{ASM}}$$

By setting operating income to zero and monitoring yield and cost, individual carriers frequently computed a break-even load factor for passenger operations which

EXHIBIT 4

Available Seat-miles, Revenue Passenger-miles, and Load Factors for All Certified U.S. Airlines, 1974–1994 Fiscal Years

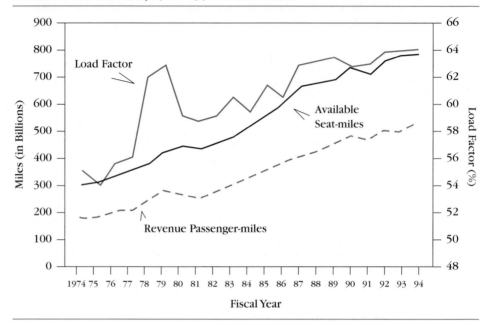

Source: U.S. Department of Transportation.

was continually compared with actual load factors. Actual load factors higher than the break-even load factor produced an operating income for passenger operations; actual load factors below a break-even load factor resulted in an operating loss.

Industry Trends Exhibit 4 charts available seat-miles, revenue passenger-miles, and load factors for all FAA certified airlines for the 1974 fiscal year through the 1994 fiscal year. While revenue passenger miles and available seat miles for the industry have shown an upward trend, load factor fluctuated due to periodic imbalances between industry capacity and passenger demand. For example, domestic airline capacity (ASMs) increased by only 1.6 percent in fiscal year 1994 while revenue passenger miles increased 6.5 percent, producing a load factor of 64.3 percent. This figure represented the highest industry load factor ever achieved on domestic routes. Domestic passenger yields evidenced a long-term downward trend for 25 years in real (adjusted for inflation) dollars. In terms of real yield (discounting fares for inflation), fares in the years 1969 to 1971 produced an average yield of 21.4 cents in 1994 dollars. By 1994, the average industry yield was 12.73 cents.

Cost per available seat mile also exhibited a downward trend since 1978 despite periodic fluctuations in fuel prices. Nevertheless, labor cost reduction and productivity improvements coupled with the gradual addition of more fuel-efficient and lower cost maintenance planes by major carriers had not kept pace with the declining yields in the industry. Efforts by major carriers to reduce labor cost, described earlier, reflected the continuing attention to reducing the cost per available seat mile.

The Airline-Within-an-Airline Concept

Only Southwest Airlines, among the major carriers, appeared able to effectively navigate the economics of air travel and avoid the financial calamity that had befallen the airline industry in the early 1990s. Operating primarily short-haul, point-to-point routes, with minimal amenities, and able to make a fast turnaround of its aircraft between flights, Southwest had much lower operating costs than other major carriers. Lower operating costs were passed on to customers in the form of consistently low fares. From 1990 through 1994, Southwest more than doubled its operating revenues and almost quadrupled its operating income. Its operating practices and financial performance prompted a 1993 U.S. Department of Transportation study to conclude: "The dramatic growth of Southwest has become the principal driving force in changes occurring in the airline industry . . . As Southwest continues to expand, other airlines will be forced to develop low-cost service in short-haul markets."[5]

With Southwest's operating practices as a blueprint, several major carriers had already explored ways to implement a low-cost airline service in short-haul markets and produce a "clone" of Southwest. An outcome of this effort was the "airline-within-an-airline" concept. This concept involved operating a point-to-point, low fare, short-haul, route system alongside a major carrier's hub-and-spoke route system.

Continental Lite Continental was the first major carrier to implement this concept. Having just emerged from bankruptcy with lower operating costs and armed with a preponderance of consumer research showing that 75 percent of customers choose an airline on the basis of flight schedule and price, Continental unveiled what came to be known as "Continental Lite" on October 1, 1993. This service initially focused on Continental routes in the eastern and southeastern United States. By December 1994, Continental had converted about one-half of its 2,000 daily flights into low-fare, short-haul, point-to-point service, but was experiencing operating difficulties. In early January 1995, with operating difficulties resulting in a sizable financial loss, the "Continental Lite" initiative began folding back into Continental's hub-and-spoke system.

Shuttle By United United, the world's largest airline in 1994, inaugurated its "airline-within-an-airline" on October 1, 1994. Branded "Shuttle By United," this initiative followed the United employee buyout in the summer of 1994 when employee wage cuts and more flexible work rules made possible a lower cost shuttle operation alongside the United hub-and-spoke route system. "Shuttle By United" was designed to be a high-frequency, low-fare, minimal amenity, short-haul flight operation initially serving destinations in California and adjacent states. If successful, United executives noted that the initiative could be expanded to 20 percent of United's domestic operations, and particularly to areas where the airline had a significant presence. One such area was the midwest, where United operated a large hub-and-spoke system out of Chicago's O'Hare Airport.

Beginning with eight routes, six of which involved United's San Francisco hub, "Shuttle By United" expanded to 14 routes by January 1995. Eight of the 14 routes involved point-to-point routes separate and apart from United's San Francisco hub. Nine of the routes competed directly with Southwest. In early December 1994, United executives reported that the initiative was exceeding expectations and some routes were profitable. "The Shuttle is working well," said its president, A. B. "Sky" Magary.[6]

---

[5] U.S. Department of Transportation press release, May 11, 1993.
[6] Quoted in Michael J. McCarty, "New Shuttle Incites a War Between Old Rivals," *The Wall Street Journal* (December 1, 1994): B1, B5.

■ SOUTHWEST AIRLINES

Southwest Airlines was the eighth largest airline in the United States in 1994 based on the number of revenue passenger miles flown. Southwest recorded net income of $179.3 million on total operating revenue of $2.6 billion in 1994, thus marking 22 consecutive years of profitable operations—a feat unmatched in the U.S. airline industry over the past two decades. According to Southwest's Chairman, President, CEO, and co-founder, Herb Kelleher, Southwest's success formula could be succinctly described as, "Better quality plus lesser price equals value, plus spiritual attitude of our employees equals unbeatable."

The Southwest Model

Southwest began scheduled service on June 18, 1971, as a short-haul, point-to-point, low-fare, high-frequency airline committed to exceptional customer service. Beginning with three Boeing 737 aircraft serving three Texas cities—Dallas, Houston, and San Antonio—Southwest presently operates 199 Boeing 737 aircraft and provides service to 44 cities primarily in the midwestern, southwestern, and western regions of the United States. Fifty-nine percent of Southwest's capacity, measured in available seat miles flown, was deployed in the western United States, 22 percent in the southwest (Texas, Oklahoma, Arkansas, and Louisiana), and 19 percent in the midwest. Exhibit 5 shows the Southwest route map in early 1995.

EXHIBIT 5

Southwest Airlines Route Map in Early 1995

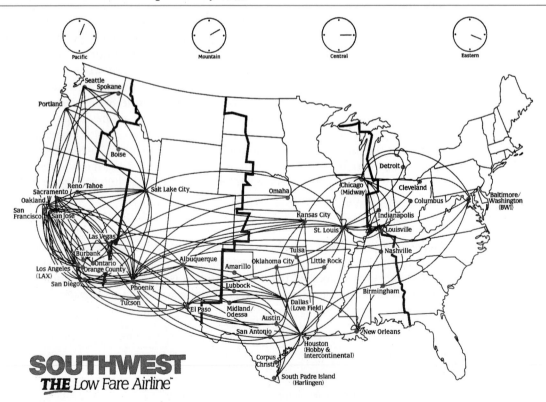

Source: Courtesy of Southwest Airlines.

Except for the acquisitions of Muse Air in 1985 and Morris Air in 1993, Southwest's management has steadfastly insisted on growing internally and refining and replicating what came to be known as the "Southwest Model" in the airline industry. This model was a mixture of a relentless attention to customer service and operations, creative marketing, and Southwest's commitment to its people. A healthy dose of fun was added for good measure.

Customer Service Southwest's attention to customer service was embodied in the attitudes of its people. According to Herb Kelleher:

> What we are looking for, first and foremost, is a sense of humor. Then we are looking for people who have to excel to satisfy themselves and who work well in a collegial environment. We don't care that much about education and expertise, because we can train people to do whatever they have to do. We hire attitudes.[7]

A sense of humor, compassion for passengers and fellow workers, a desire to work, and a positive outlook manifested themselves in customer service at Southwest. Pilots could be found assisting at a boarding gate; ticket agents could be seen handling baggage. So important was the attention to customer service that Southwest chronicled legendary achievements in an internal publication titled *The BOOK on Service: What Positively Outrageous Service Looks Like at Southwest Airlines*.

The Southwest focus on customer service also produced tangible results. In 1994, Southwest won the annual unofficial "triple crown" of the airline industry for the third consecutive year by ranking first among major carriers in the areas of on-time performance, baggage handling, and overall customer satisfaction (see Exhibit 6). No other airline had ever won the "triple crown" for even a single month.

Operations Southwest dedicated its efforts to delivering a short-haul, low-fare, point-to-point, high-frequency service to airline passengers. As a short-haul carrier with a point-to-point route system, it focused on local, not through or connecting, traffic which was common among carriers using a hub-and-spoke system. As a result, ap-

EXHIBIT 6

U.S. Department of Transportation Rankings of Major Air Carriers for 1994 by On-time Performance, Baggage Handling, and Customer Satisfaction

On-time Performance		Baggage Handling		Customer Satisfaction	
Southwest	1	Southwest	1	Southwest	1
Northwest	2	America West	2	Delta	2
Alaska	3	American	3	Alaska	3
United	4	Delta	4	Northwest	4
American	5	Alaska	5	American	5
America West	6	United	6	United	6
Delta	7	TWA	7	USAir	7
TWA	8	USAir	8	America West	8
USAir	9	Northwest	9	TWA	9
Continental	10	Continental	10	Continental	10

Source: U.S. Department of Transportation.

---

[7] Quoted in Kenneth Labich, "Is Herb Kelleher America's Best CEO?" *Fortune* (May 2, 1994): 28–35.

proximately 80 percent of its passengers flew nonstop. In 1994, the average passenger trip length was 506 miles and the average flight time was slightly over one hour. From its inception, Southwest executives recognized that flight schedules and frequency were important considerations for the short-haul traveler. This meant that Southwest aircraft had to "turn" quickly to maximize time in the air and minimize time on the ground. Turn referred to the elapsed time from the moment a plane arrived at the gate to the moment when it was "pushed back," indicating the beginning of another flight.[8] More than half of Southwest's planes were turned in 15 minutes or less while the remainder were scheduled to turn in 20 minutes. The U.S. airline industry turn time averaged around 55 minutes. A result of this difference was that Southwest planes made about ten flights per day, which was more than twice the industry average.

Southwest's operations differed from major carriers in other important ways. First, Southwest generally avoided major airline hubs in large cities. Instead, airports in smaller cities or less congested airports in larger cities were served. Midway Airport in Chicago, Illinois and Love Field in Dallas, Texas were examples of less congested airports in larger cities from which Southwest operated. Less congestion meant Southwest flights experienced less aircraft taxi time and less airport circling while awaiting landing permission. The practice of using secondary rather than hub airports also meant that Southwest did not transfer passenger baggage to other major airlines. In fact, Southwest did not coordinate baggage transfers with other airlines even in the few hub airports it served, such as Los Angeles International Airport (LAX).

Second, Southwest stood apart from other major carriers in terms of booking reservations and providing seat assignments. Rather than making reservations through computerized reservations systems, passengers and travel agents alike had to call Southwest. As a result, fewer than one-half of Southwest's seats were booked by travel agents. (Most airlines rely on travel agents to write up to 90 percent of their tickets.) Savings on travel agent commissions to Southwest amounted to about $30 million per year. Also, contrary to other major airlines, Southwest did not offer seat assignments. As Herb Kelleher said, "We still reserve your seat. We just don't tell you whether it's 2C or 38B!" Instead, reusable, numbered boarding passes identified passengers and determined boarding priority. The first 30 passengers checked in at the gate board first, then a second group of 30 (31–60) boarded, and so forth.

Third, only beverages and snacks were served on Southwest flights. The principal snack was peanuts, and 64 million bags of peanuts were served in 1994. Cookies were offered on longer flights.

Finally, Southwest flew only Boeing 737 jets in an all-coach configuration since no fare classes (first class, economy, business, etc.) existed. This practice differed from other major carriers which flew a variety of jet aircraft made by Airbus Industries, Boeing, and McDonnell Douglas, and reduced aircraft maintenance costs. Southwest's fleet was among the youngest of the major airlines at 7.6 years and had 25 new Boeing 737 aircraft scheduled for delivery in 1995. In 1994, less than one percent of Southwest flights were canceled or delayed due to mechanical incidents and Southwest was consistently ranked among the world's safest air carriers.

The combined effect of Southwest's operations was apparent in its cost structure. In 1994, Southwest's 7.08-cent cost per available seat mile was the lowest among major U.S. carriers.

---

[8] Numerous activities occurred during a turn's elapsed time. Passengers got on and off the plane and baggage was loaded and unloaded. The cabin and lavatories were tidied and the plane was refueled, inspected, and provisioned with snacks and beverages.

Marketing Creative marketing was used to differentiate Southwest from other airlines since its beginning. As Herb Kelleher put it, "We defined a personality as well as a market niche. [We seek to] amuse, surprise and entertain."

Southwest's marketing orientation was intertwined with its customer and operations orientation. In this regard, service, convenience, and price represented three pillars of Southwest's marketing effort. As with customer service and operations, Southwest's unique twist on marketing set it apart from other airlines. In the domain of pricing, for example, Southwest had always viewed the automobile as its primary competitor, not other airlines. According to Colleen Barrett, Southwest's Executive Vice President with responsibility for Customers: "We've always seen our competition as the car. We've got to offer better, more convenient service at a price that makes it worthwhile to leave your car at home and fly with us instead." In 1994, Southwest's average passenger fare was $58.44. Marketing communications continually conveyed the benefits to customers of flying Southwest. Advertising campaigns over the past 24 years featured Southwest service in "The Love Airline" campaign, convenience in "The Company Plane" campaign, and most recently, low price in "*The Low Fare Airline*" campaign (see Exhibit 7 on page 474).

Southwest offered a frequent flyer program called "The Company Club," but again with a difference. Consistent with its focus on flight frequency and short-hauls, passengers received a free ticket to any city Southwest served with eight round-trips completed within 12 months. For 50 round-trips in a 12-month period, Southwest provided a companion pass valid for one year. Having no mileage or other qualifying airlines to track, the costs of "The Company Club" were minimal compared with other frequent flyer programs and rewarded the truly frequent traveler.

Southwest also flew uniquely painted planes that signified places on its route structure. Planes were painted to look like Shamu the Killer Whale to highlight Southwest's relationship with both Sea World of California and Texas. Other planes were painted to look like the Texas state flag and called "The Lone Star Over Texas" while others, such as "Arizona One," featured the Arizona state flag (see Exhibit 8 on page 475).

People Commitment The bond between Southwest and its workers was generally regarded by the company as the most important element in the Southwest model. Herb Kelleher referred to this bond as "a patina of spirituality." He added:

> I feel that you have to be with your employees through all their difficulties, that you have to be interested in them personally. They may be disappointed in their country. Even their family might not be working out the way they wish it would. But I want them to know that Southwest will always be there for them.[9]

The close relationship among all Southwest employees contributed to Southwest's recent listing as one of the top ten best companies to work for in a recent study of U.S. firms. The study noted that the biggest plus at Southwest was that "it's a blast to work here"; the biggest minus was that "you may work your tail off."[10]

Southwest's commitment to its people was evident in a variety of forms. The company had little employee turnover compared with other major airlines and was the first U.S. airline to offer an employee profit-sharing plan. Through this plan, employees owned about 10 percent of Southwest stock. Eighty percent of promotions were internal and cross-training in different areas as well as team building were emphasized at Southwest's "People University."

---

[9] Quoted in Kenneth Labich, "Is Herb Kelleher America's Best CEO?" *Fortune* (May 2, 1994): 28–35.

[10] Robert Levering and Milton Mosckowitz, *The 100 Best Companies to Work for in America* (New York: Doubleday/Currency, 1993).

EXHIBIT 7

Representative Southwest Airlines Print Advertising Campaign

WHEN YOU WANT A LOW FARE, LOOK TO THE AIRLINE THAT OTHER AIRLINES LOOK TO.

SOUTHWEST
THE Low Fare Airline

Call your travel agent or **1-800-I-FLY-SWA**

Source: Courtesy of Southwest Airlines.

EXHIBIT 8

Southwest Airlines Aircraft

Source: Courtesy of Southwest Airlines.

Competitive and Financial Performance

Southwest's attention to customer service and efficient operations, creative marketing, and people commitment produced extraordinary competitive and financial results.

Competitive Performance According to the U.S. Department of Transportation, Southwest carried more passengers than any other airline in the top 100 city-pair markets with the most passengers in the 48 contiguous United States.[11] These 100 markets represented about one-third of all domestic passengers. In its own top 100 city-pair markets, Southwest had an average 65 percent market share compared with about a 40 percent market share for other airlines in their own top 100 city-pair markets. Southwest consistently ranked first or second in market share in more than 90 percent of its top 50 city-pair markets. In Texas, where Southwest began operations in 1971, it ranked first in passenger boardings at ten of the 11 Texas airports served and had an intra-Texas market share of 70.8 percent in mid-1994. Southwest recorded a market share of 56.4 percent in the intra-California market in mid-1994, compared with a market share of less than three percent in 1989.

Financial Performance Southwest's average revenue and income growth rate and return on total assets and stockholders' equity were the highest of any U.S. air carrier during the 1990s. Exhibit 9 provides a five-year consolidated financial and operating summary for Southwest Airlines.

Even though Southwest achieved record revenue and income levels in 1994, net income in the fourth quarter 1994 (October 1–December 31, 1994) fell 47 percent compared to the fourth quarter 1993. The last time Southwest reported quarterly earnings that were less than the same quarter a year earlier was in the third quarter of 1991. Fourth quarter 1994 operating revenues were up only three percent compared to the same period in 1993. This result was considerably less than the double-digit gains in operating revenues recorded in each of the preceding three quarters compared to 1993. Southwest's fourth quarter financial report sent the company's stock price reeling to close at a 52-week low of $15.75 in December 1994 in New York Stock Exchange composite trading, down from a record $39.00 in February 1994.

Southwest's fourth quarter 1994 earnings performance reflected the cumulative effect of numerous factors. These included the conversion of recently acquired Morris Air Corporation to Southwest's operations, competitors' persistent use of fare sales which Southwest often matched, and the airline-within-an-airline initiatives launched by Continental and United. Commenting on the fourth quarter financial and operating performance, Herb Kelleher said:

> While these short-term results will be disappointing to our shareholders, the recent investments made to strengthen Southwest Airlines are vitally important to our long-term success. We are prepared emotionally, spiritually and financially to meet our increased competition head-on with even lower costs and even better customer service.[12]

■ SOUTHWEST VS. SHUTTLE BY UNITED

The maiden flight for "Shuttle By United" departed Oakland International Airport for Los Angeles International Airport at 6:25 A.M. on Saturday, October 1, 1994. Later that morning, United's executive vice president of operations, who flew in from United's world headquarters near Chicago to mark the occasion, spoke to the media. He said:

> What we're doing is getting back into the market and getting our passengers back. We used to own Oakland and LA, and then Herb (Kelleher) came in. What we have to do is protect what's ours.[13]

---

[11] U.S. Department of Transportation press release, May 11, 1993.

[12] Quoted in Terry Maxon, "Southwest Forecasts Dip in Earnings," *The Dallas Morning News* (December 8, 1994): D1, D3.

[13] Quoted in Catherine A. Chriss, "United Shuttle Takes Wing," *The Dallas Morning News* (October 3, 1994): 1D, 4D.

EXHIBIT 9

Southwest Airlines Five-year Financial and Operating Summary (Abridged)

Selected Consolidated Financial Data[1]

(in thousands except per share amounts)	1994	1993	1992	1991	1990
Operating revenues:					
Passenger	$2,497,765	$2,216,342	$1,623,828	$1,267,897	$1,1 44,421
Freight	54,419	42,897	33,088	26,428	22,196
Charter and other	39,749	37,434	146,063	84,961	70,659
Total operating revenues	2,591,933	2,296,673	1,802,979	1,379,286	1,237,276
Operating expenses	2,275,224	2,004,700	1,609,175	1,306,675	1,150,015
Operating income	316,709	291,973	193,804	72,611	87,261
Other expenses (income), net	17,186	32,336	36,361	18,725	(6,827)[6]
Income before income taxes	299,523	259,637	157,443	53,886	80,434
Provision for income taxes[3]	120,192	105,353	60,058	20,738	29,829
Net income[3]	$179,331	$154,284[4]	$97,385[5]	$33,148	$50,605
Total assets	$2,823,071	$2,576,037	$2,368,856	$1,854,331	$1,480,813
Long-term debt	$583,071	$639,136	$735,754	$617,434	$327,553
Stockholders' equity	$1,238,706	$1,054,019	$879,536	$635,793	$607,294

Consolidated Financial Ratios[1]

Return on average total assets	6.6%	6.2%[4]	4.6%[5]	2.0%	3.5%
Return on average stockholders' equity	15.6%	16.0%[4]	12.9%[5]	5.3%	8.4%
Debt as a percentage of invested capital	32.0%	37.7%	45.5%	49.3%	35.0%

Consolidated Operating Statistics[2]

Revenue passengers carried	42,742,602[7]	36,955,221[7]	27,839,284	22,669,942	19,830,941
RPMs (thousands)	21,611,266	18,827,288	13,787,005	11,296,183	9,958,940
ASMs (thousands)	32,123,974	27,511,000	21,366,642	18,491,003	16,411,115
Load factor	67.3%	68.4%	64.5%	61.1%	60.7%
Average length of passenger haul	506	509	495	498	502
Trips flown	624,476	546,297	438,184	382,752	338,108
Average passenger fare	$58.44	$59.97	$58.33	$55.93	$57.71
Passenger revenue per RPM	11.56¢	11.77¢	11.78¢	11.22¢	11.49¢
Operating revenue per ASM	8.07¢	8.35¢	7.89¢	7.10¢	7.23¢
Operating expenses per ASM	7.08¢	7.25¢[8]	7.03¢	6.76¢	6.73¢
Number of employees at yearend	16,818	15,175	11,397	9,778	8,620
Size of fleet at yearend[9]	199	178	141	124	106

[1] The Selected Consolidated Financial Data and Consolidated Financial Ratios for 1992 through 1989 have been restated to include the financial results of Morris.

[2] Prior to 1993, Morris operated as a charter carrier; therefore, no Morris statistics are included for these years.

[3] Pro forma assuming Morris, an S Corporation prior to 1993, was taxed at statutory rates.

[4] Excludes cumulative effect of accounting changes of $15.3 million ($.10 per share).

[5] Excludes cumulative effect of accounting change of $12.5 million ($.09 per share).

[6] Includes $2.6 million gains on sales of aircraft and $3.1 million from the sale of certain financial assets.

[7] Includes certain estimates for Morris.

[8] Excludes merger expenses of $10.8 million.

[9] Includes leased aircraft.

Source: Southwest Airlines 1994 Annual Report.

At the time, Dave Ridley believed that the Oakland flight had "symbolic significance" for two reasons. First, until the late 1980s, United was the dominant carrier at the Oakland airport, but left in the early 1990s following head-to-head competition with Southwest. Second, Oakland had become the main base of Southwest's Northern California operation and was the fastest growing of California's ten major airports in terms of air traffic.

Shuttle By United[14]

Created by a team of United Airlines managers and workers over the course of a year and code-named "U2" internally, "Shuttle By United" was designed to replicate many operational features of Southwest: point-to-point service, low fares, frequent flights, and minimal amenities. Lowering operating cost was a high priority since United's cost for shorter domestic routes (under 750 miles) was 10.5 cents per available seat mile. United's targeted cost per seat mile was 7.5 cents for its shuttle operation.

Like Southwest, "Shuttle By United" featured Boeing 737 jets with a seating capacity of 137 passengers, focused on achieving 20-minute aircraft turns, and offered only beverage and snack (peanuts and pretzels) service. Management and ground crews alike had attended "enculturalization" and motivational classes that emphasized teamwork and customer service. Unlike Southwest, "Shuttle By United" provided first-class (12 seats) and coach seating. Rather than boarding passengers in groups of 30 like Southwest, a boarding process—known as WILMA for windows, middle, and aisle seat—was used for seat assignments. Passengers assigned window seats boarded first, followed by middle seat travelers, and then aisle customers. United's "Mileage Plus" frequent flyer program was available to passengers, with an option that matched Southwest's offer of one free ticket for each eight shuttle round-trips.

"Shuttle By United" was inaugurated with eight routes. Six of these were converted United routes involving the airline's San Francisco hub. Only three of the original eight routes competed directly with Southwest: San Francisco–San Diego, Oakland–Los Angeles, and Los Angeles–Sacramento. On these three routes, the "Shuttle By United" one-way, walk-up coach fare, was identical to Southwest's $69.00 "California State Fare," which was Southwest's highest fare on all seats and flights within California.[15] One-way walk-up coach fares varied on the five non-competing routes. Service from San Francisco to Burbank and to Ontario was priced at $104.00. Fares for the remaining San Francisco routes were $89.00 to Los Angeles, $99.00 to Las Vegas, and $139.00 to Seattle. The "Shuttle By United" first-class fare was typically $20.00 higher than its coach fare. "Shuttle By United" was advertised heavily using print and electronic media.

"Shuttle By United" soon expanded its route system to include six additional routes. All six routes competed directly with Southwest. Service out of Oakland included Oakland–Burbank, Oakland–Ontario, and Oakland–Seattle. Los Angeles to Phoenix and to Las Vegas and San Diego–Sacramento rounded out the new service. Except for the Oakland–Seattle route, all one-way walk-up coach fares were $69.00 for Southwest and "Shuttle By United." A one-way walk-up coach fare of $99.00 was charged on the Oakland–Seattle route by the two airlines. "Shuttle By United" also in-

---

[14] Portions of this discussion are based on Jesus Sanchez, "Shuttle Launch," *Los Angeles Times* (September 29, 1994): D1, D3; Randy Drummer, "The Not-So-Friendly Skies," *Daily Bulletin* (September 30, 1994): C1, C10; "United Brings Guns to Bear," *Airline Business* (November 1994): 10; Michael J. McCarthy, "New Shuttle Incites a War Between Old Rivals," *The Wall Street Journal* (December 1, 1994): B1, B5.

[15] Walk-up fares refer to the fare available at any time, with no restrictions, no penalties, and no advance purchase requirements.

EXHIBIT 10

Cities Served by Shuttle By United

Note: The map is not drawn to scale.

creased its flight frequency in 12 of 14 city-pair markets, primarily out of its San Francisco hub. Cities served by "Shuttle By United" appear in the map shown in Exhibit 10.

In early December 1994, United reported that the cost per available seat mile of its shuttle operation had not yet achieved its targeted 7.5 cents. In an interview, "Sky" Magary said, "We're vaguely better than halfway there."[16]

Southwest Airlines

Southwest's planning for United's initiative began months before the "Shuttle By United" scheduled October 1 launch. In June 1994, a Southwest spokesperson said the airline would "vigorously fight to maintain our stronghold in California."

Prior to the launch of "Shuttle By United," Southwest committed additional aircraft to the California market to boost flight frequencies on competitive routes. By

---

[16] Michael J. McCarthy, "New Shuttle Incites a War Between Old Rivals," *The Wall Street Journal* (December 1, 1994): B1, B5.

mid-January 1995, Southwest had deployed 16 percent of its total capacity (in terms of available seat miles flown) to the intra-California market. Thirteen percent of Southwest's total available seat-mile capacity overlapped with "Shuttle By United" by late January 1995.

Southwest also boosted its advertising and promotion budget for the intra-California market, with particular emphasis in city-pairs where "Shuttle By United" competed directly with Southwest. Southwest's *The* Low Fare Airline" advertising campaign spearheaded this effort. Southwest's walk-up fare remained at $69.00 during the fourth quarter of 1994, unchanged from the fourth quarter of 1993. However, Southwest's 21-day advance fares and other discount fares were being heavily promoted. The effect of this pricing was that Southwest's average passenger fare in the markets also served by "Shuttle By United" (excluding Oakland–Seattle) was $44.00 during the fourth quarter of 1994 and into early January 1995, compared with $45.00 in the third quarter of 1994. The average 1994 fourth-quarter fare for the Oakland–Seattle route was $51.00, down from $60.00 in the third quarter of 1994. Dave Ridley estimated that the average passenger fare for "Shuttle By United" was five to ten percent higher than the average Southwest fare in the nine markets where it competed directly with Southwest, and about $20.00 higher than the average Southwest fare in the five markets served out of San Francisco where it did not compete directly with Southwest. The difference in average passenger fares between the airlines was due to first-class seating offered by "Shuttle By United" in competitive markets and generally higher fares in non-competitive markets.

■ THE TUESDAY MEETING

The original agenda for the "Tuesday meeting" in late January 1995 focused mostly on operational issues. For example, Southwest would begin scheduled service to Omaha, Nebraska, in March 1995, and advertising, sales, promotion, and scheduling matters still required attention. Southwest's "ticketless" travel system, or "electronic ticketing" was also on the agenda. This system, whereby travelers make reservations by telephone, give their credit card number and receive a confirmation number, but receive no ticket in the mail, was scheduled to go nationwide on January 31, 1995, after a successful regional test. Final details were to be discussed.

Dave Ridley also intended to apprise his colleagues of the competitive situation in California. A staff member had prepared a report showing fourth quarter load factors by route for Southwest and estimated load factors for "Shuttle By United." He wanted to share this information with the group (see Exhibit 11), along with other recent developments. For example, a few days earlier, "Shuttle By United" had reduced its one-way walk-up coach fare on the San Francisco–Burbank route to $69.00. This fare was identical to the one charged on the Oakland–Burbank route by both airlines. In addition, Southwest's consolidated yield and load factor for January 1995 were tracking lower than the consolidated yield and load factor for January 1994. If present traffic patterns continued, Southwest's consolidated load factor would be about five points lower in January 1995 as compared to January 1994.

Unexpected news that "Shuttle By United" intended to discontinue some service and raise fares altered the original meeting agenda and posed a number of questions for Southwest executives. For instance, did the fare increase signify a major modification in United's "We're going to match Southwest" strategy? If so, what were the implications for Southwest? How might Southwest react to these changes, if at all? Should Southwest follow with a $10.00 fare increase of its own or continue with its present price and service strategy? What might be the profit impact of United's action and Southwest's reaction, if any, for each airline? And how, if at all, was United's pricing action linked to the announced withdrawal from the Oakland–Ontario market?

EXHIBIT 11

Daily Scheduled City-pair Round-trips by Southwest Airlines and "Shuttle By United" and Quarterly Load Factor Estimates

Market (City-pair)	Air Miles	Southwest Airlines Daily Round-trip Flights		Shuttle By United Daily Round-trip Flights		1994 4th Quarter Load Factor		1994 3rd Quarter Load Factor		1993 4th Quarter Load Factor	
		October–December 1994	Mid-January 1995	October–December 1994	Mid-January 1995	United	Southwest	United	Southwest	United	Southwest
San Francisco–Los Angeles	338	No Service →		31	40	66%	—	77%	—	68%	—
San Francisco–Burbank	359	No Service →		11	12	60%	—	70%	—	64%	—
San Francisco–Ontario	364	No Service →		11	12	47%	—	63%	—	64%	—
San Francisco–Las Vegas	417	No Service →		9	10	73%	—	85%	—	74%	—
San Francisco–Seattle	678	No Service →		13	16	74%	—	89%	—	77%	—
San Francisco–San Diego	417	12	12	10	12	77%	61%	87%	68%	84%	70%
Oakland–Los Angeles	338	19	25	10	15	62%	59%	—	74%	—	63%
Oakland–Burbank	326	13	16	7	11	40%	63%	—	80%	—	7 0%
Oakland–Ontario	362	12	14	7	7	32%	57%	—	68%	—	65 %
Oakland–Seattle	671	4	7	4	5	52%	66%	—	77%	—	—
Los Angeles–Sacramento	374	5	6	5	6	81%	65%	73%	53%	67%	56%
Los Angeles–Phoenix	366	25	23	9	10	48%	61%	—	60%	—	61%
Los Angeles–Las Vegas	241	13	19	10	12	61%	65%	—	73%	—	67%
San Diego–Sacramento	481	9	9	5	5	50%	68%	—	78%	—	

Source: Southwest Airlines company records. For analysis purposes, load factors can be applied to daily round-trip flights for both airlines on both legs of a round-trip.

Burroughs Wellcome Company
Retrovir

"I think that Burroughs Wellcome is very interested in getting all their money back as soon as possible, because the sun won't shine forever."[1]

Cofounder of Project Inform,
an AIDS treatment information agency (1987)

"Once the drug is out on the marketplace, the company controls the pricing."[2]

Dr. George Stanley,
Food and Drug Administration (1987)

"To make AZT accessible to everyone who should be on it, Burroughs Wellcome has an obligation to give up a significant amount of money to allow people to get access."[3]

Executive Director,
National Gay and Lesbian Task Force (1989)

"There's no plan to make another price cut."[4]

Sir Alfred Sheppard,
Chairman of the Board, Wellcome PLC (1989)

In January 1990, Burroughs Wellcome executives were under continued pressure to reduce the price of Retrovir. Retrovir brand zidovudine is the trade name for a drug called azidothymidine (AZT), which had been found to be effective in the treatment of acquired immune deficiency syndrome (AIDS) and AIDS-related complex (ARC). AIDS is a disease caused by a virus that attacks the body's immune system and damages the system's ability to fight off other infections. Without a functioning immune system, a person becomes vulnerable to infection by bacteria, protozoa, fungi, viruses, and other malignant agents, which may cause life-threatening illnesses, such as pneumonia, meningitis, and cancer. AIDS is caused by HIV (human immunodeficiency virus), a human virus first discovered in 1983. AZT is classified as an antiviral drug that interferes with the replication of HIV. As such, AZT is a treatment, not a cure, for AIDS.

In 1987, Burroughs Wellcome obtained approval from the U.S. Food and Drug Administration to market Retrovir, the first and, as of 1990, the only drug authorized for the treatment of AIDS. Soon after Burroughs Wellcome made Retrovir available for prescription sales on March 19, 1987, the company became embroiled in controversy related to the price of the drug. Critics charged that Burroughs Wellcome, which sold the drug to wholesalers at a price of $188 for a hundred 100-milligram

---

[1] "The Unhealthy Profits of AZT," *The Nation* (October 17, 1987): 407.

[2] Ibid.

[3] "AZT Maker Expected to Reap Big Gain," *New York Times* (August 29, 1989): 8.

[4] "Wellcome Seeks Approval to Sell AZT to All Those Inflicted with AIDS Virus," *The Wall Street Journal* (November 17, 1989): B4.

This case was prepared by Professor Roger A. Kerin, of the Edwin L. Cox School of Business, Southern Methodist University, with the assistance of Angela Bullard, graduate student, as a basis for class discussion and is not designed to illustrate effective or ineffective handling of an administrative situation. The case was prepared from published sources. Quotes, statistics, and published operating information are footnoted for reference purposes. Copyright © 1995 by Roger A. Kerin. No part of this case may be reproduced without the written permission of the copyright holder.

capsules, engaged in price gouging of a "highly vulnerable market." The company's President, T. E. Haigler, responded that the high price was due to the "uncertain market for the drug, the possible advent of new therapies, and profit margins customarily generated by significant new medicines."[5]

Nevertheless, the company reduced its price by 20 percent in December 1987, and again by 20 percent in September 1989. Prior to the 1989 price reduction, the Subcommittee on Health and the Environment of the U.S. House of Representatives had launched an investigation into possible "inappropriate" pricing of Retrovir. Soon after the announced price reduction in 1989, the chairman of the House subcommittee said that this was "a good first step. But I think the company can do better."[6] In November 1989, the Chairman of Wellcome PLC, the parent company of Burroughs Wellcome, was quoted as saying, "There's no plan to make another price cut."[7] However, pressure to again reduce the price continued.

■ ACQUIRED IMMUNE DEFICIENCY SYNDROME

Acquired immune deficiency syndrome can be traced to a blood sample taken and stored in the Central African nation of Zaire in 1959 (see Exhibit 1 for a chronology of important events). It was not until 1982, however, that the Centers for Disease Control and Prevention in Atlanta, Georgia, labeled the disease and warned that it

E X H I B I T   1

AIDS Chronology, 1959–1990

1959	Blood sample taken and stored in the Central African nation of Zaire. Retesting the sample in 1986, physicians discover it to be HIV-infected.
1978	Doctors determine that a child in New York died as a direct result of immune system breakdown.
1981	The Centers for Disease Control (CDC) reports breakdowns of the immune systems of several male homosexuals with the resulting occurrence of infectious diseases and cancers.
1982	CDC names the "mystery disease" acquired immune deficiency syndrome (AIDS) and warns that it may be spread by a virus in bodily fluids such as blood and semen.
1983	Scientists at the Pasteur Institute in Paris, France, isolate a suspected AIDS-causing virus.
1984	U.S. researchers identify an AIDS-causing virus as the same one isolated by the French scientists.
1985	A test is licensed to detect an AIDS-causing virus in blood.
1986	The AIDS-causing virus is named human immunodeficiency virus, or HIV.
1987	U.S. Food and Drug Administration permits sale of azidothymidine (AZT), which eases some of the symptoms of AIDS and AIDS-related complex (ARC).
1988–1990	AIDS fatalities continue to increase while the pharmaceutical industry searches for a cure.

[5] "The High-Cost AIDS Drug: Who Will Pay for It?" *Drug Topics* (April 6, 1987): 52.

[6] "How Much for a Reprieve from AIDS?" *Time* (October 2, 1989): 81.

[7] "Wellcome Seeks Approval to Sell AZT . . . ," *The Wall Street Journal* (November 17, 1989): B4.

might be spread by a virus in bodily fluids such as blood and semen. In 1983 and 1984, French and American scientists isolated a suspected AIDS-causing virus that was subsequently named human immunodeficiency virus, or HIV, in 1988. HIV is a retrovirus that can become an extra link in the genetic code, or DNA, of a cell. HIV inhibits and eventually destroys the T-4 cell, which is a key part of a person's immune system that attacks foreign germs. Without T-4 cells, people succumb to all manner of infections. The identification of HIV was a major breakthrough, especially since, prior to 1984, it was not established in the scientific community that retroviruses like HIV caused human diseases.

Incidence and Cost of HIV and AIDS

Efforts to track and forecast the incidence and cost of HIV and AIDS began in earnest in 1986. Research focused on identifying high-risk individuals, determining the geographical concentration of the disease, and arriving at estimates of the number of people afflicted with HIV and AIDS.[8] This research found that almost 90 percent of AIDS victims were homosexual men or intravenous drug users. One-half of all reported AIDS cases were in the San Francisco, Miami, New York City, Los Angeles, and Houston metropolitan areas.

Tracking and forecasting the incidence of AIDS cases and HIV infections proved to be more difficult. The CDCP reported 5,992 AIDS cases in 1984 and 35,198 cases in 1989. Estimates of HIV infections in 1990 ranged between 800,000 and 1,300,000 Americans, depending on the estimation procedure employed. The incidence of AIDS cases in the period 1981–1989 are charted in Exhibit 2. The fatality rate for persons inflicted with AIDS was about 91 percent in 1981 and 46 percent in 1989.

Treating AIDS patients has proved to be extremely expensive. According to a 1987 study by the Rand Corporation, an internationally recognized research organization, the lifetime medical costs of an AIDS patient in his thirties were estimated to be between $70,000 and $141,000. For comparison, the lifetime cost of treating a person in his thirties with digestive tract cancer was $47,000; leukemia, $29,000; and a heart attack, $67,000.

An estimated 40 percent of persons with AIDS have received care under the Medicaid Program, which is administered by the Health Care Financing Administration and funded jointly by the federal government (55 percent) and individual states (45 percent). Estimated annual costs for AIDS care and treatment funded by Medicaid ranged between $700 million and $750 million in 1988. Medicaid spending for AIDS was estimated to reach $2.4 billion in 1992. In addition, private insurers paid $250 million annually in AIDS-related medical payments.

Anti-HIV Drug Treatment

The identification of HIV in the mid-1980s prompted numerous pharmaceutical companies to search for antiviral drugs. Burroughs Wellcome led the research effort in part because of its prior development of drugs that combat viral diseases. In addition to AZT supplied by Burroughs Wellcome, other compounds were in various stages of

---

[8] Portions of this material are based on statistics reported in Brad Edmundson, "AIDS and Aging," *American Demographics* (March 1990): 28–34; Fred J. Hellinger, "Forecasting the Personal Medical Care Costs of AIDS from 1988 through 1991," *Public Health Reports* (May–June 1988): 309–319; William L. Roper and William Winkenwerder, "Making Fair Decisions about Financing Care for Persons with AIDS," *Public Health Reports* (May–June 1988): 305–308; Centers for Disease Control, "Human Immunodeficiency Virus Infection in the United States: A Review of Current Knowledge," *Morbidity and Mortality Weekly Report* (December 18, 1987): 2–3, 18–19; "Now That AIDS Is Treatable, Who'll Pay the Crushing Cost?" *Business Week* (September 11, 1989): 115–116; Centers for Disease Control, "HIV/AIDS Surveillance Report" (U.S. Department of Health and Human Services, Public Health Services: December 1990).

EXHIBIT 2

AIDS Cases, 1981–1989

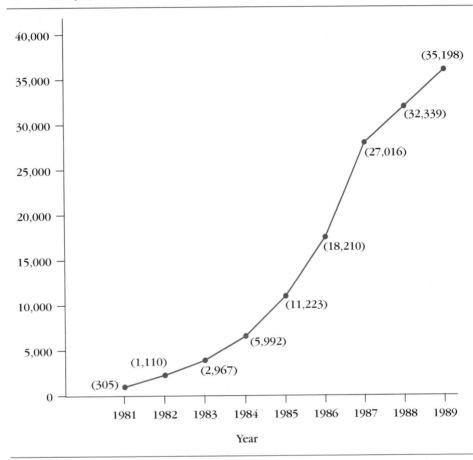

Source: Based on Centers for Disease Control and Prevention, "HIV/AIDS Surveillance Report" (U.S. Department of Health and Human Services, Public Health Services: December 1990).

development and commercialization.[9] One antiviral drug has been given limited approval by the FDA and is available to patients who have a negative reaction to AZT. This drug, produced by Bristol Myers and called DDI, is an antiviral drug that appears to inhibit reproduction of HIV and slow the damage it causes. DDI was initially studied for AIDS use by the National Cancer Institute. Like AZT, it interferes with the ability of HIV-infected cells to produce new viruses and slows the progression of HIV infection, but does not eradicate or eliminate the infection. The principal advantage of DDI over AZT is that it appears to be less toxic. DDC, developed by Hoffman-LaRoche, was in clinical trials in 1989. Other drugs produced by Glaxo and Triton Biosciences, Inc. were being tested as well. Industry analysts believed that one or more of these drugs would obtain FDA approval for prescription sales by 1991.

---

[9] Portions of this material are based on "A Quiet Drug Maker Takes a Big Swing at AIDS," *Business Week* (October 6, 1986): 32; "There's No Magic Bullet, but a Shotgun Approach May Work," *Business Week* (September 11, 1989): 118.

■ BURROUGHS WELLCOME COMPANY

Burroughs Wellcome is the American subsidiary of Wellcome PLC, an English public limited company with headquarters in London.[10] Wellcome PLC is a multinational firm with manufacturing operations in 18 countries and employs 20,000 people. Approximately 18 percent of the company's employees are engaged in research and development efforts. The company's primary business, which accounts for 89 percent of its fiscal 1989 revenue, is human health-care products, both ethical (prescription) and over the counter (nonprescription). Two ethical products account for 34 percent of its human health-care revenue: Zovirax and Retrovir. Zovirax, which is used in the treatment of herpes infection, is the company's single largest-selling product with annual sales of $492 million in 1989. Retrovir is its second largest-selling product with sales of $225 million in fiscal 1989. In addition, the company markets Actifed and Sudafed, cough and cold preparations, as over-the-counter products. These two products combined account for annual sales of $253 million. Wellcome PLC had an animal health-care business that accounted for about 11 percent of company revenue. This business was divested in late 1989.

North America represents the largest market for the products sold by Wellcome PLC, with annual sales of $997 million. Sales in the United States are roughly equivalent to 42 percent of Wellcome PLC's worldwide sales. The United Kingdom is the company's second largest market and accounts for about 10 percent of worldwide sales.

EXHIBIT 3

Selected Financial and Operating Ratios of Wellcome PLC

	Fiscal Year[a]		
	1989	1988	1987
Financial Ratios			
Gross profit margin (gross profit/sales)	70.6%	68.1%	67.5%
Return on sales (net income before tax/sales)	20.0	17.7	14.9
Return on assets (net income before tax/total assets)	20.0	18.0	15.0
Return on equity (net income before tax/common equity)	35.0	36.0	32.0
Operating Ratios			
R&D expenditures/sales	13.4	13.1	12.6
Selling, general, and administration costs/sales	36.9	36.5	39.2

[a] Fiscal year ends August 31.

Source: Wellcome PLC annual reports.

[10] Much of this material is described in Wellcome PLC's 1989 and 1990 annual reports; "Burroughs Wellcome Company," Burroughs Wellcome news release, December 13, 1990; Brian O'Reilly, "The Inside Story of the AIDS Drug," *Fortune* (November 5, 1990): 112–129. Financial figures and percentages represent approximations, since information is reported in U.S. dollars and the British pound sterling. These figures are not useful for research purposes.

EXHIBIT 4

Selected Financial and Operating Ratios for Pharmaceutical Firms in the United States, 1989

	Pharmaceutical Firm					
	Schering-Merck & Co.	Pfizer, Inc.	Abbott Labs	Upjohn	Plough	Eli Lilly
Financial Ratios[a]						
Gross profit margin	76.3%	63.6%	52.5%	69.8%	73.8%	69.9%
Return on sales	34.8	16.2	22.2	15.8	20.4	31.9
Return on assets	33.8	11.0	24.6	14.2	17.9	22.7
Return on equity	64.9	20.2	43.8	26.5	33.0	35.4
Operating Ratios						
R&D/sales	11.5	9.4	9.3	14.0	10.3	14.5
SG&A/sales	30.7	37.2	20.5	40.3	42.3	27.5

[a] See Exhibit 3 for definitions of ratios.

Source: Company annual reports.

Wellcome PLC recorded total revenues of $1.75 billion and net profit before tax of $262.1 million in fiscal 1987. Total revenues for fiscal 1989 (fiscal year ended August 31, 1989) were $2.1 billion with net profit before taxes of $475 million.[11] Selected financial and operating ratios for Wellcome PLC for the fiscal years 1987–1989 are shown in Exhibit 3. Exhibit 4 presents comparative statistics for other major firms in the U.S. pharmaceutical industry. Percentage sales and the net income growth since fiscal 1985 for Wellcome PLC are shown below:

Fiscal Years	Sales Growth	Net Income Growth
1985–1986	0.2%	7.2%
1986–1987	12.6	47.3
1987–1988	10.4	35.1
1988–1989	12.6	42.9

■ DEVELOPMENT OF RETROVIR

Burroughs Wellcome's AIDS research program began in June 1984 with an extensive search for likely drug candidates. According to Philip Furman, head of virus research, "We looked at all our known antivirals on the off chance that one would work against retroviruses."[12]

---

[11] These figures are based on the average exchange rate of $1.55 = £1 in 1987, $1.68 = £1 in 1989 (Wellcome PLC 1990 *Annual Report*).

[12] This material is based on "The Development of Retrovir," Burroughs Wellcome news release, June 1990; L. Wastila and L. Lasagna, "The History of Zidovudine (AZT)," *Journal of Clinical Research and Pharmacoepidemiology*, Vol. 4 (1990): 25–29; "The Inside Story of the AIDS Drug," *Fortune* (November 5, 1990): 112–129; "AIDS Research Stirs Bitter Fight over Use of Experimental Drugs," *The Wall Street Journal* (June 18, 1986): 26.

Laboratory Testing

Burroughs Wellcome scientists examined hundreds of compounds over a period of five months, but none proved acceptable. In November 1984, AZT was found to inhibit animal viruses in a laboratory setting. AZT had been synthesized in 1964 by a researcher at the Michigan Cancer Foundation. It was hoped then that the drug would be useful in the treatment of cancer, but when investigated, it was found to have no potential as an anticancer agent. In the early 1980s, Burroughs Wellcome scientists resynthesized AZT in their exploration of compounds with possible effectiveness against bacterial infection. This research provided information about the spectrum of the drug's antibacterial activity and its toxicity and metabolism in laboratory animals, but intensive development was not pursued. The drug was not examined again until late 1984 when it showed promise as an AIDS treatment. (Exhibit 5 details significant events in the development of Retrovir.)

Following *in vitro* demonstration of its potential by Burroughs Wellcome's scientists, 50 coded compounds including AZT were sent to Duke University, the National Cancer Institute (NCI), and the FDA for independent testing to assess their *in vitro* activity against the human retrovirus.[13] Early in 1985 these tests showed that AZT was, in fact, active against HIV in the test tube. The company then began extensive preclinical toxicologic and pharmacologic testing in the spring of 1985. At the same time, work began on scaling up synthesis of the drug in preparation for clinical testing in patients with HIV. On June 14, 1985, Burroughs Wellcome submitted an application to the FDA to obtain Investigational New Drug (IND) status for the compound, which would allow its use in a limited number of severely ill AIDS and ARC patients. A week later, the FDA notified Burroughs Wellcome that the submitted data were sufficient to allow clinical studies in humans to be initiated.

Human Testing

Retrovir was administered to patients for the first time on July 3, 1985, at the Clinical Center of the National Institutes of Health (NIH) in Bethesda, Maryland. This initial (Phase I) study, conducted under a protocol developed by Burroughs Wellcome in collaboration with scientists at the NCI, Duke University, the University of Miami, and UCLA, involved 40 patients infected with HIV. The purpose of Phase I testing was to determine how Retrovir acted in the body, the appropriate dosage, and potential adverse reactions or side effects. Initial results were encouraging. Some of the patients showed evidence of improvement, including an increased sense of well-being, weight gain, and positive changes in various measures of the immune system function. Extended treatment, however, lowered production of red blood cells and certain white blood cells in some patients who had taken high doses.

By early 1986, sufficient data on Retrovir were available to proceed with more extensive human testing. The need now was to prove that the drug could provide useful therapy for AIDS and ARC patients. More volunteers and an objective basis for comparison were essential to the conduct of the Phase II trial. A double-blind, placebo-controlled trial, conducted and financed by Burroughs Wellcome, began on February 18, 1986. A total of 281 patients participated. Safeguards built into the study provided for data to be reviewed periodically by a board of impartial experts convened under the auspices of the National Institute of Allergy and Infectious Diseases (NIAID). If either the placebo or the drug-treated group did either so poorly or so well that it would be unethical to continue the trial, the study would be stopped.

About this time, both the medical community and the general public had heard of the Phase II trial. As publicity about the trial gained momentum, AIDS patient-

---

[13] *In vitro*, a Latin phrase meaning "in glass," is used medically to mean to isolate from a living organism and artificially maintain in a test tube.

EXHIBIT 5

Retrovir Milestones, 1984–1990

June 1984	Burroughs Wellcome begins an AIDS research program to search for chemical compounds that might be effective against HIV.
November 1984	Burroughs Wellcome scientists identify AZT as potentially useful against AIDS.
Spring 1985	*In vitro* activity of AZT against HIV is confirmed by laboratories at Duke University, FDA, and NCI. This confirmatory work, requested by Burroughs Wellcome, is done on coded samples whose chemical identity is not revealed to the outside laboratories.
Spring 1985	Burroughs Wellcome continues toxicologic and pharmacologic testing of AZT. Work begins on scaling up synthesis of the drug, as the compound has never been produced beyond the few grams used for research purposes.
June 1985	FDA permits Burroughs Wellcome to begin clinical trials of AZT in humans.
July 1985	AZT is designated an "orphan drug" for the treatment of AIDS (a designation made when the affected population is less than 200,000).
July 1985	Burroughs Wellcome begins a collaborative Phase I study with NCI and Duke University to assess AZT's safety and tolerance in humans.
December 1985	Enrollment in the Phase I study, eventually involving 40 patients and investigators from NCI, Duke University, University of Miami, and UCLA, continues. Patient responses are encouraging.
February 1986	Burroughs Wellcome initiates and is the sole sponsor of a Phase II study at 12 academic centers, eventually involving 281 patients.
September 1986	The Phase II study is halted when an interim analysis by an independent data safety and monitoring board shows a significantly lower mortality rate in patients receiving AZT compared to those randomized to receive a placebo.
October 1986	Burroughs Wellcome, National Institutes of Health, and FDA establish a Treatment IND (Investigational New Drug) program as a means of providing wider access to AZT prior to FDA clearance.
December 1986	Burroughs Wellcome completes submission of a New Drug Application to FDA.
March 1987	The FDA clears Retrovir brand zidovudine (AZT) as a treatment for advanced ARC and AIDS.
February 1988	Burroughs Wellcome is issued a U.S. patent for the use of Retrovir as a treatment for AIDS and ARC based on the innovative work done by company scientists.
August 1989	Controlled clinical trials indicate that certain HIV-infected early symptomatic and asymptomatic persons can benefit from Retrovir with fewer or less severe side effects.
October 1989	Burroughs Wellcome establishes a Pediatric Treatment IND program, providing wider access to Retrovir for medically eligible children prior to FDA clearance.
January 1990	The FDA clears modified dosage guidelines for therapy with Retrovir patients with severe HIV infection.

Source: Abridged from a Burroughs Wellcome news release, "Retrovir Milestones," dated December 13, 1990.

advocacy groups became impatient with what they perceived as an overly tedious and unnecessary process. They began accusing Burroughs Wellcome and the FDA of delaying the drug's availability. These critics argued that withholding potentially effective therapy from AIDS patients was inhumane and unethical, as was the use of a placebo. David Barry, Vice President and head of the research, medical, and development divisions, defended the trial process, asserting that, if placebo controls were removed, "it could destroy the most modern and rapid clinical research plans ever devised."[14]

In September 1986, the review board recommended that the administration of the placebo be terminated. Analysis of the data had shown a significantly lower mortality rate among those patients who had received Retrovir for an average period of six months. When the trial stopped, there had been 19 deaths among the 137 patients receiving the placebo and 1 death among those patients taking Retrovir. The group receiving Retrovir also had a decreased number of infections. In addition, the weight gain, improvements in the immune system, and ability to perform daily activities noted in the Phase I trial were confirmed. However, patients involved in the Phase II trial also experienced adverse reactions similar to those reported in the earlier trial. Since it was no longer appropriate to withhold drug treatment from placebo-treated patients, all patients who had formerly received the placebo were offered Retrovir treatment with the agreement of the FDA.

Expanded distribution of the drug meant that the company would have to obtain a larger supply of thymidine, a biological chemical first harvested from herring sperm and a key raw material in AZT. In 1986, the world's supply of thymidine was 25 pounds. Recognizing that this supply would be exhausted quickly, the head of technical development at Burroughs Wellcome began a worldwide search for a thymidine supplier, recognizing that it took months and 20 chemical reactions to produce this material. This search uncovered a small German subsidiary of Pfizer, Inc., a New York-based pharmaceutical firm, which had produced thymidine in the 1960s. This company was persuaded to produce thymidine by the ton.

In March 1987, the FDA released Retrovir for treatment for adult patients with symptomatic HIV infection, those patients for whom the drug had been shown to be beneficial in clinical trials. Although no hard figures were available, it was believed that about 50,000 individuals in the United States had symptomatic HIV infection. The recommended dosage for symptomatic HIV patients was 1,200 milligrams every day, administered in 12 100-milligram capsules.

Research and Development Costs

The direct research and development costs associated with Retrovir were estimated to be about $50 million, according to industry analysts.[15] This cost was considered low, since the typical cost of developing a new drug in the United States is $125 million. Indeed, Wellcome PLC had spent $726 million for research and development on dozens of drugs in the five years preceding approval of Retrovir without producing a major commercial success. However, when the costs of new plant and equipment to produce Retrovir were also considered, total research and development cost estimates ranged from $80 million to $100 million. Furthermore, the company provided the equivalent of $10 million of the drug free to 4,500 AIDS patients and supplied free of charge a metric ton of AZT to the National Institutes of Health's AIDS Clinical Trials Group.

---

[14] David Barry, testimony before the House Committee on Government Operations Subcommittee on Intergovernmental Relations and Human Resources, July 1, 1987.

[15] Cost estimates have been made by industry analysts and have not been confirmed or denied by Burroughs Wellcome.

Burroughs Wellcome's research and development effort did benefit from AZT being designated as an "orphan drug" in 1985 under provisions of the Orphan Drug Act of 1983. This act, which applies to drugs useful in treating 200,000 or fewer people in the United States, confers special consideration to suppliers of these drugs. For example, the orphan drug designation for Retrovir provided a seven-year marketing exclusivity after its commercial introduction, tax credits, and government subsidization of clinical trials.

■ MARKETING OF RETROVIR

Initial distribution of Retrovir was limited because of its short supply in March 1987. A special distribution system was set up to ensure availability of the drug to those patients who had been shown to benefit from its use. This system remained in place until September 1987, when supplies were adequate and broader distribution was possible.

The initial price set for Retrovir to drug wholesalers in March 1987 was $188 for a hundred 100-milligram capsules. This price represented an annual cost to AIDS patients ranging from $8,528 to $9,745 depending upon wholesaler and pharmacy margins, which combined ranged from 5 to 20 percent. An immediate controversy was created, with the public, media, and AIDS patient-advocacy groups seeking justification of the price for Retrovir, a decrease in its price, or federal subsidization. Critics pointed out that, for comparison, the annual cost of interferon, a cancer-fighting drug, was only $5,000. The cofounder of Project Inform, an AIDS treatment information agency, said, "I think that Burroughs Wellcome is very interested in getting all their money back as soon as possible, because the sun won't shine forever."[16] Congressional hearings resulted in the chairman of the House Subcommittee on Health and the Environment charging that Burroughs Wellcome's "expectation was that those people who want to buy the drug will come up with the money" and that the government would "step in" to subsidize those who could not.[17] Congress subsequently created a $30 million emergency fund for AIDS patients who were unable to afford the cost of AZT.[18]

Company officials acknowledged that the pricing decision was difficult to make. According to one official, "We didn't know the demand, how to produce it in large quantities, or what competing drugs would come out in the market. There was no way to find out." Another company official said, "I guess we assumed that the drug . . . would be paid in some manner by the patient himself out of his own pocket or by third-party payers. We really didn't get into a lot of calculation along those lines."[19]

On December 15, 1987, the capsule price of Retrovir was reduced by 20 percent. The company announced that the price reduction was made possible because of cost savings achieved in the production process and an improved supply of synthetically manufactured thymidine. The company continued its research on AZT throughout 1988 into 1989, including treatments for children with HIV infection. In August 1989, this research program indicated that Retrovir produced positive results in postponing the appearance of AIDS in HIV-infected people. This development expanded the potential users of the drug to between 600,000 and 1 million people. (However, industry sources believe that fewer than one-half of the people with HIV

---

[16] "The Unhealthy Profits of AZT," *The Nation* (October 17, 1987): 407.

[17] FDC Reports—the Pink Sheet 49 (11): 5, 1987.

[18] "Find the Cash or Die Sooner," *Time* (September 5, 1988): 27.

[19] "The Inside Story of the AIDS Drug," *Fortune* (November 5, 1990): 124–125.

have been tested and told of their condition and would thus be seeking treatment.) FDA approval for marketing to this larger population was expected by March 1990.

Recognizing the expanded potential patient population and anticipated production economies, the capsule price of Retrovir was again reduced by 20 percent in September 1989. In reference to this price reduction, Burroughs Wellcome's *1989 Annual Report* noted:

> In arriving at our decision to reduce the price, we carefully weighed a number of factors. These included our responsibility to patients and shareholders, the very real remaining uncertainties in the marketplace, and the vital need to fund our continuing research and development programmes.[20]

The new price to drug wholesalers was set at $120 for a hundred 100-milligram capsules. The retail price to users was about $150 for a hundred 100-milligram capsules. Industry analysts estimated that the direct cost of manufacturing and marketing Retrovir was 30 cents to 50 cents per capsule.[21]

EXHIBIT 6

Retrovir Sales Volume, Fiscal 1987–1989

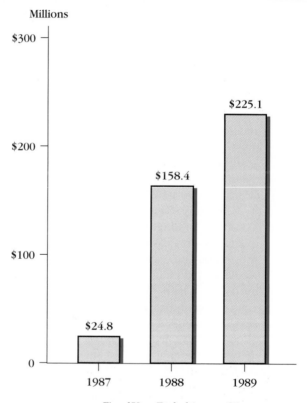

Fiscal Year Ended August 31

Note: U.S. dollar sales volume computed using average exchange rate £1 = $1.55 (1987), £1 = $1.76 (1988), £1 = $1.68 (1989).

Source: Wellcome PLC, 1990 *Annual Report.*

[20] Wellcome PLC 1989 *Annual Report*: 13.

[21] "How Much for a Reprieve from AIDS?" *Time* (October 2, 1989): 81.

Sales of Retrovir since its introduction are shown in Exhibit 6. Unit volume for Retrovir in fiscal 1990 was forecasted to be 53 percent higher than fiscal 1989 unit volume.

Patient-advocacy groups continued to criticize the pricing of Retrovir. AIDS activists chanted such slogans as "Be the first on your block to sell your Burroughs Wellcome stock" while picketing stock exchanges in London, New York, and San Francisco. The executive director of the National Gay and Lesbian Task Force said, "To make AZT accessible to everyone who should be on it, Burroughs Wellcome has an obligation to give up a significant amount of money to allow people to get access."[22] Members of Senator Edward Kennedy's staff began researching possible ways to nationalize the drug by invoking a law that allows the U.S. government to revoke exclusive licenses in the interest of national security. In addition, there were published reports that the American Civil Liberties Union was considering a suit against Burroughs Wellcome. The suit would challenge the 17-year-use patent awarded Burroughs Wellcome for Retrovir, arguing that government scientists discovered AZT's efficacy against HIV.[23] The Subcommittee on Health and the Environment of the U.S. House of Representatives, which had already launched an investigation into possible "inappropriate" pricing of the drug, continued its hearings. However, Sir Alfred Sheppard, the company's Chairman, remained firm, saying "There's no plan to make another price cut." Later in 1990, he added, "If we wrapped the drug in a £10 note and gave it away, people would say it cost too much."[24]

In January 1990, the FDA approved modified dosage guidelines for Retrovir. These guidelines reduced the recommended adult dosage to 500 milligrams per day for some symptomatic AIDS patients from the original recommended dosage of 1,200 milligrams per day established in 1987. However, some clinicians warned that lower dosages should be prescribed cautiously. Also in January, congressional lobbyists began a campaign to curb "excessive profits earned by the drug industry as a whole." Industry observers were speculating that the price of Retrovir might have to be cut again sometime in 1990 because of continued pressure from the U.S. Congress, the media, and AIDS patient-advocacy groups.[25]

[22] "AZT Maker to Reap Big Gain," *New York Times* (August 19, 1989): 8.

[23] "A Stitch in Time," *The Economist* (August 18, 1990): 21–22.

[24] "The Inside Story of the AIDS Drug," *Fortune* (November 5, 1990): 124–125.

[25] "Profiting from Disease," *The Economist* (January 27, 1990): 17–18.

Atlas Electronics Corporation

The telephone was ringing as Adrian Bartos, manager of facsimile technology engineering at Atlas Electronics Corporation, entered his office at 5:00 P.M. on January 7, 1991. The call was from the director of engineering for Mexus, Inc., who told Bartos that a competitor had underbid USS for an order on its digital converter semiconductor device for facsimile (fax) machines. Bartos was confident that the competitor's bid price was unrealistically low, since Atlas, with all its design and manufacturing experience, could meet the bid only by pricing with profit margins significantly less than those for previously produced devices. While assembling his staff and their group vice president to discuss the ramifications of the competitive bid, Bartos realized that a decision of this importance would significantly affect his company's presence as a supplier to the burgeoning fax machine industry.

■ THE FACSIMILE MACHINE INDUSTRY IN 1990

As early as 1983, the facsimile, or fax, machine was an esoteric intercompany communication device. According to industry estimates, some 50,000 fax machines were in operation in 1983, and most were housed in large *Fortune* 500 corporations. In 1990, 1.9 million fax machines were sold, representing $2.2 billion in sales. Industry forecasters were projecting unit sales of 3.2 million and dollar sales of $2.9 billion in 1993. Exhibit 1 on page 495 shows the actual and projected unit and dollar sales of stand-alone fax machines for the ten-year period 1984–1993.

Origins of the Technology

The fax machine can trace its origins to 1842 when the first primitive one was designed by a Scottish inventor, Alexander Bain. His machine had a pendulum that created a brown stain as it swung across chemically treated paper. Although not a commercial success, his original ideas sparked a number of subsequent developments in the nineteenth century. In 1902, Arthur Korn devised a photoelectric scanning system for the transmission and reproduction of photography. He developed a commercial picture-transmission system in 1907. By 1934, the Associated Press was employing a facsimile system to transmit photos and text for newspapers. After extensive use of facsimile technology by the U.S. military in World War II, the Federal Communications Commission authorized its development on a commercial basis in 1948.

Today's facsimile technology is much like the technology envisioned by Bain and successive inventors. Facsimile technology involves a scanning device that converts the optical content of a document into an equivalent electrical signal. This signal is then converted into a series of audio tones to be sent over telephone lines.

This case was prepared by Professor Roger A. Kerin, of the Edwin L. Cox School of Business, Southern Methodist University, as a basis for class discussion and is not designed to illustrate effective or ineffective handling of an administrative situation. Company names and certain market, financial, and price data have been disguised as has the focal product. Fundamental relationships, however, remain intact and are useful for analysis purposes. Copyright © 1995 by Roger A. Kerin. No part of this case may be reproduced without written permission of the copyright holder.

EXHIBIT 1

Facsimile Machine Actual and Projected Unit and Dollar Volume, 1984–1993

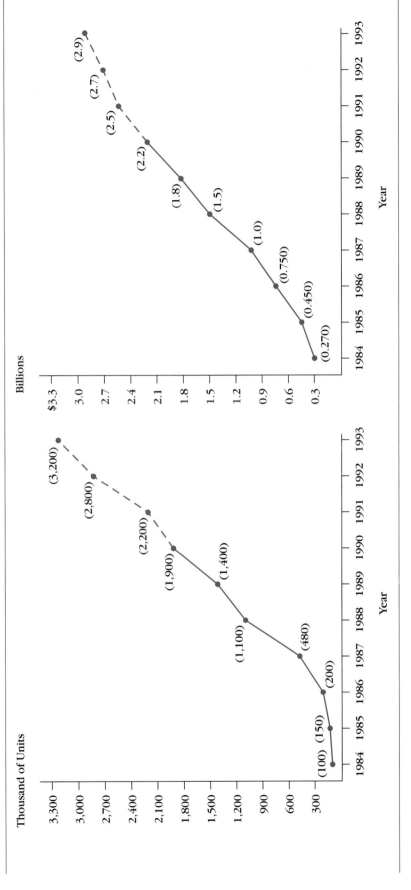

A receiving fax machine restores the tones to electrical signals and amplifies them in order to drive a printing device that reproduces the document.

Commercial Development

Commercial development of fax machines began in earnest in the 1960s. Xerox and Motorola pioneered the effort to produce commercially successful machines. In 1968, Xerox produced a machine that permitted receipt of documents by an unattended telephone, and in 1970, it introduced a lightweight portable machine that sent and received documents. In the late 1970s, four firms—Xerox, Exxon Information Systems, Burroughs, and Harris/3M (now Lanier Worldwide)—supplied 90 percent of the facsimile machines sold in the United States.

Two technical developments broadened the commercial appeal of fax machines in the early 1980s. First, the Consultative Committee on International Telephone and Telegraph (CCITT), which establishes worldwide standards for data communications, developed uniform standards to regulate transmissions from one fax machine to another. As a result, most fax machines around the world could communicate with each other. A second development was the introduction of electronic circuitry that replaced electromechanical parts in fax machines. The advent of electronics reduced transmission time from 6 minutes per page to 18 seconds, improved print quality, and provided cost savings.

Competitive and Marketing Environment

These two technical developments were followed in rapid succession by a number of changes in the competitive and marketing environments. In 1983, seven producers and nine brands composed the facsimile machine industry. By 1989, some 25 producers selling over 60 different brands competed for facsimile machine sales. The flow of new entrants into the industry resulted in rapid and often sizable fluctuations in producer market shares. Exhibit 2 illustrates the change in membership and market shares of the top five producers.

While U.S. companies dominated the market in the late 1970s and early 1980s, the top five producers in 1990 were Japanese firms. Industry analysts believed that Japanese producers would continue to dominate the industry for two reasons. First, fundamental facsimile technology, namely, printer and scanner technology, had been traditionally controlled by Japanese industry. Second, even though Japanese firms licensed printer and scanner technology, they still controlled the critical component technology. These factors gave Japanese firms a decided cost advantage and technical edge in facsimile machine production. However, industry analysts predicted that

E X H I B I T   2

Unit Volume Market Shares of Facsimile Machine Manufacturers

1982		1986		1988		1990	
Company	Share	Company	Share	Company	Share	Company	Share
Xerox	30%	Ricoh	16%	Sharp	21%	Sharp	23%
Exxon	24	Canon	13	Murata	15	Murata	17
Burroughs	17	Pitney Bowes	12	Canon	11	Canon	9
3M	14	Sharp	10	Ricoh	10	Panasonic	8
Matsushita	6	Fujitsa	7	Pitney Bowes	6	Ricoh	8
Others	9	Others	42	Others	37	Others	35
	100%		100%		100%		100%

South Korean firms, such as Daewoo, Lucky-Goldstar, and Samsung, would enter the facsimile machine market in the early 1990s using Japanese-licensed technology. It was believed that these firms could introduce models priced as low as $300.

Notable changes in marketing practices also occurred. Fax machines were originally sold exclusively by the producer's salespeople, but in 1990, 60 percent of office machine dealers sold them. Distribution was also expanded to include some discount and department stores. By late 1989, most producers relied upon multiple channels, including direct sales to large corporate accounts and retail outlets for sales to small businesses, including home offices. Investment in advertising also increased with broadened distribution. For the 12-month period ending June 30, 1989, Sharp, which is the present market leader, spent $3.7 million on media advertising, Canon spent almost $4 million, and Ricoh, $1.1 million.[1] These expenditures represented a sizable investment, since little emphasis was placed on advertising by facsimile machine producers as recently as 1985.

Product innovation efforts were also evident. Some of the more noteworthy innovations included (1) models for home office use with built-in telephones, (2) models that used plain, rather than thermal, paper for copies, (3) models that integrated telex for electronic mail purposes, and others that linked facsimile capability with large mainframe computers and minicomputers, and (4) models that allowed for secure (confidential) transmissions. In addition, the industry average price for fax machines declined from approximately $2,700 in 1984 to about $1,300 in early 1990.

Market Segmentation

The facsimile machine industry in 1990 was divided into four segments based on product price and features (see Exhibit 3 on page 498). The fastest-growing segment consisted of stripped-down machines for small businesses priced below $1,500. Murata, Canon, and Ricoh competed in this market segment as well as in the mid-range ($1,500–$3,000) segment. The high-end market segment was less price-sensitive, but more feature-driven. This segment consisted of large corporations with heavy volume needs, and Canon was its leader. Most facsimile machine producers competed in only two of these three market segments, such as low end and mid range or mid range and high end. However, some producers, for example, Sharp and Canon, competed in all three. The fourth market, the deluxe segment, represented an emerging opportunity as fax technology was fused with computer technology in large-scale corporate information systems. Few producers competed in this segment as yet. It was still in the embryonic stage with experimental, customized technology and applications being prominent.

Although estimates varied greatly because of changing model price and feature configurations, some analysts believed that facsimile industry unit volume was divided among the three major segments as follows: low-end machines accounted for 45 to 55 percent of unit volume, mid-range machines for 30 to 45 percent, and high-end machines for 10 to 15 percent.

Industry Suppliers

Over 100 different firms produced products for inclusion in fax machines. These firms included plastic molders, which supplied the cover or "box"; electromechanical firms, which manufactured mechanical controls, electric motors, and printing heads; and semiconductor firms, which produced modems, integrated circuits, analog/digital converters, logic devices, memory devices, signal processors, and other electronic components. Semiconductor devices comprised approximately 25 percent of the total material used to produce a fax machine. The remaining 75 percent

---

[1] Brian Bagot, "Brand Report: FAX Facts," *Marketing & Media Decisions* (December 1989): 129–130*ff*.

EXHIBIT 3

Facsimile Machine Market Segmentation

	Low-end Segment	*Mid-range Segment*	*High-end Segment*	*Deluxe Segment*
Price Points	Under $1,500	$1,500–$3,000	$3,000–$12,000	$25,000+
Description of segment	Small businesses and individuals	Larger businesses with higher fax volume needs	Corporate and multisite buyers with heavy volume and high-quality reproduction needs	*Fortune* 500 corporations with heavy volume needs as well as information system integration needs
Machine Features	Stripped-down, entry-level models that are operator-fed (operator must feed a single sheet at a time and wait for each sheet to be completed before feeding another)	Automatic sheet feeder, which handles 5- to 50-page transmissions, and often delayed transmission features, which allow for transmission at times when unit is unattended	Automatic sheet feeders for multi-page transmissions, technology color half-tone reproduc-tion capability, autodialing, and often simultaneous, multisite trans-mission with relay broadcasting memory capability to prevent backlogs	Integration of computers and fax transmissions
Major Competitors	Sharp Canon Toshiba Ricoh Murata	Sharp Canon Toshiba Murata Panasonic	Canon Xerox Pitney Bowes Ricoh Telautograph	Pitney Bowes Xerox

of material consisted of electric parts (25 percent) and nonelectric/electronic mater-ial and parts (50 percent).

Some 20 firms supplied semiconductor technology for fax machines. Some of these firms were vertically integrated and also produced fax machines (for example, Toshiba and Matsushita). Even though Japanese manufacturers dominated the mar-ket for fax machines, most of the semiconductors used in modems, converter chips and devices, data-compression devices, and other electronic parts were made by U.S. firms. For example, Rockwell International Corporation was estimated to supply 60 to 80 percent of the modems used in fax machines. Major well-known U.S. electron-ics firms that supplied semiconductor technology for other uses included Texas In-struments, Motorola, and National Semiconductor. Other smaller firms, such as Atlas Electronics Corporation, also competed on a selective basis.

Fax machine producers typically evaluated suppliers using a wide variety of cri-teria. These criteria included design and technical support capabilities, evidence of product quality, reliability, delivery and production flexibility, and cost. Increasingly, these criteria were being translated into requests for small-volume production to ac-commodate customization for different fax machine models, shortened cycle time from production agreement to finished product delivery, and compatibility consider-ations to allow fax machine producers to "second source" products from one or pos-sibly two other suppliers.

■ ATLAS ELECTRONICS CORPORATION

Atlas Electronics Corporation manufactured a wide variety of electrical and electronic products. The company competed in three industry segments: (1) government aerospace and defense, (2) electrical distribution products and systems, and (3) industrial control products and systems. Sales in 1990 were $263 million; operating profit before taxes was $23.4 million. An internal strategic review of company operations in mid-1990 produced five directives:

1. We will disengage from government aerospace and defense programs.
2. We will emphasize expansion of the electrical and industrial segments and contiguous new segments, taking advantage of synergy.
3. We will self-fund growth.
4. We will pursue growth through internal development of products and markets rather than through acquisitions.
5. We will pursue opportunities related to electronics, particularly when our skills can be decisive.

Operating guidelines, or "must statements," that pertained to management philosophy, budgeting, and profit expectations were also outlined:

1. We must retain and build upon our corporate philosophies and methods to manage profitable growth. Attention to the Atlas management culture through planning and control mechanisms such as Program Potential Budgeting (PPB) and Cost-Centered Design and Manufacturing (CCDM) will be emphasized.
2. Funds must be invested in major growth thrusts—that is, products that serve markets with a high growth rate and in which Atlas can develop and sustain a profitable position.
3. We must continue to increase our basic technological strengths, especially in semiconductor technology. This includes not only the design, development, and production of key components and devices, but also the application of these components to new systems.

Program Potential Budgeting System

The PPB system is the action plan for any endeavor at Atlas. A PPB program states not only what a particular endeavor expects to achieve, but also how it will be achieved and the specific actions necessary to achieve it, including the costs of design, engineering, production, and marketing. Funding is derived from a portion of operating profits intended to support a new business strategy and is controlled at the department (profit-and-loss center) level. Funding for programs is competitive in that division managers obtain input from each of the program managers and subsequently submit funding requests to a budget committee. Programs are ranked according to their growth and profitability potential by the budget committee, with funds allocated accordingly.

The annual budgeting procedure is highly refined and well controlled. Flexibility is retained, however, to modify a program definition. Programs are defined in the fourth quarter for the coming calendar year and are reviewed monthly and quarterly. The flexibility of the process is illustrated by the following reflection of Adrian Bartos on the Facsimile Technology Program:

> In 1988 the Chip Sensor Program was funded at $150,000 and the Facsimile Technology Program was allocated $75,000. In 1989, the Chip Sensor Program was allocated $180,000, while we were allocated $100,000. Then, in December 1989, a group of

vice presidents from a facsimile machine manufacturer visited us. The prospects outlined by these executives allowed for an improved Facsimile Technology Program to be developed. Funds from the Chip Sensor Program were immediately diverted to the Facsimile Technology Program, which marked the beginning of the program as it now stands.

Bartos noted that this episode was not uncommon given the corporate policy that funds should be invested in products that serve growth markets and in which the company could develop a profitable position. In the same vein, existing programs exhibiting poor profit performance could lose funding and personnel could be reassigned. Bartos was very much aware of this fact: "The sequence of events that benefited the Facsimile Technology Program could work against it unless the program sustained its profitability."

Facsimile Technology Program

Atlas traced its participation in the facsimile machine industry to the early 1980s, when electromechanical parts were being replaced with electronics. "We were involved early in the transition given our semiconductor technology," noted Bartos, "but only in a limited way since we were engaged mostly in the then more lucrative defense industry." At the time, Bartos was a project engineer for missile guidance systems.

Early Development In late 1987, Atlas was approached by ECI Corporation to prepare a proposal for a digital converter device in the amount of 10,000 units. The proposed unit price was $55. According to an Atlas executive, "A $550,000 project was relatively small potatoes, but we had excess capacity and available PPB funds. There was a general belief that we could get a footprint in the market. Moreover, technology and production synergies were present with two other programs. All three programs would benefit from the shared experience in design and engineering."

By mid-1988, it became apparent to Atlas officials that the facsimile market would double in unit volume by 1990. Adrian Bartos was assigned responsibility for the Facsimile Technology Program in late 1988. His assignment was to pursue rather than wait for business from facsimile machine producers. He sought and received PPB funding for design, engineering, marketing, and production support. It was immediately apparent to him after calling on some 15 facsimile machine producers that cost requirements imposed by these increasingly cost-conscious firms would stretch Atlas' Cost-Centered Design and Manufacturing policy. The CCDM policy required that a product be designed from the start to achieve specific performance, cost, and profit goals. In practice, this meant that design activities would focus on efforts to lower material and labor content so as to reduce the product cost necessary to perform a function.

The general guide used by Atlas in charting cost reductions was the learning (or experience) curve phenomenon, which is described in the appendix to this case. In effect, Bartos hoped that he could realize a 20 percent reduction in the cumulative average product labor cost per unit each time volume doubled for a new design. Similar curves would be developed for each proposal to facsimile machine producers and would reflect Atlas' ability to economize on material and labor content for each succeeding generation of digital converter devices. Bartos realized, however, that a practical limit existed to how much he could reduce overall costs.

Building the Business In 1989, Bartos received a call from an AMEX Electronics executive requesting that he produce a digital converter device for them. This proposal included a bid price of $45. In late February, AMEX Electronics placed a confirmed order for 50,000 units. "Suddenly we were a profitable $2 million-plus business," said Bartos.

Bartos received a call from Mexus, Inc., a Japanese firm, on November 28, 1989, asking for a proposal. A new proposal was developed to Mexus's specifications, and a price of $36 per unit was bid. The difference in the ECI, AMEX Electronics, and Mexus prices arose from manufacturing cost savings due to order size (75,000 per year for Mexus) and different product specifications, which included "off-the-shelf technology," according to Bartos.

During this period Bartos consolidated and generated a variety of data pertaining to the facsimile machine market for the purpose of assessing Atlas' potential market position and identifying possible areas of product superiority and of synergy with the company's other product development efforts. These data would serve as inputs for his PPB funding requests and preparation of financial, marketing, and production plans. It was also during this time that Bartos and his staff were recognized for their design work by the Atlas Engineering Excellence Committee. The recognition formally acknowledged their contributions to related programs, which had demonstrable effects on lowering costs.

On February 26, 1990, Bartos was notified that Mexus accepted his proposal and bid price, provided the delivery time could be shortened, which was agreed to. During the remaining spring months, Bartos directed an increasing amount of his time toward designing second-generation digital converter devices for Atlas customers and managing the production and delivery of first-generation devices. Time was also spent preparing PPB funding and planning schedules, interacting with customer engineering staffs, and making presentations to prospective buyers along with Atlas technical salespeople. During this period, Bartos submitted proposals to two other facsimile machine producers. However, neither proposal was accepted.

Mexus Second-generation Bid On November 10, 1990, Bartos was asked to bid on a more sophisticated second-generation digital converter device for Mexus. Given the nature of the bid, including customized specifications, quantity (150,000 units), and delivery time, Bartos proposed a price of $44 (see the price-cost schedule in Exhibit 4 on page 502 and supplementary material). Shortly thereafter, Bartos was advised that the competitive bid level was $42 per unit, which he met after a lengthy discussion with his group vice president and members of his staff. Then, at 5:00 P.M. on January 7, 1991, Bartos was informed that Atlas had been underbid by a competitor at a price of $37. He met with his staff and group vice president to discuss their options.

Bartos had forecast an 80 percent labor learning curve for his bid, as shown in Exhibit 4. The labor estimate for the first 1,000 units was about 1.75 hours/unit, but this cumulative average time would decrease to about 0.35 hour/unit at 150,000 units. The cumulative average time at 75,000 units was 0.44 hour/unit. That is, one-half of the unit volume would require more than 0.44 hour/unit to build, and one-half would require less. These labor hour estimates also included time for testing.

Also shown in Exhibit 4 is a 90 percent labor learning curve corresponding to the doubling of unit volume from 150,000 units to 300,000 units without redesign and major change to the configuration. Cumulative average labor hours/unit for 300,000 units would be 0.314 with the midpoint being approximately 0.33 hour/unit at the 225,000th unit produced.

Bartos did not forecast reductions in material or yield cost, since he did not foresee an interim design change that would be fruitful in the short run. Furthermore, labor cost/unit reductions, assuming that he would bid for an additional 150,000 second-generation digital converter devices within the near future, did not look promising.

Overshadowing the entire situation was the question of whether the competitor was also forecasting prices and costs on an 80 percent labor learning curve. This factor would be critical if volume doubled again for the Mexus account.

Bartos was also plagued by other considerations that emerged in his staff meeting. First, the future of cumulative facsimile unit sales volume remained a question.

EXHIBIT 4

Atlas Electronics Corporation's Second-generation Bid Price and Cost Estimate for the Digital Converter Device for Mexus, Inc.

Cost and Price Calculation

$26.50	Yielded material cost
6.36	Labor cost (0.44 hour/unit @ $14.45/hour)
$32.86	Total material, labor, and direct overhead or "manufactured cost"
11.14	25% gross margin approximation
$44.00	Unit selling price at unit volume of 150,000

Estimated Labor Learning Curve for Second-generation Digital Converter Device

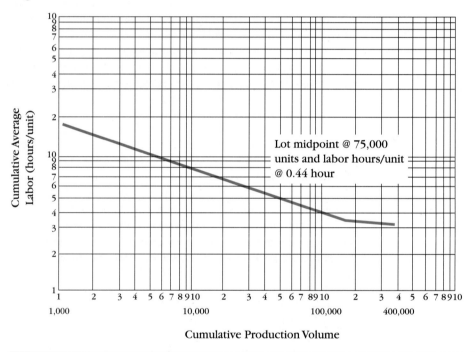

Note: 0.44 hour = lot midpoint of the 150,000-unit lot; $14.45 = hourly rate including factory overhead.

Even though industry forecasters were projecting a 16 percent increase in unit volume for 1991 and another 27 percent increase in 1992, at issue was the market share that Mexus would capture. According to one staff member, "Assuming that our device is used in all units sold by Mexus in 1991, then Mexus is roughly projecting a 1991 market share of 8 percent. This seems high, since Mexus is not one of the top fax machine marketers in market share." Bartos believed that Mexus was using multiple sources and that all Mexus facsimile machine models did contain Atlas or similar types of digital converter devices. He reminded his staff that the facsimile market was still in flux and Murata, for example, catapulted itself from tenth place in market share in 1985 to second place in 1988 and 1990 on the basis of an aggressive marketing effort. Bartos's contacts with Mexus executives indicated that Mexus had ambitious growth goals, particularly in the low-end and mid-range market segments, where it focused its sales, promotion, and distribution effort.

A second consideration dealt with delivery. Even if Atlas was awarded the contract, a possibility existed that all 150,000 units would not be shipped, since contingencies provided that Mexus could stop shipment at any time. In other words, as few as 50,000 to 75,000 units could be shipped and the order stopped. "This hasn't happened to us yet," said Bartos. "However, it has happened to others, and the probability increases as the order size increases," added the group vice president.

Profitability was a third consideration. Atlas policy held that every project must achieve the corporate net profit before tax objective (8.9 percent of net sales). Exceptions to this policy would be approved provided that (1) extraordinary short-run factors necessitated such action and (2) long-term growth potential and profitability could be demonstrated, based on competitive conditions.

The strategic capability and intent of the competitor proposing the $37 bid was a fourth consideration. Bartos was confident that the competitor was not a major semiconductor firm, such as Texas Instruments, Motorola, or National Semiconductor, but he did not know its identity. "My guess is that it's a niche player like us specializing in one or two electronic components or devices," Bartos said. "It may be buying the business, have a cost advantage, or be prepared to accept lower profitability."

At 9:00 P.M. on January 7, the meeting adjourned. The group vice president asked that Bartos and his staff prepare a recommendation with supporting documentation for his review the next morning.

■ APPENDIX

It has been observed in many industries and for a variety of products that the average manufacturing cost per unit declines by a constant percentage with every doubling of cumulative production output. This phenomenon is called the experience, or learning, effect and results from a variety of sources. Seven such factors are described below:

1. *Labor efficiency*. As workers repeat a particular production task, they become more dexterous and learn improvements and shortcuts that increase their collective efficiency. The greater the number of worker-based operations, the greater the amount of learning that can accrue from experience. This learning effect may go beyond the labor directly involved in manufacturing. Maintenance personnel, supervisors, and persons in other line and staff manufacturing positions also increase their productivity, as do people in marketing, sales, administration, and other functions.

2. *Work specialization and methods improvements*. Specialization increases worker proficiency at a given task. For instance, when two workers who formerly did both parts of a two-stage operation each specialize in a single stage, they tend to become more efficient in performing the more specialized task. Redesigning work operation methods can also result in greater efficiency.

3. *New production processes*. Process innovations and improvements can be an important source of cost reductions. The semiconductor industry, for instance, achieves learning effects from improved production technology by devoting a large percentage of its research and development effort to process improvements.

4. *Getting better performance from production equipment*. When first designed, a piece of production equipment may have a conservatively rated output. Experience may reveal innovative ways of increasing its output.

5. *Changes in the resource mix*. As experience accumulates, a producer can often incorporate different or less expensive resources in the operation. For instance, less skilled (lower-cost) workers can replace skilled (higher-cost) workers, or automation can replace labor.

6. *Product standardization*. Standardization allows the replication of tasks necessary for worker learning. Even when flexibility and/or a wider product line are important marketing considerations, standardization can be achieved by modularization. For example, by making just a few types of engines, transmissions, chassis, seats, and body styles, an auto manufacturer can achieve experience effects arising from standardization of each part. These parts in turn can be assembled into a wide variety of models.

7. *Product redesign*. As experience is gained with a product, both the manufacturer and customers gain a clearer understanding of its performance requirements. This understanding allows the product to be redesigned to conserve material, to incorporate greater efficiency in its manufacture, and to substitute less costly materials and resources for more costly ones, while at the same time improving performance. The new designs that substitute plastic, synthetic fiber, and rubber for leather in ski boots are examples of this.

The influence of these factors has been seen in reduced prices for many well-known products. For example, prices of CD players have decreased from over $900 when they were first produced to less than $200 today, and cellular telephones that sold for $4,000 are now priced as low as $99.

The Experience, or Learning, Effect

The experience, or learning, effect is amenable to measurement and has proven useful in projecting costs based on the doubling of cumulative unit production. An example of this phenomenon is tabulated in Exhibit 5, where the production growth

EXHIBIT 5

Illustration of the Experience, or Learning, Effect

Year	Annual Production	Cumulative Volume	Times Required for Doublings of Cumulative Volume	Cumulative Average Unit Cost with 15% Constant Decline
1	1,000	1,000		$100.00
			→ 1st doubling (1,000 to 2,000):	
2	1,200	2,200	1.89 years	$85.00
3	1,440	3,640		
			→ 2nd doubling (2,000 to 4,000):	
4	1,728	5,368	3.22 years	$75.25
			→ 3rd doubling (4,000 to 8,000):	
5	2,074	9,930	4.23 years	$61.41

EXHIBIT 6

Representations of the Experience, or Learning, Curve

A. A Typical 85-percent Curve Displayed on Linear Scales

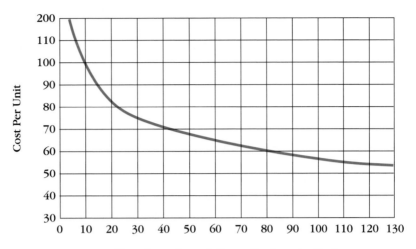

Experience (cumulative units of production)

B. A Typical 85-percent Curve Displayed on Logarithmic Scales

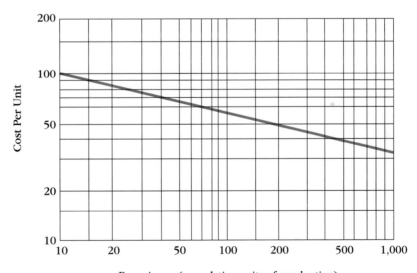

Experience (cumulative units of production)

rate is 20 percent per year, the original unit cost is $100, and the cost per unit is projected to decline at a constant rate of 15 percent with every doubling of cumulative volume. As can be seen, with an annual production growth rate of 20 percent, cumulative volume doubles three times in five years, and cumulative average unit cost, which was $100 for the first 1,000 units, declines to $61.41 for 8,000 units.

In practice, the learning effect is represented by a curve. Specifically, these curves are charted by plotting cost per unit on a vertical axis and cumulative production volume on a horizontal axis. Thus, if unit cost declines by 15 percent each time the cumulative volume of production doubles, an 85 percent curve is indicated. This means that the cumulative average cost of the 100 units produced will be about 85 percent of the cost to produce 50 units, and 200 units will be about 85 percent of the cost to produce 100 units, and so forth. An 85 percent curve is shown in Exhibit 6. Learning curves are typically drawn on double-log paper, in which both the horizontal and vertical axes are charted on a logarithmic scale. When presented in this manner, the "curve" appears as a straight line, also shown in Exhibit 6. The labor learning curve shown in the case (Exhibit 4) is plotted on a logarithmic scale.

Strategic Implications

The strategic implications of the experience, or learning, curve arise from the slope of the curve and the rate of accumulation of experience. Specifically,

> *Slope of the curve.* All things being equal, a firm that fails to achieve cost reductions along an experience or learning curve slope that are at least equivalent to those achieved by its competitors will eventually find itself at a competitive cost disadvantage.

> *Rate of experience accumulation.* All things being equal, a firm that fails to accumulate experience at least as rapidly as its competitors will find itself at a competitive cost disadvantage.

The strategic message of the learning curve is straightforward. The major-volume firm in a product market has the greatest potential for the lowest unit costs and largest profits due to cumulative production volume. As costs decline, opportunities for price reductions become available and give the firm a lower price-cost advantage that is difficult for competitors (with little cumulative volume) to match and remain profitable. Since experience, or learning, effects are most likely to occur in rapidly growing markets, frequent doubling of cumulative volume is most likely to be observed during the early stages of the product life cycle (late introductory and growth stages). These effects are less likely to be observed in later stages of the product life cycle, when unit sales increase at decreasing rates or actually decline.

Augustine Medical, Inc.
The Bair Hugger® Patient Warming System

In July 1987, Augustine Medical, Inc., was incorporated as a Minnesota corporation to develop and market products for hospital operating rooms and postoperative recovery rooms. The first two products the company planned to produce and sell were a patented patient warming system designed to treat postoperative hypothermia in the recovery room and a tracheal intubation guide for use in the operating room and in emergency medicine.

By early 1988, company executives were actively engaged in finalizing the marketing program for the patient warming system named Bair Hugger® Patient Warming System. The principal question yet to be resolved was how to price this system.

■ THE BAIR HUGGER® PATIENT WARMING SYSTEM

The Bair Hugger® Patient Warming System is a device designed to control the body temperature of postoperative patients. Specifically, the device is designed to treat the hypothermia (a condition defined as a body temperature of less than 36 degrees Centigrade or 96 degrees Fahrenheit) experienced by patients after operations.

Medical research indicates that 60 to 80 percent of all postoperative recovery room patients are clinically hypothermic. Several factors contribute to postoperative hypothermia. They are (1) a patient's exposure to cold operating room temperatures (which are maintained for the surgeons' comfort and for infection control), (2) heat loss due to evaporation of the fluids used to scrub patients, (3) evaporation from the exposed bowel, and (4) breathing of dry anesthetic gases.

The Bair Hugger® system consists of a heater/blower unit and a separate inflatable plastic/paper cover, or blanket. A photo of the system is shown in Exhibit 1 on page 508. The heater/blower unit is a large, square, boxlike structure that heats, filters, and blows air through a plastic cover. An electric cord wraps around the back of the unit for storage, and the unit is mounted on wheels for easy transport. The blower tubing attaches to the warming cover through a simple cardboard connector strap and can be retracted into the top of the unit for storage. Temperature is set by a dial with four settings on the top of the unit. A top lid opens to a storage bin that holds 12 warming covers for easy access. The disposable warming covers come packaged in 18-inch-long tubes. When unrolled, the plastic/paper cover is flat and covers an average-sized patient from shoulders to ankles. The blanket consists of a layer of thin plastic and a layer of plastic/paper material laminated into full-length

This case was prepared by Professor Roger A. Kerin, of the Edwin L. Cox School of Business, Southern Methodist University, Michael Gilbertson, of Augustine Medical, Inc., and Professor William Rudelius, of University of Minnesota, as a basis for class discussion and is not designed to illustrate effective or ineffective handling of administrative situations. Certain names and data have been disguised. The assistance of graduate students Anne Christensen, Joanne Perty, and Laurel Wichman of the University of Minnesota is appreciated. The cooperation of Augustine Medical, Inc., in the preparation of the case is gratefully acknowledged. Copyright © 1993 by Roger A. Kerin. No part of this case may be reproduced without the written permission of the copyright holder.

EXHIBIT 1

Bair Hugger® Patient Warming System

channels. Small holes punctuate the inner surface of the cover. When inflated through a connection at the feet of the patient, the tubular structure arcs over the patient's body, creating an individual patient environment. The warm air exits through the slits on the inner surface of the blanket, creating a gentle flow of warm air over the patient. The warming time per patient is about two hours.

The plastic cover was patented in 1986; there is no patent protection for the heater/blower unit.

■ COMPETING TECHNOLOGIES

Many competing technologies are available for the prevention and treatment of hypothermia. These technologies generally fall into one of two broad types of patient warming: surface warming or internal warming.

Surface-warming Technologies

Warmed hospital blankets are the most commonly used treatment for hypothermia in recovery rooms and elsewhere. An application of warmed hospital blankets consists of placing six to eight warmed blankets in succession on top of a patient. Almost all patients receive at least one application; it is estimated that 50 percent of the postoperative patients require more than one application. The advantages of warmed hospital blankets are that they are simple, safe, and relatively inexpensive. The main disadvantage is that they cool quickly, provide only insulation, and require the patient's own body heat for regenerating warmth.

Water-circulating blankets are the second most popular postoperative hypothermic treatment. Water-circulating blankets can be placed under a patient, over a patient, or both. If a blanket is placed just under the patient, only 15 percent of the body's surface area is affected. However, hospitals typically place water-circulating blankets either just over the patient or over and under the patient, forming an insulated environment that encloses 85 to 90 percent of the body's surface area. The disadvantages of water-circulating blankets are that they are heavy and expensive and can cause burns on pressure points. Moreover, although a widely used and accepted method of warming, especially for more severe cases of hypothermia, water-circulating blankets are considered only slightly to moderately effective.

Electric blankets are generally unacceptable as a hypothermic treatment because of the risk of burns to the patient and of explosion in areas where oxygen is in use.

Air-circulating blankets and mattresses are not in common use in the United States, although variations on this technology have been used in the past. This technology relies on warmed air flowing over the body to transfer heat to the patient. The advantages of warmed-air technology are that it is safe, lightweight, and theoretically more effective than warmed hospital blankets or water-circulating blankets. Products using this technology are not widely found in the U.S. market, however.

Thermal drapes, also known as reflective blankets, have recently been introduced and are gaining acceptance as a preventive measure used in the operating room. They consist of head covers, blankets, and leggings placed on the uninvolved portions of the patient's body. Their use is recommended when 60 percent of a patient's body surface can be covered. The advantages of this technology are that it is simple, safe, and inexpensive and has been shown to reduce heat loss. The disadvantage is that it merely insulates the patient and does not transfer heat to someone who is already hypothermic.

Infrared heating lamps are popular for infant use. When placed a safe distance from the body and shone on the skin, they radiate warmth to the patient. The advantages of heat lamps are that they are effective and illuminate the patient for observation or therapy. A disadvantage is that since the skin needs to be exposed, modesty prevents widespread use among adults. (They are, however, used in adult skin-graft operations.) Nurses dislike radiant heat lamps and panels because they tend to heat the entire recovery room and are uncomfortable to work under.

Partial warm-water immersion has been used in the past, especially in cases where a patient was deliberately cooled to slow down metabolism. With this method, the patient is placed in a bath of warm water and watched carefully. The advantages of this technology are that it transfers heat very effectively and it is simple. The disadvantages are that the system is inconvenient to set up and requires close monitoring of the patient, which increases labor costs. In addition, water baths must be carefully watched for bacterial growth, and they are very expensive to purchase and use.

Increasing room temperature is the most obvious way to prevent and treat hypothermia, but it is seldom used. The advantages of this method are that it is simple and relatively inexpensive and has been proven effective at temperatures of over 70 degrees Fahrenheit. The disadvantage is that warm room temperatures are not acceptable to the nurses and surgeons who must work in the environment. Furthermore, warm temperatures increase the risk of infection.

Internal-warming Technologies

Inspiring *heated and humidified air* is a fairly effective internal-warming technique currently being used with intubated patients (those having a breathing tube in the trachea). However, delivery of heated and humidified air by mask or tent to nonintubated patients is not acceptable in postoperative situations, because mask or tent delivery would interfere with observation and communication and, in the case of a tent, might increase the chance of infection. The fact that the patient must be intubated is a disadvantage, since the vast majority of postoperative patients are not intubated.

Warmed intravenous (I.V.) fluids are used in more severe hypothermic cases to directly transfer heat to the circulatory system. Warmed I.V. fluids are very effective because they introduce warmth directly into the circulatory system. The disadvantages of this technology are that it requires very close monitoring of the patient's core temperature and high physician involvement.

Drug therapy diminishes the sensation of cold and reduces shivering but does not actually increase body temperature. Although drug therapy is convenient and makes patients feel more comfortable, it does not warm them and in fact slows their recovery from anesthesia and surgery.

■ COMPETITIVE PRODUCTS

A variety of competitive products that use the above-mentioned technologies are available (see Exhibit 2). A review of competitors' sales materials and interviews with hospital personnel provided the following breakdown of competitive products.

Warmed Hospital Blankets

For treating adult hypothermia, hospitals use their own blankets, which they warm in large heating units. Many manufacturers produce heating units for hospital use. The cost of laundering six to eight two-pound hospital blankets averages $0.13 per pound. Laundering and heating costs are absorbed in hospital overhead.

Water-circulating Blankets

Several manufacturers produce water-circulating mattresses and blankets, but Cincinnati Sub-Zero, Gaymar Industries, and Pharmaseal are the major suppliers. Prices of automatic control units that measure both blanket and patient temperatures range from $4,850 to $5,295. Manual control units are priced at about $3,000, although they appear to be discounted by as much as 40 percent in actual practice.

The average life of water-circulating control units is 15 years. Reusable blankets list at from $168 to $375, depending on quality. Disposable blankets list at from $20 to $26. Volume discounts for blankets can reduce the list price by almost 50 percent.

EXHIBIT 2

Representative Competitive Products and Prices

Product	List Price	Company	Estimated Size of Company (sales; employees)	Comments
Blanketrol 200	$2,995/manual unit; $4,895/automatic unit; $165–$305/reusable blanket; $20/disposable blanket	Cincinnati Sub-Zero	$10 million; 90 employees	Hypothermia equipment is a small part of its overall business.
MTA 4700	$4,735/unit; $139/reusable blanket; $24/disposable blanket	Gaymar Industries	$17 million; 150 employees	Hypothermia equipment seems to be a major part of its business.
Aquamatic	$4,479/unit	American Hamilton (division of American Hospital Supply)	$3.3 billion; 31,300 employees	Hypothermia equipment is a very minor part of American Hospital Supply's business.
Climator	$4,000/unit	Hosworth Air Engineering Ltd.	Not available	The company could begin distribution of hypothermia equipment in the United States in 1988.

Water-circulating blanket technology has changed little over the past 20 years except for the addition of solid state controls. There is little differentiation among the products of different firms.

Reflective Thermal Drapes

O.R. concepts sells a product named the Thermadrape, which comes in both adult and pediatric sizes. Adult head covers list for $0.49 each; adult drapes list for $2.50 to $3.98, depending on size; leggings are priced at $1.50.

Air-circulating Blankets and Mattresses

Two competitors are known to provide an air-circulating product like the Bair Hugger® Patient Warming System; however, neither is currently sold in the United States. The Sweetland Bed Warmer and Cast Dryer was in use 25 years ago but is no longer manufactured. This product consisted of a heater/blower unit that directed warm air through a hose placed under a patient's blanket. The Hosworth-Climator is an English-made product that provides a controlled-temperature microclimate by means of air flow from a mattress. The Climator comes in a variety of models for use in recovery rooms, intensive care units, burn units, general wards, and patients' homes. The model most suitable for postoperative recovery rooms is priced at $4,000. This product could be distributed in the United States sometime in 1988. A summary of representative competitor products and list prices is shown in Exhibit 2.

■ THE HOSPITAL MARKET

Approximately 21 million surgical operations are performed annually in the United States, or 84,000 operations per average eight-hour work day. Approximately 5,500 hospitals have operating rooms and postoperative recovery rooms.

Research commissioned by Augustine Medical, Inc., indicated that there are 31,365 postoperative recovery beds and 28,514 operating rooms in hospitals in the United States. An estimated breakdown of the number of postoperative hospital beds and the percentage of surgical operations is shown below:

Number of Postoperative Beds	Number of Hospitals	Estimated Percentage of Surgical Operations
0	1,608	0%
1–6	3,602	20
7–11	1,281	40
12–17	391	20
18–22	135	10
23–28	47	6
29–33	17	2
>33	17	2

Given the demand for postoperative recovery room beds, the research firm estimated that hospitals with fewer than seven beds would not be highly receptive to the Bair Hugger® Patient Warming System. The firm also projected that one system would be sold for every eight postoperative recovery room beds.

Interviews with physicians and nurses, followed by a demonstration of the system, yielded a variety of responses:

1. Respondents believed that the humanitarian ethic "to make the patient feel more comfortable" is important.

2. Respondents felt that the Bair Hugger® Patient Warming System would speed recovery for postop patients.

3. Respondents wanted to test the units under actual conditions in postoperative recovery rooms. They were reluctant to make any purchase commitments without testing. A typical comment was "No one today, in this market, ever buys a pig in a poke."

4. Respondents felt that the product was price-sensitive to alternative methods. Respondents were very receptive to the notion of using the heater/blower free of charge and only paying for the disposable blankets. Physicians wanted to confer with others who would be responsible for using the product to administer the warming treatment, however, such as the head nurse in postoperative recovery rooms and the chief anesthesiologist.

5. Respondents believed that the pressure to move patients through the operating room and out of postop is greater than in the past. Efficiency is the byword.

6. Capital expenditures in hospitals were subject to budget committee approval. Although the amounts varied, expenditures for equipment over $1,500 were typically subject to a formal review and decision process.

■ AUGUSTINE MEDICAL, INC.

Augustine Medical, Inc., was founded in 1987 by Dr. Scott Augustine, an anesthesiologist. His experience had convinced him that hospitals needed and desired a new approach to warming patients after surgery. His medical knowledge, coupled with a technical flair, prompted the development of the Bair Hugger® Patient Warming System.

The Bair Hugger® Patient Warming System has several advantages over water-circulating blankets. First, warm air makes patients feel warm and stop shivering. Second, the system cannot cause burns, and water leaks around electrical equipment are

E X H I B I T   3

Sales Literature for the Bair Hugger® Patient Warming System

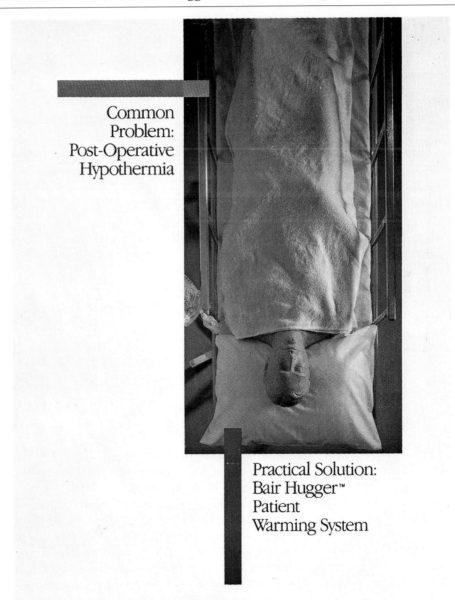

Common
Problem:
Post-Operative
Hypothermia

Practical Solution:
Bair Hugger™
Patient
Warming System

EXHIBIT 3 *(continued)*

A Warm Welcome for Your Recovery Room Patients

Augustine Medical, Inc.'s new Bair Hugger™ Patient Warming System is the most practical and comforting solution for post-operative hypothermia available today.

Every year more than 10,000,000 hospital patients experience the severe discomfort and vital signs instability associated with post-operative hypothermia. Years later, patients can still vividly recall this discomfort. Augustine Medical's new Patient Warming System is a warm and reliable solution to post-operative hypothermia.

A Practical Solution to Post-Operative Hypothermia

The Bair Hugger™ Patient Warming System consists of a Heat Source and a separate disposable Warming Cover that directs a gentle flow of warm air across the body and provides for safe and comfortable rewarming.

The Bair Hugger Heat Source uses a reliable, high efficiency blower, a sealed 400W heating element, and a microprocessor-based temperature control to create a continuous flow of warm air. There are no pumps, valves or compressors to maintain. Special features include built-in storage space for the air hose, power cord and a convenient supply of disposable Warming Covers. The Heat Source complies with all safety requirements for hospital equipment.

1. PATENTED SELF SUPPORTING DESIGN
As the tubes fill with air, the Warming Cover naturally arches over the patient's body.

2. TISSUE PAPER UNDERLAYER
The tissue paper underlayer of the Warming Cover is soft and comfortable against the patient's skin.

3. AIR SLITS
Tiny slits in the underlayer allow warm air from the Heat Source to gently fill the space around the patient.

4. SHOULDER DRAPE
The shoulder drape is designed to tuck under the chin and shoulders, trapping warm air under the cover and preventing air flow by the patient's face.

5. DISPOSABLE COVERS
The disposable Covers prevent cross contamination and reduce laundry requirements.

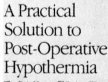

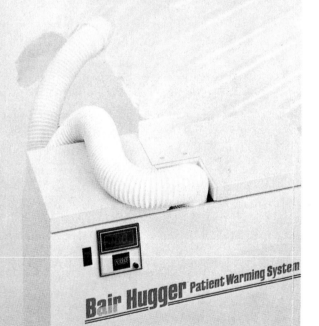

Bair Hugger Patient Warming System

---

not a problem, as they are with water-circulating blankets. Third, the disposable blankets eliminate the potential for cross-contamination among patients. Finally, the system does not require that the patient be lifted or rolled. Augustine's personal experience indicated that all of these features would be welcome by nurses and patients alike. Features and benefits of the Bair Hugger® Patient Warming System are detailed in the company's sales literature, shown in Exhibit 3 on pages 513 through 516.

Investor interest in Augustine Medical and the medical technology it provided produced an initial capitalization of $500,000. These funds were to be used for further research and development, staff support, facilities, and marketing. It was believed that this initial investment would cover the fixed costs (including salaries, leased space, and promotional literature) of the company during its first year of operation. The company would subcontract the production of the heater/blower unit and would manufacture warming covers in-house using a proprietary machine. Only minor assembly would be performed by the company.

EXHIBIT 3 *(continued)*

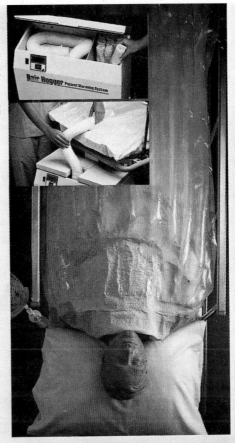

THE BAIR HUGGER™
PATIENT WARMING SYSTEM
IS SO EASY TO USE.
Remove a new Warming Cover
from the storage compartment
and unroll over the patient.

Connect the heater hose to the
inlet of the Warming Cover and
turn on the heater.

6. SIMPLE CONTROLS
A preprogrammed temperature range
and a preset high temperature limit of
110°F make the Bair Hugger safe and
simple to use.

7. INTERNAL WARMING COVER STORAGE
The storage compartment provides a
convenient supply of Warming Covers
ready for immediate use.

8. INTERNAL HOSE STORAGE
The hose retracts into its own
compartment for ready access.

9. LIGHTWEIGHT, COMPACT DESIGN
The Heat Source is designed for
convenience and portability. While in
use, it tucks under the foot of the gurney.
The unit's light weight and small size
make it simple to move and store.

10. BUILT-IN POWER CORD STORAGE
The power cord storage holds up to 12
feet of cord, making the Heat Source
portable and easy to store.

11. 5μ AIR FILTER
The air filter assures dust-free air
circulation through the Bair Hugger
Warming Cover. The filter is simple to
change when necessary.

The Bair Hugger™ Warming Cover:

The Warming Cover consists of a layer of plastic and a layer of tissue
paper laminate bonded together into long tubular channels. The
self-supporting Warming Cover is designed to arch over the patient's
body creating a warm, comfortable environment.

The Warming Cover is convenient to use because no straps, tapes or
other fasteners are required to stabilize the cover and the patient
does not have to be disturbed or moved.

When the Warming Cover is completely inflated, warm air from the
Heat Source exits the tubular channels through slits in the Cover's
soft underlayer, surrounding the patient with a gentle flow of warm air.

The Bair Hugger® Patient Warming System would be sold by and through medical products distributor organizations in various regions around the country. These distributor organizations would call on hospitals, demonstrate the system, and maintain an inventory of blankets. The margin paid to the distributors would be competitively set at 30 percent of the delivered (that is, less discounts) selling price on the heater/blower unit and 40 percent of the delivered (discounted if necessary) price on the blankets.

Preliminary estimates from subcontractors and a time-and-motion study on assembly indicated that the direct cost of the heater/blower unit would be $380. The cost of materials, manufacturing, and packaging of the plastic disposable blankets was estimated to be $0.85 per blanket.

EXHIBIT 3 *(continued)*

A Warm and Practical Discovery:
Bair Hugger™ Patient Warming System

Post-Operative Hypothermia–A Common Problem

As a practicing anesthesiologist, Dr. Scott D. Augustine observed that there was no practical treatment for the common problem of post-operative hypothermia. An extensive review of post-operative hypothermia revealed several important facts:

- Post-operative hypothermia (T<36°C or <96.7°F) occurs in 60-80% of all post-operative patients (1). This extremely common problem affects more than 10,000,000 surgical patients every year.

- Several factors contribute to post-operative hypothermia including the patient's exposure to cold operating room temperatures, heat loss due to evaporation of fluids used to scrub the patient, evaporation of moisture from exposed bowels, and the breathing of dry anesthetic gases.

- Unlike environmental hypothermia, post-operative hypothermia is not usually life threatening. However, it can have serious side effects for older or unstable patients. Negative effects include a decrease in cardiovascular stability and an increase in oxygen consumption of up to 400% during unaided rewarming, as well as severe shivering and significant patient discomfort (2).

- Patients with unstable body temperatures require intensive nursing care, which means higher costs. Recovery room time may also be prolonged due to the instability caused by post-operative hypothermia.

Variety of Treatments–Only One Practical Solution

Many methods have been used to try to warm patients after surgery including warmed hospital blankets, water mattresses and heat lamps (3). Studies have shown, though, that these methods are ineffective.

The most common method of treating hypothermia–heated hospital blankets–does not actively heat the patient. The small amount of heat retained by a cotton blanket quickly dissipates, thereby requiring patients to rewarm themselves. Because multiple blankets are typically used, this method is both inconvenient and time-consuming for nursing staff and produces large amounts of laundry.

Another common method used to try to rewarm post-operative hypothermia patients is the use of a water circulating mattress. Water circulating equipment is heavy, complex, expensive and prone to leakage. While water mattresses have been used for many years, there is no clinical evidence that documents their effectiveness (4, 5). This lack of effectiveness can be explained by the minimal body surface area in contact with the mattress, (only 15%) and the lack of blood flow to this area. The weight of the patient creates a pressure which prevents normal cutaneous blood flow. The heat in the mattress cannot be transported away from the skin and the contact surface becomes an insulator effectively minimizing potential heat transfer to the patient.

New Approach Needed

As Dr. Augustine discussed the problem of post-operative hypothermia with doctors, nurses, and industry experts he became convinced that a new approach to warming patients was needed. A survey of anesthesiologists showed that most were dissatisfied with the current technology available for treating hypothermia. A new technology was definitely needed.

As a result of his research, Dr. Augustine developed the Bair Hugger™ Patient Warming System. Numerous studies and reports have shown that increased ambient room temperatures will prevent hypothermia (6-10). Indeed, before the advent of air conditioning, the average ambient temperature of the OR was higher and hyperthermia in the peri-operative period was not uncommon. Surgical patients will predictably lose or gain heat depending on the ambient temperature of the surrounding environment. The Bair Hugger™ System simulates a warm room by surrounding the patient in a gentle flow of warm air–A Focused Thermal Environment™.

The Bair Hugger™ Patient Warming System combines the convenience and effectiveness of warm air to safely rewarm hypothermic patients. The Warming System's minimal cost is rapidly recovered in saved nursing time, reduced linen expenses and lower overall recovery room costs. There is now a practical and cost-effective solution to post-operative hypothermia.

Two-week Free Trial

To arrange for a free two-week trial of the Bair Hugger™ Patient Warming System, fill out the enclosed reply card or call us collect at (612) 941-8866.

SPECIFICATIONS HEATER/BLOWER UNIT	
Size	26" high x 14" deep x 22" wide
Weight	65 lbs.
Power Requirements	110VAC
Temperature Range	Ambient to 110°F Max
Enclosure	Enameled steel
Displayed Variables	Temperature °F
Power Cable	12 Feet long
Display	.5 inch (1.2 cm) Character LCD
COVERS	
Size	54" x 36"
Weight	8 ounces
Material	Polyethylene and tissue paper laminate.

AUGUSTINE MEDICAL INC.

PRACTICAL SOLUTIONS TO COMMON PROBLEMS IN ACUTE CARE™

10393 West 70th St., Suite 100 Eden Prairie, Minnesota 55344

References: (1) Vaughan MS, Vaughan RW, Cork RC: Anesthesia and Analgesia 60:746-751, 1981. (2) Bay J, Nunn JG, Prys-Roberts C: British Journal of Anaesthesia 40: 398-406, 1968. (3) Kucha DH, Nichols GH, Christ NM, Bynum JW: Military Medicine 139:388-390, 1974. (4) Morris RH, Kumar A: Anesthesiology 36:408-411, 1972. (5) Goundsouzian NG, Morris RH, Ryan JF: Anesthesiology 39:351-353, 1973. (6) Morris, RH: Annals of Surgery 173:230-233, 1971. (7) Morris RH, Wilkey BR: Anesthesiology 32:102-107, 1970. (8) Clark RE, Orkin LR, Rovenstine EA: JAMA 154:311-319, 1954. (9) Bigler JA, McQuistow WO: JAMA 146:551, 1951. (10) Harrison GG, Bull AB, Schmidt HJ: British Journal of Anaesthesia 40:398-406, 1960.

The central issue at this time was the determination of the list price to hospitals for the heater/blower unit and the plastic blankets, given the widespread incidence of price discounting. Immediate attention to the price question was important for at least three reasons. First, it was felt that the price set for the Bair Hugger® Patient Warming System would influence the rate at which prospective buyers would purchase the system. Second, price and volume together would influence the cash flow position of the company. Third, the company would soon have to prepare price literature for its distributor organizations and for a scheduled medical trade show, where the system would be shown for the first time.

North Pittsburgh Telephone Company

■ INTRODUCTION

In late fall 1992, Mr. Greg Sloan, Marketing Supervisor of the North Pittsburgh Telephone Company (NPT), was wondering what position to take at the next management committee meeting regarding the possible introduction of usage-sensitive pricing for NPT's new CLASS services. Greg was responsible for marketing all NPT's network services. NPT was introducing CLASS services January 1, 1993 on a subscription pricing basis, but there was some management support for offering usage-sensitive pricing for CLASS features as well. The next meeting would be critical in determining whether to offer usage-sensitive pricing and if so, how.

Greg pondered:

> This is a big decision. We've had a lot of success with other services. We've always found revenue potential in our central-office-based services and of course we try to maximize it as new opportunities come along. We always offer a full range of customer options. These central offices are a gold mine to us. That's where we make our money—toll and our network features. There has to be a big potential for revenue gains. Even so, Marketing will be held accountable for our revenue projections with or without usage-sensitive pricing.

■ NORTH PITTSBURGH TELEPHONE COMPANY

As of 1992, North Pittsburgh Telephone Company and Penn Telecom, Inc. were wholly owned subsidiaries of North Pittsburgh Systems, Inc. Founded in 1906, North Pittsburgh Telephone Company was an independent operating company, a regulated public utility, with approximately 250 employees servicing approximately 49,000 subscribers in a predominantly rural area about 15–20 miles north of Pittsburgh, Pennsylvania. NPT was ranked the 31st largest telephone company in the United States in 1992, based on access lines. NPT's area was comprised of eight exchanges in a 285 square mile (738 square km) territory. Toll-free dialing within the NPT area was available to all subscribers. Greg thought of NPT as follows:

> We're sandwiched between Bell Atlantic to the south and Sprint/United to the north. Our location relative to Bell, with Bell being so big, is always a factor in anything that we do. They are intending to go into CLASS services and they have access to all the Pittsburgh radio and TV stations. When they start flooding the market with their advertising, they can be a driver of demand in our area.

This case was prepared by Professor Michael Pearce of the Richard Ivey School of Business, copyright 1995, The University of Western Ontario.

This material is not covered under authorization from CanCopy or any reproduction rights organization. Any form of reproduction, storage or transmittal of this material is prohibited without written permission from Richard Ivey School of Business, The University of Western Ontario, London, Canada N6A 3K7. Reprinted with permission, Richard Ivey School of Business.

The main office of NPT is in Gibsonia, PA, a rural community about a 45-minute drive north from the Pittsburgh airport. Three host digital switches (Northern Telecom DMS-100) were linked to the other six remote switches, providing NPT with state-of-the-art digital switching capability. With SS7 signaling capability, fibre optics between switches, and a history of early adoption of new telecommunications technology, NPT management regarded themselves as a leading edge in the industry.

Penn Telecom was formed in 1979 as a non-regulated provider of telecommunications products and services in partnership with NPT. This organization focused on PBX, key systems, fax, and the like.

As of December 1992, NPT had 36,453 residence lines and 12,671 business lines (including payphones and foreign exchanges). The average residential customer paid $15 per month for local access and optional network services such as Custom Calling Features (Call Waiting, Call Forwarding, and Three-way Calling). Custom Calling Features (CCF) were available only on a monthly subscription basis. The monthly rates are shown in Table 1. As of December 1992, NPT had penetration rates for Custom Calling Features approaching 25 percent, as shown in Table 2.

Access lines and network features such as Custom Calling features were traditionally provided to customers on a monthly subscription basis. A customer would

Table 1
North Pittsburgh Telephone Company Pricing Information

	Custom Calling Features Monthly Subscription Rates	
	Residence	*Business*
Call Waiting	$2.00	$3.35
Call Forwarding	2.00	3.35
Three-Way Calling	2.00	3.35
Speed Calling	2.00	3.35
IdentaRing	2.00	3.35

Table 2
North Pittsburgh Telephone Company Access Line/Custom Calling Information

	12/92 Residence	*12/92* Business	*12/92* Total
Service Lines	36,453	12,671	49,124
Centrex	0	1,151	1,151
PBX Trk	0	762	762
Call Waiting	9,311	625	9,936
Call Forwarding	344	742	1,086
Three-Way Calling	170	31	201
Package	456	58	514
Speed Calling	46	5	51
IdentaRing	172	11	183
Rmt Call For	3	228	231
TOTALS	10,502	1,700	12,202

Residence Custom Calling Penetration '92—28.8%

Business Custom Calling Penetration '92—13.4%

Residence/Business Custom Calling Penetration '92—24.8%

order a service from NPT by telephone (to the Business Office in Gibsonia) or in person (by visiting their Talk Shoppe at NPT in Gibsonia). Telephone terminals were also sold, but not leased, to NPT customers at the Talk Shoppe. NPT would commence the service and then bill the customer monthly at a flat rate regardless of usage until the customer said to stop. There was no disconnection charge for terminating a service.

Such an arrangement provided the telephone company with a relatively steady stream of income, particularly as experience indicated what normal rate of churn (connects and disconnects) could be expected over time. Usage-sensitive pricing would be quite different. This approach meant establishing a flat or variable rate for each use of a service, then determining the amount to bill the customer at the end of each month.

Greg added:

> Another important thing always to think about is, of course, the local exchange competition. It's coming, it's slow in coming, but it will be here. We see it happening more and more. We've always wanted to offer our customers everything we can at the best prices with the best service. We think if we get into new services and people use them, then people will depend on them and use us. Then when our competition comes in, we'll have the competitive advantage.

■ THE INTRODUCTION OF CLASS

CLASS services referred to a new generation of network features which offered the telephone user greater control over incoming calls. NPT called these services Advanced Custom Calling Features (ACC). These features were possible because of the Northern Telecom digital DMS-100 switch. NPT had the choice of making ACC features available on demand to individual subscribers for a monthly fee, or making them universally available to everyone and then charging for each use of the feature by any individual customer. As NPT management prepared to launch these services, they felt they had little information from other phone companies about customer acceptance of ACC.

The ACC features NPT was about to introduce included the services listed below (as described in the words of their forthcoming promotional materials). Rates were to be identical for residential and business customers.

Return Call

Return Call redials your last caller and, if busy, keeps trying for up to 30 minutes. To activate this, press *69. Cost: $3.75 per month.

Select Forward

This feature lets you transfer select calls to any location. Select Forward will hold up to 12 numbers and only those calls will be forwarded to the number you choose. Press *63 and follow instructions. Cost: $3.50 per month.

Select Accept

With this feature you can program a list of up to 12 numbers from which you wish to receive a call. Numbers not on your list will be blocked and routed to a message stating that you don't wish to take the call. Press *64 and follow instructions. Cost: $3.50 per month.

Call Block

Call Block allows you to reject calls from a list of up to 12 numbers. You can add or delete numbers from your list, including the last call you received without even knowing the number. To program Call Block, press *60. Cost: $5.00 per month.

Priority Call

This feature allows you to identify up to 12 numbers by providing a distinctive ring on those incoming numbers you have programmed in. Press *61. Cost: $2.75 per month.

Repeat Call

This feature automatically redials the last number you called and keeps trying for up to 30 minutes. Repeat Call keeps dialing for you, while allowing you to make or receive other calls. Cost: $2.75 per month.

Call Trace

This feature lets you trace harassing or threatening calls. After such a call comes in, just hang up the phone, pick up the handset again and when you hear the normal dial tone, press *57. Call Trace will record the number of that call and send it directly to the phone company. Further instructions will be provided as you use the service. Trace information is provided to the local authorities.

Voice Mailbox Service (VMS) was also being introduced in January 1993. This service would provide continuous automatic telephone answering to subscribers, even when the line is busy. Customers will be able to customize their mailbox, using a personalized greeting, for example. The subscriber will be able to retrieve messages from home or remotely.

While all CLASS features would be available as of 1993, NPT decided to begin by actively promoting only three of them: Return Call, Repeat Call, and Call Block. Promotion had begun with a North Pittsburgh Telephone News bill insert in November. In the December statement, there would be a free installation offer in the bill insert. A news release was planned for the local newspapers. Meanwhile, NPT customer contact employees (Business Office, Talk Shoppe, Installation & Repair, and Telemarketing) were being trained and supported through production of customer handouts such as user guides for all ACC features. (As a regulated utility, the local PUC requirements specified how NPT was to handle customers; for example, they were required to give customers a full menu of everything available.)

Greg reflected on communicating the launch of ACC:

Marketing communications have always been difficult for us. There is no newspaper that goes out to all our customers. There are local papers, but each part of our area relies on different papers. They all have different cable companies. So, while we have no local media to speak of, the Pittsburgh media reach a lot of people we don't serve. We get ads from Bell Atlantic here that create expectations amongst our customers for what we should be doing. We try, therefore, to stay a step ahead of them in terms of what we ofer and to use direct media to reach our customer base.

We do have the regular monthly bill. We feel we are aggressive because we do things in addition to that. I don't think leaving it with just the monthly bills would give us the success we are looking for. For example, we have done a lot of technology seminars where we reach out to the business community, at least annually. We have a speaker program. It is extremely successful. We have a fellow who is a retired admiral from the U.S. Navy who does speaking for us. He knows magic so he goes out and books about two appointments a week with the Rotary, the Elks, etc. He talks about a product and does a trick that relates to the product. He leaves information and premiums for them. We get a lot of response from this. He books just about year-round. He's been with us for about four years.

NPT planned to offer subscribers monthly subscription discounts for taking more than one of any of the network features (CCF and ACC): 15 percent off for two features, 20 percent off for three, 25 percent off for four, and 30 percent off for five or more features.

NPT did not undertake regular market surveys of its customers other than those required by the PUC regulators. Those questions were along the lines of, "Did your service go in at a reasonable time?" and shed little light on likely acceptance of new net-

EXHIBIT 1

North Pittsburgh Telephone Company Forecasts by Northern Telecom

Projected percent of lines using CLASS on a usage-sensitive basis:

Year 1	18%
Year 2	22%
Year 3	26%
Year 4	30%
Year 5	30%

Projected number of (usage-sensitive) activations per month per line:

Year 1	8
Year 2	10
Year 3	12
Year 4	12
Year 5	12

Projected number of lines subscribing to CLASS on a flat rate or subscription basis:

Year 1	4%
Year 2	6%
Year 3	7%
Year 4	8%
Year 5	10%

work features. Greg recalled asking Northern Telecom for any available information about CLASS acceptance rates, but learned NPT was too early in the market process to benefit much from the experience of others. The key piece of industry wisdom was that those customers already subscribing to CCF and already "technologically advanced" in their home electronics equipment would likely be the earlier adopters of ACC.

Expectations were running high, particularly for the upscale exchanges in the western part of the territory where NPT business had been growing at 7–9 percent per year. Greg described the NPT territory:

> We have a fairly affluent population moving into our territory and many of these people are from the Pittsburgh area. The western portion of our territory is growing extremely fast. It is the fastest growing community in the state of Pennsylvania. The reason it is growing so quickly is that there are great access routes going into it. People can live out here and be in Pittsburgh in half an hour.

Previous introductions of new services had always resulted in above average response rates for all of NPT's areas, particularly the west. Greg was trying to forecast what might happen. He expected NPT's lines to grow 13.75 percent over the five-year period, maintaining the current residential/business split. He also had some estimates from Northern Telecom regarding the expected impact of usage-sensitive pricing (Exhibit 1). He was not sure of the applicability of these estimates for NPT.

■ USAGE-SENSITIVE PRICING

The NPT committee considering usage-sensitive pricing included representatives from Marketing, Network Operations, and Finance. The planning engineer, Al Weigand, was the chair of the committee. This committee had to recommend whether to offer usage-sensitive pricing for ACC, and if so, how.

Greg knew that a decision to offer usage-sensitive pricing would involve answering such questions as whether to offer both subscriptions and usage-sensitive options, what rates to charge, whether to cap the usage-sensitive fee each month at a maximum level and if so at what level, whether to price each service at the same rate, when to proceed, and how to launch the whole idea.

No capital investment would be required because all the necessary hardware had already been purchased and the approximate $1 million in additional software costs (largely for billing) would be regarded as a period expense. There would be additional expenses for training and service representatives' time in handling this new option. The remaining major foreseeable incremental costs would be in advertising and promotion. Greg expected that with some rearrangement of his budget, plus some additional money, he could expect additional costs of $35,000 to $50,000 over five years for training and promotion of usage-sensitive pricing for ACC, should they decide to launch it during 1993.

The committee knew senior management would not support any proposal to proceed that did not offer strong possibilities to at least recover all costs over a five-year period.

There was no clear consensus on what rates to charge should they proceed with usage-sensitive pricing or even whether to offer this option for all ACC features. The range of rates being considered was $0.25 to $1.00 per use. There was some agreement that $0.25 increments were best.

Another hurdle was the PUC. Greg knew the company had to be mindful about the tariffs Bell Atlantic would file. The PUC would not allow much discrepancy for the same offerings across the different utilities.

Greg was also wondering about how to communicate about usage-sensitive pricing to customers and employees. Would bill inserts and other typical approaches be appropriate?

Greg knew other telephone companies were exploring usage-sensitive pricing for CLASS. For example, Nynex had recently introduced a trial of their PHONES-MART service in the Long Island, New York serving area with usage-sensitive pricing and flat-rate pricing. The features introduced were Call Return, Repeat Dialing, Caller ID, and Call Trace, but only Call Return and Repeat Dialing were available on a per use basis. A two-month free trial was being offered to encourage use. Heavy promotion was underway using direct mail, radio, print, radio, and television. After the free trial period, per use charges were being capped at twice the monthly rate. Unfortunately, at this stage, Greg did not have any results from Nynex upon which to base his decisions. Greg viewed NPT's situation as follows:

> In previous meetings, we've talked about the capabilities and the investments, the uncertainties about getting involved in this usage-sensitive idea. We were looking for some data to help support our decision and there wasn't a lot out there about usage-sensitive. When you are one of the first into a business, there is not a lot of history. We really don't know what to expect.

The next committee meeting was due shortly. Greg knew he had to have his position clear by then.

Texas Instruments
Global Pricing in the Semiconductor Industry

Mr. John Szczsponik, Director of North American Distribution for Texas Instruments' Semiconductor Group, placed the phone back on its cradle after a long and grueling conversation with his key contact at Arrow, the largest distributor of Texas Instruments' semiconductors. With a market-leading 21.5% share of total U.S. electronic component distributor sales in 1994, Arrow was the most powerful distribution channel through which Texas Instruments' important semiconductor products flowed. It was also one of only two major American distributors active in the global distribution market.

Arrow's expanding international activities had made it increasingly interested in negotiating with its vendors a common global price for the semiconductors it sold around the world. In the past, semiconductors had been bought and sold at different price levels in different countries to reflect the various cost structures of the countries in which they were produced. Semiconductors made in European countries, for example, were usually more expensive than those made in Asia or North America, simply because it cost manufacturers more to operate in Europe than in the other two regions. Despite these differences, large distributors and some original equipment manufacturers were becoming insistent on buying their semiconductors at one worldwide price, and were pressuring vendors to negotiate global pricing terms. Szczsponik's telephone conversation with Arrow had been the third in the past month in which the distributor had pushed for price concessions based on international semiconductor rates:

> Yesterday they discovered that we're offering a lower price for a chip we make and sell in Singapore than for the same chip we manufacture here in Dallas for the North American market. They want us to give them the Singapore price on our American chips, even though they know our manufacturing costs are higher here than in the Far East. We can't give them that price without losing money!

In anticipation of increased pressure from Arrow and other large distributors, Szczsponik had organized a meeting with Mr. Kevin McGarity, Senior Vice President in the Semiconductor Group and Manager of Worldwide Marketing, to begin developing a cohesive pricing strategy. They were both to meet with Arrow executives in four days, on February 4, 1995, to discuss the establishment of common global pricing for the distributor.

Szczsponik knew that he needed to answer some basic questions before meeting with Arrow:

> Global pricing might make Arrow's job of planning and budgeting a lot easier, but our different cost structures in each region make it difficult for us to offer one price worldwide. How do we tell Arrow, our largest distributor, that we aren't prepared to

This case was developed by Profs. Per V. Jenster, CIMID, B. Jaworski, USC, and Michael Stanford as a basis for classroom discussion rather than to highlight effective or ineffective management of an administrative situation.

negotiate global pricing? Alternatively, how can we reorganize ourselves to make global pricing a realistic option? And what implications will a global pricing strategy have in relationship to other international customers?

With only two hours to go before his meeting with McGarity, Szczsponik wondered how they could respond to Arrow's request.

■ THE SEMICONDUCTOR INDUSTRY

Semiconductors were silicon chips which transmitted heat, light, and electrical charges and performed critical functions in virtually all electronic devices. They were a core technology in industrial robots, computers, office equipment, consumer electronics, the aerospace industry, telecommunications, the military, and the automobile industry. The majority of semiconductors consisted of integrated circuits made from monocrystalline silicon imprinted with complex electronic components and their interconnections (refer to Exhibit 1 for the key categories of semiconductors). The remainder of semiconductors were simpler discrete components that performed single functions.

EXHIBIT 1

Key Semiconductor Categories

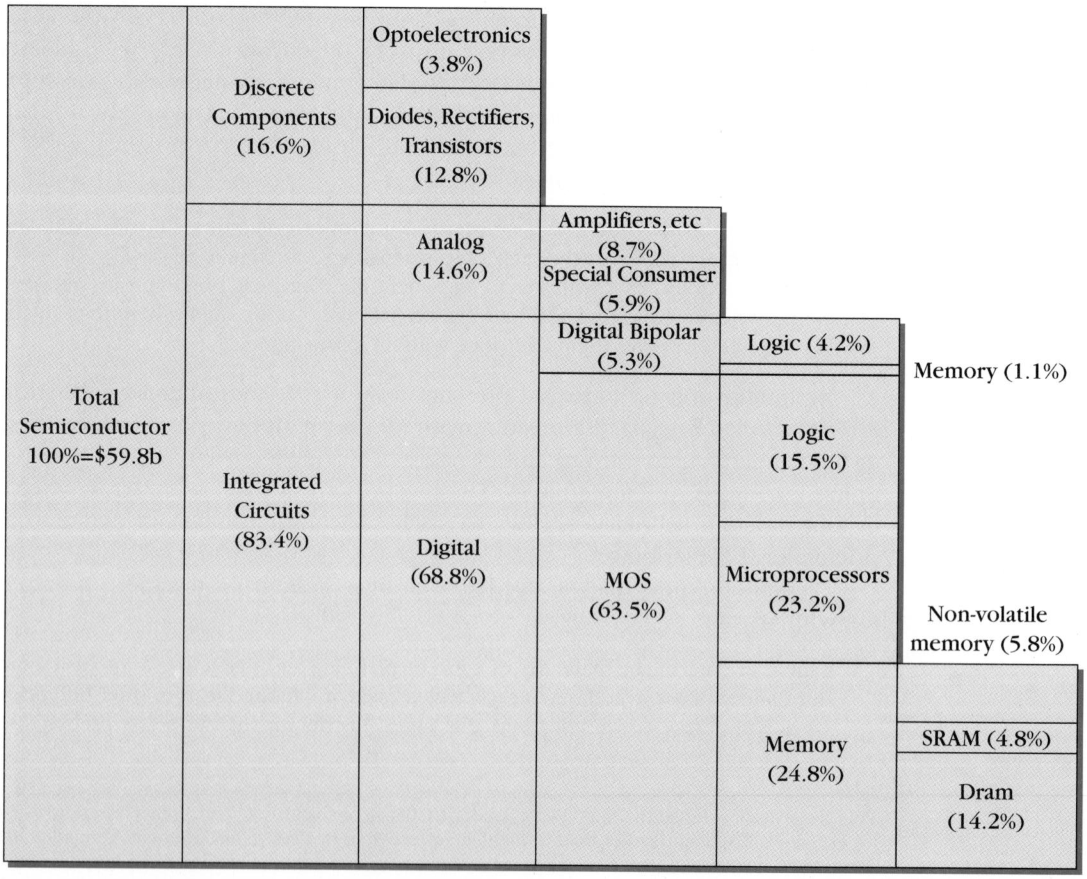

Source: Analysts' reports.

The pervasiveness of semiconductors in electronics resulted in rapidly growing sales and intense competition in the semiconductor industry. Market share in the industry had been fiercely contested since the early 1980s, when the once-dominant U.S. semiconductor industry lost its leadership position to Japanese manufacturers. There followed a series of trade battles in which American manufacturers charged their Japanese competitors with dumping and accused foreign markets of excessive protectionism. By 1994, after investing heavily in the semiconductor industry and embarking on programs to increase manufacturing efficiency and decrease production costs, American companies once again captured a dominant share of the market (refer to Exhibit 2 for the top ten semiconductor manufacturers).

In 1994, total shipments of semiconductors reached $99.9 billion, with market share divided among North America (33%), Japan (30%), Europe (18%), and Asia/Pacific (18%). The industry was expected to reach sales of $130 billion in 1995, and $200 billion by the year 2000. To capture growing demand in the industry, many semiconductor manufacturers were investing heavily in increased manufacturing capacity, although most industry analysts expected expanding capacity to reach rather than surpass demand. Combined with record low inventories in the industry and reduced cycle times and lead times, a balancing of supply and demand was causing semiconductor prices to be uncharacteristically stable. The last three quarters of 1994 had brought fewer fluctuations and less volatility in the prices of semiconductors (refer to Exhibit 3 on page 526 for a history of semiconductor price stability) despite their history of dramatic price variations.

Regardless of price stability, most semiconductor manufacturers were looking for competitive advantage in further cost reduction programs, in developing closer relationships with their customers, and in creating differentiated semiconductors which could be sold at a premium price. Integrated circuits were readily available from suppliers worldwide and were treated as commodity products by most buyers. Any steps manufacturers could take to reduce their production costs, build stronger relationships with customers, or create unique products could protect them from the price wars usually associated with commodity merchandise.

EXHIBIT 2

Top Ten Semiconductor Manufacturers

1980		1985		1990		1992	
Company	Sales $	Company	Sales $	Company	Sales $	Company	Sales $
1. Texas Instruments	1,453	NEC	1,800	NEC	4,700	Intel	5,091
2. Motorola	1,130	Motorola	1,667	Toshiba	4,150	NEC	4,700
3. Philips	845	Texas Instruments	1,661	Motorola	3,433	Toshiba	4,550
4. NEC	800	Hitachi	1,560	Hitachi	3,400	Motorola	4,475
5. National	745	National	1,435	Intel	3,171	Hitachi	3,600
6. Intel	630	Toshiba	1,400	Texas Instruments	2,518	Texas Instruments	3,150
7. Hitachi	620	Philips	1,080	Fujitsu	2,300	Fujitsu	2,250
8. Fairchild	570	Intel	1,020	Mitsubishi	1,920	Mitsubishi	2,200
9. Toshiba	533	Fujitsu	800	Philips	1,883	Philips	2,041
10. Siemens	525	Advanced Micro Devices	795	National	1,730	Matsushita	1,900

Source: Analysts' reports.

E X H I B I T   3

History of Semiconductor Stability

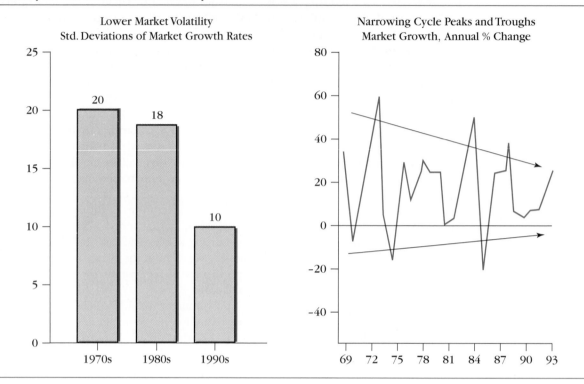

■ TEXAS INSTRUMENTS INCORPORATED

Established in 1951 as an electronics company serving the American defense industry, by 1995 Texas Instruments was a leading manufacturer of semiconductors, defense electronics, software, personal productivity products and materials, and controls. Its 1994 sales of $10.3 billion, a 21% increase from the previous year, was split among components ($6.8 billion), defense electronics ($1.7 billion), digital products ($1.66 billion), and metallurgical materials ($177 million). 1994's profits of over $1 billion came almost entirely from its components business. Components made a profit of $1.1 billion, while defense electronics made $172 million (refer to Exhibit 4 for income statements).

1994's performance was record-breaking for Texas Instruments. It marked the first time the company exceeded sales of $10 billion and over $1 billion in profit, and followed a history of volatile financial results. Although Texas Instruments was often considered the pioneer of the American electronics industry—it was one of the first companies to manufacture transistors and developed the first semiconductor integrated circuit in 1958—it struggled to maintain its position in the electronics industry through the intense competition of the 1980s. After receiving market attention with its development of such innovative consumer products as the pocket calculator and the electronic wrist watch, Texas Instruments lost its business in both markets to cheap Asian imports. Meanwhile, it struggled to keep up with orders for its mainstay business in semiconductors through the 1970s, only to see demand for its pioneer semiconductors shrink during the recession of the early 1980s. Faced with heavy losses in many of its core areas, Texas Instruments reorganized its busi-

EXHIBIT 4

Income Statements

	Texas Instruments Key Financial Numbers				
	1994	1993	1992	1991	1990
Sales ($ millions)	10,200	8,523	7,049	6,628	6,395
Operating Margin (%)	17.5	16.8	9.1	5.0	0.7
Net Profit ($ millions)	715	459	254	169	0.7
Working Capital ($ millions)	1,800	1,313	961	813	826
Long-Term Debt ($ millions)	800	694	909	896	715
Net Worth ($ millions)	2,975	2,315	1,947	1,955	2,358

nesses to foster innovation and embarked on a program of cost-cutting. By 1985, the company had refocused its efforts on its strengths in semiconductors, relinquishing market dominance in favor of greater margins. While the company continued to grow its technological leadership, it also sought to build stronger relationships with its customers.

By 1995, Texas Instruments had developed a strong position in the electronics industry, despite its reputation as a technological leader rather than a skilled marketer of its products. The company continued to remain powerful in the semiconductor industry, in part because it was the only American company that continued to manufacture dynamic random access memory chips in the face of fierce Japanese competition in the 1980s. The company had manufacturing sites spread throughout North America, Asia, and Europe, and was pursuing its strategy of increasing manufacturing capacity and developing manufacturing excellence.

The Semiconductor Group

In 1958, Texas Instruments engineer Jack Kilby developed the first integrated circuit, a pivotal innovation in the electronics industry. Made of a single semiconductor material, the integrated circuit eliminated the need to solder circuit components together. Without wiring and soldering, components could be miniaturized and crowded together on a single chip. Only a few years after Kilby's invention, electronics manufacturers were demanding these integrated circuits, or chips, in smaller sizes and at lower costs, a move that led to unprecedented innovation in the electronics industry. Soon chips became a commodity, and chip manufacturers relied on high-volume, low-cost production of reliable chips for success. Only a few manufacturers had strong positions in the production of differentiated semiconductors.

Forty years after its discovery, Texas Instruments still remained dependent on its semiconductor sales, which fell primarily in integrated circuits. The Semiconductor Group, a part of the Components Division, had total sales of $2 billion in 1994, the third consecutive year in which Texas Instruments' semiconductor revenues grew faster than the industry. The company's return to financial success in the early 1990s was based on its strong performance in semiconductor sales and profits, both of which were at record levels in 1994. Management in the company expected semiconductor sales to continue to grow strongly and was planning heavy capital expenditures on new or expanded plants in the United States, Malaysia, and Italy to increase the company's capacity.

The Semiconductor Group divided its business into two segments: standard products and differentiated products. Standard semiconductors, which accounted for 90% of the Group's sales, included products which could be substituted by competitors. Standard semiconductors performed in the market much like other products for which substitutes were readily available. Texas Instruments, like its competitors, competed for market share in these commodity products based primarily on the price it offered to original equipment manufacturers and distributors. The remaining 10% of the company's semiconductor business came from differentiated products, of which Texas Instruments was the sole supplier. Because substitutes for these products were not available in the marketplace, differentiated products commanded higher margins than their standard counterparts and were receiving greater strategic emphasis on the part of Group management. While the company continued to hold a strong position in standard semiconductors, it was searching for a strategy that would allow it to achieve a higher return on development and manufacturing investments. Managers at Texas Instruments believed that higher returns were possible only by developing more successful differentiated semiconductors.

■ ELECTRONICS DISTRIBUTION MARKET

Texas Instruments sold its semiconductors through two channels: directly to original equipment manufacturers and through a network of electronics distributors. Szczsponik estimated that 70% of the Group's U.S. customers dealt directly with Texas Instruments. The remainder bought their semiconductors through one or more of the seven major semiconductor distributors that served the North American market (refer to Exhibit 5 for information on the top electronics distributors). Whether an original equipment manufacturer dealt directly with Texas Instruments or bought from a distributor depended on the manufacturer's size. The largest original equipment manufacturers were able to negotiate better prices from semiconduc-

EXHIBIT 5

Top Electronics Distributors

Company		1994	1993	1992	1991	1990
Arrow Electronics	Sales ($ billions)	3.973	2.536	1.622	1.044	.971
	Share (%)	21.5	17.4	14.8	11.0	10.2
Avnet	Sales ($ billions)	3.350	2.537	1.690	1.400	1.429
	Share (%)	18.1	17.4	15.4	14.8	15.0
Marshall Industries	Sales ($ billions)	.899	.747	.605	.563	.582
	Share (%)	4.8	5.1	5.5	6.0	6.1
Wyle Laboratories	Sales ($ billions)	.773	.606	.447	.360	.359
	Share (%)	4.2	4.2	4.1	3.8	3.8
Pioneer Standard	Sales ($ billions)	.747	.540	.405	.360	.343
	Share (%)	4.0	3.7	3.7	3.8	3.6
Anthem	Sales ($ billions)	.507	.663	.538	.420	.408
	Share (%)	2.7	4.6	4.9	4.4	4.3
Bell Industries	Sales ($ billions)	.395	.308	.282	.257	.239
	Share (%)	2.1	2.1	2.6	2.7	2.5

Source: Lehman Brothers, "Electronic Distribution Market," December 22, 1994.

tor manufacturers than were the distributors and therefore bought directly from the manufacturers. Because mid-sized and small original equipment manufacturers were fragmented, and thus more difficult to serve, these customers were served more efficiently through the distribution channel. Szczsponik explained:

> The semiconductor market can be divided into three tiers. Fifty percent of our sales in semiconductors go to the top tier of perhaps 100 large electronics manufacturers who deal with us directly. The next 46 percent of sales come from 1,400 medium-sized companies at the next level, half of whom deal directly with us and half of whom buy through distributors. The remaining 4% of sales are to 150,000 smaller companies at the bottom tier in the market, who deal only through distributors. Distributors have a clearly defined role in servicing mid-sized and small buyers.

Distributors were considered to be clearinghouses for the semiconductor industry. Each distributor dealt with products from all the major semiconductor manufacturers. For example, Arrow Electronics sold semiconductors manufactured by Motorola and Intel as well as those made by Texas Instruments. The distributors specialized in handling logistics, material flows, sales and servicing for electronics manufacturers who were either too small to negotiate directly with the major semiconductor manufacturers or lacked sufficient expertise in logistics management. In addition, the distributors sometimes knitted packages of different products together for the smaller original electronics manufacturers as an added service. Some also performed varying scales of assembly operation.

The electronics distribution network had originally consisted of a large group of smaller companies. By 1995, however, industry consolidation had left almost 40% of the distribution market in the hands of its two largest competitors, Arrow Electronics and Avnet. The seven largest distributors captured 58% of sales in the market (refer to Exhibit 6 for the sales and market shares of the top distributors). This trend toward consolidation had had a major impact on the nature of the relationships among semiconductor manufacturers and the distributors through which they sold their products. According to Szczsponik:

> Fifteen years ago, 30 distributors were active in the industry and it was clear that the semiconductor manufacturers controlled the distribution network. With the consolidation of the distribution network into only 7 or 8 powerful players, however, power is shifting. It's hard to say if we are more important to them or they are more important to us.

EXHIBIT 6

Total Sales and Market Share of Top Distributors

		1994	1993	1992	1991	1990
Industry Total	Sales ($ billions)	16.22	12.95	10.18	9.06	9.17
Top 25	Sales ($ billions)	13.41	10.69	8.11	7.10	7.20
	Share (%)	82.7	82.5	79.7	78.4	78.5
Top 7	Sales ($ billions)	10.75	8.42	6.36	5.05	5.00
	Share (%)	58.0	57.9	57.9	53.5	52.5
Top 2	Sales ($ billions)	7.32	5.07	3.31	2.44	2.40
	Share (%)	39.6	34.8	30.2	25.8	25.2

Source: Lehman Brothers, "Electronic Distribution Market," December 22, 1994.

Price Negotiations and Global Pricing Issues

Since the vast majority of semiconductors were considered commodity products, the buying decisions of distributors were based almost entirely on price. Distributors forecast the demand for the various semiconductor products they carried and negotiated with vendors for their prices. Since semiconductor prices were notoriously volatile, the price levels negotiated between manufacturers and distributors played a vital role in the distributors' profitability. The Semiconductor Group at Texas Instruments combined the practices of forward pricing and continuous price negotiations to set prices with its distributors.

Forward Pricing The cost of semiconductor manufacturing followed a generally predictable learning curve. When a manufacturer first began producing a new type of chip, it could expect only a small percentage of the chips it produced to function properly. As the manufacturer increased the volume of its production, it both decreased the costs of production and increased the percentage of functioning chips it could produce. This percentage, termed "yield" in the industry, and the standard learning curve of semiconductor manufacturing together had a large impact on the prices semiconductor manufacturers set for their products (refer to Exhibit 7 for the price curve of semiconductor products). This yield was important to TI; a 7% increase in overall yield was equivalent to the production of an entire Wafer Fab plant, an investment of $500 million.

According to Jim Huffhines, Manager of DSP Business Development in the Semiconductor Group, managers could predict with considerable accuracy the production cost decreases and yield improvements they would experience as their production volumes increased:

> We know the manufacturing costs for any given volume of production. We also know that these costs will decrease a certain percentage and our yields will increase a certain percentage each year. These predictions are the basis of the forward prices we set with both original equipment manufacturers and distributors.

Continuous Price Adjustments Production costs and yield rates were not the only contributing factors to price levels for standard semiconductors: market supply and

EXHIBIT 7

Forward Pricing Curve

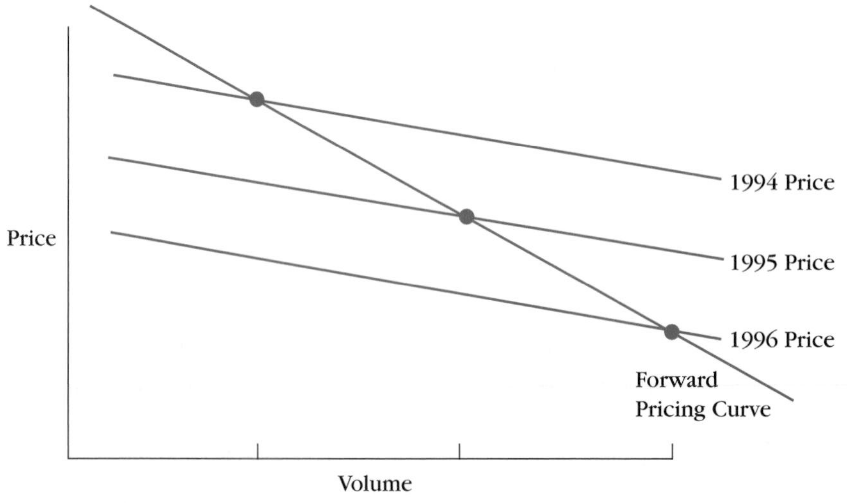

demand also played a powerful role in establishing prices. As a result of volatile prices caused by shifts in supply and demand, distributors often held inventories of semiconductors that did not accurately reflect current market rates. To protect distributors from price fluctuations, most semiconductor manufacturers offered to reimburse distributors for their overvalued inventories. Szczsponik explained:

> Semiconductor prices have fallen by 15% over the past 9 months. If Arrow bought semiconductors from me for $1.00, nine months ago, they are worth only 85¢ now. Arrow is carrying a 15% "phantom" inventory. If Arrow sells those semiconductors now, we give it price protection by agreeing to reimburse it the 15¢ it has lost per semiconductor over the past three quarters.

At the same time, distributors had at their disposal sophisticated systems for monitoring semiconductor prices from each of the major manufacturers, and were constantly in search of price adjustments from vendors when placing their orders. Szczsponik continued:

> Distributors have access to the prices of products from all the semiconductor manufacturers at any given time, and some anywhere in the world. The largest distributors have a staff of 20 to 30 people shopping around continuously for the best prices available for different types of semiconductors; add to this group a staff of accountants managing the price adjustment transactions. For example, they may call us to say that Motorola has quoted them a certain price for a semiconductor, and ask us if we can beat their price. In total, we get close to 150,000 of these calls requesting adjustments from distributors a year, and do over 10% of our sales through price adjustments. I have 10 people on my staff who negotiate price adjustments for distributors: 5 answer their calls, and 5 work with our product managers to make pricing decisions. These decisions are critical: if we make a mistake in our pricing, we lose market share in a day that can take us 3 months to recapture. At the same time, through our negotiations with distributors, we capture masses of data regarding the pricing levels of our competitors and the market performance of our different products. These data are critical to our ability to set prices.

As the distribution network consolidated into a small number of powerful companies, Szczsponik had begun to notice that his price negotiations were increasingly focused not only on beating the competition in North America, but on beating prices available around the world, including those of TI in other regions. With distributors becoming more active in the global marekt, they were more often exposed to semiconductor price levels from Europe and Asia. Industry analysts expected North American distributors to become more active in global markets as they pursued aggressive expansion campaigns in Europe and Asia. Although Texas Instruments' current contracts with its distributors prevented them from selling semiconductors outside of the region in which they were purchased, distributors were becoming insistent on access to freer global supplies and markets. While the concept may have appeared reasonable to the distributors, it was somewhat more complicated for Texas Instruments. Kevin McGarity elaborated:

> Because business is different everywhere in the world, our international distribution channels have evolved independently. They aren't subjected to the same costs, and don't operate under the same methods and calculation models. In the United States, for example, we offer a 30-day payment schedule for our customers. If they don't pay us within 30 days, we cut off their supply, no matter who they are. Italy operates under a 60-day schedule. Europeans include freight in their prices; we don't in North America. Finally, the cost of producing semiconductors varies by country. Europe tends to be more expensive than North America or Asia, simply because their infrastructure is more costly. So when one of our large distributors phones with the Singapore price for semiconductors manufactured in Düsseldorf, he is crossing boundaries that may be invisible to him but are very real to us.

Preparing for the Meeting with Arrow

With sales of almost $4 billion in 1994, Arrow Electronics was the largest semiconductor distributor in North America, of which TI products accounted for approximately 14%. Its aggressive growth had taken the company into global markets and had given it increased exposure to fluctuating price and exchange levels in different international markets. Seeking to minimize its costs, Arrow had begun to pressure semiconductor manufacturers to set standard global prices for each of their products. Motorola, one of Texas Instruments' largest competitors in the semiconductor industry, was rumored to be preparing for global pricing. Management at Texas Instruments, however, was unsure of the wisdom of moving toward global pricing. According to Szczsponik, the pros and cons to global pricing seem unevenly balanced:

> The large distributors want global pricing to reduce their costs and simplify their planning. But does it make sense for us? Right now our organization's calculation systems and costs in each country are too different for us to offer standard global prices. There are other things to consider as well. If we set global prices, we will no longer continue our price adjustment negotiations with the distributors. This may save us the cost of staffing our negotiations team, but it also takes away from us a powerful tool for gathering information on our customers' prices and our product performance. As soon as we stop negotiating price adjsutments, we lose our visibility in the market.

To prepare for his decision with McGarity and the forthcoming meeting with Arrow Electronics, Szczsponik knew TI had to make some fundamental decisions regarding global pricing. Who held the power in the relationships Texas Instruments had with its distributors? What was the source of the negotiating strength each party would bring to the meeting? Finally, what position should the Semiconductor Group take with its distributors regarding global pricing? And what organizational implications would such a decision imply?

CHAPTER 10

Marketing Strategy Reformulation: The Control Process

 Marketing strategies are rarely, if ever, timeless. As the environment changes, so must product-market and marketing-mix plans. Moreover, as organizations strive for gains in productivity, constant attention must be given to improving the efficiency of marketing efforts.

The marketing control process serves as the mechanism for achieving strategic adaptation to environmental change and operational adaptation to productivity needs.[1] Marketing control consists of two complementary activities: strategic control, which is concerned with "doing the right things," and operations control, which focuses on "doing things right." *Strategic control* assesses the direction of the organization as evidenced by its implicit or explicit goals, objectives, strategies, and capacity to perform in the context of changing environments and competitive actions. The ever-present issue of defining the fit between an organization's capabilities and objectives and environmental threats and opportunities is at the core of strategic control. *Operations control* assesses how well the organization performs marketing activities as it seeks to achieve planned outcomes. It is implicitly assumed that the direction of the organization is correct and that only the organization's ability to perform specific tasks needs to be improved.

The distinction between strategic and operations control is important to grasp. It has been noted that a "poorly executed plan can produce undesirable results just as easily as a poorly conceived plan."[2] Though undesirable results (declining sales, eroding market share, or sagging profits) may be identical, remedial actions under the two types of control will differ. Remedial efforts drawn from an operations-control perspective focus on heightening the marketing effort or identifying ways to improve *efficiency*. Alternatively, remedial efforts based on a strategic-control orientation focus on improving the *effectiveness* of the organization in seeking opportunities and mitigating threats in its environment. Improper assessment of the need for strategic versus operations control can lead to a disastrous response in which an organization pours additional funds into an ill-conceived strategy only to realize further declines in profit.

■ STRATEGIC CHANGE

Strategic change is defined here as change in the environment that will affect the long-run well-being of the organization. Strategic change may represent opportunities or threats to an organization, depending on the organization's competitive posture. For example, the gradual aging of the U.S. population represents a potential threat to organizations catering to children, whereas this change represents an opportunity to organizations providing products for and services to the elderly.

Sources of Strategic Change

Strategic change can arise from a multitude of sources.[3] One source is *market evolution*, which results from changes in primary demand for a product class and changes in technology. For example, increased primary demand for calcium in diets prompted the marketers of Tums antacid, Total cereal, and Minute Maid orange juice to promote the presence of calcium in their products. Technological change often prompts market evolution and changes in marketing techniques, as evidenced by the application of electronics to the watch industry described later in this chapter.

Market redefinition is another source of strategic change. *Market redefinition* results from changes in the offering demanded by buyers or promoted by competitors. For example, firms that provided only automatic teller machines (ATMs) for banks saw the market redefined to electronic funds transfer, with total systems rather than equipment alone being the offering purchased. Firms with systems capabilities, such as IBM and NCR, thus gained a competitive advantage in the redefined market.

Change in marketing channels is a third source of strategic change. Some recent changes in marketing channels have been prompted by *scrambled merchandising*, a trend among intermediaries to carry a wider assortment of merchandise than they did in the past (for example, 7-Eleven stores offer gasoline, and many gasoline stations now sell food items). Scrambled merchandising has led many manufacturers to reevaluate channel relationships and potential outlets for goods and services. For example, in the mid-1980s, supermarkets' share of home improvement product sales grew to over 20 percent. Firms seeing this trend benefited from the change; those that did not found themselves struggling to gain access to display space in supermarkets. Similarly, it is common today to find various electronics products, such as hand-held calculators, television sets, tape recorders, and personal computers, in general-merchandise stores as well as in specialty outlets.

Strategic Change: Threat or Opportunity?

Threat severity or opportunity potential is determined by the organization's business definition. In other words, does the threat or opportunity relate to the types of customers served by the organization, the needs of the customers, the means by which the organization satisfies these needs, or some combination of these factors?

The effects of strategic change are apparent in the transformation of the worldwide watchmaking industry.[4] Although Swiss watchmakers had dominated this industry for a century, market evolution, market redefinition, and marketing channel changes combined to spell disaster for the Swiss. While a technologically motivated market evolution changed the offering from jeweled watches to quartz and electronic watches, the primary marketing channel changed from select jewelry stores to mass merchandisers and supermarkets. Moreover, a redefinition of the term *watch* occurred. No longer was a watch defined solely in terms of craftsmanship or elegance as jewelry. Many people began to think of a watch as an economical and disposable timepiece. These changes, brought about by Timex and such Japanese firms as Seiko and Citizen, severely affected the Swiss watchmakers. Today, Swiss watchmakers have, for the most part, retreated to a highly specialized market niche, which can be identified as the prestige, luxury, artistry watch segment. For example, Swiss watches "tell you something about yourself" (Patek) and are "the most expensive in the world" (Piaget).

This example highlights how strategic change can affect an entire industry and its individual participants. In practice, several options exist for dealing with strategic change:

1. An organization can attempt to marshal the resources necessary to alter its technical and marketing capabilities to fit the market-success requirement. (Swiss watchmakers did not do this but, rather, devoted modest research funds to perfecting the design of mechanical watches, in which they had a distinctive competency. Only Ebauches S.A. invested in electronic technology and pursued the marketing opportunity available for an inexpensive, fashion watch—the Swatch.)

2. An organization can shift its emphasis to product markets where the match between success requirements and the firm's distinctive competency is clear and can cut back efforts in those product markets where it has been outflanked. (Many Swiss watchmakers chose this option.)

3. An organization can leave the industry. (Over 1,000 Swiss watchmakers selected this option, thereby eliminating more than 45,000 Swiss jobs.)

■ OPERATIONS CONTROL

The goal of operations control is to improve the productivity of marketing efforts. Because cost identification and allocation are central to the appraisal of marketing efforts and profitability, marketing-cost analysis is a fundamental aspect of operations control. This section provides an overview of marketing-cost analysis and selected examples of product-service mix control, sales control, and marketing-channel control.

Nature of Marketing-cost Analysis

The purpose of *marketing-cost analysis* is to assign or allocate costs to a specified marketing activity or entity (hereafter referred to as a *segment*) in a manner that accurately displays the financial contribution of activities or entities to the organization. Marketing segments are typically defined on the basis of (1) elements of the product-service offering, (2) type or size of customers, (3) sales divisions, districts, or territories, and/or (4) marketing channels. Cost allocation is based on the principle that certain costs are directly or indirectly assignable to every marketing segment.[5]

Several issues arise in regard to the cost-allocation question:

1. How should costs be allocated to separate marketing segments? As a general rule, the manager should attempt to assign costs in accordance with an identifiable measure of application to an entity.

2. What costs should be allocated? Again, as a general rule, costs arising from the performance of a marketing activity or charged to that activity according to administrative policy are the costs that should be allocated.

3. Should all costs be allocated to marketing segments? The answer to this question will depend on whether the manager opts for a "whole equals the sum of parts" income statement. If so, then all costs should be fully allocated. If it appears that certain costs have no identifiable measure of application to a

segment or do not arise from one particular segment, however, these costs should not be allocated.

The manager should follow two guidelines in considering the cost-allocation question. First, when costs are allocated, fundamental distinctions between cost behavior patterns should be maintained. Second, the more joint costs there are (costs that have no identifiable basis for allocation or that arise from a variety of marketing segments), the less exact cost allocations will be. In general, greater detail in cost allocation will provide more useful information.[6]

Product-Service Mix Control

Proper control of the product-service mix involves two interrelated tasks. First, the manager must assess the performance of offerings in the relevant markets. Second, the manager must appraise the financial worth of product-service offerings.

Sales volume, as an index of performance, can be approached from two directions. Growth or decline in unit sales volume provides a quantitative indicator of the acceptance of offerings in their relevant markets. Equally important is the proportion of sales coming from individual offerings in the product-service mix and how this sales distribution affects profitability. Many firms experience the "80–20 rule"— 80 percent of sales or profits come from 20 percent of the firm's offerings. For example, in the late 1980s, 20 percent of Kodak's products contributed more than 80 percent to the firm's sales.[7] Such an imbalance in the mix can have a disastrous effect on overall profitability if sudden changes in competitive or market behavior threaten the viability of this 20 percent. This happened to Kodak in the early 1990s when technological innovations such as digital imaging cameras began to redefine the photographic market. Also, Fuji proved to be an aggressive competitor in Kodak's traditional film and photographic markets.[8]

Market share complements sales volume as an indicator of performance. Market share offers a means for determining whether an organization is gaining or losing ground in comparison with competitors, provided it is used properly. Several questions must be considered when market share is used for control purposes. First, what is the market on which the market-share percentage is based, and has the market definition changed? Market share can be computed by geographical area, product type or model, customer or channel type, and so forth. In the Goodyear Tire and Rubber Company case in Chapter 8, the market share for tires was reported by geography (U.S. versus worldwide), product type (passenger car and truck), type of retail outlet (company-owned stores, discount tire stores, etc.), as well as by manufacturers' total sales. Second, is the market itself changing? For example, high market share by itself may be misleading, since overall sales in the market may be declining or growing. Finally, the unit of analysis—dollar sales or unit sales—must be considered. Because of price differentials, it is better to use unit rather than dollar volume in examining market share.

A second aspect of product-service control consists of appraising the financial contribution of market offerings. An important step in this process is the assignment of costs to offerings in a manner that reflects their profitability. However, this step is difficult and often requires astute managerial judgment. Moreover, the definition of an offering is itself illusive. For example, a "red-eye" flight (early morning or late evening) scheduled by an airline might be viewed as an offering. The decision by McDonald's and Taco Bell to open for the breakfast trade can be viewed as a market offering, the costs of which include not only the cost of producing the menu items but also the cost of being open.

From a control perspective, the manager should examine the financial worth of market offerings using a *contribution-margin approach*, in which the relevant costs charged against an offering include direct costs and assignable overhead.[9] The units

EXHIBIT 10.1

Disaggregating Service Station Costs for Product-Service Mix Control (Thousands of Dollars)

			Department	
	Total	Gasoline	General Merchandise	Automobile Service
Sales	$4,000	$2,000	$1,700	$300
Cost of goods sold and variable expenses	3,000	1,600	1,220	180
Contribution margin	1,000	400	480	120
Fixed expenses	900	500	310	90
Net income	$ 100	$ (100)	$ 170	$ 30

by which these costs are broken down should be those that contribute most meaningfully to the analysis.

Consider the situation in which the owner of a chain of gasoline service stations is examining operating performance. Exhibit 10.1 shows the operating performance before and after cost allocation by department. Examination of the total yields little managerially relevant information. When costs are disaggregated by department, however, it becomes apparent that gasoline operates at a net loss, whereas general merchandise and automobile service operate profitably. Fortunately, each department "contributes" to overhead; that is, each department's revenue exceeds its allocated variable costs.

This analysis serves a useful purpose in identifying potential trouble spots. Several alternatives exist for taking corrective action. If the owner decided to drop the unprofitable line and leave the selling space empty, then general merchandise and automobile service would have to cover the total fixed costs, which will continue. It is doubtful that this would occur. (Note that gasoline does contribute to the payment of fixed costs.) Another possibility is that the manager might expand the other departments to use the empty space. Estimates of market demand and forecasts of revenue would be needed for further consideration of this action. Moreover, a commitment of resources would have to occur that would in effect significantly alter the nature of the business.

Sales Control

Sales control directs a manager's attention to both the behavioral and the cost aspects of sales activity. The behavioral element consists of sales effort and allocation of selling time. The cost aspect consists of expenses arising from the performance and administration of the sales function.

Sales control is usually based on a performance analysis by sales territories or districts, size and type of customers or accounts, products, or some combination of these variables. Various measures used to assess sales performance include sales revenue, gross profit, sales call frequency, penetration of accounts in a sales territory, and selling and sales administration expenditures.

Consider a situation in which a district sales manager has requested a quarterly performance review of two sales personnel in a territory within the district. These individuals have failed to achieve their sales, gross profit, and profit quotas. Exhibit 10.2 on page 538 displays the representatives' performance according to customer-volume account categories. These categories were established by the national sales manager on the basis of industry norms, as were the following expected quarterly call frequencies:

EXHIBIT 10.2

Performance Summary for Two Sales Representatives

Account Category	(1) Potential Accounts in Sales District[a]	(2) Active Accounts[b]	(3) Sales Volume[c]	(4) Gross Profit[d]	(5) Total Calls[e]	(6) Selling Expenses[f]	(7) Sales Administration[g]
A	80	60	$ 48,000	$14,000	195	$18,400	
B	60	40	44,000	15,400	200	17,900	
C	40	10	25,000	12,250	50	11,250	
D	20	6	33,000	16,500	42	9,000	
Totals	200	116	$150,000	$58,550	487	$56,550	$10,000

[a] Based on marketing research data identifying potential users of company products.

[b] Current accounts.

[c] Based on invoices.

[d] Based on invoice price for full mix of products sold.

[e] Based on sales call reports cross-referenced by customer name.

[f] Direct costs of sales including allocated salaries of two sales representatives.

[g] Costs not assignable on a meaningful basis; includes office expense.

Account Definition	Expected Frequency of Quarterly Calls
A: $1,000 or less in sales	2
B: $1,000–$1,999 in sales	4
C: $2,000–$4,999 in sales	6
D: $5,000 or more in sales	8

Both representatives had an equal number of A, B, C, and D accounts.

Exhibit 10.3 shows various indices prepared by the district sales manager from the performance summary shown in Exhibit 10.2. Among the principal findings evident from Exhibit 10.3 are the following:

1. The representatives' account penetration varied inversely with the size of the account. Whereas representatives had penetrated 75 percent of the smaller A accounts, only 30 percent of the potentially large D accounts were listed as active buyers.

2. Part of the reason for this performance appears to lie in the call frequency of the representatives. The representatives exceeded the call norm on the A and B accounts, but fell short on call frequency on the C and D accounts. Moreover, their "effort" level appears questionable (487 calls ÷ 90 days ÷ 2 representatives = 2.7 calls per day).

3. The gross profit percentage derived from sales to smaller accounts was considerably lower than that derived from sales to the larger accounts, which in turn affected profitability.

4. When account sales volume is matched with gross profit and selling expenses, it becomes apparent that the smaller accounts actually produced a net contribution dollar loss.

The sales control process in this instance revealed that the two representatives were not actively calling on accounts (only 2.7 calls per day) and that their allocation of call activity focused on smaller-volume, less profitable accounts that were in fact contributing a *loss* to overhead. Redirection of effort is clearly called for in this situation.

EXHIBIT 10.3

Selected Operating Indices of Sales Performance

Sales Volume/ Active Account (Col. 3 ÷ Col. 4)	Gross Profit Active Account (Col. 4 ÷ Col. 2)	Selling Expenses/ Active Account (Col. 6 ÷ Col. 2)	Contribution to Sales Administration (Gross Profit— Selling Expenses)
A: $800	$240	$307	−$67
B: $1,100	$385	$448	−$63
C: $2,500	$1,225	$1,125	$1,375
D: $5,500	$2,750	$1,500	$1,250

Account Penetration (Col. 2 ÷ Col. 3)	Call Frequency/ Active Account (Col. 5 ÷ Col. 2)	Selling Expense per Call Col. 6 ÷ Col. 5)	Gross Profit %/ Active Account (Col. 4 ÷ Col. 3)
A: 75%	3.25	$94.36	30%
B: 67	5.0	$89.50	35
C: 25	5.0	$225.00	49
D: 30	7.0	214.29	50

Marketing Channel Control

Marketing channel control consists of two complementary processes. The manager must first assess environmental and organizational factors that may alter the structure, conduct, and performance of marketing channels. These considerations were highlighted in Chapter 8. Second, the manager must evaluate the profitability of marketing channels.

Profitability analysis for marketing channels follows the general format outlined for product-service control. Cost identification and allocation differ, however. Two types of costs—order-getting and order-servicing costs—must be identified and traced to different marketing channels. *Order-getting costs* include sales expenses and advertising allowances. *Order-servicing expenditures* include packing and delivery costs, warehousing expenses, and billing costs.[10]

Consider a hypothetical marketer of furniture polishes, cleaners, and assorted furniture improvement products. This firm uses its own sales force to sell its products through three marketing channels: furniture stores, department stores, and home improvement stores. Exhibit 10.4 on page 540 shows income statements for all three channels combined, as well as individually (general and administration costs are not allocated or included). It is apparent that when costs and revenues are traced by channel, furniture store and department store channels generate equal sales revenue; however furniture stores incur a sizable loss and department stores account for almost all of net income. Why are the returns so different?

Inspection of disaggregated costs suggest the following:

1. The gross margin percentage on the mix of products sold to department stores is 38 percent, whereas the gross margin percentage on products sold to furniture stores and home improvement stores is 30 percent. Thus, lower-margin products are being sold through furniture and home improvement stores on the average.

2. Order-getting costs (selling and advertising) run about 21 percent of sales for furniture stores, but only 7 percent for department stores and 16 percent for home improvement stores.

EXHIBIT 10.4

Disaggregated Costs of Furniture Improvement Products for Marketing Channel Control (Thousands of Dollars)

		Marketing Channel		
	Total	Furniture Stores	Department Stores	Home Improvement Stores
Sales	$12,000	$5,000	$5,000	$2,000
Cost of goods sold	8,000	3,500	3,100	1,400
Gross margin	4,000	1,500	1,900	600
Expenses				
Selling	1,000	617	216	167
Advertising	750	450	150	150
Packing and delivery	800	370	300	130
Warehousing	400	200	150	50
Billing	600	300	250	50
Total expenses	3,550	1,937	1,066	547
Net channel income (loss)	$ 450	$(437)	$ 834	$ 53

3. Order-servicing costs are 17 percent of sales for furniture stores, 14 percent for department stores, and about 12 percent for home improvement stores.

In short, a manager can conclude that the effort (reflected in costs) necessary to generate sales and service in the furniture store channel is much greater than that needed for department and home improvement stores. Moreover, furniture stores purchase products with a lower gross margin. Once these problems have been identified, efforts to remedy the situation can be explored in a more systematic fashion.

■ CONSIDERATIONS IN MARKETING CONTROL

Proper implementation of strategic and operations control requires that the manager be aware of several pertinent considerations. Three of these considerations follow.

Problems versus Symptoms

Effective control, whether at the strategic or the operations level, requires that the manager recognize the difference between root problems and surface symptoms. This means that the manager must develop causal relationships between occurrences. For example, if there is evidence of a sales decline or poor profit margins, the manager must "look behind" the numbers to identify the underlying causes of such performance and then attempt to remedy them. This diagnostic role is similar to that of a physician, who must first establish patient symptoms in order to identify the ailment.

Effectiveness versus Efficiency

A second consideration is the dynamic tension that exists between effectiveness and efficiency. Effectiveness addresses the question of whether the organization is achieving its intended goals, given environmental opportunities and constraints and organizational capabilities. Efficiency relates to productivity—the levels of output, given a specified unit of input. Suppose a sales representative has a high call frequency per day and a low cost-per-call expense ratio. The individual might be viewed favorably from an efficiency perspective. If the emphasis of the organization is on customer service and problem solving, however, this person might be viewed as ineffective.

Data versus Information

A third consideration is the qualitative difference between data and information. Data are essentially *reports* of activities, events, or performance. Information, on the other hand, may be viewed as a *classification* of activities, events, or performance designed to be interpretable and useful for decision making. The distinction between data and information was illustrated in the discussion of marketing-cost analysis techniques, where data were organized into meaningful classifications and operating ratios.

NOTES

1. For a review of the marketing control literature, see Bernard J. Jaworski, "Toward a Theory of Marketing Control: Environmental Context, Control Types, and Consequences," *Journal of Marketing* (July 1988): 23-29.

2. R. Paul, N. Donavan, and J. Taylor, "The Reality Gap in Strategic Planning," *Harvard Business Review* (May-June 1978): 126. See also Thomas Bonoma, "Making Your Marketing Strategy Work," *Harvard Business Review* (March-April 1984): 68-76.

3. These concepts were drawn from D. Abell, "Strategic Windows," *Journal of Marketing* (July 1978): 21-26.

4. This example is adapted from D. Landes, "Time Runs Out for the Swiss," *Across the Board* (January 1984): 46-55; and L. Rukeyser, "Swiss Recovery of Luxury Watch Market Provides Timely Lesson," *Dallas Times Herald* (November 12, 1989): D9.

5. Thomas Dudick, "Why SG&A Doesn't Always Work," *Harvard Business Review* (January-February 1987): 30-36.

6. B. Ames and J. Hlavacek, "Vital Truths about Managing Your Costs," *Harvard Business Review* (January-February 1990): 140-147. Dennis Weisman, "How Cost Allocation Systems Can Lead Managers Astray," *Journal of Cost Management* (Spring 1991): 4-10.

7. F. P. Strong, "Kodak: Beyond 1990," *Journal of Business & Industrial Marketing* (Fall 1987): 29-36.

8. "Kodak's New Focus," *Business Week* (January 30, 1995): 62-68.

9. Germain Boer, "In Defense of Contribution Margin Analysis," *Journal of Cost Management* (Summer 1989): 4-7.

10. For an example of cost identification in marketing channels, see Robin Cooper and Robert S. Kaplan, "Profit Priorities from Activity-Based Costing," *Harvard Business Review* (May-June 1991): 130-37.

The Circle K Corporation

The Circle K Corporation is one of the leading specialty retailers in the United States and is the nation's second largest operator and franchiser of convenience stores. From fiscal 1984 (year-end April 30), when it embarked on a significant growth strategy, to fiscal 1990, the company acquired 3,326 stores and built another 983 stores while closing 899 units. During this period, sales increased from $1 billion in fiscal 1984 to almost $3.7 billion in fiscal 1990.

On May 15, 1990, the company and its principal subsidiaries filed for protection under Chapter 11 of the United States Bankruptcy Code. This action was taken because of the company's deteriorating financial condition, due in part to increased competition, a heavy debt burden from the expansion program, and the negative effect of merchandise and price policies instituted in 1989. Shortly after the bankruptcy filing, Circle K president Robert A. Dearth, Jr., announced that he was determined to reposition the company so that it could return to profitability and pay its debt in fiscal 1991.[1] Key elements of the plan to revitalize Circle K included a change in merchandising practices, increased promotional efforts, and an aggressive pricing program, all of which were designed to improve customer service and increase sales. In addition, opportunities to close or sell unprofitable stores would be pursued. Circle K's planned turnaround strategy was scheduled for implementation in the summer of 1990. Of critical concern to Circle K management was consumer and competitive response and the profitability of the announced strategy.

■ THE COMPANY

The Circle K Corporation, which is headquartered in Phoenix, Arizona, is the 30th largest retailer in the United States according to *Fortune* magazine. The company's convenience store business was begun by Circle K Convenience Stores, Inc. in 1951. In 1980, this company became a subsidiary of the Circle K Corporation. The Circle K Corporation is a holding company, which, through wholly owned subsidiaries, operates 4,631 convenience stores in the United States and related facilities. In addition, the Circle K Corporation has approximately 1,400 licensed or joint-venture stores in 13 foreign countries.

Circle K recorded an average annual increase in sales of 25 percent since fiscal 1984. The number of stores operated by Circle K increased by 14 percent per year during the period 1984 through fiscal 1990. Most of the increase in stores came from acquisitions. In the four years prior to fiscal 1989, when Circle K incurred an

---

[1] "Circle K Squares Off with Its Creditors," *The Wall Street Journal* (May 17, 1990): A4.

This case was prepared by Professor Roger A. Kerin, of the Edwin L. Cox School of Business, Southern Methodist University, as a basis for class discussion and is not designed to illustrate appropriate or inappropriate handling of administrative situations, or to be used for research purposes. The case is based on published sources, including the Circle K Corporation annual reports and 10-K Forms. The assistance of Angela Bullard and Deborah Ovitt, graduate students, in the preparation of this case is gratefully acknowledged. Copyright © 1995 by Roger A. Kerin. No part of this case may be reproduced without written permission of the copyright holder.

operating loss of $3.8 million, the company had recorded an average annual increase in operating profit of 25 percent. Exhibit 1 and Exhibit 2 (page 544) show the Circle K Corporation's consolidated financial statements for fiscal 1988 through fiscal 1990.

Stores and Unit Expansion

Circle K stores typically have 2,600 square feet of retail selling space. Most units are located on corner sites, have parking space on one or more sides, and are equipped with modern equipment, fixtures, and refrigeration. Nearly all the stores are open seven days a week, 24 hours a day. The 4,631 stores operated by Circle K are located in 32 states. However, about 84 percent of the stores are situated in Sun Belt states ranging from California to Florida. The primary concentration of stores is in Florida

EXHIBIT 1

The Circle K Corporation's Consolidated Statement of Earnings (Thousands of Dollars)

	For the Year Ended April 30		
	1990	*1989*	*1988*
Revenues:			
Sales	$3,686,314	$3,441,384	$2,613,843
Other	50,238	53,507	42,879
Gross revenues	3,736,552	3,494,891	2,656,722
Cost of sales and expenses:			
Cost of sales	2,796,559	2,580,398	1,893,058
Operating and administrative	865,602	729,306	561,894
Reorganization and restructuring charge[a]	639,310	—	—
Depreciation and amortization	127,652	93,033	65,659
Interest and debt expense	126,799	95,912	56,608
Total cost of sales and expenses	4,555,922	3,498,649	2,577,219
Operating profit (Loss)	(819,370)	(3,758)	79,503
Gain on sale of assets[b]	—	32,323	8,198
Equity loss on foreign joint ventures	(15,064)	(1,784)	—
Earnings (loss) before federal and state income taxes and cumulative effect of accounting change	(834,434)	26,781	87,701
Federal and state income tax (expense) benefit	61,565	(11,367)	(32,790)
Net earnings (loss) before cumulative effect of accounting change	(772,869)	15,414	54,911
Cumulative effect on prior years of change in accounting for income taxes	—	—	5,500
Net earnings (Loss)	($ 772,869)	$ 15,414	$ 60,411

[a] *The company had been attempting a financial restructuring since October 1989. A review and assessment of operations by the Board of Directors resulted in a reorganization and restructuring charge of $639.3 million as of April 30, 1990. The charge includes (1) excess costs over acquired net assets and foreign investment; (2) abandonment, rejection, and reserves for fixed assets in nonperforming leased stores; (3) write-downs of real estate and other projects no longer under development, and (4) debt issuance and other costs.*

[b] *On October 31, 1988, the company sold all of its assets in connection with its manufacturing and distribution of fragmentary and block ice, sandwiches, and other fast foods. On October 27, 1987, the company sold a 50 percent interest in its wholly owned United Kingdom subsidiary.*

Source: The Circle K Corporation, Form 10-K. Fiscal Year Ended April 30, 1990; The Circle K Corporation 1989 *Annual Report.* The statement of earnings information is accompanied by extensive explanations, which are an integral part of these consolidated financial statements.

EXHIBIT 2

The Circle K Corporation's Consolidated Balance Sheet, Abridged (Thousands of Dollars)

	April 30, 1990	April 30, 1989	April 30, 1988
Current assets:			
Cash and short-term investments	$ 50,205	$ 38,488	$ 44,216
Receivables	38,138	36,265	34,446
Inventories	175,308	239,916	191,000
Other current assets	39,865	94,341	109,851
Total current assets	303,516	409,010	379,513
Property, plant, and equipment (less accumulated depreciation and amortization)	836,123	1,068,489	708,314
Other assets	134,651	567,441	447,957
Total assets	$1,274,290	$2,044,940	$1,535,784
Current liabilities:			
Due to banks	$ —	$ 91,000	$ 60,000
Accounts payable	112,111	134,944	112,144
Other current liabilities	101,504	124,501	108,463
Total current liabilities	213,615	350,445	280,607
Liabilities subject to compromise	1,206,395	—	—
Long-term debt	54,651	1,158,563	844,065
Deferred income taxes	40,496	93,045	38,133
Other liabilities	130,915	45,359	17,191
Deferred revenue	32,285	19,632	24,767
Mandatory redeemable preferred stock	42,500	47,500	47,500
Stockholders' equity	(451,567)	330,396	283,521
Total liabilities and stockholders' equity	$1,274,290	$2,044,940	$1,535,784

Source: The Circle K Corporation, Form 10-K, Fiscal Year Ended April 30, 1990; Circle K Corporation 1989 *Annual Report*. Balance sheet information is accompanied by extensive explanations, which are an integral part of these consolidated financial statements.

(846 stores), Texas (735 stores), Arizona (679 stores), California (604 stores), and Louisiana (301 stores).

The present complement of stores was an outgrowth of an aggressive acquisition program begun in December 1983 with the purchase of the nearly 1,000-store UToteM chain. This acquisition was followed in October 1984 with the purchase of Little General Stores, consisting of 435 units. In February 1985, Circle K bought 21 Day-n-Nite stores, and in September 1985, it acquired the 449-unit Stop & Go chain. The company purchased 189 units from National Convenience Stores in March 1987 and three months later bought 63 franchised 7-Eleven units from the Southland Corporation. In late 1987, Circle K's director of public relations announced that the company intended to have 5,000 stores by 1990.[2]

---

[2] "Mergers of Convenience," *Progressive Grocer* (December 1987): 50–51; "Karl Eller's Big Thirst for Convenience Stores," *Business Week* (June 13, 1988): 86, 88; Circle K Corporation 1990 10-K Form.

In April 1988, Circle K purchased the assets of 473 convenience stores, 90 closed stores, convenience store sites, stores under construction, and related facilities from the Southland Corporation. The company's last major acquisition occurred on September 30, 1988, with the purchase of the Charter Marketing Group. This transaction resulted in the addition of 538 gasoline and convenience stores. Circle K did not acquire any stores in fiscal 1990 because of its deteriorating financial condition, which led to the company's Chapter 11 bankruptcy filings. However, negotiations concerning the sale of 375 stores in Hawaii and the Pacific Northwest were initiated.

Product-Service Mix

Circle K stores sell over 3,800 different products and services. Food items include groceries, dairy products, candies, bakery items, produce, meat, eggs, ice cream, frozen foods, soft drinks, and alcoholic beverages (beer, wine, and liquor) where permitted. Fast food items, including fountain drinks, doughnuts, sandwiches, and coffee, are also sold. Non-food items sold by Circle K include tobacco products, health and beauty aids, magazines, books, newspapers, household goods, giftware, and toys. Food and non-food merchandise categories accounted for 50 percent of company revenue in fiscal 1990.

Circle K sells gasoline at 77.5 percent of its stores. Gasoline accounted for 48.6 percent of company revenue in fiscal 1990. In addition, the company provides a variety of consumer services. Consumer services include money orders, lottery tickets, game machines, and video cassette rentals. These services combined with interest income and royalty and licensing fees accounted for the remainder of company revenue.

Circle K had followed a program of continual testing and introduction of new products and services designed to appeal to a broader customer base and stimulate store traffic. According to the company's chairman of the board, Karl Eller, "We're a massive distribution system. Whatever we can push through that store, we will."[3] The addition of automatic teller machines (ATMs) or debit card programs at 1,146 stores and leased space at certain locations for Federal Express drop-off package service are recent innovations indicative of this strategy.

Efforts to sell and promote high-profit-margin products while cutting back on popular, though less profitable, merchandise proved costly for Circle K in the summer of 1989. While the gross profit margin for merchandise sales increased, dollar sales decreased (see Exhibit 3 on page 546, which details sales and gross margins for merchandise and gasoline). Traditional customers did not want these products, according to Dearth, the company's president. An integral part of his merchandising plan for fiscal 1991 included tailoring product and service offerings to the particular ethnic or socioeconomic character of each store's clientele.[4] National Convenience Stores, Inc., with its Stop & Go stores, has adopted a similar program, matching its merchandise with the demographics of surrounding neighborhoods. Early results from this merchandise program indicate that dollar sales will increase 4 to 5 percent.[5]

Advertising and Promotion Program

Circle K has historically used media advertising and special promotions to attract customers. In fiscal 1989, the company spent $4 million on advertising. This figure was down 41.2 percent from the fiscal 1988 advertising expenditures. For compari-

---

[3] Lisa Gubernick, "Stores for Our Times," *Forbes* (November 3, 1986): 40–42.
[4] "Circle K Squares Off with Its Creditors," p. A4.
[5] "Convenience Chains Pump for New Life," *Advertising Age* (April 23, 1990): 80.

EXHIBIT 3

The Circle K Corporation's Merchandise and Gasoline Sales and Gross Profit Percentage, Fiscal Years 1988–1990

Revenue Source	1990		1989		1988	
	Sales (Millions)	Gross Profit (Percentage)	Sales (Millions)	Gross Profit (Percentage)	Sales (Millions)	Gross Profit (Percentage)
Merchandise	$1,869.4	37.2%	$1,962.4	36.0%	$1,649.2	37.5%
Gasoline	1,817.0	10.8	1,479.0	10.5	964.6	10.6
Other[a]	50.2		53.5		42.9	
Total	$3,736.6		$3,494.9		$2,656.7	

[a] *Other revenues consist of commissions on game machines and lottery tickets, money order fees, interest income, royalty and licensing fees, and other items.*

Source: The Circle K Corporation, 1990 10-K Form, pp. 30–31.

son, National Convenience Stores, Inc. (with 1,100 Stop & Go stores), spends about $12 million annually on advertising. Advertising as a percent-of-sales for the convenience store industry as a whole was 0.6 percent in 1989 and 0.3 percent in 1988 and 1987.

Circle K curtailed advertising in late fiscal 1990. "Circle K is not advertising and has not been," the company's national advertising manager said in April 1990. "We're going through bad times."[6] The company's most recent promotion was a "price-buster" campaign in Florida and Arizona. This campaign came to an end in the second quarter of fiscal 1990.

More aggressive advertising and promotion efforts were the second part of the turnaround strategy planned by Circle K. The company announced that a $100 million promotion would be launched in the summer of 1990.[7] The eight-week promotion would be centered on a "We're Driving Down Prices" game, which included some 180 million instant-winner, scratch-off tickets distributed to customers who made purchases at over 3,700 Circle K stores. Game tickets would feature instant-win merchandise discounts, theme park discounts, and grand prizes such as Jeep Wranglers, round-trip Continental Airline tickets, and Bayliner Capri 17-foot speedboats.

The game would be publicized by in-store window banners, ceiling danglers, and tent cards located near checkout counters. Outdoor signage near gasoline pumps was also planned. In addition, the promotion would be supported by radio and outdoor advertising. The objective of the promotion was to communicate a change in store prices by providing Circle K customers "more value for their dollar," according to a company press release.

This new promotional program planned for the summer of 1990 would compete directly against a similar initiative launched by 7-Eleven in April 1990.[8] 7-Eleven's program involved giving away six-ounce samples of coffee, fountain drinks, and Slurpees. The company was also giving away a coupon book, valued at $250, with discounts on 7-Eleven products as well as merchandise from Sears, Roebuck and Company, Radio Shack, and Children's Palace. 7-Eleven was promoting its program through television and radio advertising.

---

[6] Ibid.

[7] "Circle K Unveils $100 Million Promotion," *Convenience Store News* (August 27–September 23, 1990): 12.

[8] "Convenience Chains Pump for New Life," p. 80.

Pricing Policy

The third leg in the Circle K strategy involved an overall price cut of 10 percent to be implemented concurrently with the $100 million promotion and the change in merchandising practices. "Before, we had the attitude of gouging the customer for what we could get," said Dearth.[9] Historically, Circle K was able to charge premium prices for food and non-food items because of convenience of location, longer hours, accessibility, and fast service without long checkout lines. Promotional pricing of high-traffic items such as cigarettes, beer, bread, soft drinks, milk, and gasoline also was used periodically. These pricing practices had provided Circle K with the highest gross-profit-margin percentages in the convenience store industry. However, due to increased competitive pressures and rising costs during fiscal 1989, the company's gross-profit-margin percentage slipped to 25 percent for the first time since fiscal 1984. In addition, the Circle K Corporation incurred its first operating loss since its incorporation in 1980.

At the beginning of the 1990 fiscal year, Circle K boosted store merchandise prices by about 6 to 7 percent. According to industry analysts, store merchandise sales volume declined 8 to 10 percent. Gasoline sales volume dropped between 1 and 6 percent.[10] In February 1990, Circle K reversed the price increases. Merchandise dollar sales for Circle K in fiscal 1990 were 4.7 percent below fiscal 1989 levels, and company gross profit dropped 3.3 percent.

■ THE CONVENIENCE STORE INDUSTRY

The convenience store industry has been one of the fastest-growing sectors of retailing over the past 20 years. Since 1977, the number of convenience stores has grown at an average annual rate of 6.5 percent. Sales volume grew at an average annual rate of 17 percent. However, sales and store growth declined in the latter half of the 1980s. In 1989, the convenience store industry generated sales of $67.7 billion through an estimated 70,200 stores nationwide.

Convenience store industry profitability has fluctuated during the past five years. The industry gross profit margin fell to its lowest level in 1989 as a result of narrowing margins on store merchandise. The industry net profit margin before income taxes decreased in each of the past five years reaching a low of 0.4 percent in 1989. Rising costs of leasing, building, equipping, insuring, and operating stores coupled with financing costs attributed to store expansion contributed to this decline, according to industry analysts. A summary of industry sales, unit growth, and profitability is shown in Exhibit 4 on page 548.

Competitors

The convenience store industry is highly fragmented. In 1989, 1,353 companies were listed as belonging to the National Association of Convenience Stores. According to Alex Brown and Sons, Inc., an investment banking firm, about 42 percent of total stores and 31 percent of industry sales were accounted for by convenience store chains with fewer than 50 stores.[11] The largest single convenience store chain is the Southland Corporation (7-Eleven). The largest U.S. convenience store operators in terms of sales and units are listed in Exhibit 5 on page 549.

---

[9] "Circle K Squares Off with Its Creditors," p. A4.

[10] Ibid.

[11] *The Convenience Store Industry* (Baltimore: Alex Brown & Sons, 1988).

EXHIBIT 4

Convenience Store Industry Summary: 1980–1989

	Year									
	1980	*1981*	*1982*	*1983*	*1984*	*1985*	*1986*	*1987*	*1988*	*1989*
Sales, Including Gasoline										
Total sales (billions of dollars)	24.5	31.2	35.9	41.6	45.6	51.4	53.9	59.6	61.2	67.7
Year-to-year change (%)	31.0	27.3	15.1	15.9	9.6	12.7	4.9	10.5	2.7	10.6
Sales, Excluding Gasoline										
Sales (billions of dollars)	17.7	21.6	23.7	25.8	29.3	33.3	36.0	39.1	39.2	40.6
Year-to-year change (%)	22.9	22.0	15.7	8.9	13.6	13.3	8.4	8.6	—	3.6
Store Data										
Total number of stores (thousands)	44.1	47.9	51.2	54.4	58.0	61.0	64.0	67.5	69.2	70.2
Year-to-year change (%)	10.0	8.6	6.9	6.3	6.6	5.2	4.9	5.5	2.5	1.4
Sales per store (thousands of dollars) (excluding gas)	394.0	450.0	463.0	474.0	511.0	544.0	564.0	579.2	567.0	578.0
Year-to-year change (%)	11.0	14.2	2.9	2.4	7.8	6.5	3.7	2.7	2.1	1.9
Profitability Data										
Gross profit margin (%)										
Merchandise						32.5	35.5	35.9	36.4	32.1
Gasoline						7.3	11.2	10.6	11.5	11.7
Total						22.8	25.1	24.4	26.2	21.8
Net profit margin before income taxes (%)						2.7	2.6	2.2	1.9	.4

Source: Based on *The Convenience Store Industry* (Baltimore: Alex Brown & Sons, 1988): 3; *The State of the Convenience Store Industry 1990* (Alexandria, VA: National Association of Convenience Stores, 1990).

Convenience store executives believe that their principal competitors are other convenience store chains, gas stations that sell food (g-stores), supermarkets, and fast food outlets. S. R. "Dick" Dole, an executive at the Southland Corporation, believed that competition for convenience stores depends on the product category:

> If you're talking about post-mix, coffee, and sandwiches, then our competition is the "fast feeders," like McDonald's and Burger King, and other convenience stores. If you're talking about beer and soft drinks, then our competition would be supermarkets, other convenience stores, and some g-stores, or a major oil company that operates a small convenience store with major emphasis on gasoline.[12]

Oil companies that operate g-stores engage in the most direct competition with convenience stores. Texaco, Chevron Corporation, Amoco Corporation, Atlantic Richfield Company, Coastal Corporation, Mobil Corporation, BP America, and Diamond Shamrock operate more than 600 g-stores each.[13] These well-capitalized companies, with the advantage of prime locations and newer stores, have become very aggressive in the creation of convenience-type stores. Although smaller than convenience stores in terms of retail selling space and number of items stocked (convenience stores stock 33 percent more items than g-stores), g-stores have focused on items traditionally viewed as convenience store staples—tobacco products, soft drinks, and beer.

---

[12] "A Conversation with S. R. 'Dick' Dole," *The Southland Family* (August 1986): 9.

[13] "Convenience Chains Pump for New Life," p. 80.

EXHIBIT 5

Largest U.S. Convenience Store Operators

Company	Key Chain(s)	Sales Volume (Millions of Dollars)	Number of Store Units (Approx.)
The Southland Corporation	7-Eleven, High's Dairy Stores, Quick Marts, Super 7	$7,950.3	7,200
The Circle K Corporation	Circle K	3,441.4	4,631
Emro Marketing Co.	Speedway, Gastown, Starvin Marvin, Bonded	1,250.0	1,673
National Convenience Stores, Inc.	Stop N Go	1,072.5	1,147
Convenient Food Mart, Inc.	Convenient Food Mart	875.0	1,258
Cumberland Farms, Inc.	Cumberland Farms	800.0	1,150

Source: Company annual reports and 10-K forms; *Convenience Store News Industry Report 1989* (New York: BMT Publications, 1989).

Supermarkets have also been aggressive in trying to attract the convenience shopper. In particular, supermarkets have targeted the "fill-in" shoppers who typically populate the "eight items and under" express counters by offering extended store hours and prepackaged foods. This segment represents about $45 billion in annual sales. Supermarkets also cater to consumers who desire prepared foods for off-premises consumption. Prepared foods sold by supermarkets now account for more than $2.4 billion in sales annually. Furthermore, industry research shows that supermarkets enjoy a better reputation among consumers for lower prices and higher-quality food than convenience stores.[14]

Convenience Store Customer and Purchase Behavior

About 90 percent of American adults (18 years or older) visit a convenience store at least once a year. Almost two-thirds of these shoppers visit a convenience store two to three times per month. The typical convenience store customer is a white male between the ages of 18 and 34 with a high school education who is employed in a blue-collar occupation. A profile of the convenience store customer is given in Exhibit 6 on page 550.

Convenience store executives are sensitive to the fact that a stereotypic convenience store customer exists. They also recognize that opportunities for future sales growth exist in attracting women generally and particularly employed women, older consumers of both sexes, and professional and white-collar workers. According to a 7-Eleven executive:

> Two important demographic groups for 7-Eleven are the increased numbers of older people and working women. The elderly, the fastest-growing segment of the population, generally are not convenience store customers. Also, working women now rep-

---

[14] "Convenience Store/Supermarket Market Segment Report," *Restaurant Business* (February 10, 1990): 125.

E X H I B I T   6

Profile of Convenience Store Customers on a Given Day

	Convenience Store Customers (Percentage)	United States Population (Percentage)
Sex		
Male	57%	48%
Female	43	52
Age		
18 to 24	21	15
25 to 34	31	24
35 to 49	25	25
50 and over	23	35
Education		
Did not finish high school	19	18
Graduated from high school	62	60
Attended college	19	22
Annual Household Income		
Less than $10,000	14	13
$10,000 to $14,999	11	10
$15,000 to $19,999	12	10
$20,000 and over	48	48
Unknown	15	19
Race		
White	83	87
Nonwhite	17	13

Source: The Gallup Organization. Used with permission.

resent 45 percent of the work force. By 1995, 80 percent of all women between the ages of 25 and 44 will be working. Right now, women represent less than one-third of our business. We must do a better job of attracting potential customers to our stores by developing programs that fit their needs.

The 24–45 age group is experiencing a tremendous growth in disposable income, which increases our need to upgrade our stores to meet their demands and tastes.[15]

Similarly, a Circle K executive said, "We feel we can appeal to other groups than the traditional blue-collar customer of the past. We'd like to skew more toward office workers and white-collar workers."[16]

Industry analysts also believe that a broadened customer base will be necessary if the convenience store industry is to prosper in the 1990s. They note that the U.S. population between the ages of 18 and 34 will actually shrink in the early 1990s. They also point out that the industry must expand its customer base to include more older, married, dual-income customers and women shoppers.

The principal purchases by the 643 customers who visit an average convenience store daily are gasoline, tobacco products, alcoholic beverages, prepared foods, and soft drinks. These five product categories account for almost 80 percent

---

[15] "A Conversation with S. R. 'Dick' Dole," pp. 9–10.

[16] "Convenience Store/Supermarket Market Segment Report," p. 134.

of convenience store sales. The average merchandise sale per customer visit was $2.29 in 1989.

Industry Trends and Concerns

Industry observers have identified several trends that are likely to affect convenience store industry growth and profitability prospects for the foreseeable future. These trends and their implications are outlined below.

The first trend relates to industry maturity and store saturation. Industry analysts cite several developments, some of which are documented in Exhibit 4.

1. Industry sales growth has slowed in recent years compared with growth rates in the 1970s and early 1980s. Similarly, the number of new stores being opened has leveled off, and consolidation is occurring as firms have elected to grow through acquisition.

2. Industry profitability has declined in recent years. The downward spiral in net profit margins has hampered the ability of firms to reinvest in their operations.

3. Store saturation is present in many geographic markets. Potentially over-stored areas include the southwestern, southeastern, and western United States. Industry forecasters predict that the demand for convenience stores is such that the market can only support 400–500 new stores per year in the period 1990–1995.

A second concern is the lack of differentiation among convenience store competitors. According to a 7-Eleven executive, "The thing to overcome is the battle of sameness."[17] The lack of differentiation has often produced costly price competition in selected markets, most notably in Florida and Texas. Efforts at differentiation reflected in new products and services have often been met with an immediate response. "We are the worst thieves around," said a Circle K executive. "As soon as one of us finds something that works, the copycats go to work."[18]

A third trend is the changing sales mix between merchandise and gasoline. In the late 1970s, roughly 82 percent of convenience store sales were merchandise. By 1989, 60 percent of sales were merchandise. The increase in gasoline sales as a percentage of total revenue has affected industry profitability because of gasoline's lower gross profit margin and often higher equipment cost. Moreover, some industry watchers believe that oil company g-stores are better equipped to deal with the lower margins. These "low-price, high-volume" g-stores, with about 80 percent of their sales coming from gasoline, and supermarkets, with a growing commitment to serving the convenience-oriented consumer, have left convenience stores "stuck in the middle," say industry analysts.[19]

■ STRATEGY CONSIDERATIONS FOR FISCAL 1991

One week prior to the announced bankruptcy filing, Karl Eller resigned as chairman, chief executive officer, and board director of the Circle K Corporation. He did so to pursue personal business opportunities and to give the company's board of directors "the latitude to establish new objectives for the future."[20]

---

[17] "Convenience Chains Pump for New Life," p. 80.

[18] "Stores for Our Times," p. 41.

[19] "Recent Events Show Plight of C-Store Chains," *National Petroleum News* (May 1990): 10.

[20] "Karl Eller Resigns as Circle K Chairman, CEO," *The Wall Street Journal and Dow Jones News Wire* (May 7, 1990).

The principal elements of the announced strategy to revitalize the Circle K Corporation included (1) an overall price reduction of 10 percent, (2) a change in merchandise practices so that individual stores could stock items reflective of the socioeconomic characteristics of their trade areas, and (3) a $100 million advertising and promotion program. As the architect of the strategy, Dearth, Circle K's president, expressed no intention of downsizing the company or laying off any of the company's 27,000 employees when the bankruptcy filing was announced.

The initial reaction to the announced strategy was mixed. According to one of Circle K's bank creditors, "We would encourage any plan that generates income. We believe this [marketing] plan probably will."[21] However, industry analysts were skeptical. Some believed that the company's troubles would force it to sell about 10 percent of its stores. By August 1990, Circle K had terminated 400 leases on stores that had been shut down. These 400 leases were estimated to cost Circle K $1 million to $1.5 million per month. Furthermore, 201 unprofitable stores were scheduled to close in August 1990. In addition, the company had deals to sell 375 stores in Hawaii and the Pacific Northwest before its bankruptcy filing. These deals were delayed pending approval by the bankruptcy court. Savings from store closings, costs associated with terminating leases, and the potential gain on the sale of stores had yet to be determined.[22]

Industry analysts also expressed doubts about the financial viability of specific elements of Circle K's turnaround strategy. Lower prices might attract customers and increase store traffic. However, gross profit margins would suffer. Furthermore, efforts to modify the merchandise mix would involve a substantial change in inventories, and the advertising and promotion program was expensive. According to a convenience store analyst, "I don't know where they will get the money."[23]

In affidavits filed with the Securities and Exchange Commission, Circle K management stated that it "believes, but has no assurances, that this plan will succeed in improving operating results." Moreover, the company "expects to continue to incur operating losses until the business plan is fully implemented and refined."[24] The question yet to be answered was "Could the announced strategy return Circle K to profitability as envisioned by its president?"

---

[21] "Circle K Squares Off with Its Creditors," p. A4.

[22] "Circle K Begins Closing 201 Unprofitable Stores," *The Wall Street Journal and Dow Jones News Wire* (August 21, 1990).

[23] "Circle K Squares Off with Its Creditors," p. A4.

[24] The Circle K Corporation, Form 10-K, for the fiscal year ended April 1990, "Management's Discussion and Analysis of Financial Condition and Results of Operations," pp. 26, 30.

Solartronics Corporation

The corporate planning process for Solartronics Corporation had just concluded, and Richard Hawly, Vice President of Marketing, was reviewing the corporate goals for 1995. Even though Hawly had participated in the deliberations and the drafting of the final document, he was impressed with the ambitious goals. For example, the corporate plan established a sales goal of $92.5 million for 1995, when sales volume for 1994 was estimated to be $67.5 million.

During the planning process, a number of fellow executives had voiced concern over whether the distribution approach used by Solartronics was appropriate for the expanded sales goals. Hawly felt that their concerns had merit and should be given careful consideration. Though he had considerable latitude in devising the distribution strategy, the final choice would have to be consistent with the overall marketing program for the company in 1995. A recommendation and supporting documentation had to be prepared in a relatively short time to permit an integrated marketing program introduction in January 1995.

◼ THE COMPANY

Solartronics Corporation was formed in 1961 by Mark Speerson, who had a Ph.D. in electrical engineering. The company introduced a stereo radio unit in 1964 and a line of television sets in 1966. By the early 1990s, the company had expanded its product line to include a full line of home entertainment equipment.

Solartronics is an assembler rather than a manufacturer of home entertainment equipment. As an assembler, the company purchases components under contract from large (usually foreign) manufacturers. These components are then identified as Solartronics Corporation products and placed in consoles or other packages for sale under the Solartronics brand name.

Solartronics distributes its products directly to 425 independent specialty home entertainment dealers and 50 exclusive dealers which are of standard industry size in terms of selling space. Combined, these 475 dealers service 150 markets in 11 western and Rocky Mountain states. The exclusive dealers, however, are the sole company representatives in 50 markets. According to Hawly, this disparity in market coverage occurred as a result of the company's early difficulty in gaining adequate distribution.[1]

---

[1] Exclusive dealerships had chosen to operate in this manner. This was not the policy of Solartronics Corporation. However, Solartronics did not pursue additional dealers in these markets for the purpose of carrying company products.

This case was prepared by Professor Roger A. Kerin, of the Edwin L. Cox School of Business, Southern Methodist University, as a basis for class discussion and is not designed to illustrate effective or ineffective handling of an administrative situation. Certain names and data have been disguised. Copyright © 1996 by Roger A. Kerin. No part of this case may be reproduced without written permission of the copyright holder.

The independent dealers typically carry ten or more brands of home entertainment equipment products, whereas the exclusive dealerships carry only Solartronics products and noncompetitive complementary products. Dealerships are located in market areas with populations of approximately 100,000 or fewer. In contrast, major competitors tend to be national in scope. Partially as a result of that—and partially because of economies of scale in advertising and distribution—these firms had been selling an increasing proportion of their products through mass merchandisers such as chain and discount stores. The overwhelming majority of these stores were located in retail trading areas with 1 million or more inhabitants.

The company employs ten sales representatives, each responsible for a territory that is generally delineated by state borders. These representatives deal primarily with the independent dealers and call on them twice a month on average.

■ THE HOME ENTERTAINMENT INDUSTRY

The home entertainment industry experienced double-digit dollar sales growth in the 1980s with the rise in consumer disposable income, changes in lifestyles, and product innovation. However, dollar sales volume growth slowed in the 1990s due in part to lower prices at both the equipment manufacturer and retail sales level. Sales growth, at manufacturer prices, was 4.5 percent between 1993 and 1994. Manufacturer dollar sales were $20.5 billion in 1994. Projected sales for 1995 were $21 million, representing a 2.4 percent increase.

Thomason (GE and RCA brands), Zenith, Matsushita (Panasonic and Quasar brands), Sony, and North American Philips (Magnavox, Sylvania, and Philco brands) account for the bulk of dollar and unit sales in the home entertainment industry. Private brands, produced by several of these companies and many others, are also important in the industry.

The product mix in the home entertainment industry consists of five major categories: television, compact disc players, videocassette players, audio systems, and tape players and recorders. Television is the largest single category in terms of dollar sales volume. These product categories vary dramatically in terms of market saturation in the United States. For example, 99 percent of U.S. households have a television set, 75 percent have a videocassette player, and 48 percent have a tape player or recorder. By comparison, 20 percent of U.S. households have a compact disc player, but only 8 percent have a portable compact disc player. Exhibit 1 shows home entertainment product unit and dollar sales for 1993 and 1994 and projected sales for 1995.

In 1990 the company commissioned a study on the socioeconomic characteristics and purchase behavior of buyers of home entertainment products. The study reported that these purchasers had household incomes above the median household income of the U.S. population as a whole. The research also revealed the following:

1. In-store demonstration, friend or relative recommendation, dealer or salesperson presentation, and advertising are dominant influences when buyers decide what brand of home entertainment products to purchase.

2. The median number of shopping trips made before purchasing home entertainment products was 2.4.

3. The most frequently shopped outlets for home entertainment products were radio/TV stores.

EXHIBIT 1

Home Entertainment Product Sales Overview and Forecast (Units in Thousands; $ Value in Millions)

Product	1993			1994			1995		
	Unit Sales	Mftrs. $ Value	Average $ Price	Unit Sales	Mftrs. $ Value	Average $ Price	Unit Sales	Mftrs. $ Value	Average $ Price
Total TV	26,499	8,889	335	27,925	9,409	337	28,920	9,708	336
Direct-view color	24,634	7,915	321	26,000	8,317	320	26,990	8,543	317
Color only	23,005	7,316	318	23,700	7,489	316	24,160	7,538	312
Stereo	9,767	4,288	439	10,665	4,533	425	11,476	4,854	423
Non-stereo	13,239	3,028	229	13,035	2,956	227	12,684	2,684	212
TV/VCR combos	1,629	599	368	2,300	828	360	2,830	1,005	355
Projection TV	465	841	1,808	535	962	1,798	585	1,038	1,775
Monochrome TV	550	40	72	530	37	70	480	33	69
LCD TV, color	300	60	200	310	61	196	320	62	195
LCD TV, mono	550	33	60	550	32	59	545	32	59
Total VCR	15,536	4,809	310	15,700	4,768	304	15,925	4,716	296
Decks	12,448	2,851	229	12,500	2,800	224	12,580	2,742	218
Stereo	3,248	997	307	3,560	1,050	295	4,200	1,218	290
Non-stereo	9,200	1,854	211	8,940	1,750	196	8,380	1,524	211
Videocassette player	449	61	135	400	52	130	360	46	127
Videodisc players	287	123	429	305	130	425	325	137	420
C-Band Sat. systems	338	395	1,170	369	406	1,100	330	330	1,000
Total audio systems	5,216	1,464	281	5,325	1,468	276	5,475	1,473	269
Rack systems	1,116	545	488	1,000	495	495	975	483	495
Compact systems	4,100	919	224	4,325	973	225	4,500	900	220
Separate components	-0-	1,635	-0-	-0-	1,750	-0-	-0-	1,790	-0-
Total CD players*	20,425	3,552	174	24,550	4,026	164	27,000	4,239	157
Portable CD players	11,276	1,289	114	14,620	1,579	108	16,540	1,720	104
Total Tape	32,343	909	29	30,940	803	26	30,285	787	26
Tape players**	15,717	397	25	15,640	375	24	15,295	367	24
Tape recorders**	16,626	501	30	15,300	428	28	14,990	420	28

*Includes portables and home decks; ** includes radio combinations.*

Source: U.S. Department of Commerce; Electronic Industries Association; Solartronics Corporation estimates.

The vast majority of home entertainment products are distributed through five types of retail outlets: (1) home furnishings/furniture stores, (2) housewares/hardware stores, (3) auto supply stores, (4) department stores/mass merchandisers (such as Circuit City), and (5) radio/TV stores. The volume of home entertainment merchandise sold by these outlets is unknown because of the variety of merchandise offered. However, selected data on the radio/TV store group with a more homogeneous product mix are available (see Exhibit 2 on page 556). These types of dealers represent all of Solartronics' accounts and operate with a gross margin of 27.5 percent.

EXHIBIT 2

Number and Retail Sales of Radio/TV Stores in the Western and Rocky Mountain States

State	Number	Sales (Thousands of Dollars)
Arizona	289	$ 412,175
California	2,375	3,952,615
Colorado	331	450,298
Idaho	86	75,073
Montana	81	96,020
Nevada	88	138,493
New Mexico	113	106,872
Oregon	286	331,815
Utah	124	143,010
Washington	457	457,482
Wyoming	59	50,630
11-state total	4,289	$6,214,483

Source: Solartronics Corporation estimate.

■ SOLARTRONICS CORPORATION PLANNING INITIATIVES FOR 1995

The following is an excerpted version of the company's planning initiatives.

General Corporate Objective

Our customer is the discriminating purchaser of home entertainment products who makes the purchase decision in a deliberate manner. To this customer we will provide, under the Solartronics brand, quality home entertainment products in the higher priced brackets that require specialty selling. These products will be retailed through reputable electronics specialists who provide good service.

Company Mission, Strategy, and Goals

The company's mission is to serve the discriminating purchaser of home entertainment products who approaches a purchase in a deliberate manner with heavy consideration of long-term benefits. We will emphasize home entertainment products with superior performance, style, reliability, and value that require representative display, professional selling, trained service, and brand acceptance—retailed through reputable electronics specialists to those consumers whom the company can most effectively service. This will be accomplished by:

1. A focused marketing effort to serve the customer who approaches the purchase of a home entertainment product as an investment.

2. Concentration on our areas of differential advantage: high-technology television, audio, and related home entertainment products with innovative features, superior reliability, and high performance levels—products that generally sell for more than $500 at retail.

3. Emphasis on products requiring display, demonstration, and product education, which must be delivered to and serviced in the home, to be sold through reputable merchants that specialize in home entertainment products and provide good service.

4. Concentration on distribution in existing markets, and general exclusion of large core cities with populations of 1 million or more.

5. Developing brand acceptance by obtaining in every market served a market position of at least $16.25 sales per capita, which our research indicates is possible.

Solartronics' 1995 marketing strategy represented a significant departure from the company's previous marketing posture. For many years the company had manufactured and marketed good-quality, medium- and promotionally priced home entertainment products. In the last few years, however, the company had begun to emphasize more expensive and more luxurious home entertainment equipment.

Although this was not stated in the overall marketing strategy, the company had also become more aggressive in its advertising. The advertising budget for 1995 included television advertising, which the company had previously eschewed in favor of local newspaper advertising on a cooperative basis with dealers. In 1995, television advertising would be allotted $7.5 million and would be directed at the 100 highest-potential markets, 50 markets served by exclusive dealers and 50 other current markets that had the next highest potential which had yet to be determined.

The overall direction of the marketing program had been reaffirmed in the recent corporate planning sessions. The sales target of $92.5 million was viewed as both ambitious and necessary. Solartronics' senior managers were of the firm belief that the company had to attain a larger, critical mass of sales volume to preserve its buying position with component suppliers, particularly with respect to component prices and discounts.

Even though there was agreement on the marketing effort and the need to expand sales volume, different viewpoints were raised concerning the capacity of present dealers to deliver $92.5 million in sales. This matter had consumed much of Hawly's time recently.

■ THE DISTRIBUTION STRATEGY ISSUE

Hawly was well aware of the value that Solartronics placed on its dealers and the importance of developing a close linkage between the company and the dealers. The company had long emphasized that dealers are an asset that must be consistently supported.

Hawly saw his charge as determining the characteristics, the number, and the locations of the dealers Solartronics would need to meet its sales goal of $92.5 million in 1995. Initially this would involve identifying the types of dealers that would satisfy the needs of the kind of customer the company sought and that would work closely with the company in meeting corporate objectives.

A number of different viewpoints had been voiced by Hawly's fellow executives. One viewpoint favored increasing the number of dealers in the markets currently served by the company. The reasoning behind this position was that it would be difficult for existing dealers to attain the sales goal specified in the corporate plan. Executives expressing this view noted that even with a 2.4 percent increase in sales following the industry trend, it would be necessary to add at least another 100 dealers. They said these dealers would be likely to be independent (nonexclusive) dealers located in the 100 markets not served by exclusive dealerships. Hawly believed that adding another 100 dealers over the next year would not be easy and would require increasing the sales force that serviced nonexclusive dealers. Executives acknowledged that this plan had more merit in the long run of, say, three to four years. However, their idea had merit as a long-term distribution policy, they thought. The incremental direct cost of adding a sales representative was $80,000 per year.

A second viewpoint favored the development of an exclusive franchise program, since 27 nonexclusive dealers had posed such a possibility in the last year. Each of these dealers represented a different market and each of these markets was considered to have high potential and be a candidate for the new advertising program. These dealers were prepared to sell off competing lines. They would sell Solartronics home entertainment products exclusively in their market for a specified franchise fee. In exchange for the dealer's contractual obligation to promote, merchandise, and service Solartronics products in a specified manner consistent with corporate objectives, Solartronics would drop present dealers in their markets and not add new dealers. Further, these dealers noted, the company's current contractual arrangements with its independent dealers allowed for cancellation by either party, without cause, with 90-days advance notification. Thus, the program could be implemented during the traditionally slow first quarter of the upcoming year. If adopted, company executives believed the franchise program in these 27 markets could be served by the television advertising program. The other 50 markets served by exclusive dealers would be unaffected, since this advertising program was already being applied. The remaining 73 markets would also be unaffected, except for increased advertising in 23 high-potential markets.

A third viewpoint called for a general reduction in the number of dealerships without granting any exclusive franchises. Executives supporting this approach cited a number of factors favoring it. First, analysis of dealers' sales indicated that 50 of Solartronics' dealers (all exclusive dealers) produced 80 percent of company sales. Second, an improvement in sales-force effort and possibly increased sales might result if more time were given to fewer dealers. Third, committing Solartronics to an exclusive franchise program would limit its flexibility in the future. Although a number had not been set, some consideration had been given to the idea of reducing the number of dealers in the 150 markets served by the company from 475 to 250. This would mean that the 50 exclusive dealers would be retained and 200 nonexclusive dealers would operate in the remaining 100 markets, of which the top 50 would benefit from the television advertising program.

A fourth viewpoint voiced by several executives was not to change either the distribution strategy or the dealers. Rather, they believed that the company should do a better job with the current distribution system. It was their opinion that additional sales personnel and the expanded television advertising budget should be sufficient. Moreover, they argued that because of slowed growth, this was not the time for major changes in distribution policy and practices.

Macon Institute of Art and History

In early 1997, Ashley Mercer, Director of Development and Community Affairs, and Donald Pate, Director of Finance and Administration, of the Macon Institute of Art and History, met to discuss what had transpired at a meeting the previous afternoon. The meeting, attended by the senior staff of the Institute and several members of the Board of Trustees, had focused on the financial status of the Institute. The Macon Institute recorded its third consecutive annual loss in 1996, and Mercer and Pate were assigned responsibility for making recommendations that would reverse the situation.

■ MACON INSTITUTE OF ART AND HISTORY

The Macon Institute of Art and History (MIAH) is a not-for-profit corporation located in Universal City, a large metropolitan area in the western United States. Founded at the turn of the century, the Institute was originally chartered as the Fannel County Museum of Fine Arts and funded by an annual appropriation from Fannel County. In the early 1980s, the name was changed to the Jonathon A. Macon Institute of Art and History to recognize the museum's major benefactor, Jonathon A. Macon. Macon, a wealthy local landowner and philanthropist, had provided the museum with a sizable endowment. According to the terms of a $25 million gift given to the museum upon his death, the museum's charter was revised and its name changed. The charter of the Institute stated that its purpose was

> To provide an inviting setting for the appreciation of art in its historical and cultural contexts for the benefit of this and successive generations of Fannel County citizens and visitors.

Randall Brent III, the Institute Director, noted that this charter differentiated the MIAH from art museums and history museums. He said:

> Our charter gives us both an opportunity and a challenge. By spanning both art and history, the Institute offers a unique perspective on both. On the other hand, a person can only truly appreciate what we have here if they are willing to become historically literate—that is our challenge.

In 1989, the MIAH benefited from a $28 million county bond election, which led to the construction of a new and expanded facility in the central business district of Universal City, the county seat of Fannel County. The location, six blocks from the museum's previous site, had extensive parking availability and access through public transportation. The site was made available for $1.00 from Jonathon Macon's real estate holdings. At the dedication of the new Institute in January 1992, Brent said:

> I will always believe that the greatest strength of our new Institute is that it was publicly mandated. The citizens of Fannel County and the vision and generosity of Jonathon Macon have provided the setting for the appreciation of art and its historical and cultural contexts. As stewards of this public trust, the Macon Institute can now focus on collecting significant works of art, encouraging scholarship and education, and decoding the history and culture of art.

■ INSTITUTE COLLECTION AND DISPLAY

The MIAH has over 15,000 works of art in its permanent collection. However, as with most museums, MIAH does not display all of its collection at the same time because of space limitations. Artworks in the collection are rotated, with some periodically loaned to other museums.

The MIAH collection includes pre-Columbian, African, and Depression-era art, as well as European and American decorative arts. The art is displayed in different portions of the Institute, where the building architecture accents the display. For example, Depression-era art is displayed in an Art Deco setting of the 1920s and 1930s; decorative and architectural art of the late nineteenth century is displayed in the Art Nouveau wing. In addition, Institute docents provide a historical context for the artworks during tours.

The MIAH collection is open for viewing Monday through Saturday from 10:00 A.M. to 6:00 P.M. and Thursday evenings until 8:00 P.M. Sunday hours are from 12:00 noon to 6:00 P.M. There is no charge for viewing the permanent collection; however, a modest fee of $3.00 to $5.00 is charged for special exhibitions. The Institute is also available for private showings and is often used for corporate, foundation, and various fund-raising events during weekday and weekend evenings. Exhibit 1 shows Institute attendance for the period 1988–1996.

EXHIBIT 1

Museum/Institute Attendance

Year	Total Institute Attendance	Special Exhibitions[a] Attendance	Proportion of Total Attendance
1988	269,786	N/A	N/A
1989	247,799	N/A	N/A
1990	303,456	N/A	N/A
1991	247,379	N/A	N/A
1992	667,949	220,867	0.33
1993	486,009	140,425	0.29
1994	527,091	227,770	0.43
1995	468,100	203,800	0.44
1996	628,472	284,865	0.45

[a] Special exhibitions attendance includes attendance at private corporation, foundation, and fund-raising events held at the Institute.

Institute Organization

The MIAH is organized by function: (1) Collections and Exhibitions, (2) Development and Community Affairs, and (3) Finance and Administration. Each function is headed by a director who reports to the Institute Director, Randall Brent III. The museum has a staff of 185 employees. In addition, 475 volunteers work at the museum in a variety of capacities.

The Collections and Exhibitions staff, headed by Thomas Crane, oversees the Institute's art collections, arranges special exhibits, is responsible for educational programming, and provides personnel and administrative support for Institute operations that directly involve the artwork. The Finance and Administration staff, headed by Donald Pate, is responsible for the daily operation of the Institute. The Institute's profit centers (the Skyline Buffet restaurant, parking, gift shop, and special exhibitions events) are also managed by this function. The Development and Community Affairs staff, under the direction of Ashley Mercer, is responsible for marketing, public relations, membership, and grants. This function engages in fund raising for the Institute, which provides supplemental funds for general operating support, endowment, and acquisitions. This function also handles all applications for foundation, federal, state, and local grants.

Institute Finances

Exhibit 2 on page 562 shows the financial condition of the MIAH for the period 1994–1996. Total Institute revenues and expenses during this period are shown below:

	1996	1995	1994
Total revenue	$10,794,110	$7,783,712	$8,694,121
Total expenses	11,177,825	7,967,530	8,920,674
Net income (loss)	($ 383,715)	($ 183,818)	($ 226,533)

The three consecutive years of losses followed seven consecutive years of either break-even or profitable status. The cumulative loss of $794,066 had depleted the Institute's financial reserves.

During a recent Board of Trustees meeting, several observations and projections were made that indicated that the Institute's financial condition needed attention:

1. The appropriation from Fannel County would decline. Whereas the county appropriated about $2 million annually to the MIAH in the early and mid-1990s, the Institute could expect no more than $1.6 million in county appropriations in 1997 and for the foreseeable future.

2. Declining interest rates in 1996 and 1997 indicated that earnings from the Institute endowment and investments would probably remain flat or decline.

3. Income from grants and other contributions in 1996 were extraordinary, and it was unlikely that the same amounts would be forthcoming in 1997.

4. Membership revenues were down for the fifth consecutive year. Membership represented the single largest source of revenue for the Institute.

5. Income from auxiliary activities—those that were intended to produce a profit—continued to show a positive contribution to Institute operations.

Special exhibitions and events were very profitable. Nevertheless, limited availability of special exhibitions in 1997, a declining number of scheduled events, and rising costs (for insurance as an example) indicated that the revenues from such activities would probably decline and costs increase in 1997. The Skyline Buffet restaurant, gift shop and parking, and the Institute Association were operating at about break-even.

EXHIBIT 2

Summary of Income and Expenses, 1994–1996

	Year Ending December 31		
Operations	*1996*	*1995*	*1994*
Income			
Appropriations by Fannel County	$1,786,929	$1,699,882	$1,971,999
Memberships	2,917,325	2,956,746	3,134,082
Contributions	338,664	221,282	42,244
Grants	763,581	281,164	645,853
Investment income	27,878	28,537	32,205
Earnings from endowment	673,805	693,625	583,612
Other	149,462	128,628	196,195
Total revenue	$6,657,644	$6,009,864	$6,606,190
Expenses			
Personnel	$1,973,218	$1,086,177	$1,681,653
Memberships	854,461	869,043	906,314
Publications/public information	594,067	404,364	441,710
Education	616,828	519,805	542,076
Administration[a]	3,777,042	3,345,153	3,389,124
Total expenses	$7,815,616	$6,224,542	$6,960,877
Operating income	($1,157,972)	($ 214,678)	($ 354,687)
Auxiliary Activities			
Revenue from auxiliary			
Special exhibitions	$1,655,200	$ 510,415	$ 451,347
Institute gift shop	1,596,775	606,503	810,123
Skyline Buffet	515,843	305,952	418,960
Institute parking	131,512	45,068	64,651
Institute Association	337,136	305,910	342,850
Revenue from auxiliary	4,236,466	1,773,848	2,087,931
Expenses from auxiliary			
Special exhibitions	814,741	313,057	137,680
Institute gift shop	1,679,294	662,685	990,090
Skyline Buffet	592,051	457,841	462,475
Institute parking	31,168	16,528	16,536
Institute Association	344,955	292,877	353,016
Expenses from auxiliary	3,462,209	1,742,988	1,959,797
Profit from auxiliary activities	$ 774,257	$ 30,860	$ 128,134
Net income	($ 383,715)	($ 183,818)	($ 226,553)

[a] *Administration expenses included mostly overhead costs, such as insurance, maintenance, utilities, equipment lease agreements, and so forth.*

■ INSTITUTE MARKETING

As Director of Development and Community Affairs, Ashley Mercer was responsible for marketing at the MIAH. Her specific responsibilities related to enhancing the image of the Institute, increasing Institute visitation, and building Institute memberships. Reflecting on her responsibilities, she said:

> In reality, Institute image, visitation, and membership are intermingled. Image influences visitation and membership. Visitation is driven somewhat by membership, but membership seems to also drive visitation and, in a subtle way, affects the image of the Institute.

Institute Image

Interest in the public image of the MIAH began soon after the new facility was dedicated in 1992. The new four-story building, situated downtown adjacent to skyscrapers, was occasionally referred to as the "marble box" by its critics, since the building facade contained Italian marble. When asked about the image of the MIAH, Brent commented:

> It is basically correct to say that, in the mind of the public, the Institute has no image. There is nothing about this [building] that says, "I'm a museum," or "Come in." There are a lot of people that are not interested in high culture and think this is a drive-in bank or an office building.
>
> Most art institutes in America have a problem with image. One of the things that makes me mad is that people think there is something wrong with the Institute. The MIAH is the most public in the country, and more heavily dependent on the membership contribution than any other [institute]. Like most, it is underendowed and underfunded from reliable public funds. This institution has chosen to be public, with free access, and this is very noble. It is wonderful that the Institute has decided not to belong to an agglomeration of very rich people.
>
> This institution has more character than it thinks it has. It has the best balanced collection between Western and non-Western art of any institute in the country. We have not chosen to sell or promote the unique aspects of this collection or the Institute's emphasis on historical context. What we have are the makings of an institution that is very different from other institutes, and we ought to be able to make that into an advantage rather than apologize for it.

Other staff members believed either that an image existed but was different for the various publics the Institute served or that the MIAH had not made a sufficient effort to create an image for itself. According to Ashley Mercer:

> Based on our marketing research, I think there are two distinctly different images. One is a non-image. People don't know what the Institute is. They also don't know what we have to offer in the way of lunch, dinner, brunch, shopping, movies, etc. They are not familiar with our collections. They are probably proud, however, that their community has a beautiful art and history institute.
>
> The other image is that we are only for specific people. This image is probably based on our membership. About 85 percent of members are college-educated (compared to 70 percent of the county population of 2.5 million), 60 percent have household incomes in excess of $60,000 (compared to 25 percent of the county population), half are over 40 years old (compared to 25 percent of the county population), and 98 percent are white (compared to 75 percent of the county population).

Janet Blake, Staff Assistant in charge of membership, noted:

> Among our membership, the MIAH is viewed as a community organization that has a cachet of class. It is exciting, educational, convenient, and inviting. It is a great place to bring visitors to our city for an afternoon of lunch and browsing.

A critic of the MIAH said:

> The MIAH has a definite image in my opinion. It's a great place to have lunch or brunch, buy an art or history book for the coffee table, and see a few things if time permits. Its parking facility is strategically located to allow its members to park conveniently for downtown shopping, particularly during the Christmas holidays.

Institute Visitation

Because there is a general belief that increased numbers of visitors lead to increased membership, Mercer's staff has historically focused its efforts on increasing the traffic through the Institute. "Social, cultural, and educational activity in the Institute is a major goal, and is not exclusive to the viewing of art," said Mercer. These efforts can be separated into general and outreach programs and programs involving special exhibitions and events.

Press Relations   The Institute continually promotes its special exhibitions and activities by sending out press releases, and it maintains a close relationship with the local media. Stories about art and history, public programs, and human interest issues are often featured in the local media. A five-year anniversary party was held at the Institute in early 1996, designed as a free special event aimed to involve the general public with the Institute.

Education and Outreach   The MIAH has many programs directed toward educating the public. Among these are public programs such as adult tours, school tours, lectures, art films, and feature films. The MIAH engages in programming to create community involvement and lends performing space to local performing arts organizations.

Special Exhibitions   Public service announcements written by the Institute are aired on local radio stations to promote special exhibitions. Advertisements are run in local newspapers in a five-county area for special exhibitions. For major special exhibitions, advertising is usually sponsored by a local corporation.

Ashley Mercer believed that these efforts increased Institute attendance. For example, periodic visitor surveys indicate that on a typical day when only the permanent collection was available for viewing, 85 percent of visitors were non-MIAH members. She added that even though less than 1 percent of nonmembers actually applied for membership during a visit, this exposure helped in the annual membership solicitation.

Institute Membership

According to Mercer:

> Institute membership and the revenue earned from membership play significant roles in the success and daily operations of the MIAH. The Institute and its members have a symbiotic relationship. Members provide the Institute with a volunteer base, without which our cost of operation would be astronomical. Member volunteers provide tours, assist at the information desk, help in the gift shop and the Skyline Buffet, and are invaluable in recruiting new members and renewing existing members.
>
> The Institute Association was created to encourage membership involvement in the Institute. The Association, with some 1,000 members, makes our volunteer effort possible—95 percent of our 475 volunteers are Association members. The Association's assistance in fund raising is critical, and we appreciate what its members have done for the MIAH. Last year alone, the Association was directly responsible for raising almost $350,000. In return, the Institute sponsors social events for Association members, offers them lectures by authorities on art and history, and provides various other privileges not available to the general membership.

Member Categories, Benefits, and Costs The MIAH has two distinct memberships: (1) personal and (2) corporate. These two memberships are further divided into categories based on dollar contributions and benefits received. There are six categories of personal membership ranging from $50 per year to $5,000 per year. Corporate memberships are divided into four categories ranging from $1,000 per year to $10,000 per year. These categories and participation levels were created in 1992 with the move to the new building. In 1996, there were 17,429 personal memberships and 205 corporate memberships.

Exhibit 3 shows the benefits received by each personal membership category. Exhibit 4 on page 566 provides a breakdown of personal memberships by category and the revenue generated by each category over the past five years. In 1996, personal memberships accounted for almost 80 percent of membership revenue.

Corporate memberships provide many of the same benefits as the $500 or higher personal memberships. In addition, corporate members are given "Employee Memberships" depending on their category. For example, corporate members that fall into the $1,000 category are given 25 "Employee Memberships"; those in the $10,000 category are given 250 such memberships.

The direct cost of benefits provided by the MIAH to personal and corporate members was estimated by the Institute's accounting firm in 1991. The Institute was required to do this because of income tax laws that limited the deductibility of membership to the difference between the direct cost of membership and the value of the benefits received. The estimated total cost of member benefits provided exceeded $1 million each year since 1991.[1] An itemized summary of benefit costs by category in 1996 is shown on page 566.

EXHIBIT 3

Membership Benefits by Membership Categories

Benefits	Membership Category					
	$50	$100	$250	$500	$1,500	$5,000
Invitations to special previews/events	*	*	*	*	*	*
Free limited parking	*	*	*	*	*	*
Free admission to special exhibits	*	*	*	*	*	*
15% discount at Skyline Buffet and gift shop	*	*	*	*	*	*
Monthly calender	*	*	*	*	*	*
Discounts on films/lectures	*	*	*	*	*	*
Reciprocal membership in other museums		*	*	*	*	*
Invitations to distinguished lectures			*	*	*	*
Listing in Annual Report			*	*	*	*
Personal tours of exhibition areas				*	*	*
Invitations to exclusive previews/events					*	*
Free unlimited parking					*	*
Unique travel opportunities					*	*
Recognition on plaques in the Institute					*	*
First views of new acquisitions					*	*
Priority on all Institute trips						*
Dinner with the Director						*

[1] The estimated cost of benefits exceeds the membership expense shown in Exhibit 2 because the cost of publications and other items is included in this estimate. These costs are allocated across several different items in Exhibit 2.

EXHIBIT 4

Personal Membership Categories and Revenues by Year, 1992–1996

Membership Category	Amount	Number of Members				
		1996	1995	1994	1993	1992
Regular	$50	13,672	12,248	13,483	16,353	17,758
Associate	$100	2,596	2,433	2,548	2,576	2,465
Collector	$250	364	325	397	461	454
Patron	$500	102	85	65	0	0
Partner	$1,500	604	638	679	741	882
Director's Club	$5,000	91	86	98	0	0
Total membership		17,429	15,815	17,370	20,131	21,559

		Membership Revenue[a]				
		1996	1995	1994	1993	1992
Regular	$50	$639,664	$556,120	611,864	$600,188	$662,631
Associate	$100	234,871	232,398	249,317	244,961	242,981
Collector	$250	81,415	76,987	97,474	108,432	105,840
Patron	$500	48,100	44,293	35,500	0	0
Partner	$1,500	815,666	958,419	968,239	1,187,728	1,041,898
Director's Club	$5,000	406,673	405,016	458,938	282,219	0
Total membership revenue[b]		$2,298,449	$2,334,583	$2,485,352	$2,451,638	$2,079,330

[a] The number of memberships times the dollar value does not equal the amounts given as the membership revenue, since some memberships are given gratis.

[b] The inconsistency between these figures and the figures shown on the income and expense statement is due to memberships given gratis.

Category	Benefit Cost
Regular ($50)	$ 631,016
Associate ($100)	81,903
Collector ($250)	64,135
Patron ($500)	39,628
Partner ($1,500)	99,567
Director's Club ($5,000)	15,975
Corporate (all categories)	125,576
Total cost	$1,057,800

The principal cost items in each category were (1) free admissions to exhibits, (2) parking, (3) the monthly calendar of Institute activities, exhibits, and events, and (4) discounts at the Skyline Buffet restaurant and gift shop.

Member Recruiting and Renewals "Recruiting new members and renewing existing members is a major undertaking," said Mercer. While some recruiting and renewals occur at the Institute during visitation, the recruitment effort mostly revolves around mail, telephone, and personal solicitations. Mail and telephone solicitations focus primarily on recruiting and renewing personal memberships in the $50 to $250 categories. Personal solicitations by the Institute Association and Friends of the MIAH are used to recruit and renew personal memberships in the $500 to $5,000 categories and corporate memberships.

The MIAH uses mailing and telephone lists obtained from other cultural organizations and list agencies. These lists are culled to target zip codes and telephone prefix numbers. Mail solicitations include a letter from the Institute Director, a brochure describing the Institute, and a membership application form. Telephone solicitations include a follow-up brochure and application form.

The economics of direct mail solicitation are illustrated below, based on an August 1996 mailing considered typical by Mercer.

Total mail solicitations	148,530
Total memberships obtained	1,532
Response rate	1.03%
Total membership revenue	$84,280.00
Total direct mail costs	$66,488.80

Two direct mail solicitations of this magnitude are conducted each year.

The solicitation process for personal memberships in larger dollar categories and corporate memberships relies on personal contact by Institute volunteers and corporate member executives. Prospective members are identified on the basis of personal contacts and from the lapsed membership roster, the society page, other organizations' membership lists, and lower-membership-level lists. Once identified, these prospects are approached on a one-to-one basis. An initial letter is sent introducing the prospect to the Institute. This first letter is followed by a personal telephone call or another letter inviting the prospect to an informal gathering at the Institute. At the gathering, the prospect is introduced to other members and is asked directly to become a member.

Renewal efforts also include mail and telephone solicitation. In addition, membership parties, special previews, and special inserts in the monthly calendar of Institute activities are used.

Institute records indicate that 70 percent of the $50 members do not renew their membership after the first year. Among those that do, 50 percent renew in each successive year. Members in the $100 to $500 categories have a renewal rate of 60 percent, and members in the $1,500 and $5,000 categories have a renewal rate of 85 percent. Mercer believed that less than 10 percent of personal members who do renew their membership increase the dollar value of their membership. Renewal rates among corporate members is about 75 percent, regardless of category.

■ CONSIDERATIONS FOR 1997

Ashley Mercer and Donald Pate met to discuss measures they might recommend to the Board of Trustees to reverse the deteriorating financial condition of the MIAH. Pate noted that at an earlier meeting with his staff, personnel reductions were discussed. Specifically, he felt that a 10 percent reduction in personnel and administration costs was possible. Furthermore, his staff estimated that the appropriation from Fannel County, contributions, grants, investment income, endowment earnings, and other income would be 15 percent below 1996 levels. A "best guess" estimate from the Director of Collections and Exhibitions indicated that special exhibitions and events would generate revenues of $1.2 million and cost $675,000 in 1997. Parking revenues and expenses resulting from nonmember visitors would remain unchanged from 1996. Rough budgets for education programs indicated that an expenditure of $500,000 for 1997 was realistic, given planned efforts. Pate said that changes in other auxiliary activities for which he was responsible, namely, the Skyline Buffet restaurant and gift shop, were not planned.

Mercer was impressed with the attention Pate had already given to the Institute's situation. She too had given consideration to matters of Institute image, visitation, and membership prior to the meeting. Unfortunately, an earlier meeting with her staff had raised more issues than hard-and-fast recommendations. Staff suggestions ranged from implementing an admission fee of $1.00 per adult (with no charge for children under 12 years old) to instituting student (ages 13–22) and senior citizen (60 and older) memberships at $30. The need for institutional advertising was raised, since the MIAH had only been promoting special exhibitions and events. Other staff members said that the benefits given to members needed to be enhanced. For example, raising discounts at the Skyline Buffet and gift shop to 20 percent was suggested. Another possibility raised was commissioning a "coffee table" book featuring major artwork at the Institute to be given with personal memberships of $500 or more.

Mercer listened to these suggestions, knowing that some were unlikely to receive Board of Trustee approval. These included any proposal to increase expenses for Publications/Public Information (for example, new books and paid institutional advertising). She had already been informed that expenses for such activities could not exceed the 1996 expenditure. Improving the member benefit package seemed like a good idea. Increasing restaurant and gift shop discounts, even though 65 percent of the business for both was already on discount, seemed like a good idea, at least at the margin. Pate said that he would give this suggestion consideration, but asked that Mercer think further about it in the context of the overall member-benefit package. Charging a nominal admission fee for nonmembers also seemed reasonable. Visitor surveys had shown that 50 percent of nonmember visitors said that they would be willing to pay a $1.00 admission fee for viewing the permanent collection (access to special exhibitions would continue to have admission fees). Furthermore, members could then be given an additional benefit, that is, free admission. However, Pate noted that the MIAH had always prided itself on free access, and he wondered how the Board of Trustees would view this suggestion. Additional membership categories below $50 and for students and senior citizens also seemed to provide new opportunities to attract segments of the population that had not typically yielded members.

Mercer and Pate believed that their initial meeting had produced some good ideas, but both thought that they had to give these matters further thought. They agreed to meet again and begin to prepare an integrated plan of action and a pro forma income statement for 1997.

3M Telecom Systems Division
Fibrlok™ Splice

It was early 1996. Dr. Dennis W. (Denny) Hamill sat back in his chair and stared at the stacks of documents in front of him on his desk. "Okay," he thought to himself, "I need to start someplace, so I might as well begin by reviewing the Fibrlok™ Splice history."

Hamill held the title of Business Director in the Telecom Systems Division of 3M Corporation, and it was his responsibility to review the performance of one of the division's most vaunted products, the Fibrlok™ Splice, a device used by telecommunications firms ("telecoms") to splice optical fibers when providing telephone service to households. Although the splice had initially exceeded the company's sales expectations, in recent years sales had leveled off, and it was Hamill's responsibility to determine if, and how, sales could be stimulated.

■ THE COMPANY

Minnesota Mining and Manufacturing Company, or 3M as it prefers to be called, is one of the best-known and most respected corporations in the world. 3M, whose stock price forms part of the Dow Jones Industrial Average, routinely makes the annual *Fortune* top-ten listing of the most admired U.S. companies, and recently it was rated as one of the best companies to work for. In 1995 3M received the National Medal of Technology® from President Clinton in recognition of its technological achievements over the past 90 years. It is, without question, a world-class corporation, one that employs 71,000 individuals in nearly 200 countries. Ranked 62nd in the *Fortune* 500 listing of the largest U.S. corporations in 1995, 3M's net revenue was nearly $13.5 billion. Exhibit 1 on page 570 contains selected financial and operating data for the company for the period 1993-1995. More than half (54 percent) of the company's revenue stream in 1995 was derived from international operations.

3M consists of 50 product divisions, subsidiaries, and departments organized into two major business sectors: Industrial and Consumer, and Life Sciences. About 62 percent of firm revenues are derived from the Industrial and Consumer sector. It is primarily a manufacturing company that produces in excess of 60,000 different products. These products range from adhesives, roofing granules, pharmaceuticals, overhead projectors, heart–lung machines, and coated abrasives to surgical drapery. 3M is unique among large corporations in that it does not focus on a single strategic core competency. Rather, 3M builds on some 30 core technologies in which it has acquired unique competencies. As such, the company follows a very decentralized management philosophy. In fact, the company can perhaps best be viewed as a com-

EXHIBIT 1

Selected 3M Operating Results, 1993–1995 (Millions of Dollars)

	1993	*1994*	*1995*
Net sales (millions)	$11,053	$12,148	$13,460
Cost of goods sold	6,344	6,839	7,713
Gross profit	4,709	5,309	5,747
Operating expenses			
Selling, general, and administrative expenses	2,918	3,219	3,446
Research and development	794	828	883
Other expenses (income)	(266)	(60)	442
Net income	1,263	1,322	976

Source: Annual reports of company.

munity of smaller business units that tend to focus on niche markets with niche products. The emphasis on "smallness" and "community" is illustrated by the fact that the average 3M factory has only 400 employees.

Company Beginning

Minnesota Mining and Manufacturing was founded in 1902 by a physician, an attorney, a merchant, and two railroad executives in Two Harbors, Minnesota, a small community on the north shore of Lake Superior. Its charter was to mine a very hard mineral, corundum, that was used in grinding wheels. When that business foundered, the company headquarters was moved to Duluth, Minnesota, with the intent of manufacturing sandpaper and abrasive wheels. In 1910, the company moved to St. Paul, Minnesota, where today it occupies a 425-acre campus with some two dozen buildings.

In 1907, William McKnight joined the company as bookkeeper. Less than seven years later he was named general manager. McKnight became the spiritual leader of the company and eventually served as chairman for more than 40 years. When he died at age 90 in 1976, McKnight was still serving on the 3M board of directors. In a 1944 speech, McKnight set forth what was to become the guiding principle of 3M: "Management that is destructively critical when mistakes are made kills initiative, and it's essential that we have many people with initiative if we are to continue to grow." This principle has been steadfastly adhered to and is embraced by the 3M corporate culture that emphasizes risk taking, teamwork, innovation, and entrepreneurship.

3M Products

One of the enduring characteristics of 3M is its continual focus on new and useful products. Consequently, 3M is legendary for the products it has pioneered. Perhaps the best-known 3M consumer products are its Scotch™-brand tapes, of which there are now hundreds of varieties. 3M also developed the first commercially viable magnetic recording tape. Other well-known 3M brands include Scotchgard™ Fabric Protector, Scotchlike™ Reflective Sheetings (for highway signs and clothing), O-Cel-O™ Stay Fresh™ Sponges, and Thinsulate™ Insulation for winter clothing. Exhibit 2 shows a breakdown of 3M's sales by general product grouping.

Bootlegging Time and Venture Teams

One of 3M's financial goals is to obtain at least 30 percent of sales every year from products less than four years old at every level in the company. Needless to say, this

EXHIBIT 2

3M Revenue by General Product Grouping (Millions of Dollars)

Product Line	Year		
	1993	1994	1995
Tape products	$1,617	$1,801	$2,042
Abrasive products	1,002	1,117	1,220
Automotive and chemical products	1,176	1,195	1,328
Connecting and insulating products	1,252	1,362	1,470
Consumer and office products	1,844	2,069	2,272
Health care products	1,876	2,002	2,221
Safety and personal care products	974	1,067	1,220
All other	1,312	1,535	1,687

Source: Annual reports.

goal has fostered innovation and entrepreneurship throughout the company, from top managers to rank-and-file employees. In fact, to encourage innovation, the company has a formal policy that allows technical and engineering staff members to spend up to 15 percent of their time (termed "bootlegging time") on projects of their own choosing. One of the most celebrated consequences of bootlegging is the Post-it® Note Pad. The note pad was developed by Art Fry, a company scientist who was searching for a solution to stop book marks from falling out of his hymnal during church services. Working on his bootlegging time, Fry found an adhesive that another 3M scientist, Spence Silver, had created but abandoned because it was not very sticky. Fry brushed the adhesive on some paper and created a product line that now annually generates sales in the hundreds of millions of dollars. Post-it® Notes currently come in 18 colors, 27 sizes, 56 standard shapes, and 20 fragrances.

In addition to providing bootlegging time, 3M fosters innovation by allowing the formation of both formal and informal new venture teams. A new venture team is essentially a task force with very special characteristics. Team members are volunteers on full-time, indefinite assignment from their normal task. They come from disciplines that include manufacturing, engineering, and marketing, and have the ability to stay together if a product proves to be successful. In such instances the product may form the nucleus of a new business unit. In keeping with the corporate spirit of entrepreneurship, venture teams are encouraged to "make a little, sell a little," which is interpreted at 3M to mean start small, learn how a business works, and then expand.

■ TELECOM SYSTEMS DIVISION

The Telecom Systems Division is a typical division at 3M. It has a 30-year history of selling products, first to telephone companies and now communication companies, all over the world. About 60 percent of the division's sales originate outside of the United States. The division has grown by concentrating first on products that help technicians and craft people (the "craft") in telephone companies splice copper cable and then protect those splices from the elements using closures and various kinds of cabinets. Over time the division built on these competencies by first adding testing equipment for copper wire and then by adding new technologies as the craft moved into fiber optics, coaxial cable, and wireless communications. Telecom Systems Division is part of the Electrical and Communications Markets Group, which in turn is part of the Industrial and Consumer Sector.

Since a large percentage of the Telecom Systems Division's sales are direct to large customers, it does not depend heavily on advertising for communicating its product offerings. Instead, the communication budget is focused on direct communication with customers, on trade shows, on press releases and success stories, and on technical articles emphasizing the benefits of the division's products. Advertising that is done (see Exhibit 3) is in very specific industry-focused trade publications.

Scotchlok™ Connector

In 1959, 3M introduced the Scotchlok™ Connector, a device for splicing copper wires used in telephone lines. This device allowed telecom technicians to splice two wires together by just inserting the wires into a connector (without stripping the insulation) and, through the use of a simple tool, snapping the connector together to make a connection between the wires that protects them from the environment. The Scotchlok™ Connector was an instant success and literally millions have been sold since its introduction. Indeed, it ultimately became the industry standard.

About 1969 3M introduced modular splicing, called MS², for splicing copper wire. MS² was a major innovation in that it allowed the telecom technician to splice 25 pairs of copper wires at a time in a single connector. Indeed, modular splicing was so popular that it has been credited with helping the telecommunications industry grow significantly over the last 20 years. At the present time 3M sells a two-wire Scotchlok™ Connector for about 5 cents; MS² sells for about $2, but it allows splicing 50 wires together very quickly, thereby improving craft productivity substantially. Presently there are about ten billion copper splices produced per year globally by 3M and its competitors.

By the mid-1980s, however, fiber optic cable was replacing copper wire in telephone lines at an increasingly rapid pace. There was a concerted effort by telecoms to replace coaxial copper wire with fiber optic cable for the "backbone" of telephone networks, that is, the "long haul" or major lines that were used to transmit long-distance telephone calls from one major point to another. Copper wire trunk lines, telephone lines that originate from a backbone and lead into a particular limited geographic location (such as a neighborhood), were also being replaced by fiber optic cable. There was considerable speculation that the major telecoms or RBOCS, as they are called (i.e., the regional operating companies resulting from the breakup of AT&T, such as Pacific Telesys and U.S. West), would soon be replacing the copper loops—the telephone lines linking a neighborhood location to a single home—with fiber optic cable.

3M's Telecom Systems Division estimated that about eight times more optical fiber would be required to replace the copper loops than was used for the backbone and trunk telephone lines. Moreover, the division estimated that the number of splices required to bring fiber optic cable into homes would be approximately 20 times greater on a per mile basis than that necessary for the backbone and trunk lines. In particular, it was expected that there would be between five and ten splices (spliced points) between a central telephone office and a home. Realizing the enormity of the task of bringing optical fiber into individual homes, telecom companies began to search for ways to minimize the expenditures required for installing, testing, and maintaining fiber optic cables to the home. These companies were joined in this quest by cable television operators, one of which estimated that the cost of running fiber to homes could be as high as $2,000 per home.

EXHIBIT 3

Typical Telecom Systems Division Trade Advertisement

From copper to fiber, you can count on 3M.

For more than 25 years, people requiring innovative solutions to their telephony or network problems have turned to 3M for answers.

3M Telecom Systems Division is a global leader in the supply of materials, components, products and services that ensure signal integrity while helping you effectively maintain the outside plant network and achieve your goals of fewer service interruptions and minimal downtime.

Copper or fiber, you can count on 3M for connections with tapes, jumpers, cable assemblies, fault finders, test sets, closures, cabinets and terminals. In fact, 3M offers thousands of products to keep your network operating day and night. And by offering this innovative blend of knowledge, hardware and skill, 3M is working to be your First Choice In Outside Plant.™

To learn more, contact your local 3M representative, fax us at 512-984-5811, or visit our Web site at www.mmm.com/telecom

3M Telecommunications

©3M

Source: 3M.

■ OPTICAL FIBER

Optical fibers are hair-thin strands of ultra-pure glass (often referred to as "light pipes") that digitally transmit voice, video, and computer data at the speed of light. A single fiber can transport up to 48 broadcast-quality video channels, whereas a 144-fiber cable can handle millions of simultaneous two-way telephone calls. Transmission is accomplished by means of light pulses through a glass fiber that has a diameter less than that of a human hair. In general, a fiber optic link consists of a light source (transmitter), fiber optic cables with connectors and/or splices, and a detector (receiver). More specifically, a fiber optic communication system consists of a transmitter that takes an electric signal, typically digital, and changes it into photons of light that are transmitted through the fiber. At various distances along the fiber are devices that amplify the light pulse. When the light pulse reaches its destination, it is detected and changed back into an electrical signal for reception. Light pulses are transmitted by total internal reflection. Consequently, the optical fibers are coated with a low refractive-index transparent material such as glass or plastic of a different type than that used in the fiber. This coating not only protects the internal reflecting surface of the fiber but also insulates adjacent fibers in a bundle.

Optical fiber was perfected in 1970 by scientists at Corning Glass Works (renamed Corning, Inc. in 1989). However, it was not until 1982 that the demand for fiber optic cable took off, spurred in part by the deregulation of the telecommunications industry. As of 1995, more than 60 million miles of optical fiber had been installed worldwide. In 1995, Corning alone produced more than 5.2 million miles of optical fiber.

There are more than one thousand suppliers of fiber optic equipment in the world. Corning, Inc. with a global market share of 32 percent, and AT&T Network Cable Systems dominate worldwide production of optical fiber. In general, the fiber optic equipment market is fiercely competitive, with firms from all over the globe competing.

Fusion versus Mechanical Splices

Properly splicing fiber optic cables is a very exacting task that requires great precision. If the splice does not result in the fiber optic cable being exactly aligned, the performance of the cable will be degraded substantially. Oversimplifying somewhat, there are two types of splicing, construction splicing and restoration splicing. The primary requirements for splices used in constructing fiber optic networks are that they be permanent and provide high performance. Cost is of secondary importance. The primary requirements for splices used in restoring (repairing) fiber optic networks are that they are easy and fast to install so that service can be restored as soon as possible.

There are essentially two methods for joining optical fiber, fusion and mechanical. Both methods of splicing accomplish the same goal in that they bring together two optical fibers and hold them in such a fashion that a light pulse can pass through the splice unhindered. Fusion splicers are a type of equipment that brings two or more optical fibers together and melts them to form a single strand. Mechanical splicers are devices that join optical fibers by aligning them and then maintaining them in alignment through the use of adhesives or epoxies or what is called elastomeric material. This material deforms under compression and can accommodate minor differences in the outside diameters of spliced fibers.

The instrument used for fusion splicing can be relatively expensive. Typical prices vary from $5,000 to $30,000 or more, and the instrument can be somewhat cumbersome when used in constrained quarters (e.g., in tunnels or false ceilings in buildings). Although a mechanical splicer does not require the large capital outlay of a fusion splicer, on average the total cost of each splice is between $7 and $20 because of the physical connector required (there is no physical connector in fusion splicing). Hence, from a cost perspective, if only a few splices are required, a mechanical splicer may be preferred. However, if many splices are to be made, a fusion splicer may be more cost effective. Moreover, fusion splicing requires highly trained technicians, whereas technicians can be easily trained to make mechanical splices. According to industry sources, the fusion splice has been widely accepted in applications requiring high volume (continuous) splicing. The mechanical splice is widely used in installations requiring relatively few splices at a time.

■ THE FIBRLOK™ SPLICE

In early 1987, Dick Patterson, a research scientist in the Telecom Systems Division, was using his bootleg time to develop a better way to splice fiber optic cable. Because he had worked on Scotchlok™ connectors, Patterson was convinced that a huge market existed for a mechanical fiber optic splice that was reasonably priced, easy to install, and resulted in high performance.

By April 1987, Patterson had formed a new venture team. The team consisted of himself as leader and Don Larson, an engineering specialist, Wes Raider, a senior design engineer, Jim Carpenter, a senior engineer, Barbara Birrell, an advanced physicist, and Al Lindh, a sales and marketing manager. As Patterson later noted, "We had a cross-functional team without knowing it." In November 1987, the team successfully tested a working optical fiber lock splice design.

The team worked literally day and night testing the mechanical splice, modifying the design, testing the modified mechanical splice, and so on. A working prototype was constructed and subjected to a myriad of engineering tests at the same time that reactions were obtained from potential customers in attempts to judge market responsiveness.

In August 1988, the Fibrlok™ Splice was introduced at a trade show in Chicago; all of the telecoms sent representatives. The splice was an inch and a half long, a quarter-inch high, and one-sixth of an inch wide. It contained a grooved aluminum element inside a plastic body with a plastic cap in the middle. A technician connecting two optical fibers would cleave and slide the ends of the fibers to be spliced into the device until they met in the center. By pressing down on the cap, the fibers would be locked into a perfectly aligned permanent splice. While the technology was complex (partly because of the high quality standards required), using the splice was easy, and telecom construction and repair workers could be taught how to use it in a short period of time. In fact, splicing could be accomplished in 30 seconds using only a simple hand-operated tool once the two ends of the fiber had been properly prepared (i.e., cleaned and cleaved), a task that would take an experienced technician one to two minutes.

Exhibit 4 on page 576 contains two diagrams of the fiber optic splice. One diagram shows the size of the splice, whereas the other shows an "exploded" schematic view of the splice. Technically, the Fibrlok™ Splice was developed to facilitate permanent splicing of standard single and multi-mode optical fibers that have 125-, 250-, or 900-micron diameters. Because any failure of the splice could have enormous loss potential for the telecom (revenue streams in the hundreds of thousands of dollars per minute can pass through a fiber optic cable) as well as 3M, great caution was observed in manufacturing and testing the Fibrlok™ Splice.

Initially, the Fibrlok™ Splice was packaged in units of five in individually sealed compartments in thermal-formed packages. Three different (color-coded) splices were available, depending on the size of the two optical fibers to be joined. To use

E X H I B I T   4

Fibrlok™ Splice Schematics

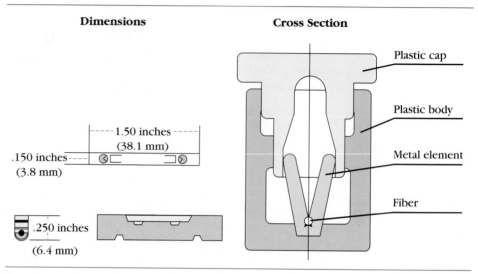

Source: Company documents.

the Fibrlok™ Splice required an assembly tool. Plans were made to market a Fibrlok™ Splice kit that included an assembly tool and 55 splices.

Similar to other Telecom Systems Division products, it was expected that the division's largest customers, such as Bell South, would buy Fibrlok™ Splices directly from 3M on a contracted price that would be negotiated. This meant that about 80 companies in the United States would buy Fibrlok™ Splices directly from 3M. The rest of the industry, literally thousands of companies, was expected to purchase Fibrlok™ Splices from 3M distributors including Anixter, Graybar, GTE Supply, and North Supply. 3M decided to price the Fibrlok™ Splice about the same regardless of whether it was sold to a distributor or to a large customer directly. Exhibit 5 contains selected information about the initial Fibrlok™ Splice offering.

The Fibrlok™ market introduction was extremely successful, with sales far exceeding projections. In October 1988, only six weeks after its introduction, sales

E X H I B I T   5

Initial Order Information and Pricing for the Fibrlok™ Splice

		Price $	
	Units/Case	*Trade*	*Distributor*
Fibrlok™ Optical Fiber Splice 250 × 250	50	16	12
Fibrlok™ Optical Fiber Splice 250 × 900	50	16	12
Fibrlok™ Optical Fiber Splice 900 × 900	50	16	12
Fibrlok™ Optical Fiber Splice Kit 250 × 250	1 each	975	755
Fibrlok™ Optical Fiber Splice Kit 250 × 900	1 each	975	755
Fibrlok™ Optical Fiber Splice Kit 900 × 900	1 each	975	755
Fibrlok™ Splice Assembly Tool	1 each	125	96.16

Source: Company records.

EXHIBIT 6

Advertisement for Fibrlok™ Splice

Take a closer look at the future of mass fiber splicing.

Signal Integrity

Fibrlok Multi-Fiber Splicing Assembly Tool

Mass fiber splicing will never be the same. With our Fibrlok Multi-Fiber Optical Splicing System, it's strip, cleave and splice – up to twelve fibers at a time. A completed splice can be assembled in less than five minutes, making the Fibrlok Multi-Fiber Splice ideal for both new construction and cable restoration applications.

Splice performance is comparable to our original Fibrlok Splice, delivering low insertion loss, low reflectance and superior thermal stability. Splicing is fast, efficient and permanent.

The Fibrlok Multi-Fiber Splice is easy to use and accommodates single-mode or multimode 125 micron fibers (individual and ribbon). The splice is available in 4-, 6-, 8-, 10- and 12-fiber configurations.

The low cost assembly tool is lightweight and portable, perfect for most real world applications.

To learn more, talk to an authorized 3M Telecom Systems distributor or your 3M representative. Or contact 3M Telecom Systems Division at 800/745 7459 or via fax at 512/984 5811.

3M *Innovation*

Source: 3M.

---

forecasts were revised. Sales were initially estimated to be approximately 85,000 units in 1989, but the early success led 3M to increase the forecast to 240,000 units. Because of the labor-intensive nature of the initial manufacturing process, a factory cost of about 50 percent of the price of each Fibrlok™ Splice was anticipated. However, it was also anticipated that significant per unit cost reductions would be achieved once manufacturing was appropriately ramped up to handle the increased demand. Exhibit 6 contains an advertisement for the Fibrlok™ Splice.

In 1995, Telecom Systems Division introduced a multi-fiber Fibrlok™ Splice. Although not much larger than the original single-fiber Fibrlok™ Splice, this new splice allowed technicians to connect up to twelve fibers at a time in a single splice. This improved craft productivity considerably. However, because taking a single fiber to the home does not necessarily require multi-fiber splicing (multi-fiber splicing occurs at points farther back in the network, such as in trunk lines where multiple fibers are in the same cable), sales of Fibrlok™ Splices did not increase substantially following the introduction of the multi-fiber Fibrlok™ Splice. Consequently, there have not been significant improvements in factory costs, and the price per fiber splice has remained fairly constant over time.

At the beginning of 1996, about 5 million single-fiber mechanical splices were being sold globally per year, with 3M's Fibrlok™ Splice holding about a 30 percent market share. Although the market for mechanical splices grew rapidly for the first three years after the Fibrlok™ Splice was introduced, in the last 7 years or so it has been relatively flat. Fusion splices still outnumber mechanical splices by about 8 to 1.

■ JANUARY 1996

With a doctorate in physics, Hamill was known for his keen analytical ability, and his tenure in the company had provided him with considerable expertise in many areas. Even so, Hamill enjoyed working with marketing-related issues because of their generally challenging nature.

As Hamill finished going through the piles of reports in front of him, he leaned back in his chair and rested his hands on his head. He thought about the division's forecast for the Fibrlok™ Splice nearly ten years ago. Back in 1987, expectations were that within five to ten years every household, at least in the United States, would either be served with fiber optic cable or have fiber "right to the curb." "Strange," he muttered to himself, "that same forecast holds today. Nothing seems to have changed. The same forecast, but it just seems to move out a year every year." Hamill was intimately familiar with the history of the Fibrlok™ Splice since one of the original venture team members, Al Lindh, indirectly reported to him.

At the beginning of 1996, there were in excess of 600 million identifiable telephone lines in the world, of which roughly one quarter were in the United States. Only a negligible proportion of these telephone lines incorporated fiber optic cable. Of the households that did have fiber optic cable, virtually all were in Japan, where the giant telecom NTT operated.

From the market research reports that he had read, Hamill calculated that new construction of telephone lines globally was running about eight percent a year (using as a base the 600 million existing telephone lines). For planning purposes Hamill assumed that three annual copper wire-to-optical fiber conversion or change-out rates were possible over the next few years—two percent, six percent, and ten percent. He assigned a .65 probability of occurrence to the two percent rate, a .25 probability to the six percent rate, and a .10 probability to the 10 percent rate.

Three Scenarios

Just as Hamill was finishing his musings, Steve Webster walked into his office. Hamill decided to bounce a couple of ideas off of Webster. "Steve, I have been thinking about the Fibrlok™ marketing strategy for 1996 and 1997, and there are three possibilities that occur to me. The first is that the market will grow very slowly. If this is the case, are we properly positioned with our existing splices, pricing, and communications to maintain the market share that we currently have without changing our current strategy?"

"But, what if we see significantly higher growth in penetration of fiber to the home? If this happens, are we still properly positioned with respect to product, price, and market support to keep our share and to be able to grow with the growing market?" Hamill paused and thought for a moment. "Finally, is it possible that we could, through significant product redesign, different pricing and cost structures, and different marketing communications or other kinds of market support, position ourselves to actually drive market growth by offering improved productivity in fiber optic mechanical splicing? What do you think, Steve?"

Webster paced the room for a few minutes before returning to his seat. "Denny," he began, "you know as well as I do that a part of the uncertainty in predicting the rate of penetration of fiber to the home is the constant change in the preferences of consumers regarding services that they want and are willing to pay for. At the same time, since copper is already installed, telephone and cable companies are increasingly finding new ways to add electronic enhancements such as ISDN, ADSL, and so on to upgrade the copper line. These enhancements allow the lines to handle more data faster. Remember, much of what is going on in the home is being driven by the Internet, fax machines, and even e-mail. Telecoms are trading off installing fiber against the cost of electronics to enhance the capability of in-place copper."

"If the last kilometer of the network remains copper to the home, enhanced by electronics, then the present model of fiber to the neighborhood will provide continued growth for fiber splicing. This growth, though, will not be the explosive growth that would occur if we can improve installation productivity by driving down the cost of splicing. Remember, telecom technicians operate at a loaded labor rate of $60 per hour. You know, Denny, without a real breakthrough in fiber splicing costs, say to under 50¢ per splice, even wireless local loop, fed by fiber to the last kilometer, moves ahead of fiber to the home."

"Well, Steve," responded Hamill, "how can we cover all options in this uncertain market? Should we invest in major cost reduction and design strategies and attempt to drive the market? Should we partner with a major end user of fiber like NTT to reduce our risk? Or should we be satisfied with a small but profitable market?"

CHAPTER 11

Comprehensive Marketing Programs

 An organization's comprehensive marketing program integrates the choice of which product or service markets to pursue with the choice of which marketing mix to use to reach target markets and, ultimately, create customers. The process of formulating and implementing a comprehensive marketing program encompasses all the concepts, tools, and perspectives described in previous chapters.

The challenge facing the manager responsible for formulating and implementing a comprehensive marketing program divides into three related decisions and actions.[1] First, the manager must decide *where to compete*. Product-market choice determines the organization's customers and competitors. This decision is often based on the organization's business definition and opportunity and target market analysis. In this regard, the manager has multiple options ranging from concentrated marketing with a focus on a single product market to differentiated marketing whereby multiple product markets are pursued simultaneously. Second, the manager must decide *how to compete*. The means a manager has available reside in the marketing-mix elements or activities. Multiple options again exist. In a simple situation with two alternatives for each of the four marketing-mix elements, 16 different marketing-mix combinations are possible. Third, the manager must determine *when to compete*. This decision relates to timing. For example, some organizations adopt a "first-to-market" posture, while others take a "wait-and-see" stance concerning market-entry decisions. Four issues are central to the design and execution of comprehensive marketing programs. First, a marketing manager must consider issues of *fit* with the market, the organization, and competition. Second, marketing-mix *sensitivities* and *interactions* must be considered as they relate to target markets. Third, issues of *implementation* must be addressed. Fourth, *organizational* issues must be taken into account. Each of these topics is discussed below.

■ MARKETING PROGRAM FIT

A successful comprehensive marketing program must effectively stimulate target markets to buy, must be consistent with organizational capabilities, and must outmaneuver competitors.[2] The fit of a program to a market is determined by the extent to which the marketing mix satisfies the unique needs and buyer requirements of a chosen target market. The fit of a program to an organization depends on the match between an organization's marketing skills and financial position, on the one hand, and the marketing mix being considered, on the other. Finally, the fit of a program to the competition relates to the strengths, weaknesses, and marketing mixes of competitors who are serving the target markets under consideration.

Establishing a program-market fit can be a daunting task. For over 20 years, DuPont explored applications for Kevlar, a synthetic fiber with five times the tensile strength of steel on an equal-weight basis. The chosen target market for Kevlar was tire makers that produced steel-belted radials. Despite Kevlar's unique qualities and $600 million of development and marketing costs, DuPont's marketing program did not persuade tire makers that Kevlar adequately satisfied their needs. Recently, DuPont's CEO announced that the company should focus "more intensely on customer needs."[3]

A comprehensive marketing program must be symbiotic with the organization implementing the program. Successful marketing programs build on an organization's strengths and distinctive competencies and avoid stressing organizational weaknesses. Failure to do this can have serious consequences. For example, Continental Airlines launched a comprehensive marketing program dubbed "Continental Lite," which centered on replicating Southwest Airlines' successful low-fare, short-flight, and point-to-point route system. However, Continental's higher operating costs and its inability to manage a short-flight, point-to-point route system produced a financial loss of almost $600 million over 15 months. The "Continental Lite" initiative was abandoned largely because it stressed organizational shortcomings rather than strengths and competencies.[4]

Finally, a successful marketing program fits the competitive realities of the marketplace. As described in Chapter 10, marketing strategies are rarely timeless. As the competitive environment changes, so must marketing programs. This is the case in the recently deregulated U.S. telecommunications industry. The Telecommunications Act of 1996 allowed long-distance telephone companies (e.g., AT&T, MCI, Sprint) to compete for local telephone service with regional telephone companies such as Bell Atlantic, U.S. West, and Nynex. It also paved the way for the merging of telephone, cellular, paging, and Internet communication technologies and services and the formation of new competitor alliances, each vying to satisfy the complete communication needs of businesses and households. These developments made obsolete marketing programs created in a near monopoly environment. These programs, which focused on a single communication technology (e.g., cellular) and service and high prices made possible by regulation, were replaced with marketing programs that focused on bundling communication technologies and services with lower prices.[5]

■ MARKETING-MIX SENSITIVITIES AND INTERACTION

Many of the case analyses thus far have implicitly or explicitly focused on target-market sensitivity to one or more elements of the marketing mix. The Jones ● Blair Company case in Chapter 4 is an example. When company management embarked on a planning effort, several views on how best to stimulate sales were voiced. One executive favored an increase of $350,000 in corporate brand advertising. Another argued for a 20 percent price reduction, and still another recommended hiring additional salespeople. Each of these executives implicitly suggested that the target market was most sensitive to the marketing-mix element he recommended.

In reality, however, the options are generally broader, and interaction effects between two or more marketing-mix elements must be considered. For instance, what would be the effect on sales of increasing corporate brand advertising *and* introducing a 20 percent price reduction? Would this action be more or less effective in stimulating sales than changing only one element of the marketing mix?

Although simultaneous consideration of marketing-mix sensitivities and interaction is a complex process, it is a necessity for the marketing manager. Consider the situation faced by John Murray, the marketing manager for DuPont's Sontara, a polyester fabric used for disposable surgical gowns and drapes used in hospital operating rooms.[6] Murray's charge was to prepare a comprehensive marketing program that would meet two objectives for Sontara: (1) maintain market share and (2) persuade garment makers that DuPont could support them in promoting Sontara to end users and would remain a strong force in the disposable fabric business.

Murray thought that if sales-force/maintenance expenditures were raised from the proposed level of $450,000 to a maximum reasonable level of $550,000 while other spending was held to proposed levels, market share could reach 35 percent of the total market. Similarly, if the other mix elements were increased to their maximum reasonable levels while the remaining expenditures were held at their proposed levels, market-share increases would be likely as well, although they would not be as dramatic. Specifically, he thought:

- If instead of spending nothing on sales-force/missionary expenses, management spent $200,000, market share would increase to 33 percent.

- If trade support/maintenance expenses were increased to $100,000, a 33 percent market share would result.

- If $100,000 were spent on trade support/missionary expenses, market share would be 33 percent.

- If advertising to intermediate users were increased to $50,000, the net effect would be a 1 percent increase in market share.

- An increase to $300,000 in advertising to end users would also result in a 1 percent share gain.

Reductions in spending were thought to have the opposite effect. Reducing sales-force/maintenance expenditures to zero while holding other spending at the proposed level was thought likely to reduce Sontara's share to 22 percent of the total market during the next 12 months. Similarly, reductions to zero spending for sales-force/missionary expenditures, trade support/maintenance, trade support/missionary, advertising to intermediaries, or advertising to end users were thought likely to reduce expected market share to 32, 27, 32, 31, or 28 percent, respectively.

As a validity check on the above estimates, Murray described what he thought would happen if all mix elements were raised simultaneously to their maximum reasonable expenditure levels or if all support was withdrawn from the product. He thought that with maximum effort a 39 percent share could be realized, although he was not sure how viable such an aggressive strategy would be for the long run. If all support was withdrawn, he estimated that market share would drop to 22 percent in the next 12 months and then decline further.

This example demonstrates the complex relationships that exist among marketing-mix elements. It also illustrates the role of assumptions and judgment in considering marketing-mix sensitivities and interactions.

Increasingly, marketing managers are turning to carefully designed market tests designed to measure marketing-mix sensitivities and interactions. By experimentally manipulating the amount and type of advertising and promotion and price levels in test markets, quantitative estimates of marketing-mix elasticities and relationships can be determined for individual products and services. For example, one consistent finding from these tests is that television advertising intensity has a far greater effect on sales volume growth for new consumer products than for products already established in the marketplace.[7] Market tests help to qualify assumptions made by marketing managers; however, they are not a substitute for judgment acquired through experience.

■ MARKETING IMPLEMENTATION

Implementation is the third leg in developing a comprehensive marketing program. Marketing managers have come to realize that poor implementation can hamper the success of an otherwise brilliantly conceived program.

Among the wide variety of subtle factors that can make or break a marketing program is timing. Failure to execute a marketing program when a window of opportunity opens can lead to failure or reduce the likelihood of success. For example, some industry observers believe that the failure of Matilda Bay Wine Cooler, introduced by the Miller Brewing Company, was due to poor timing on two counts. First, the popularity of wine coolers was declining. Second, the product was launched in the fall, typically a slow selling season.[8]

A second factor that can hamper implementation is not considering logistical aspects of a marketing program. When Holly Farms test-marketed a roasted chicken for distribution through supermarkets, consumer response was favorable. Holly Farms soon realized, however, that the roasted chicken was edible for only 18 days and it took 9 days to get the chicken from the production plant to supermarkets. As supermarkets could not be expected to sell the chicken within 9 days, Holly Farms had to halt its planned national introduction of roasted chicken.[9]

Effective execution of advertising and promotion, apart from expenditures, is a third factor in implementation. In short, the message conveyed to prospective buyers must be the right one. Revlon's Supernatural Hair Spray failed because the target market was unclear about what the product was supposed to do. Some people expected it to provide more holding power for their hair, and others expected less holding power.[10]

Finally, implementation of a price-cost plan requires careful attention and monitoring. American Express Company's aggressive marketing program for its Optima credit card resulted in a $265 million charge against company earnings in late 1991. The charge was due to credit losses and costs related to the card's operations.[11]

Formulating a comprehensive marketing program is a formidable task that demands rigorous analysis and judgment, often without the benefit of complete information. At the same time, program planning and design cannot be separated from implementation issues. "What should we do?" cannot be separated from "How do we do it?" By assigning equal importance to program formulation and program implementation, marketing managers increase the likelihood that their comprehensive marketing programs will succeed.[12]

■ MARKETING ORGANIZATION

Emphasis on marketing implementation focuses attention on organizational structure. It is often said that strategy determines structure and that organizational structure, in turn, determines whether a marketing strategy is effective and efficiently designed and implemented.[13]

A central issue in creating an effective and efficient marketing organization is finding the proper balance between centralization and decentralization of marketing activities, including strategy formulation and implementation. The strategy of regional marketing, whereby firms attempt to satisfy unique customer needs and meet competitive demands in limited geographical areas, has prompted increased decentralization of strategic marketing decisions and practices. For example, regional marketing groups at Frito-Lay design and implement region-specific marketing programs, including pricing practices and sales promotion activities. They also manage 30 percent of the company's advertising and promotion budget.[14] Efforts to "glocalize" marketing programs in the international arena have created elastic organizational structures that simultaneously strive for efficiencies through scale economies in product development and manufacturing, and for effectiveness through customization of advertising, promotion, pricing, and distribution in separate countries. As an example, Coca-Cola's concentrate formula and advertising theme are standardized worldwide, but the artificial sweetener and packaging differ across countries as do sales and distribution programs.[15] The relative emphasis on standardization versus customization in marketing strategy planning and execution ultimately manifests itself in organizational structure. For Frito-Lay and Coca-Cola, and an increasingly large number of other firms, the notion of "coordinated centralization" has produced domestic and global organizational structures that seek to foster adaptability to local conditions while preserving centralized direction in the pursuit of market opportunities and implementation of marketing programs.

NOTES

1. This discussion is based on Subhash C. Jain, *Marketing Planning and Strategy*, 5th ed. (Cincinnati, OH: Southwestern Publishing Co., 1996): 22.

2. Benson P. Shapiro, "Rejuvenating the Marketing Mix," *Harvard Business Review* (September–October 1985): 28–34.

3. Scott McMurry, "Changing a Culture: DuPont Tries to Make Its Research Wizardry Serve the Bottom Line," *The Wall Street Journal* (March 27, 1992): A1, A4.

4. Bridget O'Brien, "Continental's CALite Hits Some Turbulence in Battling Southwest," *The Wall Street Journal* (January 10, 1995): A1, A5; "Familiar Flight Plan," *Dallas Morning News* (August 10, 1996): 1F, 11F.

5. "Telecommunications," *The Wall Street Journal* (September 16, 1996): R1–R26.

6. *E. I. DuPont de NeMours & Co.: Marketing Planning for Sontara and Tyvek* (Charlottesville, VA: University of Virginia, Darden School of Business Administration).

7. Len Lodish et al., "How T.V. Advertising Works: A Meta-Analysis of 389 Real World Split Cable T.V. Advertising Experiments," *Journal of Marketing Research* (May 1995): 125–139.

8. "Miller Jumps into a Cooler Cooler Market," *Business Week* (October 26, 1987): 36–38.

9. "Holly Farms' Marketing Error: The Chicken That Laid an Egg," *The Wall Street Journal* (February 9, 1988): 36.

10. "Where's Farrah Shampoo? Next to the Salsa Ketchup," *Marketing News* (May 6, 1996): 13.

11. "Optima Backfires on American Express," *The Wall Street Journal* (October 3, 1991): B1, B2.

12. See William G. Egelhoff, "Great Strategy or Great Strategy Implementation—Two Ways of Competing in Global Markets," *Sloan Management Review* (Winter 1993): 37–50.

13. Frank V. Cespedes, *Organizing and Implementing the Marketing Effort: Text and Cases* (Reading, MA: Addison-Wesley, 1991); "The Search for the Organization of Tomorrow," *Fortune* (May 18, 1992): 92–97.

14. S. McKenna, *The Complete Guide to Regional Marketing* (Homewood, IL: R. D. Irwin, 1992).

15. John A. Quelch and Edward J. Hoff, "Customizing Global Marketing, *Harvard Business Review* (May–June 1986): 59–68; John Huey, "The World's Best Brand," *Fortune* (May 31, 1993): 44–54.

Show Circuit Frozen Dog Dinner

Executives of Tyler Pet Foods (TPF), Inc., looked forward to their meeting with representatives of Marketing Ventures Unlimited, a marketing and advertising consulting firm. The purpose of the meeting was to review the program for TPF's entry into the household dog food market in the Boston, Massachusetts, metropolitan area. TPF had sought out the consulting firm's services after discussions with food brokers who cited the tremendous potential for TPF in the household dog food market. These brokers had become aware that frozen dog food was being sold in small portable freezers in selected pet stores in a few cities in the southwestern United States. They believed these limited efforts represented a market opportunity for frozen dog food in supermarkets, where refrigerator space is more plentiful and where the majority of dog food is sold.

■ THE COMPANY AND THE PRODUCT

Tyler Pet Foods, Inc. is a major distributor of dog food for show-dog kennels in the United States. TPF has prospered as a supplier of a unique dog food for show dogs called Show Circuit Frozen Dog Dinner. Show Circuit was originally formulated by a mink rancher as a means of improving the coats of his minks. After several years of research, he perfected the formula for a specially prepared food and began feeding his preparation to his stock on a regular basis. After a short period of time, he noticed that their coats showed a marked improvement. Shortly thereafter, a nearby kennel owner noticed the improvement and asked to use some of the food to feed his dogs. The dogs' coats improved dramatically, and a business was born.

Show Circuit contains federally inspected beef by-products, beef, liver, and chicken. Fresh meat constitutes 85 percent of the product's volume, and the highest-quality cereal accounts for the remaining 15 percent. The ingredients are packaged frozen to prevent spoilage of the fresh uncooked meat.

■ PACKAGING AND DISTRIBUTION MODIFICATIONS

TPF executives recognized that modifications in the packaging of Show Circuit would be necessary to make the transition from the kennel market to the household dog food market. After some discussion, it was decided that Show Circuit would be packaged in a 15-ounce plastic tub, with 12 tubs per case. The cost of production,

The cooperation of Tyler Pet Foods, Inc. in the preparation of this case is gratefully acknowledged. This case was prepared by Professor Roger A. Kerin, of the Edwin L. Cox School of Business, Southern Methodist University, as a basis for class discussion and is not designed to illustrate effective or ineffective handling of an administrative situation. Certain names have been disguised. Copyright © 1997 by Roger A. Kerin. No part of this case may be reproduced without written permission of the copyright holder.

freight, and packaging of the meal was $6.37 per case, which represented total variable costs.

The discussions with food brokers indicated that distribution through supermarkets would be best for Show Circuit because of the need for refrigeration. Food brokers would represent Show Circuit to supermarkets and would receive for their services a 7 percent commission based on the suggested price to retailers, which had yet to be determined. Supermarkets typically receive a gross margin of 25 percent of their selling price for pet foods.

■ THE MEETING

TPF executives listened attentively to the presentation made by representatives from Marketing Ventures Unlimited. Excerpts from their presentation follow.

During the course of the meeting, TPF executives raised a number of questions. The questions were primarily designed to clarify certain aspects of the program. One question that was never asked but that plagued TPF executives was "Will this program establish a place in the market for Show Circuit?" This direct question implied several subissues:

1. Was the market itself adequately defined and segmented?
2. What position would Show Circuit seek in the market? Should the program be targeted toward all dog food buyers or toward specific segments?
3. Could the food brokers get distribution in supermarkets given the sales program?
4. What should be TPF's recommended selling list price to the consumer for Show Circuit?
5. Could TPF at least break even in the introductory year and achieve a 15 percent return on sales in subsequent years?

TPF executives realized that they had to answer these questions and others before they accepted the proposal. The total cost of the proposed plan could be $300,000 to $500,000, which TPF executives considered reasonable, although it would stretch their promotional budget.

■ PROPOSAL OF MARKETING VENTURES UNLIMITED

The following is an excerpted version of the proposal presented to TPF.

The Situation

Our goal is to introduce and promote effectively the sale of Show Circuit dog food in the Boston market area. Show Circuit is among the costliest dog foods to prepare and will be available through supermarkets.

Show Circuit is a completely balanced frozen dog food. It is of the finest quality and has been used and recommended by professional show-dog owners for years.

Yet, in spite of this history, Show Circuit is essentially a new product and is unknown to the general public. The fact that Show Circuit will be the only dog food located right next to "people food" in the frozen food section of the supermarket is an advantage that must be capitalized upon. Show Circuit's history of blue-ribbon winners is another plus. So, in essence, to market Show Circuit successfully, we must accomplish two objectives:

- Make the public aware of the brand name of Show Circuit, what the packaging looks like, and the fact that Show Circuit is a high-quality dog food.
- Direct the public to shop for dog food in the frozen food section.

The Environment

Sales of dog food will total about $5.6 billion this year at manufacturers' prices. Still, fewer than half of the dogs in the United States are regularly fed prepared dog food, which means the dog food industry has yet to tap its full potential.

Four trends indicate that this optimism is well founded. First, the dog food industry has benefited from increasing dog ownership. The U.S. dog population of 54 million, spurred on by the owners' desire for companionship or need for protection, is growing steadily and is expected to continue growing. Second, the trend toward using convenience foods in the household contributes to a lack of table scraps to be served to the dog, a fact that will only improve the prospects for selling prepared dog foods. A third important trend is that pet owners continue to invest their animal companions with human qualities and view them as members of the family. For example, a 1995 study conducted by the advertising agency, Bates USA, reported: "A person who owns a dog actually identifies with the pet, assigning human characteristics to the dog such as language, thoughts, feelings, and needs."[1] Not surprisingly, one-half of dog owners consider themselves "Mom and Dad" to their animal companions.[2] Therefore, it comes as no surprise that dog owners spend more than $5 billion annually for veterinarians' fees, medication for dogs, and dog toys, clothing, accessories, and furniture.

A fourth trend is the growth in premium and super-premium dog foods. According to an article in *Advertising Age*, these dog foods have fueled the growth in dog food sales along with the increase in pet ownership.[3]

The choice of supermarket distribution focuses on the dominant retail channel for dog food. Supermarkets dispense 55 percent of all dog food sold in the United States, which represents $3.1 billion in sales at manufacturers' prices. The other 45 percent is sold by pet superstores such as Petco and PetsMart, discount and mass merchandisers, warehouse clubs, veterinarians, and pet stores. These percentages also apply to the Boston market.

Finally, the Boston market is an ideal area for launching a new dog food. We estimate that the greater Boston area has 1.5 percent of the U.S. population (and 1.5 percent of the dog population since dog and human populations are highly correlated).

The Competition

There are about 50 dog food manufacturers and 350 dog food brands in the United States. However, eight companies—Ralston Purina, Nestlé, H. J. Heinz, Colgate-Palmolive, Mars, Doane's, Iams, and Nutro Pet Food—capture about 75 percent of dog food sales. Exhibit 1 shows the market shares of the major dog food manufacturers along with their most well-known brand.

In addition to market share, competitor advertising spending and forms of advertising used will be major considerations in planning Show Circuit's introductory marketing strategy. Total spending for advertising in the dog food industry is about 2

[1] *Pet Food Market Gets a Taste of the Good Life* (New York: Bates USA, 1995).
[2] "My Child, the Schnauzer," *American Demographics* (July 1996): 24–25.
[3] "Deluxe Brands, Pet Supers Wag the Market," *Advertising Age* (September 27, 1995): 22.

EXHIBIT 1

Top Dog Food Manufacturers in the United States

Rank	Company	Estimated Market Share	Principal Brand
1	Ralston Purina Co.	17.1%	Purina
2	Nestlé, Inc.	16.9%	Alpo
3	H. J. Heinz	13.4%	Ken-L Ration
4	Colgate-Palmolive	8.1%	Hill's Science Diet
5	Mars, Inc.	7.7%	Kal-Kan
6	Doane's	5.8%	Ol' Roy
7	Iams Co.	4.2%	Iams
8	Nutro Pet Food	2.2%	Nutro
	All Other	25.6%	
		100.0%	

percent of sales. Ralston Purina is the leading national advertiser of dog food, spending about $80 million per year, exclusive of major new product launches.[4]

The Problems and Opportunities

Introducing a New Dog Food in a New Form This is an opportunity to educate the consumer. Until Show Circuit's program breaks, dog foods fall into four categories: canned, dry, moist, and snack-type (dog treats), as shown in Exhibit 2 on page 590.

Canned dog foods average about 75 percent moisture and 25 percent solid materials. They are marketed either as complete foods or as supplementary foods.

Dry dog foods are usually produced as flakes, small pellets, or large chunks containing about 10 percent moisture and 90 percent solids. They are chewy, usually well rounded, and more economical than canned or moist foods.

Moist dog foods come in chunk or patty form and are about 25 percent moisture and 75 percent solids. They require no refrigeration and are made to look tempting to humans. This category has shown the greatest percentage increase in recent years.

Dog food treats have a wide variety of ingredients and, while tasty, are not recommended as a complete food.

All these product forms are typically marketed in the same area of the store. The consumer must now be taught to shop for dog food in another part of the store—the frozen-food section. Fortunately, some of the pioneering work has been done already. A few Boston-area supermarkets carry a frozen dog treat called Frosty Paws, which sells for $1.89 for 14 fluid ounces. This product is often placed near ice cream.

Overcoming Objections to Frozen Dog Food An objection must be anticipated regarding the requirement for thawing time and freezer space. Therefore, we should state on the container the thawing time, suggestions for quick thawing, how long the food will keep in the refrigerator, plus a gentle reminder to pull that container out of the freezer in the morning. Microwave instructions are a possibility.

Lack of Appeal of Frozen Dog Food We can quickly turn this problem into an asset in our advertising ("the first dog food made to appeal only to dogs").

---

[4] "Mega-brands of the 100 Leading National Advertisers," *Advertising Age* (September 27, 1995): 34.

EXHIBIT 2

Top Five Brands in the Four Major Dog Food Categories

Category	Share of Total Dog Food	Major Brands	Market Share
Canned	30%	Pedigree	32.4%
		Alpo	17.3
		Mighty Dog	9.2
		Skippy	6.6
		Private label	6.5
Dry	42%	Purina Dog Chow	10.5%
		Purina Puppy Chow	8.4
		Private label	7.0
		Pedigree Mealtime	6.3
		Kibbles 'n Bits 'n Bits 'n Bits	6.3
Moist	13%	Moist & Meaty	33.6%
		Ken-L Ration	25.6
		Private label	15.3
		Purina	10.6
		Gaines Burgers	9.4
Treats	15%	Milk-Bone	16.0%
		Jerky Treats	8.0
		Meaty Bone	7.4
		Private label	6.6
		Ken-L Ration Pup-peroni	5.9

Pricing We have considerable latitude in pricing as shown in Exhibit 3. Further-more, while dog owners in general are price sensitive, they are also concerned about the health and welfare of their animal companion. Show Circuit's quality suggests a premium price.

Summary of Opportunities We see Show Circuit seizing upon three opportunities:

1. The opportunity to be first to tap the vast market potential of a complete frozen dog food in supermarkets

EXHIBIT 3

Representative Dog Food Brand Prices and Package Sizes in Boston-area Supermarkets by Product Form

Canned		Dry	
Mighty Dog	$.55/5.5 oz.	Dog Chow	$9.59/22 lb.
Cycle	$.63/13.2 oz.	Gravy Train	$11.39/20 lb.
Alpo	$.63/13.2 oz.	Chuck Wagon	$8.99/20 lb.
Moist		Dog Treats	
Moist & Meaty	$9.79/13.5 lb.	Milk Bones	$2.39/26 oz.
Gaines Burgers	$6.99/6.75 lb.	Jerky Treats	$1.69/3 oz.

2. The opportunity to be among the first to claim to produce an organic dog food (Ralston Purina has introduced Nature's Course, a dry dog food positioned as "organic")

3. The opportunity to lay the groundwork for entering the frozen cat food business (cat food sales total $5.9 billion)

Creative Strategies

Positioning Show Circuit will be positioned as the finest dog food available at any price and the only thing you will want to feed a dog that is truly a member of the family.

Concentration We believe our advertising should be directed to singles and young marrieds between the ages of 21 and 30 and people 50 years old and over. The reason is that single adults, young marrieds, and childless (older) couples regard their dogs as a part of the family. The dog sleeps on the bed and has free run of the house or apartment. When children enter the picture, the dog often goes out to the back yard.

Concepts Because Show Circuit is such a unique product, there are a variety of concepts that can easily be applied, each with adequate justification:

1. The luxurious fur coat
2. The world's finest dog food
3. The guilt concept (shouldn't your dog eat as well as you do?)
4. Now your dog can eat what show champions have been eating for years.

All these will be touched on as the campaign progresses.

Creative Directions Initially, the campaign will focus attention on product identification and an introductory coupon offer.

Newspapers will supply a smaller, more retentive audience with facts to justify all claims. They will also supply the coupon, proven crucial to a successful introduction in the pet food market. The container and coupon will be prominently displayed, and the copy will emphasize Show Circuit's quality. Special-interest ads will appear in the society, sports, television, and dining-out sections. This unusual media placement is warranted by the product's unique qualities. Also, placement in these sections will pull a relatively low promotional budget out of the mass of food-section advertising.

Radio and television will provide access to a mass audience. Prime objectives are to register the brand name and the package design in the viewer or listener's memory. Because of the proven qualities of these media, an imaginative and all-important emotional approach will be taken.

Geographical Directions The entire campaign has been designed to accommodate product introduction outside the Boston market area. When the product goes national, the television spot will be ready, the introductory ads will be ready, the radio spots will be ready, and the immediate follow-up will be ready.

Sales Packet

The sales packet given to brokers should include, in the most persuasive form possible, the following categories of information:

1. Profits available in the dog food category
2. Chain store acceptance of dog food

3. Market potential

4. Suggested manufacturer's list price to consumers and quantity discount schedule

5. Information about Show Circuit

6. Information about the container

7. User endorsements

8. Promotional schedule

9. Order information

10. Reprint of ads and TV storyboard

11. Sample shelf strip

The packet should be designed to persuade the supermarket frozen-food buyer to provide freezer space to Show Circuit. Two major problems have to be overcome. Because of the organizational modes of supermarket buying departments, we will not be dealing with the regular pet food buyer. Instead, it will be necessary to persuade the frozen-food buyer to stock Show Circuit. The other major problem involves the usual higher margin for frozen foods. It will be necessary to persuade the buyer that greater product turnover will compensate for a potentially lower margin for Show Circuit.

Creative Strategy by Media

Creative strategies will differ by media. Print media will be utilized to position the product against its competition by comparing it to canned, dry, and moist categories. The print campaign will open with an attention-getting ad with a brief product history.

Television will carry the brunt of the attack. The most pressing problem is seen as the difficulty of finding the food in the supermarket, so the TV spot will emphasize location.

In order to give the campaign continuity, each ad will show the container. At the top of each of the ads designed to position the competition, the artwork reproduced on the container will be used.

No single breed of dog will be associated with the product. Both the container and the ads will show a variety of breeds from show dogs to mongrels.

The myth/fact format in newspapers will be utilized to take advantage of the current publicity dealing with the nutritional value of all-meat dog food and the continued trend toward more natural foods (see Exhibit 4).

The copy block dealing with Show Circuit will turn the problem of Show Circuit's being frozen into a product advantage.

Media Plan

Because dog food is heavily advertised, TPF must follow suit to compete.

General Media Strategy Advertising objectives are as follows:

1. Create awareness of new brand

2. Obtain distribution through grocery outlets

3. Motivate trial through coupon redemption

4. Motivate trial through emotional impact of television

Collateral Advertising Accomplishment of objective 2, getting distribution in grocery stores, is the main purpose of collateral advertising. The sales packet, containing fact sheets, shelf strips, the TV storyboard, and testimonial letters, gives the food bro-

EXHIBIT 4

Show Circuit Print Advertisement

ker an impressive story to tell to the supermarket buyer. This is recognized as the critical stage of the campaign, for without sufficient distribution, consumer advertising will be delayed.

Newspaper/Magazine The primary purpose of newspaper advertising is distribution of coupons into the market. This will be accomplished by half-page ads in major Boston newspapers. As a secondary means of distribution, full-page ads will be placed in *Better Homes and Gardens* and *Dog Fancy* magazine for distribution throughout most of the Boston market area (see Exhibit 5 on page 594). We expect that one out of ten sales will involve a coupon redemption.

The second phase of coupon distribution will be effected through 30-inch ads in the same newspapers. A final coupon distribution will be made through a 30-inch ad midway through the campaign. Newspaper insertion will be coordinated with TV flights.

Television The bulk of the budget will be placed in TV production and time. A sizable portion of the time budget will be spent on "The Late Show with David Letterman." Fixed space will be purchased within the first half-hour of the program. The remainder of the budget will reach daytime and nighttime audiences. Each flight will begin on a Monday, and newspaper advertising will be placed on Thursday of the following week.

Two basic approaches can be used for 30-second TV spots. The first approach capitalizes on the love of pet owners for their dogs. A somewhat frowzy, middle-aged, semi-greedy woman is shown enjoying a steak dinner—in contrast to an unap-

E X H I B I T   5

Show Circuit Print Advertisement

Myth:

A diet of all meat canned dog food is best for your dog

Fact:

All canned dog foods must be cooked which takes out nutrition
And they must be filled with additives and preservatives to
prevent spoilage. Also, the finest meat in the world (which
canned dog food isn't) wouldn't benefit your dog if he couldn't
digest it properly. Cereal promotes digestion of meat

SHOW CIRCUIT.
Frozen Dog Dinner

It's the perfect marriage of meat and cereal. Show Circuit is
85% federally inspected beef by-products, beef, liver, and
chicken. The other 15% is the finest cereal made. It promotes
and insures digestion of the meat, plus supplies all the vital
vitamins and minerals meat cannot. Show Circuit is
uncooked and it's frozen for freshness—there's no need for
additives or preservatives. Find Show Circuit in the
frozen food section—right next to people food

Save 10¢ on Show Circuit Frozen Dog Dinner

**This is to make the facts about dog food
a little easier for you to swallow.**

petizing cylinder of canned dog food. The spot ends on a close-up of the product. The storyboard for this spot is shown in Exhibit 6.

A second TV spot will emphasize location of the food in the supermarket. A description of the video and audio characteristics of this spot is as follows:

Video	*Audio*
Supermarket—long establishing shot of small boy with bulge under jacket	Announcer: There are many things to remember about new Show Circuit Frozen Dog Dinner.
Close-up of boy, as puppy pops out of top of jacket	Remember, although it's new to you, champion dogs have eaten it for years.
Manager walks by, boy hides dog, looks relieved	Remember, it contains all the vitamins your dog needs.
Close-up of sign indicating pet foods	Remember, Show Circuit is a perfectly balanced diet of meat and cereal. Remember, it doesn't come in a can.
Dolly shot of boy looking at competitive brands	
Close-up of boy and dog (sync)	Boy: I don't see it anywhere, Sparky.
Boy walks out of store past frozen-food compartment	Announcer: But most important, remember you find Show Circuit in the frozen (bark) food section, where you shop for other members of your family.
People turn to stare	
Tilt down and zoom in on product	

EXHIBIT 6

Show Circuit Television Spot

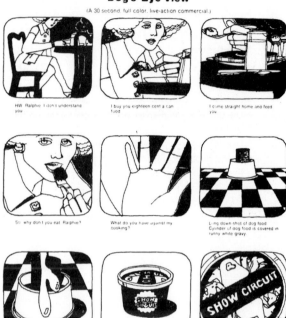

Program Budget The budget for the program described can be either $300,000 or $500,000 as shown in Exhibit 7 on page 596. We see this cost as being the only incremental cost associated with the launch in the Boston market.

We believe that this expenditure is reasonable, since most major established brands are spending $7–8 million annually for ongoing nationwide media promotion. For a new product, a higher initial expense is necessary. For instance, Heinz Pet Products spent $30 million to introduce Reward, a premium canned dog food. Ralston Purina spent $25 million to $30 million to introduce Nature's Course, a premium dry dog food. A line extension, Alpo Lite, with 25 fewer calories than regular Alpo, was launched with a $10 million advertising effort.

EXHIBIT 7

Alternative Expenditure Levels for Introductory Program

Item	Budget Levels	
	$300,000	*$500,000*
Television[a]	$159,000	$329,000
Newspapers/magazines[b]	100,500	130,500
Collateral (sales pack)	9,750	9,750
Miscellaneous	5,250	5,250
Agency fees	25,500	25,500
Total	$300,000	$500,000

[a] The difference in television cost is due to the production of a second commercial and larger television schedule.

[b] The difference in newspaper/magazine cost is due to a larger number of insertions in *Better Homes and Gardens* and *Dog Fancy* magazines.

Frito-Lay, Inc.
Sun Chips™ Multigrain Snacks

In mid-1990, Dr. Dwight R. Riskey, Vice President of Marketing Research and New Business at Frito-Lay, Inc., assembled the product management team responsible for Sun Chips™ Multigrain Snacks. The purpose of the all-day meeting was to prepare a presentation to senior Frito-Lay executives on future action pertaining to the brand.

Sun Chips™ Multigrain Snacks is a crispy textured snack chip consisting of a special blend of whole wheat, corn, rice, and oat flours with a lightly salty multigrain taste and a slightly sweet aftertaste. The product contains less sodium than most snack chips and is made with canola or sunflower oil. The chip is approximately 50 percent lower in saturated fats than chips made with other cooking oils and is cholesterol-free. According to a Frito-Lay executive, it is "a thoughtful, upscale classy chip."

The product had been in test market for ten months in the Minneapolis–St. Paul, Minnesota, metropolitan area. Even though it appeared consumer response was extremely favorable, Riskey and his associates knew their presentation to senior Frito-Lay executives would have to be persuasive. In addition to presenting a thorough assessment of test-market data, Riskey added:

> We will have to do heavy-duty selling [to top executives] because Sun Chips™ Multigrain Snacks required a new manufacturing process, carried a new brand name, and pioneered a new snack chip category. There is a huge capital investment and a huge marketing investment that could be financially justified only with a product that could be sustainable for an extended time period.

■ FRITO-LAY, INC.

Frito-Lay, Inc. is a division of PepsiCo, Inc., a New York-based diversified consumer goods and services firm. Other PepsiCo, Inc. divisions include Pizza Hut, Inc., Taco Bell Corporation, Pepsi-Cola Company, Kentucky Fried Chicken, and PepsiCo Foods International. PepsiCo, Inc. recorded net income of $1.077 billion on net sales of $17.8 billion in 1990.

Company Background

Frito-Lay, Inc. is a worldwide leader in the manufacturing and marketing of snack chips. Well-known brands include Lay's® brand and Ruffles® brand potato chips, Fritos® brand corn chips, Doritos® brand, Tostitos® brand, and Santitas® brand tortilla chips, Chee•tos® brand cheese-flavored snacks, and Rold Gold® brand pretzels.

The cooperation of Frito-Lay, Inc. in the preparation of this case is gratefully acknowledged. This case was prepared by Professor Roger A. Kerin, of the Edwin L. Cox School of Business, Southern Methodist University, and Kenneth R. Lukaska, Product Manager, Frito-Lay, Inc., as a basis for class discussion and is not designed to illustrate effective or ineffective handling of an administrative situation. Certain company information is disguised and not useful for research purposes. Copyright © 1995 by Roger A. Kerin. No part of this case may be reproduced without written permission of the copyright holder.

EXHIBIT 1

Frito-Lay, Inc.: Major Brands

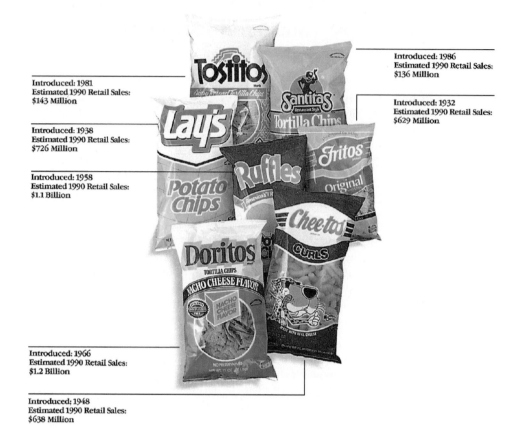

Introduced: 1981
Estimated 1990 Retail Sales:
$143 Million

Introduced: 1938
Estimated 1990 Retail Sales:
$726 Million

Introduced: 1958
Estimated 1990 Retail Sales:
$1.1 Billion

Introduced: 1986
Estimated 1990 Retail Sales:
$136 Million

Introduced: 1932
Estimated 1990 Retail Sales:
$629 Million

Introduced: 1966
Estimated 1990 Retail Sales:
$1.2 Billion

Introduced: 1948
Estimated 1990 Retail Sales:
$638 Million

Source: 1990 PepsiCo, Inc., *Annual Report*.

The company's major brands are shown in Exhibit 1 along with estimated worldwide retail sales. Other well-known Frito-Lay products include Baken-Ets® brand fried pork skins, Munchos® brand potato crisps, and Funyuns® brand onion-flavored snacks. In addition, the company markets a line of dips, nuts, peanut butter crackers, processed beef sticks, Smartfood® brand ready-to-eat popcorn, and Grandma's® brand cookies.

Frito-Lay, Inc. accounts for 13 percent of sales in the United States snack-food industry, which includes candy, cookies, crackers, nuts, snack chips, and assorted other items. The company is the leading manufacturer of snack chips in the United States, capturing nearly one-half of the retail sales in this category. Eight of Frito-Lay's snack chips are among the top ten best-selling snack chip items in U.S. supermarkets (see Exhibit 2). Doritos® brand tortilla chips and Ruffles® brand potato chips have the distinction of being the only snack chips with $1 billion in retail sales in the world.

Frito-Lay's snack-food business spans every aspect of snack-food production, from agriculture to stacking supermarket shelves. During 1990 in the United States alone, Frito-Lay used 1.6 billion pounds of potatoes, 600 million pounds of corn, and 55 million pounds of seasonings. The company has 39 manufacturing plants, more than 1,600 distribution facilities, and a 10,000-person route-sales team that calls on

EXHIBIT 2

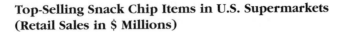

**Top-Selling Snack Chip Items in U.S. Supermarkets
(Retail Sales in $ Millions)**

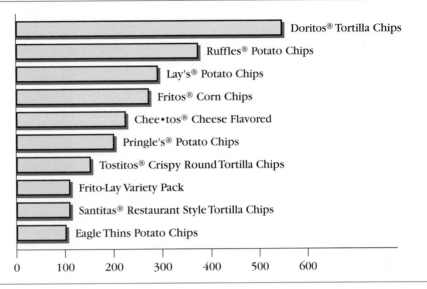

Source: 1990 PepsiCo, Inc., *Annual Report*.

more than 400,000 retail store customers each week in the United States. Frito-Lay, Inc., recorded U.S. sales of $3.5 billion in 1990.

Product-Marketing Strategies

Frito-Lay pursues growth opportunities through four product-marketing strategies.

1. *Grow established Frito-Lay brands through line extension.* Recognizing that consumers seek variety in snack tastes and sizes without compromising quality, Frito-Lay marketing executives use line extensions to satisfy these wants. Recent examples of line extension include Tostitos® brand bite-sized tortilla chips and Chee•tos® brand Flamin' Hot Cheese Flavored Snacks.

2. *Create new products to meet changing consumer preferences and needs.* Continuous marketing research at Frito-Lay is designed to uncover changing snacking needs of customers. A recent result of these efforts is evident in the launch of a low-oil light line of snack chips.

3. *Develop products for fast-growing snack-food categories.* Recognizing that snack-food categories experience different growth rates, Frito-Lay marketing executives continually monitor consumption patterns to identify new opportunities. For example, Frito-Lay acquired Smartfood® brand popcorn in 1989. In 1990, this brand became the number one ready-to-eat popcorn brand in the United States.

4. *Reproduce Frito-Lay successes in the international market.* Initiatives pursued in the United States often produce opportunities in the international arena. Primary emphasis has been placed in large, well-developed snack markets such as Mexico, Canada, Spain, and the United Kingdom. Innovative marketing coupled with product development efforts produced $1.6 billion in international snack-food sales in 1990.

■ THE SNACK CHIP CATEGORY

The United States snack-food industry recorded retail sales of $37 billion in 1990, representing a 5 percent increase over 1989. Dollar retail sales of snack chips consisting of potato, corn, and tortilla chips, pretzels, and ready-to-eat popcorn were estimated to be $9.8 billion—a 5 percent increase over 1989. A major source of growth in the snack chip category results from increased per capita consumption. In 1990, consumers in the United States bought 3.5 billion pounds of snack chips, or nearly 14 pounds per person; in 1986, snack chip per capita consumption was slightly less than 12 pounds.

Competitors

Three types of competitors serve the snack chip category: (1) national brand firms, (2) regional brand firms, and (3) private brand firms. National brand firms, which distribute products nationwide, include Frito-Lay, Borden (Guys brand potato and corn chips, and Wise brand potato chips, cheese puffs, and pretzels), Procter and Gamble (Pringles® brand potato chips), RJR Nabisco (several products sold under the Nabisco name as well as Planter's brand pretzels, cheese puffs, and corn and tortilla chips), Keebler Company (O'Boisies brand potato chips), and Eagle Snacks (a division of Anheuser-Busch Companies, Inc., which sells Eagle brand pretzels and potato and corn chips). A second category of competitors consists of regional brand firms, which distribute products in only certain parts of the United States. Representative firms include Snyder's, Mike Sells, and Charles Chips. Private brands are produced by regional or local manufacturers on a contractual basis for major supermarket chains (for example, Kroger and Safeway).

Competition

The snack chip category is very competitive. As many as 650 snack chip products are introduced each year by national and regional brand companies. Most of the products are new flavors for existing snack chips. The new-product failure rate for snack chips is high, and industry sources report that fewer than 1 percent of new products generate more than $25 million in first-year sales.

Snack chip competitors rely heavily on electronic and print media advertising, consumer promotions, and trade allowances to stimulate sales and retain shelf space in supermarkets. Pricing is very competitive, and snack chip manufacturers often rely on price deals to attract customers. The nature of the technology used to produce snack chips allows snack chip manufacturers to react swiftly to new product (flavor) introductions by competitors. Extensive sales and distribution systems employed by national brand competitors, in particular, allow them to monitor new product and promotion activities and place competing products quickly in supermarkets.

■ DEVELOPMENT OF SUN CHIPS™ MULTIGRAIN SNACKS

Sun Chips™ Multigrain Snacks resulted from Frito-Lay's ongoing marketing research and product development program. However, its taste and name heritage can be traced to the early 1970s.

Product Heritage

Frito-Lay product development personnel first explored the possibility of a multigrain product in the early 1970s when corporate marketing research studies indicated consumers were looking for nutritious snacks. A multigrain snack chip called

Prontos® was introduced in 1974 with the following positioning statement: "The different, delicious new snack made from nature's own corn, oats, and whole grain wheat all rolled into one special recipe, together in a snack for the first time from Frito-Lay." The product was only mildly successful despite advertising and merchandising support. The product was subsequently withdrawn from national distribution in 1978 due to declining sales and manufacturing difficulties. According to Frito-Lay executives, the demise of Prontos® in 1978 was driven by "non-committal" copy, a confusing name, and a product that generated appeal among too narrow a target market. Reflecting on this experience, Riskey added, "I'm not sure there were dramatic things wrong with the product design so much as difficulty with the manufacturing process. It may have been invented and introduced before its time."

The brand name for the product had an equally arduous past. The Sun Chips™ name was originally assigned to a line of corn chips, potato chips, and puffed corn snacks in the early 1970s. In 1976, the brand name was given to a line of corn chips, but by 1985, this line was also withdrawn from distribution due to poor sales performance.

Product Development: The "Harvest" Project

Early 1980s Interest in a multigrain snack was revisited in the early 1980s when Frito-Lay marketing executives began to worry whether the aging baby boomers (people born between 1946 and 1964) would continue to eat salty snacks such as potato, corn, and tortilla chips. According to Riskey:

> The aging baby boomers were a significant factor [in our thinking]. We were looking for new products that would allow them to snack. But we were looking for "better-for-you" aspects in products and pushing against that demographic shift.

In 1981, Frito-Lay marketing research and product development personnel instituted the "Harvest" project with an objective of coming up with a multigrain snack that would have consumer appeal. After several product concept tests and in-home product use tests failed to generate any consumer excitement, it was concluded that the market for wholesome snacks was not yet fully developed to accept such products. Other evidence seemed to support this view. In 1983, Frito-Lay test marketed O'Grady's™ brand potato chips. The results had been phenomenal. Projections based on test market performance indicated the brand would produce $100 million in annual sales, which it did in 1984 and 1985.

Mid-1980s The "Harvest" project continued in the mid-1980s, albeit at a slower pace due to staff changes and other responsibilities of project team members. At about this time, a change in top management and corporate objectives focused product development efforts on traditional snacks with an emphasis on flavor line extensions for established Frito-Lay brands (for example, Cool Ranch Doritos® brand tortilla chips) and low-fat versions of its potato, corn, and tortilla chips. In addition, attention was placed on cost-containment measures coupled with continuous quality-improvement initiatives using existing manufacturing facilities and existing product and process snack chip technology.

Late 1980s Development efforts on a multigrain product were renewed in early 1988. Over the following 13 months, different product formulations (for example, low oil vs. regular oil; salt content; chip shape), alternative positionings, and branding options (extension of an existing Frito-Lay brand vs. a new brand name) were extensively studied using consumer taste tests and product concept tests. The combined results of these tests yielded a multigrain rectangular chip with ridges and an exceptional taste. Further testing on brand names and flavors revealed consumer prefer-

EXHIBIT 3

Consumer Expectations and Perceptions of Snack Chips and Multigrain Snacks

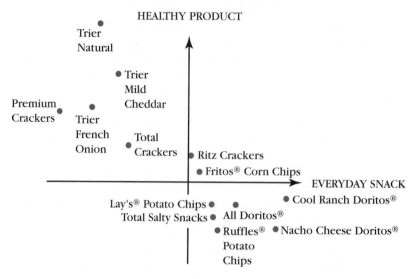

PRETRIAL PRODUCT EXPECTATIONS

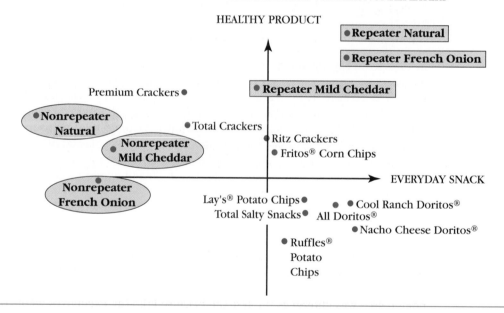

POSTUSE PERCEPTIONS: TRIER REPEATERS VS. TRIER NONREPEATERS

ences for two names (one of which was Sun Chips™) and three flavors (original/natural, French onion, and mild cheddar).

Further consumer research revealed that the multigrain product concept and assorted flavors were perceived as a "healthier product." This research also indicated that consumer expectations prior to use (that is, before initial trial of the product) were that the product would not be an "everyday snack" item. Consumers who tried the product, however, perceived the multigrain product to be an "everyday snack," at least for the natural and French onion flavors. Exhibit 3 shows a plot of pretrial consumer expectations and postuse perceptions of different flavors and representative snack chip brands and crackers. Concurrent research on brand names indicated a decided preference for the Sun Chips™ name. The name evoked positive consumer imagery and attributes of "wholesomeness, great taste, light and distinctive, and fun," according to a Frito-Lay executive.

Premarket Test

Positive consumer response to the product concept and brand name prompted an initial assessment of the commercial potential of Sun Chips™ Multigrain Snacks. A simulated test market or premarket test (PMT) was commissioned in April 1989 and conducted by an independent marketing research firm.

A PMT involves interviewing consumers about attitudes and usage behavior concerning a product category (for example, snack chips). Consumers would be exposed to a product concept using product descriptions or mock-ups of advertisements, and their responses would be assessed (see Exhibit 4 on page 604). These consumers would then be given an opportunity to receive the product if interested. After an in-home usage period of several weeks, they would be contacted by telephone and asked about their attitude toward the product, use of the product, and intention to repurchase. These data would be incorporated into computer models that would include elements of the product's marketing plan (price, advertising, distribution coverage). The output provided by the PMT would include estimates of household trial rates, repeat rates, average number of units purchased on the initial trial and subsequent repeats in the first year, product cannibalism, and first-year sales volume.[1]

The product concept tested in the PMT was priced at parity with Doritos® brand tortilla chips. Planned distribution coverage was set at levels comparable for Frito-Lay potato, corn, and tortilla chips. Two-flavor combinations (natural and French onion and natural and mild cheddar) and three advertising and merchandising expenditure levels ($11 million, $17 million, and $22 million) were tested.[2]

Results from the PMT indicated that Sun Chips™ Multigrain Snacks would produce a most likely first-year sales volume of $113 million at manufacturer's prices given the marketing plan set for the product, including a $22 million advertising and merchandising expenditure. The estimated first-year sales volume exceeded the $100 million Frito-Lay sales goal for new products. The natural and French onion flavor combination produced the lowest cannibalization (42 percent) of other Frito-Lay brands. Summary statistics for the simulated test market are shown in Exhibit 5 on page 605.

■ TEST MARKET

Positive results from consumer research and the simulated test market led to a recommendation to proceed with Sun Chips™ Multigrain Snacks and implement a test market under Dwight Riskey's direction. The Minneapolis–St. Paul, Minnesota metropolitan area was chosen as the test site because Frito-Lay executives were confident it had a social and economic profile representative of the United States. Furthermore, Minneapolis–St. Paul, in general, represented a typical competitive environment in which to test consumer acceptance and competitive behavior. The Minneapolis–St. Paul metropolitan area contained 1.98 million households that were

---

[1] Published validation data on premarket test models indicate that 75 percent of the time they are plus or minus 10 percent of actual performance when a product was introduced (see, for example, A. Shocker and W. Hall, "Pretest Market Models: A Critical Evaluation," *Journal of Product Innovation Management* 3, (1986): 86–107.

[2] Advertising and merchandising expenditures included electronic and print media advertising, consumer promotions, and trade allowances.

EXHIBIT 4

Concept Board for the Premarket Test

Introducing new SUN CHIPS™ multigrain snacks from Frito-Lay®

The great tasting snack chip for people who care about what they eat.

More and more people care about what they eat because they know that eating habits affect overall health and fitness. SUN CHIPS™ are a special blend of whole wheat, golden corn and other natural great tasting grains. These wholesome grains combined make a uniquely delicious chip with the golden goodness of corn and the nut-like flavor of wheat. They're cooked 'till lightly crisp and crunchy. Then they're lightly salted to let all that naturally good flavor come through. SUN CHIPS™ are a unique combination of great taste, great crunch, and natural goodness, all rolled into one remarkable chip.

So, try new SUN CHIPS™, the chip with the uniquely delicious taste for people who care about what they eat.

Available in these two delicious flavors:
- Natural   - French Onion

identified as users of snack chips, or 2.2 percent of the 90 million snack chip user households in the United States. Discussion among Frito-Lay marketing, sales, distribution, and manufacturing executives and the company's advertising agency indicated that the test market could begin October 9, 1989. Accordingly, a test-market plan and budget were finalized. The test market was scheduled to run for 12 months, with periodic reviews scheduled throughout the test.

Snack-food industry analysts became aware of Frito-Lay's development efforts on a multigrain snack chip soon after the company began preparation for the test market. According to one industry analyst:

EXHIBIT 5

Simulated Test-Market Results (Selected Statistics)

	Natural & Mild Cheddar Combination		Natural & French Onion Combination	
	A&M Budget $17 million	*A&M Budget $22 million*	*A&M Budget $17 million*	*A&M Budget $22 million*
Purchase Dynamics				
Brand awareness (% of households)	40	48	40	48
Cumulative first-year trial rate (%)[b]	23	27	21	25
Cumulative first year repeat rate (%)[c]	61		57	
Number of purchases in first-year per repeating household	5.9		6.2	
Volume Projections ($ millions)				
Pessimistic	87	102	86	102
Most likely	96	113	95	113
Optimistic	106	125	106	125
Incremental annual volume (%)	50		58	
Cannibalized pound volume (%) (from Frito-Lay products)	50		42	

Product and Promotion Strategy[a]

[a] The $11 million advertising and merchandising (A&M) budget for the two flavor combinations produced lower figures than those shown. For example, brand awareness was 35 percent and the cumulative first-year trial rate was 19 percent regardless of flavor combination.

[b] *Cumulative first-year trial* refers to the percentage of households that would try the product.

[c] *Cumulative first-year repeat* refers to the percentage of trier households that repurchased the product.

This is a departure from corn or potatoes. Wheat is different. Remember they departed from corn and potatoes a few years ago with Rumbles®, Stuffers®, and Toppels®, and it was a distasteful business. I'm sure they will take their time and really test it. It's not like they don't have other products, so there's no hurry.[3]

Test-Market Plan

Product Strategy Frito-Lay executives decided to introduce both the natural and French onion flavors given consumer research and simulated test-market results. Sun Chips™ Multigrain Snacks would be packaged in two sizes: a 7-ounce package and an 11-ounce package. These package sizes were identical to Doritos® brand tortilla chips. A 2 1/2 -ounce trial package would be used as well.

---

[3] "New Multigrain Chip Being Readied for Test," *Advertising Age* (June 26, 1989): 4. The products referred to were Stuffers® cheese-filled snacks, Rumbles® granola nuggets, and Toppels® cheese-topped crackers. These products were introduced in the mid-1980s, failed to meet sales expectations, and were subsequently withdrawn from the market.

EXHIBIT 6

Sun Chips™ Multigrain Snacks Packaging

EXHIBIT 6 *(continued)*

Package design was considered to be extremely important. According to a Frito-Lay executive, "We wanted distinctive, contemporary graphics which would communicate new, different and fun amidst positive images—sun and a sprig of wheat." This view materialized in a metalized flex bag with primary colors of black (natural flavor) and green (French onion flavor). Exhibit 6 shows the packages used in the test market.

Pricing Strategy Sun Chips™ Multigrain Snacks would have the same suggested retail prices as Doritos® brand tortilla chips. Research indicated these price points were consistent with consumer reference prices for snack chips and represented a

E X H I B I T   7

Sun Chips™ Multigrain Snacks Price List

Package Size	Suggested Retail Price	Frito-Lay Selling Price to Retailer
2¼ ounce	$0.69	$0.385
7 ounce	$1.69	$1.240
11 ounce	$2.39	$1.732

good value. Suggested retail prices and Frito-Lay's selling prices to retailers are shown in Exhibit 7.

Advertising and Merchandising Strategy The primary audience for Sun Chips™ Multigrain Snacks television advertising was adults between the ages of 18 and 34, since this target audience is the principal purchasers and heavy users of snack chips. A secondary audience expanded the age bracket to 49 years of age, since 34- to 49-year-olds appeared to be receptive to healthier snacks. Household members under 18 years of age would be exposed to the product through in-home usage. The advertising message would convey subtle messages, including wholesomeness, fun, and simplicity. One of the television commercials to be shown in the test market is reproduced in Exhibit 8. In addition to television advertising, the brand would be supported by in-store displays and free-standing inserts (FSIs) in newspapers (see Exhibit 9 on page 610).

Coupons placed in newspaper FSIs were to be used during the test market to stimulate trial and repeat sales. In addition, free samples would be distributed in supermarkets. Trade allowances were provided to retailers as well.

Distribution and Sales Strategy Distribution and sales of Sun Chips™ Multigrain Snacks would be handled through Frito-Lay's store-door delivery system, in which the duties of a delivery person and a salesperson are combined. Under this system, a delivery/salesperson solicits orders, stocks shelves, and introduces merchandising programs to retail store personnel. Sun Chips™ Multigrain Snacks would be sold through supermarkets, grocery stores, convenience stores, and other retail accounts that already stocked Frito-Lay's snack products.

Manufacturing Considerations Frito-Lay manufacturing personnel worked concurrently with marketing personnel on matters related to mass production of a multigrain product. While prototypes were easily developed in limited quantities, large-scale manufacturing would require a production line capable of delivering an adequate product for a market test. Since a multigrain product required different product and process technology than corn or potato products, an investment in one new production line would be necessary. Approval was granted to create a production line to produce and package 1 million pounds of the multigrain snack per year at full theoretical capacity. The production line could be in operation to ship the product in two flavors and three package sizes for the test market in September 1989.

Test-Market Budget

The advertising and merchandising budget for the test market was equivalent to a $22 million expenditure on a nationwide distribution basis. Approximately 70 percent of the budget would be spent during the first six months of the test market.

EXHIBIT 8

Sun Chips™ Multigrain Snacks Television Commercial

LEVINE, HUNTLEY, SCHMIDT
& BEAVER, INC.
CLIENT: FRITO-LAY, INC.
PRODUCT: SUNCHIPS

TITLE: "POLLY"
LENGTH: 30 Seconds
COMM'L NO.: PESU–9013

(Music under) GUY: Polly
want one?

AVO: It seems everyone who tries
new SUNCHIPS feels smarter
eating them.

POLLY: Polly wants another one.

AVO: Smarter because
they're multigrain.

POLLY: Polly wants you to fill her
water cup.

AVO: Smarter because of
the taste.

POLLY: Polly thinks you should
paint this room and this time
pick a better color.

AVO: Smarter because they're
naturally delicious.

POLLY: Polly wants to know why
one species feels it's OK to
imprison another

purely for its own entertainment.

AVO: New SUNCHIPS.

You'll feel smarter eating them.

Test-Market Results

Consumer response was monitored by an independent research firm from the beginning of the test market. Data gathered by the research firm were submitted to Frito-Lay monthly and consisted of the types of purchases, the incidence of trial and repeat-purchase behavior, and product cannibalization in the test market.

Type of Purchase Data supplied by the research firm indicated that the coupon program had a major impact on trial activity and approximately 90 percent of purchases were made in supermarkets and convenience stores. After ten months in test mar-

E X H I B I T   9

Sun Chips™ Multigrain Snacks Free-Standing Insert (FSI)

EXHIBIT 10

Household Trial and Repeat Rates for Sun Chips™ Multigrain Snacks

	Tracking (4-week Period)									
	1	*2*	*3*	*4*	*5*	*6*	*7*	*8*	*9*	*10*
Cumulative trial[a] (%)	4.7	8.2	9.8	11.3	14.1	15.7	16.5	17.4	18.5	19.9
Cumulative repeat[b] (%)	8.0	22.5	27.1	31.0	32.7	36.5	39.0	39.7	41.8	41.8

[a] Trial refers to the percentage of households that tried the product.

[b] Repeat refers to the percentage of trier households that repurchased the product.

ket, the $2\frac{1}{4}$-ounce package accounted for 15 percent of purchases, the 7-ounce package accounted for 47 percent of purchases, and the 11-ounce package accounted for 38 percent of purchases. Fifty-five percent of purchases were for the French onion flavor; 45 percent of purchases were for the natural flavor.

Trial and Repeat Rates Of critical concern to Frito-Lay executives were the incidences of household trial and repeat-purchase behavior for Sun Chips™ Multigrain Snacks. Exhibit 10 shows the cumulative trial and repeat rates for both flavors combined during the first ten months of the test market. Almost one in five households in the test market had tried the product, and 41.8 percent of these trier households had repurchased the product at least once over the 10-month period.

Equally important to Frito-Lay executives were the "depth of repeat" data supplied by the research firm. *Depth of repeat* is the number of times a repeat purchaser buys a product after an initial repeat purchase. Repeater purchasers of Sun Chips™ Multigrain Snacks purchased the product an average of 2.9 times. An estimated average purchase amount for triers was 6 ounces. Repeat and repeater households purchased an average of 13 ounces per purchase occasion.

Product Cannibalization The independent research firm also identified the incidence of product cannibalization. The research firm's tracking data indicated that 30 percent of Sun Chips™ Multigrain Snack pound volume resulted from consumers switching from Frito-Lay's potato, tortilla, and corn snack chips. About one-third of the cannibalized volume from Frito-Lay's products came from Doritos® brand tortilla chips.

The 30 percent cannibalism rate was not uncommon in new product introductions in the snack food industry. For example, when Frito-Lay introduced O'Grady's™ brand potato chips, one-third of its pound volume came from its Ruffles® brand and Lay's® brand potato chips. Even though cannibalization was an issue to be considered in evaluating test-market performance, Frito-Lay executives noted that the gross profit for Sun Chips™ Multigrain Snacks was higher than that for its other snack chips.[4] (*Case writer note*: Footnote 4 contains important information for case analysis purposes.)

---

[4] Frito-Lay, Inc. does not divulge profitability data on individual products and product lines. However, for case analysis and class discussion purposes, a multigrain snack chip can be assumed to have a gross profit of $1.30 per pound, while other snack chips (potato, tortilla, and corn) can be assumed to have a gross profit of $1.05 per pound. Gross profit is the difference between selling price and the cost of materials and manufacturing (ingredients, packaging/cartons, direct labor, other assignable manufacturing expenses, and equipment depreciation).

■ TEST-MARKET REVIEW

Riskey's presentation to senior Frito-Lay executives would conclude with his recommendation for the future marketing of Sun Chips™ Multigrain Snacks. He could recommend that the test be continued for another six months, or be expanded to other geographical areas with the same introductory strategy or some modification. Alternatively, he could recommend that Sun Chips™ Multigrain Snacks be readied for a national introduction with the strategy used in the test market or some modification in the strategy.

Planning Considerations

Numerous topics were raised in his meeting with the product management team responsible for Sun Chips™ Multigrain Snacks. Timing and competitive reaction were important issues. Riskey believed that national and regional competitors were monitoring Frito-Lay's test market. There was also a high probability that these competitors were examining the chip with the intention of developing their own version. Timing was a concern for a variety of reasons. First, if Riskey continued testing the product, a competitor might launch a similar product nationally or regionally and upstage Frito-Lay. The opportunity to be first-to-market would be lost. Second, if an expanded test market or a national introduction was considered, a decision would be needed quickly to assure adequate manufacturing capacity was in place and operating efficiently. Manufacturing capacity expansion would require a significant capital investment. Although preliminary figures represented rough estimates, manufacturing capacity capable of serving 25 percent and 50 percent of snack chip households in the United States would involve a capital expenditure recommendation of $5 million and $10 million, respectively. A full-scale national introduction would require a capital expenditure of $20 million.

Recommendations related to manufacturing capacity expansion would require a justification of the magnitude and sustainability of Sun Chips™ Multigrain Snacks sales over time. Accordingly, Riskey requested marketing research personnel to supply him with comparative brand awareness and cumulative household trial and repeat rate data for O'Grady's™ brand potato chips, since this brand was the most recent Frito-Lay product introduction to achieve $100 million in first-year sales.

Brand-awareness studies on the two brands indicated that O'Grady's™ brand potato chips achieved brand awareness among 28 percent of snack chip households during its market test compared with 33 percent for Sun Chips™ Multigrain Snacks. Exhibit 11 charts trial and repeat data for comparable test-market periods for Sun Chips™ Multigrain Snacks and O'Grady's™ brand potato chips. His interest in the sustainability of sales over time prompted a request for additional data on depth of repeat statistics for the two brands. The depth of repeat, or "repeats per repeater" for O'Grady's™ brand potato chips was 1.9 times, or about twice on an annual basis, compared with 2.9 times for Sun Chips™ Multigrain Snacks, or about three times on an annual basis.

Strategy Considerations

Several strategy options were also discussed. Some product management team members advocated increased advertising and merchandising spending if the brand was tested further or launched nationally. They believed that brand awareness would increase with additional spending and felt that spending the national introduction equivalent of $30 million could stimulate brand trial as well. Others interpreted the purchase data to mean that additional volume was possible by introducing a larger package size (for example, a 15-ounce package). They believed that a fourth, larger

EXHIBIT 11

Cumulative Trial and Repeat Rates for O'Grady's™ Potato Chips and Sun Chips™ Multigrain Snacks: 40-Week Test Market

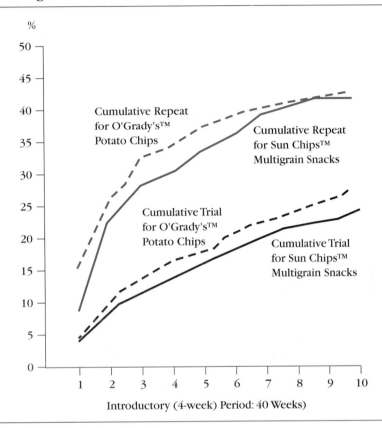

package could add about one-half ounce to the average annual purchase amount per repeat (and repeater) purchase occasion. Priced at the same price per ounce as the 11-ounce size, this action would not have a material effect on the brand's gross profit per pound. Others believed that another package size made more sense after the brand was established in the marketplace. Furthermore, the manufacturing and marketing of four sizes could stretch the production capacity, increase inventory, and challenge Frito-Lay sales personnel to get retailer shelf and display space.

Some discussion was also directed toward building the household repeat and depth of repeat business. For example, a flavor extension (for example, mild cheddar) was proposed. An advocate of this approach suggested that a flavor extension could increase the "repeats per repeater" to an average of $3^1/_2$ times per year given greater variety for consumers. However, the addition of another flavor could increase the cannibalization rate to 35 percent, some thought. Also, the mild cheddar flavor still needed to be perfected in large-scale production. Others noted that if a larger package and a flavor extension were simultaneously pursued, the number of stockkeeping units would double from six (2 flavors × 3 sizes) to twelve (3 flavors × 4 sizes). It was agreed by everyone that this action would cause severe manufacturing difficulties, since the multigrain snack process technology was still untested.

Cima Mountaineering, Inc.

"What a great hike," exclaimed Anthony Simon as he tossed his Summit HX 350 hiking boots into his car. He had just finished hiking the challenging Cascade Canyon Trail in the Tetons north of Jackson, Wyoming. Anthony hiked often because it was a great way to test the hiking boots made by Cima Mountaineering, Inc., the business he inherited from his parents and owned with his sister, Margaret. As he drove back to Jackson, he began thinking about next week's meeting with Margaret, the President of Cima. During the past month they had been discussing marketing strategies for increasing the sales and profits of the company. No decisions had been made, but the preferences of each owner were becoming clear.

As illustrated in Table 1, sales and profits had grown steadily for Cima and by most measures the company was successful. However, growth was beginning to slow as a result of foreign competition and a changing market. Margaret observed that the market had shifted to a more casual, stylish hiking boot that appealed to hikers interested in a boot for a variety of uses. She favored a strategy of diversifying the company by marketing a new line of boots for the less experienced, weekend hiker. Anthony also recognized that the market had changed, but he supported expanding the existing lines of boots for mountaineers and hikers. The company had been successful with these boots, and Anthony had some ideas about how to extend the lines and expand distribution. "This is a better way to grow," he thought. "I'm concerned about the risk in Margaret's recommendation. If we move to a more casual boot, then we have to resolve a new set of marketing and competitive issues and finance a new line. I'm not sure we can do it."

When he returned to Jackson that evening, Anthony stopped by his office to check his messages. The financial statements shown in Table 2 and Table 3 were on his desk along with a marketing study from a Denver consulting firm. Harris Fleming, Vice President of Marketing, had commissioned a study of the hiking boot market several months earlier to help the company plan for the future. As Anthony paged through the

Table 1
Cima Mountaineering, Inc. Revenues and Net Income, 1990–1995

Year	Revenues	Net Income	Profit Margin (%)
1995	$20,091,450	$857,134	4.27
1994	18,738,529	809,505	4.32
1993	17,281,683	838,162	4.85
1992	15,614,803	776,056	4.97
1991	14,221,132	602,976	4.24
1990	13,034,562	522,606	4.01

Lawrence M. Lamont is Professor of Management at Washington and Lee University. Eva Cid and Wade Drew Hammond are seniors in the class of 1995 at Washington and Lee, majoring in Management and Accounting, respectively.

Table 2
Cima Mountaineering, Inc. Income Statement (Years Ended December 31, 1995 and December 31, 1994)

	1995	1994
Net Sales	$20,091,450	$18,738,529
Cost of goods sold	14,381,460	13,426,156
Gross margin	5,709,990	5,312,373
Selling and admin. expenses	4,285,730	3,973,419
Operating income	1,424,260	1,338,954
Other income (expenses)		
Interest expense	(160,733)	(131,170)
Interest income	35,161	18,739
Total other income (net)	(125,572)	(112,431)
Earnings before income taxes	1,298,688	1,226,523
Income taxes	441,554	417,018
Net income	$ 857,134	$ 809,505

report, two figures caught his eye. One was a segmentation of the hiking boot market (see Exhibit 1 on page 617) and the other was a summary of market competition (see Exhibit 2 on page 618). "This is interesting," he mused. "I hope Margaret reads it before our meeting."

■ HISTORY OF CIMA MOUNTAINEERING

As children, Anthony and Margaret Simon watched their parents make western boots at the Hoback Boot Company, a small business they owned in Jackson, Wyoming. They learned the craft as they grew up and joined the company after college.

In the late 1960s the demand for western boots began to decline and the Hoback Boot Company struggled to survive. By 1975, the parents were close to retirement and they seemed content to close the business, but Margaret and Anthony decided to try to salvage the company. Margaret, the older, became President and Anthony became the Executive Vice President. By the end of 1976, sales had declined to $1.5 million and the company earned profits of only $45,000. It became clear that to survive, the business would have to be refocused on products with a more promising future.

Refocusing the Business

As a college student, Anthony attended a mountaineering school north of Jackson in Teton National Park. As he learned to climb and hike, he became aware of the growing popularity of the sport and the boots being used. Because of his experience with western boots, he also noticed their limitations. Although the boots had good traction, they were heavy, uncomfortable, and had little resistance to the snow and water always present in the mountains. He convinced Margaret that Hoback should explore the possibility of developing boots for mountaineering and hiking.

In 1977, Anthony and Margaret began 12 months of marketing research. They investigated the market, the competition, and the extent to which Hoback's existing equipment could be used to produce the new boots. By the summer of 1978, Hoback had developed a mountaineering and a hiking boot that were ready for testing. Several instructors from the mountaineering school tested the boots and gave them excellent reviews.

Table 3
Cima Mountaineering, Inc. Balance Sheet (Years Ending December 31, 1995 and December 31, 1994)

	1995	*1994*
Assets		
Current assets		
Cash and equivalents	$1,571,441	$1,228,296
Accounts receivable	4,696,260	3,976,608
Inventory	6,195,450	5,327,733
Other	270,938	276,367
Total	12,734,089	10,809,004
Fixed assets		
Property, plant and equipment	3,899,568	2,961,667
Less: accumulated depreciation	(1,117,937)	(858,210)
Total fixed assets (net)	2,781,631	2,103,457
Other assets		
Intangibles	379,313	568,087
Other long-term assets	2,167,504	1,873,151
Total fixed assets (net)	$18,062,537	$15,353,699
Liabilities and shareholder equity		
Current liabilities:		
Accounts payable	$4,280,821	$4,097,595
Notes payable	1,083,752	951,929
Current maturities of long-term debt	496,720	303,236
Accrued liabilities		
Expenses	2,754,537	2,360,631
Salaries and wages	1,408,878	1,259,003
Other	1,137,940	991,235
Total current liabilities	11,162,648	9,963,629
Long-term liabilities		
Long-term debt	3,070,631	2,303,055
Lease obligations	90,313	31,629
Total long-term liabilities	3,702,820	2,334,684
Other liabilities		
Deferred taxes	36,125	92,122
Other noncurrent liabilities	312,326	429,904
Total liabilities	14,672,043	12,820,339
Owner's equity		
Retained earnings	3,390,494	2,533,360
Total liabilities and owner's equity	$18,062,537	$15,353,699

The Transition

By 1981, Hoback was ready to enter the market with two styles of boots: one for the mountaineer who wanted a boot for all-weather climbing, and the other for men and women who were advanced hikers. Both styles were made of water-repellent leather uppers and cleated soles for superior traction. Distribution was secured through mountaineering shops in Wyoming and Colorado.

Hoback continued to manufacture western boots for its loyal customers, but Margaret planned to phase them out as the hiking boot business developed. How-

EXHIBIT 1

Segmentation of the Hiking Boot Market

	Mountaineers	Serious Hikers	Weekenders	Practical Users	Children	Fashion Seekers
Benefits	Durability/Ruggedness Stability/Support Dryness/Warmth Grip/Traction	Stability Durability Traction Comfort/Protection	Lightweight Comfort Durability Versatility	Lightweight Durability Good value Versatility	Durability Protection Lightweight Traction	Fashion/Style Appearance Lightweight Inexpensive
Demographics	Young Primarily male Shops in specialty stores and specialized catalogs	Young, middle aged Male and female Shops in specialty stores and outdoor catalogs	Young, middle aged Male and female Shops in shoe retailers, sporting goods stores, and mail-order catalogs	Young, middle aged Primarily male Shops in shoe retailers and department stores	Young marrieds Male and female Shops in department stores and outdoor catalogs	Young Male and female Shops in shoe retailers, department stores and catalogs
Lifestyle	Adventuresome Independent Risk taker Enjoys challenge	Nature lover Outdoorsman Sportsman Backpacker	Recreational hiker Social, spends time with family and friends Enjoys the outdoors	Practical Sociable Outdoors for work and recreation	Enjoys family activities Enjoys outdoors and hiking Children are active and play outdoors Parents are value conscious	Materialistic Trendy Socially conscious Nonhikers Brand name shoppers Price conscious
Examples of Brands	Asolo Cliff Raichle Mt. Blanc Salomon Adventure 9	Raichle Explorer Vasque Clarion Tecnica Pegasus Dry Hi-Tec Piramide	Reebok R-Evolution Timberland Topozoic Merrell Acadia Nike Air Mada, Zion Vasque Alpha	Merrell Eagle Nike Air Khyber Tecnica Volcano	Vasque Kids Klimber Nike Merrell Caribou	Nike Espirit Reebok Telos Hi-Tec Magnum
Estimated Market Share	5% Slow growth	17% Moderate growth	25% High growth	20% Stable growth	5% Slow growth	28% At peak of rapid growth cycle
Price Range	$210–$450	$120–$215	$70–$125	$40–$80	Will pay up to $40	$65–$100

Summary of Competitors

Company	Location	Mountaineering (Styles)	Hiking (Styles)	Men's	Women's	Children's	Price Range
Raichle	Switzerland	Yes (7)	Yes (16)	Yes	Yes	Yes	High
Salomon	France	Yes (1)	Yes (9)	Yes	Yes	No	Mid
Asolo	Italy	Yes (4)	Yes (26)	Yes	Yes	No	High
Tecnica	Italy	Yes (3)	Yes (9)	Yes	Yes	No	Mid/High
Hi-Tec	U.K.	Yes (2)	Yes (29)	Yes	Yes	Yes	Mid/Low
Vasque	Minnesota	Yes (4)	Yes (18)	Yes	Yes	Yes	Mid/High
Merrell	Vermont	Yes (5)	Yes (31)	Yes	Yes	Yes	Mid
Timberland	New Hampshire	No	Yes (4)	Yes	No	No	Mid
Nike	Oregon	No	Yes (5)	Yes	Yes	Yes	Low
Reebok	Massachusetts	No	Yes (3)	Yes	Yes	Yes	Low
Cima	Wyoming	Yes (3)	Yes (5)	Yes	Yes	No	High

Source: Published literature and company product brochures, 1995.

ever, because they did not completely understand the needs of the market, they hired Harris Fleming, a mountaineering instructor to help them with product design and marketing.

A New Company

During the 1980s, Hoback prospered as the market expanded along with the popularity of outdoor recreation. The company slowly increased its product line and achieved success by focusing on classic boots that were relatively insensitive to fashion trends. By 1986, sales of Hoback Boots had reached $3.5 million.

Over the next several years, distribution was steadily expanded. In 1987, Hoback employed independent sales representatives to handle the sales and service. Before long, Hoback boots were sold throughout Wyoming, Colorado, and Montana by retailers specializing in mountaineering and hiking equipment. Margaret decided to discontinue western boots to make room for the growing hiking boot business. To reflect the new direction of the company, the name was changed to Cima Mountaineering, Inc.

Cima Boots "Take Off"

The late 1980s were a period of exceptional growth. Demand for Cima boots grew quickly as consumers caught the trend toward healthy, active lifestyles. The company expanded its line for advanced hikers and improved the performance of its boots. By 1990, sales had reached $13 million and the company earned profits of $522,606. Margaret was satisfied with the growth, but she was concerned about low profitability as a result of foreign competition. She challenged the company to find new ways to design and manufacture boots at lower cost.

Growth and Innovation

The next five years were marked by growth, innovation, and increasing foreign and domestic competition. Market growth continued as hiking boots became popular for casual wear in addition to hiking in mountains and on trails. Cima and its competitors began to make boots with molded footbeds and utilize materials that reduced weight.[1] Fashion also became a factor, and companies like Nike and Reebok marketed lightweight boots in a variety of materials and colors to meet the demand for styling in addition to performance. Cima implemented a computer-aided design (CAD) system in 1993 to shorten product development and devote more attention to design. Late in 1994, Cima restructured its facilities and implemented a modular approach to manufacturing. The company switched from a production line to a system in which a work team applied multiple processes to each pair of boots. Significant cost savings were achieved as the new approach improved the profit and quality of the company's boots.

The Situation in 1995

As the company ended 1995, sales had grown to $20.0 million, up 7.2 percent from the previous year. Employment was at 425, and the facility was operating at 85 percent of capacity, producing several styles of mountaineering and hiking boots. Time-saving innovations and cost reduction had also worked, and profits reached an all-time high. Margaret, now 57, was still President, and Anthony remained Executive Vice President.

■ CIMA MARKETING STRATEGY

According to estimates, 1994 was a record year for sales of hiking and mountaineering boots in the United States. Retail sales exceeded $600 million, and about 15 million pairs of boots were sold. Consumers wore the boots for activities ranging from mountaineering to casual social events. In recent years, changes were beginning to occur in the market. Inexpensive, lightweight hiking boots were becoming increasingly popular for day hikes and trail walking and a new category of comfortable, light "trekking" shoes were being marketed by the manufacturers of athletic shoes.

Only a part of the market was targeted by Cima. Most of its customers were serious outdoor enthusiasts. They included mountaineers who climbed in rugged terrain and advanced hikers who used the boots on challenging trails and extended backpacking trips. The demand for Cima boots was seasonal, and most of the purchases were made during the summer months when the mountains and trails were most accessible.

Positioning

Cima boots were positioned as the best available for their intended purpose. Consumers saw them as durable and comfortable with exceptional performance. Retailers viewed the company as quick to adopt innovative construction techniques but conservative in styling. Cima intentionally used traditional styling to avoid fashion obsolescence and the need for frequent design changes. Some of the most popular styles had been in the market for several years without any significant modifications. The Glacier MX 350 shown in Exhibit 3 on page 620 and the Summit HX 350 boot shown in Exhibit 4, also on page 620, are good examples. The MX 350, priced at $219.00, was positioned as a classic boot for men with a unique tread design for be-

---

[1] Two processes are used to attach the uppers to the soles of boots. In classic welt construction, the uppers and soles are stitched. In the more contemporary method, a molded polyurethane footbed (including a one-piece heel and sole) is cemented to the upper with a waterproof adhesive. Many mountaineering boots use classic welt construction because it provides outstanding stability, while the contemporary method is often used with hiking boots to achieve lightweight construction. Cima used the classic method of construction for mountaineering boots and the contemporary method for hiking boots.

EXHIBIT 3

The Glacier MX 350 Mountaineering Boot

ginning mountaineers. The Summit HX 350 was priced at $159.00 and was a boot for men and women hiking rough trails. Exhibit 5 describes the items in the mountaineering and hiking boot lines, and Table 4 provides a sales history for Cima boots.

Product Lines

Corporate branding was used and "Cima" was embossed into the leather on the side of the boot to enhance consumer recognition. Product lines were also branded, and

EXHIBIT 4

The Summit HX 350 Hiking Boot

EXHIBIT 5

Cima Mountaineering, Inc. Mountaineering and Hiking Boot Lines

Product Line	Description
Glacier	
MX 550	For expert mountaineers climbing challenging mountains. Made for use on rocks, ice, and snow. Features welt construction, superior stability and support, reinforced heel and toe, padded ankle and tongue, step-in crampon insert, thermal insulation, and waterproof inner liner. Retails for $299.
MX 450	For proficient mountaineers engaging in rigorous, high-altitude hiking. Offers long-term comfort and stability on rough terrain. Features welt construction, deep cleated soles and heels, reinforced heel and toe, padded ankle and tongue, step-in crampon insert, and waterproof inner liner. Retails for $249.
MX 350	For beginning mountaineers climbing in moderate terrain and temperate climates. Features welt construction, unique tread design for traction, padded ankle and tongue, good stability and support, and a quick-dry lining. Retails for $219.
Summit	
HX 550	For experienced hikers who require uncompromising performance. Features nylon shank for stability and rigidity, waterproof inner liner, cushioned midsole, high-traction outsole, and padded ankle and tongue. Retails for $197.
HX 450	For backpackers who carry heavy loads on extended trips. Features thermal insulation, cushioned midsole, waterproof inner liner, excellent foot protection, and high-traction outsole. Retails for $179.
HX 350	For hikers who travel rough trails and a variety of backcountry terrain. Features extra cushioning, good stability and support, waterproof inner liner, and high-traction outsole for good grip in muddy and sloping surfaces. Retails for $159.
HX 250	For hikers who hike developed trails. Made with only the necessary technical features, including cushioning, foot and ankle support, waterproof inner liner, and high-traction outsole. Retails for $139.
HX 150	For individuals taking more than day and weekend hikes. Versatile boot for all kinds of excursions. Features cushioning, good support, waterproof inner liner, and high-traction outsoles for use on a variety of surfaces. Retails for $129.

alphabetic letters and numbers were used to differentiate items in the line. Each line had different styles and features to cover many of the important uses in the market. However, all boots had features that the company believed were essential to positioning. Standard features included water-repellent leather uppers and high-traction soles and heels. The hardware for the boots was plated steel, and the laces were tough, durable nylon. Quality was emphasized throughout the product lines.

Table 4
Cima Mountaineering, Inc. Product Line Sales

	Unit Sales (%)		Sales Revenue (%)	
Year	Mountaineering	Hiking	Mountaineering	Hiking
1995	15.00	85.00	21.74	78.26
1994	15.90	84.10	22.93	77.07
1993	17.20	82.80	24.64	75.36
1992	18.00	82.00	25.68	74.32
1991	18.80	81.20	26.71	73.29
1990	19.70	80.30	27.86	72.14

Glacier Boots for Mountaineering

The Glacier line featured three boots for men. The MX 550 was designed for expert all-weather climbers looking for the ultimate in traction, protection, and warmth. The MX 450 was for experienced climbers taking extended excursions, while the MX 350 met the needs of less-skilled individuals beginning climbing in moderate terrain and climates.

Summit Boots for Hiking

The Summit line featured five styles for men and women. The HX 550 was preferred by experienced hikers who demanded the best possible performance. The boot featured water-repellent leather uppers, a waterproof inner liner, a cushioned midsole, a nylon shank for rigidity, and a sole designed for high traction. It was available in gray and brown with different types of leather.[2] The Summit HX 150 was the least expensive boot in the line, designed for individuals who were beginning to hike more than the occasional "weekend hike." It was a versatile boot for all kinds of excursions and featured a water-repellent leather upper, a cushioned midsole, and excellent traction. The HX 150 was popular as an entry-level boot for outdoor enthusiasts.

Distribution

Cima boots were distributed in Arizona, California, Colorado, Idaho, Montana, Nevada, New Mexico, Oregon, Washington, Wyoming, and western Canada through specialty retailers selling mountaineering, backpacking, and hiking equipment. Occasionally, Cima was approached by mail-order catalog companies and chain sporting goods stores offering to sell their boots. The company considered the proposals, but had not used these channels.

Promotion

The Cima sales and marketing office was located in Jackson. It was managed by Harris Fleming and staffed with several marketing personnel. Promotion was an important aspect of the marketing strategy, and advertising, personal selling, and sales promotion were used to gain exposure for Cima branded boots. Promotion was directed to consumers and to the retailers that stocked Cima mountaineering and hiking boots.

Personal Selling

Cima used 10 independent sales representatives to sell its boots in the western states and Canada. Representatives did not sell competing boots, but they sold complementary products such as outdoor apparel and equipment for mountaineering, hiking, and backpacking. They were paid a commission and handled customer service in addition to sales. Management was also involved in personal selling. Harris Fleming trained the independent sales representatives and often accompanied them on sales calls.

---

[2] Different types of leather are used to make hiking boots. *Full Grain*: High-quality, durable, upper layer of the hide. It has a natural finish, and is strong and breatheable. *Split Grain*: Underside of the hide after the full-grain leather has been removed from the top. Lightweight and comfort are the primary characteristics. *Suede*: A very fine split-grain leather. *Nubuk*: Brushed full-grain leather. *Waxed*: A process in which leather is coated with wax to help shed water. Most Cima boots were available in two or more types of leather.

Mountaineering and hiking boots are made water repellent by treating the uppers with wax or chemical coatings. To make the boots waterproof, a fabric inner liner is built into the boot to provide waterproof protection and breatheability. All Cima boots were water repellent, but only those styles with an inner liner were waterproof.

Advertising and Sales Promotion

Advertising and sales promotion were also important promotional methods. Print advertising was used to increase brand awareness and assist retailers with promotion. Advertising was placed in leading magazines such as *Summit, Outside,* and *Backpacker* to reach mountaineers and hikers with the message that Cima boots were functional and durable with classic styling. In addition, cooperative advertising was offered to encourage retailers to advertise Cima boots and identify their locations.

Sales promotion was an important part of the promotion program. Along with the focus on brand name recognition, Cima provided product literature and point-of-sale display materials to assist retailers in promoting the boots. In addition, the company regularly exhibited at industry trade shows. The exhibits, staffed by marketing personnel and the company's independent sales representatives, were effective for maintaining relationships with retailers and presenting the company's products.

Pricing

Cima selling prices to retailers ranged from $64.50 to $149.50 a pair depending on the style. Mountaineering boots were more expensive because of their construction and features, while hiking boots were priced lower. Retailers were encouraged to take a 50 percent margin on the retail selling price, so retail prices shown in Figure 5 should be divided by two to get the Cima selling price. Cima priced its boots higher than competitors, supporting the positioning of the boots as the top quality product at each price point. Payment terms were net 30 days (similar to competitors), and boots were shipped to retailers from a warehouse located in Jackson, Wyoming.

■ SEGMENTATION OF THE HIKING BOOT MARKET

As Anthony reviewed the marketing study commissioned by Harris Fleming, his attention focused on the market segmentation shown in Exhibit 1. It was interesting, because management had never seriously thought about the segmentation in the market. Of course, Anthony was aware that not everyone was a potential customer for Cima boots, but he was surprised to see how well the product lines met the needs of mountaineers and serious hikers. As he reviewed the market segmentation, he read the descriptions for mountaineers, serious hikers, and weekenders carefully because Cima was trying to decide which of these segments to target for expansion.

Mountaineers

Mountain climbers and high-altitude hikers are in this segment. They are serious about climbing and enjoy risk and adventure. Because mountaineers' safety may often depend on their boots, they need maximum stability and support, traction for a variety of climbing conditions, and protection from wet and cold weather.

Serious Hikers

Outdoorsmen, who love nature and have a strong interest in health and fitness, comprise the serious hikers. They hike rough trails and take extended backpacking or hiking excursions. Serious hikers are brand conscious and look for durable, high-performance boots with good support, comfortable fit, and good traction.

Weekenders

Consumers in this segment are recreational hikers who enjoy casual weekend and day hikes with family and friends. They are interested in light, comfortable boots that provide good fit, protection, and traction on a variety of surfaces. Weekenders prefer versatile boots that can be worn for a variety of activities.

■ FOREIGN AND DOMESTIC COMPETITION

The second part of the marketing study that caught Anthony's attention was the analysis of competition. Although Anthony and Margaret were aware that competition had increased, they had overlooked the extent to which foreign bootmakers had entered the market. Apparently, foreign competitors had noticed the market growth and they were aggressively exporting their boots into the United States. They had established sales offices and independent sales agents to compete for the customers served by Cima. The leading foreign brands such as Asolo, Hi-Tec, Salomon, and Raichle were marketed on performance and reputation, usually to the mountaineering, serious hiker, and weekender segments of the market.

The study also summarized the most important domestic competitors. Vasque and Merrell marketed boots that competed with Cima, but others were offering products for segments of the market where the prospects for growth were better. As Anthony examined Exhibit 2, he realized that the entry of Reebok and Nike into the hiking boot market was quite logical. They had entered the market as consumer preference shifted from wearing athletic shoes for casual outdoor activities to a more rugged shoe. Each was marketing footwear that combined the appearance and durability of hiking boots with the lightness and fit of athletic shoes. The result was a line of fashionable hiking boots that appealed to brand- and style-conscious teens and young adults. Both firms were expanding their product lines and moving into segments of the market that demanded lower levels of performance.

■ MARGARET AND ANTHONY DISCUSS MARKETING STRATEGY

A few days after hiking in Cascade Canyon, Anthony met with Margaret and Harris Fleming to discuss marketing strategy. Each had read the consultant's report and studied the market segmentation and competitive summary. As the meeting opened, the conversation developed as follows:

MARGARET: It looks like we will have another record year. The economy is growing, and consumers seem confident and eager to buy. Yet, I'm concerned about the future. The foreign bootmakers are providing some stiff competition. Their boots have outstanding performance and attractive prices. The improvements we made in manufacturing helped to control costs and maintain margins, but it looks like the competition and slow growth in our markets will make it difficult to improve profits. We need to be thinking about new opportunities.

HARRIS: I agree, Margaret. Just this past week we lost Rocky Mountain Sports in Boulder, Colorado. John Kline, the sales manager, decided to drop us and pick up Asolo. We were doing $70,000 a year with them and they carried our entire line. We also lost Great Western Outfitters in Colorado Springs. They replaced us with Merrell. The sales manager said that the college students there had been asking for the lower-priced Merrell boots. They bought $60,000 last year.

ANTHONY: Rocky Mountain and Great Western were good customers. I guess I'm not surprised though. Our Glacier line needs another boot, and the Summit line is just not deep enough to cover the price points. We need to have some styles at lower prices to compete with Merrell and Asolo. I'm in favor of extending our existing lines to broaden their market appeal. It seems to me that the best way to compete is to stick with what we do best, making boots for mountaineers and serious hikers.

MARGARET: Not so fast, Anthony. The problem is that our markets are small and not growing fast enough to support the foreign competitors who have entered with excellent products. We can probably hold our own, but I doubt if we can do much better. I think the future of this company is to move with the market. Consumers are demanding more style, lower prices, and a lightweight hiking boot that can be worn for a variety of uses. Look at the segmentation again. The "Weekender" segment is large and it's growing. That's where we need to go with some stylish new boots that depart from our classic leather lines.

ANTHONY: Maybe so, but we don't have much experience working with the leather and nylon combinations that are being used in these lighter boots. Besides, I'm not sure we can finance the product development and marketing for a new market that already has plenty of competition. And I'm concerned about the brand image that we have worked so hard to establish over the past 20 years. A line of inexpensive, casual boots just doesn't seem to fit with the perception consumers have of our products.

HARRIS: I can see advantages to each strategy. I do know that we don't have the time and resources to do both, so we had better make a thoughtful choice. Also, I think we should reconsider selling to the mail-order catalog companies that specialize in mountaineering and hiking equipment. Last week, I received another call from REI requesting us to sell them some of the boots in our Summit line for the 1997 season. This might be a good source of revenue and a way of expanding our geographic market.

MARGARET: You're right, Harris. We need to rethink our position on the mail-order companies. Most of them have good market penetration in the East where we don't have distribution. I noticed that Gander Mountain is carrying some of the Timberland line and that L.L. Bean is carrying some Vasque styles along with its own line of branded boots.

ANTHONY: I agree. Why don't we each put together a proposal that summarizes our recommendations and then we can get back together to continue the discussion.

HARRIS: Good idea. Eventually we will need a sales forecast and some cost data. Send me your proposals and I'll call the consulting firm and have them prepare some forecasts. I think we already have some cost information. Give me a few days and then we can get together again.

■ THE MEETING TO REVIEW THE PROPOSALS

The following week, the discussion continued. Margaret presented her proposal, which is summarized in Exhibit 6 on page 626. She proposed moving Cima into the "Weekender" segment by marketing two new hiking boots. Anthony countered with the proposal summarized in Exhibit 7 on page 627. He favored extending the existing lines by adding a new mountaineering boot and two new Summit hiking boots at lower price points. Harris presented sales forecasts for each proposal and after some discussion and modification, they were finalized as shown in Table 5 on page 628. Cost information was gathered by Harris from the Vice President of Manufacturing and is presented in Table 6 on page 629. Following a lengthy discussion, in which Margaret and Anthony were unable to agree on a course of action, Harris Fleming suggested that each proposal be explored further by conducting marketing research. He proposed the formation of teams from the Cima marketing staff to research each proposal and present it to Margaret and Anthony at a later date. Harris presented his directions to the teams in the memorandum shown in Exhibit 8 on page 629. The discussion between Margaret and Anthony continued as follows:

EXHIBIT 6

Margaret's Marketing Proposal

MEMORANDUM

TO: Anthony Simon, Executive Vice President
          Harris Fleming, Vice President of Marketing
FROM: Margaret Simon, President
RE: Marketing Proposal

I believe we have an excellent opportunity to expand the sales and profits of Cima by entering the "Weekender" segment of the hiking boot market. The segment's estimated share of the market is 25 percent and according to the consultant's report it is growing quite rapidly. I propose that we begin immediately to develop two new products and prepare a marketing strategy as discussed below.

Target Market and Positioning

Male and female recreational hikers looking for a comfortable, lightweight boot that is attractively priced and acceptable for short hikes and casual wear. Weekenders enjoy the outdoors and a day or weekend hike with family and friends.

The new boots would be positioned with magazine advertising as hiking boots that deliver performance and style for the demands of light hiking and casual outdoor wear.

Product

Two boots in men's and women's sizes. The boots would be constructed of leather and nylon uppers with a molded rubber outsole. A new branded line would be created to meet the needs of the market segment. The boots (designated WX 550 and WX 450) would have the following features:

	WX 550	WX 450
Leather and nylon uppers	X	X
Molded rubber outsole	X	X
Cushioned midsole	X	X
Padded collar and tongue	X	X
Durable hardware and laces	X	X
Waterproof inner liner	X	

Uppers: To be designed. Options include brown full-grain, split-grain, or suede leather combined with durable nylon in two of the following colors: beige, black, blue, gray, green, and slate.
Boot design and brand name: To be decided.

Retail Outlets

Specialty shoe retailers carrying hiking boots and casual shoes and sporting goods stores. Eventually mail order catalogs carrying outdoor apparel and hiking, backpacking, and camping equipment.

Promotion

Independent sales representatives   Point-of-sale display materials
Magazine advertising   Product brochures
Co-op advertising   Trade shows

Suggested Retail Pricing

WX 550: $89.00
WX 450: $69.00

Competitors

Timberland, Hi-Tec, Vasque, Merrell, Asolo, Nike, and Reebok.

Product Development and Required Investment

We should allow about one year for the necessary product development and testing. I estimate these costs to be $350,000. Additionally, we will need to make a capital expenditure of $150,000 for new equipment.

E X H I B I T   7

Anthony's Marketing Proposal

MEMORANDUM

TO: Margaret Simon, President
           Harris Fleming, Vice President of Marketing

FROM: Anthony Simon, Executive Vice President

RE: Marketing Proposal

We have been successful with boots for mountaineers and serious hikers for years, and this is where our strengths seem to be. I recommend extending our Glacier and Summit lines instead of venturing into a new, unfamiliar market. My recommendations are summarized below:

Product Development

Introduce two new boots in the Summit line (designated HX 100 and HX 50) and market the Glacier MX 350 in a style for women with the same features as the boot for men. The new women's Glacier boot would have a suggested retail price of $219.99, while the suggested retail prices for the HX 100 and the HX 50 would be $119.00 and $89.00 respectively to provide price points at the low end of the line. The new Summit boots for men and women would be the first in the line to have leather and nylon uppers as well as the following features:

	HX 100	HX 50
Leather and nylon uppers	X	X
Molded rubber outsole	X	X
Cushioned midsole	X	X
Padded collar and tongue	X	X
Quick-dry lining	X	X
Waterproof inner liner	X	

The leather used in the uppers will have to be determined. We should consider full-grain, suede and nubuck since they are all popular with users in this segment. We need to select one for the initial introduction. The nylon fabric for the uppers should be available in two colors, selected from among the following: beige, brown, green, slate, maroon, and navy blue. Additional colors can be offered as sales develop and we gain a better understanding of consumer preferences.

Product Development and Required Investment

Product design and development costs of $400,000 for the MX 350, HX 100 and HX 50 styles and a capital investment of $150,000 to acquire equipment to cut and stitch the nylon/leather uppers. One year will be needed for product development and testing.

Positioning

The additions to the Summit line will be positioned as boots for serious hikers who want a quality hiking boot at a reasonable price. The boots will also be attractive to casual hikers who are looking to move up to a better boot as they gain experience in hiking and outdoor activity.

Retail Outlets

We can use our existing retail outlets. Additionally, the lower price points on the new styles will make these boots attractive to catalog shoppers. I recommend that we consider making the Summit boots available to consumers through mail order catalog companies.

Promotion

We will need to revise our product brochures and develop new advertising for the additions to the Summit line. The balance of the promotion program should remain as it exists since it is working quite well. I believe the sales representatives and retailers selling our lines will welcome the new boots since they broaden the consumer appeal of our lines.

EXHIBIT 7 *(continued)*

Suggested Retail Pricing

MX 350 for women:	$219.00
HX 100:	$119.00
HX 50:	$89.00

Competitors

Asolo, Hi-Tec, Merrell, Raichle, Salomon, Tecnica, and Vasque.

MARGARET: Once the marketing research is completed and we can read the reports and listen to the presentations, we should have a better idea of which strategy makes the best sense. Hopefully, a clear direction will emerge and we can move ahead with one of the proposals. In either case, I'm still intrigued with the possibility of moving into the mail order catalogs, since we really haven't developed these companies as customers. I just wish we knew how much business we could expect from them.

ANTHONY: We should seriously consider them, Margaret. Companies like L.L. Bean, Gander Mountain, and REI have been carrying a selection of hiking boots for several years. However, there may be a problem for us. Eventually the catalog companies expect their boot suppliers to make them a private brand. I'm not sure this is something we want to do since we built the company on a strategy of marketing our own brands that are made in the U.S.A. Also, I'm concerned about the reaction of our retailers when they discover we are selling to the catalog companies. It could create some problems.

HARRIS: That is a strategy issue we will have to address. However, I'm not even sure what percentage of sales the typical footwear company makes through the mail-order catalogs. If we were to solicit the catalog business, we would need an answer to this question to avoid exceeding our capacity. In the proposals, I asked

Table 5
Cima Mountaineering, Inc. Sales Forecasts for Proposed New Products
(Pairs of Boots)

	Project 1		Project 2		
Year	**WX 550**	**WX 450**	**MX 350**	**HX 100**	**HX 50**
2001–02	16,420	24,590	2,249	15,420	12,897
2000–01	14,104	21,115	1,778	13,285	11,733
1999–00	8,420	12,605	897	10,078	9,169
1998–99	5,590	8,430	538	5,470	5,049
1997–98	4,050	6,160	414	4,049	3,813

Note: Sales forecasts are expected values derived from minimum and maximum estimates.

Some cannibalization of existing boots will occur when the new styles are introduced. The sales forecasts provided above have taken into account the impact of sales losses on existing boots. No additional adjustments need to be made.

Forecasts for WX 550, WX 450, HX 100, and HX 50 include sales of both men's and women's boots.

Table 6
Cima Mountaineering, Inc. Cost Information for Mountaineering and Hiking Boots

	Inner Liner	*No Inner Liner*
Retail margin	50%	50%
Marketing and Manufacturing Costs		
Sales commissions	10	10
Advertising and sales promotion	5	5
Materials	42	35
Labor, overhead, and transportation	28	35

Cost information for 1997–1998 only. Sales commissions, advertising and sales promotion, materials, labor, overhead, and transportation costs are based on Cima selling prices. After 1997–1998, annual increases of 3.0 percent apply to marketing and manufacturing costs and 4.0 percent apply to Cima selling prices.

each of the teams to provide an estimate for us. I have to catch an early flight to Denver in the morning. It's 6:30; why don't we call it a day.

The meeting was adjourned at 6:35 P.M. Soon thereafter, the marketing teams were formed with a leader assigned to each team.

EXHIBIT 8

Harris Fleming's Memorandum to the Marketing Staff

MEMORANDUM

TO: Marketing Staff
CC: Margaret Simon, President
Anthony Simon, Executive Vice President
FROM: Harris Fleming, Vice President of Marketing
SUBJECT: Marketing Research Projects

Attached to this memorandum are two marketing proposals (see case Exhibits 6 and 7) under consideration by our company. Each proposal is a guide for additional marketing research. You have been selected to serve on a project team to investigate one of the proposals and report your conclusions and recommendations to management. At your earliest convenience, please complete the following.

Project Team 1: Proposal to enter the "Weekender" segment of the hiking boot market.

Review the market segmentation and summary of competition in Exhibits 1 and 2. Identify consumers that would match the profile described in the market segment and conduct field research using a focus group, a survey, or both. You may also visit retailers carrying hiking boots to examine displays and product brochures. Using the information in the proposal, supplemented with your research, prepare the following:

1. A design for the hiking boots (WX 550 and WX 450). Please prepare a sketch that shows the styling for the uppers. We propose to use the same design for each boot, the only difference being the waterproof inner liner on the WX 550 boot. On your design, list the features that your proposed boot would have, considering additions or deletions to those listed in the proposal.

2. Recommend a type of leather (from among those proposed) and two colors for the nylon to be used in the panels of the uppers. We plan to make two styles, one in each color for each boot.

EXHIBIT 8 *(continued)*

3. Recommend a brand name for the product line. Include a rationale for your choice.

4. Verify the acceptability of the suggested retail pricing.

5. Prepare a magazine advertisement for the hiking boot. Provide a rationale for the advertisement in the report.

6. Convert the suggested retail prices *in the proposal* to the Cima selling price and use the sales forecasts and costs (shown in Tables 5 and 6) to prepare an estimate of before-tax profits for the new product line covering a five-year period starting in 1997–98. Assume annual cost increases of 3.0 percent and price increases of 4.0 percent beginning in 1998–99. Discount the future profits to present value using a cost of capital of 15.0 percent. Use 1996–97 as the base year for all discounting.

7. Determine the payback period for the proposal. Assume product development and investment occurs in 1996–97.

8. Provide your conclusions on the attractiveness of these styles to mail order catalog companies and their customers. You may wish to review current mail order catalogs to observe the hiking boots featured. Assuming Cima is successful selling to mail order catalog companies, estimate the percentage of our sales that could be expected from these customers.

9. Prepare a report that summarizes the recommendations of your project team, including the advantages and disadvantages of the proposal. Be prepared to present your product design, branding, pro-forma projections, payback period and recommendations to management shortly after completion of this assignment.

10. Summarize your research and list the sources of information used to prepare the report.

Project Team 2: Proposal to extend the existing lines of boots for mountaineers and hikers.

Review the market segmentation and summary of competition in Exhibits 1 and 2. Identify consumers that match the profile described in the market segment and conduct field research using a focus group, a survey, or both. You may also visit retailers carrying hiking boots to examine displays and product brochures. Using the information in the proposal, supplemented with your research, prepare the following.

1. Designs for the hiking boots (HX 100 and HX 50). Please prepare sketches showing the styling for the uppers. We propose to use a different design for each boot, so you should provide a sketch for each. On each sketch, list the features that your proposed boots would have, considering additions or deletions to those listed in the proposal. No sketch is necessary for the mountaineering boot, MX 350, since we will use the same design as the men's boot and build it on a women's last.

2. Recommend one type of leather (from among those proposed) and two colors for the nylon to be used in the panels of the uppers. We plan to make two styles, one in each color for each boot.

3. Verify the market acceptability of the suggested retail pricing.

4. Prepare a magazine advertisement for your hiking boots. Include a rationale for the advertisement in the report.

5. Using the suggested retail prices *in the proposal*, convert them to the Cima selling prices and use the sales forecasts and costs (shown in Tables 5 and 6) to prepare an estimate of before-tax profits for the new products covering a five-year period starting in 1997–98. Assume annual cost increases of 3.0 percent and price increases of 4.0 percent beginning in 1998–99. Discount the profits to present value using a cost of capital of 15.0 percent. Use 1996–97 as the base year for all discounting.

6. Determine the payback period for the proposal. Assume product development and investment occurs in 1996–97.

7. Provide your conclusions on the attractiveness of these styles to mail order catalog companies and their customers. You may wish to review current mail order catalogs to observe the hiking boots featured. Assuming Cima is successful selling to mail order catalog companies, estimate the percentage of our sales that could be expected from these customers.

EXHIBIT 8 *(continued)*

8. Prepare a report that summarizes the recommendations of your project team, including the advantages and disadvantages of the proposal. Be prepared to present your product design, pro-forma projections, payback period and recommendations to management shortly after completion of this assignment.

9. Summarize your research and list the sources of information used to prepare the report.

Colgate-Palmolive Canada
Arctic Power Detergent

"We've got some important decisions to make on Arctic Power for 1988," said Linda Barton, Senior Product Manager for the brand. "As I see it, we can continue to develop our strong markets in Quebec, the Maritimes, and British Columbia or we can try to build market share in the rest of Canada." Ms. Barton was discussing the future of Arctic Power, one of Colgate-Palmolive Canada's leading laundry detergents, with Gary Parsons, the Assistant Product Manager on the brand.

"Not only do we have to consider our strategic direction," replied Mr. Parsons, "but we also have to think about our positioning strategy for Arctic Power. I'm for running the Quebec approach in all our markets." Mr. Parsons was referring to the Quebec advertising campaign, which positioned Arctic Power as the superior detergent for cold water cleaning.

"I'm not sure," said Ms. Barton. "We're making great progress with our current advertising in British Columbia. It might be more effective outside of Quebec. Remember, cold water washing is a newer concept for the western provinces. We have to overcome that obstacle before we can get people to buy Arctic Power. Let's go over the data again, then make our decisions."

■ THE COMPANY

Colgate-Palmolive Canada is a wholly owned subsidiary of Colgate-Palmolive, a large multinational with divisions in 58 countries. Worldwide company sales in 1986 were $4.9 billion with profits of $178 million. The Canadian subsidiary sales exceeded $250 million each year. Colgate-Palmolive Canada (CPC) manufactures a range of household, health, and personal care products. Among CPC's major brands are ABC, Arctic Power, and Fab (laundry detergents); Palmolive (dishwashing liquid); Ajax (cleanser); Irish Spring (bar soap); Ultra Brite and Colgate (toothpastes); Halo (shampoo); and Baggies (food wrap).

Under the product management system at CPC, product managers are assigned responsibility for specific brands, like Arctic Power. Their overall goals are to increase the sales and profitability of their brand. To meet these goals, the product manager supervises all marketing functions, including planning, advertising, selling, promo-

This case was prepared by Professor Gordon H. G. McDougall, of the Wilfrid Laurier University, and Professor Douglas Snetsinger, of the University of Toronto, as the basis for classroom discussion rather than to illustrate either effective or ineffective handling of an administrative situation. Names and proprietary data have been disguised, but all essential relationships have been preserved. Copyright © 1989. Used with permission.

tion, and market research. In planning and executing programs for a brand the product manager usually is assigned an assistant product manager, and they work closely together to accomplish the brand goals.

Prior to the late 1970s CPC essentially followed the strategy of nationally supporting most of its brands. The result was the CPC was spread too thin with too many brands. There were insufficient resources to properly promote and develop all of the CPC line, and profits and market share were less than satisfactory. Beginning in the late 1970s and continuing to the early 1980s the Canadian division altered its strategy. An extensive review of the entire product line was conducted, and CPC moved to what was referred to as a regional brand strategy. Where a brand had regional strength, resources were focused on that area with the objective of building a strong and profitable brand in that region. For example, Arctic Power had a relatively strong market share in Quebec and the Maritimes, where the proportion of consumers using cold water to wash clothes was considerably higher than the national average. Promotional support was withdrawn from the rest of Canada, and those resources were focused on Quebec and the Maritimes. Arctic Power was still distributed nationally but by the end of 1981, national market share was 4 percent, which consisted of an 11 percent share in Quebec, a 5 percent share in the Maritimes, and a 2 percent share in the rest of Canada. Over the next four years, marketing efforts were concentrated primarily on Quebec, and to a lesser extent, the Maritimes. This approach worked well for Arctic Power. By the end of 1985, Arctic Power's national share had increased to 6.4 percent, share in Quebec had risen to 18 percent, share in the Maritimes was 6 percent, and less than 2 percent in the rest of Canada. With the increase in sales and profitability, the decision was made to target Alberta and British Columbia for 1986. The results of these efforts exceeded expectations in British Columbia but were less than satisfactory in Alberta.

■ THE LAUNDRY DETERGENT MARKET

The laundry detergent market was mature, with unit sales increasing by approximately 1 percent annually and dollar sales increasing by about 5 percent each year (Exhibit 1 on page 634). Three large consumer packaged goods companies, Procter and Gamble, Lever Detergents, and CPC, dominated the market. All three were subsidiaries of multinational firms and sold a wide range of household and personal care products in Canada. Procter and Gamble Canada had annual sales exceeding $1 billion, and its major brands included Crest (toothpaste), Ivory and Zest (bar soaps), Secret (deodorant), Pampers and Luvs (disposable diapers), and Head & Shoulders (shampoo). P&G held a 44 percent share of the laundry detergent market in 1986, due primarily to the large share (34 percent) held by Tide, the leading brand in Canada.

Lever Detergents, with annual Canadian sales in excess of $400 million, operated primarily in the detergent, soap and toiletries categories. Major brands included Sunlight (dishwasher detergent), Close-up (toothpaste), and Dove and Lux (bar soaps). Lever held a 24 percent share of the laundry detergent market, and its leading brand was Sunlight, with a 13 percent share.

CPC was the only one of the three companies to gain market share in the laundry detergent market between 1983 and 1986. In 1986, CPC's total share was 23 percent, up from 16 percent in 1983. ABC, a value brand from CPC positioned to attract consumers interested in "value for less money," more than doubled its share between 1983 and 1986 and was the second leading brand with a 14 percent share.

EXHIBIT 1

Laundry Detergent Market—Market Shares (Percentages)

	1983	*1984*	*1985*	*1986*
Colgate				
ABC	6.0%	9.8%	11.8%	13.9%
Arctic Power	4.7	5.6	6.4	6.5
Fab	2.1	1.3	1.6	1.4
Punch	2.0	.7	.4	.3
Dynamo	1.0	.8	.6	.5
Total Colgate	15.8	18.2	20.8	22.6
Procter and Gamble				
Tide	34.1	35.1	32.6	34.1
Oxydol	4.9	4.2	4.0	3.3
Bold	4.8	4.2	3.2	2.3
Other P&G brands	4.7	4.8	4.4	4.3
Total P&G	48.5	48.3	44.2	44.0
Lever				
Sunlight	13.9	12.2	14.2	13.4
All	4.1	3.7	3.8	3.2
Surf	2.6	2.6	2.7	2.2
Wisk	3.8	4.1	4.1	4.4
Other Lever brands	.9	.8	.6	.4
Total Lever	25.3	23.4	25.4	23.6
All other brands	10.4	10.1	9.6	9.8
Grand Total	100.0	100.0	100.0	100.0
Total Market				
Tons (000s)	171.9	171.9	173.6	175.3
(% change)	2.0	0.0	1.0	1.0
Factory sales (000,000s)	$265.8	$279.1	$288.5	$304.7
(% change)	6.2	5.0	3.0	6.0

Source: Company records.

■ COMPETITIVE RIVALRY

Intense competitive activity was a way of life in the laundry detergent business. Not only did the three major firms have talented and experienced marketers, but they competed in a low-growth market where increased sales could be achieved only by taking share from competitive brands. A difficult task facing any product manager in this business was to identify the marketing mix that would maximize share while maintaining or increasing brand profitability—a task that had both long-term and short-term implications. In the long term, competitors strove for permanent share gains by building a solid franchise of loyal users based on a quality product and a strong brand image or position. These positioning strategies were primarily executed through product formulation and advertising campaigns. However, companies also competed through consumer and trade promotions (for example, coupons, feature specials in newspaper ads), tactics that were more short term in nature. Trade and consumer promotions were critical to maintain prominent shelf display and to attract competitors' customers. In virtually every week of the year, at least one brand of detergent would be "on special" in any given supermarket. The product manager's task was to find the best balance between these elements in making brand decisions.

Reformulating brands, the changing of the brand ingredients, was a frequent activity in the laundry detergent business. Reformulating a brand involved altering the amount and kinds of active chemical ingredients in the detergents. These active ingredients cleaned the clothes. Each of these cleaning ingredients was efficacious for particular cleaning tasks. Some of these ingredients were good for cleaning clay and mud from cotton and other natural fibers, while others would clean oily soils from polyesters, and yet others were good for other cleaning problems. Most detergents were formulated with a variety of active ingredients to clean in a wide range of conditions. As well, bleaches, fabric softeners, and fragrances could be included.

Thus, laundry detergents contained different *levels* and *mixes* of active ingredients. The major decision was the *amounts* of active ingredients that would be used in a particular brand. In simple terms, the greater the proportion of active ingredients, the better the detergent was at cleaning clothes. However, all detergents would get clothes clean. For example, in a recent test of 42 laundry detergents, a consumer magazine concluded, "Yes, some detergents get clothes whiter and brighter than others—but the scale is clean to cleanest, not dirty to clean."

The Canadian brands of laundry detergent contained various amounts of active ingredients. As shown in the following table, Tide and Arctic Power had more active ingredients than any other brand.

Level of Active Ingredients of Laundry Detergents*

1	2	3	4	5
Some	Bold 3	ABC	—	Arctic Power
private	Oxydol	Fab		Tide
labels	Surf	Cheer 2		
	All	Sunlight		

* The scale of active ingredients increases from 1 to 5.

In fact, Tide and Arctic Power were equivalent brands in terms of the level of active ingredients. These two, referred to as the "Cadillacs" of detergents, had considerably higher levels of active ingredients than all other detergents. While the actual *mix* of active ingredients differed between the two brands (with Arctic Power having a greater mix of ingredients that were more suited to cold water washing), the cleaning power of Tide and Arctic Power was equal.

As the amount of active ingredients in a brand increased, so did the cost. Manufacturers were constantly facing the trade-off between cost and level of active ingredients. At times they had the opportunity to reduce unit costs by switching one type of active ingredient (a basic chemical) for another, depending on the relative costs of the ingredients. In this way, the level of ingredients remained the same; only the mixture changed. Manufacturers changed the physical ingredients of a brand in order to achieve an efficient per unit cost, to provide a basis for repositioning or restaging the brand, and to continue to deliver better consumer value.

Maintaining or increasing share through repositioning or other means was critical because of the profits involved. One share point was worth approximately $3 million in factory sales, and the cost and profit structures of the leading brands were similar. While some economies of scale accrued to the largest brands, the average cost of goods sold was estimated at 54 percent of sales, leaving a gross profit of 46 percent. Marketing expenditures included trade promotions (16 percent), consumer promotions (5 percent), and advertising expenditures (5 percent), leaving a contri-

EXHIBIT 2

Share of National Media Expenditures, 1982–1986

	Percentages				
	1982	*1983*	*1984*	*1985*	*1986*
ABC	6.4	8.9	12.3	14.0	13.6
Arctic Power	6.1	6.1	6.7	7.2	9.3
Tide	21.0	17.8	19.1	16.4	29.7
Oxydol	5.1	4.5	5.9	6.6	6.4
Sunlight	14.1	10.8	10.5	9.1	11.3
All	10.3	5.5	6.9	7.7	4.0
Wisk	9.9	12.8	10.3	10.4	14.6
All other brands	27.1	33.6	28.3	28.6	12.1
Total	100.0	100.0	100.0	100.0	100.0
Total spending (000s)	$12,909	$13,338	$14,420	$13,718	$14,429
Percentage change	29.2	3.3	8.1	−4.9	5.2

Source: Company records.

bution margin of 18 percent. Not included in these estimates were management overheads and expenses (for example, product management salaries, market research expenses, sales salaries, and factory overheads), which were primarily fixed. In some instances, lower share brands were likely to spend higher amounts on trade promotions to achieve their marketing objectives.

One indication of competitive activity was reflected in advertising expenditures between 1982 and 1986. Total category advertising increased by 12 percent to $14.4 million (Exhibit 2). As well, substantial increases in trade promotions had occurred during that period. While actual expenditure data were not available, some managers felt that twice as much was being spent on trade promotions as on advertising. For example, in Montreal over a nine-month period in 1986, Tide was featured in weekly supermarket advertisements 80 times and Arctic Power 60 times. Typically, the advertisement cost for the feature was shared by the manufacturer and the retailer. At times during 1986, consumers could have purchased Arctic Power or Tide for $3.49 (regular price $5.79). There was also a strong indication that the frequency and size of price specials on detergents were increasing. The average retail price of laundry detergents (based on the volume sold of all detergents at regular and special prices) had increased by only 4 percent in the past three years, whereas cost of goods sold had increased by 15 percent during the same period.

One final observation was warranted. Between 1983 and 1986, the four leading brands—Tide, ABC, Sunlight, and Arctic Power—had increased their share from 58.7 percent to 67.9 percent of the total market. The three manufacturers appeared to be focusing their efforts primarily on their leading brands and letting the lesser brands decline in share.

Positioning Strategies

While positioning strategies were executed through all aspects of the marketing mix, they were most clearly seen in the advertising execution.

Tide was the dominant brand in share of market and share of media expenditures. Tide's strategy was to sustain this dominance through positioning the brand as superior to any other brand on generic cleaning benefits. In 1986, four national and four regional commercials were aired to support this strategy. These commercials conveyed that Tide provided the benefits of being the most effective detergent for "tough" situations, such as for ground-in dirt, stains, and bad odors. Tide also aired copy in Quebec claiming effectiveness in all temperatures. Tide's copy was usually developed around a "slice of life" or testimonial format.

Other brands in the market faced the situation of going head-to-head with Tide's position or competing on a benefit Tide did not claim. Most had chosen the latter route. CPC's ABC brand had made strong gains in the past four years, moving from sixth to second place in market share based on its value position. ABC was positioned as the low-priced, good quality, cleaning detergent. Recent copy for ABC utilized a demonstration format where the shirts for twins were as clean when washed in ABC versus a leading higher priced detergent with the statement: "Why pay more? I can't see the difference." Sunlight, a Lever brand, had for several years attempted to compete directly with Tide and build its consumer franchise based on efficacy and lemon-scented freshness. Advertising execution had been of the upbeat, upscale lifestyle approach and less of the straightforward problem solution or straight-talking approaches seen in other detergent advertising. More recently, Sunlight had been moving toward ABC's value position while retaining the lemon freshness heritage. Sunlight was positioned in 1986 as the detergent which gave a very clean fresh wash at a sensible price. The final brand which attempted to compete for the value position was All. The advertising for All also claimed that the brand particularly whitens white clothes and gives them a pleasant fragrance.

Arctic Power had been positioned as the superior-cleaning laundry detergent, especially formulated for cold water washing. For the eastern market, Arctic Power advertising had utilized a humorous background to communicate brand superiority and its efficacy in cold water. For the western market a nontraditional, upbeat execution was used to develop the cold water market.

Wisk, which had received much attention for its "ring around the collar" advertising, competed directly with Tide on generic cleaning qualities and provided the additional benefit of a liquid formulation. Tide Liquid was introduced in 1985, but received little advertising support in 1986.

Fab and Bold 3 competed for the "softergents" market. Both products, which had fabric softeners in the formulation, were positioned to clean effectively while softening clothes and reducing static cling. Another detergent with laundry product additives was Oxydol, which was formulated with a mild bleach. Oxydol was positioned as the detergent that kept colors bright while whitening whites.

The other two nationally advertised brands were Cheer 2 and Ivory Snow. Cheer 2 was positioned as the detergent that got clothes clean and fresh. Ivory Snow, which was a soap and not a detergent, was positioned as the laundry cleaning product for infants' clothes that provided superior softness and comfort.

The Cold Water Market

Every February, CPC commissioned an extensive market research study to identify trends in the laundry detergent market. Referred to as the tracking study, its findings were based on approximately 1,800 personal interviews with female heads of households across Canada each year. Among the wealth of data provided by the tracking study was information on cold water usage in Canada. Regular cold water usage was growing in Canada and, by 1986, 29 percent of households were classified as regular cold water users (Exhibit 3 on page 638). Due to cultural and marketing differences, Quebec (55 percent) and the Maritimes (33 percent) had more cold water users than the national average. A further 25 percent of all Canadian households occasionally (one to four times out of ten) used cold water for washing.

For households that washed occasionally or regularly with cold water, the most important benefits of using cold water fell into two broad categories (Exhibit 4 on

EXHIBIT 3

Proportion of Households Washing with Cold Water, 1981–1986

| | Percentages | | | | | |
	1981	1982	1983	1984	1985	1986
National	20*	22	26	26	26	29
Maritimes	23	25	32	40	32	33
Quebec	35	41	49	48	53	55
Ontario	14	13	18	16	11	17
Prairies	12	12	13	11	10	17
British Columbia	13	19	20	17	22	21

* 20 percent of respondents did five or more out of ten washloads in cool or cold water.

N = 1,800.

Source: Tracking study.

page 638). First, it was easier on or better for clothes in that cold water stopped shrinkage, prevented colors from running, let colors stay bright, and was easier on clothes. Second, it was more economical in that it saved energy, was cheaper, saved hot water, and saved electricity. Households in Quebec and the Maritimes mentioned the "economy" benefits more frequently, whereas households in the rest of Canada mentioned the "easier/better" benefit more often.

Arctic Power

Having achieved reasonable success in eastern Canada and having returned the brand to profitability, Linda Barton, Product Manager for Arctic Power, decided, for 1986, to increase the brand's share in Alberta and British Columbia. The brand plan is reported below.

EXHIBIT 4

Most Important Benefit of Cold Water Washing, 1986

Reason	National	Maritimes	Quebec	Ontario	Man./Sask.	Alta.	B.C.
Stops shrinkage	22.7%*	19.4%	5.2%	32.7%	35.4%	35.4%	30.2%
Saves energy	16.5	12.5	32.1	8.2	2.1	9.9	12.9
Prevents colors from running	11.6	17.4	0.0	21.8	21.3	9.9	2.9
Cheaper	11.1	19.4	10.4	10.2	2.8	9.3	16.5
Saves hot water	9.7	9.7	15.5	6.8	11.3	3.1	3.6
Colors stay bright	8.8	4.2	7.8	11.6	9.2	6.8	7.9
Saves on electricity	8.7	19.4	0.5	8.2	5.7	16.1	25.9
Easier on clothes	8.5	11.1	6.7	8.8	10.6	13.7	5.0

* When asked what they felt was the most important benefit of cold water washing, 22.7 percent of all respondents said, "It stops shrinking." Sample included all households that washed one or more times out of last ten washes in cold water.

N = 956.

Only the eight most frequent responses are reported.

Source: Tracking study.

■ THE 1986 BRAND PLAN FOR ARCTIC POWER

Objectives

Arctic Power's overall objective is to continue profit development by maintaining modest unit-volume growth in Quebec and the Maritimes while developing the Alberta and British Columbia regions.

Long Term (by 1996) The long-term objective is to become the number three brand in the category with market share of 12 percent. Arctic Power will continue to deliver a minimum 18 percent contribution margin. This will require

1. maintenance of effective creative/media support,
2. superior display prominence particularly in the key Quebec market,
3. continued investigation of development opportunities, and
4. cost-of-goods savings programs where possible.

Short Term The short-term objective is to sustain unit growth while building cold water washing dominance. This will require current user reinforcement and continued conversion of warm water users. Specifically, in fiscal 1986, Arctic Power will achieve a market share of 6.5 percent on factory sales of $22 million and a contribution margin of 18 percent. Regional share objectives are Maritimes—6.3 percent, Quebec—17.2 percent, Alberta—5 percent, and British Columbia—5 percent.

Marketing Strategy

Arctic Power will be positioned as the most effective laundry detergent that is especially formulated for cold water washing. The primary target for Arctic Power is women 18 to 49 and skewed toward the 25 to 34 segment. The secondary market is all adults.

Arctic Power will defend its franchise by allocating regional effort commensurate with brand development in order to maintain current users. In line with the western expansion strategy, support will be directed to Alberta and British Columbia in promoting the acceptance of cold water washing in those areas and thereby broadening the appeal among occasional and nonusers of Arctic Power.

Media Strategy

The media strategy objective is to achieve high levels of message registration against the target group through high message continuity and frequency/reach. Media spending allocation for regional television will be 75 percent on brand maintenance and 25 percent on investment for brand and cold water market development. Arctic Power will retain its number five share of media expenditure position nationally while being the number three detergent advertiser in Quebec.

		TV Spending	GRPs* per Week
1985	Plan	$1,010,000	92
	Actual	$ 990,000	88
1986	Plan	$1,350,000	95

* GRP (gross rating points) is a measurement of advertising impact derived by multiplying the number of persons exposed to an advertisement by the average number of exposures per person.

Arctic Power's 1986 media spending of $1.35 million is a 36 percent increase over 1985. This returns Arctic Power to its reach objective of 90 percent in Quebec, five points ahead of a year ago. In addition, two new television markets have been added with enhanced support in British Columbia and Alberta. Reach objectives will be achieved by skewing more of Arctic Power's spending into efficient daytime spots, which cost less than night network and are more flexible in light of regional reach objectives.

Scheduling will maintain flighting established in 1985 with concentrations at peak dealing time representing 40 weeks on-air in the east and 32 weeks in the west.[1]

Copy Strategy: Quebec/Maritimes

The creative objective is to convince consumers that Arctic Power is the superior detergent for cold water washing. The consumer benefit is that when washing in cold water, Arctic Power will clean clothes and remove stains more effectively than other detergents. The support for this claim is based on the special formulation of Arctic Power. The executional tone will be humorous but with a clear, rational explanation (Exhibit 5).

Copy Strategy: British Columbia/Alberta

The creative objective is to convince consumers that cold water washing is better than hot and to use Arctic Power when washing in cold water. The consumer benefit is that cold water washing reduces shrinkage, color run, and energy costs. The executional tone needs to be distinct from other detergent advertising in order to break through traditional washing attitudes and to do so will be young adult-oriented, light, "cool," and up-beat (Exhibit 6 on page 642).

Consumer Promotions

The objective of consumer promotions in Quebec and the Maritimes is to increase the rate of use by building frequency of purchase among existing users. The objective in B.C. and Alberta is to increase the rate of trial of Arctic Power. In total, $856,000 will be spent on consumer promotions.

Jan.	$0.50 In-pack Coupon—to support trade inventory increases and retain current customers in the face of strong competitive activity 400,000 coupons will be placed in all sizes in the Quebec and Maritimes distribution region. The coupon is for 6 L or 12 L sizes and expected redemption is 18 percent at a cost of $50,000.
April	To generate a 17 percent recent trial of regular-sized boxes of Arctic Power in B.C. and in Alberta a 500 mL salable sample prepriced at $0.49 will be distributed through food and drug stores. In addition, a $0.50 coupon for the 6 L or 12 L size will be placed on the pack of all samples. The offer will penetrate 44 percent of households in the region at a total cost of $382,000.
June	$0.40 Coupon through Free Standing Insert—to sustain interest and foster trial a $0.40 coupon will be delivered to 30 percent of homes in Alberta and B.C. The coupon is redeemable on the 3 L size and expected redemption is 4.5 percent at a cost of $28,000.
April/July	Game: Cool-by-the-Pool—five in-ground pools with patio accessories will be given away through spelling POWER by letters dropped in boxes of Arctic Power. Two letters will be placed in each box through national distribution and will coincide with high trade activity and the period in which the desirability of the prizes is highest at a cost of $184,000.

---

[1] Periodic waves of advertising, separated by periods of low activity (as opposed to continuous advertising).

EXHIBIT 5

Quebec Campaign

Arctic Power . . . is made to
work in cold water . . . some
detergents are not . . .

Look . . . Arctic Power

. . . is formulated to release
more power and energy in cold
water

. . . some detergents are
formulated to

. . . work well in hot water

. . . but

. . . put them in

. . . cold and they start to
freeze up

In cold water . . . it makes a
difference which detergent you
use . . . you want clean like this

. . . and bright like this

Look for a pack like this

. . . and you'll get more power
in cold water.

Sept. $0.75 Direct Mail National Coupon Pack (excluding Ontario)—to maximize
swing buyer volume (from competition) in Quebec and encourage trial in
the West a $0.75 coupon for the 6 L or 12 L size will be mailed to 70 percent
of households in the primary market areas, generating a 3 percent redemption rate at a cost of $212,000.

Trade Promotions

The objectives of the trade promotions are to maintain regular and feature pricing
equal to Tide and encourage prominent shelf facing. An advertising feature is expected from each key account during every promotion event run in Quebec and the
Maritimes. Distribution for any size is expected to increase to 95 percent. In the

EXHIBIT 6

Western Campaign

CLIENT: COLGATE PALMOLIVE
PRODUCT: Arctic Power
TITLE: "Cool It"
LENGTH: 30 Sec. TV

SINGERS: No!

Cool it.
Cool it.

Get some Arctic Power and
cool it.

Cold water washing that's the
way.

Up to date people save money
today . . .

they cool it.
Cool it.

Get some Arctic Power and
cool it.

You get less shrink.

You get less run.

And the laundry looks great
when you get it all done.

So cool it.
Cool it.

Get some Arctic Power and
cool it.

west, maximum effort will be directed at establishing display for the 6 L size, and four feature events will be expected from each key account. Distribution should be developed to 71 percent in B.C. and 56 percent in Alberta. Average deal size will be 14 percent off regular price or $5 per 6 L case. In addition, most trade events will include a $1 per case allowance for co-op advertising and merchandising support. The total trade budget is $3.46 million, which includes $1 million investment spending in the west. The promotion schedule is shown below.

Arctic Power 1986 Promotional Schedule

Trade Promotions	Jan.	Feb.	Mar.	Apr.	May	Jun.	Jul.	Aug.	Sep.	Oct.	Nov.	Dec.
Maritimes	X			X		X			X		X	
Quebec	X	X		X		X	X		X		X	X
Alberta/B.C.	X			X		X		X	X			
East $0.50 coupon	X	X										
West sample/ coupon				X								
West $0.40 coupon						X						
National game			X	X	X	X						
National $0.75 coupon									X			

Results of the Western Campaign

In August of 1986, during the middle of the western campaign, a "mini-tracking" study was conducted in the two provinces to monitor the program. The results of the August study were compared with the February study. (Both studies are reported in Exhibit 7 on page 644.) Market share for Arctic Power was also measured on a bi-monthly basis and the figures are shown below.

The campaign clearly had an impact—brand and advertising awareness had increased, particularly in Alberta (Exhibit 7). Brand trial within the six months had more than doubled in Alberta and was up over 25 percent in B.C. However, market share had peaked at 2.8 percent in Alberta and by the end of the year had declined to 1.9 percent. Market share in B.C. had reached a high of 7.3 percent and averaged 5.5 percent for the year.

Arctic Power Market Share

	1983	1984	1985	D/J	F/M	A/M	J/J	A/S	O/N	Total 1986
						1986				
Alberta	0.7	2.3	1.7	1.4	1.1	2.8	2.8	2.4	1.9	2.1
B.C.	3.2	4.0	3.9	4.0	4.0	6.1	6.1	7.3	5.4	5.5

In attempting to explain the different results in the two provinces, Linda Barton and Gary Parsons isolated two factors. First, B.C. had always been a "good" market for Arctic Power, with share figures around 4 percent, whereas Alberta was less than half that amount. Second, there had been a considerable amount of competitive ac-

E X H I B I T   7

Results of Western Campaign

	Prelaunch (February 1986)		Postlaunch (August 1986)	
	Alberta	*B.C.*	*Alberta*	*B.C.*
Unaided Brand Awareness[a]				
Brand mentioned total (%)	13.3	20.3	18.1	24.2
Advertising Awareness				
Advertising mentioned (unaided)[b] (%)	1.9	7.9	20.3	11.5
Advertising mentioned (aided)[c] (%)	18.5	27.9	31.4	34.6
Brand Trial				
Ever tried[d] (%)	25.0	43.0	36.3	48.0
Used (last six months)[e] (%)	6.8	15.1	17.1	19.4
Image Measure[f]				
Cleaning and removing dirt	1.0	1.2	1.2	1.5
Removing tough stains	.7	.9	.9	1.4
Being good value for the price	.5	.9	1.0	1.4
Cleaning well in cold water	1.2	1.3	1.7	1.8
Conversion to Cold Water				
Average number of loads out of 10 washed in cold water	1.8	2.2	2.0	2.3

[a] *Question*: When you think of laundry detergents, what three brands first come to mind? Can you name three more for me? *Brand Mentioned Total* is if the brand was mentioned at all. On average, respondents mentioned 4.5 brands.

[b] *Question*: What brand or brands of laundry detergent have you seen or heard advertised? *Advertising Mentioned (Unaided)* is any mention of brand advertising mentioned.

[c] *Question*: Have you recently seen or heard any advertising for *Brand? Advertising Mentioned (Aided)* is if respondent said yes when asked.

[d] *Question*: Have you ever tried *Brand*?

[e] *Question*: Have you used *Brand* in the past six months?

[f] Respondents rated the brand on the four image measures. The rating scale ranged from −5 (doesn't perform well) to +5 (performs well).

Source: Tracking study.

tivity in Alberta during the year. Each of the three major firms had increased trade and consumer promotions to maintain existing brand shares.

■ ARCTIC POWER—1987

The 1987 brand plan for Arctic Power was similar in thrust and expenditure levels to the 1986 plan. Expenditure levels in Alberta were reduced until the full implications of the 1986 campaign could be examined. Market share in 1987 was expected to be 6.7 percent up marginally from the 6.5 percent share achieved in 1986 (Exhibit 8).

Each year, every product manager at CPC conducted an extensive brand review. The review for Arctic Power included a detailed competitive analysis of the four leading brands on a regional basis and was based primarily on the tracking study. In July 1987, Linda Barton and Gary Parsons were examining the tracking information which summarized regional information on four critical aspects of the market—

E X H I B I T   8

Arctic Power Market Share and Total Volume by Region, 1983–1987E

| Region | Market Share | | | | | 1986 Total Volume* (Liters in Thousands) |
	1983	1984	1985	1986	1987E	
Maritimes	5.3	5.7	6.3	6.3	6.3	32,616
Quebec	12.3	13.8	17.7	17.5	18.0	113,796
Ontario	.9	1.1	1.1	.8	1.0	158,508
Manitoba/Saskatchewan	.2	.2	.1	.1	.1	28,440
Alberta	.7	2.3	1.7	2.1	2.0	40,644
British Columbia	3.2	4.0	3.9	5.5	6.0	32,508

1987E = Estimated.

* All laundry detergents.

brand image (Exhibit 9 on page 646), brand and advertising awareness (Exhibit 10 on page 647), brand trial and usage in past six months (Exhibit 11 on page 648), and market share and share of media expenditures (Exhibit 12 on page 649). Future decisions for Arctic Power would be based, in large part, on this information.

■ THE DECISION

Prior to deciding on the strategic direction for Arctic Power, Ms. Barton and Mr. Parsons met to discuss the situation. It was a hot Toronto day in early July 1987. Ms. Barton began the discussion. "I've got some estimates on what our shares are likely to be for 1987. It looks like we'll have a national share of 6.7 percent, broken down as follows: Maritimes (6.3 percent), Quebec (18 percent), Ontario (1 percent), Manitoba/Saskatchewan (0.1 percent), Alberta (2 percent), B.C. (6 percent)."

Mr. Parsons responded, "I think our problem in Alberta was all the competitive activity. Under normal conditions we'd have achieved 5 percent of that market. But the Alberta objective is small when you think about what we could do in our other undeveloped markets. I've been giving it a lot of thought, and we should go national with Arctic Power. We've got a brand that is equal to Tide and we've got to stop keeping it a secret from the rest of Canada. If we can duplicate our success in B.C., we'll turn this market on its ear."

"Wait a minute, Gary," said Ms. Barton. "In 1986 we spent almost $2 million on advertising and consumer and trade promotions in the west. Even though spending returned to normal levels this year, that was a big investment to get the business going, and it will be at least four years before we get that money back. If we go after the national market, you can well expect Tide to fight back with trade spending which will make our share or margin objectives even harder to achieve. On a per capita basis we'd have to spend at least as much in our underdeveloped markets as we spent in the west. We've got a real problem here. Our brand may be as good as Tide, but I don't think we can change a lot of consumers' minds, particularly the loyal Tide users. I hate to say it, but for many Canadians, when they think about washing clothes, Tide is the brand they think will clean their clothes better than any other brand. I agree that the size of the undeveloped market warrants another look. But remember, any decision will have to be backed up with a solid analysis and a plan that senior management will buy."

EXHIBIT 9

Brand Images by Region, 1986

Image Measure	National	Maritimes	Quebec	Ontario	Man./Sask.	Alberta	B.C.
Arctic Power							
• Cleaning and removing dirt	1.4	2.0	2.5	0.8	0.4	1.0	1.2
• Removing tough stains	1.1	1.6	1.9	0.7	0.3	0.7	0.9
• Being good value for the price	1.1	1.4	2.6	0.3	0.2	0.5	0.9
• Cleaning well in cold water	1.6	2.1	2.8	1.0	0.4	1.2	1.3
ABC							
• Cleaning . . . dirt	1.0	1.9	0.5	0.9	1.1	1.2	1.6
• Removing . . . stains	0.5	1.1	0.0	0.6	0.8	0.7	0.9
• Being . . . price	1.5	2.4	0.8	1.5	1.3	1.7	2.1
• Cleaning . . . cold water	0.6	1.0	0.1	0.7	0.7	0.7	0.7
Sunlight							
• Cleaning . . . dirt	2.0	1.9	1.8	2.4	1.9	1.6	1.6
• Removing . . . stains	1.6	1.6	1.5	1.9	1.4	1.2	1.2
• Being . . . price	2.0	1.7	1.9	2.4	1.8	1.7	1.5
• Cleaning . . . cold water	1.4	1.1	1.5	1.7	1.2	1.1	0.7
Tide							
• Cleaning . . . dirt	3.4	3.7	3.2	3.6	3.5	3.3	3.2
• Removing . . . stains	3.0	3.1	2.8	3.3	3.0	2.7	2.7
• Being . . . price	3.1	3.1	3.3	3.1	2.8	3.0	2.4
• Cleaning . . . cold water	2.4	2.3	2.6	2.5	2.4	2.3	1.9

Respondents rated each brand on the four image measures. The rating scale ranged from −5 (doesn't perform well) to +5 (performs well).

N = 1816.

A difference of 0.2 is likely to be significant in statistical terms.

Source: Tracking study.

EXHIBIT 10

Brand and Advertising Awareness by Region, 1986

	Percentages						
	National	Maritimes	Quebec	Ontario	Man./Sask.	Alberta	B.C.
Unaided Brand Awareness[a]							
1. Brand Mentioned First							
Arctic Power	4.4	7.0	12.5	.0	.0	1.0	2.6
ABC	8.1	18.4	4.6	7.3	4.7	8.4	12.8
Sunlight	9.3	8.4	9.6	9.3	12.0	9.1	7.9
Tide	57.9	55.5	41.9	69.7	63.1	59.7	54.4
2. Brand Mentioned Total							
Arctic Power	23.0	43.5	49.8	5.0	3.0	13.3	20.3
ABC	61.3	82.6	47.9	64.0	56.1	67.5	64.9
Sunlight	58.1	60.2	50.8	65.0	58.5	62.0	46.6
Tide	94.8	95.7	88.8	98.0	97.3	97.4	94.4
Advertising Awareness							
1. Advertising Mentioned (Unaided)[b]							
Arctic Power	7.0	10.7	17.5	.7	.0	1.9	7.9
ABC	25.2	32.8	20.8	27.0	17.3	30.5	24.9
Sunlight	8.6	4.7	5.9	13.0	5.0	6.8	8.2
Tide	44.0	40.1	32.7	55.0	46.2	48.4	35.4
2. Advertising Mentioned (Aided)[c]							
Arctic Power	29.2	38.8	55.1	15.3	5.6	18.5	27.9
ABC	56.1	61.5	55.1	56.0	51.5	60.4	53.4
Sunlight	29.9	20.1	26.4	40.3	21.3	21.1	24.9
Tide	65.3	60.9	54.8	78.0	68.1	65.3	48.4

[a] *Question*: When you think of laundry detergents, what three brands first come to mind? Can you name three for me? *Brand Mentioned First* is the first brand mentioned. *Brand Mentioned Total* is if the brand was mentioned at all. On average, respondents mentioned 4.5 brands.

[b] *Question*: What brand or brands of laundry detergent have you seen or heard advertised? *Advertising Mentioned (Unaided)* is any mention of brand advertising mentioned.

[c] *Question*: Have you recently seen or heard any advertising for *Brand*? Advertising Mentioned (Aided) means respondent said yes when asked.

N = 1816.

Source: Tracking study.

EXHIBIT 11

Brand Trial and Used in Past Six Months by Region, 1986

Brand Trial	National	Maritimes	Quebec	Ontario	Man./Sask.	Alberta	B.C.
1. Ever tried[a]							
Arctic Power	42.4	67.9	75.6	19.7	20.3	25.0	43.0
ABC	60.4	83.9	50.8	60.0	53.5	62.7	67.9
Sunlight	66.3	65.6	59.4	75.0	67.1	58.1	58.7
Tide	93.6	91.0	90.1	97.3	95.0	91.9	92.1
2. Used (past six months)[b]							
Arctic Power	19.4	29.8	46.5	4.3	2.3	6.8	15.1
ABC	37.2	56.2	34.7	32.3	29.2	39.3	47.5
Sunlight	38.3	29.8	38.0	44.3	36.2	36.7	28.5
Tide	68.1	66.6	66.0	73.3	67.8	69.5	54.8

[a] *Question:* Have you ever tried *Brand?*

[b] *Question:* Have you used *Brand* in the past six months?

Note: On average, respondents had 1.3 brands of laundry detergents in the home.

N = 1816.

Source: Tracking study.

EXHIBIT 12

Market Share and Share of Media Expenditures by Region, 1986

				Percentages			
	National	Maritimes	Quebec	Ontario	Man./Sask.	Alberta	B.C.
Market Share							
Arctic Power	6.5	6.3	17.5	.8	.1	2.1	5.5
ABC	13.9	27.8	8.6	13.8	11.6	16.1	21.5
Sunlight	13.4	7.7	12.1	16.4	14.2	10.4	11.3
Tide	34.1	24.5	28.3	39.3	40.0	36.9	28.5
All other brands	32.1	33.7	33.5	29.7	34.1	34.5	33.2
Total	100.0	100.0	100.0	100.0	100.0	100.0	100.0
Share of Media Expenditures[a]							
Arctic Power	9.3	13.1	16.1	.5	1.4	16.0	13.1
ABC	13.6	14.7	9.1	18.4	17.3	12.1	12.1
Sunlight	11.3	11.1	11.1	12.6	10.2	10.1	9.8
Tide	29.7	27.8	25.1	33.1	38.1	30.2	28.7
All other brands	36.1	33.3	38.6	35.4	33.0	31.6	36.3
Total	100.0	100.0	100.0	100.0	100.0	100.0	100.0
Total $ ('000)	$14,429	$ 695	$4,915	$4,758	$ 928	$1,646	$1,487

[a] The total amount of advertising spent by all brands was determined. The amount spent by each brand as a percentage of total spending was calculated.

Source: Company records.

"I know that even if I am right it will be a tough sell," Mr. Parsons replied. "I haven't got it completed yet, but I'm working out the share level we will need to break even if we expanded nationally."

Ms. Barton responded, "Well, when you get that done, we will talk about national expansion again. For the moment we have to resolve this positioning dilemma. I don't like a two-country approach, but it does seem to make sense in this case. I think we might still want to focus on the brand in the east and continue to develop the cold water washing market in the west."

Mr. Parsons would have preferred to continue the discussion of national expansion but realized he would have to do some work and at least produce the share estimate before he raised the subject again and so replied, "I agree that Canada is not one homogeneous market, but that perspective can be taken to extremes. I worry that all of the data we get on the regional markets is getting in the way of good marketing judgment. I prefer a unified strategy, and the Quebec campaign has a proven track record."

"Let's go over the data again, then start making our decisions," Ms. Barton concluded. "Remember, our goal is to develop a solid brand plan for 1988 for Arctic Power."

FEMSA Cerveza
SOL in the UK

In October 1994, Señor Victor Padilla, the Export Director for Cerveceria Cuauhtemoc Moctezuma (FEMSA Cerveza) was reviewing the most recent report on the brewery's European export volumes. He was particularly concerned about the collapse in exports to the United Kingdom (U.K.). The U.K. represented FEMSA Cerveza's second largest export market after the United States (U.S.), and was a critical element of the company's export strategy which sought to use export markets to protect or even increase the company's revenues. Because of the high fixed costs inherent in the brewing industry, one determinant of a brewer's success was its ability to maintain high sales volumes that translated into large revenues.

Although FEMSA Cerveza exported two brands of beer to the U.K. (SOL and Dos Equis), Señor Padilla was particularly concerned by the recent collapse in the sales of the SOL brand. Although SOL had originally done very well in the U.K. (on a volume basis), more recently, sales had declined sharply.

Señor Padilla wondered whether sales volumes could be improved by repositioning the product. He knew that to do this would require a new marketing plan, in which advertising would likely play a prominent role. There was also the question of whether it would be necessary to change the packaging, the bottle, or the color and flavor of the beer. He was also worried about the distribution channels and whether or not the company's current distribution arrangement gave it access to its target market or the group it might wish to target should it decide to reposition the product. He also wondered whether it might be more prudent for FEMSA Cerveza to abandon the U.K. altogether and to focus on other European and global markets. The declining volumes were an indication that Mexican beer might have no future in the U.K. Señor Padilla set out to review information on the U.K. market, wondering what FEMSA Cerveza's next move should be.

■ FOMENTO ECONOMICO MEXICANO, S.A. DE C.V. (FEMSA)

Mexico had a rich history in the production and sale of beer. The first brewery established in North America was founded in Mexico on December 12, 1543, through a concession granted by the King of Spain to the Spanish conquistador Alonso de Herrera. In contrast, the first U.S. brewery was founded in 1623 in Manhattan, and the first Canadian brewery was founded in 1668 in Quebec City.

This case was prepared by David Ager under the supervision of Professor Carlos Ruy Martinez and Professor John Hulland of the Richard Ivey School of Business, Copyright © 1995, The University of Western Ontario.

From 1543 through to the late 1800s, many small breweries were established throughout Mexico, most in Mexico City or in the immediate area surrounding it. In 1890, Mexico's first large-scale brewery was constructed in Monterrey, Nuevo Leon. La Fabrica de Hielo y Cerveza Cuauhtemoc, S.A., was built at a cost of 100,000 pesos.

Over the next 10 years, Cerveceria Cuauhtemoc added several local businesses to support the brewing operation. In 1899, Cerveceria Cuauhtemoc established Vidrios y Cristales de Monterrey, S.A., to manufacture glass bottles. In 1900, Fierro y Acero (later named Fundidora Monterrey) was established to manufacture steel and other metals used in the bottling (bottle caps) and packaging divisions of the company. Cerveceria Cuauhtemoc also owned factories that produced malt, corrugated carton and paper, and it founded two banks—Banco de Nuevo Leon and Banco Mercantil—to help finance its investments.

In 1936, all the company's interests were consolidated under one holding company named Valores Industriales, S.A. (VISA). By 1994, VISA had become Mexico's fifth-largest publicly traded company. FEMSA was a sub-entity of VISA, responsible for VISA's food-related activities: the production and distribution of beer and soft drinks, and the production of packaging materials used mainly in the bottled beverage industry. FEMSA was organized into four divisions: Beer, Retail, Coca-Cola FEMSA, and Packaging (see Exhibit 1).

EXHIBIT 1

FEMSA Profile (All Figures in U.S. Dollars)

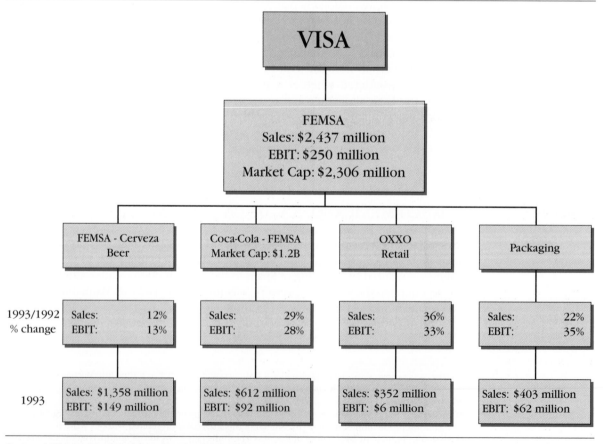

Source: A Winning North American Brewing Partnership.

EXHIBIT 2

Currency Exchange Rates, October 1994

	Canadian Dollars	U.S. Dollars	Mexican New Pesos	British Pounds
1 Canadian dollar	1.00	0.7416	2.5291	0.4689
1 U.S. dollar	1.3484	1.00	3.4094	0.6323
1 Mexican new peso	0.3954	0.2933	1.00	0.1854
1 British pound	2.1325	1.5815	5.3929	1.00

Source: *The Globe & Mail*, Thursday, October 13, 1994.

The Retail division was responsible for the management of OXXO convenience stores throughout Mexico. At the end of 1993, the company owned and operated over 700 of these stores, making it the leading operator of convenience stores in Mexico's retail sector. OXXO was also the leading distributor of beer, handling 2 percent of the total volume sold in Mexico. Unlike most other small retail operations, OXXO convenience stores offered a broad range of products and services to Mexican consumers.

Coca-Cola FEMSA was the largest Coca-Cola franchise in the world, and was responsible for the production and distribution of Coca-Cola, Sprite, and Fanta Orange throughout Mexico. The mission of the packaging division was to provide the Mexican beverage and food industries with containers and packages, at prices that were cost competitive at international levels. The packaging division's major products were beverage cans, crown bottle caps, glass bottles, labels, and cardboard boxes. The beer division, FEMSA Cerveza, was responsible for the production and distribution of beer throughout both Mexico and the rest of the world. FEMSA Cerveza's major brands in Mexico were Carta Blanca, Superior, Tecate, Tecate Light, XX Lager, Bohemia, SOL, Indio, and Heineken beers, which it distributed in Mexico on behalf of Heineken Breweries of Germany.

FEMSA Cerveza produced 20.4 million hL[1] of beer in the fiscal year ended December 31, 1993, although the division had the capacity to produce 24.4 million hL. The company operated an international beer division that exported beer to the U.S. and Europe, but more than 95 percent of its production continued to be sold in Mexico. The principal objectives of the export division were to generate volume for the company and to provide a source of foreign currency. The latter was important because some of the company's inputs needed to be acquired from outside the country. This, combined with the instability of the Mexican peso, created a need for FEMSA to develop a stable source of foreign currency.

FEMSA's consolidated net sales were N$7.571 billion[2] for fiscal year ended December 31, 1993, an increase of almost 7 percent over the previous fiscal year when consolidated sales totaled N$7.090 billion. The brewing division contributed N$4.089 billion in sales, up slightly from N$4.072 billion the previous year. FEMSA's net income for 1993 was N$684 million compared to N$552 in 1992.

---

[1] hL is the abbreviation for hectolitre. A hectolitre is equivalent to 100 litres, or 293 bottles of beer.

[2] N$ = New Peso. To help simplify foreign exchange transactions, the Mexican government introduced a new peso on January 1, 1993. The new peso was worth 1,000 of the old pesos. See Exhibit 2 for currency exchange rates between Mexico, Canada, the United States, and the United Kingdom in October 1994.

FEMSA Cerveza's Export Activities

FEMSA Cerveza operated an export division that distributed the company's products in over 55 countries around the world. FEMSA Cerveza's portfolio of brands of beer that it exported throughout the world was extensive. A list and description of the company's major export brands appears in Exhibit 3. Exhibit 4 presents the brewery's export volumes to England since 1986 and growth in volume, in percent, for selected European countries.

EXHIBIT 3

FEMSA Cerveza Brands Available for Export

Product	Description	Alcohol by Volume (Based on 12-oz Serving)
Tecate	First brewed in 1947	4.55%
	Traditionally served in a can topped with a squeeze of lime and a sprinkle of salt	
	Designed to quench big thirsts	
	Rated the #1 imported canned beer in the U.S. in 1994	
	Available in bottles	
Tecate Light	Brewed since 1992	4.10%
	Mexico's first low-calorie beer	
	Light beer with real flavor and character	
	A light extension of Tecate beer, one of Mexico's top-selling brands	
	Available in long-neck bottles and fluted, silver cans	
SOLI	Brewed since 1899	4.10%
	Golden lager beer with a smooth mellow flavor	
	Clear long-neck bottle with a painted-on label	
Bohemia	Brewed since 1900	4.80%
	A classic European-style lager beer	
	Full body, rich flavor	
Dos Equis	Brewed since 1900	4.75%
	Beautiful amber-colored beer with a rich, creamy head and smooth, mellow flavor	
	Excellent example of a traditional Vienna-style beer	
	#1 selling imported amber beer in the U.S.	
Dos Equis Special Lager	Brewed since 1983 Mellow tasting, refreshing, golden lager beer	4.45%
	Unique green glass bottle	

Source: FEMSA Cerveza marketing brochure, December 1994.

EXHIBIT 4

FEMSA Cerveza Export Volumes to the U.K. (Thousands of Cases)

	1986	1987	1988	1989	1990	1991	1992	1993	1994[a]
England	12	44	69	249	1,206	2,535	2,177	1,983	1,124

**FEMSA Cerveza Growth in Export Volumes
Selected Countries in Europe (Percent)**

	1991	1992	1993	1994[a]
France	41.3	110.3	1.7	22.5
Germany	58.8	101.9	11.9	33.1
Spain	n/a	n/a	121.4	35.5

[a] The 1994 figure is year-to-date as of the end of September 1994.

■ THE U.K. BREWING INDUSTRY

U.K. consumers spent £13.6 billion and consumed 35.3 million barrels[3] of beer in 1993. The U.K. beer industry employed 127,630 people in beer production, 9,650 in distribution, and 622,350 in the management and operation of clubs and pubs.

There were 65 brewers in the U.K., operating 95 breweries, although only nine of these were considered to operate nationally. The remainder were regional brewers, or in some cases local brewers that sold draught products to one or two small establishments. Draught beer was beer packaged and sold in a keg, drawn and delivered to the glass as needed. It was estimated that there were in excess of 1,000 brands of beer available in the U.K., although many were available exclusively in certain localities. The six largest brewers in the U.K. in 1994 were Bass, Allied, Grand Metropolitan, Whitbread, Scottish & Newcastle, and Courage. Collectively, these six brewers controlled over 75 percent of the market. This was unusual, because in many countries, such as Mexico and Canada, two national brewers controlled in excess of 90 percent of the domestic market.

Despite the appearance of a competitive environment, in reality the U.K. brewing industry had evolved into what had been termed a 'complex monopoly.' Brewers had vertically integrated their operations to include not only beer production but also wholesale and retail outlets for beer distribution. Through organization structures known as 'tied estates,' brewers owned and operated over 50 percent of all on-license[4] and less than 10 percent of all off-license[5] premises in the U.K. The tied relationship was most pervasive in the public house (pub) trade, the most preferred venue for the consumption of beer in the U.K., where nearly 75 percent of all pubs were owned by brewers.

Tied estates ranged in size from in excess of 7,000 establishments to as few as two. The tied relationship allowed brewers to control the products that were offered for sale and their prices, as well as the services, amenities, and appearances of the various premises. The result was that independent suppliers faced difficulties in mar-

---

[3] 1 barrel = 1.65 hectolitres.

[4] On-license refers to all outlets licensed to sell beer for consumption on the premises, including pubs (public houses), clubs, hotels, and restaurants.

[5] Off-license refers to all outlets licensed to sell beer to the take-home market (e.g., wine and spirits stores).

keting their products. Brewers were in turn able to keep prices high, resulting in higher margins and profits.

While beer was sold in several different formats in the U.K., draught had traditionally been the most preferred format. This phenomenon was the result of a long tradition of consuming beer in pubs. However, despite an overall increase in leisure spending in the U.K., pub-going had declined over the past four years and was expected to continue to do so in the future. With the deterioration in the U.K. economy in the early 1990s, many people had switched from consuming beer at the pub to consuming beer at home. Most of the beer consumed at home was packaged and was lower priced. The switch to at-home consumption had also led to a decline in overall consumption nationally, since the social environment of the pub led people to drink more than they would at home. Furthermore, although in a pub people generally seemed to prefer beer, at home some broadened their choices to include wine and spirits. Anti-drink-and-drive campaigns had also contributed to the decrease in beer consumption, which in 1993 was approximately 173 pints per head, down from 180 pints per head a year earlier.

Despite these trends, the on-license trade remained the predominant distribution segment for the consumption of beer in the U.K. In 1993, over 81 percent of all beer consumed in the U.K. was purchased at on-license establishments.

Imports

Imports represented approximately 6 percent of all beer consumed in the U.K.: Guinness from Ireland accounted for 3 percent, Holsten from Germany accounted for 1.5 percent, and 300 different brands competed for the remaining 1.5 percent or 529,825 barrels.[6] SOL and Dos Equis were among the 300 brands, representing FEMSA's key exports to the U.K.

The majority of imported beer was consumed in London and the southeast of the U.K., where over 25 percent of the population lived. This area of the U.K. was the site of most of the country's tourism and accounted for a disproportionate number of the country's fashion-conscious, urban professionals.

Most foreign beers available for sale in the U.K. were sold at premium prices and were lagers. Although they were of little significance in terms of market size, their general popularity with the U.K. consumer had increased, particularly with the fashion-conscious sector. Many had gained a foothold through the restaurant trade, including Kingfisher (India), Tiger (Singapore), and Dos Equis (Mexico), where customers expected to drink something exotic and authentic with their food.

Varieties of Beer

Several different types of beer were available in the U.K. The most common types were lager, ale, stout, and lite, with the latter not enjoying the same success in the U.K. as it had in the U.S. Lager was golden in color, clear and sparkling, with a crisper, more delicate flavor. The lager market in the U.K. was sub-divided into standard and premium. Generally, premium lagers had a higher alcohol content than standard lagers, although the increasingly competitive environment in the U.K. prompted some brewers to market what was technically a standard lager brand as a premium lager. More hops were added when brewing an ale, giving it a distinctive fruitiness, acidity, and a pleasantly bitter seasoning.[7] In all, ales had a more assertive, individual personality than lagers. Stouts were characterized by darkness and profundity, were either dry or sweet, and varied dramatically in alcohol content. Lite beers were low carbohydrate, low alcohol content beers.

---

[6] 1 barrel = 1.65 hectolitres and 1 hectolitre = 176 pints.

[7] Hops are one main ingredient in beer. The others are malt barley, yeast, and water.

■ BEER CONSUMPTION IN THE U.K.

The Pub

In the U.K., the pub had long been the preferred venue for the consumption of beer. In 1994, the major consideration for consumers in selecting a pub was its location. Consumers chose an outlet because it was close to home or work. Also, for many, visits to the pub were an opportunity to meet friends, and people often frequented their local (preferred establishment) to maintain social ties.

The largest segment of the pub-going population was between the ages of 18 and 34, and 61 percent of this segment had a preference for a particular locale (i.e., a regular establishment which they patronized). Exhibit 5 indicates the drink preferences of pub-goers, along with a more general profile of the drinking preferences of people in the U.K. Exhibit 6 on page 658 compares the popularity of the pub with other leisure activities.

The Lager Market

By 1993, the lager market in the U.K. had grown by 10 percent versus 1983, despite a 5 percent decrease in overall beer sales in the U.K. over the same period. Exhibit 7 on page 658 illustrates beer consumption in the U.K., by type, between 1983 and 1993. The lager market was broken down into five segments according to alcohol by volume (A.B.V.): No alcohol beer/Low alcohol beer (0%-1.2%); commodity lager (1.3%-3.3%); standard lager (3.4%-4.2%); premium lager (4.3%-7.5%); and super-strength lager (7.6%+). SOL was positioned and competed in the premium lager segment of the market.

Premium lager had increased in significance in the U.K. beer market from 20 to 30 percent of the lager market. Within the premium segment, the majority of growth had come from premium bottled lager versus canned or draught, which in 1988 represented 23 percent of the premium lager market and in 1993 represented 32 percent of the premium lager market.

EXHIBIT 5

Drink Preference of U.K. Pub-goers

	Men	*Women*
Beer	83%	37%
Spirits	10%	26%
Soft drinks	7%	37%

Source: The Brewer's Society.

Where People in the U.K. Go to Get a Beer

When?	Weekdays	Weekends
Where?	Local pub	Clubs
What?	Draught	Bottled beer (brands important)
Atmosphere?	Relaxed	Portable
	Smaller groups	Convenient
	Cheaper	Know what you're drinking
	Easygoing	Party atmosphere

Source: S. G. Warburg Securities Study on Pub Retailing, March 1994.

EXHIBIT 6

Most Popular Leisure Activities in the U.K. in 1992

Activity	% Who Visited at Least Once a Quarter
Pub	71%
Cinema	39%
Theatre	26%
Spectator sports event	23%

Source: S. G. Warburg Securities Study on Pub Retailing, March 1994.

The premium bottled lager market represented the fastest growing segment in the U.K. brewing industry, and was expected to represent 35 to 40 percent of all premium lager beer sales by the year 2000. As a result, there were many new entrants into this segment of the market, although over time very few survived. Those that did survive became stable brands and enjoyed high margins, high volumes, less diverse competition, and a long life.

A study of those brands that were considered to be stable and those products that were considered to be fads ("ephemeral") resulted in a set of characteristics for each group (see Exhibit 8).

Distribution was critical to the success of any brand in this segment of the market, particularly because of the tied estate arrangements. Exhibit 9 presents purchase trends for the off-license trade, and Exhibit 10 on page 660 presents purchase trends for the on-license trade in the U.K.

The Consumer

The premium bottled lager drinker was most often a male, between the ages of 18 and 35, whose leisure activities included cinema, shopping, and socializing in bars, clubs, and restaurants. This person was well dressed and groomed, and tended to watch television programs and read magazines that kept up with recent trends.

This individual had specific ideas about the various beer product types and formats available in the market. Draught beer was perceived as cheaper but low in taste, watery, weak, and bloating. Nonpremium bottled lager was perceived as reliable, but weak, low in taste, poor in value, and boring. Premium-bottled lager was perceived as being stronger and better flavored.

Beer that was consumed at home was purchased from off-license establishments such as liquor stores and supermarkets, where brand choice was usually influenced by consumer familiarity and special promotional offers. As well, cans were preferred over bottles because they offered better value and were more convenient.

EXHIBIT 7

Percentage Sales of All Beer Types in the U.K.

	1983	1988	1992	1993
Draught	76.5	73.3	69.5	68.5
Packaged	21.5	26.7	30.5	31.5
Total ale and stout	64.1	51.4	48.7	48.0
Total Lager	35.9	48.6	51.3	52.0

Source: Brewers and Licensed Retailers Association, London, U.K.

EXHIBIT 8

Characteristics of Beer Brands in the U.K. Market

Ephemeral	*Stable*
• Novelty	• Trusted
• Discreet	• Open
• Special	• Accessible
• One-off	• Original
• Fast burn	• Constant
• Commodity	• Brand
• Difficult	• Authentic
• Exotic	• Easy

Outside of the home, the predominant location of beer consumption for this group was the club. Here premium bottled lager was preferred for several reasons:

* It provided an alternative to draught beer that was less bloating, more refreshing, more reliable (unlike draught that could be watered down) and consistent, a cleaner drink less liable to yield a hangover.

* A bottle was much more convenient and practical than a drink in a glass for the crowded situations of clubs. The narrow mouth of a bottle reduced the amount spilled if the container was knocked over. A person could carry several by their narrow necks using hands and pockets, making it easier to buy a round for friends. They were safer, because typically the drinker held the bottle, instead of putting it down where it might get taken or knocked over.

EXHIBIT 9

Purchase Trends (Off-Trade—Great Britain, 1993)

Point of Purchase	Total Lager (%)	Premium Lager (%)	Premium Bottled Lager (%)	SOL (%)	Average Number of Brands Stocked[e]
Multiple grocers[a]	46.9	43.9	59.7	50.1	16.9
Multiple specialists[b]	20.4	27.7	22.7	29.5	12.4
Independent specialists[c]	10.9	12.4	8.1	12.5	8.5
Independent grocers[d]	16.9	13.2	7.2	6.7	5.4
Co-ops	5.0	2.8	2.3	1.2	7.2

[a] Operate more than five outlets.

[b] Operate more than five outlets and sell only alcohol.

[c] Operate fewer than five outlets.

[d] Operate fewer than five outlets and sell only alcohol.

[e] Brands refers to premium bottled lager brands.

Note: These data indicate, by percent, the volume of lager, premium lager, premium bottled lager, and SOL being purchased at each of the various off-trade segments. They also show the average number of premium bottled lager brands stocked by each of the off-trade distribution segments.

Source: STATS MR.

EXHIBIT 10

Purchase Trends (On-Trade—Great Britain, 1993)

Point of Purchase	Premium Priced Lager (%)	SOL (%)	Average Number of Brands Stocked[a]
Big 5[b]—managed	19.5	12.5	5.8
Big 5—nonmanaged	13.7	1.8	4.5
Regionals	13.7	3.8	3.4
Independent pubs	22.2	14.4	4.7
Clubs	14.4	2.7	2.6
Hotels	5.9	3.9	5.0
Other bars	7.9	15.1	4.7
Restricted (restaurants)	11.4	49.8	3.3

[a] Brands refers to premium bottled lager brands.

[b] Big 5 refers to the top five brewers in the U.K.

Note: These data indicate, by percent, the volume of premium priced lager and SOL being purchased at each of the various on-trade segments. They also show the average number of premium bottled lager brands stocked by each of the off-trade distribution segments.

Source: STATS MR.

- In clubs the customers were more quickly served at the bar because they did not need to wait for a tap to be free and the beer to be poured out.
- Bottles remained colder longer.
- Because bottled premium lager was stronger, it created the mood for socializing and dancing more quickly. The same intoxicating effect was achieved by drinking less volume, and the resulting decrease in bloating left the imbibers more comfortable for dancing.

Product and Brand Attributes

Alcoholic strength was seen as the most important attribute of premium bottled lager. Strength was what most drinkers first looked for when assessing a brand. Rather than looking for the Alcohol by Volume (A.B.V.) designation on the bottle, most people looked to other clues, in particular bottle color. Dark bottles were perceived to contain stronger beer than clear glass bottles, and brands in brown glass were perceived to be stronger than those in green glass.

Strength was viewed as important because beer was being drunk to relax and enliven the consumer, to get him or her into the right mood to cope with various social situations. Because premium bottled lager provided the same effect as draught or nonpremium bottled lager, with less volume, it could be consumed more quickly and with less bloating. Stronger beer was also thought to have a better taste and the higher strength justified the higher price. Finally, beer was being consumed primarily for intoxication; therefore, higher alcohol content delivered the desired benefit more quickly.

Although flavor was less important than strength to many beer consumers, it was more important to older drinkers and was used by all to discriminate between brands. Most drinkers were looking for a clean, crisp, smooth-tasting beer. The attribute drinkers liked least in terms of flavor was a weak or unpleasant aftertaste.

Price was a low priority except for beer bought to drink at home, in which case special offers could influence choice. Most U.K. club goers said that the point of going out was to have a good time and that they expected to pay for this. Cheap beer was thought to be a waste of money and likely to be weaker and poor in taste.

■ FEMSA CERVEZA PRODUCTS IN THE U.K.

Dos Equis

The first FEMSA Cerveza product available in the U.K. was Dos Equis. In the early 1980s, Cerveceria Moctezuma (which became part of FEMSA Cerveza in 1985 after it was merged with Cervecería Cuauhtemoc) was approached by an English person who had vacationed in Mexico, planned to open his own beer importing company in the U.K., and wanted to offer a Mexican beer as part of his product line.

Cerveceria Moctezuma granted this importer the exclusive right to import and sell Dos Equis in the U.K. As the volume of Dos Equis being sold in the U.K. increased, the importer sold his rights to Maison Caurette, a large alcoholic beverage distributor in London. Maison Caurette imported and distributed some beer products, although its primary strength was wine. As a result of this, its primary distribution strength was in the bar and club trade. In addition, Maison Caurette operated almost exclusively in the London area.

Dos Equis had maintained steady sales volumes in the U.K. since its 1982 introduction. FEMSA representatives believed that the beer was consumed by people who weren't trying to be different, who maintained a portfolio of beers from which they drank as opposed to those people who were loyal to one brand, and was mainly drunk when people went out to eat Mexican food. Advertising of Dos Equis was limited to on-premise promotions.

Market research had shown that the brand was relatively unknown, except in the occasional off-license establishment. Its Spanish-sounding name led many people to conclude that the product was from Spain. Finally, although people thought that the label looked dated and cheap, they also thought that the two Xs on the beer's label suggested strength.

SOL

In 1988, Maison Caurette approached FEMSA Cerveza looking for "something bigger for the UKs." It was at this time that a rival Mexican brewer's Corona brand was reaching the height of its popularity in the U.S. Maison Caurette explained that FEMSA Cerveza's SOL brand was sold in a clear bottle with a painted-on label, similar to the packaging of Corona. The U.K. distributor suggested that FEMSA should consider introducing SOL into the U.K. in order "to beat Corona to the punch." This recommendation made a great deal of sense, given that in the past whichever beer, SOL or Corona, had entered a particular market first, it subsequently retained the leadership position in that market. FEMSA Cerveza agreed to proceed, and in late 1988 the first cases of SOL arrived in the U.K.

The first task of Maison Caurette was to create brand awareness for SOL. The strategy used to introduce SOL to the U.K. was straightforward. Trend-setting venues in London were selected: winebars, brass clubs,[8] discos, and restaurants, places frequented by U.K. "Yuppies" and places with which Maison Caurette had an established relationship. On-premise promotions such as SOL parties, free T-shirts and caps, and happy hours with SOL were used to encourage patrons to try SOL.

---

[8] A brass club was a restaurant/bar that also provided an area for dancing.

The product was positioned as a distinctive, exotic, high-priced item. It was drunk out of a bottle with a wedge of lime positioned in the bottle's neck. In the U.K. market, SOL was a unique product and its price was integral to its image. Maison Caurette's management believed it was important for people to perceive SOL as:

> Something I can drink because I earn enough money to be able to pay the price for the product. This is a product that not everyone can afford.

In late 1989, the marketing strategy was intensified, and television advertisements teaching people how to drink the product were developed and aired almost exclusively in the London area. The Export Director commented:

> We did more advertising on the lime side than on the SOL side. In fact, I believe we sold more limes than beer.

The result was that SOL became equated with lime, and anyone who wanted a beer with a lime ordered a SOL.

Sales volumes in the U.K. began to increase rapidly in the early 1990s, with demand at times outstripping supply. In one extreme case, demand was so great that FEMSA Cerveza sent a full container of SOL by airplane from Mexico to the U.K. in order to avoid being unable to supply a key customer. Although the company had not undertaken any market research, the Export Director speculated that the principal reason for SOL's success in the U.K. was that the product was different. In fact, it was the only premium bottled lager available in a clear bottle. All other premium-priced lagers were available either in cans, or in green or brown glass bottles. In addition, SOL's introduction into the U.K. coincided with a movement among 18 to 35 year olds, who, having developed a mistrust of brewers in general, had abandoned traditional draught products and the pubs that their parents and grandparents frequented.

Advertising Proposals for SOL

By the end of 1993, the sales picture was much less encouraging. In response to declining sales volumes of SOL, in early 1994 FEMSA Cerveza hired a large global advertising agency to study the decline, and to help the company decide whether or not the product was salvageable. Furthermore, if SOL had a future in the U.K. market, the agency was asked to recommend to FEMSA Cerveza how it might go about restoring the product to its former glory.

The advertising agency undertook focus group studies to attempt to understand how SOL was perceived in the market. The following responses were those more commonly used to depict SOL:

Gimmicky	Feel like I'm drinking a Babycham
Yesterday's Fad	Not the beer to be seen drinking
Just another import	I only drink it at home
Weak	You don't hear about it anymore
Cocktail lager	Not as popular as it was two years ago when everyone drank it
A "soft" drink	You can only get it in certain bars
Drunk by "trendies"	I drink it when I can get it
For posers	

When questioned about the product, two London pub patrons commented on SOL:

> I got the mick taken out of me by my friends last night because I ordered a SOL.

> SOL is a bit superficial. It got really popular and people went away from it.

The advertising agency presented its findings to FEMSA executives, and both groups concluded that it was necessary to establish/reposition SOL less as a gimmick (i.e., something that was fashion oriented) and more as a stable brand in the premium bottled lager market. FEMSA's export group decided that they should highlight the following qualities of SOL in attempting to reposition the product: the beer was refreshing, light, easy-to-drink, it had a good, clean taste, and it came from a tropical country.

The advertising agency was convinced that it was possible to establish SOL as a stable brand within the premium bottled lager segment of the brewing industry. It had developed several advertising campaigns for television, scripts for which are found in Exhibit 11. The campaigns were intended to position SOL as a high-quality, premium product with a premium price, that was authentically Mexican.

EXHIBIT 11

Television Advertising Script

"THE USUAL"

Throughout this commercial, we would hear a swirling abstract piece of music that rises higher and higher in pitch and ends in cacophony.

This music accompanies a series of brightly colored surreal images that celebrate the unseen side of Mexico. As the pitch of the music gets higher and higher, the cuts between the images get faster and faster.
We see people in bizarre masks.

We see a shelf stacked with candy skulls.

We see a woman with live iguanas in her hair.

We see a man in a bizarre devil mask drinking a bottle of SOL.

We see two rattlesnakes fighting.

We see three Mexican Elvis impersonators.

We see a toothless old lady laughing.

We see an old bicycle turn a corner, mounted on the front is the stuffed head of a bull.

We see a cemetery at night with colorful gifts and candles placed on every grave.

We see a group of men dancing in skeleton suits.

We see two women in a bar, arm wrestling; people surround them drinking SOL.

We see a man dressed as a woman and wearing a crown.

We see a woman dressed as a man wearing another crown.

We see someone in a bar, clutching a bottle of SOL and grinning at us, displaying green teeth cut out of lime peel.

We see a 1962 Mercedes on fire.

We see a ghost.

We see people laughing as they try to lap some beer from a glass like a dog.

We see two wrestlers fighting in Mexican wrestling masks.

We see four young women dressed as angels.

The music stops and we cut to a title:
THE USUAL
We cut to a second title:
IN ORIZABA, MEXICO
We cut to a chilled bottle of SOL.

"BURRO"

This commercial is set outside a home in a Mexican suburb. Parked in the driveway is a well-kept classic American car. It's a very hot, dry day.
A Mexican man, aged 30 and dressed in normal everyday clothes, steps into frame. He holds a chilled, open bottle of SOL. He speaks directly to the camera:

EXHIBIT 11 *(continued)*

"BURRO" *(continued)*

"SOL is my favorite beer, the favorite beer of my father, and of *his* father."

He turns his head momentarily to look proudly at his bottle of beer, then looks back toward the camera:

"And for all you people who might want to be disrespectful towards it, we have a message for you."

We pull back to see the man is standing in front of two other men. Behind him on his left is an old man. Behind him on his right is an extremely old man. They begin to sing along to a rhythm played on a guitar, while performing an awkward little dance routine.

They sing:

"If you don't like the beer, kiss my burro . . ."

We cut to the face of the old man singing the last three words:

"If you don't like the beer, kiss my burro . . ."

We cut back to the men dancing, then we see the last three words sung by the young man:

"If you don't like the beer, kiss my burro . . ."

We cut back to the men dancing. This time we see the last three words sung by the oldest man.

The music stops, and we return to a close-up of the face of the youngest Mexican, who toasts us with a bottle of SOL and says:

"Remember, hombre, it's not what you think of the beer, it's what the beer thinks of you."

We say: Brewed in Orizaba, Mexico, since 1899.

"SCORPION"

In this commercial we open on a hot day outside the SOL brewery in Mexico. A worker is stacking boxes of SOL. He accidentally knocks one of them over. The box drops onto its side and the top falls open. We see a close-up of a big black scorpion scuttling across the dust and into the open box. The man, unaware, carries on stacking. Then, noticing the fallen box, he rights it, seals it, and casually places it with the other boxes.

We cut to the boxes on a dockside in Mexico waiting to be loaded onto a ship.

Then we see the boxes unloaded at a British port, and cut to them on a truck being driven down a motorway.

We then see a close-up of a single box of SOL. It's now open and resting on the bar of a typical English pub. A man is taking the bottles out two by two and putting them onto the cool shelf behind the bar. From a view inside of the box, we see his hand coming in, reaching for bottles. Two by two the bottles come out until eventually it's completely empty.

We move to a view of the pub at night. It's very busy. We see the barman's hand reach up to the shelf above the bar. We see a close-up of his fingers fumbling to reach a glass and see that his hand is about an inch away from a big, black scorpion. It's alive and well and watching the man's hand. We cut to the scorpion's view of the pub. Its tail twitches slightly.

We cut to black and see the words: SOL. Imported from Orizaba, Mexico.

"SOL DESTROYING"

The commercial is set in the apartment of a 25-year-old man. It is stylish, but obviously male in its decor.

We open on a room of people.

We hear the sound of music and laughing voices so there is obviously a party going on.

We view the action through a camera's-eye view from the floor looking skyward. The camera is focused close-up—the distant images appear out of focus.

We span the room and see the images of people.

We focus on a man whose arm comes into focus as his hand reaches out to a table and picks up and drinks from a bottle of beer. As he replaces the almost full bottle, it misses the edge and falls.

We focus on a bottle of SOL and follow it closely as it falls to the floor.

Dramatically, it explodes in slow motion just before it hits the camera.

We freeze the picture on the shattered glass.

On a fragment of it we can clearly make out the word SOL.

Alongside this word DESTROYING fades up.

EXHIBIT 11 (*continued*)

"SOL DESTROYING" (*continued*)

Followed by a voice over:
MEXICAN BORN AND BREWED SINCE 1899.

"SOL SURVIVOR"

The commercial opens on a smoke-filled room.

Dust fills the screen. We hear two men coughing.

As the dust clears we see an old-fashioned fridge charred and covered in soot.

A dirty hand opens the fridge to reveal a single bottle covered in white dust. The light in the fridge flickers as the hand brushes off the dust to reveal the SOL label.

The bottle is removed. We hear it being opened off screen and one of the men says, "Don't ever, ever do that again . . ."

The bottle is put into the screen again, a drink having been taken. Alongside the word SOL on the bottle the word SURVIVOR fades up.

This is followed by a voice-over:
MEXICAN BORN AND BREWED SINCE 1899.

"SOL WITNESS"

It's midnight and we're in a darkened room. The only light creeps through some slatted blinds and onto a woman's hands. She is slowly, deliberately removing black leather gloves. A lone cello or violin is playing a single, menacing tone.

She is being watched. We don't know by whom or by what, but whoever or whatever it is can see her shape distorted through a drinking glass.

She drops her glove into her bag, snaps it shut, and leaves. Odd that. Don't most people put on gloves when they leave?

A drink cabinet moves slowly and slightly ajar. The light from within illuminates the edge of a bottle. The door opens a little bit more to reveal a bottle of SOL. It's almost as if the bottle is peeking out of the cabinet.

Alongside the word SOL on the bottle, the word WITNESS fades up on the screen.

This is followed by a voice-over:
MEXICAN BORN AND BREWED SINCE 1899.

However, soon after viewing these proposals, FEMSA management in Mexico decided to discontinue their relationship with the advertising agency and these advertising campaigns were never used. Instead, they decided that they would conduct market research on the SOL brand in-house, and, provided that their research indicated a future for SOL in the U.K., they would work with a new advertising company to develop an appropriate campaign for SOL.

Results of In-house Market Research

The in-house marketing research indicated that SOL was a well-known, previously trendy brand, widely consumed four years earlier. SOL was still closely associated with the quarter of lime that was its trademark. However, the decline in awareness because of lack of promotion and distribution had become critical as the number of alternative brands available in the market continued to increase.

Although most people believed that SOL originated from Mexico, or possibly Spain, this fact appeared to be an unimportant component of its personality. In terms of the future viability of the product, greater importance was given to its other characteristics: good tasting, crisp, clean, smooth, refreshing, low in gas (but not flat),

EXHIBIT 12

Brand Image (Males Only)

	Is a Clean, Tasty Beer (%)	Is a Smooth Beer (%)	Is Worth Paying Extra for (%)	Is Good Quality (%)	Is an Upmarket Beer (%)	Is Attractively Packaged (%)
SOL	7	12	7	13	16	12
Beck's	55	49	32	50	37	30
Budweiser	57	47	28	52	28	36
Dos Equis	4	2	5	1	7	4
Grolsch	17	14	20	26	20	24
Holsten Pils	17	13	14	19	14	12
Labatt's Ice	21	17	9	15	12	12
Michelob	14	10	12	18	20	15
Molson	8	9	8	12	11	12

Note: Sample size was 250.

Source: Moctezuma & Cuauhtemoc Imports Ltd.

light in character, lacking after-taste, and suitable for refreshment and intoxication. Exhibit 12 presents brand image data collected from male consumers by FEMSA regarding SOL and some of the other leading premium lagers in the premium bottled lager segment of the market. Exhibit 13 presents some brand image characteristics of SOL obtained through an informal survey of both males and females.

EXHIBIT 13

Image of SOL

	Gender		Age			
	Male (%)	Female (%)	18-22 (%)	23-27 (%)	28-31 (%)	32-34 (%)
I would drink with friends	22	20	30	22	14	19
Is an upmarket beer	16	16	17	17	16	13
Is always available where you drink	14	17	16	13	15	16
Is good quality	13	15	17	12	15	10
Is a smooth beer	12	18	14	13	13	15
Is attractively packaged	12	15	17	13	17	6
Is for people who know about good lager	9	9	8	7	9	11
Is a clean, tasty beer	7	11	11	7	4	12
Is worth paying extra for	7	8	5	5	10	8
Used to be fashionable	7	5	5	6	8	6
Is a "football" lager[a]	2	2	1	3	2	1

Note: Sample size was 250.

[a] A "football" lager is a beer that you would drink with friends while watching a football game.

Source: Moctezuma & Cuauhtemoc Imports Ltd.

EXHIBIT 14

Media Expenditure Index[a] (Premium Price Lagers—Great Britain)

Brand	1991	1992	1993	1994[b]
Beck's	12.3	4.7	2.3	11.5
Budweiser	66.0	98.4	98.6	100.0
Grolsch	24.8	18.5	8.3	20.6
Holsten	70.8	33.7	63.0	79.1
Kronenberg	n/a	54.8	22.6	18.8
SOL	13.8	6.6	5.1	5.4
Stella Artois	n/a	48.4	58.6	57.9

[a] Index is chosen so that Budweiser's spending in 1994 is equal to 100.

[b] 1994 numbers are an estimate based on figures as of October 1994.

Source: Moctezuma & Cuauhtemoc Imports Ltd.

The marketing research also revealed that a product's country of origin had relevance only when it was Northern Europe or the U.S., as both regions had a strong brewing reputation with the British.

Unfortunately, the British attributed no special significance to the fact that a beer originated from Mexico. They did not perceive the country as particularly attractive, but as exotic, lively, colorful, and offering popular and interesting Mexican food. The British also saw Mexico as poor and underdeveloped, as well as unclean and dangerous. The emphasis on the Mexican origin of a product might initially have intrigued consumers, but did little in the longer term to entice them to continue consuming the product.

Competitive Reaction

In the early 1990s, Corona had entered the U.K. market, but was not particularly successful since SOL had already established itself as the bottled Mexican beer in the U.K. Some U.K. brewers developed imitations of SOL, and marketed these brands as Mexican-type beer. However, according to FEMSA Cerveza, these brands met with little success.

EXHIBIT 15

Penetration Trends Index[a] for Premium Price Lager Brands (Great Britain—On Trade)

Brand	1991	1992	1993	1994[b]
Beck's	30.6	35.6	58.6	55.0
Budweiser	36.0	61.3	82.9	100.0
Grolsch	12.6	5.4	10.4	6.8
Holsten	112.2	106.0	87.8	85.1
Kronenberg	7.7	9.0	10.8	6.3
SOL	16.2	22.6	11.3	8.1
Stella Artois	7.7	9.0	13.5	18.5

[a] Index is chosen so that Budweiser's penetration in 1994 is equal to 100.

[b] 1994 numbers are an estimate based on figures as of October 1994.

Source: Moctezuma & Cuauhtemoc Imports Ltd.

As the popularity of premium bottled lager continued to increase, so did the number of products available to consumers. It was estimated that by the end of 1994, U.K. consumers would be able to choose from over 400 brands in this category of the market. Ten years earlier no more than four brands of premium bottled lager had been available. Competition for a place in this market segment was fierce, with millions of pounds sterling being spent annually on media. Exhibit 14 on page 667 presents a media expenditure index for the more prominent premium price lagers in the U.K. Exhibit 15 on page 667 presents a penetration index for the leading premium priced bottled lagers available in the U.K.

■ THE DECISION

SOL had experienced some trying times after its entry into the U.K. brewing market, which was the world's most dynamic and competitive beer market. After having reviewed the information presented to him, Señor Padilla concluded that future opportunities existed in the U.K. for SOL, but realized that success would not come easily. With so many companies from around the world competing for a small fraction of this market, Señor Padilla knew that FEMSA Cerveza would need to develop a sophisticated marketing strategy if it planned to earn a permanent place for its SOL brand among U.K. beer consumers. As he studied the material that had been collected over the previous months, he recognized that there were a number of different ways in which he could proceed. Specifically, he needed to decide how he would position the brand; what characteristics of SOL, if any, he would modify; what new distribution channels, if any, he should pursue; and finally, what type of advertising and promotional campaign would be necessary in order to give U.K. consumers a reason to once again buy SOL.

Blair Water Purifiers India

"A pity I couldn't have stayed for Diwali," thought Rahul Chatterjee. "But anyway it was great to be back home in Calcutta." The Diwali holiday and its festivities would begin in early November 1996, some two weeks after Chatterjee had returned to the United States. Chatterjee worked as an international market liaison for Blair Company, Inc. This was his eighth year with Blair Company and easily his favorite. "Your challenge will be in moving us from just dabbling in less developed countries (LDCs) to our thriving in them," his boss had said when Chatterjee was promoted to the job last January. Chatterjee had agreed and was thrilled when asked to visit Bombay and New Delhi in April. His purpose on that trip was to gather background data on the possibility of Blair Company entering the Indian market for home water purification devices. Initial results were encouraging and prompted the second trip.

Chatterjee had used his second trip primarily to study Indian consumers in Calcutta and Bangalore and to gather information on possible competitors. The two cities represented quite different metropolitan areas in terms of location, size, language, and infrastructure—yet both suffered from similar problems in terms of water supplied to their residents. These problems could be found in many LDCs and were favorable to home water purification.

Information gathered on both visits would be used to make a recommendation on market entry and on elements of an entry strategy. Executives at Blair Company would compare Chatterjee's recommendation to those from two other Blair Company liaisons who were focusing their efforts on Argentina, Brazil, and Indonesia.

■ INDIAN MARKET FOR HOME WATER FILTRATION AND PURIFICATION

Like most aspects of India, the market for home water filtration and purification took a good deal of effort to understand. Yet despite expending this effort, Chatterjee realized that much remained either unknown or in conflict. For example, the market seemed clearly a mature one, with four or five established Indian competitors fighting for market share. Or was it? Another view portrayed the market as a fragmented one, with no large competitor having a national presence and perhaps 100 small, regional manufacturers, each competing in just one or two of India's 25 states. Indeed, the market could be in its early growth stages, as reflected by the large number of product designs, materials, and performances. Perhaps with a next generation product and a world-class marketing effort, Blair Company could consolidate the market and stimulate tremendous growth—much like the situation in the Indian market for automobiles.

This case was written by Professor James E. Nelson, University of Colorado at Boulder. He thanks students in the Class of 1996 (Batch 31), Indian Institute of Management, Calcutta, for their invaluable help in collecting all data needed to write this case. He also thanks Professor Roger Kerin, Southern Methodist University, for his helpful comments in writing this case. The case is intended for educational purposes rather than to illustrate either effective or ineffective decision making. Some data as well as the identity of the company are disguised. Copyright © 1997 by James E. Nelson. Used with permission.

Such uncertainty made it difficult to estimate market potential. However, Chatterjee had collected unit sales estimates for a 10-year period for three similar product categories—vacuum cleaners, sewing machines, and color televisions. In addition, a Delhi-based research firm had provided him with estimates of unit sales for Aquaguard, the largest selling water purifier in several Indian states. Chatterjee had used the data in two forecasting models available at Blair Company along with three subjective scenarios—realistic, optimistic, and pessimistic—to arrive at the estimates and forecasts for water purifiers shown in Exhibit 1. "If anything," Chatterjee had explained to his boss, "my forecasts are conservative because they describe only first-time sales, not any replacement sales over the 10-year forecast horizon." He also pointed out that his forecasts applied only to industry sales in larger urban areas, which was the present industry focus.

One thing that seemed certain was that many Indians felt the need for improved water quality. Folklore, newspapers, consumer activists, and government officials regularly reinforced this need by describing the poor quality of Indian water. Quality suffered particularly during the monsoons because of highly polluted water entering treatment plants and because of numerous leaks and unauthorized withdrawals from water systems. Such leaks and withdrawals often polluted clean water after it had left the plants. Politicians running for national, state, and local government offices also reinforced the need for improved water quality through election campaign promises. Governments at these levels set standards for water quality, took measurements at thousands of locations throughout the nation, and advised consumers when water became unsafe.

During periods of poor water quality, many Indian consumers had little choice but to consume the water as they found it. However, better educated, wealthier, and more health-conscious consumers took steps to safeguard their family's health and often continued these steps year around. A good estimate of the number of such

EXHIBIT 1

Industry Sales Estimates and Forecasts for Water Purifiers in India 1990–2005 (Thousands of Units)

Year	Unit Sales Estimates	Unit Sales Forecast Under . . .		
		Realistic Scenario	Optimistic Scenario	Pessimistic Scenario
1990	60			
1991	90			
1992	150			
1993	200			
1994	220			
1995	240			
1996		250	250	250
1997		320	370	300
1998		430	540	400
1999		570	800	550
2000		800	1,200	750
2001		1,000	1,500	850
2002		1,300	1,900	900
2003		1,500	2,100	750
2004		1,600	2,100	580
2005		1,500	1,900	420

households, Chatterjee thought, would be around 40 million. These consumers were similar in many respects to consumers in middle- and upper-middle-class households in the United States and the European Union. They valued comfort and product choice. They saw consumption of material goods as a means to a higher quality of life. They liked foreign brands and would pay a higher price for such brands, as long as purchased products outperformed competing Indian products. Chatterjee had identified as his target market these 40 million households plus those in another four million households who had similar values and lifestyles, but as yet took little effort to improve water quality in their homes.

Traditional Method for Home Water Purification

The traditional method of water purification in the target market relied not on any commercially supplied product but instead on boiling. Each day or several times a day, a cook, maid, or family member would boil two to five liters of water for 10 minutes, allow it to cool, and then transfer it to containers for storage (often in a refrigerator). Chatterjee estimated that about 50 percent of the target market used this procedure. Boiling was seen by consumers as inexpensive, effective in terms of eliminating dangerous bacteria, and entrenched in a traditional sense. Many consumers who used this method considered it more effective than any product on the market. However, boiling affected the palatability of water, leaving the purified product somewhat "flat" to the taste. Boiling also was cumbersome, time consuming, and ineffective in removing physical impurities and unpleasant odors. Consequently, about 10 percent of the target market took a second step by filtering their boiled water through "candle filters" before storage. Many consumers who took this action did so despite knowing that water could become recontaminated during handling and storage.

Mechanical Methods for Home Water Filtration and Purification

About 40 percent of the target market used a mechanical device to improve their water quality. Half of this group used candle filters, primarily because of their low price and ease of use. The typical candle filter comprised two containers, one resting on top of the other. The upper container held one or more porous ceramic cylinders (candles) which strained the water as gravity drew it into the lower container. Containers were made of either plastic, porcelain, or stainless steel and typically stored between 15 and 25 liters of filtered water. Purchase costs depended on materials and capacities, ranging from Rs.350 for a small plastic model to Rs.1,100 for a large stainless steel model.[1] Candle filters were slow, producing 15 liters (one candle) to 45 liters (3 candles) of filtered water each 24 hours. To maintain this productivity, candles regularly needed to be removed, cleaned, and boiled for 20 minutes. Most manufacturers recommended that consumers replace candles (Rs.40 each) either once a year or more frequently, depending on sediment levels.

The other half of this group used "water purifiers," devices that were considerably more sophisticated than candle filters. Water purifiers typically employed three water processing stages. The first removed sediments, the second objectionable odors and colors, and the third harmful bacteria and viruses. Engineers at Blair Company were skeptical that most purifiers claiming the latter benefit actually could deliver on their promise. However, all purifiers did a better job here than candle filters.

---

[1] In 1996, 35 Indian Rupees (Rs.) were equivalent to U.S. $1.00.

Candle filters were totally ineffective in eliminating bacteria and viruses (and might even increase this type of contamination), despite advertising claims to the contrary. Water purifiers generally used stainless steel containers and sold at prices ranging from Rs.2,000 to Rs.7,000, depending on manufacturers, features, and capacities. Common flow rates were one to two liters of purified water per minute. Simple service activities could be performed on water purifiers by consumers as needed. However, more complicated service required units to be taken to a nearby dealer or an in-home visit from a skilled technician.

The remaining 10 percent of the target market owned neither a filter nor a purifier and seldom boiled their water. Many consumers in this group were unaware of water problems and thought their water quality acceptable. However, a few consumers in this group refused to pay for products that they believed were mostly ineffective. Overall, Chatterjee believed that only a few consumers in this group could be induced to change their habits and become customers. The most attractive segments consisted of the 90 percent of households in the target market who either boiled, boiled and filtered, only filtered, or purified their water.

All segments in the target market showed a good deal of similarity in terms of what they thought important in the purchase of a water purifier. According to Chatterjee's research, the most important factor was product performance in terms of sediment removal, bacteria and virus removal, capacity (either in the form of storage or flow rate), safety, and "footprint" space. Purchase price also was an important concern among consumers who boiled, boiled and filtered, or only filtered their water. The next most important factor was ease of intallation and service, with style and appearance rated almost as important. The least important factor was warranty and availability of financing for purchase. Finally, all segments expected a water purifier to be warranted against defective operation for 18 to 24 months and to perform trouble free for five to ten years.

■ FOREIGN INVESTMENT IN INDIA

India appeared attractive to many foreign investors because of government actions begun in the 1980s during the administration of Prime Minister Rajiv Gandhi. The broad label applied to these actions was "liberalization." Liberalization had opened the Indian economy to foreign investors, stemming from recognition that protectionist policies had not worked very well and that western economies and technologies—seen against the collapse of the Soviet Union—did. Liberalization had meant major changes in approval requirements for new commercial projects, investment policies, taxation procedures, and, most importantly, attitudes of government officials. These changes had stayed in place through the two national governments that followed Gandhi's assassination in 1991.

If Blair Company entered the Indian market, it would do so in one of three ways: (1) joint working arrangement, (2) joint venture company, or (3) acquisition. In a joint working arrangement, Blair Company would supply key purifier components to an Indian company which would manufacture and market the assembled product. License fees would be remitted to Blair Company on a per unit basis over the term of the agreement (typically five years, with an option to renew for three more). A joint venture agreement would have Blair Company partnering with an existing Indian company expressly for the purpose of manufacturing and marketing water purifiers. Profits from the joint venture operation would be split between the two parties per the agreement, which usually contained a clause describing buy/sell procedures available to the two parties after a minimum time period. An acquisition entry would have Blair Company purchasing an existing Indian company whose operations then would be expanded to include the water purifier. Profits from the acquisition would belong to Blair Company.

Beyond understanding these basic entry possibilities, Chatterjee acknowledged that he was no expert in legal aspects attending the project. However, two days spent with a Calcutta consulting firm had produced the following information. Blair Company must apply for market entry to the Foreign Investment Promotion Board, Secretariat for Industrial Approvals, Ministry of Industries. The proposal would go before the Board for an assessment of the relevant technology and India's need for the technology. If approved by the Board, the proposal then would go to the Reserve Bank of India, Ministry of Finance, for approvals of any royalties and fees, remittances of dividends and interest (if any), repatriations of profits and invested capital, and repayment of foreign loans. While the process sounded cumbersome and time consuming, the consultant assured Chatterjee that the government usually would complete its deliberations in less than six months and that his consulting firm could "virtually guarantee" final approval.

Trademarks and patents were protected by law in India. Trademarks were protected for seven years and could be renewed on payment of a prescribed fee. Patents lasted for 14 years. On balance, Chatterjee had told his boss that Blair Company would have "no more problem protecting its intellectual property rights in India than in the United States—as long as we stay out of court." Chatterjee went on to explain that litigation in India was expensive and protracted. Litigation problems were compounded by an appeal process that could extend a case for easily a generation. Consequently, many foreign companies preferred arbitration, as India was a party to the Geneva Convention covering Foreign Arbitral Awards.

Foreign companies were taxed on income arising from Indian operations. They also paid taxes on any interest, dividends, and royalties received, and on any capital gains received from a sale of assets. The government offered a wide range of tax concessions to foreign investors, including liberal depreciation allowances and generous deductions. The government offered even more favorable tax treatment if foreign investors would locate in one of India's six Free Trade Zones. Overall, Chatterjee thought that corporate tax rates in India probably were somewhat higher than in the United States. However, so were profits—the average return on assets for all Indian corporations in recent years was almost 18 percent, compared to about 11 percent for United States corporations.

Approval by the Reserve Bank of India was needed for repatriation of ordinary profits. However, approval should be obtained easily if Blair Company could show that repatriated profits were being paid out of export earnings of hard currencies. Chatterjee thought that export earnings would not be difficult to realize, given India's extremely low wage rates and its central location to wealthier South Asian countries. "Profit repatriation was really not much of an issue, anyway," he thought. Three years might pass before profits of any magnitude could be realized; at least five years would pass before substantial profits would be available for repatriation. Approval of repatriation by the Reserve Bank might not be required at this time, given liberalization trends. Finally, if repatriation remained difficult, Blair Company could undertake crosstrading or other actions to unblock profits.

Overall, investment and trade regulations in India in 1996 meant that business could be conducted much easier than ever before. Hundreds of companies from the European Union, Japan, Korea, and the United States were entering India in all sectors of the country's economy. In the home appliance market, Chatterjee could identify 11 such firms—Carrier, Electrolux, General Electric, Goldstar, Matsushita, Singer, Samsung, Sanyo, Sharp, Toshiba, and Whirlpool. Many of these firms had yet to realize substantial profits, but all saw the promise of a huge market developing over the next few years.

■ BLAIR COMPANY, INC.

Blair Company was founded in 1975 by Eugene Blair, after he left his position in research and development at Culligan International Company. Blair Company's first product was a desalinator used by mobile home parks in Florida to remove salts from brackish well water supplied to residents. The product was a huge success, and markets quickly expanded to include nearby municipalities, smaller businesses, hospitals, and bottlers of water for sale to consumers. Geographic markets also expanded, first to other coastal regions near the company's headquarters in Tampa, Florida, and then to desert areas in the southwestern United States. New products were added rapidly as well and, by 1996, the product line included desalinators, particle filters, ozonators, ion exchange resins, and purifiers. Industry experts generally regarded the product line as superior in terms of performance and quality, with prices higher than those of many competitors.

Blair Company sales revenues for 1996 would be almost $400 million, with an expected profit close to $50 million. Annual growth in sales revenues averaged 12 percent for the past five years. Blair Company employed over 4,000 people, with 380 having technical backgrounds and responsibilities.

Export sales of desalinators and related products began at Blair Company in 1980. Units were sold first to resorts in Mexico and Belize and later to water bottlers in Germany. Export sales grew rapidly, and Blair Company found it necessary to organize its International Division in 1985. Sales in the International Division also grew rapidly and would reach almost $140 million in 1996. About $70 million would come from countries in Latin and South America, $30 million from Europe (including shipments to Africa), and $40 million from South Asia and Australia. The International Division had sales offices, small assembly areas, and distribution facilities in Frankfurt, Germany; Tokyo, Japan; and Singapore.

The Frankfurt office had been the impetus in 1990 for development and marketing of Blair Company's first product targeted exclusively to consumer households—a home water filter. Sales engineers at the Frankfurt office began receiving consumer and distributor requests for a home water filter soon after the fall of the Berlin wall in 1989. By late 1991, two models had been designed in the United States and introduced in Germany (particularly to the eastern regions), Poland, Hungary, Romania, the Czech Republic, and Slovakia.

Blair Company executives watched the success of the two water filters with great interest. The market for clean water in LDCs was huge, profitable, and attractive in a socially responsible sense. However, the quality of water in many LDCs was such that a water filter usually would not be satisfactory. Consequently, in late 1994, executives had directed the development of a water purifier that could be added to the product line. Engineers had given the final design in the project the brand name "Delight." For the time being, Chatterjee and the other market analysts had accepted the name, not knowing if it might infringe on any existing brand in India or in the other countries under study.

■ DELIGHT PURIFIER

The Delight purifier used a combination of technologies to remove four types of contaminants found in potable water—sediments, organic and inorganic chemicals, microbials, or cysts, and objectionable tastes and odors. The technologies were effective as long as contaminants in the water were present at "reasonable" levels. Engineers at Blair Company had interpreted "reasonable" as levels described in several

World Health Organization (WHO) reports on potable water and had combined the technologies to purify water to a level beyond WHO standards. Engineers had repeatedly assured Chatterjee that Delight's design in terms of technologies should not be a concern. Ten units operating in the company's testing laboratory showed no signs of failure or performance deterioration after some 5,000 hours of continuous use. "Still," Chatterjee thought, "we will undertake a good bit of field testing in India before entering. The risks of failure are too large to ignore. And, besides, results of our testing would be useful in convincing consumers and retailers to buy."

Chatterjee and the other market analysts still faced major design issues in configuring technologies into physical products. For example, a "point of entry" design would place the product immediately after water entry to the home, treating all water before it flowed to all water outlets. In contrast, a "point of use" design would place the product on a countertop, wall, or at the end of a faucet and treat only water arriving at that location. Based on cost estimates, designs of competing products, and his understanding of Indian consumers, Chatterjee would direct engineers to proceed only with "point of use" designs for the market.

Other technical details were yet to be worked out. For example, Chatterjee had to provide engineers with suggestions for filter flow rates, storage capacities (if any), unit layout and overall dimensions, plus a number of special features. One such feature was the possibility of a small battery to operate the filter for several hours in case of a power failure (a common occurrence in India and many other LDCs). Another might be one or two "bells or whistles" to tell cooks, maids, and family members that the unit indeed was working properly. Yet another might be an "additive" feature, permitting users to add fluoride, vitamins, or even flavorings to their water.

Chatterjee knew that the Indian market would eventually require a number of models. However, at the outset of market entry, he probably could get by with just two—one with a larger capacity for houses and bungalows and the other a smaller capacity model for flats. He thought that model styling and specific appearances should reflect a western, high-technology school of design in order to distinguish the Delight purifier from competitors' products. To that end, he had instructed a graphics artist to develop two ideas that he had used to gauge consumer reactions on his last visit (see Exhibit 2 on page 676). Consumers liked both models but preferred the countertop design over the wallmount design.

■ COMPETITORS

Upwards of 100 companies competed in the Indian market for home water filters and purifiers. While information on most of these companies was difficult to obtain, Chatterjee and the Indian research agencies were able to develop descriptions of three major competitors and brief profiles of several others.

Eureka Forbes

The most established competitor in the water purifier market was Eureka Forbes, a joint venture company established in 1982 between Electrolux (Sweden) and Forbes Campbell (India). The company marketed a broad line of "modern lifestyle products" including water purifiers, vacuum cleaners, and mixers/grinders. The brand name used for its water purifiers was "Aquaguard," a name so well established that many consumers mistakenly used it to refer to other water purifiers or to the entire product category. Aquaguard, with its 10-year market history, was clearly the market leader and came close to being India's only national brand. However, Eureka Forbes

EXHIBIT 2

Delight Water Purifier Wallmount and Countertop Designs

Wallmount Design	*Countertop Design*

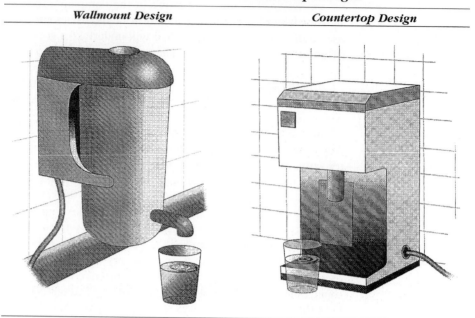

had recently introduced a second brand of water purifier called "PureSip." The Pure-Sip model was similar to Aquaguard except for its third stage process, which used a polyiodide resin instead of ultraviolet rays to kill bacteria and viruses. This meant that water from a PureSip purifier could be stored safely for later usage. Also in contrast to Aquaguard, the PureSip model needed no electricity for its operation.

However, the biggest difference between the two products was how they were sold. Aquaguard was sold exclusively by a 2,500 person salesforce that called directly on households. In contrast, PureSip was sold by independent dealers of smaller home appliances. Unit prices to consumers for Aquaguard and PureSip in 1996 were approximately Rs.5,500 and Rs.2,000, respectively. Chatterjee believed that unit sales of PureSip were much smaller than unit sales for Aquaguard but growing at a much faster rate.

An Aquaguard unit typically was mounted on a kitchen wall, with plumbing required to bring water to the purifier's inlet. A two-meter-long power cord was connected to a 230-volt AC electrical outlet—the Indian standard. If the power supply were to drop to 190 volts or lower, the unit would stop functioning. Other limits of the product included a smallish amount of activated carbon that could eliminate only weak organic odors. It could not remove strong odors or inorganic solutes like nitrates and iron compounds. The unit had no storage capacity and its flow rate of one liter per minute seemed slow to some consumers. Removing water for storage or connecting the unit to a reservoir tank could affect water quality, like a candle filter.

Aquaguard's promotion strategy emphasized personal selling. Each salesman was assigned to a specific neighborhood and was monitored by a group leader who, in turn, was monitored by a supervisor. Each salesman was expected to canvass his neighborhood, select prospective households (e.g., those with annual incomes exceeding Rs.70,000), demonstrate the product, and make an intensive effort to sell the product. Repeated sales calls helped to educate consumers about their water quality and to reassure them that Aquaguard service was readily available. Television commercials and advertisements in magazines and newspapers (see Exhibit 3) sup-

EXHIBIT 3

Aquaguard Newspaper Advertisement

DON'T JUST GUARD YOUR FAMILY THIS MONSOON.

AQUAGUARD IT.

The monsoons bring a welcome relief from the long hot summer. But they also bring along some of the most dangerous water-borne diseases. Like cholera, dysentry, gastro-enteritis and jaundice. Which is why you need an Aquaguard Water Purifier, to safeguard your family.

Today, Aquaguard is synonymous with clean, pure and safe drinking water.

Aquaguard is a 3 stage water purification system using the latest Ultra Violet technology, which destroys disease causing bacteria and virus in the water. It also has a unique

Electronic Monitoring System which stops water flow automatically if the purification level falls below pre-determined standards.

In addition, with Aquaguard you have the Eureka Forbes guarantee of After-Sales-Service at your doorstep.

So install an Aquaguard today. And help your family enjoy the monsoons better.

For a free demonstration at your home call the friendly man from Eureka Forbes or write to us at the addresses given below

Aquaguard
EUREKA FORBES LTD.

Calcutta: Mani Tower, Block Uttara, 1st Flr., 31/41 Vinoba Bhave Rd., Calcutta - 700 038. Tel: 4786845/5444. * 27 A, Lal Mohan Bhattacharjee Rd., 2nd Flr., Calcutta - 700 014. Tel: 2451548/2325. * 12 D, Chakraberia Rd. (North), Calcutta - 700 020. Tel: 746411/5326. * 177, Raja Dinendra Street, Opp. Desbandhu Park, Shyam Bazar, Calcutta - 700 004. Tel: 5545729/7248. * 21 G, Deodar Street, Calcutta - 700 019. * Guwahati: G.N.B.Rd., Silpukhuri, Above Jungle Travels, Near Goswami Service Station, Guwahati - 781 003. Tel: 31574. * Howrah: 105/106 A Panchsheel Apt., 1st Flr., 493, B.G.T. Road (South), Howrah - 711 102. Tel: 6606042. * Siliguri: 521 Swamiji Sarani, 1st Flr., Hakimpara P.O., Siliguri, Dist. Darjeeling. Tel: 26332.

ported the personal selling efforts. Chatterjee estimated that Eureka Forbes would spend about Rs.120 million on all sales activities in 1996 or roughly 11 percent of its sales revenues. He estimated that about Rs.100 million of the Rs.120 million would be spent in the form of sales commissions. Chatterjee thought the company's total advertising expenditures for the year would be only about Rs.1 million.

Eureka Forbes was a formidable competitor. The salesforce was huge, highly motivated, and well managed. Moreover, Aquaguard was the first product to enter the water purifier market and the name had tremendous brand equity. The product itself was probably the weakest strategic component—but it would take much to convince consumers of this. And, while the salesforce offered a huge competitive advantage, it represented an enormous fixed cost and essentially limited sales efforts to large urban areas. More than 80 percent of India's population lived in rural areas, where water quality was even lower.

Ion Exchange

Ion Exchange was the premier water treatment company in India, specializing in treatments of water, processed liquids, and waste water in industrial markets. The company began operations in 1964 as a wholly owned subsidiary of British Permutit. Permutit divested its holdings in 1985 and Ion Exchange became a wholly owned Indian company. The company presently served customers in a diverse group of industries, including nuclear and thermal power stations, fertilizers, petrochemical refineries, textiles, automobiles, and home water purifiers. Its home water purifiers carried the family brand name, ZERO-B (Zero-Bacteria).

ZERO-B purifiers used a halogenated resin technology as part of a three-stage purification process. The first stage removed suspended impurities via filter pads, the second eliminated bad odors and taste with activated carbon, and the third killed bacteria using trace quantities of polyiodide (iodine). The latter feature was attractive because it helped prevent iodine deficiency diseases and permitted purified water to be stored up to eight hours without fear of recontamination.

The basic purifier product for the home carried the name "Puristore." A Puristore unit typically sat on a kitchen counter near the tap, with no electricity or plumbing hookup needed for its operation. The unit stored 20 liters of purified water. It sold to consumers for Rs.2,000. Each year the user must replace the halogenated resin at a cost of Rs.200.

Chatterjee estimated that ZERO-B captured about 7 percent of the Indian water purifier market. Probably the biggest reason for the small share was a lack of consumer awareness. ZERO-B purifiers had been on the market for less than three years. They were not advertised heavily nor did they enjoy the sales effort intensity of Aquaguard. Distribution, too, was limited. During Chatterjee's visit, he could find only five dealers in Calcutta carrying ZERO-B products and none in Bangalore. Dealers that he contacted were of the opinion that ZERO-B's marketing efforts soon would intensify—two had heard rumors that a door-to-door salesforce was planned and that consumer advertising was about to begin.

Chatterjee had confirmed the latter point with a visit to a Calcutta advertising agency. A modest number of 10-second TV commercials soon would be aired on Zee TV and DD metro channels. The advertisements would focus on educating consumers with the position, "It is not a filter." Instead, ZERO-B is a water purifier and much more effective than a candle filter in preventing health problems. Apart from this advertising effort, the only other form of promotion used was a point of sale brochure that dealers could give to prospective customers (see Exhibit 4).

On balance, Chatterjee thought that Ion Exchange could be a major player in the market. The company had over 30 years' experience in the field of water purification and devoted upwards of Rs.10 million each year to corporate research and development. "In fact," he thought, "all Ion Exchange really needs to do is to recognize the market's potential and to make it a priority within the company." However, this might be difficult to do, given the company's prominent emphasis on industrial markets. Chatterjee estimated that ZERO-B products would account for less than two

EXHIBIT 4

ZERO-B Sales Brochure

percent of Ion Exchange's 1996 total sales, estimated at Rs. 1,000 million. He thought the total marketing expenditures for ZERO-B would be around Rs.3 million.

Singer

The newest competitor to enter the Indian water purifier market was Singer India Ltd. Originally, Singer India was a subsidiary of The Singer Company, located in the United States, but a minority share (49 percent) was sold to Indian investors in 1982. The change in ownership had led to construction of manufacturing facilities in India for sewing machines in 1983. The facilities were expanded in 1991 to produce a broad line of home appliances. Sales revenues for 1996 for the entire product line—sewing machines, food processors, irons, mixers, toaster, water heaters, ceiling fans, cooking ranges, and color televisions—would be about Rs.900 million.

During Chatterjee's time in Calcutta, he had visited a Singer Company showroom on Park Street. Initially he had hoped that Singer might be a suitable partner to manufacture and distribute the Delight purifier. However, much to his surprise, he was told that Singer now had its own brand on the market, "Aquarius." The product was not yet available in Calcutta but was being sold in Bombay and Delhi.

A marketing research agency in Delhi was able to gather some information on the Singer purifier. The product contained nine stages (!) and sold to consumers for Rs.4,000. It removed sediments, heavy metals, bad tastes, odors, and colors. It also killed bacteria and viruses, fungi, and nematodes. The purifier required water pres-

sure (8 PSI minimum) to operate but needed no electricity. It came in a single countertop model that could be moved from one room to another. Life of the device at a
flow rate of 3.8 liters per minute was listed as 40,000 liters—about four to six years
of use in the typical Indian household. The product's life could be extended to
70,000 liters at a somewhat slower flow rate. However, at 70,000 liters, the product
must be discarded. The agency reported a heavy advertising blitz accompanying the
introduction in Delhi—emphasizing TV and newspaper advertising, plus outdoor
and transit advertising as support. All 10 Singer showrooms in Delhi offered vivid
demonstrations of the product's operation.

Chatterjee had to admit that photos of the Aquarius purifier shown in the Calcutta showroom looked appealing. And a trade article he found had described the
product as "state of the art" in comparison to the "primitive" products now on the
market. Chatterjee and Blair Company engineers tended to agree—the disinfecting
resin used in Aquarius had been developed by the United States government's National Aeronautics and Space Administration (NASA) and was proven to be 100 percent effective against bacteria and viruses. "If only I could have brought a unit back
with me," he thought. "We could have some test results and see just how good it is."
The trade article also mentioned that Singer hoped to sell 40,000 units over the next
two years.

Chatterjee knew that Singer was a well-known and respected brand name in India. Further, Singer's distribution channels were superior to those of any competitor
in the market, including those of Eureka Forbes. Most prominent of Singer's three
distribution channels were the 210 company-owned showrooms located in major urban areas around the country. Each sold and serviced the entire line of Singer products. Each was very well kept and staffed by knowledgeable personnel. Singer products also were sold throughout India by over 3,000 independent dealers, who
received inventory from an estimated 70 Singer-appointed distributors. According to
the marketing research agency in Delhi, distributors earned margins of 12 percent of
the retail price for Aquarius while dealers earned margins of five percent. Finally,
Singer employed over 400 salesmen who sold sewing machines and food processors
door-to-door. Like Eureka Forbes, the direct salesforce sold products primarily in
large urban markets.

■ OTHER COMPETITORS

Chatterjee was aware of several other water purifiers on the Indian market. The Delta
brand from S & S Industries in Madras seemed a carbon copy of Aquaguard, except
for a more eye-pleasing, countertop design. According to promotion literature, Delta
offered a line of water-related products—purifiers, water softeners, iron removers, desalinators, and ozonators. Another competitor was Alfa Water Purifiers, Bombay. The
company offered four purifier models at prices from Rs.4,300 to Rs.6,500, depending
on capacity. Symphony's Spectrum brand sold well around Bombay at Rs.4,000 each
but removed only suspended sediments, not heavy metals or bacteria. The Sam Group
in Coimbatore recently had launched its "Water Doctor" purifier at Rs.5,200. The device used a third stage ozonator to kill bacteria and viruses and came in two attractive
countertop models, 6- and 12-liter storage. Batliboi was mentioned by the Delhi research agency as yet another competitor, although Chatterjee knew nothing else
about the brand. Taken all together, unit sales of all purifiers at these companies plus
ZERO-B and Singer probably would account for around 60,000 units in 1996. The remaining 190,000 units would be Aquaguards and PureSips.

At least 100 Indian companies made and marketed candle filters. The largest of
these probably was Bajaj Electrical Division, whose product line also included water

heaters, irons, electric light bulbs, toasters, mixers, and grillers. Bajaj's candle filters were sold by a large number of dealers who carried the entire product line. Candle filters produced by other manufacturers were sold mostly through dealers who specialized in small household appliances and general hardware. Probably no single manufacturer of candle filters had more than five percent of any regional market in the country. No manufacturer attempted to satisfy a national market. Still, the candle filters market deserved serious consideration—perhaps Delight's entry strategy would attempt to "trade-up" users of candle filters to a better, safer product.

Finally, Chatterjee knew that sales of almost all purifiers in 1996 in India came from large urban areas. No manufacturer targeted rural or smaller urban areas and at best, Chatterjee had calculated, existing manufacturers were reaching only ten to fifteen percent of the entire Indian population. An explosion in sales would come if the right product could be sold outside metropolitan areas.

■ RECOMMENDATIONS

Chatterjee decided that an Indian market entry for Blair Company was subject to three "givens," as he called them. First, he thought that a strategic focus on rural or smaller urban areas would not be wise, at least at the start. The lack of adequate distribution and communication infrastructure in rural India meant that any market entry would begin with larger Indian cities, most likely on the west coast.

Second, market entry would require manufacturing units in India. Because the cost of skilled labor in India was around Rs.20 to Rs.25 per hour (compared to $20 to $25 per hour in the United States), importing complete units was out of the question. However, importing a few key components would be necessary at the start of operation.

Third, Blair Company should find an Indian partner. Chatterjee's visits had produced a number of promising partners: Polar Industries, Calcutta; Milton Plastics, Bombay; Videocon Appliances, Aurangabad; BPL Sanyo Utilities and Appliances, Bangalore; Onida Savak, Delhi; Hawkins India, Bombay; and Voltas, Bombay. All companies manufactured and marketed a line of high-quality household appliances, possessed one or more strong brand names, and had established dealer networks (minimum of 10,000 dealers). All were involved to greater or lesser degrees with international partners. All were medium-sized firms—not too large that a partnership with Blair Company would be one-sided, not too small that they would lack managerial talent and other resources. Finally, all were profitable (15 to 27 percent return on assets in 1995) and looking to grow. However, Chatterjee had no idea if any company would find the Delight purifier and Blair Company attractive or if they might be persuaded to sell part or all of their operations as an acquisition.

Field Testing and Product Recommendations

The most immediate decision Chatterjee faced was whether or not he should recommend a field test. The test would cost about $25,000, placing 20 units in Indian homes in three cities and monitoring their performance for three to six months. The decision to test really was more than it seemed—Chatterjee's boss had explained that a decision to test was really a decision to enter. It made no sense to spend this kind of time and money if India were not an attractive opportunity. The testing period also would give Blair Company representatives time to identify a suitable Indian company as either a licensee, joint venture partner, or acquisition.

Fundamental to market entry was product design. Engineers at Blair Company had taken the position that purification technologies planned for Delight could be "packaged in almost any fashion as long as we have electricity." Electricity was needed to operate the product's ozonator as well as to indicate to users that the unit was functioning properly (or improperly, as the case might be). Beyond this requirement, anything was possible.

Chatterjee thought that a modular approach would be best. The basic module would be a countertop unit much like that shown in Exhibit 2. The module would outperform anything now on the market in terms of flow rate, palatability, durability, and reliability, and would store two liters of purified water. Two additional modules would remove iron, calcium, and other metallic contaminants that were peculiar to particular regions. For example, Calcutta and much of the surrounding area suffered from iron contamination, which no filter or purifier now on the Indian market could remove to a satisfactory level. Water supplies in other areas in the country were known to contain objectionable concentrations of calcium, salt, arsenic, lead, or sulfur. Most Indian consumers would need neither of the additional modules, some would need one or the other, but very few would need both.

Market Entry and Marketing Planning Recommendations

Assuming that Chatterjee recommended proceeding with the field test, he would need to make a recommendation concerning mode of market entry. In addition, his recommendation should include an outline of a marketing plan.

Licensee Considerations If market entry were in the form of a joint working arrangement with a licensee, Blair Company financial investment would be minimal. Chatterjee thought that Blair Company might risk as little as $30,000 in capital for production facilities and equipment, plus another $5,000 for office facilities and equipment. These investments would be completely offset by the licensee's payment to Blair Company for technology transfer and personnel training. Annual fixed costs to Blair Company should not exceed $40,000 at the outset and would decrease to $15,000 as soon as an Indian national could be hired, trained, and left in charge. Duties of this individual would be to work with Blair Company personnel in the United States and with management at the licensee to see that units were produced per Blair Company's specifications. Apart from this activity, Blair Company would have no control over the licensee's operations. Chatterjee expected that the licensee would pay royalties to Blair Company of about Rs.280 for each unit sold in the domestic market and Rs.450 for each unit that was exported. The average royalty probably would be around Rs.300.

Joint Venture/Acquisition Considerations If entry were in the form of either a joint venture or an acquisition, financial investment and annual fixed costs would be much higher and depend greatly on the scope of operations. Chatterjee had roughed out some estimates for a joint venture entry, based on three levels of scope (see Exhibit 5). His estimates reflected what he thought were reasonable assumptions for all needed investments plus annual fixed expenses for sales activities, general administrative overhead, research and development, insurance, and depreciation. His estimates allowed for the Delight purifier to be sold either through dealers or through a direct, door-to-door salesforce. Chatterjee thought that estimates of annual fixed expenses for market entry via acquisition would be identical to those for a joint venture. However, estimates for the investment (purchase) might be considerably higher, the same, or lower. It depended on what was purchased.

Chatterjee's estimates of Delight's unit contribution margins reflected a number of assumptions—expected economies of scale, experience curve effects, costs of Indian labor and raw materials, and competitors' pricing strategies. However, the most

EXHIBIT 5

Investments and Fixed Costs for a Joint Venture Market Entry

	Operational Scope		
	Two Regions	Four Regions	National Market
1998 Market potential (units)	55,000	110,000	430,000
Initial investment (Rs.000)	4,000	8,000	30,000
Annual fixed overhead expenses (Rs.000)			
Using dealer channels	4,000	7,000	40,000
Using direct salesforce	7,200	14,000	88,000

important assumption was Delight's pricing strategy. If a skimming strategy were used and the product sold through a dealer channel, the basic module would be priced to dealers at Rs.5,500 and to consumers at Rs.5,900. "This would give us about a Rs.650 unit contribution, once we got production flowing smoothly," he thought. In contrast, if a penetration strategy were used and the product sold through a dealer channel, the basic module would be priced to dealers at Rs.4,100, to consumers at Rs.4,400, and yield a unit contribution of Rs.300. For simplicity's sake, Chatterjee assumed that the two additional modules would be priced to dealers at Rs.800, to consumers at Rs.1,000, and would yield a unit contribution of Rs.100. Finally, he assumed that all products sold to dealers would go directly from Blair Company to the dealers (no distributors would be used).

If a direct salesforce were employed instead of dealers, Chatterjee thought that prices charged to consumers would not change from those listed above. However, sales commissions would have to be paid in addition to the fixed costs necessary to maintain and manage the salesforce. Under a skimming price strategy, the sales commission would be Rs.550 per unit and the unit contribution would be Rs.500. Under a penetration price strategy, the sales commission would be Rs.400 per unit and the unit contribution would be Rs.200. These financial estimates, he would explain in his report, would apply to 1998 or 1999, the expected first year of operation.

Skimming versus penetration was more than just a pricing strategy. Product design for the skimming strategy would be noticeably superior, with higher performance and quality, a longer warranty period, more features, and a more attractive appearance than the design for the penetration strategy. Positioning, too, most likely would be different. Chatterjee recognized several positioning possibilities: performance and taste, value for the money/low price, safety, health, convenience, attractive styling, avoiding diseases and health-related bills, and superior American technology. The only position he considered "taken" in the market was that occupied by Aquaguard—protect family health and service at your doorstep. While other competitors had claimed certain positions for their products, none had devoted financial resources of a degree that Delight could not dislodge them. Chatterjee believed that considerable advertising and promotion expenditures would be necessary to communicate Delight's positioning. He would need estimates of these expenditures in his recommendation.

"If we go ahead with Delight, we'll have to move quickly," thought Chatterjee. "The window of opportunity is open but if Singer's product is as good as they claim, we'll be in for a fight. Still, Aquarius seems vulnerable on the water pressure requirement and on price. We'll need a product category 'killer' to win."

Preparing a Written Case Analysis

Chapter 3 outlined an approach to marketing decision making and case analysis. The purpose of this appendix is to provide a more detailed description of what is involved in a thorough written case analysis through the use of an example. The following case—Republic National Bank of Dallas: NOW Accounts—describes an actual problem encountered by bank executives. The case is accompanied by a student analysis in the format described in Chapter 3. The student analysis shows how to organize a written case and the nature and scope of the analysis, which includes both qualitative and quantitative analyses. You should read and analyze the case before examining the student analysis.

Republic National Bank of Dallas
NOW Accounts

■ INTRODUCTION

In early 1977, Ruth Krusen, marketing officer for Republic National Bank of Dallas (RNB), was asked to assess the impact on Republic Bank of offering NOW (negotiable order of withdrawal) accounts if they became legal nationwide. Specifically, she was asked to:

The cooperation of Republic National Bank of Dallas in the preparation of this case is gratefully acknowledged. This case was prepared by Professor Roger A. Kerin, of the Edwin L. Cox School of Business, Southern Methodist University, as a basis for class discussion and is not designed to illustrate effective or ineffective handling of an administrative situation. Certain data have been disguised.

1. Determine the impact on profits that Republic National Bank could anticipate from NOW accounts

2. Recommend a NOW account marketing strategy

NOW accounts, which are effectively interest-bearing checking accounts, have been in use since 1972 in New England. In early 1977, however, a bill was introduced into Congress that would allow commercial banks and thrift institutions in all 50 states to provide this service.[1] Despite some opposition in Congress, observers were of the opinion that legislation enabling NOW accounts would be passed by the first quarter of 1978 and would become effective January 1979.

BANKING IN TEXAS

Texas is a "unit banking" state. This means that individual banks cannot operate branch banks. The regulation that limits a bank to a single location was specified in the state constitution of 1876. In 1971, however, amendments to the Bank Holding Act allowed individual banks to acquire smaller institutions if the identity of the acquired bank was maintained. Since 1971, large banks in Texas have formed holding companies to improve their lending capability in order to better serve large commercial accounts. By 1977, 33 bank holding companies were operating in Texas. Holding companies owned 250 of the state's 1,360 banks and held about 55 percent of the state's total bank deposits in 1977.

Three of the largest bank holding companies in Texas are based in Dallas. Each operates its largest bank in downtown Dallas. First International Bancshares, which operates First National Bank, is the largest bank holding company in Texas. Republic of Texas Corporation operates the Republic National Bank of Dallas and is the second-largest holding company. Mercantile Texas Corporation operates Mercantile National Bank and is the fifth-largest bank holding company in terms of total assets.

Banking activity in Texas generally corresponds to pockets of urban and commercial growth. Accordingly, banking activity is concentrated in the Dallas–Fort Worth and Houston metropolitan areas. The San Antonio metropolitan area has shown a dramatic increase in banking activity due in part to population growth and increased economic growth.

COMPETITIVE SITUATION IN DALLAS

The Dallas banking market consists of 57 banks in the city of Dallas and an additional 43 banks in Dallas County. At the end of 1976, the 57 banks in the city of Dallas recorded total deposits of $13.27 billion. The 43 banks in Dallas County recorded deposits of about $1.25 billion.

Three large downtown banks dominate the Dallas banking market. At the end of 1976, Republic National Bank, First National Bank, and the Mercantile National Bank accounted for approximately 78 percent of total bank deposits in the city of Dallas and 71 percent of Dallas County bank deposits. Republic National Bank was the leader with approximately $4.6 billion in deposits, followed closely by First National Bank with $4.4 billion. Mercantile National Bank recorded total deposits of about

---

[1] Thrift institutions include mutual savings banks, cooperative banks, credit unions, and savings and loan associations. Thrift institutions differ from commercial banks in that only banks have the authority to accept demand deposits or checking accounts or offer commercial loans.

$1.3 billion at the end of 1976. These three banks are located within walking distance of one another, as well as of some 12 other banks.

Competitive activities of Dallas banks have historically focused on retail (consumer) or wholesale (business) bank account development. Banks located in suburban areas typically emphasized the retail business, whereas downtown banks emphasized the wholesale business. Nevertheless, the Dallas competitive environment in recent years has been characterized by aggressive bank marketing efforts on both fronts. According to one observer of the Dallas banking scene:

> The competitive marketing furor is fierce, and it's not just the catchy advertising themes. . . . There's a scramble going on to repackage consumer services, put forth new services, cross-sell services, and woo corporate customers. There's Saturday banking, extended hours banking, 24-hour tellers, foreign currency sales, cash machines, no-charge checking package deals, automatic payroll deposits, pension fund management services, computer billing services, specially arranged travel tours, traveler's checks to spend on travel tours, equipment leasing, credit card loans, loan syndications, lock boxes, and on and on. First National Bank in Dallas alone lists more than 400 different bank "products" in its inventory of services.[2]

Krusen confirmed the observation that the Dallas banking market was competitive. She noted that RNB continues to be competitive in banking services, but "the question of how aggressive we should be has not been resolved at least as regards retail account marketing." RNB has at least as many bank services for customers as competitors do, if not more services than are offered by the vast majority of commercial banks in Dallas.

In addition to commercial banks, savings and loan associations (S&Ls) also compete for passbook savings accounts among Dallas County residents. At the end of 1976, deposits of the 22 Dallas County-based savings and loan associations were $2.85 billion. Dallas Federal Savings was the largest savings and loan association with about $909.6 million in deposits, or about 32 percent of total deposits. Texas Federal Savings and First Texas Savings combined accounted for approximately $992 million in deposits, or 35 percent of total deposits. Dallas-based savings and loan associations operated approximately 150 offices in Dallas County. Savings and loan associations based outside Dallas County also operated about 50 offices in the county.

Savings and loan associations have aggressively sought deposits in recent years. Dallas-based associations have historically outpaced the national average for savings and loan deposit volume growth. Savings associations have emphasized two competitive advantages in their passbook savings marketing programs. First, they could pay $5^1/_4$ percent on passbook savings, whereas commercial banks were limited by law to 5 percent on passbook savings. Second, they could develop branch operations with a common name, whereas commercial banks were limited to a single location in Texas.

Savings and loan associations have placed greater emphasis on consumer, or installment, loans in recent years. Texas is unique among states in that it allows savings associations to provide installment loans, and some associations have used this opportunity to attract deposit volume. According to an industry observer, "S&Ls have historically attracted older customers. Installment loans are a useful service to bring in younger customers, introduce them to S&Ls, and get them to open a passbook savings account."

Credit unions also represent a competitive force in the Dallas market. By the end of 1976, 218 credit unions were located in the city of Dallas and its immediate

---

[2] Dave Clark, "A Big Pitch for Bucks," *Dallas–Fort Worth Business Quarterly* 1, no. 2.

environs. These credit unions operated 232 offices. Combined, credit unions held over $666 million in assets and served almost one-half million members.

Credit unions compete effectively in the Dallas market in three ways. First, they offer consumer, or installment, loans to their members at competitive interest rates. They hold a significant share of the automobile loans in the Dallas market. Second, credit unions hold substantial funds in member savings accounts. Third, credit unions provide share drafts to their members. A *share draft* is a withdrawal document that permits credit union members to make payments from interest-bearing savings accounts. These drafts resemble checks but are actually drafts drawn on a credit union and payable through a bank.

■ REPUBLIC NATIONAL BANK

Republic National Bank was founded in 1920. At that time, the bank was called Guaranty Bank and Trust, and it held a state banking charter. After several name changes, the present name was adopted in 1937, and RNB obtained a national bank charter. Today, RNB is the largest member of the Republic of Texas Corporation bank holding-company system. By the end of 1977, RNB would be ranked twenty-first in the United States in total assets and deposits and would be the largest bank in Texas and the South in terms of total assets, deposits, loans, and equity capital. Also by the end of 1977, RNB would be ranked 150th among the 500 largest banks in the non-Communist world, according to *American Banker* magazine. RNB had total assets exceeding $6 billion and a net income of approximately $36.3 million by that time.

Retail Account Marketing

Although figures are not available for competing banks, RNB is considered to have one of the largest, if not the largest, retail account bases in the Dallas area. According

E X H I B I T   1

Estimated Distribution of Personal Checking Account Balances in Early 1977

Account Size	*Percentage of Accounts*	*Percentage of Total Checking Account Deposits*
Under $200	32%	3%
$200–$499	23	3
$500–$999	14	4
$1,000–$4,999	18	13
$5,000–$9,999	7	11
$10,000–$24,999	3	13
$25,000–$100,000	2	20
Over $100,000	1	33
	100%	100%

Number of personal checking accounts: 45,000

Personal checking account deposits: $150 million

Note: Figures reported in this exhibit reflect approximations drawn from *1977 District Bank Averages: Functional Cost Analysis* (Dallas: Federal Reserve Bank of Dallas, 1977).

to Krusen, this occurred as a result of RNB's historic position of "taking chances on the little guy and community service." It was estimated that about 55 percent of RNB's retail checking accounts in 1977 were under $500. Exhibit 1 shows the distribution of accounts by account size.

This philosophy is communicated in RNB advertising. Beginning in the late 1960s with its "Silver Star Service" campaign and continuing with the "Star Treatment" advertising campaign, RNB communicated to present and potential customers that they were special and that RNB had a number of special services to provide them. In early 1977 the "Republic National Bank *Is* Dallas" campaign was launched, with Orson Welles narrating television and radio advertising spots and the Dallas Symphony playing the theme music. This campaign was designed to reflect the mutual traditions of RNB and Dallas residents as progressive and growth-oriented, as well as emphasize the interdependence of banking leadership and service with the prosperity and quality of Dallas life. Marketing research has shown that RNB has had the highest "top-of-mind awareness" of any bank in the Dallas area since 1975.

Retail Account Services

RNB retail account marketing efforts have resulted in a variety of traditional as well as innovative bank services for its customers. For example, RNB provides its Teller 24® Service, which is an automatic bank teller/cash machine. This service operates 24 hours a day at 26 locations around the city of Dallas and in six other Texas cities. Another innovation, the *Starpak* Account, is a complete package of banking services provided to customers for a fixed monthly fee of $3. Exhibit 2 on page 690 gives a description of this service. RNB personal checking is highly competitive in the Dallas market, with no service charge for accounts that maintain a minimum monthly balance of $400. A $1 charge accrues to accounts with a minimum monthly balance of $300, a $2 charge with a minimum monthly balance of $200, and a $3 charge with no minimum balance requirement.

Retail Checking Account Revenue and Cost Estimates

In the course of preparing her report, Krusen contacted the RNB Controllers Division to obtain revenue and cost data on retail checking accounts. The Controllers Division report, based largely on Federal Reserve statistics, indicated that approximately 85 percent of retail checking account deposits were investable. In other words, about 15 percent of checking account deposits must be held in reserve. Ninety-six percent of savings account balances were investable.

The Controllers Division also indicated that RNB would realize an average yield on loans and securities of about 7.5 percent in 1977. Krusen noted that this figure was the lowest experienced by RNB in recent years. In 1974 RNB had realized an average yield of 10.59 percent. Other figures obtained directly from Federal Reserve statistical averages for commercial banks with total deposits of over $200 million were as follows:

Service and handling charge revenue per account per month:	$1.56
Account cost per month (including checks, deposits, and other assignable overhead):	$5.24

EXHIBIT 2

Components of Republic National Bank's Starpak Account

1. *Unlimited Checking*—There's no minimum balance requirement, no per check charge, and no limit on the number of checks you write when you have a Starpak personal checking account.

2. *Free Personal Checks*—They're prenumbered and personalized with your name, address, and phone number, and you can order as many as you need any time you need them.

3. *Reduced Loan Rates*—With this feature alone, many people make Starpak pay for itself. At the end of the loan period, we'll refund 10 percent of the total interest you paid on installment loans of $1,000 or more, when the loan has been repaid as agreed. Of course, your loan is subject to normal credit approval.

4. *No Bank Charge for Traveler's Checks*—Or for Money Orders or Cashier's Checks when you show us your Starpak Account Card.

5. *Free Safe Deposit Box*—We'll give you the $5 size free. Or take $5 off the rent for a larger size.

6. *Combined Monthly Statement*—Your monthly statement can include status reports on any or all of the accounts you and your spouse have at Republic. You select the accounts you want the Combined Statement to cover. We can include your checking, savings, personal certificates of deposit, and even personal loans. Yes, you'll also receive separate regular statements on each of your Republic accounts you include in the Combined Statement.

7. *Numerical Check Listing*—Your monthly statement will report each check in the order written. That makes it much easier to reconcile your statement each month.

8. *Automatic Overdraft Protection*—This optional service gives you additional peace of mind and the opportunity to take advantage of an exceptional bargain. It works this way. If the checks you write exceed your balance, we'll cover the overdrafts up to the limit of your Republic Master Charge or VISA Credit. Finance charges for deferred payment will apply at the normal rate. Repayment will be through your monthly Master Charge or VISA account payment.

9. *Teller 24® Service*—You can get cash from your Starpak Checking Account, or your Republic Master Charge or VISA Card, at any of 26 Teller 24 machines located in Dallas and six other Texas cities, and at 12,000 banks nationwide. With Teller 24 your money is available 24 hours a day, 7 days a week.

10. *Automatic Loan Repayment*—If you have an installment loan at Republic, we will, at your request, withdraw your monthly loan payment from your Starpak Checking Account. It's a good way to make sure you can take advantage of the 10 percent interest refund.

11. *Automatic Savings Account Deposits*—If you've never been able to save before, this plan solves the problem. Just tell us how much and on what day of the month. On the date you specify, we'll automatically transfer the amount you select from your checking to your savings account. Then, to help your savings grow even faster, we'll pay the highest interest rates allowable.

12. *Starpak Account Card*—It identifies you as a preferred customer of Republic National Bank, entitled to the privileges and special savings available with your Starpak Account.

13. *No Separate Charges*—All these Starpak services are available for the flat monthly fee of $3. There's no separate charge.

Plus these other services available to all Republic National Bank customers—We pay postage both ways when you bank by mail. We'll validate your in-bank parking stub when you bank. And you'll have a personal banker assigned to your accounts so that you can call for advice or assistance with any banking need.

Source: Bank brochure.

■ NOW ACCOUNTS

NOW accounts came into being as the result of the attempt of a Massachusetts mutual savings bank to circumvent the prohibition against thrift institutions' offering checking accounts. After a two-year regulatory and legal battle, Consumer Savings Bank of Worcester, Massachusetts, won its case and in June 1972 began to offer a savings account on which checklike instruments called negotiable orders of withdrawal could be written. Other mutuals in Massachusetts and New Hampshire soon followed suit.

Although regulatory authorities persist in regarding the NOW account as a savings account on which checks can be written, from a consumer point of view (and from an operational point of view) it is a checking account that pays interest. As consumers gradually became educated about NOWs, commercial banks began to lose customers to this attractive type of account, with which they were unable to compete. In response, federal and state laws were passed permitting commercial banks as well as mutuals and S&Ls in Massachusetts and New Hampshire to offer NOW accounts starting in January 1974. As of March 1976, financial institutions in the other New England states were granted the same powers. In two of the states (Connecticut and Maine), state-chartered thrifts had been empowered to offer checking accounts a few months earlier.

In New England, NOW accounts may be offered to individuals and to nonprofit organizations (except that in Connecticut, thrifts can offer NOWs only to individuals).[3] A uniform rate ceiling of 5 percent applies to all institutions. Excerpts from a report prepared by the RNB Marketing Division on the development of NOW accounts in New England are presented in the appendix at the end of this case.

■ NOW ACCOUNT MARKETING STRATEGY

The task facing Krusen was difficult for a number of reasons. First, the only NOW account information available pertained to the New England experience. Although this information would be useful in gauging the rate of adoption of NOW accounts, it was not entirely clear how the Dallas-area banks and thrift institutions would react. Second, several contingency plans would have to be charted. If NOW accounts were not deemed appropriate for RNB by top management, then Krusen would have to recommend a strategy to maintain the RNB customer base. This strategy would depend on whether a "free" NOW account program became popular in the Dallas area or a more conservative approach was adopted by competitors. If the NOW account was adopted by RNB, she realized, the NOW account package (separate account or part of an existing bank service) and the price (service charges, if any) would have to be defined. The package and price would be, in part, determined by the competitive environment that developed and the cost of NOW accounts.

Timing was a third consideration. Should RNB be a leader and set the competitive tenor in the market or take a "wait and see" stance? Finally, if RNB decided to adopt the NOW account, then a question of communications would arise. For example, should RNB quietly inform present customers of NOW account availability or actively communicate availability to the Dallas market as a whole via an advertising program?

---

[3] At the time of this case and for analysis purposes, only retail (personal and nonprofit) checking accounts were affected by NOW accounts in the Dallas area.

■ **APPENDIX: NOW ACCOUNTS IN NEW ENGLAND, A REPORT PREPARED BY THE MARKETING DIVISION OF REPUBLIC NATIONAL BANK OF DALLAS**

The objectives of this investigation of NOW accounts in New England were

1. To learn the speed and magnitude of NOW account impact as a basis for estimating the impact on RNB

2. To identify and evaluate various marketing strategies and their possible relevance to our own market

Penetration of NOWs

Reaction of New England financial institutions given the power to offer NOWs is shown in Exhibit A.1. It indicates the percentages of thrifts and commercial banks that were offering NOWs by August 1976 and the market shares of commercial banks. By August 1976 mutual savings banks in Massachusetts and New Hampshire had been able to offer NOWs for 50 months, commercial banks for 30 months. In the other states, all institutions had been able to offer them for only 6 months.

Despite the resistance of commercial banks in Massachusetts and New Hampshire to offering NOWs, Exhibit A.1 shows that a substantial majority are now providing them. In the other New England states, commercial banks have moved more quickly to adopt NOW accounts. This is one of the reasons that they have a larger share of NOW accounts and balances than do commercial banks in Massachusetts and New Hampshire. Nevertheless, even in the latter states, commercial banks have captured more of the total NOW balances than have thrifts.

One conclusion supported by the data is that the competitiveness of financial institutions is directly related to the degree to which the state's population is concentrated in large urban markets.

The additional data on Massachusetts and New Hampshire shown in Exhibit A.2 indicate the substantial impact of NOWs in the personal payment account market. Exhibit A.2 shows that after four years, 72 percent of checking account balances in New Hampshire have been converted to NOWs and 44 percent have been converted in Massachusetts. Thrifts have captured 27 percent of this market in New Hampshire and 21 percent in Massachusetts.

EXHIBIT A.1

NOW Account Adoption in New England as of August 1976

	Percentage of Institutions Offering		Commercial Banks' Share of NOW Market	
	Thrifts	Commercial Banks	Percentage of Accounts	Percentage of Balances
Massachusetts	94[a]	72	32	52
New Hampshire	81[a]	64	43	62
Connecticut	69	53	35	74
Maine	32	40	68	81
Vermont	23	29	89	93
Rhode Island[b]	25	75	83	85

[a] Mutual savings banks only; in each state two-thirds of the savings and loans also offer NOWs.

[b] Rhode Island has a unique situation of affiliated mutual savings banks and commercial banks. Figures in exhibit refer only to unaffiliated thrifts and commercial banks. NOWs are offered by 66 percent of the affiliated group.

EXHIBIT A.2

Personal Payment Accounts, August 1976

	Personal Payment Balances	
	Percentage in NOWs	*Percentage in Thrifts*
New Hampshire	72%	27%
Massachusetts	44	21

Note: Personal payment accounts consist of all checking balances plus 80 percent of NOW balances. The 20 percent of NOW balances estimated to have come from savings accounts have been deducted.

Marketing Strategies

Massachusetts and New Hampshire As simple as the concept of an interest-bearing checking account appears to be, NOW account introduction in New England produced an initial confusion of positioning, pricing, and marketing strategies.

Positioning. For a variety of reasons, thrifts initially positioned NOWs as savings accounts with a special convenience feature in getting access to funds. Consumers who opened them did not regard them as checking accounts and there was relatively low account activity. Adding to the confusion, when banks began to offer NOWs, some of them were very negative in their presentations. They told customers, in effect, "We have NOW accounts, but you don't really want to spend your savings, do you?"

In time, thrifts and then banks became more daring in presenting NOWs as accounts that were identical in function to checking accounts but paid interest. NOWs are by now recognized as a substitute for checking accounts, are opened instead of checking accounts (or an existing checking account is closed when it is realized that it is no longer needed), and have virtually the same level of activity as checking accounts.

Pricing. Pricing was initially fairly conservative. In New Hampshire, NOWs were usually offered at a lower rate of interest than a savings account, while in Massachusetts per-item charges were prevalent. Then a price war began and increasing numbers of institutions offered free NOWs—that is, maximum rate of interest, no service or item charges, and no minimum balance requirements.

The proportion of institutions offering free NOWs increased until mid-1975, but since then the trend has been reversed, largely because late entrants into the field have offered less generous terms. It has also been true that some institutions that previously offered free NOWs have imposed charges or minimum balance requirements.

The free NOW resulted from a variety of causes and motives:

1. At the time of introduction, money market rates were so high that the cost of NOW funds might still allow a margin of profit.
2. Thrifts were inexperienced in the costs involved in servicing checking accounts.
3. Some thrifts were determined to establish a good market share early, regardless of short-run lack of profitability.
4. In the major market areas, there was a free checking environment.

Price and service package. Pricing structures on NOWs in New England are as varied as checking account charges have historically been. The possibility of competing through the interest rate paid is the only new element. When NOW accounts are not free, some variant of the following occurs:

1. *Interest rates.* Initially, some institutions paid less than the maximum rate on savings accounts. However, under competitive pressure, rates rose to the 5 percent ceiling in all major markets. However, some institutions do not pay on a day-of-deposit to day-of-withdrawal basis. While very few now pay only on collected balances, several large banks are contemplating going in that direction. A few banks pay only on minimum balances.

2. *Balance requirements.* Balances above which the NOW account is "free" range from $200 to $1,000. In most cases, this is the minimum balance, although one large bank, Shawmut, has an average balance requirement.

   What happens when the balance that goes below the minimum varies.

   In some cases, no interest is paid; in others, a transaction or service fee is imposed; and in some cases, both. In some isolated markets, fees are imposed on all accounts, but in competitive major markets, NOWs become free at some balance level.

3. *Transaction charges.* Charges per check range from 10 to 25 cents. Usually, the charge is levied on all checks if the balance is below the required level. In some cases, a certain number of checks are free (5 to 15 per month), and in some other cases the number of free checks is related to balances (for example, 5 checks per $100 of average balance).

4. *Service charge.* Some banks charge flat fees rather than per-transaction charges. Fees generally are $1 or $2.

Other New England States By the time NOW accounts were authorized in the other New England states, both thrifts and commercials had had the opportunity to assess the cost and competitive impact of NOWs in the two original states, and money market conditions had changed. These facts are reflected in the response of financial institutions in offering NOWs. Commercial banks have moved more rapidly than they did in Massachusetts and New Hampshire. At the same time, both thrifts and commercial banks have been more conservative in pricing.

Connecticut. Thrifts have moved aggressively to offer both checking accounts and NOWs. Although free checking prevails in major Connecticut markets and although about one-third of the thrifts offer free NOWs, large Connecticut banks have offered NOWs on conservative terms (high minimum balances with transaction charges for lower-balance accounts). The effect of this strategy is reflected in the high average balances of commercial bank NOWs—over $4,000.

Rhode Island. The financial market is highly concentrated in a very few institutions. Six months after NOWs became legal, six of the nine commercial banks affiliated with thrift institutions, six of the eight unaffiliated banks, and one of the four unaffiliated thrifts were offering NOWs. None of them offered free NOWs. As in the checking account market in this state, relatively high minimum balances are required. It should be noted that because of the thrift commercial bank affiliations, a majority of thrifts have in effect been able to offer checking accounts to their customers.

Maine. Thrifts have concentrated harder on selling checking accounts than on offering NOWs. Neither thrifts nor commercial banks have moved very fast to offer NOWs. Few offer them free.

Vermont. This state shows the slowest gain in institutions offering NOWs. None offers them free.

Republic National Bank of Dallas

NOW Accounts

■ STRATEGIC ISSUES AND PROBLEMS

Ruth Krusen, marketing officer for RNB, has been given responsibility for (1) determining the profit impact RNB could anticipate from NOW accounts and (2) recommending a contingency plan for a NOW account marketing strategy. Her task involves a number of important factors. She must assess the likelihood that the Dallas competitive environment will be liberal or conservative in its marketing of NOW accounts. An important consideration is RNB's role in affecting this environment, given its dominant position in the Dallas market and its posture regarding aggressiveness in retail account marketing. Ultimately, she must make a "go-no go" decision. A "go" decision requires a recommendation on the form of the service, its target market, its price reflected in service charges, and promotion. A "no go" decision must take into consideration RNB's competitive position without NOW accounts and measures to minimize their impact. The problem facing RNB is how to retain its dominant competitive position given an environmental threat (NOW accounts) while at the same time preserving profitability and its customer base.

■ INSIGHTS FROM THE NEW ENGLAND EXPERIENCE

The NOW account experience, based on the data in the report of the marketing division, reveals the following:

1. The faster commercial banks move to adopt NOW accounts, the larger their share of NOW accounts and NOW account balances.

2. Cannibalization of checking accounts occurs when NOW accounts are available; 72 percent of checking account balances in New Hampshire have been converted to NOW accounts, and 44 percent of checking accounts in Massachusetts have been converted to NOWs. These figures developed over 50 months (four years) after the NOW introduction (see Exhibit A.2).

3. Exhibit 1 in the case provides some evidence that NOW account balances are high. This could mean that those individuals with high checking account balances are more likely to switch to NOWs. Alternatively, the Connecticut experience would indicate that minimum balance requirements increase NOW account balances. Data for Massachusetts and New Hampshire—both of which experienced "free NOWs"—would tend to support the point that individuals with high account balances convert to NOWs.

4. NOW account usage activity approaches checking account activity; hence checking account costs are merely transferred to managing NOW accounts.

5. Competitive activity, reflected in the NOW package provided, reveals that "free NOWs" were initially provided. Financial institutions subsequently offered less generous terms, however.

6. NOW account packages differ greatly with respect to minimum balances, service charges, and positioning against checking and savings accounts.

Results from the New England experience suggest that three scenarios are possible in the Dallas market.

Environment	*Environment Description*
No NOW adoption:	Financial institutions refrain from adoption.
Liberal NOW adoption:	NOWs are adopted with no minimum balance, service charges, 5 percent interest, an active promotion/communication program.
Conservative NOW adoption:	NOWs are adopted with some form of minimum service charges, less than 5 percent interest, little promotion or communication.

Numerous factors will affect the likelihood of each environment's developing in the Dallas market.

Factors in favor of a no-NOW environment:

1. The New England experience suggests that a no-win possibility exists for all financial institutions. For example, banks will have to pay interest on previously interest-free funds, and S&Ls and credit unions will incur costs not previously encountered.

2. Money market rates are quite low at present, suggesting little spread to make an adequate profit margin.

Factors in favor of a NOW environment:

1. The New England experience suggests that where NOWs are legalized, they are adopted in some form, by someone.

2. If the Dallas market is competitive *and* various financial institutions are vying for deposits, then NOWs offer a means to attract deposits. Moreover, the New England experience suggests that "getting in first" is crucial. "Followership" is not rewarded.

3. S&Ls are poised to take some advantage of NOWs in that their interest rate paid on deposits will fall from $5^1/_4$ percent to 5 percent, assuming a 5 percent ceiling level.

Factors in favor of a liberal NOW environment:

1. Thrifts might view NOWs as a way of gaining deposits quickly.

2. S&Ls will benefit from NOWs even if 5 percent interest is offered on NOW accounts, since they are currently paying $5^1/_4$ percent on savings.

3. Share drafts provided by credit unions have characteristics similar to those of NOWs; NOW accounts would seem like a logical extension.

Factors in favor of a conservative NOW environment:

1. This appears to be the trend in New England states.

2. Dallas banks do not generally offer free checking.

3. Money market rates are low.

It would seem that a potential determinant of how the NOW environment evolves will be the decision of RNB, given its dominance in the Dallas banking market. RNB's dominant position would seem to affect the environment *only* if RNB acts immediately with a well thought out NOW account program. NOWs are probably inevitable—that is, the no-NOW environment seems unlikely. The question, then, is whether a liberal or a conservative NOW environment will develop. The environment could be influenced by RNB.

■ REPUBLIC NATIONAL BANK

RNB dominates the Dallas financial market. Its assets alone ($6 billion) are almost ten times *total* assets of all credit unions ($666 million). RNB's deposits ($4.6 billion) exceed the total for *all* S&Ls ($2.85 billion). RNB has the largest deposit base of all Dallas banks *and* the largest retail account deposit base in Dallas.

Nevertheless, RNB management apparently has not resolved how aggressive the bank should be in retail account marketing efforts. The aggressiveness issue would seem to be related to the bank's emphasis on the wholesale rather than the retail business.

Exhibit 1 in the case indicates that about 55 percent of RNB's checking accounts are under $500. However, 96 percent of total checking account balances are accounted for by accounts of $500 and up, and 53 percent of total deposits are accounted for by accounts of over $25,000. The average account size is $3,333 ($150 million in deposits divided by 45,000 accounts). A profitability analysis of checking account sizes reveals that RNB loses money on accounts that are less than $500 on an annual basis (see Exhibit 1 in this analysis). This profitability analysis indicates that accounts below $500 produce a *loss* of $519,210 annually:

Accounts under $200:	14,400 accounts × ($24.24)	= ($349,056)
Accounts $200-$499:	10,350 accounts × ($16.44)	= ($170,154)
Loss		= ($519,210)

EXHIBIT 1

RNB Retail Account Profit Analysis (Based on Exhibit 1 in the Case)

Account Size	Average Interest Revenue per Account[a]	+	Average Service/ Handling Revenue per Account[b]	=	Average Revenue per Account	−	Account Cost[b]	=	Profit/ (Loss)
Less than $200	$19.92		$18.72		$38.64		$62.88		$(24.24)
$200-$499	27.72		18.72		46.44		62.88		(16.44)
$500-$999	60.71		18.72		79.43		62.88		16.55
$1,000-$4,999	153.47		18.72		172.19		62.88		109.31
$5,000-$9,999	333.93		18.72		352.65		62.88		289.77
$10,000-$24,999	920.83		18.72		939.55		62.88		876.67
$25,000-100,000	2,125.00		18.72		2,143.72		62.88		2,080.84
Greater than $100,000	7,083.00		18.72		7,101.72		62.88		7,038.84

[a] Computed as follows: $\dfrac{\text{Account size deposit volume}}{\text{Number of accounts in category}} \times 85\% \times 0.075$.

For an account size of $200, using Exhibit 1 data: $\dfrac{\$4.5 \text{ million}}{14,400} \times 0.85 \times 0.075 = \$19.92$

[b] Annualized average account revenue and cost given in the case where service/handling charge revenue per account per month = $1.56; account cost per month = $5.24.

More important, this analysis provides important data on the pricing of NOW accounts and the form of the service, as will be discussed later.

■ PLAN OF ACTION

There are two primary alternatives open to RNB: to offer NOWs or not to offer NOWs. If NOWs are considered, then the form, price, and promotion must be determined. The alternatives are:

1. Do not offer NOW accounts.

2. Offer NOW accounts with no conditions and promote them heavily or modestly.

3. Offer NOW accounts with conditions and promote them heavily or modestly.

The advantages and disadvantages of the options available to RNB can be outlined as follows:

1. Not offering NOW accounts:

   Advantages

   - RNB is dominant and has the resources to wait and see what will happen.

   - The impact on revenue of offering NOWs would be too severe. Assuming that *all accounts* are cannibalized by NOWs and the interest yield drops from $7\frac{1}{2}$ percent to $2\frac{1}{2}$ percent because of 5 percent interest on NOWs, the interest revenue lost will be about $6.0 million.

Checking Deposits		*Percent Investable*		*Investable Deposits*
$150 million	×	85%	=	$127.5 million
				Interest Revenue
$127.5 million	×	0.075	=	9,562,500
$144 million	×	0.025	=	−3,600,000
Interest revenue lost				$5,962,500

   Note that NOW accounts are viewed as savings accounts, and 96 percent of deposits are investable.

   Disadvantages

   - RNB will lose an opportunity to be an innovator or the "first to market," which has been shown in New England to be advantageous.

   - Erosion of accounts may occur, as individuals switch to institutions offering NOW accounts. This factor is particularly important if *large* accounts switch, and they are most likely to do so, since they stand to benefit most from NOW accounts.

2. Offering NOW accounts with no conditions:

   Advantages

   - Nonconditional NOWs will have a dramatic impact on the Dallas banking market. Banks offering them will most likely attract deposits and accounts in great numbers, particularly since they are a better deal than checking accounts with minimum balances or service charges, *plus* they give interest!

   - Nonconditional NOW accounts will set the competitive tenor of the market; retail banks not offering them may be unable to compete.

- By offering nonconditional NOWs, RNB will keep current accounts from being attracted to competitors (preemptive cannibalism).

Disadvantages

- This strategy could be very expensive. As noted earlier, in addition to the account costs, a loss of interest of $6 million is possible.
- This strategy will cannibalize checking accounts almost totally.

3. Offering NOW accounts with conditions:

Advantages

- A minimum-balance condition would allow RNB to accept only those accounts on which it can make money.
- A service/handling charge condition would also result in greater account selectivity.
- A break-even analysis shows how RNB can determine a minimum balance given current service charge and account costs per year. The break-even point is the point at which total revenues (interest plus handling/service charges) minus total costs (account cost per month) equals zero. Since RNB will net 2.5 percent in account interest revenue, has an $18.72 handling and service revenue per account per year ($1.56 × 12 months), and has an annual account cost of $62.88 ($5.24 × 12 months), solving for the minimum account balance reveals the following:

$$\text{Profit} = \frac{\text{acct. interest}}{\text{revenue}} + \frac{\text{handling/}}{\text{service charge}} - \frac{\text{acct.}}{\text{cost}}$$

$$0 = 0.025X + \$18.72 - \$62.88$$

$$\$44.16 = 0.025X$$

$$\$1,766.40 = X$$

Thus, RNB breaks even at an account size of $1,766.40, given existing handling/service revenue per account and account maintenance costs. This minimum balance level would be a condition that from 80 percent to 90 percent of RNB's accounts could meet (see Exhibit 1 in the case).

Disadvantages

- This strategy leaves RNB open to being undercut by competitors if conditions are too stringent.
- Overly complex conditions and the likelihood of customers' being unexpectedly hit with service charges could hurt goodwill, particularly among larger balance account holders.

■ RECOMMENDED NOW ACCOUNT MARKETING STRATEGY

The previous analysis indicates that RNB can shape the NOW account environment in Dallas. The following NOW account marketing strategy will ensure that this will happen.

Goals and Objectives

1. RNB should pioneer NOW accounts in the Dallas market to set the competitive tone and create a "rational" NOW environment.

2. RNB should focus on achieving 85% customer retention.

3. RNB should break even on NOW accounts.

Target Market

The target market for NOW accounts should be current customers with large account balances. Specifically, current customers with an account size of $1,800.00 is the primary target market. This market represents almost all of RNB's current accounts. There is little to gain from attracting new customers for NOW accounts.

Marketing Mix

Product Strategy NOW accounts will be included with an existing service bundle—the Starpak Account. It is expected that NOW accounts will cannibalize existing accounts. RNB's focus on current customers is a form of preemptive cannibalism necessary to retain existing customers.

Price Strategy NOW accounts should carry a service charge. The recommended charge is $18.75 per account. This service charge, given the account cost, account interest revenue, and an account interest revenue, will allow RNB to break even on estimated minimum account balance of $1,766.40.

Distribution and Sales NOW accounts will be provided at all locations by the New Account staff. Training for the New Account RNB staff should begin immediately. Documentation for the Starpak Account should be immediately modified to incorporate NOW accounts.

Advertising and Promotion A modest advertising and promotion (A&P) program is recommended for NOW accounts. The A&P program should focus on current customers via a direct mail program and specifically inserts in monthly statements. Starpak print and TV advertising should incorporate reference to NOW accounts.

Advertising opportunity. Conditions suggesting that a product or service would benefit from advertising. They are (1) favorable primary demand for the product or service category, (2) the product or service to be advertised can be significantly differentiated from its competitors, (3) the product or service has hidden qualities or benefits that can be portrayed effectively through advertising, and (4) there are strong emotional buying motives for the product or service.

Brand equity. The added value a brand name bestows on a product or service beyond the functional benefits provided.

Brand extension strategy. The practice of using a current brand name to enter a completely different product class.

Break-even analysis. The unit or dollar sales volume at which an organization neither makes a profit nor incurs a loss. The formula for determining the number of units required to break even is: unit break-even = total dollar fixed costs ÷ (unit selling price − unit variable costs).

Bundling. The practice of marketing two or more product or service items in a single "package" with one price.

Business mission. Describes the organization's purpose with reference to its customers, products or services, markets, philosophy, and technology.

Cannibalism. The process whereby the sales of a new product or service come at the expense of existing products (services) already marketed by the firm.

Chain ratio method. A technique for estimating market sales potential that involves multiplying a base number by several adjusting factors that are believed to influence market sales potential.

Channel captain. A member of a marketing channel with the power to influence the behavior of other channel members.

Channel conflict. A situation that arises when one channel member believes another channel member is engaged in behavior that is preventing it from achieving its goals.

Co-branding. The pairing of two brand names of two manufacturers on a single product.

Contribution. The difference between total sales revenue and total variable costs, or, on a per-unit basis, the difference between unit selling price and unit variable cost. Contribution can be expressed in percentage terms (contribution margin) or dollar terms (contribution per unit).

Cost of goods sold. Material, labor, and factory overhead applied directly to production.

Cross-elasticity of demand. The responsiveness of the quantity demanded of one product or service to a price change in another product or service.

Distinctive competency. An organization's unique strengths or qualities, including skills, technologies, or resources that distinguish it from other organizations. These competencies are imperfectly imitable by competitors and provide superior customer value.

Diversification. A product-market strategy that involves the development or acquisition of offerings new to the organization and the introduction of those offerings to publics (markets) not previously served by the organization.

Dual distribution. The practice of distributing products or services through two or more different marketing channels that may or may not compete for similar buyers.

Effective demand. The situation when prospective buyers have both the willingness and ability to purchase an organization's offerings.

Exclusive distribution. A distribution strategy whereby a producer sells its products or services in only one retail outlet in a specific geographical area.

Fighting brand strategy. The practice of adding a new brand whose sole purpose is to confront competitive brands in a product class being served by an organization.

Fixed cost. Expenses that do not fluctuate with output volume within a relevant time period (usually defined as a budget year), but became progressively smaller per unit of output as volume increases. Fixed costs divide into programmed costs, which result from attempts to generate sales volume, and committed costs, which are those required to maintain the organization.

Flanker brand strategy. The practice of adding new brands on the high or low end of a product line based on a price-quality continuum.

Full-cost price strategies. Those that consider both variable and fixed cost (total cost) in the pricing of a product or service.

Gross margin (or gross profit). The difference between total sales revenue and total cost of goods sold, or, on a per-unit basis, the difference between unit selling price and unit cost of goods sold. Gross margin can be expressed in dollar or percentage terms.

Harvesting. The practice of reducing the investment in a business entity (division, product) to cut costs or improve cash flow.

Integrated marketing communications. The practice of blending different elements of the communication mix in mutually reinforcing ways.

Intensive distribution. A distribution strategy whereby a producer sells its products or services in as many retail outlets as possible in a geographical area.

Life cycle. The plot of sales of a single product or brand or service or a class of products or services over time.

Market. Prospective buyers (individuals or organizations) who are willing and able to purchase the existing or potential offering (product or service) of an organization.

Market-development strategy. A product-market strategy whereby an organization introduces its offerings to markets other than those it is currently serving. In global marketing, this strategy can be implemented through exportation, licensing, joint ventures, or direct investment.

Market evolution. Changes in primary demand for a product class and changes in technology.

Market-penetration strategy. A product-market strategy whereby an organization seeks to gain greater dominance in a market in which it already has an offering. This strategy often means capturing a larger share of an existing market.

Market redefinition. Changes in the offering demanded by buyers or promoted by competitors.

Market sales potential. The maximum level of sales that might be available to all organizations serving a defined market in a specific time period given (1) the marketing-mix activities and effort of all organizations, and (2) a set of environmental conditions.

Market segmentation. The breaking down or building up of potential buyers into groups on the basis of some sort of homogeneous characteristic(s) (e.g., age, income, geography) relating to purchase or consumption behavior.

Market share. Sales of a firm, product, or brand divided by the sales of the served "market."

Market targeting (or target marketing). The specification of the specific market segment(s) the organization wishes to pursue. Differentiated marketing means that an organization simultaneously pursues several different market segments, usually with a different strategy for each. Concentrated marketing means that only a single market segment is pursued.

Marketing audit. A comprehensive, systematic, independent, and periodic examination of a company's or business unit's marketing environment, objectives, strategies, and activities with a view of determining problem areas and opportunities and recommending a plan of action to improve the company's marketing performance.

Marketing-cost analysis. The practice of assigning or allocating costs to a specified marketing activity or entity in a manner that accurately displays the financial contribution of activities or entities to the organization.

Marketing mix. Those activities controllable by the organization and include the product, service, or idea offered, the manner in which the offering will be communicated to customers, the method for distributing or delivering the offering, and the price to be charged for the offering.

New-brand strategy. The development of a new brand and often a new offering for a product class that has not been previously served by the organization.

Net profit margin (before taxes). The remainder after cost of goods sold, other variable costs, and fixed costs have been subtracted from sales revenue, or simply, total revenue minus total cost. Net profit margin can be expressed in dollar or percentage terms.

Offering. The sum total of benefits or satisfaction provided to target markets by an organization. An offering consists of a tangible product or service plus related services, warranties or guarantees, packaging, etc.

Offering mix or portfolio. The totality of an organization's offerings (products and services).

Operating leverage. The extent to which fixed costs and variable costs are used in the production and marketing of products and services.

Operations control. The practice of assessing how well an organization performs marketing activities as it seeks to achieve planned outcomes.

Opportunity analysis. The process of identifying opportunities, matching the opportunity to the organization, and evaluating the opportunity.

Opportunity cost. Alternative uses of resources that are given up when pursuing one alternative rather than another. Sometimes referred to as the benefits not obtained from not choosing an alternative.

Payback period. The number of years required for an organization to recapture its initial investment in an offering.

Penetration pricing strategy. Setting a relatively low initial price for a new product or service.

Positioning. The act of designing an organization's offering and image so that it occupies a distinct and valued place in the target customer's mind relative to competitive offerings. A product or service can be positioned by (1) attribute or benefit, (2) use or application, (3) product or service user, (4) product or service class, (5) competitors, and (6) price and quality.

Price elasticity of demand. The percentage change in quantity demanded relative to a percentage change in price for a product or service.

Product-development strategy. A product-market strategy whereby an organization creates new offerings for existing markets through product innovation, product augmentation, or product line extensions.

Pro forma income statement. An income statement containing projected revenues, budgeted (variable and fixed) expenses, and estimated net profit for an organization, product, or service during a specific planning period, usually a year.

Product-line pricing. The setting of prices for all items in a product line. It involves determining (1) the lowest-priced product price, (2) the highest-priced product, and (3) price differentials for all other products in the line.

Pull communication strategy. The practice of creating initial interest for an offering among potential buyers, who in turn demand the offering from intermediaries, ultimately "pulling" the offering through the channel. The principal emphasis is on consumer advertising and consumer promotions.

Push communication strategy. The practice of "pushing" an offering through a marketing channel in a sequential fashion, with each channel representing a distinct target market. The principal emphasis is on personal selling and trade promotions directed toward wholesalers and retailers.

Regional marketing. The practice of using different marketing mixes to accommodate unique preferences and competitive conditions in different geographical areas.

Relevant cost. Expenditures that (1) are expected to occur in the future as a result of some marketing action and (2) differ among marketing alternatives being considered.

Sales forecast. The level of sales a single organization expects to achieve based on a chosen marketing strategy and an assumed competitive environment.

Scrambled merchandising. The practice of wholesalers and retailers to carry a wider assortment of merchandise than they did in the past.

Selective distribution. A distribution strategy whereby a producer sells its products or services in a few retail outlets in a specific geographical area.

Situation analysis. The appraisal of operations to determine the reasons for the gap between what was or is expected and what has happened or will happen.

Skimming pricing strategy. Setting a relatively high initial price for a new product or service.

Strategic change. Environmental change that will affect the long-run well-being of the organization.

Strategic control. The practice of assessing the direction of the organization as evidenced by its implicit or explicit goals, objectives, strategies, and capacity to perform in the context of changing environments and competitive actions.

Strategic marketing management. The analytical process of (1) defining the organization's business, mission, and goals; (2) identifying and framing organizational opportunities; (3) formulating product-market strategies; (4) budgeting marketing, financial, and production resources; and (5) developing reformulation and recovery strategies.

Success requirements. The basic tasks that must be performed by an organization in a market or industry to compete successfully. These are sometimes "key success factors," or simply KSFs.

Sunk cost. Past expenditures for a given activity that are typically irrelevant in whole or in part to future decisions. The "sunk cost fallacy" is an attempt to recoup spent dollars by spending still more dollars in the future.

SWOT analysis. A formal framework for identifying and framing organizational growth opportunities. SWOT is an acronym for an organization's *Strengths* and *Weaknesses* and external *Opportunities* and *Threats*.

Trade margin. The difference between unit sales price and unit cost at each level of a marketing channel. Trade margin is usually expressed in percentage terms.

Trading down. The process of reducing the number of features or quality of an offering and lowering the purchase price.

Trading up. The practice of improving an offering by adding new features and higher quality materials or augmenting products with services and raising the purchase price.

Value. The ratio of perceived benefits to price for a product or service.

Variable cost. Expenses that are uniform per unit of output within a relevant time period (usually defined as a budget year); total variable costs fluctuate in direct proportion to the output volume of units produced. Variable cost includes cost of goods sold and other variable costs such as sales commissions.

Variable-cost price strategies. Those that consider only direct (variable) cost associated with the offering in pricing a product or service.

Working capital. The dollar value of an organization's current assets (such as cash, accounts receivable, prepaid expenses, inventory) *minus* the dollar value of current liabilities (such as short-term accounts payable for goods and services, income taxes).

Subject Index

Company Index

Brand Index